*SAT
FOR
DUMMIES®
8TH EDITION

*SAT FOR DUMMIES® 8TH EDITION

by Geraldine Woods with Peter Bonfanti and Kristin Josephson

WILEY

John Wiley & Sons, Inc.

*SAT For Dummies,® 8th Edition

Published by
John Wiley & Sons, Inc.
111 River St.
Hoboken, NJ 07030-5774
www.wiley.com

Copyright © 2012 by John Wiley & Sons, Inc., Hoboken, New Jersey

Published simultaneously in Canada

For general information on our other products and services, please contact our Customer Care Department within the U.S. at 877-762-2974, outside the U.S. at 317-572-3993, or fax 317-572-4002.

For technical support, please visit www.wiley.com/techsupport.

Wiley publishes in a variety of print and electronic formats and by print-on-demand. Some material included with standard print versions of this book may not be included in e-books or in print-on-demand. If this book refers to media such as a CD or DVD that is not included in the version you purchased, you may download this material at http://booksupport.wiley.com. For more information about Wiley products, visit www.wiley.com.

Library of Congress Control Number: 2011927304

ISBN: 978-1-118-02608-3 (pbk); 978-1-118-10207-7 (ebk); 978-1-118-10208-4 (ebk); 978-1-118-10248-0 (ebk)

Manufactured in the United States of America

10 9 8 7 6 5 4 3

WILEY

About the Authors

Geraldine Woods has prepared students for the SAT, both academically and emotionally, for the past three decades. She also teaches English and directs the independent-study program at the Horace Mann School in New York City. She is the author of more than 50 books, including *English Grammar For Dummies*, 2nd Edition; *English Grammar Workbook For Dummies*, 2nd Edition; *Grammar Essentials For Dummies; Research Papers For Dummies; College Admission Essays For Dummies; AP English Literature & Composition For Dummies;* and *AP English Language & Composition For Dummies,* all published by Wiley. She lives in New York City with her husband and two parakeets.

Peter Bonfanti has taught high school math in New York City since 1996. Before that, he lived in Pennsylvania and was a monk. Before that, he went to school in New Jersey, where he was born and hopes to return someday.

Kristin Josephson survived the college admissions process only to drop out of MIT 16 months later to attend circus school in San Francisco. While there, she studied flying trapeze, trampoline, and acrobatics. Kristin discovered her passion for teaching while she was tutoring in the Bay Area, a passion that led her to complete her degree at Colorado College. Kristin eventually landed at the Horace Mann School, where she has been teaching high school mathematics since 2007.

Dedication

For Linda, friend of 40 years; for Gillian, an honorary New Yorker; and for Jacqueline, kindness personified.

Authors' Acknowledgments

Geraldine Woods: I would like to thank Peter Bonfanti and Kristin Josephson, good friends and accomplished mathematicians, who created the math explanations and examples for this book. I also thank Albert Wu, a former student and aspiring comedy writer, who came up with the idea for mock SAT questions and graciously allowed me to use it. I appreciate the efforts of Georgette Beatty, Christy Pingleton, Megan Knoll, and Lindsay Lefevere of Wiley, as well as those of my agent, Lisa Queen, and the technical reviewers, Cindy Kaplan and Amy Nicklin.

Peter would like to thank his parents, for making it possible for him to get up every morning, and Lorraine, for making it worth his while. (Also his brother, Paul, who put up with sharing a room with him for many of those mornings.)

Kristin Josephson: I'd like to thank my friends, loved ones, teachers, and students for kindness, compassion, interest, and hilarity. I especially want to thank my mother, Lynn, who regularly astonishes me and who inspired me to be the teacher I am today, and my father, Marc, who lifted me up to the full moon as an infant and who has never missed an opportunity to teach me something new.

Publisher's Acknowledgments

We're proud of this book; please send us your comments at http://dummies.custhelp.com. For other comments, please contact our Customer Care Department within the U.S. at 877-762-2974, outside the U.S. at 317-572-3993, or fax 317-572-4002.

Some of the people who helped bring this book to market include the following:

Acquisitions, Editorial, and Vertical Websites

Senior Project Editor: Georgette Beatty
(*Previous Edition: Tim Gallan*)

Executive Editor: Lindsay Sandman Lefevere

Copy Editors: Christine Pingleton, Megan Knoll
(*Previous Edition: Amanda M. Langferman, Caitlin Copple*)

Assistant Editor: David Lutton

Technical Editors: Cindy Kaplan, Amy Nicklin

Editorial Manager: Michelle Hacker

Editorial Assistants: Rachelle S. Amick, Alexa Koschier

Cover Photo: © iStockphoto.com/Steve Shepard

Cartoons: Rich Tennant (www.the5thwave.com)

Composition Services

Project Coordinator: Sheree Montgomery

Layout and Graphics: Carrie A. Cesavice, Nikki Gately, Erin Zeltner

Proofreaders: Melissa D. Buddendeck, Lauren Mandelbaum

Indexer: Steve Rath

Publishing and Editorial for Consumer Dummies

Kathleen Nebenhaus, Vice President and Executive Publisher

Kristin Ferguson-Wagstaffe, Product Development Director

Ensley Eikenburg, Associate Publisher, Travel

Kelly Regan, Editorial Director, Travel

Publishing for Technology Dummies

Andy Cummings, Vice President and Publisher

Composition Services

Debbie Stailey, Director of Composition Services

Contents at a Glance

Table of Contents

Introduction

First, lower your shoulders. Now unclench your knees and take a deep breath. No, I'm not a yoga instructor. I'm giving you these directions because if you're like most people, the very thought of the SAT makes you huddle into a basic turtle shape. As you may already know, the dreaded test asks you to read and write, to identify and use correct grammar, and to solve both simple and complex math problems. Are you really surprised that your head tends to tuck protectively close to your chest whenever you contemplate the SAT?

But you don't have to turn into a candidate for physical therapy just because a standardized test looms in your future. I have a little secret: The SAT isn't as bad as you think, especially now that you've shown wisdom and foresight in buying this book. (Yes, I count modesty as one of my many virtues.) The SAT *is* horrible in some ways. For one thing, the test kills a perfectly good weekend morning, when you could be sleeping or doing something noble, such as discovering a cure for nail fungus. Yet, although it is challenging, the SAT isn't any harder than your everyday school tests; in fact, in a lot of ways, it's easier.

Did I really just use a form of the word *easy* to describe the SAT? Yes, I did, but "easy" doesn't mean you can throw away this book and forget about preparation. You can't go cold to the SAT and expect to give it your best shot. A little preparation goes a long way (all upward), and your score will climb nicely if you invest just a small portion of your life in getting acquainted with the ultra-annoying exam. Don't you at least want to be prepared so the directions and format aren't a surprise on SAT day? Furthermore, a little practice can help you avoid the SAT's tricks and traps after you discover how to spot them. Working with *SAT For Dummies,* 8th Edition, will ensure that when everyone else's shoulders rise with tension, you'll be poised and relaxed, ready to show the world (well, the part of the world that most concerns you at this stage in your life — the colleges) how brilliant you are.

About This Book

The SAT is one of the standardized tests that fall like mudslides on almost everyone applying to a college or university in the United States and to some English-speaking institutions abroad. A few schools don't require any standardized tests, preferring instead that their applicants concentrate on answering questions like "Why breathe?" and "Peanut butter — inevitable or technological?" If you're planning to attend one of those schools, I offer my congratulations. You can put this book down now and go bowling or dancing (or do whatever it is that makes you happy). But if your college — the one that you hope will be your college someday — requires a standardized test, you're probably facing either the SAT or the ACT. I'm assuming the SAT because you plunked down the cash for this book. (What? You charged it to Grandma's trust fund? No matter. The point remains the same: You're reading this book because you have to take the SAT.) If you just love tests and want to take both (in which case you should seriously consider getting a life), check out *ACT For Dummies,* 5th Edition, by Lisa Zimmer Hatch and Scott Hatch (Wiley).

In theory, the SAT gives colleges a way to measure your ability to succeed in their hallowed halls. Although the test itself doesn't really determine whether you'll excel in the world of higher education, it does give the admissions people a number (a set of numbers, actually) with which to compare you to all their other applicants. In case you didn't know, if you have a high SAT score, you have a better chance of getting into Really-Wanna-Go-There University.

Just to make your life a little more confusing, two SATs are out there, waiting to torture you:

✔ The biggest and the one most colleges require is the SAT, formerly known officially (and still occasionally) as the SAT I or the SAT Reasoning Test. That's the one I prepare you for in this book.

✔ The other SAT, cleverly named the SAT Subject Test and formerly known as the SAT II, is a set of exams geared to subjects in school — languages, sciences, math, history, and so on. *SAT For Dummies,* 8th Edition, doesn't deal with those tests, though you may want to check out some other *For Dummies* titles (such as *Algebra I For Dummies,* 2nd Edition, and *Algebra II For Dummies* by Mary Jane Sterling; *Biology For Dummies,* 2nd Edition, by Rene Fester Kratz and Donna Rae Siegfried; and so forth, all published by Wiley) to get a good review without a lot of hassle.

SAT For Dummies, 8th Edition, takes you through each section of the SAT, explaining what the test makers are looking for and how you can deliver it. In this book, you find a few easy ways to increase your vocabulary as painlessly as possible, because, as Yogi Berra (famous Yankee catcher and language wrecker) didn't say, "Nine tenths of the SAT game is half vocabulary." As a bonus, I scatter SAT words and definitions throughout the book, including in paragraphs that have nothing to do with vocabulary *per se.* (By the way, **per se** means "as such" or "for itself.") In addition, I include a quick but effective review of the math and grammar essentials that tend to pop up on the exam.

To help you step up your game on the SAT, throughout this book I include in-depth analysis and sample sets of each type of question that the SAT dumps on you — sentence completions, math grid-ins, and so forth. And to kill still more of your free time (and help you improve your SAT-tested skills), I include a detailed explanation with each answer so you know what you answered right and wrong, and why. To help you get a feel for how ready you are to take the real SAT, I give you five practice tests that you can take under true-test conditions. (No, they're not real SATs because the company that produces the actual test is sitting on those rights and making a ton of cash by doing so. The test you get on test day may not have exactly the same number of questions in exactly the same order as the ones I provide here. But the tests in this book are as close as anyone can come without invoking lawyerly attention, and they'll do the job.) Finally, I tuck plenty of extra practice questions into other chapters so you can party it up with math, critical reading, and multiple-choice writing whenever you're in the mood.

Just as in every *For Dummies* book, you don't have to read this book from cover to cover. No, I don't mean that you should skip the entire book. (Pause for a shudder of horror at such a thought.) Instead, pick and choose just what you need from the wide range of topics in *SAT For Dummies,* 8th Edition. For example, if you're a whiz at reading comprehension but math sends you screaming into the night, don't bother focusing much on Part II. Instead, concentrate on Part IV. Check out the table of contents to see what areas you want to focus on and then start chugging away. You can also check out the intro bullets at the beginning of each chapter under the heading "In This Chapter" to see specifically what you can accomplish by spending your precious time going through that text. Be selective and take your time as you move through this book, and you'll be prepared for the exam *and* caught up on your sleep — and homework — when you face the SAT. As a bonus, you may also find that your schoolwork improves as you increase your vocabulary, sharpen your grammar skills, and practice math problems.

Conventions Used in This Book

To help you navigate this book, I use the following conventions:

✔ *Italics* have two different duties:

  • To introduce new terms, particularly in the math and writing chapters

  • To emphasize a particular word or point

- ✔ *This font* highlights vocabulary words that I define in the text. (Pay attention to these terms because increasing your store of words can really improve your score on the SAT.)

- ✔ **Boldface** indicates the action part of numbered steps and the main items in bulleted lists.

- ✔ `Monofont` denotes Web addresses.

  When this book was printed, some Web addresses may have needed to break across two lines of text. If that happened, rest assured that I haven't put in any extra characters (such as hyphens) to indicate the break. When using one of these Web addresses, just type in exactly what you see in this book, ignoring any line breaks you encounter.

What You're Not to Read

Like many teachers, I love trivia, but I understand that useless facts are an acquired taste, and you may have something better to do than read about the development and use of the SAT. Nevertheless, I couldn't resist throwing in some interesting information about the exam, which you can find in some of the gray boxes, called *sidebars,* and which I cleverly disguise as SAT questions. Skip them, unless you're trying to take your mind off your next dental appointment or your last big breakup. You don't need to know anything about the exam except how to ace it. And if you memorized the dictionary when you were 12, feel free to skip the vocabulary-specific sidebars, too!

Foolish Assumptions

I recently met a graduate of a university famous for the ivy climbing over its brick walls who told me that he had taken the SAT an extra time — *after* he had already been accepted — just to see whether he could achieve an even higher score. As I gave him a discreet once-over, checking for other signs of mental illness, he added, "I like taking tests."

In writing this book, I assume several things about you, including that you have nothing at all in common with my friend, who is actually quite sane, despite his love for sharpened No. 2 pencils.

My other assumptions include the following:

- ✔ You hate standardized tests but want to achieve a high score on the SAT.

- ✔ You have plenty of better things to do with your time than to plow through a ton of useless information. For you, then, I put in what you need to know and what you need to practice, and nothing else except for a few lame jokes, but hey, humor me (no pun intended).

- ✔ You've taken the usual math and language arts courses in elementary, middle, and early high school — through, say, algebra, geometry, and sophomore English. So even though I review the basics of those subjects, I'm not actually trying to teach you something you've never seen before.

If you know that English grammar is a pitfall for you, feel free to increase my profit margin by purchasing *English Grammar For Dummies,* 2nd Edition, which provides a complete tour through the wonderful world of nouns, commas, and all that stuff. You can find tons of grammar practice in the *English Grammar Workbook For Dummies,* 2nd Edition, which I also wrote. Those of you who are math challenged will find these books helpful: *Algebra I For Dummies,* 2nd Edition, and *Algebra II For Dummies* by Mary Jane Sterling and *Geometry For Dummies,* 2nd Edition, by Mark Ryan. Wiley publishes all these titles.

I hope (but don't count on the fact) that the SAT you've signed up to take *isn't* less than 12 hours or more than two years away. This book is useful to would-be SAT takers who think planning ahead involves putting your foot on the floor a nanosecond before standing up, as well as those who are sitting around watching their teeth just in case they get a cavity someday. In Chapter 2, I provide a schedule for the obsessively late, the obsessively early, and the normal crowd in between.

Finally, though a lot of the silly jokes in this book arise from interactions with my teenage students, I don't base everything on that age group. If you're hitting college after living a little, good for you. This book can help you find your groove, too. (You'll have to handle the all-nighters yourself.)

How This Book Is Organized

You don't need any extra chores if you're in the last year or two of high school. You're at maximum warp in sports or other extracurricular activities, and you've finally figured out how to impress the freshmen. Now's the time to enjoy life. Nor do you need a million-hour SAT prep course if you're holding down a job or burping a baby (or doing both simultaneously). Luckily, this book doesn't take a thousand hours of your life. In fact, this book should claim only about 25 or 30 hours or perhaps even less of your valuable time, depending on how fast you read and how often you stop to check your instant messages. (Chapter 2 gives you a couple of possible schedules, geared to when you're starting your SAT prep and how harried your life is.) The following sections outline what's where in this book.

Part 1: Surveying the Field: An Overview of the SAT

This part provides an overview of the SAT so you know what's facing you. It's the spot for practical stuff: what to expect on test day, what you're permitted to bring into the test room, how to order (or cancel) score reports, and so on. It includes a bowl of alphabet soup (ACT, SAT, SAT Subject, PSAT/NMSQT), as well as information on what colleges expect and how they interpret your scores. This part also helps students with special needs (foreign students, students needing special accommodations, and so on) navigate the exam and tells everyone how and when to study for it.

Part II: Comprehending the SAT: The Critical Reading Sections

Part II takes you through the wonderful world of reading comprehension, explaining the four types of questions you'll find on the Critical Reading sections (sentence completions, short reading passages, paired passages, and long passages) and the best strategies for each. Tons of practice questions get your reading muscles in shape and ready for the real SAT.

Part III: Getting the "Write" Answers: The Writing Sections

Part III opens the grammar toolbox so you can tackle the Multiple-Choice Writing sections of the SAT. It explains how to apply grammar rules to error-recognition questions as well as to sentence- and paragraph-revision questions. It also describes the best approach for succeeding on the essay portion of the test and shows you how to beat the clock when you write your own essay.

Part IV: Take a Number, Any Number: The Mathematics Sections

Time to fire up the calculator — either the one in your head or the little plastic doodad with batteries. This part takes you on a whirlwind tour of the concepts most likely to help you answer the questions on the SAT Math section. It includes a ton of sample problems (no, not the "I wouldn't date you if you were the last person on earth" type but the "what is the value of x" sort) and shows you the most efficient way to solve them, with or without a calculator, which you're allowed to bring to the test.

Part V: Where the Rubber Meets the Road: Practice Tests

This part contains five practice tests that prepare you well in terms of style and content for the SAT. However, the number of questions and the placement of sections (whether the Mathematics or Critical Reading section appears as Section 2, for example) may vary on the real SAT. No matter. If you practice with the sample tests I give you in Part V, you'll be well prepared to face the big, ugly SAT come test day.

So sharpen your pencil, lock the door, turn off the DVD player, and prepare for take-off!

Part VI: The Part of Tens

Ah, the famous *For Dummies* Part of Tens. In this part, I include two quick, light-hearted chapters about how to de-stress and what to double-check when you're taking the SAT. I also include an appendix that shows you how to score your practice SAT exams so you can get an idea of how ready you are for the real test.

Icons Used in This Book

Icons are those cute little pictures that appear in the margins of this book. They indicate why you should pay special attention to the accompanying text. Here's how to decode them:

This icon points out helpful hints about strategy — what the all-star test takers know and the rookies want to find out.

This icon identifies the sand traps that the SAT writers are hoping you fall into as you take the test. Take note of these warnings so you know what to do (and what not to do) as you move from question to question on the real SAT.

When you see this icon, be sure to file away the information that accompanies it. The material will come in handy as you prepare for (and take) the SAT.

This icon identifies questions that resemble those on the actual SAT. (Be sure to read the answer explanations that always follow the questions.)

Where to Go from Here

Okay, now that you know what's what and where to find it, you have a choice. You can read every single word I've written (I love you! I'd marry you if I weren't already hitched!), or you can check out only the parts of the book that address your "issues," as they say on daytime talk shows. In other words, if you feel confident with your math skills but panicky about the critical reading questions, hit Part II first and give Part IV a pass, at least for now. Or, if vocabulary is your personal monster, read the long-range vocabulary-building tips in Chapter 2 and flip through the whole book, scanning all the vocabulary words that look like *this*. Another good way to start is to take one of the sample tests in Part V, score it using the appendix, and then focus on your weak spots.

No matter what you do next, start by doing something simple: Lower your shoulders. Calm down, stay loose, and score big on the SAT.

Part I
Surveying the Field: An Overview of the SAT

"I always get a good night's sleep the day before a test so I'm relaxed and alert the next morning. Then I grab my pen, eat a banana, and I'm on my way."

In this part . . .

As an SAT candidate, you need to follow one cardinal rule as you prepare to take what is perhaps the most important test of your life to this point: Know your adversary. In this case, your adversary is a little paper booklet with a deceptively innocent appearance. Don't be fooled; the SAT holds one key to your future. To make your fight with the SAT fair, you must tour the SAT's native habitat and figure out how to speak its language.

Part I is a field guide to the SAT: what it tests, when you can and should take it, where you can find it, and how it affects your chances for admission to college. Part I also explains when to guess and what to do to stay calm on SAT day.

Chapter 1

Pouring Your Brain into Little Ovals: The SAT

You may be wondering why you're stuck with the SAT. Unbelievable as it may seem, the test was established to help, not *annihilate* (wipe out completely) students. Right about now you're probably thinking that I'm giving you the old *it's for your own good* line that authority figures always use when they're about to drop you off a cliff. But the SAT was created to level the playing field — to predict the likelihood of academic success of students, regardless of family background, connections, and other privileges. The SAT has never actually succeeded in this lofty goal, and the college admissions playing field still resembles the Alps more than the Great Plains. However, the SAT does give colleges a *number* for each student that, theoretically at least, measures the ability of everyone who takes it without regard for the dollar value of trust funds sitting in the vault.

In this chapter — whether you have a trust fund or not — you can find the ABCs of the SATs: why you need to take the exam; when, where, and how often to take it; where to send your scores; and how to deal with special needs. Chapter 1 also provides a peek into the structure of the exam itself.

Sitting for the SAT Rather Than ACTing Up

Most college applicants pass through one of two giant gates on their way into U.S. colleges and some foreign schools. One is the ACT, and the other is the SAT. Most colleges accept scores from either test; check with the admissions office of the colleges on your list to be sure you're taking the tests they prescribe. (A good general rule for college admissions is give them what they want, when they want it.) The SAT and the ACT tests are roughly the same in terms of difficulty. Unless you're really obsessed, don't bother to take both. Because you're reading *SAT For Dummies,* 8th Edition, rather than downloading the latest rap song, presumably you're taking the SAT. But if you're also taking the ACT, don't forget to check out *ACT For Dummies,* 5th Edition, by Lisa Zimmer Hatch and Scott Hatch (Wiley).

Don't confuse the SAT with the SAT Subject Tests. You may have heard different names for both kinds of tests, including SAT I and SAT II, but those terms are now officially *obsolete* (outdated, so yesterday) because the company that makes them has renamed them the SAT and SAT Subject Tests. (Just to make life a little bit harder, the testing company sometimes calls the SAT the SAT Reasoning Test.) Whatever you call them, be sure you know the difference. The SAT tests the proverbial three Rs — reading, 'riting, and 'rithmetic (but clearly not spelling). The SAT Subject Tests cover biology, history, math, and a ton of other stuff. Depending on the schools you apply to, you may have to take one or more Subject Tests or none at all.

Many libraries and nearly all bookstores have college guides — 20-pound paperbacks describing each and every institution of higher learning you may apply to. Check out the colleges on your list to see which tests they accept or require. Be sure to check the copyright date of the guide — the SAT went through some major changes in 2005, so earlier books may not be accurate. You may also visit individual college Web sites for the most up-to-date requirements. The official Web site of the College Board (the makers of the SAT) also lists popular colleges and the tests they want to *inflict* (impose) on you.

If college isn't in your immediate future, you may want to take the SAT just to see how you do. If your plans include a stint in the armed forces or hitchhiking through Borneo before hitting higher education, you can keep your options open by taking the SAT before you go. Also, if you take the SAT while formal "book-learning" is still fresh in your mind, you may do better. Then when you retire your thumb or trigger finger, you have some scores to send to the college of your choice, though if a long period of time has passed, the colleges may ask for an updated score. How long is *a long period of time?* It depends on the college you're applying to. Some may ask for an updated SAT after only a couple of years; others are more lenient. Obviously, whether you took three years off to work on the world's deepest tan or ten years to decipher the meaning of an obscure archaeological site also influences the admissions office's decision on SAT scores. Check with the college(s) you're interested in and explain your situation.

Getting Set for the SAT: Registering for the Right Test at the Right Time

The SAT is given at select high schools throughout the United States and in English-speaking schools in many other countries. Even home-schoolers can take the SAT, though not in their own living rooms. To find the test center nearest you or to request a registration form, ask the college or guidance counselor at your high school. If you're home-schooled, call the nearest public or private high school. Or, you may register through the SAT Web site (www.collegeboard.com). If you're hitting the SAT for a second time, you can register by phone. Call the College Board's Customer Service center (within the U.S.: 866-756-7346; outside the U.S.: 212-713-7789). Hearing-impaired test takers can call the TTY Customer Service number (within the U.S.: 888-857-2477; outside the U.S.: 609-882-4118). If you're stranded on a desert island without a phone, the Internet, or a school office (in which case the SAT is the least of your problems), try writing to the College Board SAT Program, P.O. Box 025505, Miami, FL 33102 for the forms you need. The SAT costs $47, though fee waivers are available for those experiencing financial difficulties, and extra services — additional score reports, for example — cost more. (See "Meeting Special Needs" in this chapter for more information.)

In high-stress situations — Martian invasions, nuclear meltdowns, the cancellation of your favorite TV show — rumors *abound* (grow and thrive). So too with the SAT. You've probably heard that certain versions of the SAT — the ones given in October or November or the ones given in a particular state — are easier than others. Not so. The SAT makers include a section in the test that serves as a statistical tool to ensure that all the SAT tests, regardless of when or where they're given, are equal in difficulty. This part of the test, called the *equating* section, is the one section that you must answer that counts for absolutely nothing (for you). No matter how well you do on the equating section, or (if you're having a bad day) how badly you blow it, the equating section won't affect your score. However, because the equating section isn't labeled, you have to take every section seriously.

The SAT pops up on the calendar seven times a year. You can take the exam as often as you want. If you're a *masochist* — you enjoy pain — you can take all seven tests, but most people stick to this schedule:

Autumn of junior year (about 1¾ years before college entrance): Time to take the PSAT/NMSQT.

Spring of junior year (about 1¼ years before college entrance): Take the SAT strictly for practice, though you can send your scores in if you're pleased with them.

Autumn of senior year (a bit less than a year before entrance): The SAT strikes again. Early-decision candidates prefer taking the test in October or November; regular applicants may choose from any of the three autumn dates, including December.

Winter of senior year (half-year before entrance): Some SAT-lovers take the exam in autumn and again in winter, hoping that practice will make perfect, at least in the eyes of the colleges. The high scores won't hurt (and you probably will improve, just because the whole routine will be familiar), but don't put a lot of energy into repeated bouts of SAT fever. Your grades and extracurriculars may suffer if you're too fixated on the SAT, and you may end up hurting your overall application.

If you're transferring or starting your college career midyear, you may sit for the SAT in January, March, May, or June. Check with your counselor or with the college of your choice and go with that recommendation.

Everyone takes the SAT on Saturday except for those students who can't for religious reasons. If you fall into that category, your SAT will be on Sunday. Get a letter from your cleric (religious leader) on letterhead and mail it in with your registration form.

In terms of test sites, the early bird gets the worm. (Do you ever wonder why no one ever deals with the worm's fate? He got up early, too, and look what happened to him.) When you register, you may request a test site, but if it's filled, you'll get an alternate. So don't delay; send in the form or register online as soon as you know when and where you want to take the exam.

Meeting Special Needs

If you have a learning disability, you may be allowed to take the SAT under special conditions. The first step is to get an Eligibility Form from your school counselor. (Home-schoolers, call the local high school.) You may also want to ask your college counseling office for a copy of the *College Board Services for Students with Disabilities Brochure* (pamphlet). If your school doesn't have one, contact the College Board directly (609-771-7137, TTY 609-882-4118) or check the testing agency's Web site (www.collegeboard.com). File the form well in advance of the time you expect to take the test. Generally, if you're entitled to extra test time in your high school, you'll be eligible for extra time on the SAT. What does *extra time* really mean? Extra time equals 1½ the usual amount for each section. So if regular test takers have 20 minutes for a section, extended-timers get 30 minutes.

¡Atención! What every foreign student needs to know about the SAT

First, welcome to the U.S.'s worst invention, the Seriously Annoying Test (SAT), which you're taking so that you can attend an American institution. Getting ready for this exam may make you consider another American institution, one with padded rooms and bars on the windows. But a high SAT score is certainly within reach for individuals who have studied English as a second language. Here's one secret: The SAT's formal vocabulary is actually easier than American conversational English and slang. So even if you look up at the sky in puzzlement when someone asks, "What's up?" you should be able to decode an SAT question. (By the way, "What's up?" is a general inquiry into your state of mind, current occupation, and plans for the immediate future.) As a foreign student, pay special attention to the vocabulary words in this book. You may want to keep a notebook or a computer file of new words you encounter as you work through the sample questions.

Also turn your concentration up to "totally intense" in the math section (see Part IV) of this prep book because arithmetic doesn't change from language to language. Neither does geometry or algebra. If you can crack the basic language used to put forth the problem, you should be able to rack up a ton of points.

At no additional charge, the SAT also provides wheelchair accessibility, large-print tests, and other accommodations for students who need them. The key is to submit the Eligibility Form early so that the SAT makers — the College Board — can ask for any extra documentation and set up appropriate test conditions for you. You can send paper documentation, or, beginning in 2010, file an Eligibility Form via the Internet. Check out www.collegeboard.com for details.

Questions about special needs? Your local high school's counselor or principal can help, or you can e-mail the College Board (ssd@info.collegeboard.org).

If your special need resides in your wallet, you can apply for a fee waiver, which is available to low-income high school juniors and seniors who live in the United States, Puerto Rico, and other American territories. Ask your school counselor for an application. (As with everything to do with the SAT, if you're a home-schooler, call the local high school for a form.) And be careful to avoid extra fees when you can. You'll run into extra charges for late or changed registration and for some extras — super-speedy scores, an analysis of your performance, and the like. (See the section "Scoring on the SAT" later in this chapter for more information on score-reporting options.)

Measuring Your Mind: What the SAT Tests

Statistically, the SAT tests whether or not you'll be successful in your first year of college. Admissions officers keep track of their students' SAT scores and have a pretty good idea which scores signal trouble and which scores indicate clear sailing. Many college guides list the average SAT scores of entering freshmen.

That said, the picture gets complicated whenever the wide-angle lens narrows to focus on an individual, such as you, and admissions offices are well aware of this fact. How rigorous your high school is, whether you deal well with multiple-choice questions, and how you feel physically and mentally on SAT day (fight with Mom? bad romance? week-old sushi?) all influence your score. Bottom line: Stop obsessing about the SAT's unfairness (and it is unfair) and prepare.

The college admission essay is a great place to put your scores in perspective. If you face some special circumstances, such as a learning disability, a school that doesn't value academics, a family tragedy, and so on, you may want to explain your situation in an essay. No essay wipes out the bad impression created by an extremely low SAT score, but a good essay gives the college a way to interpret your achievement and to see you, the applicant, in more detail. For help with the college admission essay, take a look at *College Admission Essays For Dummies,* published by Wiley and written by yours truly.

The SAT doesn't test facts you studied in school; you don't need to know when Columbus sailed across the Atlantic or how to calculate the molecular weight of magnesium in order to answer an SAT question. Instead, the SAT takes aim at your ability to follow a logical sequence, to comprehend what you've read, and to write clearly in standard English. The math portion checks whether you were paying attention or snoring when little details like algebra were taught. Check out the next sections for a bird's-eye view of the three SAT topics.

Critical Reading

This topic pops up three times per SAT, in terms of what counts toward your score. (All SATs include an extra section in either reading or math that the SAT makers use for research only.) You face two 25-minute sections and one 20-minute section of Critical Reading, a fancy term for reading comprehension. Each section contains sentence completions and reading comprehension passages that are either short (about 100 words) or long (600 to 800 words). You also see a set of paired passages — a double-take on one topic from two different points of view.

Sentence completions

The sentence completions are just fill-ins. You will encounter three sets of five, six, or eight questions. Sentence completions test vocabulary and your ability to decode the sentence structure, as in the following:

The SAT sentence-completion section is guaranteed to give you a headache, so the test makers thoughtfully provide _____ with each exam.

(A) aspirin

(B) dictionaries

(C) answer keys

(D) tutoring

(E) scalp massage

The answer is Choice (A). Given that the sentence specifies *headache,* your best choice is *aspirin,* at least in SAT world. In real life you may prefer a day at the spa, but the test makers haven't included that option. Choice (E) is a possibility, too, but the SAT goes with the best answer, not the only answer.

Reading comprehension

Reading comprehension questions are a mixture of literal (just the facts, ma'am) and interpretive/analytical. You may be asked to choose the meaning of a word in context or to assess the author's tone or point of view. Passages may be drawn from the natural and social sciences, humanities, or fiction, as in the following:

Tim was frantic to learn that the first GC-MP8 handheld was already in circulation. And here he was wasting his time in college! The degree that he had pursued so doggedly for the past three years now seemed nothing more than a gigantic waste of time. The business world, that's where he belonged, marketing someone else's technology with just enough of a twist to allow him to patent "his" idea.

In this passage, the word *his* is in quotation marks

(A) because it's a pronoun

(B) because the reader is supposed to hiss at Tim, whom everyone hates

(C) to show that the idea really came from someone else

(D) to demonstrate that the idea really came from a female masquerading as a male

(E) because the typesetter had some extra quotation marks

The answer is (C). These quotation marks refer to Tim's claim to "someone else's technology." Although he isn't quoted directly, the quotation marks around *his* imply that Tim says that a particular invention is his, when in fact it isn't.

Writing

To the *chagrin* (disappointment or embarrassment) of English teachers everywhere, the SAT Writing sections contain only a sliver of actual writing: one 25-minute essay on a topic that you've never seen before, plus 35 minutes' worth of short answers. Why so little writing? As those of us who sit with 4-foot-high piles of essays on our laps know, it takes a long time to read student prose. The SAT test makers must pay people to read and score essays — a much more expensive and time-consuming proposition than running a bubble sheet through a scanner. The multiple-choice questions check your ability to recognize errors in grammar, punctuation, and word use and to make sentence revisions. You also see a couple of *pseudo* (fake) first drafts of student essays and answer some questions about the writer's intentions. In these longer passages, you again have to select the best revisions.

Error recognition

Error-recognition questions are long sentences (they have to be long to allow enough room for four possible errors) with underlined portions. You choose the portion with a mistake or select (E) for *no error*.

Flabberton <u>denounced his lover</u> for her <u>work with</u> the Revolutionary <u>Band, he</u> had a new
        A   B   C

bass guitarist lined up whose musical talents <u>were, he</u> said, "awesome." <u>No error.</u>
                                                D   E

The correct choice is (C). Each half of the sentence can stand alone, so a comma alone can't join them. You need a semicolon or a word such as *and* or *so* to glue the two parts together.

Sentence revision

In these questions, the test gurus underline one portion of a sentence and provide four alternatives. Choice (A) always repeats the original wording.

Having been turned down by 15 major league baseball teams, Flabberton changed to basketball, and he succeeded <u>in his goal where he was aiming to be a professional athlete</u>.

(A) in his goal where he was aiming to be a professional athlete

(B) in that he reached his goal of aiming to be a professional athlete

(C) where he became a professional athlete

(D) in his goal of becoming a professional athlete

(E) because he wanted million-dollar sneaker ads

The answer is (D). Just kidding about (E), though an endorsement contract actually was Flabberton's motivation.

Paragraph revision

These questions throw you into the mind of a fairly competent student writer who has had only enough time to complete a first draft of an essay on a general topic. Some of the questions ask you to combine sentences effectively; others resemble the sentence-revision section — an underlined portion with possible improvements or alternate versions of entire sentences.

Essay

This section is the only spot in the Writing section where you actually get to write something. And I do mean *write*. For those of you who have keyboards permanently implanted under your fingernails, this section may be a handwriting challenge. And thanks to ever-evolving technology, an image of your essay — inkblots, saliva drools, and all — will be available on the Web to the college admission offices that are reviewing your applications. Start practicing your penmanship.

In terms of what you write, the essay is a standard, short discussion of a general topic that the SAT makers provide. You have to take a stand and defend it with evidence (from literature, history, and/or your own experience or observation). The main challenge is time: You have only 25 minutes to think, write, and revise.

Mathematics

SAT math questions rely on Algebra II and some advanced topics in geometry, statistics, and probability. Your SAT contains two 25-minute Math sections and one 20-minute section that count toward your score (and perhaps one equating section that the SAT uses for its own statistical analysis only). Almost all the questions are multiple choice, in which you choose the answer from among five possibilities. Ten are *grid-ins* in which you supply an answer and bubble in the actual number, not a multiple-choice letter (check out Chapter 11 for more on these). Here's a sample multiple-choice problem:

If $xy - 12 = z$, and the value of x is 2, which of the following must be true?

(A) $z =$ the number of days since you've had no homework

(B) $y = 12 + z$

(C) $z = 2y - 12$

(D) $2y - z = 100$

(E) $y >$ the number of hours you have to spend studying SAT math

The answer is (A). Just kidding. It's actually (E). Oops, kidding again. The correct choice is (C).

Scoring on the SAT

No, I'm not talking about *that* kind of scoring. I'm talking academics here, or at least the SAT's version of academics. The maximum SAT score is 2,400 (with a top score of 800 on each of the three main sections: Critical Reading, Writing, and Math).

You get one point for each correct answer you supply on the SAT, and for everything but the essay and math grid-ins, you lose ¼ point for each incorrect answer. (If you make a mistake on a grid-in, you receive no points, but nothing is deducted.) Two (severely underpaid) English teachers who have undergone special training in SAT scoring standards read your essay. Each reader awards it 1 to 6 points. If the readers disagree by more than one point, which happens in about 6 percent of the essays, a third super-expert reader weighs in. When you get your Writing score, you see a score of 20 to 80 for the multiple-choice questions and an essay subscore of 2 to 12. The multiple-choice score counts for 70 percent of your total Writing score, and the essay for 30 percent.

The SAT isn't curved, but raw scores are converted to a number between 200 and 800. You receive 200 just for showing up, and an 800 — the highest score — can be achieved even if you've made a few errors. How did the test makers settle upon this score range? I have no idea!

To guess or not to guess; that is the question. The answer is a definite *maybe*. On the grid-ins, always guess because you won't get a penalty for a wrong answer. If you have no clue on the grid-ins, bubble in your birthday or the number of cavities you had during your last checkup. For the other five-answer, multiple-choice questions, try to eliminate obviously wrong answers. If you can dump one, you have a one in four chance of guessing correctly. Go for it. If you can't eliminate anything, leave the question blank. Always guess if you can eliminate two of the five choices because the odds favor you. Students who make this sort of educated guess usually score higher on the SAT than they would have if they'd left more blanks.

The basic fee for the test is $47, with the first four score reports being free, but you pay about $10 extra for additional score reports. (Prices, of course, are always subject to change, and don't expect any to go down. Check the College Board Web site for pricing changes.) You can request additional score reports on the (how do they think of these names?) Additional Score Report Request Form, which you can download from the Web site.

For a higher fee ($12.50), you can get a detailed analysis of your test performance — how many of each sort of question you answered right and wrong and how difficult each question was. Then you can tailor your prep hours to the stuff that's hard for you. Ask for the *Student Answer Service* when you register. For even more money ($18), the SAT sends you a copy of the questions and your answers, along with a form you can use to order a copy of your answer sheet, but only for certain test dates. Look for the *Question and Answer Service* when you register.

If you're planning to take another SAT, spring for the *Student Answer Service*. Seeing what you got wrong gives you a blueprint for review.

Score reports arrive at your high school about five weeks after you take the test. (Home-schooled? Call your local high school for results.) If you're the antsy type and are willing to fork over a few more dollars, you can find out the good news by phone. Call Customer Service (within the U.S.: 866-756-7346; outside the U.S.: 212-713-7789; TTY 888-857-2477 for the U.S. or 609-882-4118 for outside the U.S.). Have a credit card, your registration number, and your birth date ready. If you have access to the Internet, you can create a free (yes, something's actually free!) account on the College Board Web site (www.collegeboard.com). Look for *My SAT Online Score Report.* It tells you your 200–800 scores in Critical Reading, Writing, and Mathematics, and some information on how well you did on various types of questions.

Chapter 2

Getting Ready, Set, and Going: Preparing for the SAT

In This Chapter

▶ Tailoring SAT prep to your life

▶ Making the most of the time remaining before the test

▶ Handling last-minute nerves

▶ Working effectively on the morning of the test

*W*hat? You've discovered how to tie your shoelaces and you still haven't started to prepare for the SAT? Tsk, tsk. You're in trouble. You should have begun to study *in utero* (before birth) by having your mother play vocabulary tapes next to her stomach. And all that time you wasted in kindergarten playing with blocks when you could have been studying square roots! You'll have to give up sleeping to make up for lost time. And don't even *think* about that party.

Does the preceding paragraph sound like the voice inside your head? If so, you need to take a deep breath and release that anxiety. SAT prep can start at many different points in your life and still be effective. In this chapter, you find long-term and short-term strategies for SAT prep, as well as medium-length prep for the Average Joe and Josephine. And for those of you who suddenly realized that The Test is next week, I provide a panic-button scenario. Lastly, I explain what to do to maximize your score the night before the test (speaking of panic) as well as the morning of SAT day.

Flying with the Early Bird: A Long-Range Plan

Okay, so you're the type of person who buys summer clothes in December. (By the way, thanks a lot. Because of you, all the department stores feature bikinis when I'm trying to buy a sweater.) To put it another way, you're not in diapers, but the test isn't coming up within the next year. Congratulations. Check out the following long-range SAT prep plan:

✔ **Sign up for challenging courses in school.** If you're in high school, *eschew* (reject) courses such as "The Poetry of Greeting Cards" and "Arithmetic Is Your Friend." Go for subjects that stretch your mind. Specifically, stick it out with math at least through Algebra II and Geometry. If high school is in your rearview mirror, check out extension or enrichment adult-ed courses.

✔ **If possible, take a vocabulary-rich course.** When I say that a good vocabulary is key to SAT success, I'm not indulging in *hyperbole* (exaggeration). If your school offers classes with a lot of reading, go for them. Some schools even have whole courses devoted to vocabulary (mine has a course in Greek and Latin roots). These classes may not be as exciting as "Cultural Interpretations of Music Videos," but they pay off.

✔ **Get into the habit of reading.** Cereal boxes, Internet pop-up balloons, and 1,000-page novels — they're all good, though they're not all equal. The more you read, and the more difficult the material you read, the more your reading comprehension improves.

✔ **Do a daily crossword puzzle in your newspaper or check out *Crossword Puzzle Challenges For Dummies* by Patrick Berry (Wiley).** I know. Crossword puzzles seem like a good way to become a candidate for Nerds Anonymous. But you can discover a lot by *pondering* (thinking deeply about) language on a daily basis. Plus, some people (me, for example) actually enjoy crossword puzzles. But then I never claimed to be anything other than a nerd.

✔ **Write letters or e-mails to the editor.** The editor of anything. Find a point of view and start sending off your prose — to the school or local paper, to national magazines, to radio or television stations. The SAT essay calls upon you to make a case for your point of view. The more you get used to creating a written argument, the easier the essay will be. As a side benefit, you may have a civic impact.

✔ **Keep your math notebooks.** Resist the urge to burn your geometry text the minute the last class is over. Keep your math notebooks and folders of homework papers. From time to time, go over the important concepts. The notebook may *evoke* (call to mind) the context in which you studied right triangles or square roots. For example, if you see a stain next to an explanation of factoring, it may take you back to that immortal day when Herbie threw a spitball at you while the teacher was working out a factoring problem on the board. If you're mentally back in the class, you may find that you remember more of the mathematical explanation the teacher gave. (Of course, if you spent the rest of the class lobbing spitballs back at Herbie instead of paying attention, you're out of luck. Turn to Part IV for a general math review.)

✔ **Look through the chapters in this book that explain the structure of each type of SAT question.** When SAT day dawns, you shouldn't be facing any surprises. Be sure that you're familiar with the directions for each section so that you don't have to waste time reading them during the actual exam.

✔ **Take all five practice exams in Part V of this book.** After you identify your weak spots (not that you actually have any — just areas where you could be even more excellent), hit the practice chapters for the types of questions that bother you.

✔ **Take the PSAT/NMSQT.** This "mini-SAT" gives you a chance to experience test conditions. It may also open the door to a pretty snazzy scholarship, the National Merit.

As the SAT approaches, you long-range planners can relax. You're in a fine position to *condescend* (act superior) to all the goof-offs who didn't even begin to think about the exam until junior year in high school. (What? You're one of those goof-offs? Never fear. I offer you some hope and help in the next section.)

Hitting the Golden Mean: A Medium-Range Plan

In this category you're conscientious but not obsessive. You have a bit less than a year before SAT day (in high school terms, you're a junior), and you have a reasonable amount of time to devote to SAT prep. You're in fine shape, though you may have to take some ribbing from the "I've got a career plan even though I'm not old enough for working papers" types. Here's your strategy:

- ✔ **Do all you can to extract maximum vocabulary growth from your last school year before the SAT.** Make friends with words. Listen to talk radio (the stations with on-air fundraisers, not the drive-by call-in shows that feature a hot discussion of the Yankees' chances for a three-peat) or watch sophisticated talk shows on television (not the shows that feature oatmeal addicts and the men and women who love them). Take some thick books out of the library and use them for more than missiles to hurl at your annoying little sister. *Peruse* (read thoroughly, scrutinize) the newspaper every day, preferably one that stays away from extensive coverage of celebrity Botox.

- ✔ **Work on your writing.** If your school offers an elective in nonfiction writing, go for it. Or volunteer to write for the school newspaper. Write letters or e-mails to the editor (see a fuller explanation in the section "Flying with the Early Bird: A Long-Range Plan"). Become comfortable with the sort of writing that makes a case for a particular point of view because that's what you have to do on the SAT.

- ✔ **Get a math study-buddy.** I'm not talking about a tutor. Yes, you can find out a lot from someone who dreams quadratic equations. But you can also profit from studying with someone who is on your own level of ability. As the two of you work together, solving problems and figuring out formulas, you can pound the knowledge firmly into your brain. All teachers know that you learn best what you have to explain to someone else. Plus, a study-buddy probably can explain what he or she knows in a different way. If the teacher's explanation didn't do it for you, your friend's may.

- ✔ **Resurrect your Algebra II book or borrow one from a friendly math teacher.** Look through the chapters that made you tear your hair out the first time you went through the book. Refresh your memory with a sample problem or two.

- ✔ **Look through *SAT For Dummies*, 8th Edition.** Read the explanations of each type of question. Be sure that you know the directions and format by heart.

- ✔ **Take one of the practice exams in Part V of this book.** After you know which sort of question is likely to stump you, do all the relevant practice questions.

- ✔ **Take the PSAT/NMSQT.** You can't pass up a chance to experience the exam in its native habitat (a testing center), even if the test is shorter than the real SAT.

If you follow this plan, you Golden Meaners should be in fine shape for the SAT. (I refer to the ancient Greek ideal, the Golden Mean, also known as the perfect middle. If this expression makes you say, "It's all Greek to me," you may want to read some Greek mythology. References to those stories show up all the time on the SAT.)

Controlling the Panic: A Short-Range Plan

The SAT is next month or (gulp!) next week. Not ideal, but not hopeless either. Use the following plan to get through it alive:

- ✔ **Read Chapter 1 of this book carefully.** Find out what sort of questions are on the exam and when guessing is a good idea. Take a quick look at the chapters that explain each type of question.

- ✔ **Do one complete practice exam from Part V.** Yes, I know. Nearly four good hours gone forever. But you should hit one exam, just so you know what the SAT experience is like.

- ✔ **Work on at least some of the practice questions for all your trouble spots.** Obviously, the more practice the better, but even a little can go a long way in SAT prep.

- ✔ **Clear the deck of all unnecessary activity so you can study as much as possible.** I don't recommend that you skip your sister's wedding (or your physics homework), but if you can put something off, do so. Use the extra time to hit a few more practice questions.

Should you take an SAT prep course?

Complete this sentence: SAT prep courses

(A) don't make a huge difference in your score

(B) employ Ivy League graduates who are paying off college loans until their film deals come through

(C) provide jobs for unemployed doctoral candidates finishing dissertations on the sex life of bacteria

(D) keep underpaid high school teachers from total *penury* (poverty)

(E) are great places to pick up prom dates

The answer: All of the above. I won't explain (B) through (E), because unless you're desperate for a prom partner, you're probably interested only in (A). The company that makes the SAT has studied the effects of SAT prep courses and found that in general they have a minimal effect on your score — about 10 points for verbal and 15 to 20 points for math. A few long-term courses do make a slightly bigger difference (25 to 40 points combined verbal and math), but because you have to devote 40-plus hours to them, you get approximately one extra point per hour of study. Not a very efficient use of your time! You've already proved your brilliance by purchasing *SAT For Dummies,* 8th Edition. If you work your way through the book with some care, you'll have done enough.

I teach seniors, and every year I see at least a couple of students put themselves in danger of failing English 12 because they're spending all their homework time on SAT prep. Bad idea. Yes, you want to send good scores to the colleges of your choice, but you also want to send a decent high school transcript. Prepare for the test, but do your homework too.

Snoozing through the Night Before

No matter what, don't study on SAT day minus one. The only thing that last-minute studying does is make you more nervous. What happens is simple: The closer you get to test day, the more you take notice of the stuff you don't know. On the eve of the test, every unfamiliar vocabulary word is outlined in neon, as is every *obscure* (not well known, hidden) math formula. And every time you find something that you didn't know — or forget something that you did know at one time — your heart beats a little faster. Panic doesn't equal a good night's sleep, and eight solid hours of snoozing is the best possible prep for three-plus hours of multiple-choice questions.

Also, resist the urge to call your friends who are also taking the test. Chances are they're nervous. The old saying, "Misery loves company," definitely applies to the SAT. Instead, place everything you need on The Morning in one spot, ready and waiting for use. Lay out some comfortable clothes, preferably layers. If the test room is too cold, you want to be able to add a sweater. If it's too hot, you may find removing a jacket or sweater helpful without getting arrested for indecent exposure.

After you set up everything for SAT day, do something that's fun . . . but not too much fun. Don't hit the clubs or party down with your friends. Find an activity that eases you through the last couple of pre-SAT waking hours. Go to sleep at a reasonable hour (after setting your alarm clock) and dream of little, penciled ovals patting you gently on the shoulder.

Getting there is half the fun

On the morning of the SAT, what should you avoid more than anything?

(A) a relaxing session of your favorite cartoons

(B) a two-hour detour on the road to the test center

(C) a kiss from Grandma

(D) a slurp from your dog

(E) a swim with your pet goldfish

The answer is (B). Did you ever watch an old sitcom on television, one with a pregnancy plotline? Inevitably the mad dash to the hospital is lengthened by a detour, a traffic jam, or a wrong turn. On SAT day, you don't want to be in that old sitcom. Make sure that your journey to the test center is event-free. Try the route there at least once before test day, preferably at the same time and on the same day of the week (that is, Saturday morning, unless you're taking the test on Sunday because of religious observances) so you know what sort of traffic to expect. Leave the house with plenty of time to spare. The idea is to arrive rested and as relaxed as someone who is facing 200-plus minutes of test can be.

Sailing through SAT-Day Morning

SAT day isn't a good time to oversleep. Set the alarm clock and ask a reliable parent/guardian/friend to verify that you've awakened on time. If you're not a morning person, you may need a few additional minutes. Then, no matter how nutritionally challenged your usual breakfast is, eat something healthful. Unless it upsets your stomach, go for protein (eggs, cheese, meat, tofu, and so on). Stay away from sugary items (cereals made primarily from Red Dye No. 23, corn syrup, and the like) because sugar gives you a surge of energy and then a large chunk of fatigue. If you think you'll be hungry during the morning, throw some trail mix, fruit, or other noncandy snacks into your backpack. Then hit the road for the test center.

If disaster strikes — fever, car trouble, little brother's arrest — and you can't take the SAT on the appointed day, call the College Board and request that they transfer your fee to the next available date.

Bringing the right stuff

Be sure to have these items with you:

- **Admission ticket for the SAT:** Don't leave home without it! You can't get in just by swearing that you "have one at home on top of the TV."

- **Photo identification:** The SAT accepts drivers' licenses, school IDs, passports, or other official documents that include your picture. The SAT doesn't accept Social Security cards or library cards. If you're not sure what to bring, ask your school counselor or call the College Board directly.

- **No. 2 pencils:** Don't guess. Look for the No. 2 on the side of the pencil. Take at least three or four sharpened pencils with you. Be sure the pencils have usable erasers or bring one of those cute pink rubber erasers you used in elementary school.

✔ **Calculator:** Bringing a calculator is optional. You don't absolutely need a calculator to take the SAT, but it does help on some questions. A four-function, scientific, or graphing calculator is acceptable. Anything with a keyboard (a minicomputer, in other words), a phone, or a handheld PDA (personal digital assistant) is barred, as are electronic writing pads and devices that use a stylus to input information. So is any device that needs to be plugged in or that makes noise. If you're the type of person who wears both suspenders and a belt, just in case one fails, bring a backup calculator and extra batteries. Also, be sure to bring a calculator that you've used before. Test day isn't the time to acquaint yourself with a new device!

✔ **Handkerchief or tissue:** I add this one because as an experienced proctor, I know that absolutely nothing is more annoying than a continuous drip or sniffle. Blow your nose and do the rest of the room — and yourself — a favor!

✔ **Watch:** In case the wall clock is missing, broken, or out of your line of vision, a watch is crucial. Don't bring one that beeps because the proctor may take it away if it disturbs other test takers.

After you arrive at the test center, take out what you need and stow the rest of the stuff in a backpack under your seat. Don't forget to turn off your cellphone or beeper, if you have one.

The test proctor doesn't allow scrap paper, books, and other school supplies (rulers, compasses, highlighters, and so on) in the test room, so be sure to leave these items behind. Also, no iPods or other music devices. You have to swing along to the tune inside your head.

Handling test tension

Unless you have ice cubes where everyone else has emotions, you're probably nervous when you arrive at the test center. Try a couple of stretches and head shakes to *dispel* (chase away) tension. During the exam, wriggle your feet and move your shoulders up and down whenever you feel yourself tightening up. Some people like neck rolls (pretend that your neck is made of spaghetti and let your head droop in a big circle). If you roll your neck or move your head to either side, however, be sure to close your eyes. Don't risk a charge of cheating. Just like an Olympic diver preparing to go off of the board, take a few deep breaths before you begin the test and anytime during the test when you feel nervous or out of control.

You get one break per hour, which you probably want to spend in the bathroom or out in the hallway near the test room. During breaks, *stay away* from your fellow test victims, including your best friend. You don't want to hear someone else's version of the right answer. ("Everything in Section 2 was (B)! I got negative 12 for that one! You didn't? Uh oh.") If you like pain, allow yourself to talk over the test with your friends *after* the whole thing's over — great SAT-day night date talk, if you never want to see your date again. After you finish the exam, you can obsess about wrong answers until the cows come home. (Where do cows go? To the mall? To the office? I'm from New York City, so the only cows I see are pictures on milk cartons.)

Starting off

The test proctor distributes the booklets with, I always think, a *vindictive* thump. (*Vindictive* means "seeking revenge," the sort of attitude that says, "Ha, ha! You're taking this awful test and I'm not! Serves you right!") Before you get to the actual questions, the proctor instructs you how to fill in the top of the answer sheet with your name, date of birth, Social Security number, registration number, and so forth. Your admission ticket has the necessary information. You also have to copy some numbers from your test booklet onto the answer sheet. You must grid in all those numbers and letters. Filling in bubbles with a pencil is such a fun way to spend a weekend morning, don't you think?

Don't open the test booklet early. Big no-no! You'll be sent home with a large *C* (for Cheater) engraved on your forehead. Just kidding about the forehead, but *not* kidding about the sent-home part. The proctor can can (no, not can-can) you for starting early, working after time is called, or looking at the wrong section.

The proctor announces each section and tells you when to start and stop. The proctor probably uses the wall clock or his/her own wristwatch to time you. When the proctor says that you're starting at 9:08 and finishing at 9:33, take a moment to glance at the watch you brought. If you have a different time, reset your watch. Marching to a different drummer may be fun, but not during the SAT. You want to be on the same page and in the same time warp as the proctor.

Focusing during the test

Keep your eyes on your own paper, except for quick glimpses at your watch. No, I'm not just saying so because cheating is bad and you'll get busted. Keeping your eyes where they belong is a way to concentrate on the task at hand. If you glance around the room, I guarantee you'll see someone who has already finished, even if only three nanoseconds have elapsed since the section began. You'll panic: *Why is he finished and I'm only on Question 2? He'll get into Harvard and I won't!* You don't need this kind of idea rattling around in your head when you should be analyzing the author's tone in passage three.

If your eye wants to run around sending signals to your brain like *I glimpsed number 15 and it looks hard,* create a window of concentration. Place your hand over the questions you've already done and your answer sheet over the questions you haven't gotten to yet. Keep only one or two questions in eye range. As you work, move your hand and the answer sheet, exposing only one or two questions at a time.

You aren't allowed to use scrap paper, but you *are* allowed to write all over the test booklet. If you eliminate a choice, put an *X* through it. If you think you've got two possible answers but aren't sure which is best, circle the ones you're considering. Then you can return to the question and take a guess. (See Chapter 1 for a full explanation of when to guess and when to skip.)

I had an uncle who always buttoned his sweater so that he had two extra buttonholes left at the bottom. As you grid in your answers, avoid ending up like my uncle. When you choose an answer, say (silently, to yourself), "The answer to number 12 is (B)." Look at the answer sheet to be sure you're on line 12, coloring in the little (B). Some people like to answer three questions at a time, writing the answers in the test booklet and *then* transferring them to the answer sheet. Not a bad idea! The answer sheet has alternating stripes of shaded and nonshaded ovals, three questions per stripe. The color helps you ensure that you're putting your answers in the correct spot. Take care not to run out of time, however. Nothing from your test booklet counts; only the answers you grid in add to your score.

Pacing yourself

The SAT makers do all kinds of fancy statistical calculations to see which questions fool most of the people most of the time, and which are the equivalent of "How many points are awarded for a three-point field goal?" (That was an actual question on an athlete's final exam in one college, no kidding. Needless to say the athlete was considered a top prospect for the school's basketball team.) After the test makers know which questions are easy, medium, and hard, they place them more or less in that order on the exam (except on the reading comprehension passages).

What this means is that as you move through a particular section, you may find yourself feeling more and more challenged. What this also means is that you should be sure to answer (and grid in) everything from the beginning of a section. As you approach the end, don't worry so much about skipping questions. You get the same amount of credit (one point) for each right answer from the "easy" portion of the test as you do for a correct response in the "hard" section.

When you talk about easy and hard, one size doesn't fit all. A question that stumps 98 percent of the test takers may be a no-brainer for you. So look at everything carefully. Don't assume that you can't answer a question at the end of a section; nor should you assume that you know everything in the beginning and panic if you don't.

Should you take the PSAT/NMSQT?

Complete this sentence: The PSAT/NMSQT is

(A) what you see on the bottom of the bowl when you don't eat all the alphabet soup

(B) the noise you make slurping the aforementioned soup

(C) a test that prepares you for the SAT and screens scholarship applicants

(D) the average tile selection when I play word games

(E) a secret government agency that investigates music downloads from the Internet

The answer is (C). The PSAT used to be short for the *Preliminary Scholastic Aptitude Test,* back when the initials SAT actually meant something. Now PSAT just means *Pre-SAT.* The NMSQT part still stands for something —

National Merit Scholarship Qualifying Test. Though it has a two-part name, the PSAT/NMSQT is just one test, but it performs both the functions described in Choice (C). If you're a super brain, the PSAT/NMSQT may move you into the ranks of semifinalists for a National Merit Scholarship, a *prestigious* (high-status) scholarship program. You don't have to do anything extra to apply for a National Merit Scholarship. Just take the test, and if you make the semifinals, the National Merit Scholarship Program sends you an application. Even if you think your chances of winning a scholarship are the same as Bart Simpson's passing the fourth grade, you should still take the PSAT/NMSQT. The PSAT changed along with the SAT and mirrors the SAT, though the PSAT is slightly shorter and doesn't include an essay. Taking the PSAT gives you a feel for the SAT itself — the test conditions, the format, and (I hate to admit) the pressure.

Part II
Comprehending the SAT: The Critical Reading Sections

The 5th Wave   By Rich Tennant

"Your buddy says the two of you were peripheral to the incident in question. You just said you were superficial to the incident. Now which is it, peripheral or superficial?!"

In this part . . .

The SAT Critical Reading section isn't the place for you to make comments such as "Paragraph two is a bit boring. A little dialogue would spice it up." Instead, it's the place to show SAT makers and colleges alike that you have what it takes to comprehend college-level prose. Not that the exam actually fulfills its goal, mind you, but it does measure your ability to register facts, make inferences, and pick up *nuances* (subtleties) of tone and style.

Part II helps you sail through the SAT's sea of *verbiage* (a mess of words with only a little content). Specifically, Chapter 3 describes each type of question you have to answer in the Critical Reading section and provides some helpful hints for understanding passages from each subject area the SAT addresses — social and natural sciences, humanities, and literary fiction. Chapter 4 hits you with a ton of practice passages, and Chapters 5 and 6 address sentence completions.

Chapter 3

Reading between (and on) the Lines: The Critical Reading Section

Two seconds after Ugh the Cave Dweller first carved some words on a rock wall, a prehistoric teacher-type asked, "What does *Mastodon eat you* imply?" and the critical reading exam was born. Your test may be a bit tougher than Ugh's, but don't worry. In this chapter, I help you polish some critical reading skills that help you get through passage-based comprehension questions with flying colors. (Turn to Chapter 5 for lots of details on sentence-completion questions.) I also show you how to read faster and how to zero in on the questions you're more likely to answer correctly.

Getting Acquainted with the Critical Reading Section

In their infinite wisdom, the SAT test makers have determined that 70 minutes of highly artificial reading tells colleges how equipped you are to plow through 50 or 60 pounds of textbooks each semester. To test your reading abilities, they throw the following three types of questions at you, generally mixed together in three sections:

✔ **Single passages:** Some consist of as many as 700 to 800 words; some have only 100 words.

✔ **Paired passages:** The paired word count may total 700 to 800 words, but it may also be only 200 words.

✔ **Sentence completions:** See Chapter 5 for more details.

Note: You may *encounter* (meet; run into) four Critical Reading sections on your test if you've been chosen to take a reading *equating section,* which the SAT makers use to try out new questions. The equating section looks exactly like any other Critical Reading section, and it isn't labeled as an equating section. When you apply your brain to an equating section, you're basically working for the SAT — even though you pay a test fee instead of receiving a paycheck. How unfair.

Meeting SAT single passages

Long single passages are accompanied by 10 to 14 questions, and short passages are followed by only 2 questions. These questions cover everything from the passage's main idea, the author's tone and attitude, the facts stated in the passage, the meaning of certain words, and the implications of various statements. (Find out more on each type of question in the later section "Conquering Passage-Based Questions.")

The SAT attempts to mimic reading that you'll actually face in college, though I personally have never had a course that required me to read random bits of information on a topic I've never seen before, don't care about, and will never see again. (Oh wait. I *have* had courses like that.) Because students of all majors take the SAT, the reading passages come from all areas of study, with the exception of math word problems, which get their very own section on the SAT. (See Part IV for all the details about that section of the test.)

Doubling your trouble: Paired passages

Every SAT contains at least one set of paired passages. In it, you may find one passage written by an immigrant about his or her life and one written by a historian who has studied immigration and its effect on the economy. Or, you may find an excerpt from a scientist's biography paired with an explanation of the significance of that scientist's discovery. The two passages together may reach 850 words and be followed by ten or more questions, though the SAT often gives you a pair of 100-word passages followed by only four questions. Most paired-passage questions resemble those attached to single passages, but you also face paired-passage questions about the differences between the two passages in point of view, attitude, and tone.

Completing sentences

Sentence-completion questions are sentences that contain gaps into which you need to place the best word or phrase. These questions rely on your ability to construct a bridge when faced with a gap between two ideas. Some sentence-completion questions contain two blanks rather than only one, but regardless of how many blanks they have, they all require you to make a logical deduction with the help of word clues in the sentence and common sense. Chapter 5 explains in detail how to ace the sentence-completion questions.

Conquering Passage-Based Questions

When you enter Critical Reading Passage World, be sure to take weapons — not whips and machine guns, but logic and comprehension skills. This section shows you how to answer the difficult SAT reading questions, whether they're attached to long or short passages.

Speaking factually

It never hurts to have some real-world knowledge in your test-taking tool box, but don't panic when you encounter a passage and several fact-based questions about a topic you've never heard of. The SAT critical reading questions never require you to know anything beyond what's presented in the passage. So even though you once blew up the chemistry lab, you can still master all the questions related to a passage about toxic waste.

TIP

Cracking all types of passages

Because the SAT makers assume that you'll read something in every subject area when you're in college, they throw passages from many areas of academia at you. Check out these hints for approaching science, social-science, humanities, and fiction passages.

When you're attacking a science passage, try these tactics:

✔ **Look carefully for the author's stance.** Whatever the subject, figure out what the author is *advocating* (making a case for). These passage questions often ask about the author's point of view.

✔ **Don't worry about technical vocabulary.** If you see a tough word, the definition is probably tucked into the sentence. Look for it, but don't stress about not knowing exactly what technical words mean.

✔ **Identify the argument.** Many science passages, and especially paired passages, present a dispute between two viewpoints. The SAT questions may zero in on the evidence for each theory or make you identify each author's stance.

✔ **Notice the examples.** The SAT science passages are chock-full of examples. The questions may require you to figure out what the examples prove.

If you're poring over a social-science passage (anthropology, sociology, education, cultural studies, and so on), keep these tips in mind:

✔ **Go for the positive.** The SAT doesn't criticize anyone with the power to sue or contact the media. So if you see a question about the author's tone or viewpoint, look for a positive answer unless the passage is about war criminals or another crew unlikely to be met with public sympathy.

✔ **Take note of the structure.** The social-science passages frequently present a theory and support it with sets of facts or quotations from experts. If you're asked about the significance of a particular detail in a passage, the detail is probably evidence in the case that the author is making.

✔ **Look for opposing ideas.** Experts like to argue, and human nature — the ultimate subject of social-science passages — provides plenty of arguable material. Many SAT passages present two viewpoints, in the paired passages and elsewhere. Look for the opposing sides, or identify the main theory and the objections to it.

If you face a humanities passage on the SAT (one dealing with art history, history, literature and the arts, culture, and language), keep in mind the following tips:

✔ **Notice the details.** Humanities passages often contain a great deal of description, as in "The sculpture is carved from solid maple and displayed on a base of pancakes." Don't let your attention wander; take note of the small stuff.

✔ **Stay attuned to word choice.** A passage dealing with the humanities may contain an excerpt from a *memoir* (someone's memories, written from a personal point of view). Memoirs are perfectly suited to questions about the author's tone (bitter, nostalgic, fond, critical, and so forth). Pay attention to *connotation* — not the dictionary definition but the feelings associated with a word.

✔ **Keep in mind the big picture.** Humanities questions frequently single out one example and ask you to explain its context or significance. Think about the big picture when you get to one of these questions. How does the detail fit into the whole?

SAT literary fiction is rare, but it does show up occasionally. Follow these tips to reach a higher score:

✔ **Forget about plot.** Plot isn't important in fiction passages because not much can happen in 750 words. Concentrate on identifying scene, character traits, tone, point of view, and symbols.

✔ **Think metaphorically.** Every word in the passage is there for a reason, and never more so than in literary fiction. If Line 5 says that the banana was rotten, you can bet the banana is a metaphor for society or some such concept.

✔ **Listen to a literary passage.** Of course, you can't make any noise while taking the SAT, but you can let the little voice in your head read expressively, as if you were acting it out. Chances are you'll pick up some information from your mental reenactment that you can use when answering the questions.

✔ **Cut your losses if you're lost.** Literary passages are the *mavericks* (the loners) of the SAT world. They can be about anything and in any style. If you start to read one and feel totally lost, skip it and go back to it later, time permitting.

Fact-based questions zero in on statements in the passage. They test whether you comprehend the meaning of what you're actually reading. For example, in a descriptive paragraph, a fact-based question may ask whether the neighborhood is crowded or sparsely populated. In a science passage, you may be asked the result of an experiment.

Never skip a fact-based question because it's almost impossible to get wrong. Amazingly enough, the test makers often refer you to the very line in the passage that contains the answer.

SAT fact-based questions *do* have a couple of traps built in. Sometimes the test writers word the passage in a confusing way. Successfully decoding a question's meaning depends on your ability to pick up the word clues embedded in the passage. Here are a few of the words SAT makers love to use to keep you on your toes and some explanations of what they really mean. (You may want to memorize these words so they're in neon lights in your brain.)

- ✔ **Except, but, not, in contrast to, otherwise, although, even though, despite, in spite of:** These words indicate contrast, identifying something that doesn't fit the pattern.

- ✔ **And, also, in addition to, as well as, moreover, furthermore, not only . . . but also, likewise, not the only:** When you see these clue words, you're probably looking for something that does fit the pattern.

- ✔ **Therefore, because, consequently, hence, thus, accordingly, as a result:** Now you're in cause-and-effect land. Look for something that causes or leads to something else (or something caused by something else).

- ✔ **Than, like, equally, similarly:** Time to compare two ideas, two quantities, two people, two actions — you get the idea.

- ✔ **Until, after, later, then, once, before, since, while, during, still, yet, earlier, finally, when:** You're watching the clock (or calendar) when you see these clue words. Think about the order of events.

It's time to pull out your secret decoder ring so you can attack the following sample question, based on a nonexistent passage that I would actually love to read.

According to the passage, the distinction between "Mustard Yellow" (Line 11) and "Hot Dog Pink" (Line 55) is

(A) Picasso was extremely fond of hot dogs laced with mustard.

(B) Both colors are created with the same artificial chemicals.

(C) Mustard Yellow is found in nature, but Hot Dog Pink is found only in baseball stadiums.

(D) Neither color will ever reach the wall of the author's living room.

(E) Mustard Yellow belongs to the blue family.

The correct answer is Choice (C). Okay, I'm kidding in this question (what else is new?), but I actually tuck in a few real points about SAT fact questions. Notice that the question asks you to find a *distinction,* or difference. Right away you can rule out Choices (B) and (D) because they state common characteristics. The sneaky SAT makers play tricks on people who read the question too quickly. You can also rule out Choice (A) because it doesn't mention either color. That choice represents another SAT maker's habit; throwing in an answer that may be true according to the passage (which contains a whole section on Picasso's eating habits as they related to his color choices) but that is irrelevant in terms of the question. The test makers are hoping you choose Choice (A) because you remember the bit about Picasso's favorite snack, ignoring the fact that (A) doesn't address the color issue. (By the way, I made this up. For all I know Picasso was a vegetarian.) Choice (E) may be okay if the passage emphasizes the color families and tells you that Mustard Yellow can party down with the Blues while Hot Dog Pink can't. The passage doesn't, so Choice (C) is your best bet. This choice clearly states a distinction, which is what the question calls for.

Identifying word clues is especially crucial in the 100-word passages. Because test makers can't rely on lengthy discussions of boring ideas to trick you — or to put you to sleep, which amounts to the same thing — they choose little words to trip you up. If you see one of the words or phrases from the previous bulleted list, underline it and take it into account when you're choosing an answer.

Clue words show up in the questions, too, so be *vigilant* (on your guard) when reading the questions, not just while perusing the reading passage itself.

Defining as you read

Many SAT questions ask you to define a word as it's used in the passage. Teacher-types like me call this exercise *vocabulary in context.* Never skip a vocabulary-in-context question because chances are the answer is right there in the sentence the word appears in. Even if the definition isn't right there, figuring it out is easy to do. Here's an example:

In Line 12, "snoggled" means . . .

Perhaps you've never heard of *snoggled* — not surprising because I made it up. But doesn't it sound like something the school nurse would warn you about? "Snoggling leads to uncontrolled movements of the eyebrows. . . ." Even without a dictionary definition, you can figure out the meaning of the word from its context. For example, look at the rest of the paragraph on the test:

> Overcome by passion the moment he snoggled her perfume, Oxford trailed Lympia pathetically around the house.

Okay, now you can clearly see that *snoggled* has something to do with sniffing, scenting, or otherwise catching a whiff of. If one of your choices is *smelled* or a synonym of *smelled,* you're home free.

Vocabulary-in-context questions do contain one big sand trap, though. Many of these questions ask you for the definition of a word you probably already know. But — and this is a big *but* — the passage may use the word in an odd or unusual way. And, of course, one of the choices is usually the word's definition that you know, just sitting there waiting for the unwary test taker to grab it. For example:

In Line 55, the word "deck" means

(A) to hit so hard that the receiver of the blow falls over

(B) a floor of a ship

(C) the compartment at the rear of an automobile

(D) a wooden structure built onto the side of a house

(E) to adorn with decorations

If you selected Choice (E), go to the head of the class, because Line 55 was a lyric from a famous Christmas carol, "*Deck* the Halls." Bottom line: Always answer a vocabulary-in-context question because the answer is usually right there in the passage, but never answer one without actually checking the context.

Decoding symbols and metaphors

Appearances often deceive on the SAT. The passage may contain one or more symbols or metaphors that have a deeper meaning. For example, the questions may resemble the following:

✔ In the second paragraph, the author compares his trip to Shea Stadium to a treasure hunt because . . .

✔ The fly ball mentioned in Line 8 symbolizes . . .

✔ The long wait for hot dogs (Line 12) primarily serves to illustrate . . .

The best strategy for answering symbol- or metaphor-based questions is to form a picture in your brain. Refer to the preceding questions and pretend that you're playing a videotape of the trip to Yankee Stadium featuring the fly ball or the wait for a hot dog. Then ask yourself *why* the author wanted to place that picture in your brain. Perhaps the trip to the ballpark (on your internal videotape) is bathed in golden light and accompanied by mellow violins. The comparison to a treasure hunt may show you that the author was searching for his lost youth, which he found unexpectedly at a baseball game. Or, when you run the tape of the fly ball smacking into the author's forehead, you may realize that the incident embodies the shock of his realization that baseball is no longer the idyllic sport he once played.

The SAT writers use metaphor-based questions to check whether or not you can grasp the big picture. For example, once when I was in high school, the teacher compared voting rights to a set of milk bottles. If everyone's rights were respected, the milk bottle was full. If some people were *disenfranchised* (not allowed to vote), the milk bottle was only half full. In a dictatorship, the milk bottle was empty. As the teacher blathered on about democracy and full milk bottles, one student's hand waved in the air. "Milk doesn't come in bottles anymore," she remarked. "It's all cartons now." Clearly this student was missing the big picture. She was focusing on the detail, but she wasn't grasping what the teacher was trying to convey.

When faced with a symbol- or metaphor-based question, experience the moment (but only for a moment, because time is short on the SAT) and feel its purpose.

Identifying the attitude

An *attitude* in a reading passage goes way beyond the "don't take that attitude with me" comment that parents repeat with depressing regularity. In SAT jargon, an attitude can be critical, objective, indifferent, and so forth. The following clue words may pop up in the answer choices:

✔ **Pro, positive, in favor of, leaning toward,** *laudatory* **(praising), agreeable,** *amenable* **(willing to go along with), sympathetic:** The author is *for* a particular topic or argument.

✔ **Doubtful, offended, anti, resistant to, contrary to, counter to,** *adversarial* **(acting like an enemy), opposed, critical of, disgusted with:** The author is *against* a particular topic or argument.

✔ **Objective, indifferent, noncommittal, impartial,** *apathetic* **(not caring), unbiased,** *ambivalent* **(can't decide either way or has mixed feelings):** The author is *neutral* on a particular topic or argument.

To answer an attitude question, first decide where the author lands — for, against, or neutral — in relation to the topic. Check for clue words that express approval or disapproval.

Even in a dry-as-dust passage about the low water table in some country you've never heard of, the author has an attitude, and the SAT may ask you to identify it. Check out these examples:

✔ The author's attitude toward the Water Minister's statement in Line 88 can best be described as . . .

✔ In response to the proposed law on water table measurement, the author's comments are . . .

If you're looking for a positive answer in an attitude question, start by crossing out all the negative or neutral choices. In the preceding water table law question, for example, you can instantly dump *argumentative, condemning,* and similar words if you know that the author favors the law.

A variation of the attitude question asks you to identify the author's *tone.* Tone and attitude overlap a little, but tone is closer to what you would hear if the passage were the words of someone speaking directly to you. You can use some of the same clues you use for attitude to help you figure out the author's tone. Just remember that tone questions include emotions, so check for irony, amusement, nostalgia, regret, and sarcasm.

Understanding examples

Quite a few critical reading questions ask you to figure out why an author used a particular example. Here are a few examples:

- The example of the fish scaler demonstrates that . . .
- The author's statement that the fish smelled "putrid" (Line 2) serves to . . .
- The quotation from the hotel clerk about the choice of movies rented exemplifies . . .

The key to this sort of question is to get inside the writer's mind. "Why did the author put that particular example in that particular place?" The example may be a small detail in a paragraph full of details. If so, try to decide what title you would give to the paragraph. Suppose that the fish scaler is in a paragraph describing kitchen tools. Depending on the paragraph's contents, you may choose "Stuff in my kitchen that I never use" or "Stuff in my kitchen I can't do without" as a good title for the list. After you get the title, you should be able to choose the answer choice that best explains why the writer chose to use the fish scaler as an example in the passage. The fish scaler example may lead you to a statement like "Many people buy kitchen utensils they never use" or "The proper tool makes any job easier."

Alternatively, the example may be one complete paragraph out of many in the passage. In that case, what title would you give this passage? Chances are giving the passage a fitting title can lead you to the correct response.

Covering all your bases: The main idea

In reading terms, the questions on the SAT that address the main idea of a particular passage give you choices that fall into the too-broad, too-narrow, off-base, or just-right categories. A just-right choice includes all the supporting points and details in the passage, but it isn't so broad as to be meaningless.

You frequently get at least one main idea–related question that applies to the entire passage. Think of the main idea as an umbrella protecting you from a driving rain as you walk down a street. If the umbrella is too large, the wind will blow you away. If it's too small, you'll get wet. You need one that fits perfectly. Imagine for a moment that you're trying to find a main idea for a list that includes the following: jelly, milk, waxed paper, light bulbs, and peaches. A main idea that fits is *things you can buy at the supermarket.* One that is too broad is *stuff.* A too-narrow choice is *food* because very few people like the taste of light bulbs — and everyone who does is locked up in a padded room somewhere. A completely off-base main idea is *canned goods.*

A variation on the main idea–related question asks about the main ideas in a paragraph, not the passage as a whole. Use the same guidelines you use to identify the main idea of a passage to choose the correct answer.

Making inferences

You make inferences every day. (An *inference* is a conclusion you reach based on evidence.) Perhaps you come home and your mother is chewing on the phone bill and throwing your bowling trophies out the window. Even though she hasn't stated the problem, you can guess that the call you made to the bowling team in Helsinki wasn't included in your basic monthly calling plan.

The SAT Critical Reading section has tons of that kind of inference. You get a certain amount of information, and then you have to stretch it a little. The questions may resemble the following:

- ✔ What may be inferred from the author's statement that she is "allergic to homework" (Line 66)?
- ✔ The author implies in Line 12 that small stuffed animals . . .
- ✔ The author would probably agree with which of the following statements?

To crack an inference question, act like a Sherlock Holmes clone. You have a few clues. Perhaps you have a set of statements about small stuffed animals: Very young kids tend to eat these little stuffed animals; unmarred stuffed animals fetch high prices on eBay; children seldom appreciate presents for more than a few moments after receiving them. You get the picture? Then ask yourself what sort of conclusion you can come to, given the evidence. Stretching the stuffed animal example, you may think that buying and selling stuffed animals for a profit is better than ignoring your little nephew's birthday. After you reach a conclusion, check the choices to see which one best matches your conclusion.

If you're asked to infer, don't look for a statement that is actually in the passage. By definition, inferences reside between the lines. If a statement is in the passage, it's the wrong answer.

Skipping When You're at the End of Your Rope

When you're barreling through a Critical Reading section on the SAT, time is your *foe* (enemy). To maximize your score, you need to concentrate on questions you're fairly certain you can answer correctly. Unlike sentence-completion questions, which the SAT test makers place in order of difficulty (from easy to more difficult), the passage-based questions don't move from easy to hard. Instead, the order of the questions attached to the passages follows the organization of the passage itself. Question 1 may ask about Lines 12 through 14, Question 2 about Lines 24 through 28, and so forth. Questions about the entire passage (the author's attitude or tone, main idea, and so forth) may be anywhere but are often at the beginning or at the end of the question set.

Because the questions referring to the SAT Critical Reading passages aren't in order of difficulty, you need to make some quick decisions about what to answer and what to skip, particularly as you get to the end of the time allotted. In general, follow these steps:

1. **Answer the factual questions. (See the section "Speaking factually.")**

2. **Go to the vocabulary-in-context type of question. (See the section "Defining as you read.")**

3. **Start with the questions that ask you to interpret the author's tone or purpose. (See the section "Identifying the attitude.") If anything is unclear, skip it.**

4. **If the test makers ask questions about the main ideas, relationships between paragraphs, and inferences, do the ones that seem obvious to you and skip the rest. (See the sections "Covering all your bases: The main idea" and "Making inferences.") Go back if you have time for the tough ones.**

5. **In paired passages, answer all the Passage I questions that you know immediately and then all the Passage II questions that you can ace with no trouble. (See the section "Doubling your trouble: Paired passages.") Then tackle the shared-passage queries.**

No matter which questions you answer first, remember one important rule: You get as many points for a correct answer to an easy question as you do for a correct answer to a hard question. I know, it's not fair. But then again, this is the SAT. Fairness *isn't* part of the deal. Also, remember that you get no points for a skipped question, but you *lose* a quarter point for a wrong answer. Don't guess wildly. (For a detailed explanation of scoring, see Chapter 1.)

Making a Long Story Short: Reading Quickly

When I was in high school, my health teacher — just out of college and not much older than the students she was teaching — was afraid to assign the sex-education chapter of the text-book. Maybe she feared angry calls from the PTA, or maybe she just didn't want to face the two-dozen sets of teenage giggles. So she dropped the birds and the bees and instead taught us how to speed-read. I was annoyed at the time (after all, who's not interested in sex?), but reading fast does come in handy, especially in pressured situations like the SAT.

You don't have to set your sights on becoming a Kentucky Derby winner, but if you usually plow through paragraphs at a turtle's pace, a few simple tricks may make a big difference in how many questions you have a chance to answer and, thus, how high you score on the SAT.

A few SAT prep courses advise you to save time by reading only bits of the passages in the Critical Reading section. Bad idea, in my humble opinion. At least some of the questions in this section ask you to assess the entire piece, pinpointing the author's tone or overall point of view. If time is a problem, work on reading faster, not on reading less.

To increase your reading speed, try these techniques:

- **Wind sprint.** If you're a track star, you run a lot at a steady pace, but occasionally you let out all the stops and go as fast as possible for a short period of time. When you're reading, imitate the runners. Read at a steady pace, but from time to time push yourself through a paragraph as fast as you possibly can. After a couple of minutes, go back to your normal reading speed. Soon your "normal" speed will increase.

- **Read newspaper columns.** When you read, your eyes move from side to side. But you have *peripheral* (on-the-edge) vision that makes some of those eye movements unnecessary. To practice moving your eyes less (and, thus, speeding up your progress), read a narrow newspaper column. Try to see the entire column width without moving your eyes sideways. If you practice a couple of times, you can train your eye to grasp the edges as well as the center. Bingo! Your speed will increase.

- **Finger focus.** If you're reading something wider than a newspaper column, you can still reap gains from the peripheral-vision training described in the preceding bullet point. Just place your finger underneath the line you're reading, about a third of the way in. Read the first half of the line in one stationary glance. Then move your finger to about two-thirds of the way across. Take in the second half of the line in just one more glance. There you go! Your eyes are moving less, you're staying focused, and you're reading faster.

- **Hit the high spots.** People who make a living analyzing such things as paragraph organization (can you imagine a more boring career?) have determined that nearly all paragraphs start with a topic sentence. If you want to get a quick overview of a passage, read the topic sentence of each paragraph slowly. Then go back and zoom through the details quickly. Chances are you can get everything you need.

The *mis*-ing link

Adding the *mis* family of words to your vocabulary is a surefire way to score higher on the SAT. Do you sometimes make a *mis*take and *mis*behave in front of the *mis*anthropic teacher who has a long, thick ruler and isn't afraid to use it because she totally hates people? Don't *mis*construe (misunderstand) my meaning: I'm not that sort of teacher. I do, however, *mis*manage my time, especially when I've been out partying when I should've been home marking essays.

Welcome to the *mis* family, known for its bad manners and wrong ways. When you *mis*take, you take something wrong. When you *mis*behave, you behave badly. Here are a few more relatives in the *mis* family:

- *Misalign:* To deviate from the straight, or aligned course. A walk down a bumpy path illustrates what happens when the construction crew runs late and misaligns the paving stones.

- *Misanthropes:* Those who think people are basically bad. Picture a hermit on top of an alp, hiding in a cave. (*Misanthropic* is the adjective.)

- *Misconstrue:* A twin of misapprehend, meaning "misunderstand," as in "Hard-of-hearing Horatio misapprehended the command to blow his horn and instead saluted the captain by sewing a thorn."

- *Misnomer:* A wrong term, or wrong name, as in "Calling him *Honest Abe* is a misnomer, given that he has been arrested 569 times."

- *Misogynist:* Rounds out the I-hate-you category. A misogynist is someone who thinks women are bad and (in my experience) does everything possible to show it.

Deciding Which to Read First: The Passage or the Question

Every time I tutor for the SAT (and I tutor a lot), my students ask me whether they should read the passage or the questions first. A variation of this query is whether to read the passages at all. (For the record: I don't recommend skipping the passages. Ever.) As for which to read first, you should make the decision based on your personal style. Are you good at keeping details in your head? If so, go for the read-the-question-first option. Don't read all the choices; just glance at the *tag line* (the beginning of the question) so you have a rough idea of what the testers are focusing on.

If you feel that your head is filled with too many facts already, settle in with the passage before you look at the questions. Keep your pencil handy and circle anything that looks particularly important. Write a word next to each paragraph, summing up its main idea ("hot dog line," "argument for the designated hitter," and so on). Then hit the questions and locate the answers. Many students who scored high on the SAT took margin notes during the test, so give it a try!

Whether you read the passage or question first, never skip the italicized introduction to a passage. Many SAT passages are preceded by a short italicized description along the lines of *This passage comes from the diary of a 16th-century maniac* or *The author of this passage was locked in an SAT test site for 14 days before being rescued.* This description orients you to the passage and may help you decide the author's tone. For example, after being locked in an SAT exam room, the author probably isn't going to write a hymn of praise to your favorite test. The maniac reference alerts you to the fact that the narrator may be unreliable. You won't see a factual question based on the italicized introduction, but you may be sure that the SAT doesn't waste words, and whatever the test writers say in italics is useful in some way.

Chapter 4

Practicing Critical Reading Passages: Reading for Points

My seventh-grade teacher used to thump around the classroom yelling, "Read! Read! Read!" as she slapped a metal ruler on the desks and occasionally on the heads of inattentive students. Whenever I remember her, I think (a) these days she'd probably get sued for the ruler hits, and (b) she was right about the reading. The only way to become a better reader is to practice. And the only way to become a better SAT *critical reader* is to practice (guess what!) Critical Reading passages.

In this chapter, I provide the raw material, first for single passages and then for paired passages. I finish up with some short passages. You just stir in the brainpower for a higher score. (Turn to Chapter 3 for more info on any of the topics covered in these practice questions.)

Hitting the Singles Scene: Full-Length Passages

Most SAT passages are singles; their only companions are ten or so questions, which follow the order in which information is presented in the passage, not the order of difficulty. In this section, I provide two full-length, single, stand-alone, practice Critical Reading passages with a sampling of typical questions. In the first set, I give you the answer and an explanation after each question. When you get to the second set, which is set up like the real test, you're on your own — just until you complete the passage and its questions. The answers and explanations follow the set.

Set 1

In this passage from *The Secret Life of Dust* (Wiley), author Hannah Holmes discusses some airborne particles called diatoms.

Line   Flying diatoms don't add significantly to the airborne vegetable matter, in terms of simple tonnage. But when these glass-shelled algae do take a spin through the atmosphere, they raise interesting questions. They seem to defy the size limit for far-flying dust, for one thing. And they may sometimes fly with a purpose.

(05)   Michael Ram, a professor of physics at the University of Buffalo, has become an expert at teasing these tiny organisms out of ice cores from Antarctica and Greenland. Deep glaciers preserve thousands upon thousands of fine layers, each representing a year. And trapped in each layer is a sprinkling of fallen desert dust, stardust, volcanic ash, pollen, insect parts — and diatoms. Ram melts a bit of ice, then puts the remaining sediment under a microscope.

(10)   The diatoms, he says, stand out due to their geometric perfection. Desert dust, under the microscope, resembles shattered rock. But diatoms often resemble delicately etched pill-boxes or broken shards of the same.

Most diatoms spend their brief lives adrift in rivers, ponds, lakes, and oceans. And when they die, their little shells sink. Ram says the ideal source of diatom dust is a shallow lake

(15)   that shrinks in the dry season, exposing the sediment at its edges to the wind. Africa and the western United States are both pocked with excellent candidates.

Ram originally intended to use the diatoms he found to trace the source of the dust and diatoms in each sample: if the ice of one century was rich in North American diatoms, and the next century's ice held African diatoms, he could conclude that the prevailing wind had

(20)   shifted. This might reveal something about the dynamics of climate change. But Ram's diatoms proved coy about their place of origin. Many of them look alike. Scientists with more diatom expertise are pursuing this line of inquiry.

And Ram's diatoms have caused additional head scratching. Generally, scientists don't expect things much larger than a few hundredths of a hair's width to fly long distances. But

(25)   Ram has seen disks as wide as a hundred, or even two hundred, microns — that's a whopping two hairs in diameter. "These diatoms are large, but they have a large surface area, and they're light," Ram speculates in the accent that remains from his European upbringing. "They're like Frisbees. They're very aerodynamic."

The size of the diatoms may also relate to the strength of the wind that lifted them. An

(30)   uncommonly strong wind can lift uncommonly large dust, as a survey of hailstone cores has suggested. Carried up into a storm cloud and then coated in ice until they fell again have been such "dusts" as small insects, birds, and at least one gopher tortoise. Perhaps a large diatom is not such a challenge.

But a third source of puzzlement is what appears to be a complete colony of diatoms that

(35)   evidently dwelled smack atop the Greenland glacier about four hundred years ago. It is common for living diatoms to blow into melt pools at the edges of glaciers and there start a family. But the founder of the little clan Ram discovered apparently flew all the way to the center of the immense island before dropping into a puddle. And that pioneer was still in good enough shape to launch a modest dynasty.

1. The phrase that most nearly describes "flying diatoms" (Line 1) is

   (A) living or dead algae that may be transported through the air

   (B) single-celled animals that can fly

   (C) glass-shelled, winged animals

   (D) living algae imprisoned in glass

   (E) dead algae borne through the air by wind

The tough part about this question is that most of the choices have some element of truth in them. But in SAT Land, some isn't enough. Line 14 states that "the ideal source of diatom dust is a shallow lake that shrinks in the dry season, exposing the sediment at its edges to the wind." The last paragraph talks about "living diatoms" that "blow into melt pools at the edges of glaciers," so (D) and (E) drop out. Because they "fly" with the aid of wind, (B) and (C) aren't correct, as these choices imply or directly specify wings. All that's left is (A) the correct answer.

2. The word "teasing" (Line 6) in this context may best be defined as

   (A) mocking

   (B) coaxing

   (C) annoying

   (D) disentangling

   (E) shredding

Surprisingly, all the other choices are in fact definitions of teasing, but the one that fits here is *disentangling*. The correct answer is (D).

3. Diatoms puzzle researchers because

   (A) they sometimes appear in unexpected places

   (B) they have glass shells

   (C) their surface is extremely small, given their weight

   (D) they may be carried by wind after death

   (E) none of the above

Choices (B) and (D) are true, but not puzzling, and Choice (C) is untrue. Choice (A) is correct because Lines 34–39 discuss the *puzzlement* of the colony in the Greenland glacier.

4. The title that best expresses the contents of this passage is

   (A) Characteristics of Algae

   (B) The Lives of Diatoms

   (C) A Scientific Study of Diatoms

   (D) Michael Ram's Life and Work

   (E) Windborne Diatoms

Titles, like the swimsuits you tried on last summer, may be too big, too small, or just right. In this set of answers, Choices (A) and (B) are too big, which in reading terms means too general. Choices (C) and (D) are too small, or too specific. They focus on one part of the passage, instead of on the whole. Choice (E) is the best because it takes into account all the contents except Paragraph 3, which is clearly inserted as background information, creating a context for the rest of the information about diatoms.

5. Which statement may be inferred from Lines 17–22?

   (A) Winds from North America and from Africa blow in the same direction.

   (B) Ram's analysis showed that all diatoms from Antarctica and Greenland ice originate in the same shallow lakes.

   (C) Ram does not know enough about diatoms to differentiate one type from another.

   (D) Diatoms change over the course of a century.

   (E) Diatoms originating in Greenland differ from diatoms originating in Antarctica.

Ram was hoping to find a wind shift, so wind from North America and wind from Africa must blow from different directions. Hence, Choice (A) isn't the prizewinner here. Choices (B) and (D) are wrong, based on the passage, which also says that Ram couldn't tell the diatoms apart. Someone with *more diatom expertise* was needed for this task, so Choice (C) is the best answer.

6. The example of hailstone cores (Line 30) primarily

    (A) shows how dust is examined

    (B) illustrates wind direction

    (C) explains what weather conditions diatoms face

    (D) reinforces the idea that wind can carry heavy particles

    (E) contrasts with the methods used to study diatoms

The preceding paragraph says that the distances diatoms travel solely via wind power puzzle scientists. Line 30 says that "uncommonly strong wind can lift uncommonly large dust," and the hailstone core example reinforces this point. Choice (D) is the correct answer.

After you finish the first practice passage, profile your strengths and weaknesses by checking which type of question stumped you. Here's the key: Questions 1 and 3 were fact-finding missions, Question 2 tackled vocabulary, 4 hit the main idea, and 5 required you to make an inference or to interpret a metaphor. Question 6 concerned the significance of an example. For help with any of these question types, check out the corresponding section in Chapter 3.

Set 2

> In this excerpt from Dickens's 19th-century novel Great Expectations, *the narrator recalls a Christmas dinner.* **Note:** *"bobbish" means "hungry," and "Sixpennorth of halfpence" is a nickname referring to a very small quantity of British money of the period. "N.B." means "note well."*

Line I opened the door to the company — making believe that it was a habit of ours to open that door — and I opened it first to Mr. Wopsle, next to Mr. and Mrs. Hubble, and last of all to Uncle Pumblechook. N.B., I was not allowed to call him uncle, under the severest penalties.

(05) "Mrs. Joe," said Uncle Pumblechook: a large hard-breathing middle-aged slow man, with a mouth like a fish, dull staring eyes, and sandy hair standing upright on his head, so that he looked as if he had just been all but choked, and had that moment come to; "I have brought you, as the compliments of the season — I have brought you, Mum, a bottle of sherry wine — and I have brought you, Mum, a bottle of port wine."

(10) Every Christmas Day he presented himself, as a profound novelty, with exactly the same words, and carrying the two bottles like dumb-bells. Every Christmas Day, Mrs. Joe replied, as she now replied, "Oh, Un-cle Pum-ble-chook! This IS kind!" Every Christmas Day, he retorted, as he now retorted, "It's no more than your merits. And now are you all bobbish, and how's Sixpennorth of halfpence?" meaning me.

(15) We dined on these occasions in the kitchen, and adjourned, for the nuts and oranges and apples, to the parlour; which was a change very like Joe's change from his working clothes to his Sunday dress. My sister was uncommonly lively on the present occasion, and indeed was generally more gracious in the society of Mrs. Hubble than in other company. I remember Mrs. Hubble as a little curly sharp-edged person in sky-blue, who

(20) held a conventionally juvenile position, because she had married Mr. Hubble — I don't know at what remote period — when she was much younger than he. I remember Mr. Hubble as a tough high-shouldered stooping old man, of a sawdusty fragrance, with his legs extraordinarily wide apart: so that in my short days I always saw some miles of open country between them when I met him coming up the lane.

(25) Among this good company I should have felt myself, even if I hadn't robbed the pantry, in a false position. Not because I was squeezed in at an acute angle of the table-cloth, with the table in my chest, and the Pumblechookian elbow in my eye, nor because I was not allowed to speak (I didn't want to speak), nor because I was regaled with the scaly tips of the drumsticks of the fowls, and with those obscure corners of pork of which the pig, when living,

(30) had had the least reason to be vain. No; I should not have minded that, if they would only have left me alone. But they wouldn't leave me alone. They seemed to think the opportunity lost, if they failed to point the conversation at me, every now and then, and stick the point into me. I might have been an unfortunate little bull in a Spanish arena, I got so smartingly touched up by these moral goads.

1. Which statement may be inferred from Lines 1–2?

(A) The door that the narrator opens is normally locked.

(B) The door that the narrator opens is never used for company.

(C) The narrator is not normally allowed to open the door for visitors.

(D) Different doors are used on special occasions and for everyday entries.

(E) The doors in the narrator's house are always kept open.

2. The author's attitude toward Uncle Pumblechook and Mrs. Joe in Paragraphs 2 and 3 (Lines 5–14) may best be characterized as

(A) mildly critical

(B) approving

(C) admiring

(D) ambivalent

(E) sharply disapproving

3. The move from the kitchen to the parlour is compared to Joe's change of clothes because

(A) Mrs. Joe is uncomfortable with both

(B) both take place only on special occasions

(C) the narrator is confused by each of these actions

(D) Mrs. Hubble is always present for both of these actions

(E) Joe insists upon both of these changes

4. The details in Paragraph 5 (Lines 25–34) serve to

(A) show how the author enjoys Christmas dinner

(B) explain the behavior of the dinner guests

(C) describe a 19th-century Christmas celebration

(D) make the case that the narrator is not treated well

(E) illustrate 19th-century child-rearing practices

5. The metaphor of "an unfortunate little bull in a Spanish arena" (Line 33) means that

(A) the narrator, like a bull in a bullfight, is a target of teasing attacks

(B) the narrator's table manners are more like those of an animal than a polite child

(C) the narrator did not participate actively in the conversation

(D) the dinner guests were the targets of the narrator's mocking comments

(E) the dinner resembled a festive sporting event

6. The author of this passage would most likely agree with which statement?

(A) Children should be seen and not heard.

(B) The narrator has a happy life.

(C) Holiday gatherings may be joyous occasions.

(D) People often show off during holiday gatherings.

(E) Holiday celebrations should be abolished.

Answers to Set 2

1. **D.** Lines 1–2 contain the statement that the narrator was "making believe that it was a habit of ours to open that door." *That door* implies a contrast with another door, so you can rule out Choices (A), (C), and (E). The two remaining choices present no real puzzle. Because company is arriving, Choice (B) can't be correct. Bingo — (D) is your answer.

2. **A.** The description of Uncle Pumblechook (isn't that one of the all-time greatest names?) clearly shows that Choices (B) and (C) won't do, because *a mouth like a fish* isn't an approving or admiring comment. Choice (D) is possible, because clearly the author isn't *sharply disapproving*, given that the negative comments are quite tame (**ambivalent** means "of two opinions"). But Choice (A) is the best. If the two characters are pretending to do something that they've never done before and do so every year, the author is critical of them, but only mildly so.

3. **B.** Mrs. Joe is *uncommonly lively,* so Choice (A) is out. The passage gives no indication that Joe insists on anything, so you can rule out (E). Mrs. Hubble isn't really a factor, and the narrator's general confusion isn't specifically connected to clothes or location. The best is (B), because Joe's change is referred to as *Sunday dress* and (B) refers to special occasions.

4. **D.** The author is certainly *not* enjoying dinner, so Choice (A) is out. The dinner guests' behavior (B) is possible, but the details tell you more about how the narrator is treated than about the guests' general behavior. Choices (C) and (E) are too general. Choice (D) is the only one to make the cut.

5. **A.** The guests are described as unwilling to leave the narrator alone, so you can rule out (D) and (E) because the narrator isn't the attacker — there goes (D) — and the dinner isn't a fun occasion — goodbye (E). Choice (C) is true but has no relationship to the bullfighting image, and neither does the statement about table manners. The narrator is, however, described as the target of attacks by the guests' statements, just as the bull faces attacks in a bullfight. Thus, (A) is the correct answer.

6. **D.** The change from one room to another, the use of a special door, the ceremonial exchange of gifts — all these details prove that the characters in this passage are showing off, putting on airs, pretending to be better than they really are, and in general acting like contestants on a reality show. Choice (D) fills the bill.

 Time for a checkup. Look at everything you got wrong and figure out your weak spots — facts, inference, main idea, and so on. Here's the key: Questions 1, 4, and 6 are about inference; 2 is about attitude; 3 is about symbolism; and 5 is about metaphor. After you know what to work on, turn to Chapter 3 for some tips.

Doing Double Duty: Paired Passages

Paired passages double your trouble, but if you approach them the right way, they also double your score. Twice as many chances to get the answer right! Expect some questions on Passage I, some on Passage II, and a couple that address the similarities or differences between both passages. Work through the first set, checking the answers and explanations that follow each question, and then fly solo through the second set, which is set up like the real test. The answers to the second set are at the end. Good luck!

Set 1

The first passage discusses the relationship between geography and human culture. The second passage comes from *The Secret Life of Dust* by Hannah Holmes (Wiley). The author addresses climate change. *Note:* An *oviraptor* is a type of dinosaur. Mount Pinatubo was a volcano that erupted in 1991.

Passage 1

Line
Human culture is invariably rooted in the site in which it flourishes. Thus human history is also the study of land and water formations, climate, and characteristics of the physical world. Climate, of course, is neither a constant nor a sole factor in human development. The earth's climate has undergone many variations in its long history. So too are there shifts in
(05) civilizations. Today's fertile soil, verdant forests, and prosperous empire may very well be tomorrow's ruins, as the fall of classic Mayan civilization following a prolonged drought in the ninth century illustrates.

Acknowledging the influence of climate, scientists today study the gradual rise in average temperature, preparing for major shifts in trade, population density, and political affinity.
(10) Modern science has in some sense inherited the mantle of ancient seers. One historian declared that climatologists have taken up the role of ancient priests — those in Egypt, for example, whose prayers to the gods were designed to ensure that the annual flood of the Nile River was sufficient for agriculture but not so extensive as to cause damage to settlements.

Yet anyone studying the effect of climate change on human culture must also take into
(15) account the consistency and resiliency of human life. Archaeologists at some sites have found similarities in artifacts and settlement patterns before and after major climate changes. More than 73,000 years ago, for example, the eruption of Mt. Toba, a volcano in Indonesia, ejected so much dust into the atmosphere that sunlight was dimmed and the earth entered an ice age. If climate change is such a powerful force, how is it that humanity
(20) survived this period with its culture largely intact?

Passage II

One very clear message in the ice is that the Earth's climate is naturally erratic. According to the dust and gases trapped in the ice, the climate is always — always — in flux. If it's not getting warmer, it's getting colder. Year to year the shifts may be masked by an El Niño, a La Niña, a Mount Pinatubo, or some other temporary drama. But decade to decade, century to
(25) century, the world's temperature is in constant motion.

On a grand scale our moderate, modern climate is abnormal. Through most of the dinosaur era the planet's normal state was decidedly steamier. When the oviraptor perished in the Gobi Desert, the world may have been eleven to fourteen degrees hotter, on average.

Then, just 2.5 million years ago, the planet entered a pattern of periodic ice ages, punctu-
(30) ated by brief warm spells. The ice caps, as a result, have taken to advancing and retreating intermittently. The glaciers have ruled for the lion's share of time, with the warm "inter-glacials" lasting roughly ten thousand years each. We inhabit an interglacial known as the Holocene, which ought to be coming to an end any day now. The thermometer, however, does not seem poised for a plunge.

(35) All things being equal, no climatologist would be surprised if the Holocene persisted for another few thousand years — climate change is that erratic. But all things are not equal. Human industry has wrought profound changes in the Earth's atmosphere since the last warm period.

1. Based on the statements in the first paragraph (Lines 1–7) of Passage I, which position would the author most likely support?

    (A) History is intertwined with geography.

    (B) Human beings shape their environment, not the other way around.

    (C) Climate and prosperity are completely unrelated.

    (D) Dramatic climate changes always cause dramatic cultural shifts.

    (E) Climate is the most important factor in the creation of an empire.

    Most of the choices are as extreme as a category-five hurricane, but the author's position is closer to a moderate summer breeze. Lines 1–3 make clear that *the site* (that is, the geography and climate) where people live is a factor in human culture, a belief expressed by (A). Did Choice (D) entrap you? Lines 5–7 refer to the fall of the Mayan Empire because of extreme drought, but Line 3 firmly asserts that climate isn't the *sole factor* determining the stability of a civilization.

2. In the context of Line 4, what is the best definition of *shifts*?

    (A) transfers

    (B) modifications

    (C) swings

    (D) working periods

    (E) gears

    Lines 3–5 tell you that climate *has undergone many variations* and *[s]o too* have there been *shifts* in civilizations. The word *too* tells you that you're looking for a synonym of *variations*, which Choice (C) provides. Choice (B) is close, but a *modification* usually refers to a small change to an existing thing, and the paragraph describes more extreme changes.

3. The example of the Mayan civilization serves to

    (A) emphasize the importance of water conservation

    (B) clarify how history and climate are related

    (C) show that no empire is immune to climate change

    (D) reveal how human behavior influences climate

    (E) explain that political power depends upon a wealth of natural resources

    The Mayan empire fell because of *a prolonged drought* (Line 6), so you can immediately eliminate Choices (C) and (D). To choose among the remaining three answers, examine the whole paragraph, which discusses the effect of climate on human culture. In that context, Choice (B) is the best answer.

4. Which of the following best expresses the meaning of this statement: "Modern science has in some sense inherited the mantle of ancient seers" (Line 10)?

    (A) Much scientific knowledge is as imprecise as magic.

    (B) Scientific knowledge isn't accessible to ordinary people.

    (C) Science attempts to predict future events.

    (D) Scientists today are expected to understand the past.

    (E) The ancients understood science very well.

    Ancient seers tried to predict the future, and Lines 8–9 tell you that today's scientists are "preparing for major shifts in trade, population density, and political affinity" — future trends, in other words. Hence, Choice (C) is the answer you seek.

5. The author mentions Mt. Toba (Lines 17–19)

   (A) as an example of extreme climate change

   (B) to warn of the dangers of natural forces

   (C) to show that volcanoes can do damage

   (D) as an illustration of the way human behavior changes when climate changes

   (E) to explain how ice ages occur

The third paragraph of Passage I (Lines 14–20) talks about climate and culture. The passage states that the eruption of Mt. Toba brought on an ice age, but — and this is an important *but* — human culture survived *intact* (not damaged or broken). Therefore, Choice (A) is your best answer here.

6. In Passage II, the author mentions the oviraptor (Line 27) to illustrate

   (A) the difference between human and animal responses to climate

   (B) how living creatures adapt to many climates

   (C) a creature that became extinct because of climate shifts

   (D) how the dinosaurs were affected by climate

   (E) a dinosaur that lived during a warm period

The author doesn't develop the *oviraptor* example. Choices (A), (B), (C), and (D) are out because they call for a more extensive discussion of the dinosaur in question. Choice (E) is the correct answer.

7. In Passage II, which phrase most nearly defines "any day now" (Line 33)?

   (A) within a week

   (B) within a month

   (C) within a year

   (D) during our lifetime

   (E) within a thousand years

The author of Passage II certainly takes the long view. Paragraph 4 specifically says that even a few thousand years would be possible, but that amount of time is labeled as *erratic*, or without a consistent pattern. So the best answer is (E).

8. Compared to the authors of Passage I, the author of Passage II

   (A) describes volcanic eruptions as more important factors in climate change

   (B) believes that climate change has less effect on human behavior

   (C) is more concerned with human beings' effect on climate than the effect of climate on human beings

   (D) sees climate as having greater historical importance

   (E) thinks that the Earth's climate will change more rapidly

Lines 37–38 state that "[h]uman industry has wrought profound changes in the Earth's atmosphere since the last warm period." Thus the author considers how human beings affect climate, not the other way around, as is the case in Passage I. Go for Choice (C).

9. Evidence from both passages supports the idea that

    (A) climate change is inevitable

    (B) human beings cannot withstand radical climate changes

    (C) human activity affects climate

    (D) climate changes very little

    (E) climatologists must study human behavior to understand temperature patterns

    Passage I makes a point of stating that climate isn't *a constant* (Line 3) and Passage II flat out tells you that climate is always changing (Lines 21–22). Therefore, Choice (A) fits perfectly. Choice (C) may have lured you because the author of Passage II does state that human activity is a factor; Passage I, however, ignores the human effect on the weather.

10. The title that best fits both passages is

    (A) Global Warming

    (B) Climate Change

    (C) Volcanoes and Climate

    (D) Human Effects on Climate

    (E) Climate's Effects on Humans

    Choice (A) is out because Passage I talks about Mt. Toba, an example of colder temperatures, and Passage II doesn't really deal with volcanoes, so (C) is also out. Passage I ignores human effects on climate, so the answer can't be (D), and (E) is out because Passage II mentions the climate's effects on human beings only in passing. As a result, (B) is the correct answer.

Set 2

> The first passage is an excerpt from The Ancient Egyptians For Dummies *by Charlotte Booth (Wiley). The second passage comes from a 19th-century guide to Egyptian archaeology.*

Passage 1

Line Egyptian art is not a photograph. When considering Egyptian art, modern viewers must remember that the Egyptians rarely recorded "the truth" — a realistic depiction of an object or person. Although the images can never be viewed as portraiture or a true rendition, every element of a composition is designed to tell you something
(05) about the person, event, or ritual. This notion explains the lack of perspective and three-dimensional qualities in Egyptian art, as well as the somewhat bizarre (to our eyes at least) representations of people, animals, and gods. Everything in ancient Egyptian art is presented from the most recognizable viewpoint in an effort to eliminate ambiguity.

Passage II

(10) The wrestlers of the Beni Hasan tombs, the dancers and servants of the Theban catacombs, attack, struggle, posture, and go about their work with perfect naturalness and ease. These, however, are exceptions. Tradition, as a rule, was stronger than nature, and the Egyptian masters continued to deform the human figure. Their men and women are actual monsters from the point of view of the anatomist; and yet, after

(15)   all, they are neither so ugly nor so ridiculous as might be supposed by those who have seen only the wretched copies so often made by our modern artists. The wrong parts are joined to the right parts with so much skill that they seem to have grown there. The natural lines and the fictitious lines follow and complement each other so ingeniously, that the former appear to give rise of necessity to the latter. The conventionalities of Egyptian art once

(20)   accepted, we cannot sufficiently admire the technical skill displayed by the draughtsman.

1. According to Passage I, which of the following statements about Egyptian art is not true?

(A) Egyptian art was valid only if the viewer recognized the people or things it depicted.

(B) Though objects were sometimes distorted, people were always drawn in lifelike proportions.

(C) In Egyptian art, clarity was more important than realism.

(D) Egyptian art does not present three-dimensional images.

(E) The subjects of Egyptian art may be natural or supernatural.

2. According to Passage II, Egyptian art

(A) sometimes depicts natural figures

(B) always follows a set tradition

(C) relies heavily upon a knowledge of anatomy

(D) is inferior to the work of modern artists

(E) frequently incorporates mythological monsters

3. With which statement would the authors of both passages agree?

(A) Only the original artworks are worth viewing.

(B) In Egyptian art, supernatural images are more important than natural ones.

(C) Egyptian artists did not understand basic anatomy.

(D) The historical context of Egyptian art is irrelevant.

(E) Modern viewers must understand Egyptian art in order to appreciate it.

4. Compared to Passage I, Passage II is

(A) more critical of Egyptian art

(B) more general

(C) more specific

(D) more concerned with history than aesthetics

(E) less descriptive

Answers to Set 2

1. **B.** When you're checking for an answer that *isn't* true, go through the answers in order. With any luck, the false statement will be high up in the pack, and you won't have to bother with the answers that follow. In this question, Choice (A) is clearly true, because Lines 7–9 tell you that "Everything in ancient Egyptian art is presented from the most recognizable viewpoint in an effort to eliminate *ambiguity*" (two possible meanings). Choice (B), on the other hand, immediately makes the lie-detector jump: The passage specifically refers to "bizarre . . . representations of people" (Lines 6–7). Bingo: you've found the false statement, so you're done.

2. **A.** Passage II opens with a description of specific tombs, where paintings of wrestlers "go about their work with perfect naturalness" (Line 11). The passage also explains that the wrestlers are *exceptions* (Line 12) to the usual style. Therefore, Egyptian art "sometimes *depicts* [shows] natural figures" — Choice (A).

3. **E.** In Passage I, the art is described as "bizarre (to our eyes, at least)" (Lines 6–7), but the author also says that "every element of a composition is designed to tell you something about the person, event, or ritual" (Lines 4–5). Passage II explains that once "the conventionalities of Egyptian art" (Line 19) are accepted, the artists' technical skill is evident. Thus, both authors agree that *modern viewers* may need some background in Egyptian artistic style in order to appreciate it, as Choice (E) states.

4. **C.** Passage I discusses Egyptian art in a general way, explaining the principles underlying its style. While Passage II also contains some general statements, it begins with two specific examples, "the wrestlers of the Beni Hasan tombs and the dancers and servants of the Theban catacombs" (Lines 10–11), making Choice (C) the best response.

Abbreviating the Agony: Short Passages

The 100-word (give or take a sentence) Critical Reading passages are short but *not* sweet. Don't be fooled by their length; sometimes the questions attached to these little devils are harder than those based on longer passages because more is implied than stated in a tiny slice of text. Still, you can conquer short passages after you've practiced them. Here are two sets: One takes you step by step, and the second, which is set up like the real test, sends you out alone, with answers at the very end.

Set 1

This excerpt from a 19th-century novel describes a female tavern owner's dilemma.

Passage 1

Line To maintain the discipline of the tavern, nevertheless, the presence of a man was desirable; she understood this. Besides, the condition of an old maid did not seem to her at all inviting, and she did not care to wait the epoch of a third youth, before making a choice. But what would the unsuccessful candidates say? Would not this decision be at the risk of kin-
(05) dling a civil war, of provoking perhaps a general desertion? Then, too, accustomed as she was to command, the idea of giving herself a master alarmed her.

1. According to the passage, the narrator

(A) wants to hire three youths to help in the tavern

(B) is deciding whether to hire a youth or an old maid

(C) is confused about running a tavern

(D) understands that a man will help keep order in the tavern

(E) does not like giving orders

Choice (D) is correct. The clue is in Sentence 1. The narrator *understood* that the *presence of a man was desirable* in order to *maintain the discipline of the tavern.* You can dump Choice (A) because she did not care to wait for a third youth, so she's not hiring three people. Choice (B) bites the dust because she's worried about becoming an old maid herself, not thinking about hiring one. The passage directly contradicts (C) and (E).

2. Who is most likely to participate in the "civil war" referred to in Line 5?

(A) candidates who lose an election

(B) someone not chosen to run the tavern

(C) people who drink at the tavern

(D) soldiers from a local fort

(E) old maids

Choice (B) is correct. Check out the reference to *a third youth* in Line 3. The author implies that a man is present, ready to work in the tavern, but a third youth may arrive as competition for the role of helper. A *civil war* may break out between the two male candidates for the position, including someone not chosen to run the tavern, also known as (B).

This passage is an excerpt from *The Hidden Universe,* a science text by Roger J. Tayler (Wiley).

Passage 11

Astronomy is very different from other sciences in that it is observational rather than exper-
Line   imental. Almost all of the information that an astronomer gathers about the Universe is in
the form of electromagnetic waves, such as light and radio waves, which travel to the Earth
from distant objects. From the properties of these waves an attempt is made to understand
the structure and evolution of the Universe. At the outset there is one major problem. The
(05)   observations can only be interpreted by use of the laws of physics, but these laws of physics have only been established through experiments on the Earth and in its immediate
neighborhood at the present time.

3. The passage implies that the laws of physics

    (A) may not be the same away from the Earth

    (B) can never change

    (C) are a problem for scientists because they cannot be the subject of any experiments

    (D) apply only to waves

    (E) have been verified in environments away from the Earth

The passage contains a couple of clue words — *different* (Line 1) alerts you to a contrast, and "only . . . on the Earth . . . at the present time" (Lines 7–8) puts you on notice that anything away from the Earth is doubtful. The enticing-but-wrong answer here is Choice (C) because the passage does describe the problem of not being able to verify the laws of physics — away from the Earth. The laws of physics may certainly be verified *on Earth,* including the law that whenever I drop a sandwich it will land jelly side down. Choice (A) is correct.

4. In the context of Line 5, what is the best rephrasing of "at the outset"?

    (A) when one gathers data

    (B) when one analyzes data

    (C) the first consideration is

    (D) historically

    (E) in the early days of astronomy

Choice (C) is for *correct* in this question. Although the passage refers to a process, and all processes take place over time, the statement that "At the outset there is one major problem" (Line 5) takes into account the study of astronomy, not the gathering or analysis of data. Nor does the phrase refer to an earlier stage of scientific knowledge.

This excerpt from *The House of Science* by Philip R. Holzinger (Wiley) discusses world population growth in relation to food supply.

Passage III

Line Given the present growth rate of 1.6 percent, the world's population will more than double in your lifetime. But is this rate of growth likely to remain the same? With a significant portion of the world's population currently malnourished or undernourished, can the earth sustain a population more than twice the size it has now? Some scientists think it can, but a great many

(05) think it is unlikely, given our present resources and technology. We have made strides in feeding the world's population. For example, scientists have come up with new strains of wheat, rice, and other crops that produce a good deal more per plant than the old strains did. These new strains are part of what is known as the Green Revolution.

5. What assumption does the author make about the rate of population growth?

   (A) Scientists should work to increase the rate of population growth.

   (B) The Green Revolution will lower the growth rate of population.

   (C) The present growth rate of population must change as the number of people on earth increases.

   (D) Without adequate food, the rate of population growth will slow.

   (E) A growth rate of 1.6 percent is ideal.

The clue is the question pair in Lines 2–4. Placing them together implies a cause-and-effect relationship. Another clue is the description of agricultural improvements. Plopping them in a paragraph about population links the two. Choice (D) is correct.

6. In this passage, the "Green Revolution" (Line 8) refers to

   (A) changes in the way plants are harvested

   (B) new types of plants

   (C) plants that yield more food, in addition to other advancements in agriculture

   (D) an increased concern for ecology

   (E) population control through food rationing

The passage talks about new crops and then throws you the label *Green Revolution,* so the revolution has to have something to do with food and/or plants, so you can eliminate (D) and (E). Choice (C) wins the race because the last sentence in the passage says *part* of the Revolution, so other factors must exist.

This paragraph about food safety comes from *Basic Statistics* by Olive Jean Dunn (Wiley).

Passage IV

Line [A] newspaper article several years ago stated that it is safer to eat in restaurants than in homes or at private affairs. The statistical basis for this conclusion was that health departments receive fewer reports of food poisoning from restaurants than from picnics, private parties, and private homes. The conclusion that restaurant meals are safer than home

(05) meals does not follow from the fact that more reports of food poisonings come from picnics, private parties, and private homes than come from public eating places. First, we would have to know the number of meals served in each type of eating place in order to compare them. Second, food poisoning from a restaurant meal is often difficult to trace to the restaurant, so that restaurants *may* be less safe than private homes even though fewer

(10) cases of food poisoning are reported per meal served.

7. The author believes that statistics

    (A) should be used to evaluate the safety of restaurants

    (B) prove that restaurant meals are safer on the whole than most people think

    (C) accurately measure the safety of picnic food

    (D) can easily be misinterpreted by the media

    (E) are the media's most valuable source of information

The SAT writers tuck a bunch of false clues in these choices, hoping to distract you. The passage criticizes the newspaper article that evaluated the safety of restaurant meals. Choices (D) and (E) deal with media, so they're both in the running. Choice (E) loses the race, however, because of its vagueness. Choices (A) and (C) are contradicted by the passage, and (B) falls away because of the word *prove*. Thus, (D) is right.

8. In Line 9 the word *may* is italicized because the author

    (A) thinks that restaurants are more dangerous than most people believe

    (B) wants to emphasize that no valid conclusion about the safety of restaurants may be drawn without more information

    (C) is confused about the safety of various food sources

    (D) believes that many cases of food poisoning are not reported

    (E) is emphasizing how little is known about restaurant meals

An italicized word nearly always creates emphasis, as in "The SAT is an *awful* test." So Choices (B) and (E) are the best bets, with (E) voted off the island because it says nothing about safety. If you selected (B), pat yourself on the back.

After you're done, add up your score. If you answered more than four right, you're doing great. Take the night off. If only one or two made it into your correct column, hit the next set.

Set 2

> *This passage about leadership comes from* The Transformational Leader, *by Noel M. Tichy and Mary Anne Devanna (Wiley).*

Passage 1

Line   In the United States there is a continuing shift in the demographics of the workforce. In 1985 white males became a minority in the workforce, yet they continue to hold virtually all the positions of power in large organizations. Similar pressures are emerging in Japan as women look for a more meaningful role in society. No society is immune
(05)   to this growing hunger for opportunity and equity. Laws and sanctions to correct inequity are formulated by the government but they are implemented by organizations. And it is in the implementation that the debate about equity begins. The core challenge is to mobilize an increasingly pluralistic workforce where many groups have no significant decision-making role. This tends to set up the dynamic for con-
(10)   frontation rather than collaboration.

1. The authors imply that

   (A) women have too many decision-making roles in international organizations

   (B) Japanese women are discontent with traditional roles

   (C) white males in the United States hold too little power in the workplace

   (D) laws to change the ethnic or gender balance of power are easy to put into effect

   (E) white males are now a minority in the American workforce

2. What is the meaning of "sanctions" in Line 5?

   (A) blessings

   (B) praise

   (C) approval

   (D) penalties

   (E) actions

This selection from Physical Science in the Middle Ages *by Edward Gran (Wiley) describes the origins of universities in Western Europe.*

Passage 11

Line [T]he spontaneous emergence of universities was intimately associated with the new learning that had been translated into Latin throughout the course of the twelfth century. Indeed the university was the institutional means by which Western Europe would organize, absorb, and expand the great volume of new knowledge; the instru-
(05) ment by which it would mold and disseminate a common intellectual heritage for generations to come. While the universities of Paris and Oxford became renowned as centers of philosophy and science and Bologna for its schools of law and medicine, all three . . . shaped the university into a form that has persisted to this day.

3. According to the passage, once many works had been translated into Latin,

   (A) Latin could more easily be taught in universities

   (B) universities were formed to translate more books

   (C) knowledge could be shared among scholars

   (D) the language was not understood by university students

   (E) scholars could no longer appreciate the knowledge gained by past generations

4. The author implies that

   (A) all true universities teach philosophy, science, law, and medicine

   (B) the establishment of universities was the result of a carefully planned effort

   (C) law and medicine were not appreciated in Paris and Oxford

   (D) today's universities should have an international student body

   (E) today's universities owe much to an intellectual effort in the 12th century

> *In this passage from a 19th-century novel, the narrator reminisces about a childhood friend.*

Passage III

Line Ratsey was always kind to me, and had lent me a chisel many a time to make boats, so I stepped in and held the lantern watching him chink out the bits of Portland stone with a graver, and blinking the while when they came too near my eyes. The inscription stood complete, but he was putting the finishing touches to a little sea-piece
(05) carved at the top of the stone, which showed a schooner boarding a cutter. I thought it fine work at the time, but know now that it was rough enough; indeed, you may see it for yourself in Moonfleet churchyard to this day, and read the inscription too, though it is yellow with lichen, and not so plain as it was that night.

5. The carving referred to in the passage

(A) was probably a tombstone

(B) was primarily created by the author

(C) contained only words

(D) has hardly aged at all

(E) was intended to protect eyesight

6. A schooner and a cutter (Line 5) are

(A) carving tools

(B) names carved on the stone

(C) types of stone

(D) associated with the sea

(E) mineral formations

> *This passage from* Rogue Asteroids and Doomsday Comets *by Duncan Steel (Wiley) describes the damage that may be caused by the impact of an asteroid (chunk of space rock) on our planet.*

Passage IV

Line A 500-meter asteroid crashing into a desert — for example, the Outback of Australia or the Sahara — would devastate an area of about 160,000 square kilometers and cause substantial damage over a far greater region. For example, if the asteroid fell in the Outback, all of the cities in Australia would almost surely be shaken flat. This
(05) would not, however, be the worst-case scenario. The consequences of the same asteroid arriving a few hours earlier and perhaps landing in the Pacific Ocean between New Zealand and Tahiti would be far worse. This is because the impact would generate an enormous tsunami (a huge ocean wave), often caused by earthquakes.

7. According to the passage, which of the following is true of both earthquakes and collision with an asteroid?

(A) Neither shakes cities so strongly that buildings are flattened.

(B) Both may generate tsunamis.

(C) Both have the power to devastate deserts and oceans.

(D) Both originate in the Southern Hemisphere.

(E) Australia is less affected by earthquakes and asteroid collisions than New Zealand and Tahiti are.

8. The passage mentions the Outback of Australia because

(A) it is most likely to be hit by an astero'

(B) it has been hit by asteroids in the

(C) the Outback is a source of tsur

(D) it serves as an example of a

(E) Australia has felt the eff mis but not asteroids

Answers to Set 2

1. **B.** The false positive in this question is Choice (E) because the passage states that white males are a minority in the American workforce. So anyone who zoomed through the question got this one wrong. Why? Because the question asks what the authors *imply*, not what they actually say. The statement in Lines 3–4 about Japanese women's search for *a more meaningful role* is the clue that nails down (B) because no one searches if he or she is already content.

2. **D.** A vocabulary-in-context question is usually a cinch, as long as you take the time to read the context. The passage says, "Laws and sanctions to correct inequity are formulated by the government." The law doesn't give blessings or praise, and approval is rare, so Choices (A), (B), and (C) are all wrong. Besides, you can't correct a mistake with approval. Choice (E) is too vague. Two cheers for (D).

3. **C.** The clue in Sentence 1 intimately associates learning and Latin. Because the universities are sharing learning, you need take only one tiny step from Latin to learning to universities, where you find — in addition to keg parties and tailgate parties — *scholars.* Choice (C) is correct.

4. **E.** Zero in on Lines 5–6, where you find *generations to come,* and Line 8, which mentions a form that "has persisted to this day . . ." which, by the way, is Tuesday. (Just kidding.) Now you can check out Choices (D) and (E), which talk about *today's universities.* Choice (E) relates to the rest of the passage, the 12th-century part.

5. **A.** You're in a churchyard, carving, and the carving stays around long enough to gather *lichen* (little fungi) and blur its words. Think *tombstone* or *monument,* and only tombstone is an option. Bingo! Choice (A) is right.

6. **D.** Even if you're unfamiliar with the words (which name types of boats), Line 4 tells you that the carving is a *sea-piece.* Choice (D) is the only one that deals with the sea.

7. **B.** The appealing-but-wrong choice is (C) because although both earthquakes are described in the passage as devastating, giant waves don't hit the desert. Thus, Choice (B) is a better bet.

8. **D.** This question is a rule-out, as in rule out the wrong answers and what's left is correct. You can't justify Choice (A) because the odds of an asteroid hitting the desert are never discussed. Ditto for (B) and (E) — the passage doesn't tell you whether an asteroid or a giant wave once hit the Outback. Choice (C) is just plain wrong. Opt for (D).

Chapter 5

Filling In the Blanks: Sentence Completions

New York City subways used to display signs advertising a school for shorthand. "If u cn rd ths, u cn gt a gd job," they declared. I never did try for the "good job" they were dangling in front of me, even though I "could read this" easily. But I did have fun watching people puzzle out the missing letters. SAT sentence completions are only a little more complicated than the missing-letter ads on the subway. The words you see have all their letters — always a plus in reading! Also, the test makers tuck some clues into the sentence so you can figure out what's missing. The hardest questions include words known only by people who eat dictionaries for breakfast (low carb, but not very tasty).

On the SAT you find from five to eight sentence completions in each Critical Reading section. The usual SAT scoring applies: one point for each correct answer, no points for a skipped question, and a quarter-point deduction for each error. In this chapter, I explain how to approach the easy and mid-level sentence completions. I also provide strategies for the tough questions, including when to guess and when to skip.

Sampling the Sentence Completion Menu

If you're having a small anxiety attack right now worrying about sentence completions, take a deep breath and relax. In this section, you discover how to identify the different types of sentence completions, the first step toward solving them.

Sentence completions come in a few basic forms:

✔ Simple vocabulary, one blank
✔ Simple vocabulary, two blanks
✔ Tough vocabulary, one or two blanks

Each Critical Reading section on the SAT has some single-blank and so[m]e ~~double~~ questions. Don't assume that the doubles are harder. Some are actua[lly easier than the] ~~sin~~gles because more words give you more clues. Continue reading t[o see what these] types look like and to find out some general tips on solving these l[ittle guys.]

In the following sections, I provide some sentence-completion questions that are similar to those on the real SAT, though mine (she said modestly) are marginally funny and the SAT has no sense of humor whatsoever. I also provide solutions and the reasoning that I used to determine the answers. (Check out the "Completing the Sentence: Steps That Work" section later in this chapter for different strategies to help you ace the sentence-completion section on your SAT.)

Simple vocabulary, one blank

Several sentence-completion questions throw you the vocabulary equivalent of a softball, though you may not know every single word in them. However, easy vocabulary doesn't mean that the sentence is a cinch. Fortunately, the SAT gremlins do play fair to the extent that they scatter word clues for the observant reader. Check this one out:

Because she was upset by the security guard's close attention, Suzy Sunshine stormed out of the lingerie store and remained _____ for the rest of the day.

(A) braless

(B) serene

(C) annoyed

(D) joyful

(E) hungry

The answer is (C). Here's the deal: Upon reading the sentence, you immediately think of an innocent shopper tailed too closely by a security guard. You picture little Suzy abandoning the piles of luxury underwear and heading home. Real-world experience tells you that Suzy is probably annoyed or even indignant. As you check for clues in the sentence, you notice *because* and *stormed*. The *because* tells you to focus on answers that would be consequences of Suzy's experience in the store. *Stormed* tells you about Suzy's mood. Several words pop into your head when you think about the blank — *grouchy, mad, angry,* and so forth. When you check the choices, you see (C), *annoyed,* and that's the answer.

Sometimes clue words are omitted, but you can figure out the logic of the sentence anyway. (The sentence in the preceding question, for example, makes sense even if *because* is left out.)

> Upset by the security guard's attention, Suzy Sunshine stormed out of the lingerie store and remained _____ for the rest of the day.

To answer these questions, be aware of what the sentence implies as well as what it states.

Here's the same sentence with a twist:

Although she was upset by the security guard's close attention and stormed out of the lingerie store, Suzy Sunshine remained _____ for the rest of the day.

(A) braless

(B) serene

(C) annoyed

(D) joyful

(E) hungry

The answer is (B). The word *although* sets up a contrast. Because she *stormed,* you know Suzy was annoyed upon leaving the store. The *although* tells you that her mood changed and that (C) is the opposite of what you want. Choosing your own fill-in, you may opt for *peaceful.* (When you create your own fill-in, don't worry about grammar or proper English. Just concentrate on the meaning.) *Serene,* or peaceful, is the choice that fits best.

Suppose you create your own fill-in but nothing matches it? For instance, in the preceding question you may have said *alone* or *secluded.* Not bad, but not on the answer list. Either create a new fill-in or check out the choices and see what appeals.

Note: More than one choice may work. In the preceding example, *joyful* contrasts with *stormed.* However, *stormed* has an element of anger in it, so *serene* is better.

Simple vocabulary, two blanks

Two for the price of one. What could be bad about that deal? Plenty. However, not as much as you think. The two-blank question is often easier than its single cousin because you get extra hints about the right choice. Take a look at this example:

Despite her _____ mood, Suzy Sunshine put on a _____ face when she faced the tabloid reporter.

(A) positive . . . cheerful

(B) unpleasant . . . friendly

(C) thoughtful . . . interested

(D) grouchy . . . irritable

(E) depressed . . . sad

The answer is (B). Even if you've never been a celebrity, life in the 21st century has probably given you the impression that tabloid reporters can grasp the tiniest thread and turn it into a rope strong enough to hang a naïve interview subject. So (A), (B), and (C) are all possibilities, unless Suzy is going for the sympathy vote, in which case (E) makes the cut. But the word clue *despite* tells you to search for opposites. You can rule out (A), (D), and (E) because they're closer to synonyms. Choice (B) quickly emerges as the best choice — an opposite that also matches real-world clues.

If you're fairly sure that you know the correct word for either one of the blanks, zero in on the choices that fit and ignore the rest. But don't jump on an answer simply because it fits one of the blanks. Go for something that fits both because a shortcut may easily lead you astray. As a matter of fact, the SAT writers are crossing their fingers and hoping that you select the quick — but wrong — answer.

If you see a sentence completion with relatively simple words, read extra carefully. Be s that you understand the meaning of the sentence before choosing an answer. To mak life even more miserable than usual, the SAT writers usually place one very appeali answer among the five choices in this sort of sentence completion. If you space c a second or if you overlook one picky little detail, you may fall headfirst into a

Tough vocabulary

If your caregiver had the foresight to shout vocabulary words at ' played in, you may find these questions easy. For normal people the "tough-vocabulary" sentence completions are a challenge — but bility. (For tips on improving your vocabulary, see Chapter 2.)

The best method of attack is to eliminate the choices that contain words you have never seen before and then concentrate on the remaining answers. Follow the same strategy in reading the sentence that you followed for simple-vocabulary questions: Check for real-world links and look for word clues. Then examine your possible answers. If one fits, go for it. If nothing that you recognize makes sense, turn your attention to the *I-have-no-idea-what-these-words-mean* choices. Use the usual guessing rule. If you have eliminated one or more of the five choices, take a stab and move on to another question. If not, leave it blank and forget about it.

Many tough-vocabulary questions have the definition right there in the sentence. Look for the definition and see if it jars anything loose in your brain. For instance, suppose the sentence reads as follows:

In her _____ mood, Suzy Sunshine sat frowning and took pleasure in nothing.

(A) affable

(B) jocund

(C) jovial

(D) morose

(E) narcissistic

Okay, the test makers have given you one break. The entire second half of the sentence is a definition; you just have to find the word that fits. *Frowning* and *taking pleasure in nothing* mean "depressed." Now you just have to find a word that means "depressed." Reread the five choices. Anything register? If so, go for it. Or if you know that some of the words *don't* mean "depressed," rule them out. Then apply the guessing rules. In the preceding example, by the way, *morose* means "depressed," so the answer is (D). The other words are as follows: *affable* means "friendly," *jocund* means "joking," *jovial* means "joyous," and *narcissistic* means "egotistical, thinks he's/she's the center of the universe."

Want to increase your vocabulary, fast? Keep a notepad or a stack of index cards near you when you're reading. When you come across an unfamiliar word, take a moment to jot down the sentence. Later, check the word's meaning. You can use the dictionary, a computer, a handy teacher, or even a parent. Note the meaning. Don't write *all* the possible definitions, just the one that fits the sentence. From time to time, review your word/sentence list (or index cards) — your personal dictionary. The words will stick in your mind because you didn't memorize a random list; you got them from something you were actually reading. The context helps keep the new words in your memory bank. (For more long-term vocabulary-building tips, check out Chapter 2.)

Uncovering Word Clues

Sentences fall into a small number of recognizable patterns. Sentences may follow chronological order, relate cause and effect, explain similarities, or add examples. They also contrast ideas or things and name exceptions to the rule. Certain words are clues to sentence structure. After you identify those words, you've solved the riddle. Take a look at the most prevalent clue words you may encounter on the SAT and example sentences:

- ✔ **After:** *Barney ate three dried fish after he went to the movies.* (The sentence doubles back in time from the fish to the movies.)

- ✔ **And, also:** *Brunhilda added three new ants to her all-bug baseball team, and she also acquired a terrific centipede pitcher that had recently cleared waivers.* (The sentence adds examples.)

- ✔ **But:** *Barbara bellowed for help for seven straight hours, but Bella barely whimpered her distress.* (The sentence contrasts two Viking warriors.)

🖝 **So:** *Bettina's aardvark wouldn't stop eating her pet ants, so she slapped him.* (The sentence moves logically from cause to effect.)

🖝 **Then:** *Trini went to the movies and then ate two bags of popcorn.* (The sentence proceeds in a straight line chronologically from the movies to the snack.)

In addition to the five preceding common SAT clue words, check out the following list for other clue words you may encounter:

🖝 **Cause and effect:** Because, for, therefore, consequently, hence, thus, accordingly, as a result, ergo (only in truly boring academic writing, the type that should be banned from the planet, if not the solar system)

🖝 **Comparison:** Than, equally, like . . . as, similarly, similar to, like

🖝 **The exception to the rule (contrasting idea):** On the other hand, in contrast to, however, despite, in spite of, nevertheless, nonetheless, otherwise, although, though, even though

🖝 **More of the same:** And, also, as well, in addition, not only . . . but also, furthermore, moreover, besides, likewise, not the only, such as, for example, for instance, showing, illustrating

🖝 **Time marches on (or back):** Then, once, before, after, since, while, during, still, yet, until, up until, later, earlier, finally, in the end, when, originally

No! No! A thousand times *no!* Not to mention *never, but, nor, neither,* and other *negative* words. These word gremlins pop up frequently in sentence completions, a trap for the unwary. When you see a negative word, give yourself an extra moment to be sure you understand the sentence's meaning. A Grand Canyon-size difference separates *Fiona wanted to polish Nick's teeth more than anything else in the world* and *Fiona didn't want to polish Nick's teeth more than anything else in the world.* Also, be careful of double negatives. The SAT has good grammar, so you won't find a sentence completion saying something like *He didn't want no vegetables.* However, you may find this sentence: *Because Mattie didn't understand Martian, she had no interest in that newspaper.* Okay, maybe not that exact sentence, but one with a similar structure. Be sure to decode both parts of the sentence before choosing a completion answer.

Applying Real-Life Experience

You can decode a few of the SAT sentence completions with a fast reference to your own, normal, happens-to-every-human experience. For example, suppose you're reading this passage:

> Al, weary and depressed by the idea of still another meaningless date with Ella instead of an evening with the love of his life, Marcia, begged off by feigning a headache.

Okay, imagine that the word *feigning* is new to you. No big deal. Everyone's been in Al's shoes, signed up to have dinner with a loser because the person he or she really wants to date has basically said, "Not in this universe" to all requests for romantic attention. So what do you do when you really can't take it anymore? You pretend to have a headache. There you go. *Feigning* means "pretending." Of course, if you're just reading, you probably don't take the time to say explicitly, "*Feign* is a fancy way of saying pretend." You just go on your gut instinct and keep reading, hoping to find out how Ella reacts to her 20th straight rejection. By the way, you probably didn't stop to look up *explicitly* in the dictionary. You decoded the sentence without that word, which means "openly or clearly, stated upfront" as in "My mother never explicitly told me to take out the garbage so she can't punish me just because half of the kitchen looks like a toxic waste dump."

After you uncover the word clues and apply real-life logic, you probably have a pretty good idea what the sentence is trying to say. Now you're ready to complete it and be on your way to a high score in the sentence-completion section.

Completing the Sentence: Steps That Work

For both simply worded and vocabulary-laden questions, follow these steps to come up with the right answer:

1. **Read the entire sentence.**

   This step sounds too obvious to state, but some people actually try to choose an answer after reading only a couple of words. The SAT test makers are ready for these "partial readers." They take care to provide a choice that looks fine but is the verbal equivalent of the halfway point in a dive into a waterless swimming pool.

2. **Check for clue words.**

   If you find any, underline them. (Not sure what a clue word is? Check out the section "Uncovering Word Clues" earlier in this chapter.)

3. **Decide what the sentence is trying to say.**

   You may not be able to get the whole meaning yet, but you should have some idea what target the sentence is aiming at. Don't look at the answer choices yet.

4. **If possible, make up a word or phrase that fits the blank(s).**

   You can't always do so, but if you can, you're nearly home free. Check the answers to see whether any choice matches your idea. If so, take that option and move on. If not, think about whether the answer is likely to be a positive or a negative word. Put a little plus or minus sign in the blank to remind you of the type of answer you're searching for.

5. **Eliminate the nonstarters.**

   You may be able to rule out some choices right away. For example, if you know that the blank indicates a change in direction for the sentence — a contrast, perhaps — you can dump all the choices that seem similar to the idea expressed in the rest of the sentence. If you've placed a plus sign in the blank, dump the negative words.

6. **Check the remaining answers for the best match.**

   Even if you weren't able to come up with a possible fill-in, the answer choices may give you some ideas. Plug each remaining choice into the sentence until one fits snugly. If more than one answer is possible, go for the one that matches a clue in the sentence. In the SAT sentence completions, you're always looking for the best answer, not just any old answer that may be okay.

If you have absolutely no idea what some of the words mean, follow the general rule on guessing. If you can eliminate one choice, take a guess. If you can't eliminate any choices, skip the question. No matter what, don't waste brain cells on a question that relies on a bunch of words that have never crossed your path. Move on to the questions that you have a better shot at getting right. (See Chapter 1 for the complete lowdown on guessing.)

Chapter 6

Practicing Sentence Completions

. . . .

In This Chapter

▶ Getting comfortable with some guided sentence completions

▶ Analyzing your strengths and weaknesses by solving sentence completions on your own

. . . .

Practice may not make perfect, but when it comes to sentence completions, practice definitely leads to higher scores. As you get comfortable with this type of question, you can quickly zero in on the clue words and maneuver around the SAT's favorite tricks.

In this chapter, you find two sets of SAT-style sentence completions, arranged in increasing level of difficulty. After you finish each question in the first set, check the explanation that directly follows the question. No peeking! If you're too tempted, place a sheet of paper over the answer. Even if you get the correct answer, read the whole explanation. You may discover some new vocabulary and tricks of the trade. The answers to the second set, which is set up like the real test, are in their own section following the last question in the set. No peeking there either! (For more info on answering sentence completions, check out Chapter 5.)

Level of difficulty is always an individual decision, so you may find some of the earlier sentences more difficult and some of the later sentences a walk in the park. But in general, look especially hard for traps in the last three sentence completions, including the ones in this chapter. Follow the guessing rules that I outline in Chapter 1.

Set 1: Tackling Some Guided Questions

1. Audrey Vazquez, who acknowledges Cervantes as a _____, takes inspiration from his famous windmill episode but raises the comedy to a new level.

   (A) model

   (B) descendant

   (C) obstacle

   (D) tragedian

   (E) contradiction

   The key word here is *inspiration*. If Audrey Vazquez takes *inspiration* from Cervantes, Cervantes has to be something positive, and he has to come before Audrey's time. Boom! You can eliminate *descendant* and *obstacle*. Because the *famous windmill episode* is comedy, you can dump *tragedian*. *Contradiction* doesn't make much sense, so *model* is best. Choice (A) is correct.

2. The labor leader's foray into astrology has been ignored by all but the most inclusive biographers, and even they tend to _____ this period in his life.

   (A) investigate

   (B) explain

   (C) fabricate

   (D) emphasize

   (E) minimize

   The clue that cracks this sentence is *even*. You know you're going to continue the same idea from the beginning of the sentence, which tells you that the period is *ignored*. What fits with *ignored*? *Minimize* means "to pay as little attention to as possible." Choice (E) is correct.

3. The central achievement of *Macbeth* is Shakespeare's ability to _____ the politics of his day and _____ the interplay of ambition and conscience.

   (A) uncover . . . synthesize

   (B) dissect . . . reveal

   (C) penetrate . . . rearrange

   (D) analyze . . . confuse

   (E) idealize . . . downgrade

   Think about the relationship between the two blanks. The first does something to *politics*, and the second relates to *ambition* and *conscience*. If you fill in the blanks with the first thing that comes into your head, you may say "dig into" the politics and "show" the ambition/conscience connection. So you can immediately knock out (D) and (E) because *confuse* and *downgrade* aren't achievements. (A), (B), and (C) are all possible until you get to the second blank because *uncover, dissect,* and *penetrate* all tell you that Shakespeare is getting into politics. But only (B) fits when you hit the second blank. *Synthesize* means "to pull lots of loose ideas into a whole" or "to manufacture." *Rearrange* doesn't make sense. Choice (B) has it all: If Shakespeare *dissects* politics, he slices into it and examines the pieces in detail, thus *revealing* the way ambition and conscience relate to each other. Three cheers for (B).

4. _____ that intentions have some _____ in a discussion of poetry, let us refer to the journal of Alex Plug, which clearly states that his sonnet "On Homework" was written to express disgust with the last biology assignment.

   (A) Denying . . . importance

   (B) Acknowledging . . . ambiguity

   (C) Granting . . . validity

   (D) Reiterating . . . irrelevance

   (E) Disproving . . . interest

   You can rule out (A) because if you *deny* that intentions have *importance,* why bother listening to the author's explanation of how he wrote "On Homework"? You can drop (D) and (E) for the same reason. (B) leaves the playing field because Plug's journals *clearly* make a point, and *ambiguity* implies that more than one interpretation is possible. Thus, Choice (C) is correct.

5. The failure of the parent to control his child's behavior meant that the entire streetcar had to endure a flow of meaningless _____ from a youngster barely old enough to talk.

   (A) prattle

   (B) joviality

   (C) criticism

   (D) maledictions

   (E) maladies

   You know the sentence refers to a problem because the streetcar riders must *endure,* or put up with something, so you can rule out *joviality* (fun, jolliness). "Barely old enough to talk" tells you that the problem concerns words; time to dump *maladies* (ills) and *maledictions* (curses). *Criticism* could be verbal trouble, but tiny little kids seldom lecture on the flaws in Spielberg's latest movie. *Prattle* — meaningless chatter — fits best. Pat yourself on the back if you said Choice (A).

6. Although _____ images of the region persist, the area in fact has witnessed a _____ of economic and social activity.

   (A) photographic . . . mutation

   (B) sordid . . . devastation

   (C) illusory . . . decline

   (D) geographic . . . predominance

   (E) negative . . . resurgence

   The clue word *although* tips you off: The sentence contrasts two ideas. Choice (E) gives you opposite directions — *negative* is on the way down, and *resurgence* (resurrection or rebirth) is on the way up. No other pair contains this contrast, so Choice (E) is correct.

7. The most controversial section is Ms. Haldock's frank _____ on patriotism.

   (A) platitude

   (B) metamorphosis

   (C) consensus

   (D) treatise

   (E) neologism

   The clues are the words *controversial* and *frank* — concepts usually applied to ideas in written or oral form. Choices (A), (D), and (E) may refer to words (*platitude* means "soothing proverb or saying," *treatise* means "a written discussion of ideas," and *neologism* means "newly coined word"). Of the three, only *treatise* fits with *controversial,* an adjective applied to things that people argue about. Choice (D) is correct.

 Now that you've completed a set, look at the questions you answered incorrectly. Decide why you made a mistake. Was it an issue of vocabulary? Missing a word clue? Eliminating clearly wrong answers and then making a bad guess? After you examine your pattern of errors, you know what you need to work on. If it's vocabulary, check out Chapter 2 for some tips. Also look at the words that look like *this* (and their accompanying definitions) that I tuck into this and all chapters. If word clues trip you up, take a look at Chapter 5.

Set 2: Practicing Some Questions on Your Own

1. His expression was _____ at every game; I don't think I saw him smile even when his team scored a hundred points.

    (A) downcast

    (B) affable

    (C) joyful

    (D) pert

    (E) mirthful

2. The king's _____ was evident when he declined to increase the tax rebate for his loyal but _____ subjects.

    (A) benevolence . . . poverty-stricken

    (B) greed . . . undertaxed

    (C) laziness . . . stubborn

    (D) popularity . . . aged

    (E) miserliness . . . needy

3. The judges who select the recipients of Woodron Fellowships _____ the purpose of the foundation when they financed Edward Ebert's research on the origin of mathematics, a project that is sure to _____ that topic successfully.

    (A) violated . . . describe

    (B) exonerated . . . delineate

    (C) contravened . . . explicate

    (D) honored . . . illuminate

    (E) supported . . . obfuscate

4. The comedian's _____ body made his emergence from the narrow chimney appear ridiculous and nearly impossible.

    (A) wizened

    (B) lithe

    (C) rotund

    (D) sooty

    (E) emaciated

5. Agnell's submission is in stark contrast to her growing awareness of the value of _____ speech.

    (A) impromptu

    (B) controversial

    (C) rebellious

    (D) protective

    (E) timorous

6. The beauty queen received her award primarily for her _____.

    (A) protocol

    (B) pulchritude

    (C) luminescence

    (D) integrity

    (E) chicanery

7. The _____ spectator did not hesitate to offer his opinion on every aspect of the game, even though he knew very little about sporting events.

    (A) inhibited

    (B) vociferous

    (C) credulous

    (D) brusque

    (E) judicious

8. The approaching rain gave us a(n) _____ excuse to escape the _____ party.

    (A) ubiquitous . . . jovial

    (B) unsolicited . . . riotous

    (C) plausible . . . boring

    (D) multifarious . . . elegant

    (E) intrinsic . . . obligatory

Answers to Set 2

1. **A.** You're looking for a downer, and the only word that doesn't apply to the can't-stop-grinning types is *downcast*, so (A) is the correct answer. *Affable* means "friendly," as in your basic chat-over-the-back-fence neighbor. *Pert* (also known as a shampoo) means "chirpy," as in your basic kid-sister-on-a-good-day attitude. *Mirth* means "laughter," so you can figure out *mirthful* yourself.

2. **E.** The clues in the sentence concern the tax rebate. If the king *declined* (refused) to increase the *rebate*, he didn't lower taxes. So (A), the trap in this question, is out because if the king displayed *benevolence*, he'd take less money from his poor subjects. On the other hand, if he showed *miserliness*, he counted every penny and didn't return any more than he absolutely had to, even though his subjects were *needy*. Choice (E) is right.

3. **D.** Use real-world knowledge to get a foothold here. Fellowships are fancy scholarships and are designed to add to the body of knowledge. So any positive word in the first blank must be matched by a positive word in the second blank. Or both blanks can be negative. The word *successfully* implies that you're aiming for positive, so you can rule out (A) and (C), in which the first choices are negative, and (E), in which the second choice is negative. Choice (B) falls away because you don't *exonerate* a purpose (prove that the purpose is guiltless), though you can exonerate the officers of the Woodron Fellowship if you can prove that they didn't spend a month in the Bahamas snorkeling away the scholarship money. Choice (D) is correct.

4. **C.** What makes an entry through a narrow chimney nearly impossible? A fat body. Hence Choice (C) is the answer you seek: *Rotund* is a word for those who shop for pants with 60-inch waists. The other choices don't fit: *wizened* means "shriveled up," *lithe* means "graceful" (think ballerina), and *emaciated* means "thin to the point of starving." Choice (D) is meant to distract you because soot does come from chimneys. However, because soot comes from chimneys, a sooty body is the opposite of *nearly impossible* for anyone who has slithered down one.

5. **C.** You need a contrast to *submission*, so you can rule out *impromptu* (off the cuff, unplanned), *protective*, (serving to shield or defend) and *timorous* (fearful, shy). *Controversial* is a possibility, but to *rebel* is the opposite of *to submit*, so *rebellious* is a better choice. Choice (C) is your best bet here.

6. **B.** Okay, *pulchritude* sounds like something you'd get arrested for, but it actually means "beauty." The next closest is *luminescence* because beautiful people tend to shine, but this word is better for things that really light up, like 40-watt bulbs. *Protocol* (the rules of diplomacy) and *integrity* (honesty) don't win beauty crowns, though *chicanery* (trickery) might. Still, (B) is best.

7. **B.** *Vociferous* people talk a lot and loudly — just the sort of spectators who think they know everything. *Inhibited* people are restrained and quiet. *Credulous* (believing too easily, as in "You'll sell me the Brooklyn Bridge? Great!") and *judicious* (wise) don't fit; neither does *brusque* (rude, abrupt). Choice (B) is right.

8. **C.** This relatively easy sentence becomes a killer when you look at the word choices, which are strictly for the "I read the whole thesaurus last night" set of people. But you can take an educated guess on the second blank. If you're talking about an *excuse* and an *escape*, the party is probably *boring*, which is Choice (C). Then real-world clues help. You want to get out of a boring party? Plead weather, and you'll be believed because your excuse is *plausible*, or believable. The other choices don't come close, though (B) may have caught your eye because rain is *unsolicited* (not asked for) and parties may be *riotous* (the neighbors may call the cops). Choice (C) is correct.

Getting the lowdown on sentence completions

Finish this sentence: SAT sentence completions

(A) are best when buttered lightly and eaten with globs of strawberry jelly

(B) should be sent for a very long walk on a short pier jutting into any convenient ocean

(C) are tough even for those with good vocabulary and reading skills

(D) make up a bit less than a third of the Critical Reading portion of the SAT

(E) may be answered only if you're in touch with your inner thesaurus

The correct answer is Choice (A). Just kidding. Though I do like strawberry jelly and I wouldn't mind dunking these questions in the Atlantic (Choice B). The real clinkers here are (C) and (E). True, if you've been working on your vocabulary (see Chapter 2 for hints), you already have a leg up on SAT sentence completions. But even if you haven't been buttering pages of the dictionary and eating them with a dab of strawberry, you can still do well on this section if you stay alert to reading clues. Choice (D), by the way, is the correct answer.

Part III

Getting the "Write" Answers: The Writing Sections

The 5th Wave   By Rich Tennant

PRONOUNS   AMATEURNOUNS

YOU   YOUS
             YAWL
THEY   WHOZITS
HE
SHE
IT

In this part . . .

The Sumerians scratched on wax and clay, the Egyptians penned on papyrus or carved on stone, and medieval monks bent over parchment. You get a bunch of green ovals and a sheet of lined paper. Welcome to the SAT Writing section.

This instrument of torture provides you with four ways to display your authorial prowess. One is an essay, which you have to write quickly under conditions that would send the best writer screaming into the night. Another is error recognition, in which you recognize, but don't correct, grammatical faults. Next up is sentence revision: The SAT writers underline a section of a sentence and give you a selection of ways to change it, for better or worse. Finally, the testers throw a couple of student compositions at you and ask how to improve the writing.

In this part, I take you through each of these tasks, steering you away from common pitfalls and toward winning techniques that will help you do your best on this section of the test.

Chapter 7

Writing Your Way to a High Score: The Essay

In This Chapter
▶ Responding to the essay prompt
▶ Collecting your thoughts quickly
▶ Drafting and revising your essay for maximum points
▶ Evaluating your essay according to SAT standards

*W*hen you open the SAT booklet, the first thing you see is the essay-writing section, which you have 25 minutes to complete. Why do you have such a short time limit? Keep in mind that the SAT writers have to pay teachers to read and grade essays. They can't just run the essays through a scanning machine that works 24/7 without bathroom breaks. Short essays mean less teacher-marking time.

Tiny masterpieces aren't easy to write, but don't worry. In this chapter, I explain how to start, how to finish, and what to do in the middle when you're writing an SAT essay. I also explain what the graders look for as they grade your essay and show you how to score your own essay so you have a sense of how you'd do on the first writing section of the real SAT.

Answering Promptly: Writing about the Right Topic in Your Essay

The essay portion of the SAT starts off with an essay *prompt* — a couple of short para-graphs that act as the starting gun for the essay race. This prompt consists of one or two quotations or paraphrased statements from writers, politicians, philosophers, and the like. Following the prompt is the question, which directs you to reflect on the topic and to write an essay based on your own experience, observation, and/or knowledge that you've piled up during all those years in school. Check out the following sample prompt, drawn from my own feverish brain and not from anything written by the (fictitious) Mary Oxblood:

"To admit responsibility is to enter the world of adulthood, for true maturity comes from facing the consequences of one's actions. On the other hand, Bart Simpson's famous comment, "I didn't do it; nobody saw me do it; you can't prove anything," resembles the defense of most modern politicians when faced with justifiable accusa-tions of improper behavior." — Mary Oxblood, "I'm Innocent"

How should people respond when they are justly accused of wrongdoing? To support your ideas, give one or more examples from literature, the arts, science, history, current events, or your own experience and observation.

The essay prompt is meant to mimic the sort of question a college professor might give on an exam. However, the SAT conveniently ignores two facts:

- No college test is only 25 minutes long.

- College professors tend to ask questions based on their coursework, not on general observation and knowledge.

Because students arrive at the SAT with a diverse array of courses and life experiences, the essay prompt has to be extremely general in order to be accessible to every student who takes the test. So although a college professor of history may ask you to discuss the causes of the Peloponnesian War, knowing that you're supposed to have read three pounds of books on the subject, the SAT sticks to vague, abstract prompts. Look for essays on secrecy, loyalty, the future, the value of controversy, the impact of one's childhood, and other general concepts.

Because the SAT prompts are broad, you can probably adapt any number of life experiences to the question. Plus, tons of different literary works or current events can provide suitable evidence. Before the exam, look through your high school English and history textbooks and spend some time on an Internet site or two that cover current events. That way, you have some supporting evidence fresh in your mind when you face the test.

Some students write and memorize an entire, general essay before the exam. Then when they get to the exam room, they write as much as they can remember of the prepared work and adapt it to the prompt by tacking on a new topic sentence. Bad idea. True, you can twist many different subjects and literary works to fit a given prompt. However, the fastest way to fail the essay (yes, you *can* fail) is not to answer the question being asked in the prompt. In fact, the principal *criterion* (standard; plural form is *criteria*) a scorer considers when grading an essay is whether or not the essay addresses the assigned topic. So if SAT writers ask you about a response to wrongdoing (see the sample question earlier in this section), don't write about the value of democracy. Write about responses to wrongdoing in a democratic system, if you wish, but tailor your essay to the specific topic in the question. Otherwise, you may find yourself receiving a zero on this section of the SAT.

Organizing Your Thoughts — Timing Is Everything

All you get is 25 minutes — that's right, not even a half-hour — to write one of the most important essays of your academic career up to this point. So when the SAT proctor tells you to start the essay, you should pick up your pen and begin to scribble furiously, right? Wrong. I know that my advice goes against your *innate* (inborn) urge to string words together for the entire time allotted. But you'll do better if you spend 2 or 3 minutes gathering your thoughts. To shock you even more, I now have to tell you to stop early and spend the last 2 or 3 minutes revising your work. That's right, folks. Given 25 minutes, you should write for no more than 20 and spend the extra 5 on sound writing process. (Check out the "Mastering the Writing Process" section for more details.)

Follow this approach for the best results when writing your 25-minute essay:

- **First 2 or 3 minutes:** Read the question, gather your thoughts, jot down a couple of ideas, and then number them (first idea, second idea, third, and so on).

- **Next 18 to 20 minutes:** Create an introductory paragraph with a strong *thesis statement* (the main idea you're putting forth), write the body paragraph(s), and come to a conclusion. (For more information, read the "Writing" section later in this chapter.)

- **Last 2 or 3 minutes:** Reread your prose, correcting spelling and grammar.

Have you awakened from your faint yet? Good, because you need to take a few moments to check out the following reasons why process is crucial when you're writing under time and SAT pressure:

✔ If you begin to write your essay immediately, you may end up crossing out so much that the essay becomes illegible. You have only one answer sheet and must write on it by hand, unless you're allowed to use a keyboard because of a documented learning disability, such as *dysgraphia*, the fancy term for difficulty in producing readable penmanship.

✔ You can't possibly produce a good, organized essay unless you take a moment to envision the logical structure.

✔ You risk forgetting to include the specific facts or ideas that bring your essay to life if you don't write down your ideas before you start writing. Even though you may remember the main ideas of your example(s), some details will elude you unless you gather your thoughts before writing. While you write words on the page, you have to think about grammar, spelling, and all those other things that English teachers care about. You don't have time to recall all the important details you wanted to include in your essay.

✔ If you don't leave time at the end to reread your essay, you risk not fixing the simple errors in mechanics (spelling *aren't* without the apostrophe, for example, or omitting a period from a sentence) that you may make as you write your essay.

Mastering the Writing Process

Tons of famous writers have written about their approach to stringing words together. Though the individual details vary, just about everyone agrees that good writing comes from a sound process — one that allows you to gather ideas, order and express them as you write, and revise your work. Moving through this process will help you be successful on the essay portion of the SAT. The following sections explain each stage of the writing process in more detail.

Prewriting

Prewriting is everything you do before your pen hits the answer sheet. To illustrate the prewriting process, here's a sample prompt (from a fictitious book by a nonexistent author):

"An ancient proverb claims that a journey of a thousand miles begins with a single step, but that step is difficult to take in scuba flippers. Nevertheless, the traveler must not be discouraged by whatever obstacles fate places in the path to glory." — Al McCloud, *How I Swam the Pacific Ocean and Made a Lot of Money Blogging about It*

Many human journeys, both literal and metaphorical, nearly fail because the first step is too hard or too frightening for the traveler, but much may be gained by overcoming obstacles and continuing onward. Comment on this statement based on your own experience or literary, scientific, or historical knowledge.

You start your prewriting by zooming through the prompt and deciding what the SAT writers are asking about. The sample prompt I provide here concerns journeys and the idea that some of them almost don't happen because beginnings are so hard. (Perhaps the test makers were thinking of essay writing itself when they chose this prompt.) After you crack the prompt, run through your mental index for journeys you or someone else almost didn't take. Don't forget to consider journeys of the spirit in which people take a hesitant step toward friendship, journeys of the mind in which a scientist, perhaps, takes the first step toward a discovery, and other nonliteral trips.

Don't even think about touching the answer sheet until you have all your thoughts in order. The SAT test booklet is a fine spot for prewriting. Remember, however, that nothing you write on the test booklet counts toward your essay. Only the answer sheet is graded.

Imagine that you decide to write your essay on a "journey" you took toward the thumb-wrestling team two years ago. You almost didn't show up for tryouts because you were afraid that your friends would laugh at you. (They were all on the chess team.) But you went, you demonstrated good thumb technique, you made the team, and now your thumb is champion of the Northern Hemisphere. After you select this idea, concentrate on jotting down a few details of that first, eventful day:

- ✔ Tryouts during lunch
- ✔ Wrestled five thumbs in all
- ✔ Pizza day
- ✔ Thumb a little sore from piano practice the day before
- ✔ Didn't know the coach
- ✔ Couldn't believe the thrill of victory
- ✔ Asked to join the team
- ✔ Herbie helped me find the room
- ✔ Won the second and third matches

When you're brainstorming ideas, don't worry about putting them in the appropriate order. Just write down whatever comes to mind about your chosen topic. Remember, you're spending only two or three minutes on this part of the writing process!

After you get these basic facts on paper, number them so you know which one to use first, second, third, and so forth. In the preceding list, I'd number the items this way: 1, 6, 2, 5, 4, 8, 9, 3, and 7. Other sequences are possible, but this one begins with your thinking about the tryouts (they're during lunch and you'll miss the pizza), moves to your arrival at the tryouts (finding the room and worrying about an unknown coach and a sore thumb), continues through your performance during the tryouts (you won two of the five matches and felt great doing so), and ends with the result (you made the team).

Setting the order of your ideas is similar to outlining a paper, which is something your grade school teachers probably made you do, although they likely insisted on a complicated system of margins and numbering. You don't have time for that sort of outline when you're taking the SAT. Just think about the order of your ideas, throw numbers on the scrap paper, and get ready to write.

Writing

In 25 minutes, you probably won't be able to create a fully formed, exquisitely detailed essay (unless, of course, your name is Shakespeare). The best you can hope for is an organized, reasonably specific piece. For that you need an introduction and a conclusion, with the meat of the essay — the supporting evidence — in the middle.

When you're referring to your own ideas and experiences, you may use *I* and *me* (what English teachers call *first person*) in your essay. However, when you're writing about science, literature, history, or current events, you may be more comfortable using *third person* — no references to yourself, just statements about other people, events, or things. The choice is yours.

Note: As you can probably tell from the sample introduction, body, and conclusion that follow, I'm having some fun here. You, however, shouldn't have much fun when you write the SAT essay. Yes, you want to avoid boring the essay graders to death if you can, but don't inflict your humor on them. They're looking for clear, fluent writing for *college,* not comedy clubs.

Introductory paragraph

Just a couple of sentences long, the introductory paragraph lets the reader know what the rest of your essay is about. For SAT purposes, make clear how your topic connects to the essay prompt. Also try to include something that draws the reader's interest because SAT graders read for hours at a time and look kindly on students who take the writing even a millimeter away from terminal boredom. Here's a sample introduction for the thumb-wrestling essay I develop earlier in the "Prewriting" section:

> The most difficult step in a journey may be the very first, as I found out the day I tried out for the thumb-wrestling team. Beset by hunger pangs and tempted by the tangy scent of pizza wafting from the cafeteria, I almost didn't attend the tryouts. But something — perhaps a desire to prove myself and to give my thumb a chance at excellence — drove me to the door of room 221 that day. I am very glad I did.

The preceding introductory paragraph accomplishes the basic tasks. Notice the direct connections to the question in Sentences 1 and 2: "The most difficult step in a journey may be the very first" and "I almost didn't attend." The introduction also makes the writer's position on the topic clear: "I am very glad I did." The paragraph isn't as thrilling as a Hollywood movie trailer, but it does engage the reader with a couple of mildly intriguing details — the pizza and the desire to prove the thumb's excellence.

You don't need to refer specifically to the quotation from the prompt in your essay, nor should you bother rewriting it. Just be sure that you address the issue the quotation and the accompanying question present. A good introduction lets the reader know what the essay is about and what position the writer is taking on the issue at hand. If the reader is puzzled at the end of Paragraph 1, you're in trouble.

Body paragraphs

In the extremely short time frame you have to write your SAT essay, you can't come up with more than one or two body paragraphs. Make the most of them! Present the specifics of your argument clearly and concisely. (In the example I use throughout this section, these specifics are the details of the thumb-wrestling tryouts.) Here's a sample body for the thumb-wrestling essay:

> The tryouts were held during lunch hour, and because I had missed school the previous day to attend my piano recital, I wasn't even sure where the event was taking place. I had actually walked into the cafeteria, convinced that thumb wrestling wasn't in my future, when I spied my friend Herbie. Herbie urged me to attend and offered to escort me to room 221. Outside the door I nearly turned back. I didn't know the coach, and my thumb was throbbing as a result of four hours of piano practice for the recital.

> The first match against a thumb at least twice as big as mine was a washout. Fortunately, the next two matches went to me. As I savored the thrill of victory, I saw the coach eyeing me thoughtfully. Next he sent over his best wrestler. I played him twice, and twice I went down in defeat. I was sure my thumb-wrestling career was over. To my surprise and delight, the coach welcomed me to the team anyway!

Okay, so it's not Dickens's *A Tale of Two Cities.* No matter. It includes enough detail to bring the reader into the writer's experience. To bring the thumb-wrestling experience (or journey) back to the question, however, you need a conclusion.

Concluding paragraph

Conclusions are a real pain. When you get all the way to the end of your evidence, you just want to put the pen down and relax a little, at least until the next section of the SAT begins. Instead, you have to come up with still another paragraph. How annoying.

Without the conclusion, though, your essay doesn't do its job, which (apart from getting you into college) is to show the reader the significance of everything you've written thus far. Think of the conclusion as the final nail in the poster advertising your point of view on the essay prompt. Without that nail, the poster will fall off the wall, and you certainly don't want that! Here's a sample conclusion for the thumb-wrestling essay:

> Now I'm the North American Thumb-Wrestling Champ (high school, under 4-inch division). My sport has taken me to China, Japan, Uruguay, and downtown Peoria. None of the wonderful experiences I've had at thumb-wrestling tournaments would have happened had I not walked, sore thumb and all, to the tryout room two years ago. I can only imagine the number of human accomplishments that the world would be without if people allowed themselves to be frightened by the first step in their journeys.

Take a close look at what this conclusion accomplishes. It refers to the question ("first step") and the author's point of view ("None of the wonderful experiences . . . would have happened"). In the last sentence, the conclusion also takes the essay's ideas 1 millimeter forward by referring to what the world would lack if others were deterred by the difficulty of the first step.

Also notice what the conclusion does *not* include: repetition of the material in the essay, a label like "in this essay I have proved that," or a completely new, unrelated idea like "I love pizza days."

Sometimes the conclusion isn't a separate paragraph. It may be no more than a killer last sentence placed at the end of your final example. Just be sure the reader has a sense of *finality* — of reaching a logical endpoint.

Polishing

Put the dust cloth away, but take out your best grammar and spelling knowledge. It's time to review and revise your essay. After the whole essay is on the page, reread it at least once. Neatly cross out any errors (the grammar review in Chapter 9 helps with this task) and write the corrections legibly in the space above the line.

Don't try to skip this step in the writing process so that you have more time for the actual writing because a grammatically correct essay (even one with a few cross-out marks) will score more points than an unedited, mistake-filled draft. Remember, anyone can make a ~~mitak~~ mistake, but only the smartest test takers correct their errors.

Scoring the Essay: Rubrics without the Cube

The SAT pays desperate-for-cash or have-no-life English teachers (some fall into both categories) to score the essays. The graders used to sit in windowless rooms, scoring essays until their eyeballs went on strike. Now modern technology allows them to sit in their very own living rooms, where their eyeballs still fry. An image of each essay is also posted on the Web, where colleges that you apply to can view it, warts and all (yet another reason why it's so important to write neatly).

So what do the essay graders look for as they score your essay? Read the following sections to find out, and then be sure to try your hand at scoring your own practice essays using the guidelines provided here. (See Chapter 8 for some practice essay prompts; and don't forget to score the essays you write during the practice tests in Chapters 20, 22, 24, 26, and 28.)

How graders score the essays

The essay graders give each essay that answers the question 1 to 6 points. An off-topic essay (one that doesn't address the given prompt) receives no points at all. Two graders score each essay, and your essay's final score is the sum of the two graders' scores. In other words, you get between 2 and 12 points for your essay. If the scores for a single essay are more than one point apart (one reader gives you a 6 and another gives you a 3, perhaps), the essay goes to a super-reader, who decides your score.

The score for the SAT essay is *holistic* (meaning that it's seen as one in its entirety; it isn't broken into parts). So the graders don't award a tenth of a point for grammar, a half-point for organization, and so on. They just read the essay and plop a number on the whole thing.

The number isn't random or based solely on the reader's preference, however. The SAT graders follow a *rubric* — a set of standards — in awarding points. They consider several factors, including the following, as they read and score your essay:

✔ **Does the essay answer the question?** The answer here must be "yes," or your essay receives no points. In better essays (those scoring 4, 5, or 6), the connection between your ideas and the prompt is easy to see. In weaker essays (those scoring 1, 2, or 3), the grader has to poke around a little to figure out how your ideas relate to the question.

✔ **Does the essay demonstrate a thoughtful consideration of ideas (what the SAT calls "critical thinking")?** A good SAT essay (a 5 or 6, perhaps) weighs alternatives and acknowledges complexity. A bad essay (say, a 2 or 1) reduces ideas to the simplest level. Thoughtfulness, of course, is a *continuum* (a range), not an either/or quality. Many essays fall into the middle range (a 3 or 4), indicating that the graders see some maturity but also identify room for improvement.

I once proctored a test (not the SAT but a school exam) with just one question: "Describe your ideal society." No doubt the teacher was expecting her students to mull over the rights of the group versus the rights of individuals and other important issues. Sadly, half of the students wrote something like "An ideal society is one in which everyone is happy." Not much thinking went into that answer, and it surely wouldn't have scored well on the SAT!

✔ **Does the essay make a case for the writer's point of view by providing appropriate evidence?** Think of your SAT essay grader as a defense attorney, waiting to *contradict* (challenge, disagree with) you. You have to prosecute your case by presenting evidence. In a well-written essay (a 4, 5, or 6), you have specific examples to back up your ideas. In a poorly written essay (a 1, 2, or 3), on the other hand, you include only a little evidence, or the evidence is too general to support your assertions.

✔ **Is the essay organized? Does it move logically from one idea to the next?** Great SAT essays (those that score 5s or 6s) are like guided tours; readers never have to wonder where they are or how they got there. One paragraph leads cleanly to the next. A middle-of-the-road essay (a 3 or 4) has a dead end or a wrong turn in it. A poor essay (a 1 or 2) leaves readers wandering around without a clue.

✔ **Is the vocabulary appropriate?** You don't need to plop a dictionary into your essay, but your word choice needs to show some variety (warranting a score of 4 or higher), and at least some of the words need to have more than one syllable. (An essay grade of 2 reflects elementary school–level vocabulary.)

✔ **Is the writing fluent, with varied sentence structure?** An essay that scores a 6 matches sentence structure and meaning. Less important ideas, for example, show up in subordinate clauses or verbals, and main ideas appear in independent clauses. An essay that scores a 4 or 5 strays occasionally from the usual subject-verb-object pattern. In an essay that scores a 2 or 1, the sentences sound short and choppy.

✔ **Is the writing grammatical, with good spelling and punctuation?** The idea here is simple: Follow the rules of Standard English, and your score rises. The better essays (those that score 4s, 5s, and 6s) have some mistakes — but not enough to make a lasting impression on the reader. Weaker essays (those that score 1s, 2s, and 3s) would draw a lot of red ink from the graders' pens, if they actually corrected your work. (If grammar isn't your *forte*, or strong point, turn to Chapter 9 for help.)

After considering each of these factors, the SAT graders rate your essay on a scale from 1 to 6 with 6 meaning outstanding, 5 meaning effective, 4 meaning competent, 3 meaning inadequate, 2 meaning seriously limited, and 1 meaning fundamentally lacking. Keep in mind that even the "outstanding" essays may have a couple of errors in them, and the "fundamentally lacking" pieces may have a few good points hidden in them somewhere. An essay's score simply represents its overall content and quality. To get a better idea of what each score means, check out Chapter 8 for some sample essays — a 5, a 3, and a 1 — along with an explanation of how each essay earned its number.

How you can score your practice essays

Scoring your own essay is difficult but not impossible. After you finish the practice tests in Chapters 20, 22, 24, 26, and 28, reread each of your essays, keeping in mind the four main categories that follow. Start with a perfect score of 6 and then measure your essay against this scoring guide:

✔ **Mechanics:** If you have only a couple of grammar, spelling, and punctuation errors, give yourself full credit for this category. If you have three or four mistakes in each paragraph, deduct one point. If you find even more than three or four mistakes per paragraph, deduct two points.

✔ **Organization:** Check your essay's structure. Does it proceed logically from idea to evidence to conclusion? If so, you're good to go. If the logical thread breaks anywhere or if you skipped a step — the conclusion, perhaps — deduct one point for each break in organization.

✔ **Evidence:** You need to have at least three or four details in each body paragraph or one piece of evidence that is described at length. Your body paragraphs should be heavy on specifics and light on general statements. If you find several general statements in the body of your essay, deduct one point — not for each general statement, just one point overall. If you have strong, numerous details, give yourself full credit for this quality.

By the way, the SAT writers don't care where your evidence comes from, as long as you provide support for your thesis. Essay graders are under orders not to give more credit to writers who cite history or literature instead of personal experience. So if you want to discuss, say, the time you peeked out the window and broke your nose, go for it — as long as it supports your main argument.

✔ **Fluency:** This quality is hard to describe but easy to *discern* (detect). Read the essay aloud. Does the language flow freely, easily, and naturally? Can you imagine reading it in a book? Or is it choppy and disjointed? Fluid language means no deduction. Choppy or awkward language throughout the essay means a one-point deduction.

After you come up with a score, double it. That's your essay's total grade. A 12 means you can go dancing; a 2 indicates that you have some work to do. Turn to Chapter 8 for additional practice with scoring essays.

Chapter 8

Practicing Essays

In This Chapter

▶ Looking at examples to see what's good, bad, and just so-so

▶ Trying your hand at some sample essay prompts

Lock the dog in the rumpus room. Put your little brother down for a nap. Turn off the phone. Set a kitchen timer for 25 minutes and tear out two sheets of lined paper from a notebook. (Loose-leaf is also acceptable.) Sharpen a No. 2 pencil. (The SAT doesn't allow you to write with a pen.) It's time to practice essay writing so you aren't bowled over on SAT day. This chapter contains eight SAT-style essay prompts. Some contain quotations from famous writers; a few contain quotations from my very own, semi-sane mind. (Asterisks — * — mark the semi-sane ones. Don't look for these authors in your local bookstore.)

I suggest you write essays for three prompts. If you have the energy and drive to write all eight essays, don't write them all at one sitting. To give you a peek into an SAT grader's mind, this chapter starts with three sample essays (scored 5, 3, and 1) and explains why each earned its score.

Spying Some Samples: SAT Essays and Evaluations

You can't hit a target if you're blindfolded, so to give you a general idea of what to shoot for, here are three SAT essays (written, I must confess, not by real test takers but by yours truly). The first earns a score of 5, almost but not quite the top score. The second hits the middle — a 3. The last, in more ways than one, is a 1 — a subpar essay that you *won't* write on SAT day because you've had the foresight to practice with the prompts in this chapter.

The prompt

"But if success I never find, / Then come misfortune, I bid thee welcome."
—Robert Burns, "Fickle Fortune"

"Success is not the only goal in life, but it is the most important." —Angelo Eliott*

Consider the consequences of success and failure. Can success ever be a disadvantage? May failure be a benefit? Referring to history, literature, or your own experiences and observations, discuss the possible consequences of success and failure.

The good: Looking at a "5" essay

Here's a fine essay, one that merits a 5 from an SAT grader:

It's only human to desire success, but it's also human to fail. Columbus set off to find a route to the "Indies," and he stumbled upon the Americas. His "failure" led to immense benefits for the European powers, though of course his actions brought many disadvantages to Native Americans. But that's the point. Success and failure are interrelated. Neither is totally good or totally bad. The way a person deals with success or failure is much more important than the result itself.

In Charles Dickens' novel Great Expectations, the main character, Pip, wants to become a gentleman. He isn't content to work as a blacksmith, his original goal in life, after he meets a "gentlewoman," Estella, who treats him badly. Through a series of complicated plot twists, Pip does become a gentleman. He benefits from increased finances and education, but his "success" also alienates Pip from his loving stepfather, Joe, and from his friend Biddy. It's only when Pip loses all his money — when he fails — that Pip recovers his common sense and reconnects with his family and true friends. Dickens even rewards Pip with a romantic connection to Estella, all after Pip has picked himself up from his failure.

Similarly, failure and success are entwined in my own life. In my physics class, I worked with a team to set up an experiment to measure the momentum of an object of a fixed weight on various slopes. My goal was to figure out the formula without consulting a textbook. Day after day, lunch hour after lunch hour, my teammates and I sent a little cart rolling down a track. We timed and measured, counted and calculated. At the end of the week, we had still not found the answer. Technically we had failed. However, we had learned many things, such as how hard it is to measure a short time span with limited equipment, how good it is to share ideas with each other, and how sticking with a project can be very rewarding. If that's failure, give me more of it, because failure looks surprisingly similar to success.

This essay receives a 5 for several reasons:

- ✔ It answers the question and takes a stand: Success and failure are two sides of the same coin, and attitude is more important than result. The reader doesn't have to search for these ideas; they are communicated immediately in the first paragraph.

- ✔ The writer provides evidence for the assertions in the essay. The writer gives three examples to support her stance — Columbus, Dickens, and physics. They convey the complicated nature of success and failure very well, though the Columbus example is not described in depth. Had the writer devoted more attention to Columbus — similar to the amount of space given to Dickens and physics, the essay may have approached a score of six.

- ✔ The essay is well organized. The first paragraph explains the writer's *thesis,* or main idea. Next come two paragraphs devoted to supporting examples. The last example concludes with a short but appropriate statement: "If that's failure, give me more of it, because failure looks surprisingly similar to success." That sentence serves as a conclusion.

- ✔ The use of language is sophisticated (*alienated, reconnect,* and so on). The sentences show variety, and the grammar and spelling are good. Slightly more sophisticated vocabulary and sentence structure would have raised this essay to the top score.

The not-too-bad: Examining a "3" essay

Check out the middle of the pack, an essay that earns a score of 3:

Angelo Eliot said that, "Success is not the only goal in life, but it is the most important. I agree with Mr. Eliot because success is everyone's goal. Who starts out in the morning trying for something else? Yes, people fail, but not one really wants that. Instead, we all try for success, probably sucess is hard-wired into human nature as a goal.

When imigrants leave their native land, they are almost always looking for a more success-ful life. In New York City, where I live, I see people from every place in the world. They come here for success. They want more than they had before. They want their children to be suc-cessful too. Even if they have some disadvantages, such as they miss their home country and their families if left behind, imigrants mostly feel that it is worth it to be more success-ful. This is the American Dream. Everyone wants to have a good house, a good job, and to earn more money than they did before. I have talked with many imigrants, and they agree that success is the most important goal.

In conclusion, Mr. Eliot is right. You can fail and still pick yourself up, but that doesn't make failure good. It makes you try harder to reach success, which is what Mr. Eliot talked about.

Why is this essay a 3? Read on:

- ✔ The writer takes a clear stand on success and failure, and that stand is easy to *discern* (recognize, detect) in Paragraph 1. The question, "Who starts out in the morning trying for something else?" draws the reader's attention nicely. The statement that a desire for success may be *hard-wired* shows some sophistication.

- ✔ The example of immigrants (which, by the way, is spelled with two *m*'s) is a good one. However, the statements in Paragraph 2 are somewhat general. Also, the writer repeats the same ideas several times. Cutting repetition and adding more specifics would improve this paragraph a lot.

- ✔ The essay is organized, but a little too simply. The first paragraph explains the writer's stance on the success/failure issue. So far so good! The middle paragraph provides evi-dence to support the writer's view — also good. The last paragraph is meant to be a conclusion, but really it's just a restatement of ideas from the introduction. That sort of ending places this essay firmly in the middle range because more mature writers stretch a bit at the end of an essay. (Compare the last paragraph of this essay to the "5" essay earlier in this chapter to see what I mean.)

- ✔ The language isn't terrible, but the vocabulary is fairly simple. The sentences vary somewhat in their patterns — a good feature of this essay. The writer made some spell-ing and grammar mistakes (*Eliott* is the name, not *Eliot,* and *sucess* needs an extra *c* in Paragraph 1). A good proofreading would have moved this essay up a notch.

The not-so-good: Checking out a "1" essay

Here's the bottom of the barrel, except for blank or off-topic essays, which receive no points at all:

You can't find success, Robert Burns says you should welcome bad fortune. But "Success is not the only goal in life, but it is the most important says Angelo Eliott. You should try to succeed, but if you fail you should never give up and try again. I think that bad fortune isn't what any body wants. Nobody likes to fail. Success is a goal too.

Once when a general went to war, he lost. He didn't give up though. He tried the next battle. Everyone must have a goal in life so you should not try for bad fortune, ever, no matter how disscourageing it is for you.

Oh boy. Big trouble here. Let me count the ways:

- ✔ This essay makes reference to both quotations in the prompt, but there's no clear statement of what this writer believes about success and failure, just a bunch of disconnected sentences. The closest the writer comes to a thesis is "Nobody likes to fail."

- ✔ The only example (the general) doesn't say much about the relative benefits of success and failure. This example should have been much more specific (which general? what happened in the next battle?). Also, with a little work, the example could have made a point — that failure sometimes motivates people or that early success makes people *complacent* (a little too satisfied and comfortable).

- ✔ The essay doesn't have a clear, recognizable structure, mostly because it doesn't have enough material to organize. The reader should move from thesis to evidence to conclusion, but this essay has only a lame attempt at a thesis (see the first bullet point) and a vague, general statement at the end of the second paragraph.

- ✔ The language is clumsy, and the writer has several run-on sentences and spelling mistakes.

Practicing What I Preach: Your Turn to Write

In the previous sections, you see examples of essays ranging from pretty darn good to pretty darn bad, so now's the time for you to get some practice writing them yourself. Unfortunately, the SAT writers don't give you a choice of essay topics on SAT day, so don't read all eight of the following prompts and go for the one that immediately appeals to you. Pick a number from one to eight at random — your birthday month (unless you were born after August), how often you had ice cream yesterday, the number of people in your family — and settle in with that question. When the 25 minutes are up, put your pencil down, shake the cramp out of your hand, and put the essay away. Later, when your brain has recovered from its fried state, look at the essay objectively. Score it according to the grading criteria in Chapter 7.

If your essay refers to literature, remember this rule: Underline the titles of full-length works (books or plays). Place the titles of shorter works (articles or poems) inside quotation marks.

Essay Prompt 1

"'It is a truth universally acknowledged, that a single man in possession of a good fortune, must be in want of a wife,' wrote Jane Austen in her masterful work, *Pride and Prejudice.* Austen's characters act on assumptions about human behavior, and frequently these assumptions are proved wrong." —Ray Bann, "Mr. Darcy's Error"*

"'Assume that their goals are the same as ours; they want peace, security, and reasonable happiness.' That's the advice the president offered to his negotiating team just hours before the cease-fire talks. With his statement in mind, we approached the enemy." —Dolvin Eddlesworth, *Negotiating for Fun and Profit*

What effect do assumptions have on human behavior? Draw upon your own experience or upon your knowledge of literature or world affairs in discussing whether assumptions are a positive, negative, or mixed factor.

Essay Prompt 2

"Nineteenth-century author Sydney Smith wrote that truth is justice's handmaid. The Freedom of Information Act has opened the workings of the American government to public scrutiny, and justice has been served accordingly." —Predieu Orant, *American Democracy in the Age of Instant Messaging**

"Justice is truth in action." —Benjamin Disraeli, 19th-century British Prime Minister

Comment on the relationship between truth and justice, supporting your ideas with evidence from literary works, current affairs, history, or your own experience.

Essay Prompt 3

"American poet Henry Wadsworth Longfellow wrote of 'the divine Insanity of noble minds' that creates 'what it cannot find.' Three centuries earlier, William Shakespeare related 'the lunatic' to the poet because both create new realities." —Gerbel Hamstar, "The Relation Between Craziness and Creativity"*

Is realism the enemy of creativity? Must an artist or scientist ignore what is already known in order to move beyond established boundaries? Refer to your knowledge of art, literature, science, or personal experience to discuss the relationship between reality and creativity.

Essay Prompt 4

"Where silence once reigned, the cellphone now interrupts. 'Computer error' is blamed for almost every glitch in modern life, from erroneous weather forecasts to ridiculous tax bills. Modern life has become enslaved to technology." —Lobelia Closper, *Free Yourself from Machines**

Technology has not made our lives easier. Agree or disagree with this statement, supporting your position with references to your life or your reading.

Essay Prompt 5

"Dionysius the Elder, being asked whether he was at leisure, replied, 'God forbid that it should ever befall me!'" —Plutarch, Roman historian

"Cultivated leisure is the aim of man." —Oscar Wilde, British writer

Is leisure time a blessing or a curse? Take a position on this issue and support your view with evidence from literature, history, current events, or your own observations and experiences.

Essay Prompt 6

"Ignorance, the root and stem of all evil." —Attributed to Plato, Greek philosopher

"Ignorance is bliss." —Thomas Gray, British poet

Should ignorance ever be preferred to knowledge? Discuss your views, supporting your ideas with reference to your life or reading.

Essay Prompt 7

"As a young man, Lyndon B. Johnson wrote about how uncomfortable it is to have ambition. The ambitious person, said Johnson, is discontented and restless. However, according to Johnson, ambition is what makes us strive for 'better things in the future.'" —Woefield Cowbus, *Life with LBJ**

How much ambition is too much? Discuss your answer to this question with evidence from your observation, your life experience, or your reading.

Essay Prompt 8

"Science is fast outrunning ethics. Almost as soon as society decides whether a new medical technique may be justified, the procedure is outmoded. Cloning, the artificial prolongation of life, the ability to alter one's appearance or design one's offspring — what used to be the stuff of science fiction is fast becoming science fact. And science has implemented its discoveries without undergoing the necessary examination of its rights and obligations." —Crewly Kind, "The Scientists' Dilemma"*

Who should decide how and when, if ever, a scientific discovery should be implemented? Support your position with evidence from your knowledge of science, literature, history, current events, or from your firsthand experience of life.

Chapter 9

Joining the Grammar Police

. . . .

. . . .

If you've ever had the urge to tear a grammar book into tiny little pieces, take heart. The SAT multiple-choice writing questions aren't horribly difficult. Expect two sections, or three if you've been saddled with an equating section. (An *equating section* makes you an unsalaried employee of the College Board. Your work on an equating section gives the test makers statistical data but doesn't affect your score.) In this chapter, I explain the three types of questions you face in SAT multiple-choice writing, show sample questions from each, and explain the best approach to solving them. I also review some basic grammar rules. (If you need a full-scale grammar course, check out my books [she said modestly], *English Grammar For Dummies,* 2nd Edition, and *English Grammar Workbook For Dummies*, 2nd Edition, both published by Wiley.)

Surveying Multiple-Choice Writing Questions

Before you jump into multiple-choice writing questions, you need to know a little bit about what you're getting into. This SAT section hits you in three different ways:

✔ Error recognition

✔ Sentence revision

✔ Passage revision

These three types of questions check word choice, verb tense, pronouns, and all the other thorny details that English teachers love. You'll also find questions that address style — whether you can write *concisely* (without extra words) and smoothly.

Bubbling the wrong answer: Error-recognition questions

These SAT questions call for the wrong answer. And if you're wrong, you're right. No, I haven't overdosed on super-caffeinated lattes. I'm talking about error-recognition questions, a bunch of which show up in the SAT Writing section. Here's an example:

Mary Sue, broke and bewildered, wandered away from her keepers, however, she soon
          A   B

found a campaign manager and successfully ran for governor. No error.
          C   D   E

The correct answer is Choice (B). *However* can't legally join two sentences, according to the grammar cops. (See the section "Nailing Nouns and Capturing Commas: The SAT Grammar Review" later in this chapter for more on specific grammar rules.) The comma in front of *however* should be a semicolon.

The key to error-recognition questions is to pretend for a moment that the underlining doesn't exist. Just read the sentence to see what sounds wrong, and then look for the letter. If nothing pops up on first reading, check each underlined portion carefully. Still no mistake? Go for (E), which is always *no error*. The following helpful do's and don'ts can make answering error-recognition questions much easier:

- ✔ **Do keep an eye open for incorrect punctuation.** Always check apostrophes and commas.

- ✔ **Do look for vocabulary mistakes.** Error-recognition sentences sometimes contain mistakes in vocabulary. Words that are commonly confused (*affect* and *effect,* for example) or nonexistent but still popular (such as *irregardless*) may show up.

- ✔ **Don't worry about spelling and capitalization mistakes.** They never appear in the error-recognition sentences. Assume that the words are spelled correctly and that the capital letters are in the right spots.

- ✔ **Do watch out for verbs.** Verb tense is a big deal, as is subject-verb agreement (choosing a singular or plural verb).

- ✔ **Do pay attention to pronouns.** The SAT-ists often mix singular and plural forms incorrectly.

- ✔ **Don't worry about the parts of the sentence that aren't underlined.** They're always correct.

- ✔ **Don't waste time figuring out how to correct the error.** Just find it and bubble it in.

- ✔ **Do skip the sentence if the answer is a complete mystery.** The SAT deducts a quarter point for a wrong answer and no points for a blank. If you can eliminate one choice, cut your losses and move on to the next question.

Don't be afraid to choose *no error* if you can't find anything wrong. Everybody makes a mistake sometimes, but everybody gets it right sometimes, too.

Improving sentences: Sentence revisions

One set of Writing section questions — sentence revisions — presents you with sentences that have a portion underlined. Choice (A) is the equivalent of "no error" — the underlined portion as it appears in the sentence. The other four choices, (B) through (E), change the original a little or a lot. Take a look at this sample question:

James spent his free time tearing up SAT prep books, setting fire to grammar texts, and diligent study.

(A) tearing up SAT prep books, setting fire to grammar texts, and diligent study

(B) tearing up SAT prep books and setting fire to grammar texts and diligent study

(C) in SAT prep book tearing, grammar test firing, and diligent study

(D) tearing up SAT prep books, setting fire to grammar texts, and studying diligently

(E) tearing up SAT prep books, setting fire to grammar texts, and he studied diligently

The correct answer is Choice (D). All items in a list should be in the same form. *Diligent study* doesn't match *tearing* and *setting*.

Notice that each choice varies only a little from the original. You may find a question that needs a lot of changes to reach perfection, but in general, this part is the pickiest on the exam. Focus on details and keep the following in mind:

- ✔ **Check for homonyms.** These are words that sound the same but are spelled differently (*who's* and *whose, here* and *hear,* for example).

- ✔ **Don't overlook punctuation.** Check all the commas, semicolons, and other punctuation marks.

- ✔ **Focus only on the underlined text.** You can't change anything in the sentence that isn't underlined.

- ✔ **Keep in mind verb tense and parallel structure.** Verb tense is a big deal in this type of question. Also check that everything that is doing the same job in the sentence has the same grammatical identity — what English teachers call *parallel structure.* If you listen to the sentence in your head and you hear a pattern break, you may have found an error. See the sections "Tensing up" and "Staying between the parallel lines" later in this section for help with these grammar issues.

- ✔ **Look for the best answer.** The SAT asks for the best answer, not the right answer. The distinction between these two is subtle. On this sort of question, you may find two choices that are grammatically correct, but one is more concise than the other. Go for the shortest version that gets the job done.

Some test takers find it helpful to read the original sentence, reword it mentally, and then look for a choice that matches.

Revising for fun and profit: Passage revisions

Do you have any old compositions stuffed in a drawer somewhere? Perhaps something that you wrote a few years ago? If so, you have ready-made SAT practice material. Take out those sheets of paper and see how you could have improved the writing. Now you're ready for SAT passage-revision questions.

The SAT passage revision presents you with what the SAT writers call "a typical student's first draft" of an essay. The sentences in the passage are numbered and followed by a batch of questions. You may be asked to fix one sentence or to consider the transition between two paragraphs. Other questions deal with organization (is everything in the best place? does one paragraph lead logically to another?), repetition, and sentence combination. Other questions address the author's purpose. The idea is to find out how you'd create a second draft without the hassle of actually writing a second draft. (Remember, hand-scored writing costs a lot.)

Here's a sample with a couple of questions to go with it:

[1] When parents and teens argue, it tends to get ugly. [2] Teens are sometimes not trustful of their parents, and parents wish that their sons and daughters are more respectful. [3] This does not have to be the case.

4 Just the other day I asked my mother to withdraw me from the SAT prep course.

5 With all that I have to do, you don't need any extra work. 6 She immediately got on my case and asked me if I wanted a smack in the mouth. 7 I said, No, I'm not disrespectful.

8 Then we argued. 9 We argued for two hours. 10 Finally we came to an agreement.

11 She would not smack me in the mouth and I would attend the SAT prep course one more time. 12 Then she would allow me to be withdrawn if I promised to work on the *SAT For Dummies,* 8th Edition which is better anyway.

13 You may find yourself in this situation one day. 14 If you do, remember that smacking someone in the mouth is not a good alternative. 15 Ask yourself who's at fault before you strike. 16 Also, don't assume that you know everything.

1. What is the best revision of Sentence 1?

    (A) Parents and teens arguing can be ugly.

    (B) Parents and teens are ugly when they argue.

    (C) Arguments between parents and teens tend to veer out of control.

    (D) Parents arguing with teens are ugly.

    (E) Parents and teens argue, and it isn't pretty.

    Choice (C) is correct. Choices (A) and (E) have grammar mistakes; you need an apostrophe after *teens* in (A), and you should eliminate the vague *it* in (E). Choices (B) and (D) change the meaning.

2. What is the best way to combine Sentences 8–10?

    (A) We argued for two hours before finally coming to an agreement.

    (B) We argued for two hours, finally we came to an agreement.

    (C) Arguing for two hours, an agreement was finally reached.

    (D) We argued and agreed for two hours.

    (E) For two hours we argued and then agreed.

    Choice (A) is correct. The others, apart from sounding clunky (don't you love those technical terms?), have errors in grammar or meaning.

3. Which of the following statements best describes the purpose of Paragraph 3?

    (A) to alert child protection agencies about a bad home situation

    (B) to give an example of a parent/teen conflict that was worked out successfully

    (C) to show how annoying teens can be

    (D) to show how unreasonable adults can be

    (E) to advertise my book

If you selected (B), you're right on target, though I admit that (E) has some truth in it. Choices (C) and (D) are easy to eliminate: The SAT avoids criticizing groups. Choice (A) is from another universe, as "child protection agencies" aren't in the passage.

Don't expect to be thrilled by the subject matter or the writing in passage-revision questions. The material is boring, but the questions are reasonably easy. Keep these strategies in mind, and the experience may not be so agonizing:

- **Read the whole passage before you hit the questions.** Don't skip over any text because you may miss something essential.

- **Generally ignore everything the SAT writers don't ask you about.** Even if you're itching to make a particular sentence better, don't. But when you choose the best revision for something they *do* ask you about, be sure that your new sentence fits well with the sentences before and after it.

- **Don't forget to check for wordiness.** If more than one answer choice looks good, go for the more concise revision, as long as it maintains the meaning of the original.

- **Remember that SAT passages have very simple organization.** Check for an introduction that tells the reader the topic and the writer's stance, a body that gives examples or that presents the situation's complexity, and a conclusion that sums up and extends the main idea slightly. If any of these parts are missing or out of order, take note. You may find a question addressing these issues.

- **Start with the easier questions.** Questions that refer to one sentence are easier, in general, than questions that refer to the entire passage. If you're pressed for time, go for the one-sentence questions first. You can always go back later to the whole-passage or whole-paragraph questions.

Nailing Nouns and Capturing Commas: The SAT Grammar Review

Okay, don't worry. I make sure this grammar review is quick and painless, and if you're pretty good at grammar, you can ignore this section entirely. Here I touch on the most commonly tested topics on the SAT.

Agreeing with the grammar cops

Stop nodding your head! I'm not talking about comments like "Yes, I also think we should defrost Antarctica." I'm talking about matching singular to singular, plural to plural. In the grammar world, you can't mix singular and plural without risking war.

In terms of agreement, the SAT loves to ask you about

- Subject-verb pairs
- Pronoun-antecedent pairs

Subject-verb agreement

A *verb* expresses action or state of being; the *subject* is whoever or whatever is *doing* the action or *in* the state of being. Think of the subject-verb pair as a marriage: The two have to be compatible, or potted plants start sailing across the room. In grammarland, compatibility means that a singular subject takes a singular verb and a plural subject takes a plural verb. Check out these examples:

> *Felicia flounders* in the face of an SAT test. (*Felicia* is a singular subject; *flounders* is a singular verb.)

> All Felicia's *friends* happily *help* her. (*Friends* is a plural subject; *help* is a plural verb.)

The SAT doesn't spend much time on the simple subject-verb pairs. Instead, the exam concentrates on the ones that may be confusing, such as the following:

- ✔ *There/here*: Neither of these words are subjects. The real subject comes *after* the verb. Match the verb to the real subject.

  "Here are three crayons." *Crayons* is the subject.

- ✔ *Either/or* and *neither/nor*: These words join two subjects. Match the verb to the closest subject.

  "Neither Mary nor her parakeets are eating that leftover lettuce." *Parakeets* is the closest subject.

- ✔ **Interrupters between the subject-verb pair:** If a description or an addition without the word *and* comes between the subject and the verb, ignore it.

  "Barry, not his parakeets, likes honey-flavored seed." *Not his parakeets* is an interrupter.

Don't ignore anything tacked on with *and*. Two singular words joined by *and* make a plural subject. ("Frank and his partners are investing in that bird-cage factory." *Frank and his partners* is a plural subject.)

Pronoun-antecedent agreement

An *antecedent* is a word that a pronoun replaces. In the sentence "Mary told John that he was a drip," *he* is a pronoun and *John* is the antecedent because *he* stands for *John*. The rule on antecedents is super simple: Singular goes with singular and plural with plural. You already know all the easy applications of this rule. In the *Mary/John* sentence, you'd never dream of replacing *John* with *they*. The SAT makers, however, go for the confusing spots, and so do I.

- ✔ **Pronouns containing *-one*, *-thing*, or *-body* are singular.** Match these pronouns with other singular pronouns.

  "Everyone brought his or her teddy bear to the SAT." *His or her* is singular.

- ✔ *Either, neither, each,* and *every* are singular. These words are sometimes followed by phrases that sound plural (*either of the boys* or *each father and son*), but these words are always singular.

  "Neither of the boys has brought his teddy bear to the SAT." *His* is singular.

- ✔ **Sentences with *the only one who* and *one of the few . . . who* need special attention.** The expression *the only one who* (or *the only one that*) is singular and calls for a singular verb and singular pronoun, and *one of the few . . . who* (or *one of the few or many . . . that*) is plural and calls for a plural verb and plural pronoun.

  "George is the only one of the SAT takers who gnashes his teeth." Or "George is one of the many SAT takers who gnash their teeth."

As in the preceding examples, when you're deciding singular or plural for a pronoun, you may be deciding the same issue for a verb. Check both!

Tensing up

On the SAT Writing section, tense isn't just what's happening to your muscles. *Tense* is the quality of verbs that indicates time. The English language has a ton of rules regulating tense. To check tense on the SAT, make a timeline. You don't have to write down the events; just use your reading comprehension skills to figure out what happened when. Then remember these rules:

- ✔ **The helping verbs *has* and *have* connect present and past actions.** When you see these helping verbs, something started in the past and is still going on. ("Rodney has been bubbling in SAT answers for about ten minutes.")

- ✔ **The helping verb *had* places one past action before another past action.** ("Rodney had bubbled only three answers when the proctor called time.")

- ✔ **Don't change tenses without a reason.** Especially in the paragraph-revision portion of the exam, you may see a sentence that veers suddenly from past to present or vice versa. If the meaning justifies the shift, fine. If not, you've found an error.

Verbs also have moods. The only mood you have to worry about on the SAT is subjunctive (forget the name) and in only one situation: condition contrary to fact. Look for sentences that make statements that aren't true. ("If I were making the SAT, I would dump all the grammar questions. If I had known about the grammar, I would not have burned my English textbook.") The *if* part of the sentence — the untrue part — gets *were* or *had*, and the other part of the sentence features *would*. The SAT makers like to place a *would* in the *if* part of the sentence in order to trip you up.

Casing the joint

Pronouns, bless their little hearts, have case. *Case* makes the difference between *me* and *I*, *him* and *his*, and (gasp) *who* and *whom*, not to mention *whose*. The rules are actually quite easy. Use a subject pronoun (*I, he, she, we, they, who, whoever*) when you need a subject. Object pronouns (*me, him, her, us, them, whom, whomever*) cover almost everything else. To show possession, try *my*, *his*, *her*, *its*, *our*, *your*, *their*, and *whose*. Naturally, the SAT tries to throw you curveballs, but the following strategies help you keep everything straight:

- ✔ **Isolate the pronoun and check the sentence.** By placing pronouns with nouns (in a list, perhaps), the pronoun gets lost. You have a better chance of "hearing" the correct pronoun if you ignore the distractions.

  For example, if you see "The proctor gave the test to three boys and I," you may not notice the error. Cut out "the three boys," however, and you have "The proctor gave the test to I." Now the error may be easier to spot: The sentence should read "to the three boys and me."

- ✔ **Make sure every verb has a subject.** This tip is especially helpful with who/whom dilemmas. If you have a verb flapping around without a subject, you probably need *who* or *whoever* — the subject pronouns. ("The proctor gave a No. 2 pencil to whoever needed one." Whoever is the subject of needed.) If the who/whom issue shows up in a question, change the question to a statement and then make the pronoun decision.

- ✔ **Pronouns and nouns preceding *-ing* words such as *swimming, skiing, crying*, and so forth should be possessive.** The possessive shifts the emphasis to the *-ing* word. ("Gonzo's parents did not object to *his* taking the SAT 15 times.")

Between you and I is a common error, so the SAT writers like placing it on the test. The correct phrase is *between you and me*.

One cardinal rule of pronouns: Confusing pronouns (*she* in a sentence with two female names, perhaps) are a no-no. Also avoid plopping *this, that,* or *which* into a sentence to refer to a subject-verb combination. Pronouns aren't allowed to refer to subject-verb combinations (*clauses,* in grammar lingo).

Punctuating your way to a perfect score

Not many punctuation problems show up on the SAT, but you do find a couple of common errors. These rules help keep you on your toes:

- **Sentences must be joined together legally.** Sometimes a comma and a joining word — *and, or, but,* and *nor,* for example — do the job, and sometimes you need a semicolon. Some tricksters *(consequently, therefore, nevertheless, however)* look strong enough to join two sentences, but they really aren't. When you have one of these guys stuck between two sentences, add a semicolon.

- **Be careful to punctuate descriptions correctly.** If the description is essential to the meaning of the sentence — you don't know what you're talking about without the description — don't use commas. ("The play that George wrote makes no mention whatsoever of the SATs.") If the description is interesting but nonessential, place commas around it. ("George's first and only play, which he called *The SAT Blues,* flopped at the box office.")

- **Check apostrophes.** You may find a missing possessive form in front of an *-ing* word. (See the section "Casing the joint" for more information.) You may also find an apostrophe where it doesn't belong. The pronouns *whose* and *its* are possessives, and they don't need apostrophes. (*Who's* means "who is" and *it's* means "it is.")

No possessive pronoun (*whose, its, theirs, his, hers, ours,* and so on) ever has an apostrophe in it.

Choosing the right word

The SAT makers love to throw words at you that are almost right. Unfortunately, in grammarland, not quite right is completely wrong. In this section, I take you on a quick tour of the most common sights in the SAT Writing section, at least in terms of word choice.

- **Affect and effect:** The SAT *affects* your life; its influence is inescapable. The *effect* of all this SAT prep is a high score. See the difference? The first is a verb and the second a noun. But — and the SAT loves this trick — *effect* can sometimes be a verb meaning "to bring about" as in "Pressure from the colleges effects change."

- **Continuous and continual:** The first of this pair describes something that never stops, and the second describes something that stops and starts. So a baby needs *continuous* care, but a refrigerator's freezing cycle is *continual.*

- **Disinterested and uninterested:** The first means fair, as in *the SAT is supposed to be a disinterested measure of your ability.* The second means you're yawning because you couldn't care less.

- **Except and accept:** I *accept* all the awards offered to me *except* the one for Nerd of the Year.

- **Farther and further:** *Farther* is for distance and *further* for time and intensity.

- **Fewer and less:** *Fewer* is for stuff you can count (shoes, pimples, cavities) and *less* for stuff you measure (sugar, ability, toothache intensity).

- **Good and well:** *Good* describes nouns, and *well* describes verbs. To put it another way, a person or thing is *good,* but you do something *well.* The SAT is *good,* and you study *well* for the exam.

- **Lie and lay:** Two words created by the devil. You *lie* down when you plop yourself on the sofa, and you *lay* a book on a shelf. But in the past tense, you *lay* down for a few hours yesterday, and you *laid* your SAT prep book on the bonfire. With present and past participles, you have *lain* (yes, *lain!*) awake all night worrying about the SAT because you had *laid* your SAT prep book on the bonfire before going to bed.

- **Like and as:** The first one can be used with a noun but not with a subject-verb pair. (Think *like* a pro when you take the SAT.) The second is the one you want for a subject-verb pair. (Do *as* you *like.*)

- **Sit and set:** *Sit* is what you do to yourself, and *set* is what you do to something else. Therefore, "May sits down as soon as Al sets a chair on the floor."

Along with these pairs of commonly confused words, be on the lookout for the following "words" or phrases that you should never use because they don't exist in Standard English:

- Irregardless (use *regardless*)

- Different than (the correct version is *different from*)

- The reason is because (should be *the reason is that*)

- Could of/should of/would of (use *could have, would have, should have*)

This list obviously doesn't contain all the errors you may encounter on the SAT tests, because English has thousands and thousands of words and a lot can go wrong. But now that you've read this section, these tricky words won't trap you on the SAT.

Staying between the parallel lines

A favorite SAT question concerns *parallelism,* the way a sentence keeps its balance. The basic principle is simple: Everything doing the same job in a sentence must *be* the same type of grammatical element. You can't "surf and soak up sun and playing in the sand" because *playing* breaks the pattern. You can "surf and soak up sun and play in the sand" without any problems — well, without any grammatical problems. I'd slather on some sunblock, if I were you. To parallel park in the high-score spots, keep these ideas in mind:

- **Look for lists.** Whenever you have two or three things bunched together, they probably have the same job. Make sure they match.

- **Be wary of paired conjunctions.** Conjunctions are joining words. Three common paired conjunctions are *either/or, neither/nor,* and *not only/but also.* When you encounter one of these pairs, examine what follows each conjunction. If a subject-verb combo follows *either,* a subject-verb combo should follow *or.* ("Either I will go to the store or I will order it online.") If only a noun follows *either,* only a noun should follow *or.* ("Either the store or the Internet will have the sweater I want.")

- **When two complete sentences are joined together, usually the verbs are both active or both passive.** In an active-verb sentence, the subject is doing the action or is in the state of being expressed by the verb. ("Archie flies well." "Archie is happy.") In a passive-verb sentence, the subject receives the action of the verb. ("The window was broken by a high-speed pitch.") A parallel sentence generally doesn't switch from active to passive or vice versa.

Chapter 10

Practicing Grammar Problems: Recognizing Your Mistakes

This chapter helps you get in the mood (terminally bored, ready to have a root canal rather than think about grammar *one more minute*) for the SAT multiple-choice writing sections. Here, you find error-recognition, sentence-revision, and paragraph-revision sample questions. All are accompanied by answers and explanations, and I promise not to say, "Because I said so," when I explain why a particular answer is correct.

After each answer explanation in this chapter, I state in parentheses which grammar principle is being tested. If you need a more complete review, turn back to Chapter 9 and review the relevant section. If your grammar skills need more than a touch-up, feel free to inflate my ego by consulting *English Grammar For Dummies,* 2nd Edition, and *English Grammar Workbook For Dummies,* 2nd Edition (Wiley), both by yours truly.

Examining Error-Recognition Questions

The SAT (Slow And Time-consuming) directions tell you to choose an underlined portion of the sentence that contains an error and to bubble in the corresponding letter. The last choice — (E) — always stands for *no error*. As you work on these sample problems, keep in mind that you're checking for grammar, punctuation, and word use. Forget about capitalization and spelling, which aren't covered on this exam. Also, assume that everything that's *not* underlined is correct. In the first set, the answer immediately follows each question, so use a piece of paper to cover up the answer while you work on the question. In the second set, which is set up like the real test, the answers are all together at the end.

Set 1

1. At least a year <u>before the race,</u> Kaitlin, <u>as well as</u> all the other drivers, <u>need to assemble</u> a

             A   B   C

   staff of qualified <u>mechanics who</u> can assist her in preparing the vehicle. <u>No error.</u>

                   D   E

The portion of the sentence set off by commas *(as well as all the other drivers)* is an interrupter. Ignore it when matching a subject to a verb. If you examine the sentence without the interrupter, you see the naked subject-verb pair: *Kaitlin* need. Sounds wrong, right? *Kaitlin* is singular and takes the singular verb *needs*. Choice (C) is correct. (subject-verb agreement)

2. According to our friends at the Internal Revenue Service, the problem with uncollected
     A   B

   taxes is when other taxpayers have to pay more. No error.
     C   D   E

The verb *is* acts as a giant equal sign, so the stuff on each side of *is* must match. Grammatically, *problem* is the important word in front of *is* because *problem* is the subject. *Problem* should match *that*, not *when*, because *problem* is a general word — a noun — and doesn't refer specifically to time. *When* is a time word. The correct sentence would read *the problem with uncollected taxes is that* . . . Choice (C) is correct. (parallel structure)

3. Awed by the power of the New York Yankees, Dan, whom everyone believes is the most
                                                 A

   committed fan, purchased a banner proclaiming the fact that "Bombers Rule!" No error.
          B   C   D   E

Who is for subjects and *whom* takes on all the other jobs in the sentence (direct object, bricklayer, dental-floss untangler, and so forth). Every verb in the sentence has to have a subject. The subject-verb pairs are *everyone believes, who is,* and *Dan purchased.* Choice (A) is correct. (pronoun case)

4. If I would have known about the possibility of a volcanic eruption, I would have stayed away
      A   B   C   D

   from the area. No error.
            E

This sentence falls into a category labeled "condition contrary to fact" because the speaker in the sentence did not know about the eruption. In a contrary-to-fact sentence, use *had* or *were* in the *if* part of the sentence and *would* in the other part of the sentence. The correct version: *If I had known about.* . . . Choice (A) is correct. (verb tense and mood)

5. Larry donated the violins to the senior orchestra members and to we freshmen so that all
                                          A   B   C

   talented musicians could play with top-notch instruments. No error.
                  D   E

Take your fingers and cover *the senior orchestra members* and *freshmen.* Now read the sentence. *Donated the violins to* . . . *we?* I don't think so. *Donated* . . . *to us* sounds better. The grammatical explanation: *To* is a preposition and needs an object pronoun. *Us* is an object pronoun; *we* is a subject pronoun. Choice (B) is right. (pronoun case)

6. Sitting on the dock, the patient boy watched his father row the boat toward the shore.
      A   B   C   D

   No error.
     E

Choice (E) is correct. No error. When a sentence begins with a verb form that acts as a description, the verb form (a participle, if you want to get technical) must describe the subject of the sentence. In Question 6, the *patient boy* is the subject and he's sitting *on the dock,* so no error appears. (placement of descriptions)

7. Valuing honesty, Phil sent the package to the Post Office, and he explains that the package

A   B   C

belonged to someone else. No error.

D   E

   When you start off telling a story in past tense, you should stay in past tense unless the content justifies a shift. *Phil sent* starts you off in past tense, and *he explains* is in present tense. Choice (C) is the error you're looking for. (verb tense)

8. Irregardless of your feelings about museum visits, you must take the time to see the new

A   B   C   D

exhibit on the Byzantine Empire. No error.

                         E

   Regardless of what you think, *irregardless* isn't a word. Choice (A) is correct. (word choice)

9. The teachers couldn't determine who's homework was missing, despite the

            A   B   C

principal's efforts to keep track of students' paperwork. No error.

D   E

   The contraction *who's* means "who is," and this sentence calls for a possessive pronoun *(whose)*. Choice (B) is correct. (pronouns)

10. There are less shoes today in that cabinet than there were yesterday because the

   A   B   C   D

shoemaker has taken some to be repaired. No error.

                           E

    Less is for stuff you measure (air, loneliness, mustard) and *fewer* is for stuff you count. Choice (B) is right. (word choice)

Okay, if you correctly answered about 50 percent, you're on track for a fairly good score. Of course, keep at it and aim for higher. Analyze your mistakes, reread the appropriate explanations in Chapter 9, and then hit the second set.

Set 2

1. That store is selling wool sweaters at a

              A   B

large discount, Kirsten may purchase one

           C

pullover for each day of the week. No error.

            D   E

2. The complete affect of global warming

            A

on the environment is still unknown;

               B   C

nevertheless, the nation must take steps to

D

reduce carbon fuel consumption. No error.

                          E

3. Did the commission really state that someone should change their vote on that issue?

A   B

one should change their vote on that issue?

        C   D

No error.

   E

4. Defiant to the end, the convicted revolutionary refuses to except his fate. No error.

A   B

tionary refuses to except his fate. No error.

         C   D   E

5. The packet of multicolored jellybeans, won
   A
   by our combined efforts, should be divided
   B
   between you and I and not shared with the
   C
   slackers who skipped the final competition.
   D
   No error.
   E

6. Ashley gave a portion of salad to we men
   A   B
   and then began to distribute the napkins
   C
   and forks. No error.
   D   E

7. Distressed by rumors about a large
   A
   number of fatal crashes, her parents firmly
   B
   objected to Alexa's skydiving without a
   C   D
   generous insurance policy. No error.
   E

8. Annie feels badly about the mistake
   A
   she made when preparing oxtail stew
   B   C
   for her friends. No error.
   D   E

9. Miranda, to her amazement, is the only one
   A
   of the many freshmen attending this year's
   B
   French Day Festival who is able to pro-
   C
   nounce her teacher's name correctly.
   D
   No error.
   E

10. Whom shall I say is calling, assuming that
    A   B   C
    I agree to relay the message? No error.
    D   E

Answers to Set 2

1. **C.** You can't glue together two complete sentences with just a comma. Question 1 is a run-on sentence, so (C) is the answer you seek. (punctuation)

2. **A.** *Affect* means "to influence" and *effect* means "a result." In this sentence, *effect* is called for. Ring one up for (A). (word choice)

3. **D.** *Someone* is singular and should be paired with the singular pronouns *his* or *her,* not with the plural *their.* Choice (D) is correct. (agreement)

4. **D.** *Except* means "all but" and *accept* means "to receive willingly." In this sentence, *accept* makes more sense. Three cheers for (D). (word choice)

5. **C.** The correct expression is *between you and me. Between* is a preposition and must be followed by an object, not a subject pronoun. Choice (C) is right. (pronoun case)

6. **B.** Cover *men* with your finger and read the sentence. *To we?* Uh uh. *To us?* Yup. *To us* is correct. Choice (B) is correct. (pronoun case)

7. **E.** Everything is hunky-dory in this statement! Choice (E) is correct here. Did I catch you with (D)? The parents don't object to Alexa, just to her skydiving, so possessive is called for here. (pronoun case)

8. **A.** *Badly* describes an action and *bad* describes a person or thing. In this sentence, you need *bad* to explain Annie's mood. Choice (A) is correct. (word choice)

9. **E.** Nothing wrong with this statement, so (E) is correct. The trap here is (C). Because Miranda is *the only one,* the pronoun *who* is singular and takes the singular verb *is.* (agreement)

10. **A.** Rearranged and corrected, the sentence reads, "I shall say who is calling." The pronoun *who* serves as the subject of *is calling.* Choice (A) is correct. (pronoun case)

TIP
Once more onto the analyst's couch: Check what type of question tripped you up and go back over the explanations in Chapter 9.

Solving Sentence-Revision Questions

In this sort of question you're not just looking for grammar mistakes; you're also aiming for style. Choice (A) is always the underlined part of the sentence, repeated without any changes. If you think the sentence sounds fine, bubble in (A) and be done with it. Otherwise, reword the sentence in your mind and try to find an answer that fits. If nothing fits your imaginary revision, check out the SAT's offerings and choose the one that sounds best. Set 1 gives you the answers after each question; Set 2, which is set up like the real test, gives you the answers at the end.

Even after you've found the correct answers, squeeze out a couple of seconds to review the explanations that follow the questions. I have taken care to include a couple of frequently tested ideas in this section that didn't merit a full-blown discussion in Chapter 9. Reading the explanations will help you pick up grammar issues that may show up on the real SAT.

Set 1

1. Dancing in local productions, singing in the homecoming show, <u>and music lessons all</u> paved the way for her career in the arts.

   (A) and music lessons all

   (B) as well as music lessons all

   (C) and teaching music, all

   (D) and teaching music all

   (E) and lessons in music

   All the items in a list should resemble each other, at least in terms of grammar. *Dancing* and *singing* should be matched with *teaching*. No comma is needed at the end of a list, so (C) hits the reject pile. Choice (D) is correct. (parallel structure)

2. <u>In the newspaper it says that</u> the egg hunt will be held outdoors only if the weather cooperates.

   (A) In the newspaper it says that

   (B) According to the newspaper, it says that

   (C) According to the newspaper,

   (D) In the newspaper it reports that

   (E) The newspaper says that

   The *newspaper* doesn't *say,* and neither does *it.* Choice (C) is right. (word choice)

3. The plot of the drama was so intriguing that Annie didn't realize until the final curtain <u>how much time it was that had passed</u>.

   (A) how much time it was that had passed

   (B) how much time it was that passed

   (C) how much time passed

   (D) how much time had passed

   (E) how late it had been

First of all, you don't need *it,* so you can immediately rule out (A), (B), and (E). Of the two remaining, (D) is better because the *realizing* and the *passing* take place at two separate times in the past. To show that the *passing* was earlier, use *had.* Choice (D) is correct. (verb tense)

4. Stirring the batter vigorously, <u>a tasty cake will result, even for amateur bakers</u>.

   (A) a tasty cake will result, even for amateur bakers

   (B) even amateur bakers can make a tasty cake

   (C) a tasty cake will be made by amateur bakers

   (D) amateur bakers will result in a tasty cake

   (E) a cake that tastes good will be the result for amateur bakers

   The sentence begins with a verb form *(stirring),* but the subject that follows it — *a tasty cake* — obviously isn't doing the stirring. By the laws of grammar, a verb form beginning a sentence must be an action performed by the subject. Choices (A), (C), and (E) are out on those grounds. Choice (D) bites the dust because it doesn't make sense. Give it up for (B). (placement of descriptions)

5. <u>Either the puppies or the dog trainer is</u> to be commended for the excellent behavior of the pack.

   (A) Either the puppies or the dog trainer is

   (B) Either the puppies or the dog trainer are

   (C) The puppies, along with the dog trainer is

   (D) The dog trainer, and the puppies too, is

   (E) Either the puppies, or the dog trainer is

   When you're confronted with an *either/or* sentence, match the verb to the closest subject. In this sentence, the closest subject is *trainer,* which pairs nicely with *is.* Also, avoid separating two subjects with commas, as in (E). Choice (A) is right. (subject-verb agreement)

6. The mayor told us citizens that the responsibility for public safety <u>was to be shouldered by him</u>.

   (A) was to be shouldered by him

   (B) he was to shoulder

   (C) he would have shouldered

   (D) was his

   (E) was to be his

   What's with the shoulders? Choices (A), (B), (C), and (E) are overly long. Go for the most economical version wherever possible. Choice (D) is correct. (conciseness)

7. Alex told us that <u>there is a good reason for him accepting</u> blame for the fire.

   (A) there is a good reason for him accepting

   (B) there is a good reason for he not accepting

   (C) there is a good reason, he accepts

   (D) he has a good reason to accept

   (E) there is good reason, for him to accept

   There is helps out in some sentences, but often it's unnecessary. Choice (D) does the job in fewer words. (conciseness)

8. That art historian maintains that only the painter <u>can interpret his work, consequently</u> the art gallery must use the catalog the scholar prepared or nothing at all.

    (A) can interpret his work, consequently

    (B) can interpret his work; consequently

    (C) can have interpreted his work; consequently

    (D) can have interpreted his work, and consequently

    (E) can be interpreting his work; consequently

Consequently, a nice mouthful that looks important, is actually a weak, never-goes-to-the-gym sort of word. The rules of grammar don't allow *consequently* to join two complete sentences. If you want to glue two sentences together, you need a semicolon or a conjunction — a true joining word — in front of *consequently.* Choice (A) is out. Choices (C), (D), and (E) lose the race because the verb tense is wrong. If you selected (B), pat yourself on the head. (complete sentences)

Set 2

1. The business executive <u>spoke continually for seven hours with whomever</u> would listen until the problem with the company's cash shortage was resolved.

    (A) spoke continually for seven hours with whomever

    (B) spoke continuously for seven hours with whomever

    (C) spoke continually for seven hours with whoever

    (D) spoke continuously for seven hours with whoever

    (E) had spoken continually for seven hours with whoever

2. My sister, barely able to speak and sniffing furiously, <u>told me that she has a cold</u>.

    (A) told me that she has a cold

    (B) has told me that she has a cold

    (C) told me that she had a cold

    (D) will have told me that she had a cold

    (E) told me, that she had a cold

3. Everyone <u>should have brought their best</u> clothes to the dance competition in order to make a good impression on the judges.

    (A) should have brought their best

    (B) should of brought his or her best

    (C) should have brought his or her best

    (D) could've brought their

    (E) should've brought their

4. The trophy should be awarded to the best athlete, <u>the same standards applying to everyone who plays on the team</u>.

    (A) the same standards applying to everyone who plays on the team

    (B) all athletes playing on the team meeting the same standards

    (C) with the same standards applying to every player on the team

    (D) applying the same standards to everyone on the team

    (E) and the same standards apply to everyone on the team

5. <u>When one is ready to enter college, you</u> should have the ability to write a good essay.

    (A) When one is ready to enter college, you

    (B) When you are ready to enter college, you

    (C) When one is ready to enter college you

    (D) When one is ready to enter college, they

    (E) When one is ready to enter college they

6. Mary told her aunt that <u>she should not wear black because it</u> is a gloomy color.

    (A) she should not wear black because it

    (B) she should not wear black, because it

    (C) her aunt should not wear black, it

    (D) her aunt should not wear black it

    (E) her aunt shouldn't wear black because it

7. The <u>principle of the school must maintain an attitude</u> of dignity, even when pupils misbehave.

(A) principle of the school must maintain an attitude

(B) principal of the school must maintain an attitude

(C) principle of the school should maintain an attitude

(D) principle of the school, he must maintain an attitude

(E) principal of the school he must maintain an attitude

8. <u>Having read the report, John immediately took</u> steps to correct the problem.

(A) Having read the report, John immediately took

(B) Reading the report, John immediately had taken

(C) Reading the report John immediately took

(D) Having read the report, John immediately will take

(E) Having read the report John immediately will take

Answers to Set 2

1. **D.** *Continually* means "stopping and starting endlessly." *Continuously* means "ongoing without a pause." In this sentence the executive (who now has a severe case of laryngitis) didn't stop talking at all for seven hours. Hence (B) and (D) are in the running, but (D) wins because *whoever* is needed as the subject of *would listen*. (pronoun case, word choice)

2. **C.** When you relate what someone said, use past tense unless you're stating something that is always true (the sort of thing you'd read in an encyclopedia). Choice (C) is correct. (verb tense)

3. **C.** *Should of* (along with its pals *could of* and *would of*) is a big no-no. Strike these expressions from your vocabulary. The *of* should be *have,* as in *should have, could have, would have. Everyone* is singular, so *their* changes to *his* or *her.* Choice (C) is right because it's the only choice that avoids both problems. (word choice, pronoun-antecedent agreement)

4. **C.** In the original sentence, everything after the comma isn't grammatically attached to the portion of the sentence preceding the comma. Choice (C) creates a prepositional phrase that gives more information about the verb *(should be awarded).* Choice (E) is also grammatically correct, but (C) is a little more sophisticated, so it's the best answer. (sentence completeness, style)

5. **B.** A shift in a car gives you the right gear at the right time. A shift in a sentence is a grammatical *faux pas* (error). Grammar rests upon a basis of consistency. This sentence has a shift from *one* to *you.* Oops. Gotta go to (B), which stays with *you.* (parallel structure)

6. **E.** The original sentence doesn't tell you who needs the pink scarf instead of funeral colors — Mary or the aunt? Choices (C), (D), and (E) clarify the situation, but (C) and (D) are *run-on sentences* (two sentences glued together without a legal joining word or a semicolon). Choice (E) is correct. (pronouns, punctuation)

7. **B.** The *principal* is your *pal,* so you need to dump (A), (C), and (D). Choice (E) adds an unnecessary *he.* Choice (B) is correct. (word choice)

8. **A.** Verb tense and commas are both issues in this sentence. Verb-tense errors rule out (B), (D), and (E). The tenses in (A) and (C) are okay, but (C) is missing a comma. Choice (A) is correct. (verb tense, punctuation)

After you check the answers, take note of your problem areas (flabby abs? saddlebag thighs?) and turn back to the corresponding explanations in Chapter 9. Because this sort of question checks style as well as grammar, not every answer has a corresponding section in Chapter 9. (Fortunately for you, I tell you why something's right or wrong in the explanation.)

Paragraph-Revision Questions

This type of question presents a piece of writing that a fellow student may have produced. As a first draft, it has some grammar and style problems. Each sentence is numbered, and the whole thing is followed by a set of questions with answers and explanations. Take a crack at the first set, which provides the answer after each question, review your problem areas, and then hit the second set, which is set up like the real test and provides all the answers at the end.

Set 1

[1] When I was about two years old, my mother made me eat lima beans, which apparently annoyed me so much that I frowned at her the rest of the day. [2] That's what my family says, as I don't remember myself. [3] Now I like lima beans, therefore my tastes have changed. [4] Your preferences one day may be different at another time. [5] No one can tell what they will think in the future, so everyone should be careful not to rule out the possibility of change.

[6] This is particularly important in the world of ideas. [7] If someone presents an idea that you don't like, you shouldn't put it aside and never think about it again. [8] After all, new information may change your mind. [9] Different experiences can also change the way you think. [10] Many ideas that were once accepted by almost everyone — slavery, the absolute right of a king to rule his country and other ideas — are now considered wrong.

[11] Being in a democracy, openness to ideas is more important than anything else. [12] A political candidate may seem too radical or too conservative the first time you listen, but later they start to appear more logical. [13] Thinking and probing for information makes the difference. [14] Last election day when I went to the polls, I had thought before about whom to vote for and why. [15] If I would have chosen without thought, I would not have done my duty as a citizen. [16] Like lima beans, ideas can grow on you. [17] So everyone has the obligation to be open and thoughtful.

1. Which of the following is the best revision of the underlined portion of Sentence 1?

   When I was about two years old, my mother made me eat <u>lima beans, which apparently annoyed me so much that</u> I frowned at her the rest of the day.

   (A) lima beans that apparently annoyed me so much that I

   (B) lima beans. I was so annoyed that

   (C) lima beans, however they annoyed me so much that

   (D) annoying lima beans, and

   (E) lima beans, apparently annoyed me so much that

   Pronouns may replace nouns and pronouns but *not* subject-verb combinations. In the original sentence, *which* is replacing an expression containing a subject-verb pair *(my mother made me eat)*. Penalty box. Changing *which* to *that* in (A) doesn't solve the problem because *that* is also a pronoun. Choice (C) is a run-on because *however* isn't a legal joining word. Choices (D) and (E) are awkward. Choice (B) is correct. (pronouns)

2. In the context of the first paragraph, how should Sentence 5 be revised?

   (A) You can't tell what you will think in the future, so you should be careful not to rule out the possibility of change.

   (B) No one can tell what he or she will think in the future, so everyone should be careful not to rule out the possibility of change.

   (C) What you think might be a mystery tomorrow, so don't rule out change.

   (D) You may change in ways you can't foresee, don't rule out new ideas.

   (E) No one knows how they will change, especially in terms of ideas.

   One and *they* are a mismatch because *one* is singular and *they* is plural. Also, the rest of the paragraph — and the question specifically tells you to look at the rest of the paragraph — deals with *you*. A paragraph needs consistency, and shifting from *one* or *they* to *you* is inconsistent. Go for (A) instead of (C) or (D) because (A) keeps the original meaning of the sentence. (parallel structure)

3. How may Sentences 8 and 9 best be combined?

   (A) After all, new information may change your mind and different experiences can also change the way you think.

   (B) After all, new information may change your mind, and different experiences can also change the way you think.

   (C) After all, new information may change your mind; different experiences can also change the way you think.

   (D) After all, new information and experiences may change the way you think.

   (E) After all, new information may change your mind, like different experiences do.

   Wordiness is a pain. Why? Have you ever sat through a 20-minute speech containing three minutes' worth of information? Choice (D) is the most concise. (conciseness)

4. What is the best revision of Sentence 11?

   (A) Being in a democracy, openness to ideas are more important than anything else.

   (B) Openness to ideas is more important than anything else because of democracy.

   (C) Being in a democracy, you should have openness to ideas more than anything else.

   (D) In a democracy, openness to ideas is an extremely important quality.

   (E) Being in a democracy, openness to ideas is needed more than anything else.

Being is a verb form, and when you begin a sentence with a verb form, the subject of the sentence should be doing the action expressed by the verb form. Choices (A) and (E) bite the dust because *openness* isn't the person who is *being* in a democracy. Choices (B) and (C) are wordy and awkward. Choice (D) is correct. (placement of descriptions)

5. What is the best revision of Sentence 15?

   (A) If I would choose without thought, I would not have done my duty as a citizen.

   (B) If I had chosen without thought, I would not have done my duty as a citizen.

   (C) Choosing without thought had been wrong, as a citizen.

   (D) If I would have chosen without thought, I should not have done my duty as a citizen.

   (E) Had I chosen without thought, my duty as a citizen would not have been done.

Sentence 15 expresses what grammarians call *condition contrary to fact* — something that isn't true. In this sort of sentence, the "if" part should have *were* or *had* as part of the verb, never *would.* The *would* belongs in the other half of the sentence. Choice (B) is right. (verb tense and mood)

6. The writer's reference to lima beans in the third paragraph is intended to

   (A) show personal growth

   (B) introduce a note of humor

   (C) compare election choices to food

   (D) relate to the reader's personal experience

   (E) unify the passage by bringing it full circle

A fine design for essays is that of a circle, to end where you began. Very deep and philosophical, also unified! Choice (E) is correct. (logical organization of ideas)

Set 2

⬛1⬛ The famous writer, Franz Kafka, once said that anything that has lasting value always comes from within. ⬛2⬛ I agree with Kafka because he was right to value inner qualities, not possessions. ⬛3⬛ I am not opposed to owning material things, and everyone should have whatever they need to survive, plus more as well. ⬛4⬛ Just imagine a life without museums filled with beautiful art or a town without stores selling beautiful objects. ⬛5⬛ These things have value, and they are possessions that can be bought and sold.

⬛6⬛ However, Kafka was right in saying that lasting value always comes from within, and art proves his point. ⬛7⬛ The great paintings we see in museums and even the best of fashion (things you keep and pass on to your children and their children) come from creativity, the expression of human genius. ⬛8⬛ A museum shows visitors what they can achieve and also displays the culture of a society. ⬛9⬛ It shows the traditions of a people. ⬛10⬛ You can sell a painting and become rich. ⬛11⬛ You can't put a price on the meaning of art. ⬛12⬛ No one can buy or sell culture.

[13] Kafka's quotation is the ultimate motivation for creating art. [14] We as a society spend a lot of time and money on consumer goods. [15] If we paid more attention to our creative spirit, we would be better off. [16] Working from within ourselves, as Kafka said, creates lasting value.

1. What is the best revision of Sentence 2?

    (A) (no change)

    (B) Kafka was right to not value possessions but to value inner qualities instead.

    (C) Kafka rightly values inner qualities more than possessions.

    (D) Kafka, not valuing possessions, values inner qualities.

    (E) Inner qualities, not possessions, are valued by Kafka.

2. Which of the following is the best change to Sentence 3?

    (A) (no change)

    (B) Omit "I am not opposed to owning material things, and."

    (C) Change "they need" to "he or she needs."

    (D) Add a comma and "such as art" to the end of the sentence.

    (E) Change "material things" to "art."

3. In the context of the essay, what is the function of Sentence 6?

    (A) to introduce a new topic

    (B) to give examples that contradict Kafka's ideas

    (C) to concede that criticism of Kafka is partly justified

    (D) to expand upon the example provided in the first paragraph

    (E) to explain the limits of Kafka's argument

4. Which sentence in the second paragraph (Sentences 6–12) may be omitted without weakening the writer's argument?

    (A) 6

    (B) 9

    (C) 10

    (D) 11

    (E) 12

5. How may Sentences 10 and 11 best be combined?

    (A) You can sell a painting and become rich, but you can't put a price on the meaning of art.

    (B) Selling a painting and becoming rich, you can't put a price on the meaning of art.

    (C) You can sell a painting, but you can't put a price on the meaning of art, even if it makes you rich.

    (D) Selling a painting, you become rich, and you can't put a price on the meaning of art.

    (E) As you sell a painting and become rich, you can't put a price on the meaning of art.

6. What is the best way to improve the third paragraph (Sentences 13–16)?

    (A) (no change)

    (B) Omit Sentence 13.

    (C) Add "because he explains the value of art" to the end of Sentence 13.

    (D) Combine Sentences 14 and 15.

    (E) Add a sentence that does not refer to art as an example of Kafka's ideas.

Answers to Set 2

1. **C.** Sentence 2, in its original form, is repetitive. *I agree* and *he was right* make the same point. Choices (B) and (D) are also unnecessarily repetitive *(value, valuing)*. Choice (C) is streamlined but gets the point across. Choice (E) shifts to passive voice *(are valued)* for no reason. Go with (C). (conciseness)

2. **C.** The pronoun *they* is plural, but *everyone* (which *they* refers to) is singular. Therefore, *they* should change to the singular *he or she*. Choice (C) is right. (agreement)

3. **D.** The first paragraph lays out an idea *(lasting value comes from within)* but concedes that material possessions are necessary, including art. The second paragraph continues the discussion of art, showing how its creation is the product of an inner quality *(human genius)*. Sentence 6, which begins the second paragraph, doesn't introduce a new idea. Therefore, Choice (A) is wrong. Nor does it contradict or modify what was said in the first paragraph, so Choices (B), (C), and (E) don't work. Choice (D) is the best answer. (logical organization of ideas)

4. **B.** The *culture of a society* in Sentence 8 is the equivalent of *the traditions of a people* in Sentence 9, so you can drop Sentence 9 without losing anything. Choice (B) is correct. (conciseness)

5. **A.** Sentences 10 and 11 work in opposing directions. Sentence 10 talks about making money, and Sentence 11 talks about a priceless experience. Thus (A), in which *but* signals a change in direction, is best. (word choice)

6. **B.** Kafka's quotation may explain the value of art, but it says nothing about the motivation for creating it. Hence Sentence 13 adds very little to the writer's argument. True, cutting Sentence 13 makes the last paragraph very short. However, a short paragraph in which everything makes sense is better than a long paragraph with *erroneous* (wrong) statements. Go with (B). (conciseness)

Here's looking at *Eu, Anthro*

The *eu* family has nothing in common with *ew*, the sound you make when a bug crawls up your sleeve. *Eu* is a Greek prefix that means *good* or *pleasant*. Easy-listening tunes are **euphonious** (they sound good) and **eulogies** are speeches in which all (and only) good things are said about someone (they're usually given in honor of the deceased at a funeral or memorial service). A **euphemism** is a more pleasant term that may substitute for a word you don't like to say, such as the substitution of *restroom* for toilet.

The *anthros* are the family of man (and woman). An **anthropologist** studies human behavior and society, but a **misanthrope** hates people. If you dress your dog in little dresses (pause for a shudder and a call to the humane society), you're guilty of **anthropomorphism** — projecting human qualities onto nonhumans.

Part IV
Take a Number, Any Number: The Mathematics Sections

The 5th Wave   By Rich Tennant

©RICHTENNANT

"The math portion of that test was so easy. I figure I've got a 7 in 5 chance of acing it."

In this part . . .

In my experience, two types of people inhabit the world: those who say disdainfully, "Math? My accountant will take care of that stuff!" and those who gleefully declare, "Ooh, more numbers!" No matter which camp you belong to, after you read this part, you'll find SAT math approachable and, perhaps, easier than you anticipated.

This part begins with a brief fly-by of the exam's Math section, all 70 glorious minutes of it, and moves on to more in-depth analysis and techniques for each topic covered on the test. To ruin just a tiny bit more of your life, I also include practice questions that are very similar to the ones you'll see on test day.

Chapter 11

Meeting Numbers Head-On: The SAT Math Sections

In This Chapter

▶ Surveying the mathematics portion of the SAT

▶ Choosing the right calculator and using it efficiently during the exam

▶ Tackling time constraints

▶ Getting good at grid-ins

▶ Adopting the best strategies for SAT math questions

*I*f you're one of those people who whined to your ninth-grade math teacher, "No one in the real world *ever* has to calculate the value of $6x - y$," the SAT is about to prove you wrong. You can't get much more real world than a test that helps to determine where you go to college and maybe even what sort of job you get afterward. And on the SAT, the value of $6x - y$ is fair game. So are absolute value (and I'm not talking about the great price you got on that orange sweater), exponential growth (the kind your tuition payments will display), and plenty of other fun stuff. In this chapter, I show you what's where, how to prepare, and most important, how to survive the SAT Math section.

Having Fun with Numbers: SAT Math 101

The SAT booklet you open with sweaty, trembling fingers one morning in the near future will contain three sections of math that count toward your score: two 25-minute sections and one 20-minute section. You may also encounter an equating section that allows the SAT makers to try out new questions. You pay them to let you take the test, and they treat you like a lab rat. Nice, huh?

The equating section doesn't count toward your final score, but because you never know which section is equating, don't blow off anything. You may end up ignoring a section that matters.

Each Math section begins with a little gift basket: a set of formulas to help you solve the problems — the area and circumference of a circle, the area of a square, the angles and sides of "special" triangles, and so forth. As you plod through an SAT Math section, look back whenever you need this information so you're sure that your nerves haven't changed, say, the area of a rectangle from $a = lw$ to $a = lw^2$.

The SAT Math sections are mostly five-answer multiple-choice questions. Ten questions are *grid-ins,* which require you to bubble in the numbers you come up with, thus, giving you no hint whatsoever about the correct answer. (Check out the section "Knowing When to Grid and Bear It" later in this chapter for everything you need to know about these questions.) Expect to see problems relating to topics commonly covered in the first three years of high school math. In other words, you'll see questions on numbers and operations, algebra and functions, geometry, statistics, probability, and data interpretation. For more specifics, read on.

Numbers and operations

Nope. I'm not talking about the $100,000 you pay a surgeon to have your insides adjusted. The category of numbers and operations, which counts for 20 to 25 percent of your SAT Math score, includes the following:

- **Arithmetic:** You have to add, subtract, divide, and multiply and show understanding of even and odd numbers, positive and negative numbers, and primes.

- **Arithmetic sequences:** If you get 20, 24, 28, 32, and 36 on your five most recent math quizzes, what will you get on the next one, assuming that the sequence stays the same? (Not included in this section: Will you ever *not* be grounded again in this lifetime after your parents see your report card?)

- **Exponential growth sequences, also known as geometric sequences:** These questions require you to multiply by a certain number in order to get to the next term in the sequence. For example, the number of bent wire hangers at the bottom of my closet on consecutive days is 4, 12, 36, 108, 324 . . . you get the idea. You may be asked to create a mathematical statement expressing the way my wire hanger collection grows.

- **Percents:** How much will you have to pay if your book bill increases by 4,000 percent?

- **Ratios and proportions:** If the ratio of tuba players who try out for Prestigious University to those that get in is 2,000 to 3, how many tuba players are accepted out of the 4,000 that apply?

- **Sets, including union, intersection, and elements:** The set of all the parakeet treats I buy and the set of all the parakeet treats that my birds will actually eat (instead of strew around my living room) overlap slightly. The SAT may ask you to identify common elements or ask other questions about two or more sets.

Algebra and functions

Now you're in "what is the value of x" territory, which accounts for 35 to 40 percent of the problems in the Math section. Look for these types of questions:

- **Absolute value:** How far away from a particular point on the number line is another number? That's the absolute value, which may show up in equations or functions.

- **Equations and inequalities:** It's time to have fun with equal signs, as in $3q + 4$ = the number of hours you groan while learning stuff like this. This category also includes quadratic equations, which have things like x^2 in them, such as $x^2 + 8x + 15$.

- **Exponents:** These little numbers tell you how many times to multiply something by itself, as in x^4. You may see positive, negative, and fractional exponents.

- **Factoring:** Factoring is the math equivalent of extracting the cocoa powder and flour from a brownie after it's baked. Here's a typical factoring problem: If a rectangle has a length of $x + 3$ and an area of $x^2 + 8x + 15$, what is its width, in terms of x?

- **Functions:** I'm talking not about my cousin Thelma's fundraiser for impoverished bee-keepers, but about problems in which you take a number, do some stuff to it, and end up with a new number. Functions, which are written as *f(x)*, appear in a number of guises, including the graphs of linear and quadratic functions.

- **Special symbols:** These strange figures have been created just for the SAT; in other words, they don't exist in *normal* math. You have to figure out, given the definition, how to manipulate these symbols.

Geometry

True confession: When I was in high school, I *loved* geometry class. Maybe it was all those squares and triangles that attracted me, or perhaps the reliance on logic. Whether you love it or hate it, you face the following types of geometry problems, which occupy 25 to 30 percent of SAT Math real estate:

- **Areas and perimeters:** This topic covers the basic how-much-carpet-and-baseboard-to-buy question for common shapes as well as weird forms. Also, you may find questions on volume.

- **Coordinate geometry:** The SAT asks about slopes of lines, including parallel and perpendicular lines. Also, if point *G* has the coordinates (x_1, y_1) and point *W* has coordinates (x_2, y_2), what is the midpoint when I spread cream cheese on a bagel? Just joking about the bagel, but you do have to know midpoints. You may also have to interpret the graph of a function and to answer questions about transformations of a function. An example: If *f(x)* measures how much time Gloria spends on her cellphone, how will *f(x)* change the day after her unlimited calling plan starts?

- **Parallel and perpendicular lines:** This topic questions you about what parallel and perpendicular lines do when they're alone in the dark, what kind of angles cut into them, how they behave under pressure (when they have to take the SATs, for example), and so forth.

- **Quadrilaterals and other polygons:** The SAT folks may throw you a quadrilateral quiz or a polygon problem.

- **Triangles:** You find everything you ever wanted to know about triangles, especially the properties of right, isosceles, equilateral, and "special" ones. (Why are they "special"? Because they're on the SAT. Just kidding. Check out Chapter 16 for the lowdown on special triangles.)

Statistics, probability, and data interpretation

This category, which counts for 10 to 15 percent of the SAT Math section, includes graphs, charts, and other fun topics, including the following:

- **Averages:** Make friends with the three *M*s — median, mode, and mean.

- **Geometric probability:** If I'm hanging a picture on my kitchen wall, what's the probability that I'll drive the nail right through a hot-water pipe?

- **Logic:** This topic covers those horrible problems you never see in real life, such as *What is the seating plan if Mr. Green can't sit next to Ms. Red but must sit across from Violet and behind Orchid or he throws popcorn . . .* Wait, I just flashed back to the seating plan at my wedding. You *do* use this stuff in real life!

- **Probability:** If you wash and dry 12 pairs of black socks and a pair of white socks, what is the likelihood that you'll match two socks right out of the dryer?

✔ **Scatterplots:** No, the term doesn't refer to incompetent mystery writers. *Scatterplots* are bits of data represented on a graph. The test writers may show you a bunch of dots, where the *x*-axis represents the amount of time spent reading this book and the *y*-axis shows students' SAT scores. You may have to answer questions about the data, such as exactly how brilliant you were to buy *SAT For Dummies,* 8th Edition.

Anything in the preceding list resemble a foreign language? Probably, because math is a kind of language. If you need to brush up on one or more of these topics, check out the relevant chapters in Part IV for review and practice problems.

Calculating Your Way to SAT Success

When *pundits* (wise guys, like the intellectuals sitting around tables discussing politics on TV) blather on about the decline of civilization, they often mention the fact that students today are allowed to bring calculators to the SAT and other standardized tests. "In our day," they say, "we had to work with our heads, not with machines." Yeah, right. As if any of them even knows how to turn on a calculator, let alone figure out the square root of 324. (P.S. It's 18.)

So you can bring a calculator. Big deal. The SAT makers declare that you can solve every problem on the test with brainpower alone, and they're right. But you're not allergic to a little help, are you? In fact, a calculator may not be the absolute number-one requirement for doing well on the Math section, but it's pretty high on the list. Let me tell you a little secret of success: Become best friends with your calculator *before* the exam. Don't waste time on SAT day trying to find the right buttons.

You're allowed to bring a battery-operated, four-function, graphing, or scientific calculator to the exam. The test makers recommend a scientific calculator. In addition to the four functions (addition, subtraction, multiplication, and division), a scientific calculator also lets you figure out cool stuff like square roots, combination problems involving π, and more. Most also calculate fractions, so adding ¼ and ½ is less traumatic. You aren't allowed to bring anything with a raised keyboard or anything that connects to the outside world. (For more information on what's prohibited, turn to Chapter 2.)

In addition to doing everything a scientific calculator accomplishes, a graphing calculator also lets you draw graphs. If you have one you're comfortable with, bring it along to the test. If you don't own a graphing calculator, don't rush out and buy one because the instruction manual is about 100 pages long (I'm not joking) and you don't really need graphing capability on the SAT.

All calculators come with instruction manuals. After you find your manual, read it. Practice the more complicated-looking procedures with problems from a math book or from this book. Fractions, decimals, and percents should be first on your list. If you're not getting the right answers, ask a fellow student or your math teacher for help. Knowing in advance how to push the right buttons can save you time and give you more right answers, and that's why you're taking the test.

If you've lost your manual, get a copy from the manufacturer. (Check the calculator's serial number and the Web site or information telephone line of the company that made it.) Or buy a new calculator if you can possibly afford one. Spending a few bucks on a new calculator now will pay off big time when you receive your scores.

If you don't own a calculator, don't worry. Although the SAT doesn't supply calculators, some schools do provide loaners to students who don't have their own. Talk with your math teacher. (Home-schoolers, call the local high school to inquire about access to their supply.) The most important thing is that you're familiar with the calculator you plan to take to and use on the test.

Knowing when *not* to use a calculator is almost as important as knowing how to tap in numbers. Sometimes a question presents you with a long string of numbers. You *can* find the answer with a calculator, *if* you type in everything accurately and *if* you have time to do so. But often you can solve the long-string-of-numbers question much more quickly, without a calculator, by noticing a pattern or by carrying out a simple math operation in your head or with paper and pencil. (As you work out the practice problems in Part IV, read the explanations that accompany the answers, even if you correctly answered the problem. Tucked into the explanation you may find a statement telling you how a calculator could have helped or wasn't really needed.)

If your batteries run out during the test, too bad. Don't expect the proctor to plunk a triple-A on your desk. Moral of the story: Have fresh batteries in your calculator before SAT-day morning.

Taking Your Time versus Getting It Right

Finishing every problem on the Math section of the SAT in the time you're given is certainly possible. However, finishing every question the SAT makers hit you with *and* getting them all correct is extremely unlikely. Furthermore, if you're in a mad rush to finish a section, you're going to make some mistakes that you would never have made had you worked at a slower pace.

Right now, resolve that you're not going to worry about getting to all the problems. Decide instead to spend as much time as you need on each problem to be reasonably sure that you answer it correctly. Also, cut your losses. Give up on a problem if you spend two or three minutes on it without getting anywhere. Finally, if a problem makes absolutely no sense to you, skip it. Put a big circle around the question in the booklet, and take pains to skip the proper line on the answer sheet. If you find yourself with an extra nanosecond at the end of the section, go back to the problems you skipped. Follow the usual guessing rules to come up with a reasonable answer. (See Chapter 1 for more information on guessing.)

Is it just me, or are there more exponents on the bottom of the page?

Complete this sentence: SAT math problems are placed in order

(A) so that the answer letters spell out the name of the test maker's boyfriend

(B) with the hardest topics first

(C) by grade level, with 9th-grade material first and 11th-grade material last

(D) by throwing the questions down a flight of stairs

(E) from easiest to hardest

The correct answer is (E). The SAT makers arrange the problems roughly in the order of difficulty. (How do they know what's difficult and what's easy? They make you slog through equating sections and gather data on the number of wrong answers, that's how.) Don't assume that all the arithmetic questions are easy and all the third-year math problems are tough. The SAT makers try to include varying levels of difficulty for each topic, regardless of when it shows up in your high school curriculum.

Take a shot at all the questions in the first third of each math set and attempt to figure out the middle third, if you can. Hit the last third of a set of problems only as time allows.

Knowing When to Grid and Bear It

Ten of the most fun questions (just kidding — they're as boring as everything else on the exam) are grid-ins. Sadly, you don't get five convenient multiple choices for a grid-in. On the other hand, you don't lose any points for a wrong answer, so guess as much as you want. Figure 11-1 shows a sample blank grid-in.

Figure 11-1:
A blank
grid-in.

The grid-in problems are normal questions of any type and all levels of difficulty. After you solve the problem, you have to darken the ovals that correspond to your answer. (Notice that the SAT makers cleverly avoid spending money on graders who could actually evaluate your ability to solve a math problem.) Before you start filling in those little ovals, you need to take note of some built-in traps. Beware of the following:

- **Write your answer and then darken the ovals.** Grid-ins have little boxes in which you can write your answer, but the scanner doesn't read the boxes, just the darkened ovals. But even though only the bubbles are scored, don't skip the writing part because you may "bubble" inaccurately.

- **You can't grid in negative numbers.** The grid has no minus sign. Hence, all answers are positive.

- **Gridding in mixed numbers is impossible.** If you grid in 5½, the scanner reads "51 over 2," not "five and one half." Solution: Convert your answer to an improper fraction (one that has absolutely no manners and behaves scandalously on Saturday night). In the preceding example, grid in ¹¹⁄₂ (11 over 2), as shown in Figure 11-2a. You may also choose to grid your answer as a decimal.

- **You can start from the extreme left or right, and the middle, too.** Just be sure that you have enough boxes for the answer you want to record.

- **Don't place zeroes before a decimal point.** If your answer is .5, darken the oval for the decimal point and the five, not 00.5 (Figure 11-2b).

- **If your answer is a repeating decimal, fill in all the boxes, rounding off the last number only.** In other words, darken the ovals for .333 or .667 (⅓ and ⅔ expressed as decimals), not .3 or .67 (Figure 11-2c).

- **If your answer isn't a repeating decimal (.4, for example), you don't have to fill in all the boxes.** Just darken a decimal point and a 4.

Don't agonize over *the* perfect, correct answer. Some grid-ins have several possible right answers. (Usually those problems say something like "a possible value for *x* is . . .") Just find one of them and you're all set. Also be aware that when there are several possible correct answers, sometimes the problem will ask for the *least* or *greatest* answer.

Figure 11-2:
Three grid-ins, properly filled in.

Planning for the Battle: Some Math Strategies That Work

In other chapters in Part IV, I show you the best way to attack each type of question in the SAT Math section. But some general math strategies help you get off on the right foot. Try these on for size:

- **Read the question and figure out what the SAT makers want to know.** Circle significant words such as *greater than, percentage,* and so forth.

- **Use the booklet as scrap paper.** Write your calculations in the extra blank space, but no matter what, take time to bubble in your answers. Even though the proctor collects the test booklet, the information in it doesn't count toward your score.

- **Don't overuse the calculator.** See if a simple math approach gets you to the right answer.

- **Keep an eye on the clock.** You get as many points for each correct answer to an easy question as you do for a correct answer to a hard question. Don't spend five minutes on one hard question and skip 11 easy questions because you run out of time.

- **Follow the guessing guidelines I outline in Chapter 1.** You lose a quarter point for each incorrect multiple-choice answer. Grid-ins take nothing away from your score if you're wrong, so guess as much as you want on those questions.

- **Try out the multiple-choice answers and see which one works.** If the SAT writers ask something like "Which number is divisible by both 13 and 14?" start plugging in the answers until one of them works. SAT multiple-choice answers are usually in order from smallest to largest. When you plug in, start with Choice (C), and check whether you end up above or below the target. Then try (B) or (D), depending on the direction you need to go.

- **Think of realistic answers.** The SAT Math section isn't tied tightly to the real world, but it's not from Mars either. If you're looking for a weight, don't choose "5,098 pounds" unless you have a truck on the scale. Think about the range of human body sizes and concentrate on answers in that category. Similarly, if you're looking for a discount and come up with a negative sale price, you've done something wrong. Try again.

- **Don't assume that the provided diagram will solve the problem.** SAT figures aren't created purposely to deceive you, but they may not be drawn to scale. (Look for a note stating this fact.)

- **Be sure to answer the question being asked.** Often in your calculations, you may derive an intermediate answer that may appear as an answer choice but isn't the final answer to the question asked.

Multiplying your vocabulary

Basic number operations multiply your vocabulary skills:

✔ *Multi*-plying and *div*-iding. Think *multiply* when you encounter ***multinational*** (many nations involved), ***multilateral*** (many sides), ***multifarious*** (many different types, various) and any other *multi* word. Similarly, *division* will help you tackle ***diversify*** (to split or to branch out into many paths) and ***divergent*** (splitting in different directions, differing, contradictory).

✔ Sub*traction* has a root word — *trac* or *tract* — which means "to pull." With the same root word, you've got ***contract*** (to pull together, to shrink in on itself), ***retract*** (literally, "to pull back"; to take back words you've already said), ***detract*** (literally, "to pull down"; to take away from someone's reputation), and ***extract*** (to pull from, the way a dentist *extracts* your teeth).

> ✔ **Even if you're not Picasso, draw little figures to illustrate problems when you need help visualizing them.** For example, the classic "Evelyn was traveling east at 60 miles an hour and Robert was moving toward her at 30 miles an hour" sort of problem cries out for arrows and lines like the ones shown in Figure 11-3.

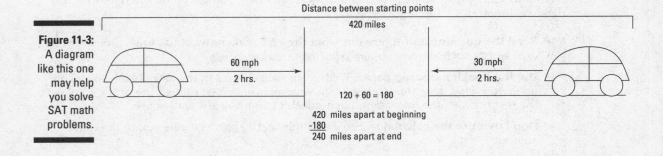

Figure 11-3: A diagram like this one may help you solve SAT math problems.

Distance between starting points
420 miles
60 mph
2 hrs.
30 mph
2 hrs.
120 + 60 = 180
420 miles apart at beginning
−180
240 miles apart at end

Chapter 12

Numb and Numbering: The Ins and Outs of Numbers and Operations

*O*nce upon a time you could take care of all the numbers you needed for school purposes with ten fingers and, in a pinch, a couple of toes. Sadly, life has changed. For the SAT, you need to know what's prime and what's not, as well as how to calculate and manipulate percents, ratios, means, and the like. Not to mention sets and sequences! Never fear. Even though you've moved way beyond body-part math, this chapter tells you everything you need to know about numbers and operations, at least as they appear on the SAT.

Meeting the Number Families

Mathematics starts with numbers, which come in various "flavors." You need to nibble on several types of numbers before you hit SAT day, so in this section I present a buffet of numbers.

You may be wondering why you need a vocabulary lesson to do well on SAT math. The fact of the matter is the SAT makers love to tuck these terms into the questions, as in "How many prime numbers are . . ." or "If the sum of three consecutive integers is 102, what is . . ." and the like. If you don't know the vocabulary, you're sunk before you start.

Check out this "menu" of *toothsome* (good-tasting) numbers:

✔ **Whole numbers:** *Whole numbers* aren't very well named because they include 0, which isn't a whole lot of anything. The whole numbers are the ones you (hopefully) remember from grade school: 0, 1, 2, 3, 4, 5, 6 . . . you get the idea. Whole numbers, by definition, don't include fractions or decimals.

Whole numbers can be even or odd. *Even numbers* are divisible by 2, and *odd numbers* aren't.

✔ **Prime numbers:** *Prime numbers* are divisible only by themselves and by 1. The first few prime numbers are 2, 3, 5, 7, 11, 13, 17, and 19. Zero and 1 aren't prime numbers. They're considered "special." (The kids in grade school said that about me, too.) Two is the only even prime number. No negative number is ever prime because all negative numbers are divisible by −1.

One common misconception is that all odd numbers are prime. Don't fall into that trap. Tons of odd numbers (9 and 15, for example) aren't prime because they're divisible by another number.

✔ **Composite numbers:** Anything that's not prime or special is *composite.* If you can divide a number by some smaller number (other than 1) without getting a remainder, you have a composite number. A few composite numbers are 4, 6, 8, 9, 10, 12, 14, 15, 16, 18, 20, 21, and so on. (I could go on to add zillions more, but you get the idea.)

Speaking of divisibility, remembering these points will win you SAT points:

- All numbers whose digits add up to a multiple of 3 are also divisible by 3. For example, the digits of 789 add up to 24 (7 + 8 + 9 = 24); because 24 is divisible by 3, so is 789.

- Ditto for multiples of 9. If the digits of a number add up to a multiple of 9, you can divide the number itself by 9. For example, the digits of 729 add up to 18; because 18 is divisible by 9, so is 729.

- All numbers ending in 0 or 5 are divisible by 5.

- All numbers ending in 0 are also divisible by 10.

These divisibility rules work backward, too. Consider the number 365. It's not even, so it can't be divided by 2. Its digits add up to 14, which isn't divisible by 3 or 9, so it's not divisible by either 3 or 9. Because 365 ends in 5, it's divisible by 5. Because it doesn't end in 0, it's not divisible by 10.

✔ **Integers:** The whole numbers and all their opposites — also known as *negative numbers* — are *integers.* The whole numbers go all the way up to infinity, but the integers are even more impressive. Integers reach infinity in both directions, as the number line in Figure 12-1 shows.

Figure 12-1:
Integers go
on forever
and ever.

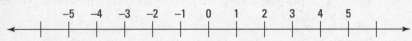

When you're asked to compare integers, remember that the farther to the right a number is, the greater it is. For example, 3 is greater than −5. Also, −4 is greater than −20.

✔ **Rational numbers:** Numbers for whom a padded room without a view isn't necessary. Just kidding. All integers are *rational numbers.* In addition, any number that can be written as a fraction — proper or improper — is a rational number. (In a *proper fraction,* the number on top is smaller than the number on the bottom, and in an *improper fraction,* the top number is greater than the bottom number.) Plus, any decimal that either ends, like 0.23 (the decimal for ²³⁄₁₀₀), or repeats like $0.1\overline{6}$, the decimal for ⅙, or $0.\overline{142857}$, the decimal for ⅐, is a rational number. The following are also rational: −2, 0.234, ⁷³⁵⁄₁₃, $5.8\overline{53}$.

✔ **Irrational numbers:** *Irrational numbers* are decimals that never end or repeat. Practically speaking, you need to worry about only two kinds of irrational numbers:

- Radicals (such as $\sqrt{2}$ and $\sqrt{3}$)

- π, which you've probably heard of because it appears in the formula for the area of a circle. (Like Mom's apple dessert, π is in a class by itself.)

Every type of number I mention in this chapter is a *real* number. Right about now you're probably wondering, "Are some numbers *not* real?" The bad news: Yes, and you may have to figure them out some day, perhaps at the college you're sending your SAT scores to. The good news: That day isn't today because every number on the SAT is real.

Getting Your Priorities Straight: Order of Operations

How many times has your mom told you to turn off the Wii and start on your homework because you "have to get your priorities straight." I'm not going to comment on the annoyance that authority figures generate, especially when they're right, but I am going to tell you that in math, priorities matter.

Consider the problem $3 + 4 \times 2$. If you add $3 + 4$, which of course equals 7, and multiply by 2, you get 14. Nice answer, but wrong, because you forgot about Aunt Sally. "Aunt Sally," or more accurately, "**P**lease **E**xcuse **M**y **D**ear **A**unt **S**ally," or *PEMDAS,* is a mnemonic (memory) device you can use to help you remember what mathematicians call *order of operations.* When faced with a multipart problem, just follow the order of operations that "Aunt Sally" calls for. Note the italicized letters in the following step list, which tells you what "Aunt Sally" really means:

1. Do everything in *p*arentheses.
2. Calculate all *e*xponents.
3. *M*ultiply and *d*ivide, from left to right.
4. *A*dd and *s*ubtract, from left to right.

Back to the sample problem, $3 + 4 \times 2$. No parentheses or exponents, so the first operations up are multiplication and division. Because there's no division, you're left with 4×2, which equals 8. Onward to addition and subtraction (in this problem, subtraction isn't present, so forget about subtracting). Just add 3 to 8, at which point you arrive at 11, the correct answer.

Many calculators know the "Aunt Sally" rules, but on older ones, sometimes you have to input the numbers according to the "Aunt Sally" rules to ensure the right answer. Be sure to figure out which kind of calculator you have before test day.

Aunt Sally's lonely, so here's another chance to visit her:

The expression $20 - (40 \div 5 \times 2) + 3^2$ is equal to

(A) −5

(B) 7

(C) 10

(D) 13

(E) 25

The answer is (D). Start with what's in the parentheses: $40 \div 5 \times 2$. Don't fall into the trap of multiplying 5×2 first; proceed from left to right: $40 \div 5 = 8$ and $8 \times 2 = 16$. Next, tackle the exponent: $3^2 = 9$. At this stage, you have $20 - 16 + 9$. Again, resist the temptation to start by adding; just go left to right ($20 - 16 = 4$ and then $4 + 9 = 13$).

Playing Percentage Games

The SAT loves percentages, perhaps because math teachers who are sick of the question "Am I ever going to use this stuff in real life?" actually write the math portion of the exam. With percentages, the answer is yes if you're taking out a loan (interest rates) or investing the earnings from your part-time job in mutual funds (still interest, but this time it's a good thing). *Percents* represent how much of each hundred you're talking about.

Taking a percentage of a number is a simple task if you're using a calculator with a "%" button. Just hit the "%" and "×" buttons. For example, to find 60 percent of 35, multiply 60% by 35. The answer is 21. If you're not blessed with such a calculator, you can turn a percent into a decimal by moving the decimal point two spaces to the left, as in 60% = 0.60. (Other examples of percents include 12.5% = 0.125, 0.4% = 0.004, and so on.) Or, turn the percent into a fraction. The "cent" in *percent* means hundred, so 60 percent = $^{60}/_{100}$.

For more complicated problems, fall back on the formula you mastered in grade school:

$$\frac{is}{of} = \frac{\%}{100}$$

Suppose you're asked "40% of what number is 80?" The number you're looking for is the number you're taking the percent *of*, so x will go in the *of* space in the formula:

$$\frac{80}{x} = \frac{40}{100}$$

Now cross-multiply: $40x = 8,000$. Dividing by 40 gives you $x = 200$.

A particularly annoying subtopic of percentages is a problem that involves a percent increase or decrease. A slight variation of the percentage formula helps you out with this type of problem. Here's the formula and an example problem to help you master it:

$$\frac{amount\ of\ change}{original\ amount} = \frac{\%}{100}$$

The value of your investment in the winning team of the National Spitball League increased from \$1,500 to \$1,800 over several years. What was the percentage increase of the investment?

(A) 300

(B) 120

(C) 83⅓

(D) 20

(E) 16⅔

The correct answer is (D). The key here is that the number 1,800 shouldn't be used in your formula. Before you can find the *percent* of increase, you need to find the *amount* of increase, which is 1,800 – 1,500 = 300. To find the percentage of increase, set up this equation:

$$\frac{300}{1,500} = \frac{x}{100}$$

Cross-multiply to get $1,500x = 30,000$. Dividing tells you that $x = 20$ percent.

The SAT makers often try to confuse you by asking about something that doesn't appear in the original question, as in this example:

At one point in the season, the New York Yankees had won 60 percent of their games. The Yanks had lost 30 times and never tied. (As you know, there are no ties in the world's noblest sport, baseball. No crying either.) How many games had the team played?

(A) 12

(B) 18

(C) 50

(D) 75

(E) 90

The answer is (D). Did you find the catch? The winning percentage was 60 percent, but the question specified the number of losses. What to do? Well, because ties don't exist, the wins and losses must have represented all the games played, or 100 percent. Thus the percentage of losses must be 100% − 60%, which is 40%. Put the formula to work:

$$\frac{30}{x} = \frac{40}{100}$$

As always, cross-multiply: $40x = 3{,}000$, and $x = 75$.

Keeping It in Proportion: Ratios

After you know the tricks, ratios are some of the easiest problems to answer quickly. I call them "heartbeat" problems because you can solve them in one throb. Here are the points to remember:

> ✔ A ratio is written as $\frac{of}{to}$ or of:to.
>
> • The ratio *of* sunflowers *to* roses = $\frac{sunflowers}{roses}$.
> • The ratio *of* umbrellas *to* heads = umbrellas:heads.
>
> ✔ A possible total is a multiple of the *sum* of the numbers in the ratio.

You may have to confront a proportion problem like this on the test:

> At a party, the ratio of blondes to redheads is 4:5. What could be the total number of blondes and redheads at the party?

This one's mega-easy. Just add the numbers in the ratio: 4 + 5 = 9. The total must be a multiple of 9, such as 9, 18, 27, 36, and so on. If this "multiple of" stuff is confusing, think of it another way: The sum must divide evenly into the total. That is, the total must be divisible by 9. Can the total, for example, be 54? Yes, 9 goes evenly into 54. Can it be 64? No, 9 doesn't go evenly into 64.

Check out another example.

Trying to get Willie to turn down his stereo, his mother pounds on the ceiling and shouts. If she pounds seven times for every five times she shouts, which of the following can be the total number of poundings and shouts?

(A) 75

(B) 57

(C) 48

(D) 35

(E) 30

The correct answer is (C). Add the numbers in the ratio: 7 + 5 = 12. The total must be a multiple of 12. (It must be evenly divisible by 12.) Here, only 48, Choice (C), is evenly divisible by 12. Of course, 75 and 57 try to trick you by using the numbers 7 and 5 from the ratio.

Notice how carefully I've been asking what *can be* the *possible* total. The total can be *any* multiple of the sum. If a question asks you which of the following is the total, you have to answer, "It cannot be determined." You know only which *can be* true.

Another ratio headache strikes when you're given a ratio and a total and asked to find a specific term. To find a specific term, do the following, in order:

1. **Add the numbers in the ratio.**

2. **Divide that sum into the total.**

3. **Multiply that quotient by each term in the ratio. (The *quotient* is the answer you get when you divide.)**

4. **Add the answers to double-check that they sum up to the total.**

Pretty confusing stuff. Take it one step at a time. Look at this example problem:

Yelling at the members of his team, whose record was 0 for 21, the irate coach pointed his finger at each member of the squad, calling everyone either a "wimp" or a "slacker." If he had 3 wimps for every 4 slackers, and every member of the 28-man squad was either a wimp or a slacker, how many wimps were there?

Here's how to solve it:

1. **Add the numbers in the ratio: 3 + 4 = 7.**

2. **Divide that sum into the total:** $^{28}\!/_7$ = 4.

3. **Multiply that quotient by each term in the ratio: $4 \times 3 = 12$; $4 \times 4 = 16$.**

4. **Add to double-check that the numbers sum up to the total: 12 + 16 = 28.**

Now you have all the information you need to answer a variety of questions: How many wimps were there? 12. How many slackers were there? 16. How many more slackers than wimps were there? 4. How many slackers would have to be kicked off the team for the number of wimps and slackers to be equal? 4. The SAT writers can ask all sorts of things, but if you have this information, you're ready for anything they throw at you.

The SAT writers often throw in extra numbers that aren't used at all to solve the problem. In the preceding example, the team's not-quite-World-Series-quality 0 and 21 win/loss record is interesting but irrelevant in terms of the question you're answering. Don't get distracted by extra information.

Getting DIRTy: Time, Rate, and Distance

Time to dish the dirt, as in D.I.R.T. **D**istance **I**s **R**ate × **T**ime. or D = *RT*. When the SAT throws a time, rate, and distance problem at you, use this formula. Make a chart with the formula across the top and fill in the spaces on the chart. Here's an example to help you master this formula:

> Jennifer drives 40 miles an hour for 2½ hours. Her friend Ashley goes the same distance but drives at 1½ times Jennifer's speed. How many *minutes* longer does Jennifer drive than Ashley?

Don't start making big, hairy formulas with *x*s and *y*s. Make the DIRT chart using the distance formula: Distance = Rate × Time.

When you fill in the 40 mph and 2½ hours for Jennifer, you can calculate that she went 100 miles. Think of it this way: If she goes 40 mph for one hour, that's 40 miles. For a second hour, she goes another 40 miles. In a half-hour, she goes ½ of 40, or 20 miles. (See? You don't have to write down 40 × 2½ and do all that pencil-pushing; use your brain, not your yellow No. 2 pencil or your calculator.) Add them together: 40 + 40 + 20 = 100. Jennifer drives 100 miles.

	Distance	=	Rate	×	Time
Jennifer	100		40 mph		2½ hours

Because Ashley drives the same distance, fill in 100 under distance for her. She goes 1½ times as fast. Uh-uh, put down that calculator. Use your brain! 1 × 40 is 40; ½ × 40 is 20. Add 40 + 20 = 60. Ashley drives 60 mph. Now this gets really easy. If she drives at 60 mph, she drives one mile a minute (60 minutes in an hour, 60 miles in an hour). Therefore, to go 100 miles takes her 100 minutes. Because your final answer is asked for in minutes, don't bother converting this to hours; leave it the way it is.

	Distance	=	Rate	×	Time
Ashley	100		60 mph		100 minutes

Last step. Jennifer drives 2½ hours. How many minutes is that? Do it the easy way, in your brain. One hour is 60 minutes. A second hour is another 60 minutes. A half-hour is 30 minutes. Add them together: 60 + 60 + 30 = 150 minutes. If Jennifer drives for 150 minutes and Ashley drives for 100 minutes, Jennifer drives 50 minutes more than Ashley.

	Distance	=	Rate	×	Time
Jennifer	100		40 mph		150 minutes
Ashley	100		60 mph		100 minutes

Be careful to note whether the people are traveling in the same direction or opposite directions. Suppose you're asked how far apart drivers are at the end of their trip. If you're told that Jordan travels 40 mph east for 2 hours and Connor travels 60 mph west for 3 hours, they're going in opposite directions. If they start from the same point at the same time, Jordan has gone 80 miles one way, and Connor has gone 180 miles the opposite way. They're 260 miles apart. The trap answer is 100 because careless people (not *you*!) simply subtract 180 − 80.

Demonstrating the Value of Radicals

Knowing how to manipulate radicals can help you get around in Berkeley, California. Radical knowledge also helps with the SAT. In math-speak, a *radical* is a square root, as well as the symbol indicating square root, $\sqrt{\ }$. The *square root* of number x, written $\sqrt{x}$, is the positive number which, multiplied by itself, gives you x. As a classic example, $\sqrt{9} = 3$, because $3 \times 3 = 9$. If only radicals were always that easy. Unfortunately, most numbers have square roots that are decidedly not pretty. $\sqrt{7}$, for example, equals approximately 2.645751311.

The rules for multiplication and division of radicals are simple. Just multiply and divide the numbers normally:

$$\sqrt{5} \times \sqrt{6} = \sqrt{30} \text{ or } \sqrt{55} \div \sqrt{5} = \sqrt{11}$$

Addition and subtraction are trickier. You can't just add and subtract the numbers and plop the result under a square root sign. For example, $\sqrt{3} + \sqrt{5}$ doesn't equal $\sqrt{8}$. You can add or subtract radicals only if they have the same number under the symbol, so $\sqrt{27} + \sqrt{12}$ is impossible as written. However, you can break down some radicals by factoring out a perfect square and simplifying it, so $\sqrt{27} = \sqrt{9}\sqrt{3} = 3\sqrt{3}$, and $\sqrt{12} = \sqrt{4}\sqrt{3} = 2\sqrt{3}$; then, $3\sqrt{3} + 2\sqrt{3} = 5\sqrt{3}$.

A few squares show up all the time on the SAT. Scan Table 12-1 so you're familiar with these numbers when you see them.

Table 12-1				Simple Square Roots								
Numbers	$-x$	-1	0	1	2	3	4	5	6	7	8	9	x
Squares	x^2	1	0	1	4	9	16	25	36	49	64	81	x^2

Notice how the square of both x and $-x$ is x^2? Conveniently, when you multiply two negative numbers, the result is positive, as it is when you multiply two positive numbers. So the square of the same negative and positive number is always the same: $(-8)^2 = 64$ and $(+8)^2 = 64$.

Computing Absolute Value

Absolute value is a simple concept that's annoyingly easy to mess up. *Absolute value* is the number, shorn of its positive or negative value. The symbol looks like a Superman phone booth without a roof. The absolute value of 3 is written $|3|$, which equals 3; the absolute value of -3 is written $|-3|$, which also equals 3.

On the SAT, you may see a number or algebraic expression inside the absolute value symbol. If you do, follow these steps:

1. **Simplify whatever is inside the absolute value symbol, if possible.**

2. **If the answer is negative, switch it to positive.**

Some people have the (incorrect) idea that absolute value changes subtraction to addition. Nope. If you're working with $|3-4|$, don't change the quantity to $3 + 4$. Calculate whatever is inside the absolute value symbols first, $|3-4| = |-1|$, and only *then* change the result to a positive number, in this case 1.

Finding the Pattern

Math sometimes involves recognizing patterns and seeing where those patterns lead. The SAT occasionally asks you to play mathematician with two types of patterns: *arithmetic* and *geometric*. The math word for pattern, by the way, is *sequence.*

Check out this arithmetic sequence: 2, 5, 8, 11, 14, . . . Notice how each number is obtained by adding 3 to the previous number? In an arithmetic sequence, you always add or subtract the same number to the previous term to get the next term. Another example of an arithmetic sequence is 80, 73, 66, 59, . . . In this one, you're subtracting 7 from the previous term.

A geometric sequence is similar to an arithmetic sequence, but it works by multiplication or division. In the sequence 2, 6, 18, 54, . . . every term is multiplied by 3 to get the next term. In 100, 50, 25, 12½, . . . each term is divided by 2 to get the next term.

Often, the best way to solve these problems is just to make a list and follow the pattern. However, if the test writers ask you for something like the 20th term of the sequence, this process can take forever. Each type of sequence has a useful formula, which is worth memorizing if you have the time and the room in your head:

✔ For an arithmetic sequence, the nth term = the first term + $(n - 1)d$, where d is the difference between terms in the sequence. In the sequence 2, 5, 8, 11, 14, the difference between terms is +3, because you add 3 each time. What would be the 20th term? Take 2, the first term, and add 3 19 times, so it's $2 + 19(3) = 2 + 57 = 59$.

✔ For a geometric sequence, the nth term = the first term $\times r^{(n-1)}$, where r is the ratio of one term to the next. Huh? Well, you probably remember that taking something to a power (that's what the exponent stands for) means multiplying it by itself a bunch of times. For example, 4 to the 5th power = $4 \times 4 \times 4 \times 4 \times 4$, which equals 1,024. (Powers get big really fast.) You can do powers on most calculators by using either the "y^x" or the "^" button. On mine, I do 4 to the 5th by typing: 4 "y^x" 5 = .

Check out this sequence: 2, 6, 18, 54. The ratio is 3 because you multiply by 3 each time. To find the 10th term (the 20th would be way too big to handle), take 2×3^9 (that's 3 to the 9th power). $3^9 = 19,683$, and $2 \times 19,683 = 39,366$, so that's the answer.

To find the nth term, you always use $n - 1$, no matter what kind of sequence it is. That's because $n - 1$ is how many steps it takes to get from the first term to the nth term.

As if your life weren't tough enough, the SAT folks often hide these sequences inside a word problem, such as the following:

The bacteria population in my day-old wad of chewing gum doubles every 3 hours. If there are 100 bacteria at 12:00 noon on Friday, how many bacteria will be present at midnight of the same day?

(A) 200

(B) 300

(C) 800

(D) 1,600

(E) 409,600

The right answer is (D). To solve this problem, make a chart. Because the population doubles every 3 hours, count off 3-hour intervals, doubling as you go:

12:00 (noon) = 100 bacteria

3:00 p.m. = 200 bacteria

6:00 p.m. = 400 bacteria

9:00 p.m. = 800 bacteria

12:00 (midnight) = 1,600 bacteria

And here's another example in which the formulas come in handy:

Author A, an extraordinarily fast writer who zips through a chapter a day, gets paid $100 for her first chapter, $200 for her second, $300 for her third, and so on. Author B, also a member of the chapter-a-day club, gets paid $1 for his first chapter, $2 for his second, $4 for his third, $8 for his fourth, and so on. On the 12th day,

(A) Author A is paid $76 more.

(B) Author B is paid $24 more.

(C) They are paid the same amount.

(D) Author A is paid $1,178 more.

(E) Author B is paid $848 more.

The correct answer is (E). Author A's plan is an arithmetic sequence, increasing by $100 each time, so on the 12th day she's paid $100 + 11(100) = 100 + 1,100 = \$1,200$. Author B's plan is a geometric sequence, multiplied by 2 each time, so on the 12th day, he's paid $1 \times 2^{11} = 1 \times 2,048 = \$2,048$. So Author B is paid $848 more.

Setting a Spell

A *set* is just a collection of things — shrunken heads, leftover hockey pucks, Barbie outfits, whatever. In math, a set is a collection of *elements,* usually numbers, which you find inside brackets: { . . . }. For example, the set of whole numbers less than 6 is a set with six elements: {0, 1, 2, 3, 4, 5}. Some sets go on forever, and three dots at the end tell you so. The set of positive odd numbers is {1, 3, 5, 7, . . . } because it reaches infinity. A set may have nothing inside of it; this is the "empty set," and it's written either { } or (more commonly) Ø.

For the SAT, you need to know about two specific things when it comes to sets — the union and the intersection of sets. The *union* of two sets is just the two sets put together; thus, the union of {1, 2, 3} and {5, 7, 8} is {1, 2, 3, 5, 7, 8}.

Even if something shows up in both sets, it shows up only once in the union. Thus, the union of {2, 3, 4} and {3, 4, 5} is {2, 3, 4, 5}, *not* {2, 3, 4, 3, 4, 5}. The following steps help you find the number of elements in the union of two sets:

1. **Add up the number of elements in each set.**

2. **Subtract the number of elements that show up in both.**

In the preceding example, 3 + 3 = 6; but because 3 and 4 show up in both sets, you have to subtract 2. The union has 4 elements. The *intersection* of two sets, on the other hand, contains only those elements that show up in both of them. The intersection of {1, 2, 4} and {4, 6, 7} is {4}; the intersection of {3, 5, 7} and {2, 4, 6} is Ø, also known as "empty."

Chapter 13

Practicing Problems in Numbers and Operations

In This Chapter

▶ Trying your hand at SAT questions involving numbers and operations

▶ Figuring out which problems give you the most trouble

*T*hat old saying, "Practice makes perfect," is annoying yet true. In this chapter, I hit you with two sets of numbers and operations questions along with explanations of the answers. After you practice each question in the first set, check your answers and read the explanations for any questions you answered incorrectly. (The answers immediately follow each question. Use a piece of paper to cover the answers as you work.) If you're confused about any point, turn back to Chapter 12 for more details on the kind of problem that's stumping you. The second set is set up like the real test: You do all the problems and then check your work with the answer key that follows the last question.

Set 1: Trying Out Some Guided Questions

1. If you invest $2,000 for one year at 5% annual interest, the total amount you would have at the end of the year would be

(A) $100

(B) $2,005

(C) $2,100

(D) $2,500

(E) $3,000

Solve the question like this: 5% = 0.05, so 5% of 2,000 = $0.05 \times 2,000 = 100$. But wait! Before you choose 100 as your answer, remember that you still have the $2,000 that you originally invested, so you now have 2,000 + 100 = $2,100. You can also solve this problem using the is/of method I discuss in Chapter 12. You're basically being asked, "What *is* 5% *of* 2000?" so you write $\frac{x}{2,000} = \frac{5}{100}$. Cross-multiplying gives you $100x = 10,000$, so $x = 100. Of course, you still need to add in the original $2,000 to get your answer, so Choice (C) is correct.

2. Which number is an element of the set of prime numbers but not of the set of odd numbers?

   (A) 0

   (B) 1

   (C) 2

   (D) 3

   (E) 9

   Because 2 is the only prime number that isn't odd, Choice (C) is correct.

3. 100 percent of 99 subtracted from 99 percent of 100 equals

   (A) –1

   (B) 0

   (C) 0.99

   (D) 1

   (E) 1.99

   Keep in mind that 100 percent of anything is itself, so 100 percent of 99 is 99. Ninety-nine percent of 100 equals $0.99 \times 100 = 99$ (not a big surprise because percent means "out of one hundred"). And $99 - 99 = 0$, so Choice (B) is the correct answer.

4. The tenth number of the sequence 50, 44.5, 39, 33.5, . . . would be

   (A) –4

   (B) 0.5

   (C) 1

   (D) 1.5

   (E) 6

   The numbers decrease by 5.5 every time. The simplest way to do this problem is to continue the pattern: 50, 44.5, 39, 33.5, 28, 22.5, 17, 11.5, 6, 0.5. You can also use the following formula to find the tenth term: the nth term = the first term + $(n - 1)d$, where d is the difference between terms in the sequence. Therefore, $50 + 9(-5.5) = 50 - 49.5 = 0.5$. Hooray for Choice (B), the correct answer.

5. If E represents the set of even numbers and N represents the set of numbers divisible by 9, which number is in the intersection of E and N?

   (A) 99

   (B) 92

   (C) 66

   (D) 54

   (E) 9

   An element is in the intersection of two sets only if it's in both of them. You can go through the choices until you find the right one: 99 isn't even; 92 isn't divisible by 9; 66 isn't divisible by 9; 54 is even *and* divisible by 9; 9 isn't even. Thus, 54 is the only one that works, and Choice (D) is the right answer.

6. The first three elements of a geometric sequence are 1, 2, and 4. What is the eighth element of the sequence?

    (A) 14

    (B) 16

    (C) 29

    (D) 128

    (E) 256

    The formula for geometric sequences tells you that the answer is $1 \times 2^7 = 1 \times 128 = 128$. (Remember that in this formula the exponent is one less than the number of the term you're being asked for.) Three cheers for Choice (D).

7. The expression $3^2 - 4 + 5(\frac{8}{2})$ equals

    (A) −27

    (B) −15

    (C) 5

    (D) 22

    (E) 25

    Aunt Sally to the rescue! (See Chapter 12 for the lowdown on my favorite relative.) First, do the operation in parenthesis, $\frac{8}{2} = 4$, and then calculate 3^2, which equals 9. That leaves you with $9 - 4 + 5(4)$. Next, multiply $5 \times 4 = 20$. Now the expression is $9 - 4 + 20$. You have a trap to avoid: Did you see it? Don't do addition before subtraction; just go left to right: $9 - 4 = 5$, and $5 + 20 = 25$. Give it up for Choice (E).

8. Which of the following numbers is rational?

    (A) π

    (B) 0.12112111211112 . . .

    (C) $\sqrt{8}$

    (D) $\sqrt{9}$

    (E) $\sqrt{10}$

    To do this problem, you need to remember the definitions of rational and irrational numbers. π is irrational by definition. (Yes, it's worth memorizing this fact.) The number 0.12112111211112 . . . is irrational because the decimal never ends or repeats. (For those of you who are still awake, it doesn't repeat because the number of 1s keeps increasing.) All radicals are irrational if the number underneath isn't a perfect square: So $\sqrt{8}$ and $\sqrt{10}$ are both irrational. However, because $\sqrt{9} = 3$, it's rational. Choice (D) is correct.

9. Given that there are 30 days in April, the ratio of rainy days to sunny days during the month of April could *not* be

    (A) 5:3

    (B) 3:2

    (C) 5:1

    (D) 4:1

    (E) 3:7

The rule for ratios states that the total must be divisible by the sum of the numbers in the ratio. Because 5 + 3 = 8, and 30 isn't divisible by 8, Choice (A) is correct. Just to be thorough, of course, you should check that all the other possible sums do go into 30. (They do, I promise. But check anyway!)

10. At a sale, a shirt normally priced at $60 was sold for $48. What was the percentage of the discount?

(A) 12%

(B) 20%

(C) 25%

(D) 48%

(E) 80%

Use the percentage formula, $\frac{is}{of} = \frac{\%}{100}$ but, as always, be extra careful. The problem asks for the percentage of the discount, so don't just plug in 48. Instead, first figure out the amount of the discount, which was 60 − 48 = 12. Using 12, write $\frac{12}{60} = \frac{p}{100}$, where p is the percentage of the discount. Cross-multiplying, you get 1,200 = 60p, and p = 20. You can still get the right answer using 48. If you use 48 in the formula, you get 80%. Because the shirt now costs 80% of what it used to, the discount is 100% − 80% = 20%. Choice (B) is correct either way.

Set 2: Practicing Some Questions on Your Own

Note: Two questions (2 and 6) are grid-ins. On the blank grids in this section, write and bubble in your answers. (See Chapter 11 for the proper way to bubble in your answers for grid-in questions.)

1. The total number of even three-digit numbers is

(A) 49

(B) 100

(C) 449

(D) 450

(E) 500

2. Evaluate $\left|10 - \left(42 \div |1 - 4|\right)\right|$.

3. A disease is killing the fish in a certain lake. Every 8 days, half of the fish in the lake die. If there are 1,000 fish alive on March 3, how many are still alive on March 27?

   (A) 0

   (B) 100

   (C) 125

   (D) 250

   (E) 500

4. If a number n is the product of two distinct primes, x and y, how many factors does n have, including 1 and itself?

   (A) 2

   (B) 3

   (C) 4

   (D) 5

   (E) 6

5. Which number is 30% greater than 30?

   (A) 27

   (B) 30.9

   (C) 33

   (D) 36

   (E) 39

6. A recipe for French toast batter calls for ½ teaspoon of cinnamon for every 5 eggs. How many teaspoons of cinnamon would be needed if a restaurant made a huge batch of batter using 45 eggs?

7. Which of the following is not equivalent to $\sqrt{40}$?

   (A) $2\sqrt{10}$

   (B) $\sqrt{30} + \sqrt{10}$

   (C) $\sqrt{5}\sqrt{8}$

   (D) $\sqrt{90} - \sqrt{10}$

   (E) $\sqrt{160} \div 2$

8. Janice wrote down all the numbers from 11 to 20. Darren wrote down all the positive numbers less than 30 that are divisible by 6. How many numbers are in the union of their two lists?

   (A) 2

   (B) 12

   (C) 14

   (D) 15

   (E) 16

9. Elena drove for one hour at 60 miles per hour, and for half an hour at 30 miles per hour. Returning home along the same route, she maintained a constant speed. If the journey home took the same total amount of time as the original drive, what was her speed on the journey home?

   (A) 40 miles per hour

   (B) 42 miles per hour

   (C) 45 miles per hour

   (D) 50 miles per hour

   (E) 54 miles per hour

$$\begin{array}{r} ABC \\ + \ 6BC \\ \hline 1B5A \end{array}$$

10. In the correctly solved addition problem above, A, B, and C all stand for different numbers from 1 to 9. The value of C must be

   (A) 8

   (B) 7

   (C) 6

   (D) 5

   (E) 4

Answers to Set 2

1. **D.** Counting all the even three-digit numbers would take a really long time, so try to figure out this question logically. The three-digit numbers start with 100 and end with 999. How many numbers do you have? It's 900, not 899. (Yes, there is a formula you can use here: Subtract the numbers and add 1. Works every time.) How many of these numbers are even? Well, because even and odd numbers alternate on this list, half of them are even, and half are odd. So you have 450 of each type. Choice (D) is right.

2. **4.** When doing an absolute value problem, treat the absolute value symbols as parentheses when trying to figure out the order of operations. Because this problem has a bunch of parentheses and absolute values, work from the inside out:

$$\left|10-\left(42 \div |1-4|\right)\right|$$

$$\left|10-\left(42 \div |-3|\right)\right|$$

$$\left|10-\left(42 \div 3\right)\right|$$

$$\left|10-(14)\right|$$

$$|-4|$$

$$4$$

3. **C.** On March 3, 1,000 fish are alive. On March 11, 500 fish are alive. On March 19, 250 fish are left. And on March 27, 125 fish are left. Choice (C) is correct.

4. **C.** Prime numbers have only two factors: 1 and themselves. Pretend in your problem that $x = 5$ and $y = 7$. Then $n = 5 \times 7 = 35$. The factors of 35 are 1, 5, 7, and 35. Because you can't break down 5 or 7, there are no other factors. As long as you pick prime numbers for x and y, you'll always get four factors for n. Choice (C) is correct.

5. **E.** Solve it like this: 30% of 30 = $0.30 \times 30 = 9$. Because the answer is 30% greater than 30, add 30 + 9 = 39. Three cheers for Choice (E).

6. **4.5 or ⁹⁄₂.** If you set up a ratio, you'd write $\dfrac{\text{cinnamon}}{\text{eggs}} = \dfrac{\text{cinnamon}}{\text{eggs}}$ or $\dfrac{\frac{1}{2}}{5} = \dfrac{x}{45}$.

   Cross-multiplying gives you $22.5 = 5x$, and $x = 4.5$. You can also reason as follows: The number of eggs was multiplied by 9, so the amount of cinnamon should be, too. Okay, ½ × 9 = 4½ = ⁹⁄₂ or 4.5. The answer is 4.5 or ⁹⁄₂. (Don't grid in 4½.)

7. **B.** You could use a calculator to figure out what each choice equals, but this problem gives you a chance to practice working with radicals. Start with $2\sqrt{10}$. This doesn't equal $\sqrt{20}$ because you can't multiply a whole number and a radical. In order to multiply these, you must turn 2 into $\sqrt{4}$; now, $\sqrt{4}\sqrt{10} = \sqrt{40}$. On to (B): It's "illegal" to add radicals that don't have the same number inside (penalty = 5 to 10 years of multiplication tables). Also, there's no way to break down $\sqrt{30}$ or $\sqrt{10}$, because no perfect square goes into either one. So you're stuck on this one. In (C), $\sqrt{5}\sqrt{8} = \sqrt{40}$. In (D), you can break down $\sqrt{90}$ to $\sqrt{9}\sqrt{10} = 3\sqrt{10}$. Then $3\sqrt{10} - \sqrt{10} = 2\sqrt{10}$ (remember that $\sqrt{10}$ has an "invisible" 1 in front of it). And you saw in (A) that $2\sqrt{10} = \sqrt{40}$. For (E), use the same trick as in (A): Change 2 into $\sqrt{4}$, so $\sqrt{160} \div 2 = \sqrt{160} \div \sqrt{4} = \sqrt{40}$. Bottom line: They all equal $\sqrt{40}$, except for (B). If you check it out on a calculator, $\sqrt{40} \approx 6.32$, but $\sqrt{30} + \sqrt{10} \approx 8.64$. Thus, (B) is correct.

8. **B.** Janice's list has 10 numbers: {11, 12, 13, 14, 15, 16, 17, 18, 19, 20}. Darren's list has 4 numbers: {6, 12, 18, 24}. Now, don't fall into the trap of thinking that there are 14 numbers in the union; even though 12 and 18 show up in both sets, you're not allowed to count them twice in the union. The total number of elements in the union is 14 − 2 = 12. Thus, (B) is correct.

9. **D.** The original trip took 1½ hours. Elena traveled 60 miles plus half of 30, which is 60 + 15 or 75 miles. And 75 divided by 1½ equals 50. Choice (D) is correct.

Hitting a vocabulary Homer

Had enough math for the moment? Take a TV break. Have you ever seen anyone less *hirsute* (hairy) than Homer Simpson? This famous *gourmand* (someone who loves to eat and drink a large quantity) isn't exactly a fan of *gourmet* cooking (featuring excellent or high-quality food and drink). Homer spends so much time gobbling down doughnuts that he's made himself *rotund*, or *obese*, and not at all *agile* or *lithe*. (The first two mean "fat" and the second two mean "graceful in movement.") Homer's also *gullible* (he'll believe anything) and *indolent* (don't wake him up when he's "working"). Two words you'll never use to describe Homer: *svelte* (fashion-model thin) and *emaciated* (thin to the point of starvation).

10. **A.** We know that

$$
\begin{array}{r}
ABC \\
+\ 6BC \\
\hline
1B5A
\end{array}
$$

A must be an even number because you get it by adding $C + C$, but *A* can't be 2 because then the two numbers wouldn't add up to something bigger than 1,000. So $A = 4, 6,$ or 8.

Now look at the tens column. The sum of $B + B$ can't be 5 unless you carried a "1" from the ones column. That means that $C + C = 14, 16,$ or 18, so $C = 7, 8,$ or 9.

What about *B*? $B + B + 1$ (you carried, remember) gives you 5. So *B* could be either 2 or 7, because $7 + 7 + 1 = 15$. But if $B = 7$, then the hundreds column makes no sense. (Try it and you'll see why.) So *B* must be 2. Because $B = 2$, *A* must $= 6$ to make the hundreds column work, and that makes $C = 8$. Check the original problem:

$$
\begin{array}{r}
628 \\
+\ 628 \\
\hline
1256
\end{array}
$$

It works! Choice (A) is correct.

Chapter 14

X Marks the Spot: Algebra and Functions

In This Chapter
▶ Working through expressions with exponents
▶ Using factoring to find solutions
▶ Unraveling equations to get to the right answer
▶ Understanding functions and knowing how to solve them

*I*f x is the value of the present your mom expects for her birthday and y is the amount of money in your piggybank, what equation best represents your chances of staying on her good side this year? Don't worry. This problem won't appear on the SAT, but it's a good example of why I love algebra: You get to play with little letters, even though you're solving a math problem.

If you love algebra, or even if you'd prefer to shred the pages of your algebra text, this chapter's for you. Here, you find a quick-and-dirty review of the basics of SAT algebra, plus a spin through functionland, where $f(x)$ rules.

Note: Throughout this chapter and this book, I use the $\times$ multiplication symbol in problems that involve two or more numbers; whenever the problem involves variables, I use the $\cdot$ multiplication symbol.

Powering Up: Exponents

Many SAT questions require you to know how to work with bases and exponents. Here's the lowdown on some of the most important concepts:

✔ The *base* is the big number (or letter) on the bottom. The *exponent* is the little number (or letter) in the upper-right corner.

- In x^5, x is the base; 5 is the exponent.

- In 3^y, 3 is the base; y is the exponent.

✔ A base to the zero power equals one.

- $x^0 = 1$

- $129^0 = 1$

I could give you a long, *soporific* (sleep-causing) explanation as to why a number to the zero power equals one, but you don't really care, do you? For now, just memorize the rule.

✔ A base to the first power is just the base. In other words, $4^1 = 4$.

✔ **A base to the second power is** *base* × *base*.

- $x^2 = x \cdot x$
- $5^2 = 5 \times 5 = 25$

✔ **The same is true for bigger exponents.** The exponent tells you how many times the number repeats. For example, 5^6 means that you write down six 5s and then multiply them all together.

- $5^6 = 5 \times 5 \times 5 \times 5 \times 5 \times 5$, which equals 15,625.

  - Remember that an exponent tells you to multiply the base times itself as many times as the exponent, so 2^3 does *not* equal 6 ($2 \times 2 \times 2 = 8$).

On most calculators, you can do powers with either the "y^x" or the "^" button. Just type the base, the appropriate button, the exponent, and the good ol' "=" button.

✔ **A base to a negative exponent is the reciprocal of the base to a positive exponent.**

This one is a little more confusing. A *reciprocal* is the upside-down version of something. (Here's a *conundrum*, or riddle: Is the North Pole the reciprocal of the South Pole?) When you have a negative exponent, just put base and exponent under a 1 and make the exponent positive again.

- $x^{-4} = \dfrac{1}{x^4}$
- $5^{-3} = \dfrac{1}{5^3} = \dfrac{1}{125}$

The answer isn't negative. When you flip it, you get the reciprocal, and the negative just sort of fades away. Don't fall for the trap of saying that $5^{-3} = -\dfrac{1}{5^3}$ or $-\dfrac{1}{125}$.

✔ **A base to a fractional exponent is a root of the base.** Ah, more confusion. You're already familiar with the standard square root of a number: $\sqrt{25} = 5$ because $5^2 = 25$. Because it takes two 5s to make 25, we can also write $25^{1/2} = 5$.

It works the same way with other powers. $5^3 = 5 \times 5 \times 5 = 125$, so you can say that $125^{1/3} = 5$. And $64^{1/6} = 2$ because $2^6 = 64$.

You can also do fractional powers on your calculator, either by using "^" and typing the fraction (in which case you *must* place the fraction in parentheses), or by using the "$\sqrt[x]{y}$" button, which is usually accessed by using the second function key.

✔ **To multiply like bases, add the exponents.**

- $x^3 \cdot x^2 = x^{(3+2)} = x^5$
- $5^4 \times 5^9 = 5^{(4+9)} = 5^{13}$
- $p^3 \cdot p = p^3 \cdot p^1 = p^{(3+1)} = p^4$
- $129^3 \times 129^0 = 129^{(3+0)} = 129^3$

You can't multiply *unlike* bases. Think of it as trying to make dogs and cats multiply. All you end up with is a miffed meower and a damaged dog.

- $x^2 \cdot y^3 = x^2 \cdot y^3$ (no shortcuts)
- $5^2 \times 129^3 = 5^2 \times 129^3$ (you actually have to work it out)

✔ **To divide like bases, subtract the exponents.** You can divide two bases that are the same by subtracting the exponents.

- $x^5 \div x^2 = x^{(5-2)} = x^3$
- $5^9 \div 5^3 = 5^{(9-3)} = 5^6$
- $q^3 \div q^5 = q^{(3-5)} = q^{-2} = \dfrac{1}{q^2}$
- $129^4 \div 129^0 = 129^{(4-0)} = 129^4$

(Did I get you on that last one? It should make sense. Any base to the zero power is 1. Any number divided by 1 is itself.)

Did you look at the second example, $5^9 \div 5^3$, and think that it was 5^3? Falling into the trap of dividing instead of subtracting is easy, especially when you see numbers that just beg to be divided, such as 9 and 3. Keep your guard up.

✔ **Multiply exponents that appear inside and outside of parentheses.** Here's what I mean:

- $\left(x^2\right)^3 = x^{(2 \cdot 3)} = x^6$
- $\left(5^3\right)^3 = 5^{(3 \times 3)} = 5^9$

✔ **To add or subtract like bases to like powers, add or subtract the numerical coefficient of the bases.** The *numerical coefficient* (a great name for a rock band, don't you think?) is simply the number *in front of* the base. Notice that it isn't the little exponent in the right-hand corner but the full-sized number to the left of the base.

- $31x^3$: 31 is the numerical coefficient.

- $-8y^2$: -8 is the numerical coefficient.

- x^3: What is the numerical coefficient? It's 1 because any number is itself times 1; the 1 isn't always written out. Good trap.

- $37x^3 + 10x^3 = 47x^3$: Because the bases are the same and the exponents are the same, just add the numerical coefficients: $37 + 10 = 47$.

- $15y^2 - 10y^2 = 5y^2$: Just subtract the numerical coefficients: $15 - 10 = 5$.

You can't add or subtract terms with like bases with different exponents. In other words, $13x^3 - 9x^2$ isn't equal to $4x^3$ or $4x^2$ or $4x$. All it is equal to is $13x^3 - 9x^2$. The bases and exponents must be the same for you to add or subtract the terms.

You can't add or subtract the numerical coefficients of unlike bases.

Putting It Together and Taking It Apart: FOIL and Factoring

One of the most common tasks that you probably remember from algebra class is the multiplication of expressions. (What? You were playing fantasy baseball that Thursday? Well, because it was baseball, you're forgiven!) These expressions come in several varieties:

✔ **One term times one term:** To multiply two terms, multiply their coefficients and *add* the powers of any common variables being multiplied; for example, $(3a^3)(-2a) = (3 \times -2)(a^{3+1}) = -6a^4$. Check out the section "Powering Up: Exponents" for more details about exponents.

✔ **One term times two (or more) terms:** Use the familiar distributive law: Multiply the single term by each of the terms in parentheses. Be sure to take your time and work out each product individually before combining them for the final answer.

To do $3b^3(2b^2 - 5)$, write

$$3b^3 \cdot 2b^2 = 6b^5$$

$$3b^3 \cdot -5 = -15b^3$$

And your answer is $6b^5 - 15b^3$.

✔ **Two terms times two terms:** Now, use my favorite four-letter word starting with *f*. Shame on you! I mean FOIL, of course. Multiply in the order *First, Outer, Inner, Last*.

To work out $(x - 3)(2x + 5)$:

1. Multiply the ***First*** terms: $x \cdot 2x = 2x^2$.

2. Multiply the ***Outer*** terms: $x \cdot 5 = 5x$.

3. Multiply the ***Inner*** terms: $-3 \cdot 2x = -6x$.

4. Multiply the ***Last*** terms: $-3 \times 5 = -15$.

5. Combine like terms: $5x + -6x = -1x$ or $-x$.

And your solution is $2x^2 - x - 15$.

Memorize the following two special cases of FOIL. Don't bother to work them out every time you see them. If you know them by heart, you can save valuable SAT minutes on test day.

✔ **$(a + b)(a - b) = a^2 - b^2$.** You can use this shortcut only when the two terms are exactly the same *except for their signs*. For example, $(x + 5)(x - 5) = x^2 - 5^2 = x^2 - 25$. Because this method uses only the first and the last terms from FOIL, I like to call it the FL method.

✔ **$(a + b)^2 = (a + b)(a + b) = a^2 + 2ab + b^2$.** If I had a nickel for every time a student has messed this one up, I wouldn't need the meager cash I'm making from writing this book. (Of course, I'd still be writing it; I'm here for you!) Check out the following example to see the rule in action.

The expression $(x - 3)^2$ is equivalent to

(A) $x^2 - 9$

(B) $x^2 + 9$

(C) $x^2 + 6x - 9$

(D) $x^2 - 6x + 9$

(E) $x^2 - 6x - 9$

The correct answer is (D). Say it with me: FL doesn't work here! Answer choices (A) and (B) are just wrong. If you do FOIL the long way, you get $(x - 3)(x - 3) = x^2 - 3x - 3x + 9 = x^2 - 6x + 9$. Or you could just use the formula: $(x - 3)^2 = x^2 + 2(-3)x + (-3)^2 = x^2 - 6x + 9$.

Now that you know how to do algebra forward, are you ready to do it backward? You need to be able to factor down a quadratic equation, taking it from its final form back to its original form of two sets of parentheses.

For example, given $x^2 + 13x + 42 = 0$, solve for x.

Take this problem one step at a time:

1. **Set up your answer by drawing two sets of parentheses.**

   $(\ )(\ ) = 0$.

2. **To get x^2, the *first* terms have to be x and x. Fill those in.**

   $(x\ )(x\ ) = 0$.

3. **Look now at the *last* term in the problem.**

   You need two numbers that multiply together to be +42. Well, there are several possibilities such as 42×1, 21×2, or 6×7. You can even have two negative numbers: -42×-1, -21×-2, or -6×-7. You aren't sure which one to choose yet. Go on to the next step.

4. Look at the *middle* term in the problem.

You have to add two values to get +13. What's the first thing that springs to mind? Probably 6 + 7. Hey, that's one of the possibilities in the preceding step! Plug it in and try it.

$$(x + 6)(x + 7) = x^2 + 7x + 6x + 42 = x^2 + 13x + 42.$$

Great, but you're not done, yet. The whole equation equals zero, so you have $(x + 6)(x + 7) = 0$. Because any number times zero equals zero, either $(x + 6) = 0$ or $(x + 7) = 0$. Therefore, x can equal –6 or –7, *not* +6 or +7.

You may also have to factor an expression like $y^2 - 49$. This sort of problem probably looks familiar to you if you remember the FL formula (which I discuss earlier in this section): $(a + b)(a - b) = a^2 - b^2$. The expression $y^2 - 49$ is known as a *difference of squares* because it equals $y^2 - (7)^2$. Any difference of squares can be factored into an FL product; in this case, $y^2 - 49 = (y + 7)(y - 7)$.

Solving Equations: Why Don't They Just Tell Me What X Is?

You've probably spent a lot of time in school solving the two most basic types of equations: *linear* (for example, $3x + 5 = 5x - 7$, whose solution is $x = 6$) and *quadratic* (for example, $x^2 + 13x + 42 = 0$, which I solve in the preceding section using factoring). Every once in a while, the SAT makers also hit you with more complex algebraic equations: absolute value equations, rational equations, and radical equations. This section provides you a brief overview of these topics so they look familiar if you run into any of them on SAT day.

Remember that most of the SAT is a multiple-choice test. When you're presented with an equation that you're not sure how to solve, you can always fall back on the ancient strategy of plugging in the answers one at a time.

Absolute value

Absolute value presents you with a number stuck inside a roofless phone booth. I explain absolute value in Chapter 12. Here I tell you what to do when one pops up in an equation. Check out this problem:

The equation $|x - 4| = 3$ has the solution(s)

(A) 7 only

(B) 1 only

(C) –1 only

(D) 7 and 1

(E) 7 and –1

The correct answer is (D). Because an absolute value symbol turns everything into a positive number, the expression inside the absolute value could equal either 3 or –3. This is the key to solving an equation with an absolute value. If $|something| = n$, then either *something* = n or *something* = $-n$. You must solve each of these equations separately to get two answers.

But there's a catch: You also must check each answer in the original equation. Only solutions that make the original equation true count in your final answer.

Now back to the preceding example:

$$|x - 4| = 3$$
$$x - 4 = 3 \quad \text{or} \quad x - 4 = -3$$
$$+4 \quad +4 \qquad\qquad +4 \quad +4$$
$$x = 7 \quad \text{or} \qquad x = 1$$

Check:

$$|(7) - 4| = 3 \qquad |(1) - 4| = 3$$
$$|3| = 3 \qquad\qquad |-3| = 3$$
$$3 = 3 \qquad\qquad\quad 3 = 3$$

Because both checks work, your answer is (D): 7 and 1.

You could, of course, just plug in the choices to solve the problem. Remember those pesky grid-ins, though! Because not every problem is multiple choice, take the time to figure out how to solve each type of equation from scratch.

Radical equations

No, *radical equations* aren't a fringe group of equations the FBI is keeping an eye on; they're equations that contain square roots. Check out this example, with a handy radical.

Find the solution to the equation $3\sqrt{x} + 5 = 17$.

Because this question isn't multiple choice (yep, it's a grid-in), you have to solve this problem the long way. In a normal linear equation, you start by isolating x; here, you must first isolate $\sqrt{x}$:

$$3\sqrt{x} + 5 = 17$$
$$\phantom{3\sqrt{x} + } -5 \quad -5$$
$$\frac{3\sqrt{x}}{3} = \frac{12}{3}$$
$$\sqrt{x} = 4$$

Now don't make the mistake of thinking that x should be 2; $\sqrt{2}$ doesn't equal 4. Instead, x is 16, because $\sqrt{16} = 4$.

Rational equations

Rational equations have fractions in them. Sometimes, when the denominators of the fractions contain only numbers, removing the fractions and dealing with a simpler problem is easier. To solve $\frac{x}{3} + 1 = \frac{x}{2} - 3$, you multiply every term by 6 because that's the smallest number that eliminates both the 2 and the 3 (officially, 6 is the *least common denominator,* or LCD, of 2 and 3). Assuming you cancel correctly, your new equation is $2x + 6 = 3x - 18$, and x equals 24. (I'm letting you do the steps by yourself; practice makes perfect scores.)

When the denominator contains variables, your best bet is to combine terms with like denominators and then cross-multiply:

$$\frac{12}{x} + \frac{15}{x-1} = \frac{25}{x-1}$$
$$\quad -\frac{15}{x-1} \quad -\frac{15}{x-1}$$
$$\frac{12}{x} = \frac{10}{x-1}$$

Cross-multiplying gives you $12(x-1) = 10x$. Then $12x - 12 = 10x$, and x equals 6. If you plug back into the original equation, you get $\frac{12}{6} + \frac{15}{5} = \frac{25}{5}$, or $2 + 3 = 5$, which means that your answer checks out.

Direct and inverse variation

In a direct or inverse variation problem, instead of being given an equation to work with, the SAT makers tell you that two quantities "vary directly" or "vary inversely." These expressions represent two specific types of equations that you're already familiar with under other names.

A *direct variation* problem is just another type of ratio problem. If a and b vary directly, then the ratio $\frac{a}{b}$ is always equal to a certain constant. Thus, you can solve a direct variation problem by setting up the ratio $\frac{a_1}{b_1} = \frac{a_2}{b_2}$, cross-multiplying, and solving as usual, as you do in this example:

> x and y vary directly. If $x = 10$ when $y = 6$, what does x equal when $y = 21$?

Let $x_1 = 10$ and $y_1 = 6$. Then x_2 is what you're looking for, and $y_2 = 21$. Set up the ratio $\frac{x_1}{y_1} = \frac{x_2}{y_2}$ or $\frac{10}{6} = \frac{x_2}{21}$, and cross-multiply to get $6x_2 = 210$, so $x_2 = 35$.

Notice that when one variable increases, the other variable increases as well. This feature of direct variation problems helps you do a common-sense check of your answer.

When two variables vary *inversely,* their product is always equal to the same number. For example, suppose that p and q vary inversely, and $p = 3$ when $q = 12$. Because $pq = (3)(12) = 36$ in this case, pq must equal 36 for all values of p and q. When $p = 2$, $q = 18$ (and vice versa); when $p = 6$, $q = 6$, as well. This strategy works for all inverse variation problems.

Barely Functioning

By the time you get to functions on the SAT, you may think that you can't . . . function, that is. But think of a function as a simple computer program: You give it an input and it produces an output. For example, $x \rightarrow 2x - 1$ is a function. The arrow means that you put in a number for x (5, for example), and get out one less than twice that number as the result (9, in this case). The input and output can then be written as an ordered pair: (5, 9) is a member of this function, as are the pairs (1, 1) and (0.5, 0), along with many others.

You're most likely to see functions written as $f(x)$. This expression, pronounced "eff of x" is somewhat misleading because it looks as though multiplication of some sort is going on, which isn't necessarily the case. For example, $f(x) = x - 4$ is a function for which $f(9) = 5$, $f(4) = 0$, and $f(1) = -3$. When you put in 9 for x, you get out 5; when you put in 4, you get out 0; and when you put in 1, you get out −3. Notice that $f(x)$ and y are the same thing.

Notice that the number replaces x when evaluating the function. That is, $f(9) = (9) - 4 = 5$. Some students like the notation $f(\square) = \square - 4$, because the box shows where the input goes. This is especially useful for complicated-looking functions, such as $f(x) = 3x^2 - 2^x + x$. What's $f(3)$ in this case? Well, if you write $f(\square) = 3\square^2 - 2\square + \square = 3(3)^2 - 2^{(3)} + (3) = 3(9) - 8 + 3 = 27 - 8 + 3 = 22$, you have the answer.

On the SAT, you may be given a function and be asked what *can't* go into it. Keep in mind two things that you can't do in a function:

✔ Divide by zero.

✔ Take the square root of a negative number.

So if you see a function like $y = \sqrt{x-4}$, numbers like 4, 5, 6, and so on are okay, but numbers less than 4 aren't because then you'd have a negative number under the radical. For a function like $f(x) = \dfrac{x+2}{(x-4)(x+1)}$, x could be any number except 4 or –1 because plugging in those numbers gives you a denominator of zero, which is a no-no. Notice, by the way, that plugging in –2 is fine because it's okay for the *numerator* of a fraction to be zero.

Functioning at a Higher Level

At this point, you may be wondering, "Why are functions such a big deal?" After all, functions seem like a pretty abstract concept. However, it turns out that a huge number of real-life situations can be modeled using functions. To do well on the Math section of the SAT, you definitely want to be good friends with two of the most common types of functions: linear and quadratic.

Figuring out linear functions

You've probably worked a lot with linear functions, especially in graphing. All linear functions have the form $y = mx + b$ or $f(x) = mx + b$. In graphing terms, m represents the slope of the line being drawn, while b represents its y-intercept. Take a look at this example:

If $f(x)$ is a linear function with a slope of 2, passing through the point (–2, –3), $f(x)$ must also pass through the point

(A) (1, 2)

(B) (1, 3)

(C) (2, 2)

(D) (2, 3)

(E) (0, 2)

The correct answer is (B). The best way to solve this problem is to draw a graph. To get it right, you have to remember the meaning of slope: Slope $= \dfrac{\text{rise}}{\text{run}}$. A slope of ⅖, for example, tells you to move 2 spaces up (the rise) and 5 spaces to the right (the run). The function in this problem has a slope of 2, which is the same as ⅖. Starting at (–2, –3) and following these directions yields this graph:

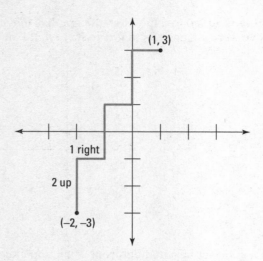

Instead of simply giving you numbers, the SAT writers may present a real-world situation and ask you to model it with a function. For example, if an express mail package costs $1.50 plus 40 cents per pound, you can write $c = 1.50 + 0.40p$, where c is the cost, and p represents the number of pounds.

Thinking through quadratic functions

Quadratic functions, on the other hand, have the form $y = ax^2 + bx + c$ or $f(x) = ax^2 + bx + c$. Graphically, they're represented by a *parabola,* a shape that resembles the basic roller coaster hump. You certainly won't be asked to graph any of these, but you may be asked some graph-based questions. Keep these points in mind as you work with quadratic functions:

✔ The roots or solutions of a function are the x-values that make $f(x) = 0$. On a graph, the roots are the points where the graph crosses the horizontal x-axis.

✔ The number of solutions of $f(x) = a$ is the number of points where the graph has a height of a. On the following graph, $f(x) = 3$ twice, at the marked points.

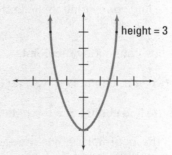

✔ If a number is added to a function, the graph is moved up that many units. If the function above were changed from $f(x)$ to $f(x) + 4$, the new graph would be

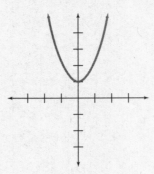

Note that subtracting a number from a function moves the graph down.

✔ If a number is added to x in a function, the graph is moved that many units *to the left*. This rule is tricky because you may have guessed the graph moved the other way. If the original function were changed to $f(x + 4)$, it would look like the following graph. Notice that this rule is used when you're adding to x, not to the whole function. As you may guess, if you were to graph $f(x - 4)$, you'd move four units to the right.

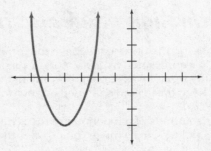

Some graphing problems don't involve equations; instead, you may be given a pair of points and be asked about the line connecting them. In these types of problems, three formulas are crucial:

✔ The slope of the line connecting the points (x_1, y_1) and (x_2, y_2) is $\dfrac{y_2 - y_1}{x_2 - x_1}$

✔ The distance between the points (x_1, y_1) and (x_2, y_2) is $\sqrt{(x_2 - x_1)^2 + (y_2 - y_1)^2}$

✔ The midpoint of the line connecting the points (x_1, y_1) and (x_2, y_2) is $\left(\dfrac{x_2 + x_1}{2}, \dfrac{y_2 + y_1}{2} \right)$

You probably learned these formulas some time ago. They're not exciting, but they are useful. Try using them on the points $(-1, 2)$ and $(5, -6)$:

$$\text{Slope} = \frac{(-6) - (2)}{(5) - (-1)} = \frac{-8}{6} = -\frac{4}{3}$$

$$\text{Distance} = \sqrt{((5) - (-1))^2 + ((-6) - (2))^2} = \sqrt{(6)^2 + (-8)^2} = \sqrt{36 + 64} = \sqrt{100} = 10$$

$$\text{Midpoint} = \left(\frac{(5) + (-1)}{2}, \frac{(-6) + (2)}{2} \right) = \left(\frac{4}{2}, \frac{-4}{2} \right) = (2, -2)$$

Thanks, you've been *grat*

Did your favorite grandparent send you a lucky rabbit's foot (from a very unlucky rabbit) to insure success on the math portion of the SAT? If so, you probably expressed your *gratitude* (thanks) because you were *grateful* (thankful) and not an *ingrate* (someone who thinks the whole world owes him or her a living and, therefore, never appreciates anything). Waiters and bartenders, on the other hand, always appreciate *gratuities* (tips). Other *grat* words include *gratis* (free — you'll be thankful for the gift, right?) and *gratuitous* (given freely but not necessary, like your mom's criticism of your latest dating partner). You may find the *grat* family *gratifying* (filling one's needs or desires) when they show up on the SAT.

Decoding symbolism

One of the most popular (to the test makers, that is) types of function problems on the SAT involves symbolism. In these problems, the SAT makers create a new symbol for a function. Look over this example, which uses < and > as symbols.

If $<n> = n^2 - n$, then which of the following is equal to $<3> + <3>$?

(A) $<3>$

(B) $<4>$

(C) $<6>$

(D) $<9>$

(E) $<12>$

Choice (B) is the answer. This problem is just like a normal function problem, except that instead of writing $f(n) = n^2 - n$, the problem uses the symbol $<n>$. This example is also one of those annoying problems in which you have to try out all the possibilities until one of them works:

$<3> = 3^2 - 3 = 9 - 3 = 6$

$<4> = 4^2 - 4 = 16 - 4 = 12$ (This looks like the answer, because it equals 6 + 6.)

$<6> = 6^2 - 6 = 36 - 6 = 30$

$<9> = 9^2 - 9 = 81 - 9 = 72$

$<12> = 12^2 - 12 = 144 - 12 = 132$

Because $<3> + <3> = <4>$, the answer is (B).

Chapter 15

Practicing Problems in Algebra and Functions

....

In This Chapter

▶ Practicing algebra and functions with some guided problems

▶ Troubleshooting your problem areas with some independent-practice questions

....

In this chapter, you hone your skills for SAT algebra and function problems. Try ten, see how you do, and then try ten more if you're a glutton for punishment (or algebra, which in some people's minds is the same thing).

Be sure to check all your answers against mine. Don't neglect the explanations, which may help you understand what went wrong. In the first practice set, each answer immediately follows the question. Don't cheat. Cover the answer with a piece of paper until you're ready to read the explanation. The second set is set up like the real test: You go through all the questions and then check your answers in the next section. For more information on any of the topics I cover in these practice questions, check out Chapter 14.

Set 1: Getting Started with Some Guided Questions

Note: Question 3 is a grid-in, so you don't get any answers to choose from. See Chapter 11 for details on answering grid-ins correctly.

1. If k is a positive integer, which of the following is a possible value for k^2?

(A) −1

(B) 0

(C) 2

(D) 6

(E) 9

Choice (A) is impossible because any number, when squared, is positive. Choice (B) is zero squared, but the problem said that the original number had to be positive. Choices (C) and (D) aren't perfect squares; no number multiplied by itself gives you 2 or 6 as an answer. That leaves you with (E), which is 3^2.

2. If $y = \frac{x+5}{2}$, then increasing the value of y by 2 will increase x by

    (A) 1

    (B) 2

    (C) 3

    (D) 4

    (E) 5

This problem is good for picking your own numbers. For example, say that y was originally 10; then you would have $10 = \frac{x+5}{2}$. Multiplying both sides by 2 gives you $20 = x + 5$, or $x = 15$. Now the problem tells you to increase y by 2, making it 12. If you do the math (I'm trusting you here), you find that x is now 19, so it increased by 4. This result makes sense because the equation tells you that you need to divide $x + 5$ by 2 to get y; y increases half as quickly as x. Thus, your answer is (D).

3. In his will, a man left his land to his three children: ⅔ of the estate to his oldest child, ¼ to his middle child, and 15 acres to his youngest. How many acres were in the original estate?

A word problem? With no multiple-choice answers? And fractions? Okay, deep breaths. Now get to work. In any word problem, list the various things you need to know to solve the problem. Four important things pop up in this one: the original estate and the amount left to the three children. Because the original estate is what you're looking for, call it x. Remembering that the word *of* usually indicates multiplication, you can then make a list:

x = original estate

$\frac{2}{3}x$ = oldest child

$\frac{1}{4}x$ = middle child

15 = youngest child

Because the three children's shares made up the whole estate, you can write $\frac{2}{3}x + \frac{1}{4}x + 15 = x$.

With a common denominator of 12:

$$\frac{8}{12}x + \frac{3}{12}x + 15 = x$$

$$\frac{11}{12}x + 15 = x$$

$$-\frac{11}{12}x \qquad -\frac{11}{12}x$$

$$15 = \frac{1}{12}x$$

Finally, multiplying both sides by 12, you get $x = 180$.

That's a lot of work for one problem. If you're a visual person, you may prefer to solve it with a graph:

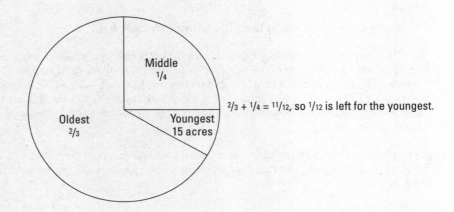

$2/3 + 1/4 = 11/12$, so $1/12$ is left for the youngest.

4. If x and y are both integers, $x > 3$, and $y < 2$, then $x - y$ could be

(A) 3

(B) 2

(C) 1

(D) 0

(E) −1

After the last problem, this one's a breeze. x is an integer greater than 3, so it must be at least 4. y is an integer less than 2, so it must be at most 1. $4 - 1 = 3$, so (A) is correct. Notice that making x bigger or y smaller would make $x - y$ bigger than 3, so all the other choices are impossible.

5. If n and p vary directly, and $n = 12$ when $p = 9$, which of the following pairs is a possible set of values for n and p?

(A) $n = 9, p = 12$

(B) $n = 18, p = 15$

(C) $n = 18, p = 6$

(D) $n = 20, p = 15$

(E) $n = 10, p = 8$

When quantities vary directly, their ratio — in this case x/p — must always remain the same. There are two ways to solve this problem. One way is to set up the ratios one at a time, cross-multiplying to see which answer works. For example, for (A), write $12/9 = 9/12$. Cross-multiplying gives you $144 = 81$, so this answer doesn't work. Repeating this process shows that (D) works.

The other way to solve this problem is to find the original ratio on your calculator. $12/9 = 1.3333\ldots$ or $4/3$. Trying all the other pairs shows you that only $20/15$ gives you the same ratio.

6. If $a^2 - b^2 = 40$ and $a - b = 10$, then $a + b =$

   (A) 4

   (B) 10

   (C) 14

   (D) 30

   (E) It cannot be determined from the information given.

Well, (E) sure looks tempting, but you can do better. When you see a quadratic expression in a problem, see if it can be factored. $a^2 - b^2$ should look familiar to you. (If not, turn to Chapter 14.) Keep in mind that $a^2 - b^2$ factors out to $(a - b)(a + b)$. Because $a^2 - b^2 = 40$ and $a - b = 10$, $(10)(a + b) = (40)$, so $a + b = 4$. Notice that you didn't even have to figure out the value of the variables to solve the problem; that situation actually happens a lot on the SAT. Three cheers for (A).

7. A copying service charges \$2.50 to copy up to 20 pages, plus 5 cents per page over 20. Which formula represents the cost, in dollars, of copying c pages, where c is greater than 20?

   (A) $2.50 + 5c$

   (B) $2.50 + 0.05c$

   (C) $(2.50)(20) + 0.05c$

   (D) $2.50 + 0.05(c - 20)$

   (E) $0.05(2.50 + c)$

As is often the case, one good approach is to pick a number for c and then see which formula works. Try $c = 28$. (Remember, c has to be greater than 20). The cost for 28 pages would be \$2.50 for the first 20, plus \$0.05 times the 8 remaining pages, which is \$0.40, for a total of \$2.90. Plugging 28 into the various formulas (using a calculator, of course) yields \$142.50 for (A), \$3.90 for (B), \$51.40 for (C), \$2.90 for (D), and \$1.53 for (E). Choice (D) is correct.

8. Let a be defined as one more than a if a is odd, and as one less than a if a is even. Which of the following would result in the smallest number?

   (A) –2

   (B) –1

   (C) 0

   (D) 1

   (E) 2

Test out each answer choice. Choice (A), –2, is even, so one less than –2 is –3. The other choices give you 0, –1, 2, and 1, in that order. Thus, Choice (A) is correct.

9. If $(2g - 3h)^3 = 27$, then $(2g - 3h)^{-2} =$

(A) 9

(B) ⅙

(C) ⅑

(D) –6

(E) –9

First, give up on trying to figure out the values of g and h. The key is the expression $(2g - 3h)$, which shows up in both parts of the problem. Replace it with something simpler, like q. (I get tired of using x all the time.) So you know that $q^3 = 27$. A little trial and error (or your calculator) reveals that $q = 3$. Now you need to find $q^{-2} = (3)^{-2} = \dfrac{1}{(3)^2} = \dfrac{1}{9}$. Choice (C) is correct.

10. A party supplier charges a flat rate, plus a certain amount for each person. If supplies for 12 people cost \$140, and supplies for 20 people cost \$180, then supplies for 40 people would cost

(A) \$220

(B) \$280

(C) \$300

(D) \$360

(E) \$400

The setup for this problem is a classic linear equation. The flat rate is the y-intercept, while the amount per person is the slope. Therefore, you can write $y = mx + b$, using the number of people as x and the cost as y. When you're solving a problem like this, find the slope first, using the formula $m = \dfrac{y_2 - y_1}{x_2 - x_1} = \dfrac{180 - 140}{20 - 12} = \dfrac{40}{8} = 5$. Bingo, the cost per person is \$5. You can now figure out b by using either pair of numbers. Because supplies for 12 people cost \$140, and \$5 × 12 people = \$60, the flat rate is \$80. (You'd get the same answer if you used 20 people and \$180.) Your equation is $y = 5x + 80$. Plugging in 40 for x gives you $y = 280$. Choice (B) is correct.

By the way, another way to do this problem is to play "find the pattern." When the number of people went up by 8 — from 12 to 20 — the cost went up by \$40. You could make a chart like this one:

People	12	20	28	36	44
Cost	\$140	\$180	\$220	\$260	\$300

The cost for 40 people would be halfway between \$260 and \$300 — in other words, \$280.

Set 2: Practicing Some Questions on Your Own

Note: Question 1 is a grid-in. Turn to Chapter 11 for help on answering that type of question.

1. If $(x + 2)^2 + (x - 1)^2 = ax^2 + bx + c$, find the value of b.

2. The pressure of a gas and its volume vary inversely. If a certain gas has a pressure of 120 kilopascals (kPa) when its volume is 250 cubic centimeters (cc), what is its pressure when its volume is 200 cc?

   (A) 170 kPa

   (B) 150 kPa

   (C) 100 kPa

   (D) 96 kPa

   (E) 70 kPa

3. Given the function $f(x) = \dfrac{5x}{x^2 - 4x + 4}$, which number is not a possible value for x?

   (A) −4

   (B) −2

   (C) 0

   (D) 2

   (E) 4

4. Below is the graph of the equation $y = -x^2$.

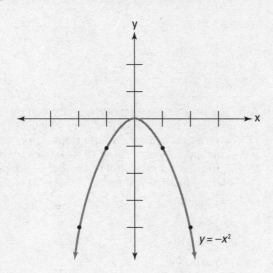

Which of the following choices represents the graph of $y = -x^2 + 4$?

(A)

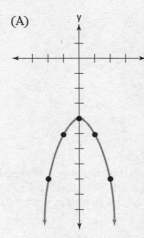

(B)

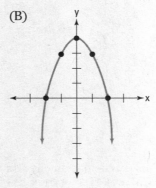

(C)

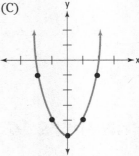

(D)

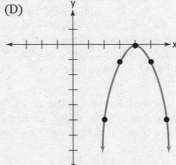

(E)

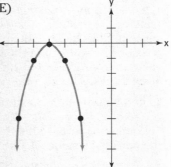

5. The solution set to the equation
$|w| - 6 = 2w$ is

(A) {6}

(B) {6, –6}

(C) {–6}

(D) {–2, –6}

(E) {–2}

6. If $f(x)$ is a linear function passing through the points (2, 5) and (6, 3), then the y-intercept of $f(x)$ is

(A) 7

(B) 6

(C) 5

(D) 4

(E) 3

7. If $x \backslash\backslash y$ is defined as $x^2 - y$, which statement is always true?

(A) $0 \backslash\backslash y = y$

(B) $x \backslash\backslash 1$ is positive

(C) $x \backslash\backslash 4 = x \backslash\backslash (-4)$

(D) $x \backslash\backslash y = y \backslash\backslash x$

(E) $4 \backslash\backslash y = (-4) \backslash\backslash y$

8. If $k^{1/2} - 3 = 5$, then $k =$

(A) 64

(B) 16

(C) 8

(D) 4

(E) 2

9. The population of a certain city can be modeled by the function $p(y) = 20,000(2)^{y/20}$, where $p(y)$ represents the population, and y measures years since 1976. If the city had a population of 32,490 in 1990, then its population in 2030 will be

(A) 30,000

(B) 64,980

(C) 80,000

(D) 108,000

(E) 129,960

10. The solution set to the equation
$$5 - \frac{2x+2}{x+1} = \frac{9}{x+1} \text{ is}$$

(A) { }

(B) {–1}

(C) {–1, 2}

(D) {2}

(E) {8}

Answers to Set 2

1. **2.** The answer is 2. This problem is an easy one to mess up, but not if you remember the formulas I explain in Chapter 14: $(a + b)^2 = a^2 + 2ab + b^2$. It's also fine to just do FOIL, rewriting the problem as $(x + 2)(x + 2) + (x - 1)(x - 1)$. Either way, the problem becomes $x^2 + 4x + 4 + x^2 - 2x + 1$, which equals $2x^2 + 2x + 5$, so $b = 2$.

2. **B.** When two quantities *vary inversely,* their product is always the same number. Usually, finding that number is the key to getting the right answer. You're told that a pressure of 120 corresponds to a volume of 250, and $120 \times 250 = 30,000$. Thus, your missing pressure (call it p), times 200, must equal 30,000. Solving $200p = 30,000$ gives you $p = 150$. Common-sense double-check: If quantities vary inversely, one of them should go up when the other goes down. Notice that the volume went down from 250 cc to 200 cc and that the pressure went up from 120 kPa to 150 kPa. Whenever possible, take a second to make sure your answer makes sense. Choice (B) is correct.

3. **D.** In this problem, you know that dividing by 0 is against the rules. The denominator can be factored to $(x - 2)(x - 2)$, which means that 2 is the only number that would make the denominator zero, so it's the only number that's not in the *domain* (the fancy name for "all the possible x-values"). Choice (D) is correct.

4. **B.** Adding 4 to a function raises its graph by four units, so Choice (B) is correct.

5. **E.** You could just plug in all the choices, but, for practice, try to go through the official steps:

Isolate the absolute value: $|w| - 6 = 2w$

$$\begin{array}{cc} +6 & +6 \\ \hline |w| = 2w + 6 \end{array}$$

Create two equations: $w = 2w + 6$ $w = -2w - 6$
$$\begin{array}{cc} -2w \quad -2w & \text{or} \quad +2w \quad +2w \end{array}$$

Solve: $\dfrac{-w}{-1} = \dfrac{6}{-1}$ $\dfrac{3w}{3} = \dfrac{-6}{3}$
  $w = -6$ $w = -2$

Check: $|(-6)| - 6 = 2(-6)$ $|(-2)| - 6 = 2(-2)$
  $6 - 6 = -12$ $2 - 6 = -4$
  $0 = -12$ $-4 = -4$
  No   Yes

So the only answer that works is –2. Choice (E) is correct.

6. **B.** If you find a sketch helpful (I know I do), draw something like the following graph:

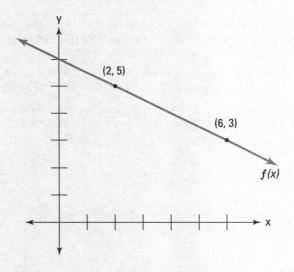

The graph can convince you that the answer is either (A) or (B). To be sure, use your formula for linear equations, $y = mx + b$. First, find the slope of your line:

$$m = \frac{y_2 - y_1}{x_2 - x_1} = \frac{3 - 5}{6 - 2} = \frac{-2}{4} = -\frac{1}{2}$$

So the equation is $y = -\frac{1}{2}x + b$. Use (2, 5) to find b:

$5 = -\frac{1}{2}(2) + b$

$5 = -1 + b$

$\underline{+1 \quad +1}$

$6 = b$

So your y-intercept is 6, and the answer is (B).

7. **E.** No cool solving methods here. You just have to check all the possibilities.

   Choice (A): $0\backslash\backslash y = (0)^2 - y = 0 - y = -y$. Nope. Onward to (B): $x\backslash\backslash 1 = (x)^2 - 1 = x^2 - 1$. This is usually positive, but if x is zero (or a fraction), then it's negative. Moving on to (C): $x\backslash\backslash 4 = (x)^2 - 4 = x^2 - 4$, and $x\backslash\backslash(-4) = (x)^2 - (-4) = x^2 + 4$. They're not equal. Now for (D): $x\backslash\backslash y = x^2 - y$, and $y\backslash\backslash x = y^2 - x$. These don't look equal, and plugging in two different numbers for x and y should convince you that they're not. Which leaves (E): $4\backslash\backslash y = (4)^2 - y = 16 - y$, and $(-4)\backslash\backslash y = (-4)^2 - y = 16 - y$. At last!

8. **A.** Here's the official way to solve the problem:

   $$k^{1/2} - 3 = 5$$
   $$\phantom{k^{1/2}} +3 \quad +3$$
   $$k^{1/2} = 8$$

   Because $k^{1/2}$ means $\sqrt{k}$, square both sides:

   $$k = 8^2 = 64$$

   So (A) is correct. Of course, you can also just plug in all the choices to see which one works. The key is knowing what $k^{1/2}$ means.

9. **E.** When you're given a problem like this one, it helps to pause for a moment to see whether you can figure out what the function really means. This function is an exponential growth situation. The initial population (in 1976) was 20,000, and the function doubles (the growth factor is 2) every 20 years. If you understand this concept, you can figure out the answer without actually plugging the numbers into the function. Because the population doubles every 20 years, it doubles from 1990 to 2010 and doubles again from 2010 to 2030. $32{,}490 \times 2 \times 2 = 129{,}960$, so Choice (E) is correct.

   You can also solve the problem by plugging the right numbers into your calculator. Because $2030 - 1976 = 54$ years, plug in 54 for y. $20{,}000(2)^{54/20} = 20{,}000(2)^{2.7} = 20{,}000(6.4980) = 129{,}960$.

10. **D.** The best way to do this problem is to start by noticing that the two fractions have common denominators. Therefore, they can be combined if you get them on the same side:

    $$5 - \frac{2x+2}{x+1} = \frac{9}{x+1}$$
    $$+\frac{2x+2}{x+1} \quad +\frac{2x+2}{x+1}$$
    $$5 = \frac{9}{x+1} + \frac{2x+2}{x+1}$$
    $$5 = \frac{2x+11}{x+1}$$

    Now, if you multiply by $x + 1$ on both sides:

    $$(x+1)5 = \frac{2x+11}{x+1}(x+1)$$
    $$5x+5 = 2x+11$$
    $$-2x \qquad -2x$$
    $$3x+5 = 11$$
    $$-5 \quad -5$$
    $$\frac{3x}{3} = \frac{6}{3}$$
    $$x = 2$$

    Choice (D) is correct.

Chapter 16

Checking More Figures Than an IRS Agent: Geometry Review

*T*hink of geometry as a mini art lesson. The key to doing well on geometry problems is this: Draw and label a diagram for every geometry problem that you face. Include every measurement that you know on the diagram, and use a variable to label anything you're looking for.

After you get a nice little illustration on paper, you're ready to rumble through the problem. Without that drawing, you're primed for a fall, so even if you think a problem is incredibly easy, draw a quick diagram anyway. Beauty isn't what counts; getting the right answer is.

I'm giving you fair warning: This chapter includes a lot of information to memorize. But don't panic: I have some good news for you, too. A lot of what I review in this chapter appears in the direction text box that's printed at the beginning of every math section on the real SAT. Here's what the text box looks like:

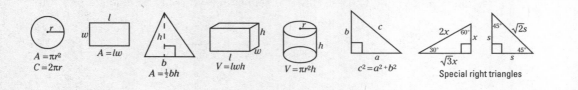

There are 360 degrees of arc in a circle.

There are 180 degrees in a straight line.

There are 180 degrees in the sum of the interior angles of a triangle.

Playing the Angles: Knowing What Makes One Angle Different from Another Angle

Angles are a big part of the SAT geometry problems, so pay attention to this section. Finding an angle is usually a matter of simple addition or subtraction, provided you remember the key facts I cover here.

When it comes to angles, the following three rules generally apply to the SAT:

- There are no negative angles.

- There are no zero angles.

- Fractional angles rarely appear on the test. For example, an angle is unlikely to measure 45½ degrees or 32¾ degrees.

Now that you know what you won't find in the SAT geometry questions, take a look at the important facts you need to remember for the problems you will find:

- **Angles that equal 90 degrees are called *right angles*.** They're formed by perpendicular lines and are indicated by a box in the corner of the two intersecting lines.

A common SAT trap is to have two lines appear to be perpendicular. Don't assume you're looking at a right angle unless you see one of the following:

- The words "This is a right angle" in the question

- The perpendicular symbol (⊥), which indicates that the two lines form a 90-degree angle

- The box in the corner of the two intersecting lines

If you don't see one of these three "disclaimers," you may be headed for a trap!

Not necessarily a right angle

- **The sum of the angles around a point is 360 degrees.** Think of the angles as forming a complete circle around a center point.

360 degrees

✔ **Angles that are opposite each other are *congruent* (they have equal measures) and are called *vertical angles.*** Note that vertical angles may actually be horizontal. Just remember that vertical angles are across from each other, whether they're up and down (vertical) or side by side (horizontal).

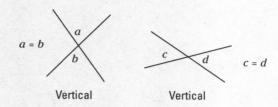

Vertical   Vertical

✔ **Angles in the same position — called *corresponding angles* — around two parallel lines and a transversal have the same measures.** When you see two parallel lines and a *transversal* (a line that crosses them), number the angles. Start in the upper-right corner with 1 and go clockwise. For the second batch of angles, start again in the upper-right corner with 5 and proceed clockwise. The numbers will help you keep track of the angles. Note that all the odd-numbered angles are congruent and all the even-numbered angles are congruent, as long as the question and/or diagram tells you that the lines are parallel.

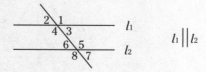

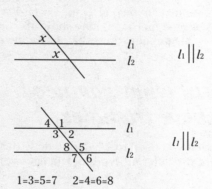

1=3=5=7   2=4=6=8

Be careful not to zigzag back and forth when numbering, like this:

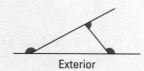

If you zig when you should've zagged, you can no longer use the tip that all even-numbered angles equal one another and all odd-numbered angles equal one another.

✔ **The *exterior angles* of any figure are supplementary to the interior angles and sum up to 360 degrees.** Exterior angles can be very confusing; keep in mind that they *always* sum up to 360 degrees, no matter what type of figure you have.

Exterior

To be called an exterior angle, an angle must be *supplementary* to an interior angle; in other words, the two angles must form a straight line with a side of the figure. The following example isn't an exterior angle:

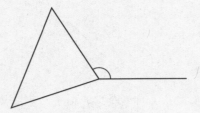

Increasing Your Polygon Knowledge: Triangles, Quadrilaterals, and More

A fair number of math problems you face when you take the SAT deal with *polygons* — figures with three or more noncurved sides. Triangles take a star role on the test, but quadrilaterals (four-sided shapes) also appear fairly regularly, and a more exotic figure (a pentagon or a hexagon, perhaps) may show up, too. Never fear: This section prepares you for all sorts of polygon questions that may appear on the SAT.

Figuring out what you need to know about triangles

Before I explain what you need to be able to do with triangles on the SAT, you need to familiarize yourself with the different types of triangles you may see on the test. The key points are as follows:

- A triangle with three equal sides and three equal angles is called *equilateral*.

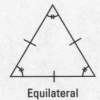

Equilateral

- A triangle with two equal sides and two equal angles is called *isosceles*.

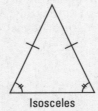

Isosceles

✔ **Angles opposite equal sides in an isosceles triangle are also equal.**

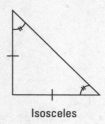

Isosceles

✔ **A triangle with no equal sides and no equal angles is called** *scalene*.

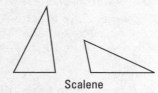

Scalene

✔ **In any triangle, the largest angle is opposite the longest side.** Similarly, the smallest angle is opposite the shortest side, and the medium angle is opposite the medium-length side.

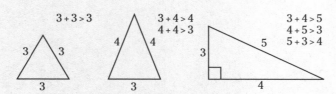

✔ **In any triangle, the sum of the lengths of two sides must be greater than the length of the third side (an idea often written as** *a* + *b* > *c*, **where** *a*, *b*, **and** *c* **are the sides of the triangle).**

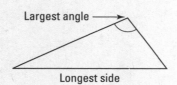

✔ **In any type of triangle, the sum of the interior angles is 180 degrees.**

  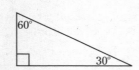

✔ **The measure of an exterior angle of a triangle is equal to the sum of the two remote interior angles.**

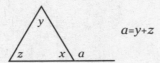

When you think about this rule logically, it makes sense. The sum of supplementary angles is 180 degrees. The sum of the angles in a triangle is 180. Therefore, angle $x = 180 - (y + z)$ or angle $x = 180 - a$. Thus, $a = y + z$.

Identifying what makes two triangles (or other figures) similar

Another concept that SAT writers love to test you on is figure similarity, particularly triangle similarity. What makes two figures *similar?* They must have all their angles in common, and their sides must be in proportion. The following rules pertain to all similar figures, including triangles:

✔ **The sides of similar figures are in proportion.** For example, if the heights of two similar triangles are in a ratio of 2:3, then the bases of those triangles are in a ratio of 2:3, as well.

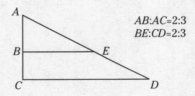

✔ **The ratio of the areas of similar figures is equal to the square of the ratio of their sides.** For example, if each side of Figure A is ⅓ the length of each side of similar Figure B, then the area of Figure A is ⅑ — which is $(⅓)^2$ — the area of Figure B.

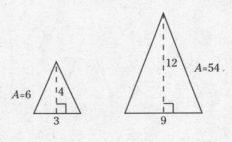

Figure A   Figure B

Time to apply the rules to the test. Take a crack at the following example to see whether you've been paying attention.

Two similar triangles have bases of 5 and 25. Which of the following expresses the ratio of the areas of the two triangles?

(A) 1:5

(B) 1:15

(C) 1:25

(D) 2:15

(E) It cannot be determined from the information given.

The answer is (C). The ratio of the sides is ⁵⁄₂₅ = ⅕. The ratio of the areas is the square of the ratio of the sides: ⅕ × ⅕ = ¹⁄₂₅. Note that (E) is a trap for the unwary. You can't figure out the exact area of either figure because you don't know the height (the area of a triangle is ½ base × height). However, I didn't ask you for an area, only for the ratio of the areas, which you can find.

Tired yet? I hope not, because you can travel this logical road a bit farther: What do you suppose is the ratio of the volumes of two similar figures? Because you find volume in cubic units, the ratio of the volumes of two similar figures is the cube of the ratio of their sides. If Solid A has a base of 5 and similar Solid B has a base of 10, then the ratio of their volumes is 1:8 — (½)³, which is ½ × ½ × ½ = ⅛.

Don't assume that any figures on the SAT are similar; either the problem must tell you they're similar, or (if they're triangles), they must have the exact same angles.

Calculating the area of triangles

The formula for finding the area of a triangle is: A = ½ base × height. The height (officially known as the *altitude*) is always a line perpendicular to the base. It may be a side of the triangle, as in a right triangle:

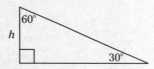

The height may be inside the triangle, in which case it is often represented by a dashed line and a small 90-degree box:

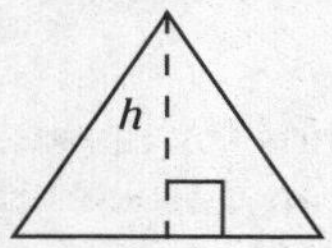

Or the height may be outside the triangle. This configuration is very confusing, but you may find it in trick questions. On the plus side, the problem will usually show you the altitude, as in this drawing:

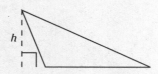

Using the Pythagorean Theorem

You have probably studied the *Pythagorean Theorem* (known colloquially as *PT*) at some point in your math career. The theorem says that in any right triangle, you can find the lengths of the sides using the PT formula: $a^2 + b^2 = c^2$, where a and b are the legs of the triangle and c is the hypotenuse. The hypotenuse is always opposite the 90-degree angle and is always the longest side of the triangle.

Keep in mind that the Pythagorean Theorem works only on right triangles. If a triangle doesn't have a right or 90-degree angle, you can't use it.

Simplifying things with Pythagorean triples

Going through the whole PT formula every time you want to find the length of a side in a right triangle is a pain in the posterior. To help you simplify your work, memorize the following four very common PT ratios:

- **Ratio 3:4:5.** In this ratio, if one leg of the triangle is 3, the other leg is 4, and the hypotenuse is 5.

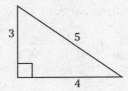

  Because this is a ratio, the sides can be in any multiple of these numbers, such as 6:8:10 (two times 3:4:5), 9:12:15 (three times 3:4:5), 27:36:45 (nine times 3:4:5), and so on.

- **Ratio 5:12:13.** In this ratio, if one leg of the triangle is 5, the other leg is 12, and the hypotenuse is 13.

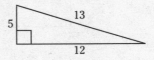

  Because this is a ratio, the sides can be in any multiple of these numbers, such as 10:24:26 (two times 5:12:13), 15:36:39 (three times 5:12:13), 50:120:130 (ten times 5:12:13), and so on.

- $s : s : s\sqrt{2}$, **where s stands for the side of the figure.** Because two sides are congruent, this formula applies to an isosceles right triangle, also known as a 45-45-90 triangle. If one side is 2, then the other leg is also 2, and the hypotenuse is $2\sqrt{2}$.

This formula is great to know for squares. If a question tells you that the side of a square is 5 and wants to know the diagonal of the square, you know immediately that it is $5\sqrt{2}$. Why? A square's diagonal cuts the square into two isosceles right triangles (isosceles because all sides of the square are equal; right because all angles in a square are right angles). What is the diagonal of a square with sides of 64? $64\sqrt{2}$. What is the diagonal of a square with sides of 12,984? $12,984\sqrt{2}$.

✔ $s : s\sqrt{3} : 2s.$ This ratio is a special formula for the sides of a 30-60-90 triangle.

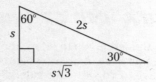

This type of triangle is a favorite of the test makers. The important thing to keep in mind here is that the hypotenuse is twice the length of the side opposite the 30-degree angle. If you get a word problem saying, "Given a 30-60-90 triangle of hypotenuse 20, find the area" or "Given a 30-60-90 triangle of hypotenuse 100, find the perimeter," you can do so because you can find the lengths of the other sides:

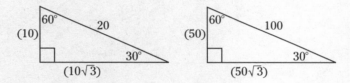

Two 30-60-90 triangles are formed whenever an equilateral triangle is cut in half. If an SAT question mentions the altitude of an equilateral triangle, you almost always have to use a 30-60-90 triangle to solve it.

Time to stretch those mental triangular muscles. Try this sample problem:

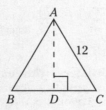

In this equilateral triangle, the length of altitude *AD* is

(A) 6

(B) 9

(C) $6\sqrt{2}$

(D) $6\sqrt{3}$

(E) 12

The answer is (D). Look at the 30-60-90 triangle formed by *ACD*. The hypotenuse is 12, the original side of the equilateral triangle. The base is 6 because it's half the hypotenuse. That makes the altitude $6\sqrt{3}$, according to the ratio.

TIP

Remember that the 45-45-90 and 30-60-90 triangle patterns are included in the formula box at the beginning of each math section, in case you forget them. Don't hesitate to look back at the direction text as you move through the math sections.

Taking a quick look at quadrilaterals

Think you know everything there is to know about squares and rectangles? Well, think again! I'm here to give you a few more oh-so-interesting rules to add to your geometry toolbox. These rules all have to do with four-sided figures, or *quadrilaterals:*

- ✔ **Any four-sided figure is called a *quadrilateral*.** The sum of the interior angles of any quadrilateral equals 360 degrees. Any quadrilateral can be cut into two 180-degree triangles.

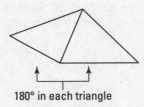

180° in each triangle

- ✔ **A *square* is a quadrilateral with four equal sides and four right angles.** The area of a square is: side^2.

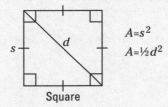

$A = s^2$

$A = \frac{1}{2}d^2$

Square

- ✔ **A *rhombus* is a quadrilateral with four equal sides and four angles that aren't necessarily right angles.** A rhombus looks like a square that's slipping sideways. The area of a rhombus is: $\frac{1}{2}d_1 d_2$ ($\frac{1}{2}$ diagonal$_1$ × diagonal$_2$).

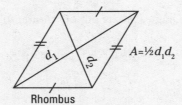

$A = \frac{1}{2}d_1 d_2$

Rhombus

✔ A *rectangle* **is a quadrilateral with four equal angles, all of which are right angles.** The top and bottom sides are equal, and the right and left sides are equal. All angles in a rectangle are right angles. (The word *rectangle* means "right angle.") The area of a rectangle is length × width (which is the same as base × height).

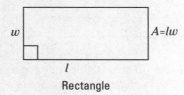

Rectangle

✔ A *parallelogram* **is a quadrilateral with two opposite and equal pairs of sides.** The top and bottom sides are equal, and the right and left sides are equal. Opposite angles are equal but not necessarily right. The area of a parallelogram is: base × height. (**Note:** The height is always a perpendicular line from the tallest point of the figure down to the base.)

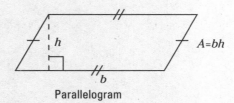

Parallelogram

✔ A *trapezoid* **is a quadrilateral with two parallel sides and two nonparallel sides.** The area of a trapezoid is: ½ (base$_1$ + base$_2$) × height. It makes no difference which base you label base$_1$ and which one you label base$_2$ because you're adding them together anyway. Just be sure to add them *before* you multiply by ½.

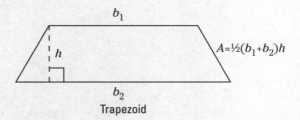

Trapezoid

Considering some other polygons

Triangles and quadrilaterals are the most common polygons tested on the SAT; however, they're certainly not the only ones out there. Table 16-1 notes a few other polygons you may see on the test.

Table 16-1	Some Polygons
Number of Sides	**Name**
5	Pentagon
6	Hexagon (think of *x* in six and *x* in hex)
8	Octagon

A polygon with all equal sides and all equal angles is called *regular*. For example, an equilateral triangle is a regular triangle, and a square is a regular quadrilateral.

The SAT writers won't ask you to find the area of any of these polygons, but they may ask you to find the *perimeter*, which is just the sum of the lengths of all the sides. They may also ask you to find the exterior angle measure, which is always 360 degrees. If they ask you about other angles, divide the shape up into triangles, as I do in the following figure. Then try your hand at the sample question that follows the illustration.

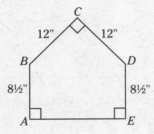

As the diagram shows, an official major league home plate has the shape of a pentagon. Given the measurements shown, the length of *AE*, to the nearest inch, must be

(A) 10

(B) 12

(C) 15

(D) 17

(E) 20

The answer is (D). The key to solving this problem is in shape *BCD*, which is an isosceles right triangle. As you know, an isosceles right triangle is a 45-45-90 triangle, which has the ratio $s : s : \sqrt{2}s$. Therefore, the hypotenuse, or *BD*, must be $12\sqrt{2}$, which multiplies out to 16.97, or 17. Because *ABDE* is a rectangle, *AE* has the same length.

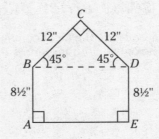

Sometimes you have to use several different shapes to solve a problem, especially when the SAT throws a strange diagram at you and asks you to find the area of a shaded section, a very popular question (popular with the test makers, not with the test takers). In the following diagram, a circle of radius 7 is surrounded by a square. How would you find the area of the shaded section?

In any problem like this one, the shaded area is equal to the area of the larger shape minus the area of the smaller shape — in this case, the area of the square minus the area of the circle. Because the circle has a radius of 7, its diameter is 14, which must be the same as the side of the square. The area of the square, then, equals $14 \times 14 = 196$. You can find the circle's area using the formula $\pi r^2 = \pi(7)^2 = 49\pi$. The shaded area, then, equals $196 - 49\pi$, or 42.06, if you're using decimals.

Getting the Lowdown on Circles

The SAT makers love testing you on circles, and, believe me, they toss in enough of them for a three-ring circus. But don't panic. Problems involving circles are easy to do as long as you keep in mind the following points:

- ✔ **A *radius (r)* goes from the center of a circle to its outer edge.** (The plural of *radius* is *radii,* in case you're curious.)

Radius

- ✔ **A *diameter (d)* connects two points on the outside or edge of the circle, going through the center.** A diameter is equal to two radii.

Diameter

- ✔ **The perimeter of a circle is called the *circumference*.** The formula for circumference is $2\pi r$ or πd (logical because 2 radii = 1 diameter).

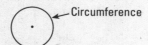

Circumference

You may encounter a wheel question in which you're asked how much distance a wheel covers or how many times a wheel revolves. The key to solving this type of question is knowing that one rotation of a wheel equals one circumference of that wheel. (Try your hand at the wheel-related example problem later in this section.)

✔ **The area of a circle is πr^2.**

✔ **A *chord* connects any two points on a circle.** The longest chord in a circle is the diameter.

✔ **A *tangent* is a line that touches the circle at exactly one point.** When a tangent line meets a radius of the circle, a 90-degree angle is formed.

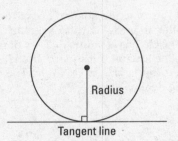

✔ **An *arc* is a portion of the circumference of a circle.** The degree measure of an arc is the same as its central angle. (In case you're wondering what a *central angle* is, it's an angle that has its endpoints on the circumference of the circle and its center at the center of the circle.)

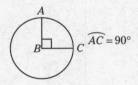

The SAT sometimes asks you to find the length of an arc. To do so, follow these steps:

1. **Find the circumference of the entire circle.**

2. **Put the degree measure of the arc over 360 and reduce the fraction.**

3. **Multiply the circumference by the fraction.**

✔ **A *sector* is a portion of the area of a circle.** To find the area of a sector, do the following:

1. **Find the area of the entire circle.**

2. **Put the degree measure of the sector over 360 and reduce the fraction.**

3. **Multiply the area by the fraction.**

Finding the area of a sector is very similar to finding the length of an arc. The only difference is in the first step. Whereas an arc is a part of the circle's circumference, a sector is a part of the circle's area.

Now that all these rules are circling in your head (pun intended!), try your hand at a few example problems.

A child's wagon has a wheel of radius 6 inches. If the wagon wheel travels 100 revolutions, approximately how many feet has the wagon rolled?

(A) 325

(B) 314

(C) 255

(D) 201

(E) 200

The answer is (B). One revolution is equal to one circumference: $C = 2\pi r = 2\pi(6) = 12\pi$ = approximately 37.68 inches. Multiply that by 100 = 3,768 inches, and 3,768 inches ÷ 12 = 314 feet.

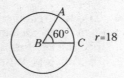

Find the length of arc *AC*.

(A) 36π

(B) 27π

(C) 18π

(D) 60

(E) 6π

The answer is (E). Take the steps one at a time. First, find the circumference of the entire circle: $C = 2\pi r = 36\pi$. Don't multiply π out; problems usually leave it in that form. Next, put the degree measure of the arc over 360. The degree measure of the arc is the same as its central angle, $60° = {}^{60}\!/_{360} = \frac{1}{6}$. The arc is ⅙ of the circumference of the circle. Multiply the circumference by the fraction: $36\pi \times \frac{1}{6} = 6\pi$.

Be very careful not to confuse the degree measure of the arc with the length of the arc. The length is always a portion of the circumference, always has a π in it, and always is in linear units. If you chose (D) in this example, you found the degree measure of the arc rather than its length.

What's the area of the shaded sector?

(A) 0.25π

(B) 16π

(C) 24π

(D) 64π

(E) 90π

The answer is (B). To do this problem, first, find the area of the entire circle: $A = \pi r^2 = 64\pi$. Second, put the degree measure of the sector over 360. The sector is 90 degrees, the same as its central angle. $\frac{90}{360} = \frac{1}{4}$. Third, multiply the area by the fraction: $64\pi \times \frac{1}{4} = 16\pi$.

Avoiding Two-Dimensional Thinking: Solid Geometry

From time to time, the SAT writers like to make an effort to include "real-world math" on the test. Now, if it were really about the real world, you'd see questions like "If a student wakes up 20 minutes before school begins and it takes him 10 minutes to run there at top speed, how many students are going to want to sit near him in class?" But where was I?

Now I remember. The real world is three-dimensional (3-D). To reflect that simple fact, almost every SAT has a problem or two dealing with a box, a cylinder, or (rarely) some other three-dimensional shape. The key formulas you need to know regarding these 3-D figures are included in the direction text at the start of each math section, but I also offer you a quick review here.

Volume

The volume of any polygon is: Area of the base × height. If you remember this formula, you don't have to memorize the following more-specific formulas, but I include them here to help you visualize the three most common 3-D shapes and their volumes:

✔ **Volume of a cube:** s^3

Cube

A cube is a 3-D square. Think of a die (one of a pair of dice). All a cube's dimensions are the same; that is, length = width = height. In a cube, these dimensions are called *edges*, or *sides*. The volume of a cube is side × side × side = side^3 = s^3.

✔ **Volume of a rectangular solid:** $l \cdot w \cdot h$

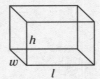

Rectangular solid

A rectangular solid is a box. The base of a box is a rectangle, which has an area of length × width. Multiply that area by height to fit the original volume formula: Volume = area of base × height, or $V = l \cdot w \cdot h$.

✔ **Volume of a cylinder:** $\pi r^2 \cdot$ height

Cylinder

Think of a cylinder as a can of soup. The base of a cylinder is a circle. The area of a circle is πr^2. Multiply that number by the height of the cylinder to get this formula: area of base × height = $\pi r^2 \cdot$ height. Note that the top and bottom of a cylinder are identical circles. If you know the radius of either the top base or the bottom base, you can find the area of the circle.

Surface area

On rare occasions, the SAT writers may ask you to find the surface area of a solid object. The surface area is, sensibly enough, the total area of all the sides (surfaces) of the object. To find the surface area of a box with six sides, calculate the area of each of the rectangles that forms a side, and then add them all up. If the test makers were in a particularly bad mood when they wrote the test, you might see a problem like the following example:

Find the surface area of the square-based pyramid shown below:

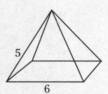

(A) 24

(B) 60

(C) 84

(D) 96

(E) 120

Choice (C) is the right answer. The area of the square is just 6 × 6 = 36. You know that the area of one of the triangular sides can be found by using the formula area = ½ base × height, but you don't yet know the height of each triangle. So take a moment to draw one of the triangular sides by itself:

The dashed line is the height, which makes a right angle with the base and cuts it in half. Thus, you have a right triangle with a leg of length 3 and a hypotenuse of 5. Does that sound familiar? Of course: It's a 3-4-5 triangle! So the height is 4, making the area of one triangle $\frac{1}{2} \times 6 \times 4 = 12$. And because there are four such triangles, their total area is $4 \times 12 = 48$, which you can now add to the 36 from the base to get Choice (C), or 84.

I don't know about you, but I think I deserve a nap after that problem!

Chapter 17

Practicing Problems in Geometry

● ●

In This Chapter

▶ Practicing a few guided geometry problems

▶ Focusing on angles, shapes, and distances in some sample questions

● ●

*E*ven if you'd rather squash a polygon than calculate its measurements, bite the bullet and check out at least some of the practice questions in this chapter. You get two sets. In the first set, move through each problem by solving it and then immediately checking your answer using the explanation I provide. Don't cheat. Cover the answers with a blank sheet of paper until you come up with your own solutions. If you (gasp) stub your toe on any of these geometry problems, try your hand at the second set, which is set up like the actual test. In that set, solve all the questions before checking your answers with the explanations I offer in the section that follows the questions. (Turn to Chapter 16 for more information on any of the topics covered in these practice questions.)

The following diagrams appear at the beginning of each math section of the SAT to help you work through the geometry problems. Don't hesitate to use them as you answer the practice problems in this chapter.

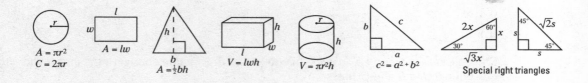

Set 1: Getting Started with Some Guided Questions

Note: Questions 3 and 6 are grid-ins, so you don't get any answers to choose from. See Chapter 11 for a quick review of grid-ins.

1. In the following square, what is the length of side *s*?

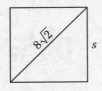

(A) 8

(B) $8\sqrt{2}$

(C) $8\sqrt{3}$

(D) 16

(E) $16\sqrt{2}$

Choice (A) is correct. When you cut a square in half, you get a 45-45-90 triangle, with the square's diagonal as the hypotenuse. The freebie information at the beginning of each math section (nice of them to help you, don't you think?) tells you that in a 45-45-90 triangle, the length of the hypotenuse equals $\sqrt{2}s$, where *s* is the length of a side of the square. Because the hypotenuse equals $8\sqrt{2}$, the side equals 8.

2. If the distance between points *A* and *B* is 5, and the distance between points *B* and *C* is 7, then the distance between points *A* and *C* may not equal

(A) 1

(B) 2

(C) 3

(D) 6

(E) 7

Choice (A) is correct. To answer this question, draw a line connecting *A* and *B* and another one connecting *B* and *C*, like so:

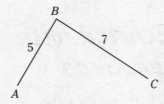

Now you can use a little thing called the *triangle inequality*. The distance from *A* to *C* forms the third side of a triangle, and a law was made a distant eon ago that the sum of two sides of a triangle must be greater than the third side. That law makes it impossible for *AC* to equal 1 because 1 + 5 = 6, which isn't bigger than 7. Before moving on, take a minute to make sure the other four answers *do* satisfy the triangle inequality (or I'm in a lot of trouble).

Beware of making assumptions in geometry problems. The first thing to realize when you look at Question 2 is that *A*, *B*, and *C* don't have to make a straight line, though they could. Most people assume that the three points must be on the same line.

3. In the following drawing, $\overline{BE} \| \overline{FI}$. Find the measure, in degrees, of the angle marked x.

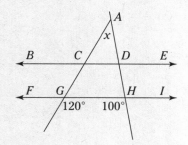

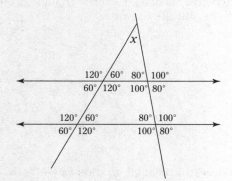

Because this drawing contains parallel lines cut by transversals (the two lines meeting at point A), you can fill in a whole lot of angles right off the bat. Each transversal creates eight angles, and these angles come in two groups of four equal angles each. Here they are, filled in:

After you determine the angles, the problem becomes simpler. Because ACD is a triangle, its angles must add up to 180 degrees. With a 60-degree and an 80-degree angle already accounted for, the missing angle must be 40 degrees — your correct answer.

Don't grid-in the degree symbol; just do the number.

4. What is the sum of the angles marked *a*, *b*, *c*, and *d* in the following diagram?

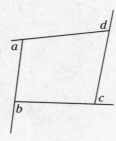

(A) 180 degrees

(B) 360 degrees

(C) 540 degrees

(D) 720 degrees

(E) It cannot be determined from the information given.

Choice (B) is correct. This one you just have to memorize. The sum of the exterior angles of any shape is always 360 degrees. Remember that fact.

5. If an equilateral triangle has sides of length 6, then its altitude has a length of

(A) 3

(B) $2\sqrt{3}$

(C) $3\sqrt{2}$

(D) $3\sqrt{3}$

(E) $6\sqrt{3}$

Choice (D) is correct. This one's a special-triangle problem in disguise. Here's the equilateral triangle with its altitude drawn:

(Of course, you drew this triangle as soon as you were done reading the problem, right?) Each half of the original triangle forms a 30-60-90 triangle. Making a second drawing just to be clear is worth your time.

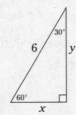

From the formulas I provide at the beginning of this chapter, you know that the side marked x must be half of 6, or 3, which means that y, the altitude, must equal $3\sqrt{3}$. Thus, (D) is correct.

6. In the following diagram, O is the center of the circle, and angles A and B have the same measure. Find the measure of the angle marked x in degrees.

The easiest way to think about this problem is to chop the dart shape in the circle into two triangles, like so:

Notice that the line segments OA, OB, and OC are all radii, which makes them all the same length. That means both triangles are isosceles. In any isosceles triangle, the base angles must have equal measures; because you were told that A and B have the same measure, all the angles marked below are congruent:

You're almost to the solution. Because angle AOB is 90 degrees, the other side of the angle (dark line below) must measure 270 degrees to make 360 degrees around a point. That means that half of 270, or 135 degrees, is the top angle of the isosceles triangle. That leaves 45 degrees for the other two angles. And, because two of these angles together made up x, x must equal 45. Whew!

Set 2: Practicing Some Questions on Your Own

Note: Refer to the diagrams I provide at the beginning of this chapter to help you answer these questions. Remember that those diagrams appear at the beginning of the math sections on the real SAT.

1. In this triangle, the measure of angle *x* is greater than the measure of angle *y*. Which of the following statements must be false?

    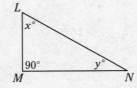

    (A) $MN > LM$

    (B) $(LN)^2 - (LM)^2 = (MN)^2$

    (C) $LN > MN$

    (D) $LN - LM = MN$

    (E) $m\angle y < 45°$

2. A car has wheels with a radius of 1.5 feet. If the car is backed down a driveway that is 95 feet long, about how many complete turns will the wheels make?

    (A) 10

    (B) 13

    (C) 14

    (D) 20

    (E) 32

3. In the following diagram, *O* is the center of the circle, and $\overline{AP}$ and $\overline{CP}$ are tangents. If $OA = 8$ and $BP = 9$, find *CP*.

    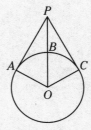

    (A) $\sqrt{17}$

    (B) 9

    (C) $\sqrt{145}$

    (D) 15

    (E) 17

4. In the following diagram, a square is inscribed in a circle. If one side of the square has a length of 10, then the shaded area equals

    (A) $100\pi - 100$

    (B) $50\pi - 100$

    (C) $100\pi - 50$

    (D) $100 - 25\pi$

    (E) $50\pi - 50$

5. In the following drawing, *ACDE* is a parallel-ogram with an area of 36. Find the length of *AC*.

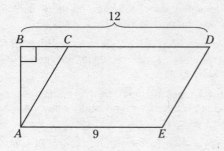

(A) 3

(B) $2\sqrt{2}$

(C) 4

(D) 5

(E) $4\sqrt{3}$

6. This cylindrical gas tank, originally empty, has a radius of 2 m and a height of 3 m. At 11 a.m., gas starts being added to the tank at a rate of 10 m³ per hour. The tank will be completely full closest to

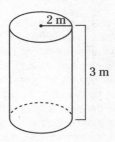

(A) 2 p.m.

(B) 2:30 p.m.

(C) 3 p.m.

(D) 3:30 p.m.

(E) 4 p.m.

Answers to Set 2

1. **D.** As you often should do in this type of problem, go through the answers one by one. Choice (A) is true because, in any triangle, the shortest side is opposite the smallest angle. Because *y* is smaller than *x* and both of them must be smaller than 90 degrees, *y* is the smallest angle and *LM* is the shortest side. Choice (B) is just a fancy way of writing the Pythagorean Theorem. Because *LN* is the hypotenuse of a right triangle, $(LM)^2 + (MN)^2 = (LN)^2$, so $(LN)^2 - (LM)^2 = (MN)^2$. Choice (C) is true for essentially the same reason as (A): *LN* must be the longest side of the triangle because it's across from 90 degrees, the largest angle. Choice (D) wins the "False Award" because of the triangle inequality. In any triangle, the sum of the two short sides must be *greater* than the sum of the longest side. That fact means that *LM* + *MN* > *LN*, so *LN* − *LM* can't equal *MN*. You could stop there, but just to be thorough, check out the last one. Choice (E) is true. Because the sum of the angles of any triangle is 180 degrees, the measures of *x* and *y* must add up to 90 degrees. Because *x* is larger than *y*, *x* must be greater than 45 degrees, and *y* must be less than 45 degrees. The correct answer — the false statement — is (D).

2. **A.** This one is a classic SAT problem. The key is knowing that one complete rotation equals the circumference of the wheel. Because circumference = $2 \times \pi \times$ radius, you have *C* = 2(3.14)(1.5) = 9.42 feet. Dividing 95 by 9.42 gives you 10.08, so your answer is 10. Give it up for (A).

3. **D.** Because $\overline{AP}$ and $\overline{CP}$ are tangents, the angles at *A* and *C* must be right angles. (If this fact is a surprise, turn back to Chapter 16. I can almost guarantee that this concept will show up in some form on the test.) Triangles *OPC* and *OPA* are right triangles, so the Pythagorean Theorem comes into play (and hits the ball out of the park). Because *OA* = 8, *OB* and *OC* are also 8 because all radii are equal. That makes *OP* = 8 + 9 = 17. *OP* is the hypotenuse, *OC* is a leg, and *CP* is a leg. So $(CP)^2 + (8)^2 = (17)^2$; $(CP)^2 + 64 = 289$; $(CP)^2 = 225$; and *CP* = 15. Choice (D) is correct.

Circling in on a better vocabulary

Lots of vocabulary words — the kind you may find in reading comprehension passages or even in normal conversation — pop out of math lessons and land in the real world. For example, the line that touches a circle but doesn't pierce it (a *tangent*) gives rise to the expression *going off on a tangent* (moving away from the main topic to something that is only marginally related at best), as in "Coop went off on a tangent about eggs when he was supposed to be discussing feather boas." A related word, *tangential,* shows up in sentences such as "The dry cleaners' association and the United Featherworkers of America criticized Coop's tangential remarks."

You probably know how to find the *circumference* of a circle (the distance around the edge). Well, the following words are all in the same family:

✔ *Circumlocution:* To talk around by speaking indirectly and avoiding a clear statement, as in "Answering controversial questions in an election year, politicians favor circumlocutions."

✔ *Circumnavigate:* To sail around, as in "Bob circumnavigated the globe in a leaky washtub."

✔ *Circumscribe:* To limit; picture a warden drawing a circle around someone and forbidding him or her to cross the line.

✔ *Circumspect:* Cautious; think of an imaginary circle around yourself that you venture beyond only with extreme care.

✔ *Circumvent:* To go around, as in "Bruckner circumvented the door alarm by breaking through the wall."

A distant cousin of the *circum* family is *circuitous,* an adjective that may describe the sort of route taxi drivers take with tourists in the back seat (round and round, just to drive up the fare).

4. **B.** This one is a shaded-area problem, so your answer must be the circle's area minus the square's area. The square's area is pretty simple to figure out: It's $(10)^2 = 100$. To find the circle's area, you need to know its radius. You can make a diameter by drawing the diagonal of the square, like so:

Look familiar? The diagonal of a square creates a 45-45-90 triangle, so the length of the diagonal is $10\sqrt{2}$. (The SAT makers love special triangles.) The radius is half of the diameter, $10\sqrt{2}$, or $5\sqrt{2}$. Bingo. The area of the circle is $\pi\left(5\sqrt{2}\right)^2 = \pi\left(5\right)^2\left(\sqrt{2}\right)^2 = \pi\left(25\right)\left(2\right) = 50\pi$. So your answer is $50\pi - 100$, Choice (B).

5. **D.** The area of a parallelogram uses the same formula as a rectangle: base × height. Because the base, *AE,* is 9, and the area is 36, the height, *AB,* must be 4. (Don't be fooled into thinking that *AC* is the height. The height is always perpendicular to the base, never slanted.) Meanwhile, *BC* = 12 – 9 = 3. This is yet another right triangle, so you can use the Pythagorean Theorem to get *AC* = 5. Even better, if you remember the 3-4-5 right triangle, you just know that the answer is 5 without having to do all the work. Choice (D) is your final answer.

6. **C.** The volume of a 3-D figure equals the area of its base times its height. Because the base is a circle, its area is $\pi r^2 = \pi(2)^2 = 4\pi$, or about 12.56 m². Multiplying by 3, the height, gives you a volume of 37.68 m³. Dividing 37.68 m³ by 10 m³ per hour gives you 3.768 hours to fill the tank. This answer is a little bit closer to four hours than to 3.5 hours (3.75 would be exactly halfway), so you can round up to 4 hours. Four hours after 11 a.m. is 3 p.m. Choice (C) is correct.

Chapter 18

Playing the Odds:
Statistics and Probability

1f you take the SAT 25 times, what are the odds that you'll die of boredom before entering college? Your SAT proctor, even more bored than the 25 test takers in front of him, launches an ink-filled balloon into the 30-square-foot classroom. What is the probability that it will miss you and land on the mouth-breather in the next row?

Questions like these — similar but humorless — confront you on the SAT. To increase the odds that you'll ace the topic of statistics and probability, read on. Also peruse this chapter to get the lowdown on the three *m*s (mean, median, and mode) and scatterplots and other graphs, as well as logic questions.

Working with the Odds: Probability

The *probability* of an event (or the odds that it will occur) is almost always defined as a fraction. So in many probability situations, you have to compute two separate numbers, one for the numerator and one for the denominator of the fraction. What do these numbers stand for? Well, here's the formula:

$$\text{the probability of an event} = \frac{\text{the number of ways for the event to occur}}{\text{the total number of possible outcomes}}$$

Say that you have a jar containing 6 red, 4 yellow, and 8 blue marbles. The probability of picking a blue marble $= \dfrac{8 \text{ blue marbles}}{6+4+8 = 18 \text{ total marbles}}$, which can be reduced to ⁴⁄₉.

Probability can also be written as a percentage. The easiest way to compute the percentage is with your calculator. Suppose the probability that a major label will sign your garage band is ⅝. (In your dreams, by the way. The real probability is ⁵⁄₈₈₉,₃₀₀,₉₂₃.) Enter 5 ÷ 8 on your calculator to get 0.625. Now move the decimal two places to the right. Bingo. The probability that you and your bandmates will ride to the MTV studio in a limo is 62.5%.

REMEMBER

An event that is certain to happen has a probability of 1, or 100%. An event that is impossible has a probability of zero. Nothing can ever have a probability greater than one or less than zero. Another way to say the second fact: Negative probability doesn't exist.

When you calculate probability, remember the number 1. All the possible events must have probabilities that add up to 1 (or 100%). That fact leads to a useful rule, which may be stated in three ways:

- ✔ The probability that an event won't happen equals 1 minus the (decimal or fractional) probability of the event.

- ✔ The probability that an event won't happen equals 100% minus the (percent) probability of the event.

- ✔ The probability that an event won't happen equals

$$\frac{\text{total number of possibilities} - \text{number of ways for the event to happen}}{\text{total number of possibilities}}$$

Imagine that you're sitting in class with 19 other students, and your teacher decides to pick one student at random to stay after school for a round of eraser cleaning. What's the chance that she picks you? It's $\frac{1}{20}$: Out of 20 students, there's only one you.

So what's the chance that she doesn't pick you? Figure it out all three ways:

- ✔ $1 - \frac{1}{20} = \frac{20}{20} - \frac{1}{20} = \frac{19}{20}$

- ✔ Because $\frac{1}{20} = 5\%$, $100\% - 5\% = 95\%$

- ✔ Because there are 20 total possibilities (20 students), $\frac{20-1}{20} = \frac{19}{20}$

The following sections discuss two variations of the typical SAT probability problem.

Psyching out multiple-probability questions

Not surprisingly, the SAT writers have found plenty of ways to make probability problems harder. One of their favorite torture devices is to ask you about a probability involving multiple events. When a problem involves multiple events, the total number of possibilities is the product of the number of possibilities for each event. If, for example, you open your closet on laundry day and find two clean shirts and three pairs of pants, the total number of outfits you can make is $2 \times 3 = 6$ (assuming you're not a fashionista and don't care about little things like complementary colors). This rule is known as the *counting principle,* although the "multiplication principle" may be a better name for it. This method works whether you're using whole numbers, percentages, or fractions.

Multiple-probability questions on the SAT may resemble the following example:

Jenny arranges interviews with three potential employers. If each employer has a 50% probability of offering her a job, what's the probability that she gets offered all three?

(A) 10%

(B) 12.5%

(C) 20%

(D) 25%

(E) 100%

The answer is (B). Applying the counting principle to Jenny's situation, you can say that the probability of her being offered all three jobs is $50\% \times 50\% \times 50\%$, or $\frac{1}{2} \times \frac{1}{2} \times \frac{1}{2} = \frac{1}{8}$ (12.5%).

Surviving geometric probability

Unbelievably, those SAT writers sometimes expect you to combine your knowledge of two different areas of mathematics: geometry and probability. (Turn to Chapter 16 for a geometry review.) Check out this example:

A dart is thrown at the dartboard below. If the radius of the circle is 5 inches, then the probability that the dart lands in the square but not in the circle is closest to

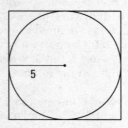

(A) 21%

(B) 22%

(C) 50%

(D) 78%

(E) 79%

The answer is (A). You may recognize this question as a variation of the shaded-area problem. (Check out Chapter 16 for more info on shaded areas.) Because the problem asks about the four corner regions of the diagram, first you have to figure out the area of these regions. The area of the circle is $\pi r^2 = \pi(5)^2 = 25\pi$ square inches. Because a side of the square equals the circle's diameter, which is 10, the square's area is $10^2 = 100$ square inches. That makes the total area of the corner regions equal to $100 - 25\pi = 100 - 78.54 = 21.46$. Because the square's area is 100, the probability that the dart lands in one of the corners is $^{21.46}/_{100} = 21.46\%$.

Saying "MMM": Mean, Median, and Mode

Sometimes the SAT writers give you a group of numbers and ask you to find their average (officially called their *mean*, or sometimes *arithmetic mean*). This sort of problem is probably familiar to you, especially if you're into computing your grade-point average or your favorite baseball player's batting average. To find the average, just add up the numbers and divide the total by the number of numbers you just added. For example, to find the average of 2, 4, and 9, add those three numbers (total = 15) and divide by three. The average is 5.

When you calculate an average, don't fall into the trap of dividing by 2 all the time. You must divide by the number of terms you're averaging.

If a group of numbers is evenly spaced, the mean is the middle number (assuming there is one). Suppose you're asked to find the arithmetic mean of the numbers from 1 to 19. Even with a calculator, adding up all the numbers and then dividing is time-consuming, not to mention easy to mess up. But the 19 numbers are evenly spaced (all 1 apart), and 10 is the middle number. No matter which way you start, from 1 or from 19, you find nine numbers evenly spaced on either side of 10. Therefore, 10 is the average, the mean, and the arithmetic mean. (Use any term you want.)

Remember that this trick works only when the numbers are evenly spaced. If you're told to find the average of 3, 5, 7, 12, and 18, you have to compute the long way. And despite what common sense may tell you, only an *odd* number of numbers has a middle number. For example, this trick doesn't work for a list like 3, 4, 5, 6, 7, 8; this list has an even number of terms, so it doesn't have a middle term. Remember, you can still find the average by adding up all the numbers and dividing by the total number of numbers. You just can't use the middle term as a shortcut.

Moving beyond mean (to nice and friendly, or **affable** and **amiable**, which are variations on the nice/friendly theme), SAT mathematicians also want you to understand *median*. The *median,* as those of you with drivers' licenses already know, is the strip down the middle of the road. In math, the *median* is defined as the middle number in a list, when the list is in numerical order. That last bit is important because you may have a list like 2, 5, 3, 7, 8 and need to find the median. It's not 3, but 5. When you put the numbers in order, the list reads 2, 3, 5, 7, 8, with 5 sitting right in the middle.

If you have an even number of numbers (say, 3, 5, 6, 7, 8, 10), the list has no middle number, so mathematicians cheat a little. The median is the mean of the two numbers closest to the middle. In this example, the two numbers in question are 6 and 7, so the median is 6.5.

The last of the three *m*s is the *mode*, the easiest to find. In a mixed bag of numbers, the *mode* is the number or numbers that pop up most frequently. So if you have a set with three 4s and three 8s, plus pairs of a bunch of other numbers, you have two modes, 4 and 8, in that set. You can also have a set with no mode at all if everything shows up the same number of times.

Which of the following is true for the set of numbers 3, 4, 4, 5, 6, 8?

(A) mean > mode

(B) median > mean

(C) mode > median

(D) median = mode

(E) median = mean

The answer is (A). If you average the terms, you get 30 ÷ 6, or 5, which is the mean. The median is 4.5 (halfway between the third and fourth terms), and the mode is 4. So (A) is the only one that fits.

Reading Graphs

Some of the math questions on the SAT are called *data interpretation*. Sounds important, huh? Actually, it's just a pompous name for "reading a graph," something you've been doing for years. Don't let graph problems intimidate you. Here are the three most common types of graphs you're likely to see on the SAT:

- Bar graph
- Circle or pie graph
- Two-axes line graph

I explain these graphs in more detail in the following sections. Because the SAT writers sometimes try to trip you up by asking you to compare statistics in two different graphs, I cover that topic here, as well.

Bar graphs

A *bar graph* has vertical or horizontal bars. The bars may represent actual numbers or percentages. If a bar goes all the way from one side of the graph to the other, it represents 100 percent.

Circle or pie graphs

The *circle* or *pie graph* represents 100 percent. The key to this graph is determining the total that the percentages are part of. Below the graph you may be told that in 1994, 5,000 students graduated with PhDs. If a 25-percent segment on the circle graph is labeled "PhDs in history," you know that the number of history PhDs is 25 percent of 5,000, or 1,250.

Two-axes line graphs and scatterplots

A typical *line graph* has a bottom and a side axis. You plot a point or read a point from the two axes. A special kind of two-axes graph is the *scatterplot*. A scatterplot contains a bunch of dots scattered around a two-line graph. Here's an example:

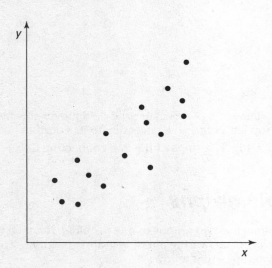

Notice how the points seem to follow a certain trend, getting higher as you move to the right. When a trend is present, drawing a line that estimates the behavior of the points is possible. This line is known as a *line of best fit*. On the test, you may be given a scatterplot and have to choose the line of best fit from a list of choices, or you may have to estimate the slope of the line of best fit.

For the following data set, the line of best fit would have a slope that is closest to

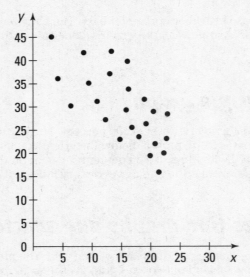

(A) –2

(B) –1

(C) 0

(D) 1

(E) 2

The correct answer is (A). Because the data moves downward, it must be (A) or (B). If you look at the top left point, you can estimate its coordinates as (5, 45). The bottom right point is around (20, 15). The slope of the line connecting these points would be $\frac{15-45}{20-5} = \frac{-30}{15} = -2$.

Multiple graphs

Some questions use two graphs in one problem. No need to fret! I'm here to help you through the art of answering multiple-graph questions. To get started, run your eyeballs over the two graphs that follow.

You must read these graphs together. The second graph is a bar graph going from 0 to 100 percent. Read the graph by subtracting to find the appropriate percentage. For example, in 1990, "Grandparents won't donate a building" begins at 20 percent and goes to 50 percent, a difference of 30 percent. You've fallen into a trap if you say that "Grandparents won't donate a building" was 50 percent. In 1993, "Just felt like it" goes from 80 percent to 100 percent, which means it was actually 20 percent.

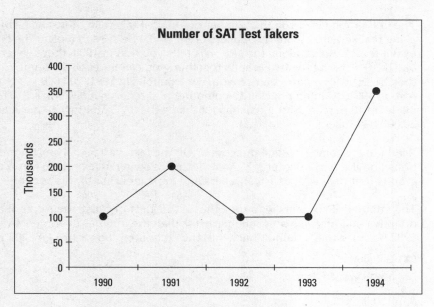

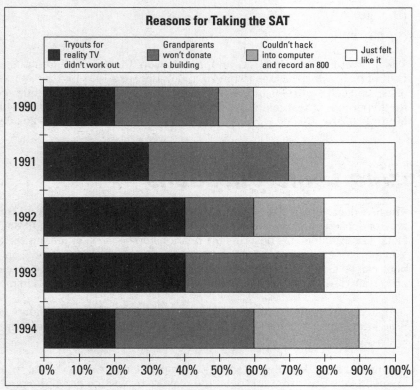

The first graph gives you the number of SAT test takers in thousands. (By the way, I'm not using real statistics from the makers of the SAT.) Be sure to look at the labels of the axes. For example, *Thousands* along the side axis tells you that in 1990, there weren't 100 test takers but 100,000. Using the two graphs together, you can find out the number of test takers who took the SAT for a particular reason. For example, in 1991, 200,000 students took the test. Also in 1991, "Couldn't hack into computer and record an 800" (from 70 to 80, or 10 percent) made up 10 percent of the reasons for taking the SAT. Multiply 10 percent or $0.10 \times 200,000 =$ 20,000 test takers.

Ready to try some practice questions? On the test, you usually encounter three to five questions about a particular graph. Answer the following question based on the two practice graphs that deal with SAT test takers and appear earlier in this section.

The number of students who took the SAT in 1994 because their grandparents wouldn't donate a building was how much greater than the number of students who took the SAT in 1992 because they couldn't hack into the computer and record an 800?

(A) 250,000

(B) 140,000

(C) 120,000

(D) 100,000

(E) 20,000

The answer is (C). In 1994, "Grandparents won't donate a building" accounted for 40 percent of test-taking reasons (from 20 to 60). Because 1994 had 350,000 test takers, multiply $0.40 \times 350,000 = 140,000$. In 1992, "Couldn't hack into computer and record an 800" counted for 20 percent of test-taking reasons (60 to 80). In 1992, 100,000 students took the test. Multiply $0.20 \times 100,000 = 20,000$. The correct answer is $140,000 - 20,000 = 120,000$, or (C).

Analyzing Logic Questions

The SAT occasionally tosses you a logic question, disguised as a simple math question. This type of question has two parts. First is the set of statements or conditions, sometimes called the facts. These statements describe the relationship between or among people, items, or events. You may, for example, be given statements about students at a school and then be asked which ones can be assigned to the same classes. You may be told facts about events that can happen on certain days of the week or about what different combinations of items are possible.

A logic question often takes a long time to solve. Make the decision whether you have the time — and the patience! — to do it properly. If not, skip the question and come back to it later, if you can. Don't rush yourself.

Before you start doodling to solve a logic problem, be sure you know all the people or items involved. Make a "program" of all the players by writing down the pool of people or events. For example, if the question talks about five teachers, Mahaffey, Negy, O'Leary, Plotnitz, and Quivera, use initials and jot down M, N, O, P, and Q on the test booklet.

What not to call the umpire

Mathematicians love baseball — or at least baseball stats. So take a moment to rest from your math labors and watch your favorite team. You can call the ump *disinterested* (fair) but not *uninterested* (bored out of his skull). Unless you want to go down on strikes, also avoid calling him *pusillanimous* (cowardly) and *mendacious* (lying). Whatever you think of the pay scale, stay away from *mercenary* (in it only for the money, as opposed to in it for the love of the game) and *partial* or *partisan* (taking sides). Nor would an umpire appreciate being labeled *iniquitous* (evil) or *intemperate* (excessive, extreme).

To gain the ump's favor, try calling him *judicious* (showing good judgment) and *discerning* (sharp, perceptive). Describing the umpire's calls as *sonorous* (deep and pleasant in sound) may also get you to first base.

Next, use a diagram to show the relationship between people or events. Here are a few of the most common diagrams.

- ✓ **Calendar:** Draw a simple calendar and fill in the events that happen on particular days.

- ✓ **Ordering or sequencing:** You may have a relationship problem in which some people are taller or heavier than others. Write a line of people, with A above B if A is taller than B, C at the bottom if she is the shortest, and so on.

- ✓ **Grouping or membership:** This problem asks you which items or people could belong to which group. For example, membership in a club may require four out of five characteristics. Often this type of question doesn't require a graph, but it does require a lot of *if . . . then* statements, such as "If A is in the group, then B isn't."

Try your hand at this logic-based example:

Five spices — lemon pepper, marjoram, nutmeg, oregano, and paprika — are aligned next to one another between the left and right sides of a kitchen cabinet. Their arrangement must conform to the following conditions:

The marjoram is immediately to the right of the paprika.

The oregano is either all the way to the left or second from the left.

The lemon pepper is farther left than the nutmeg.

Which of the following could *not* be true?

(A) The paprika is second from the left.

(B) The marjoram is to the right of the lemon pepper.

(C) The nutmeg is exactly in the middle.

(D) The lemon pepper is exactly in the middle.

(E) The nutmeg is all the way to the right.

The answer is (D). To help keep track of the information, write out initials for the roster of spices — L, M, N, O, and P — and make five simple dashes to represent the five positions of the spices:

— — — — —

The easiest condition to accommodate is the one that indicates that the oregano must be first or second from the left. Draw these two possibilities:

O __ __ __ __

__ O __ __ __

The next thing to note is that the paprika and marjoram must always move together. So test out the answer choices, making sure to also fulfill the third condition. Choice (A) is fine, because you can write O, P, M, L, N and meet all conditions. Choice (B) also works, because you can write O, L, P, M, N. And for (C), you can write either O, L, N, P, M or L, O, N, P, M.

Choice (D) is no good, though. If L is in the middle, you have to put P and M to its right because they always travel together. But that doesn't leave room to put N to the right of L, so you can't fulfill the third condition. Take a moment to check that (E) works. (It does, with one option being O, L, P, M, N.) Choice (D) is the only option that doesn't work, so that's your answer.

Chapter 19

Practicing Problems in Probability, Statistics, and Logic

In This Chapter

▶ Practicing some guided questions about probability, statistics, and logic
▶ Poring over some sample questions on your own

You can count on at least a couple of probability, statistics, and logic problems showing up on your particular version of the SAT. Don't freak out! Now's the time to practice with the help of the two sets in this chapter. After you complete each question in the first set, check your answers and read the explanations of any problem you answered incorrectly. (The answers immediately follow each question.) Don't cheat, though! Use a piece of paper to cover the answers as you work through the problems. Then, if you need more practice, hit Set 2, which is set up more like the real test, with the answers coming in a section separate from the questions themselves. Turn to Chapter 18 for a refresher course in any topic that stumps you in either set.

Set 1: Trying Your Hand at Some Guided Questions

Note: Questions 1 and 7 are grid-ins, which means you don't get any answers to choose from. See Chapter 11 for tips on answering grid-ins.

1. A school cafeteria offers two soups, three main dishes, and four desserts. Find the total number of possible meals consisting of one soup, one main dish, and one dessert.

The correct answer is 24. Using the counting principle, $2 \times 3 \times 4 = 24$.

2. The chance of rain tomorrow is ¼. As a percentage, what is the probability that it will not rain tomorrow?

(A) 4%

(B) 25%

(C) 40%

(D) 75%

(E) 96%

As a percentage, ¼ = 25%. The probability of an event not happening equals 100% minus the probability of it happening, and 100% − 25% = 75%. Choice (D) is correct.

3. In a special deck of 20 cards, 8 cards are red on both sides, 7 cards are blue on both sides, and the other 5 cards are red on one side and blue on the other side. If a student picks a card and places it on his desk, what is the probability that the side facing up is blue?

(A) ¹⁹⁄₄₀

(B) ¹²⁄₂₀

(C) ⁷⁄₄₀

(D) ⁷⁄₂₀

(E) ¹²⁄₄₀

This one's a little tricky. Even though there are 20 cards, the question asks only about the side of the card facing up, and there are 20 × 2 = 40 possible sides. The 7 cards that are blue on both sides represent 7 × 2 = 14 blue sides, and there are 5 cards with one blue side. 14 + 5 = 19, so the probability is ¹⁹⁄₄₀. Choice (A) is correct.

Problems 4, 5, and 6 use the following graphs:

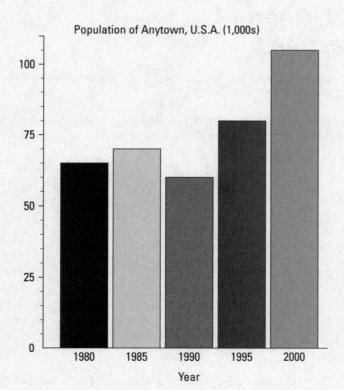

Population of Anytown, U.S.A. (1,000s)

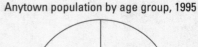

Anytown population by age group, 1995

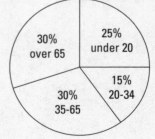

4. In 1990, what was the approximate number of Anytown residents over the age of 65?

   (A) 55,000

   (B) 50,000

   (C) 25,000

   (D) 14,000

   (E) It cannot be determined from the graphs.

   Don't trip over this one. You can tell from the bar graph that in 1990 Anytown had approximately 60,000 total residents, but the pie graph tells you only about the ages of the residents in 1995. You have no way to determine anything about the ages of Anytown residents in 1990, so Choice (E) is correct.

5. During which five-year period did Anytown have the greatest percent increase in population?

   (A) 1980–1985

   (B) 1985–1990

   (C) 1990–1995

   (D) 1995–2000

   (E) It cannot be determined from the graphs.

   You can throw out (B) right away because the population decreased. Don't get fooled by (D); although the population went up by 25,000 people, the percent change was 25,000 ÷ 80,000 = 0.3125, or 31%. But from 1990 to 1995, the population increased by 20,000 from an original population of 60,000. That's 20,000 ÷ 60,000 = 0.3333, or 33%. Thus, (C) is correct.

6. In 1995, roughly how many Anytown residents were between the ages of 20 and 65?

   (A) 45

   (B) 15,000

   (C) 30,000

   (D) 36,000

   (E) 45,000

   A look at the pie chart tells you that 30 + 15, or 45% of the residents were between 20 and 65 in 1995. Because there were 80,000 residents, change 45% into 0.45, and 0.45 × 80,000 = 36,000. Give it up for (D).

7. A bag contains red, blue, and green marbles. The probability of picking a red marble is ½; the probability of picking a blue marble is ⅓. If the bag holds seven marbles that are green, find the total number of marbles in the bag.

Your answer here is 42. To do this one, you need a little algebra. Because the probability of picking a red marble is ½, half of the marbles are red. Similarly, ⅓ of the marbles must be blue. So ½ of the marbles, plus ⅓ of the marbles, plus the seven green marbles, is the number you're looking for. If you let x represent the total number of marbles, you can write $\frac{1}{2}x+\frac{1}{3}x+7=x$.

Because fractions are annoying, multiply everything by 6 to get $3x + 2x + 42 = 6x$. This equation gives you $5x + 42 = 6x$, so $x = 42$. Another way to think about this question: The red and blue marbles represent ½ + ⅓ = ⅚ of the marbles. That leaves 1 – ⅚ = ⅙ of the marbles to be green, and 7 is ⅙ of 42.

8. If a student picks a square at random on the following grid, what is the probability that he picks a square that is not shaded?

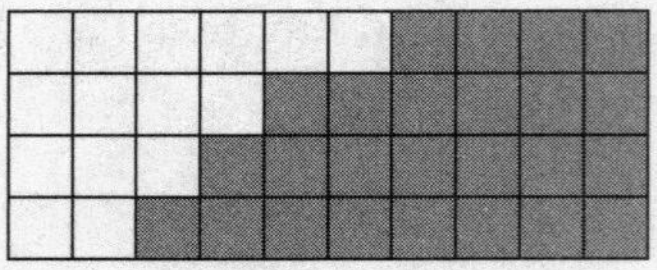

(A) ⅗

(B) ⅜

(C) ⅖

(D) ⅝

(E) 3/10

Twenty-five of the 40 squares are shaded, leaving 40 – 25 = 15 unshaded. 15/40 reduces to ⅜. Choice (B) is correct.

9. Which graph could represent the line of best fit for this scatterplot?

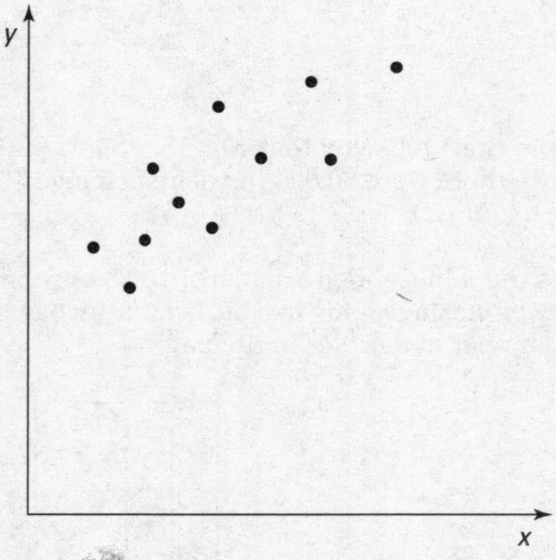

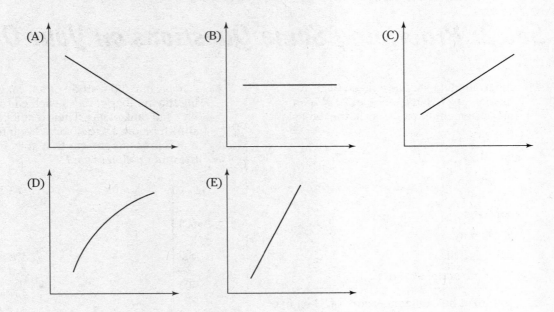

As long as you remember what the "line of best fit" means, this one is easy (see Chapter 18 if you don't). Choice (C) is correct.

10. Adrianna, Bob, Chris, and Darrell all arrive at school between 7:30 and 8:00.

    Chris was late to school, but Bob was not.

    Darrell arrived ten minutes after Adrianna.

    Bob didn't see Adrianna when he came into school.

Based on this information, which student(s) could have arrived at exactly 7:30?

(A) only Adrianna

(B) only Bob

(C) either Adrianna or Bob

(D) only Chris

(E) none of them

You don't know what time the school day starts, but the first clue tells you that Chris must have arrived later than Bob, so Chris couldn't have arrived at 7:30, but (from this clue) Bob could have. The same logic applies to the second clue: Darrell arrived after Adrianna, so Darrell couldn't have been there at 7:30, but Adrianna could have. The third clue is just the SAT makers (okay, me) messing with you; Adrianna might have already been in the building, or she might not have been, but we just can't tell. So Choice (C) is correct because either of them might have arrived at 7:30; in fact, they might have both arrived then, if the school has more than one door.

Set 2: Practicing Some Questions on Your Own

1. A certain data set has a mean of 20, a median of 21, and a mode of 22. Which measurement must occur in the data set?

   I. 20

   II. 21

   III. 22

   (A) I only

   (B) II only

   (C) III only

   (D) II and III

   (E) none of the above

2. A student has a median score of 83 on five tests. If she scores 97 and 62 on her next two tests, her median score will

   (A) increase to 90

   (B) decrease to 82

   (C) decrease to 79.5

   (D) remain the same

   (E) It cannot be determined from the information given.

3. Alicia picks a number from the set {1, 2, 3, 4, 5, 6}. Michelle picks a number from the set {3, 4, 5, 6, 7, 8}. What is the probability that they select the same number?

   (A) ⅙

   (B) ⁴⁄₃₆

   (C) ⅚

   (D) ¹⁶⁄₃₆

   (E) ⅝

4. A magazine did a study of ten cars, comparing the number of miles each car could go on a full tank of gas. Their results are shown below. Of the labeled points, which one represents the car that goes the farthest per gallon of gas?

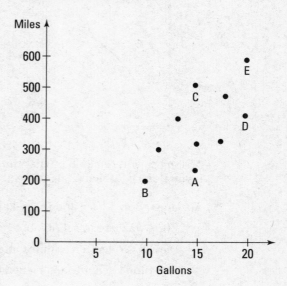

   (A) A

   (B) B

   (C) C

   (D) D

   (E) E

5. If a two-digit number is picked at random, what is the probability that the number chosen is a perfect square?

   (A) ⁶⁄₉₀

   (B) ¹⁰⁄₁₀₀

   (C) ⁷⁄₉₁

   (D) ⁶⁄₈₉

   (E) ⁹⁄₉₉

6. A class contains five boys and seven girls. In how many ways can a teacher line up two boys and two girls, in that order?

(A) 35

(B) 140

(C) 210

(D) 840

(E) 1,225

7. A junior is choosing her classes for senior year. If she takes calculus, she can also take either history or English, but not both. If she takes psychology in the first semester, she cannot take sociology or creative writing. If she takes psychology in the second semester, she cannot take calculus, but can take any elective she wants during the first semester. Based only on this information, which of the following is *not* a possible choice of courses for her?

(A) English, calculus, psychology, statistics

(B) History, sociology, psychology, English

(C) Creative writing, psychology, history, English

(D) Calculus, psychology, creative writing, history

(E) Psychology, sociology, English, statistics, creative writing

8. The following dartboard consists of three circles with the same center. If the circles have radii of 6, 8, and 10 inches, what is the probability that a dart that hits the board lands in the shaded ring?

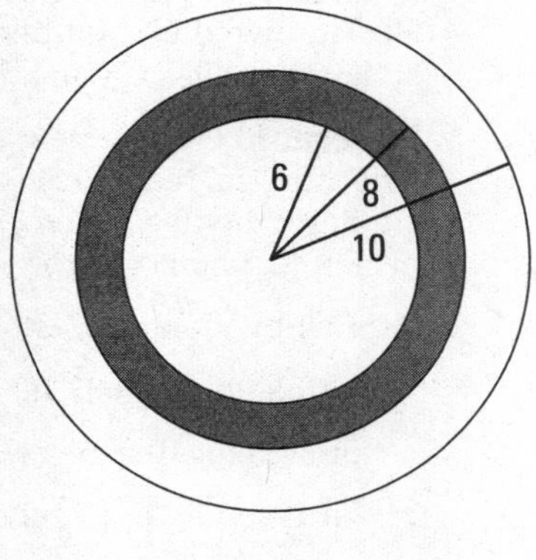

(A) $\frac{7}{25}$

(B) $\frac{4}{5}$

(C) $\frac{3}{4}$

(D) $\frac{9}{16}$

(E) $\frac{16}{25}$

9. A student has taken three tests, with an average (arithmetic mean) of 82. What grade must she receive on her next test in order to have an overall average of 85?

(A) 85

(B) 88

(C) 90

(D) 94

(E) 97

Answers to Set 2

1. **C.** If you remember how to compute the three *m*s, you'll realize that the mean and median don't have to be in the data set. (Look in Chapter 18 for more on mean, median, and mode.) But because the mode is the most common measurement, it must be in the set. Thus, Choice (C) is correct.

2. **D.** The median is the score in the middle. If 83 is in the middle, adding a 97 on one side and a 62 on the other side doesn't change where the middle is. The correct answer is (D).

3. **B.** First determine the total number of possibilities. Using the counting principle, you know you have $6 \times 6 = 36$ possibilities. Because the two sets overlap at 3, 4, 5, and 6, the girls may pick the same number in only four ways. Hence, the answer is $\frac{4}{36}$. (Notice that the fraction isn't always reduced in probability questions.) Choice (B) is correct. Another way to look at it: The first girl has a $\frac{4}{6}$ chance of picking a number that the second girl could match. If the first girl picks a number that can be matched, the second girl has a $\frac{1}{6}$ chance of picking the same number. The math: $\frac{4}{6} \times \frac{1}{6} = \frac{4}{36}$.

4. **C.** Car C travels approximately 500 miles on 15 gallons, for $^{500}/_{15}$ or around 33 miles per gallon. Although Car E goes almost 600 miles, it needs 20 gallons, so it gets less than 30 miles per gallon. The other cars all travel fewer than 30 miles per gallon. Choice (C) is correct.

5. **A.** As usual in a probability question, you need to start by determining the total number of two-digit numbers. The two-digit numbers run from 10 to 99. The formula you can use here is as follows: The total is one more than the difference of the two numbers, or $99 - 10 + 1 = 90$. The two-digit numbers that are perfect squares are 16, 25, 36, 49, 64, and 81. Pat yourself on the back if you answered (A).

6. **D.** Because cloning people isn't a reality just yet, the teacher can't pick the same person twice. So the teacher has five choices for the first boy, but only four left for the second. Similarly, he has seven choices for the first girl and six for the second. Using the counting principle, you know the answer is $5 \times 4 \times 7 \times 6 = 840$. Choice (D) is correct.

7. **D.** Start by making a list of combinations that are impossible:

   Calculus, English, history

   First-semester psychology, sociology

   First-semester psychology, creative writing

   Second-semester psychology, calculus

   Now consider the choices: Choice (A) is fine, if she takes psychology in the first semester. Choice (B) is okay if she takes psychology in the second semester. Choice (C) is fine, if she takes psychology in the second semester. Choice (D) is a problem. If she takes psychology in the first semester, then creative writing is out. But if she takes it in the second semester, then calculus is out. Choice (E) is fine if she takes psychology in the second semester. Choice (D) is the correct answer.

8. **A.** The shaded ring has an outer radius of 8 and an inner radius of 6. So the area of the shaded ring is the area of the radius-8 circle minus the area of the radius-6 circle, or $\pi(8)^2 - \pi(6)^2 = 64\pi - 36\pi = 28\pi$. The entire dartboard has a radius of 10, so its area is $\pi(10)^2 = 100\pi$, and the probability equals $^{28\pi}/_{100\pi} = ^{28}/_{100} = ^{7}/_{25}$. Choice (A) is correct.

9. **D.** The formula *average score $\times$ number of scores = total score* helps you answer this problem. The student wants to end up with an average score of 85 on four tests, for a total score of $85 \times 4 = 340$. The student's total number of points on the first three tests is $82 \times 3 = 246$. So to make up the difference, she needs $340 - 246 = 94$ points on her next test to get (1) the car keys and (2) permission to stay out past 7 p.m. Choice (D) is correct.

Part V

Where the Rubber Meets the Road: Practice Tests

The 5th Wave

By Rich Tennant

Brad felt foolish letting a fly on the wall distract him from his SAT.

In this part . . .

Time for a reality check. The first time you sit in a silent room facing an SAT test shouldn't be the morning of your test day. By that time, you should have at least one practice exam under your belt, fortifying you like a hearty breakfast for the rigors of SAT reasoning. Yes, working through a practice exam does kill a perfectly fine morning (or evening or middle of the night — whenever you prefer to practice), but the investment of time will pay off.

In this part, I thoughtfully (and humbly) provide not just one but five (count 'em if you don't believe me) full-length SATs. In the interests of full disclosure (I'm the mother of a lawyer), I must tell you that I, not the College Board, wrote them. Your test may differ slightly in number and order of questions from the real SAT. Also, because I'm kind-hearted, I haven't included the extra, nonscored section that you'll find on the real test. (The SAT makers always throw in a section that doesn't count toward your official score. This section helps them devise future tortures — er, I mean *tests*.)

I promise you that the tests in this part do prepare you nicely for whatever the SAT makers throw at you. Try one, score it, review whatever was tough for you (the answers and explanations follow each exam), and then, if you have time, try out another one. You may be bored now, but you'll be smart and prepared come SAT day.

Chapter 20

Practice Exam 1

• •

*T*he first paragraph is usually where you find my lame jokes, but in this chapter, you need to be as serious as you can be. Clear out your room or find a sheltered spot in the public library. Place a watch in front of you, or sit where you can see a wall clock. Tear out the answer sheet that follows this page and gather two lined sheets of loose-leaf paper and a No. 2 pencil. Allot yourself the official amount of time you have to take each section (I tell you how much time you get at the beginning of each section), and get to work.

If you finish a section early, go back and recheck it. But don't even think about looking at other sections. If you do so on the actual exam, the proctor will invalidate your whole test, and you'll get a big fat zero for all your hard work! If you run out of time, put your pencil down and move on to the next section. Take a ten-minute break between Sections 3 and 4 and another ten minutes off between Sections 6 and 7.

No matter how tempted you are, resist the urge to turn to Chapter 21, where the answers and explanations for this practice test reside. Save them for later! And good luck.

Note: The real SAT will have ten sections, instead of the nine you see here because the College Board throws in an "equating section" that doesn't count toward your score but allows the testers to evaluate new questions. The SAT doesn't tell you which section is useless (to you). Because I'm here to help you score high on the SAT, I don't include an equating section in any of the practice tests in this book. Nice of me, huh?

Answer Sheet

For Section 1, use two loose-leaf or lined notebook pages to write your essay. (On the real exam, the answer booklet contains two lined sheets.) For Sections 2 through 8, use the ovals and grid-ins provided with this practice exam to record your answers. Begin with Number 1 for each new section. If any sections have fewer than 35 questions, leave the extra spaces blank.

Section 2: Critical Reading

1. Ⓐ Ⓑ Ⓒ Ⓓ Ⓔ   8. Ⓐ Ⓑ Ⓒ Ⓓ Ⓔ   15. Ⓐ Ⓑ Ⓒ Ⓓ Ⓔ   22. Ⓐ Ⓑ Ⓒ Ⓓ Ⓔ   29. Ⓐ Ⓑ Ⓒ Ⓓ Ⓔ
2. Ⓐ Ⓑ Ⓒ Ⓓ Ⓔ   9. Ⓐ Ⓑ Ⓒ Ⓓ Ⓔ   16. Ⓐ Ⓑ Ⓒ Ⓓ Ⓔ   23. Ⓐ Ⓑ Ⓒ Ⓓ Ⓔ   30. Ⓐ Ⓑ Ⓒ Ⓓ Ⓔ
3. Ⓐ Ⓑ Ⓒ Ⓓ Ⓔ   10. Ⓐ Ⓑ Ⓒ Ⓓ Ⓔ   17. Ⓐ Ⓑ Ⓒ Ⓓ Ⓔ   24. Ⓐ Ⓑ Ⓒ Ⓓ Ⓔ   31. Ⓐ Ⓑ Ⓒ Ⓓ Ⓔ
4. Ⓐ Ⓑ Ⓒ Ⓓ Ⓔ   11. Ⓐ Ⓑ Ⓒ Ⓓ Ⓔ   18. Ⓐ Ⓑ Ⓒ Ⓓ Ⓔ   25. Ⓐ Ⓑ Ⓒ Ⓓ Ⓔ   32. Ⓐ Ⓑ Ⓒ Ⓓ Ⓔ
5. Ⓐ Ⓑ Ⓒ Ⓓ Ⓔ   12. Ⓐ Ⓑ Ⓒ Ⓓ Ⓔ   19. Ⓐ Ⓑ Ⓒ Ⓓ Ⓔ   26. Ⓐ Ⓑ Ⓒ Ⓓ Ⓔ   33. Ⓐ Ⓑ Ⓒ Ⓓ Ⓔ
6. Ⓐ Ⓑ Ⓒ Ⓓ Ⓔ   13. Ⓐ Ⓑ Ⓒ Ⓓ Ⓔ   20. Ⓐ Ⓑ Ⓒ Ⓓ Ⓔ   27. Ⓐ Ⓑ Ⓒ Ⓓ Ⓔ   34. Ⓐ Ⓑ Ⓒ Ⓓ Ⓔ
7. Ⓐ Ⓑ Ⓒ Ⓓ Ⓔ   14. Ⓐ Ⓑ Ⓒ Ⓓ Ⓔ   21. Ⓐ Ⓑ Ⓒ Ⓓ Ⓔ   28. Ⓐ Ⓑ Ⓒ Ⓓ Ⓔ   35. Ⓐ Ⓑ Ⓒ Ⓓ Ⓔ

Section 3: Mathematics

1. Ⓐ Ⓑ Ⓒ Ⓓ Ⓔ   8. Ⓐ Ⓑ Ⓒ Ⓓ Ⓔ   15. Ⓐ Ⓑ Ⓒ Ⓓ Ⓔ   22. Ⓐ Ⓑ Ⓒ Ⓓ Ⓔ   29. Ⓐ Ⓑ Ⓒ Ⓓ Ⓔ
2. Ⓐ Ⓑ Ⓒ Ⓓ Ⓔ   9. Ⓐ Ⓑ Ⓒ Ⓓ Ⓔ   16. Ⓐ Ⓑ Ⓒ Ⓓ Ⓔ   23. Ⓐ Ⓑ Ⓒ Ⓓ Ⓔ   30. Ⓐ Ⓑ Ⓒ Ⓓ Ⓔ
3. Ⓐ Ⓑ Ⓒ Ⓓ Ⓔ   10. Ⓐ Ⓑ Ⓒ Ⓓ Ⓔ   17. Ⓐ Ⓑ Ⓒ Ⓓ Ⓔ   24. Ⓐ Ⓑ Ⓒ Ⓓ Ⓔ   31. Ⓐ Ⓑ Ⓒ Ⓓ Ⓔ
4. Ⓐ Ⓑ Ⓒ Ⓓ Ⓔ   11. Ⓐ Ⓑ Ⓒ Ⓓ Ⓔ   18. Ⓐ Ⓑ Ⓒ Ⓓ Ⓔ   25. Ⓐ Ⓑ Ⓒ Ⓓ Ⓔ   32. Ⓐ Ⓑ Ⓒ Ⓓ Ⓔ
5. Ⓐ Ⓑ Ⓒ Ⓓ Ⓔ   12. Ⓐ Ⓑ Ⓒ Ⓓ Ⓔ   19. Ⓐ Ⓑ Ⓒ Ⓓ Ⓔ   26. Ⓐ Ⓑ Ⓒ Ⓓ Ⓔ   33. Ⓐ Ⓑ Ⓒ Ⓓ Ⓔ
6. Ⓐ Ⓑ Ⓒ Ⓓ Ⓔ   13. Ⓐ Ⓑ Ⓒ Ⓓ Ⓔ   20. Ⓐ Ⓑ Ⓒ Ⓓ Ⓔ   27. Ⓐ Ⓑ Ⓒ Ⓓ Ⓔ   34. Ⓐ Ⓑ Ⓒ Ⓓ Ⓔ
7. Ⓐ Ⓑ Ⓒ Ⓓ Ⓔ   14. Ⓐ Ⓑ Ⓒ Ⓓ Ⓔ   21. Ⓐ Ⓑ Ⓒ Ⓓ Ⓔ   28. Ⓐ Ⓑ Ⓒ Ⓓ Ⓔ   35. Ⓐ Ⓑ Ⓒ Ⓓ Ⓔ

Section 4: Critical Reading

1. Ⓐ Ⓑ Ⓒ Ⓓ Ⓔ   8. Ⓐ Ⓑ Ⓒ Ⓓ Ⓔ   15. Ⓐ Ⓑ Ⓒ Ⓓ Ⓔ   22. Ⓐ Ⓑ Ⓒ Ⓓ Ⓔ   29. Ⓐ Ⓑ Ⓒ Ⓓ Ⓔ
2. Ⓐ Ⓑ Ⓒ Ⓓ Ⓔ   9. Ⓐ Ⓑ Ⓒ Ⓓ Ⓔ   16. Ⓐ Ⓑ Ⓒ Ⓓ Ⓔ   23. Ⓐ Ⓑ Ⓒ Ⓓ Ⓔ   30. Ⓐ Ⓑ Ⓒ Ⓓ Ⓔ
3. Ⓐ Ⓑ Ⓒ Ⓓ Ⓔ   10. Ⓐ Ⓑ Ⓒ Ⓓ Ⓔ   17. Ⓐ Ⓑ Ⓒ Ⓓ Ⓔ   24. Ⓐ Ⓑ Ⓒ Ⓓ Ⓔ   31. Ⓐ Ⓑ Ⓒ Ⓓ Ⓔ
4. Ⓐ Ⓑ Ⓒ Ⓓ Ⓔ   11. Ⓐ Ⓑ Ⓒ Ⓓ Ⓔ   18. Ⓐ Ⓑ Ⓒ Ⓓ Ⓔ   25. Ⓐ Ⓑ Ⓒ Ⓓ Ⓔ   32. Ⓐ Ⓑ Ⓒ Ⓓ Ⓔ
5. Ⓐ Ⓑ Ⓒ Ⓓ Ⓔ   12. Ⓐ Ⓑ Ⓒ Ⓓ Ⓔ   19. Ⓐ Ⓑ Ⓒ Ⓓ Ⓔ   26. Ⓐ Ⓑ Ⓒ Ⓓ Ⓔ   33. Ⓐ Ⓑ Ⓒ Ⓓ Ⓔ
6. Ⓐ Ⓑ Ⓒ Ⓓ Ⓔ   13. Ⓐ Ⓑ Ⓒ Ⓓ Ⓔ   20. Ⓐ Ⓑ Ⓒ Ⓓ Ⓔ   27. Ⓐ Ⓑ Ⓒ Ⓓ Ⓔ   34. Ⓐ Ⓑ Ⓒ Ⓓ Ⓔ
7. Ⓐ Ⓑ Ⓒ Ⓓ Ⓔ   14. Ⓐ Ⓑ Ⓒ Ⓓ Ⓔ   21. Ⓐ Ⓑ Ⓒ Ⓓ Ⓔ   28. Ⓐ Ⓑ Ⓒ Ⓓ Ⓔ   35. Ⓐ Ⓑ Ⓒ Ⓓ Ⓔ

Section 5: Mathematics

1. Ⓐ Ⓑ Ⓒ Ⓓ Ⓔ   8. Ⓐ Ⓑ Ⓒ Ⓓ Ⓔ   15. Ⓐ Ⓑ Ⓒ Ⓓ Ⓔ   22. Ⓐ Ⓑ Ⓒ Ⓓ Ⓔ   29. Ⓐ Ⓑ Ⓒ Ⓓ Ⓔ
2. Ⓐ Ⓑ Ⓒ Ⓓ Ⓔ   9. Ⓐ Ⓑ Ⓒ Ⓓ Ⓔ   16. Ⓐ Ⓑ Ⓒ Ⓓ Ⓔ   23. Ⓐ Ⓑ Ⓒ Ⓓ Ⓔ   30. Ⓐ Ⓑ Ⓒ Ⓓ Ⓔ
3. Ⓐ Ⓑ Ⓒ Ⓓ Ⓔ   10. Ⓐ Ⓑ Ⓒ Ⓓ Ⓔ   17. Ⓐ Ⓑ Ⓒ Ⓓ Ⓔ   24. Ⓐ Ⓑ Ⓒ Ⓓ Ⓔ   31. Ⓐ Ⓑ Ⓒ Ⓓ Ⓔ
4. Ⓐ Ⓑ Ⓒ Ⓓ Ⓔ   11. Ⓐ Ⓑ Ⓒ Ⓓ Ⓔ   18. Ⓐ Ⓑ Ⓒ Ⓓ Ⓔ   25. Ⓐ Ⓑ Ⓒ Ⓓ Ⓔ   32. Ⓐ Ⓑ Ⓒ Ⓓ Ⓔ
5. Ⓐ Ⓑ Ⓒ Ⓓ Ⓔ   12. Ⓐ Ⓑ Ⓒ Ⓓ Ⓔ   19. Ⓐ Ⓑ Ⓒ Ⓓ Ⓔ   26. Ⓐ Ⓑ Ⓒ Ⓓ Ⓔ   33. Ⓐ Ⓑ Ⓒ Ⓓ Ⓔ
6. Ⓐ Ⓑ Ⓒ Ⓓ Ⓔ   13. Ⓐ Ⓑ Ⓒ Ⓓ Ⓔ   20. Ⓐ Ⓑ Ⓒ Ⓓ Ⓔ   27. Ⓐ Ⓑ Ⓒ Ⓓ Ⓔ   34. Ⓐ Ⓑ Ⓒ Ⓓ Ⓔ
7. Ⓐ Ⓑ Ⓒ Ⓓ Ⓔ   14. Ⓐ Ⓑ Ⓒ Ⓓ Ⓔ   21. Ⓐ Ⓑ Ⓒ Ⓓ Ⓔ   28. Ⓐ Ⓑ Ⓒ Ⓓ Ⓔ   35. Ⓐ Ⓑ Ⓒ Ⓓ Ⓔ

9.   10.   11.   12.   13.

14.   15.   16.   17.   18.

Section 6: Multiple-Choice Writing

1. Ⓐ Ⓑ Ⓒ Ⓓ Ⓔ   8. Ⓐ Ⓑ Ⓒ Ⓓ Ⓔ   15. Ⓐ Ⓑ Ⓒ Ⓓ Ⓔ   22. Ⓐ Ⓑ Ⓒ Ⓓ Ⓔ   29. Ⓐ Ⓑ Ⓒ Ⓓ Ⓔ
2. Ⓐ Ⓑ Ⓒ Ⓓ Ⓔ   9. Ⓐ Ⓑ Ⓒ Ⓓ Ⓔ   16. Ⓐ Ⓑ Ⓒ Ⓓ Ⓔ   23. Ⓐ Ⓑ Ⓒ Ⓓ Ⓔ   30. Ⓐ Ⓑ Ⓒ Ⓓ Ⓔ
3. Ⓐ Ⓑ Ⓒ Ⓓ Ⓔ   10. Ⓐ Ⓑ Ⓒ Ⓓ Ⓔ   17. Ⓐ Ⓑ Ⓒ Ⓓ Ⓔ   24. Ⓐ Ⓑ Ⓒ Ⓓ Ⓔ   31. Ⓐ Ⓑ Ⓒ Ⓓ Ⓔ
4. Ⓐ Ⓑ Ⓒ Ⓓ Ⓔ   11. Ⓐ Ⓑ Ⓒ Ⓓ Ⓔ   18. Ⓐ Ⓑ Ⓒ Ⓓ Ⓔ   25. Ⓐ Ⓑ Ⓒ Ⓓ Ⓔ   32. Ⓐ Ⓑ Ⓒ Ⓓ Ⓔ
5. Ⓐ Ⓑ Ⓒ Ⓓ Ⓔ   12. Ⓐ Ⓑ Ⓒ Ⓓ Ⓔ   19. Ⓐ Ⓑ Ⓒ Ⓓ Ⓔ   26. Ⓐ Ⓑ Ⓒ Ⓓ Ⓔ   33. Ⓐ Ⓑ Ⓒ Ⓓ Ⓔ
6. Ⓐ Ⓑ Ⓒ Ⓓ Ⓔ   13. Ⓐ Ⓑ Ⓒ Ⓓ Ⓔ   20. Ⓐ Ⓑ Ⓒ Ⓓ Ⓔ   27. Ⓐ Ⓑ Ⓒ Ⓓ Ⓔ   34. Ⓐ Ⓑ Ⓒ Ⓓ Ⓔ
7. Ⓐ Ⓑ Ⓒ Ⓓ Ⓔ   14. Ⓐ Ⓑ Ⓒ Ⓓ Ⓔ   21. Ⓐ Ⓑ Ⓒ Ⓓ Ⓔ   28. Ⓐ Ⓑ Ⓒ Ⓓ Ⓔ   35. Ⓐ Ⓑ Ⓒ Ⓓ Ⓔ

Section 7: Critical Reading

1. Ⓐ Ⓑ Ⓒ Ⓓ Ⓔ	8. Ⓐ Ⓑ Ⓒ Ⓓ Ⓔ	15. Ⓐ Ⓑ Ⓒ Ⓓ Ⓔ	22. Ⓐ Ⓑ Ⓒ Ⓓ Ⓔ	29. Ⓐ Ⓑ Ⓒ Ⓓ Ⓔ
2. Ⓐ Ⓑ Ⓒ Ⓓ Ⓔ	9. Ⓐ Ⓑ Ⓒ Ⓓ Ⓔ	16. Ⓐ Ⓑ Ⓒ Ⓓ Ⓔ	23. Ⓐ Ⓑ Ⓒ Ⓓ Ⓔ	30. Ⓐ Ⓑ Ⓒ Ⓓ Ⓔ
3. Ⓐ Ⓑ Ⓒ Ⓓ Ⓔ	10. Ⓐ Ⓑ Ⓒ Ⓓ Ⓔ	17. Ⓐ Ⓑ Ⓒ Ⓓ Ⓔ	24. Ⓐ Ⓑ Ⓒ Ⓓ Ⓔ	31. Ⓐ Ⓑ Ⓒ Ⓓ Ⓔ
4. Ⓐ Ⓑ Ⓒ Ⓓ Ⓔ	11. Ⓐ Ⓑ Ⓒ Ⓓ Ⓔ	18. Ⓐ Ⓑ Ⓒ Ⓓ Ⓔ	25. Ⓐ Ⓑ Ⓒ Ⓓ Ⓔ	32. Ⓐ Ⓑ Ⓒ Ⓓ Ⓔ
5. Ⓐ Ⓑ Ⓒ Ⓓ Ⓔ	12. Ⓐ Ⓑ Ⓒ Ⓓ Ⓔ	19. Ⓐ Ⓑ Ⓒ Ⓓ Ⓔ	26. Ⓐ Ⓑ Ⓒ Ⓓ Ⓔ	33. Ⓐ Ⓑ Ⓒ Ⓓ Ⓔ
6. Ⓐ Ⓑ Ⓒ Ⓓ Ⓔ	13. Ⓐ Ⓑ Ⓒ Ⓓ Ⓔ	20. Ⓐ Ⓑ Ⓒ Ⓓ Ⓔ	27. Ⓐ Ⓑ Ⓒ Ⓓ Ⓔ	34. Ⓐ Ⓑ Ⓒ Ⓓ Ⓔ
7. Ⓐ Ⓑ Ⓒ Ⓓ Ⓔ	14. Ⓐ Ⓑ Ⓒ Ⓓ Ⓔ	21. Ⓐ Ⓑ Ⓒ Ⓓ Ⓔ	28. Ⓐ Ⓑ Ⓒ Ⓓ Ⓔ	35. Ⓐ Ⓑ Ⓒ Ⓓ Ⓔ

Section 8: Mathematics

1. Ⓐ Ⓑ Ⓒ Ⓓ Ⓔ	8. Ⓐ Ⓑ Ⓒ Ⓓ Ⓔ	15. Ⓐ Ⓑ Ⓒ Ⓓ Ⓔ	22. Ⓐ Ⓑ Ⓒ Ⓓ Ⓔ	29. Ⓐ Ⓑ Ⓒ Ⓓ Ⓔ
2. Ⓐ Ⓑ Ⓒ Ⓓ Ⓔ	9. Ⓐ Ⓑ Ⓒ Ⓓ Ⓔ	16. Ⓐ Ⓑ Ⓒ Ⓓ Ⓔ	23. Ⓐ Ⓑ Ⓒ Ⓓ Ⓔ	30. Ⓐ Ⓑ Ⓒ Ⓓ Ⓔ
3. Ⓐ Ⓑ Ⓒ Ⓓ Ⓔ	10. Ⓐ Ⓑ Ⓒ Ⓓ Ⓔ	17. Ⓐ Ⓑ Ⓒ Ⓓ Ⓔ	24. Ⓐ Ⓑ Ⓒ Ⓓ Ⓔ	31. Ⓐ Ⓑ Ⓒ Ⓓ Ⓔ
4. Ⓐ Ⓑ Ⓒ Ⓓ Ⓔ	11. Ⓐ Ⓑ Ⓒ Ⓓ Ⓔ	18. Ⓐ Ⓑ Ⓒ Ⓓ Ⓔ	25. Ⓐ Ⓑ Ⓒ Ⓓ Ⓔ	32. Ⓐ Ⓑ Ⓒ Ⓓ Ⓔ
5. Ⓐ Ⓑ Ⓒ Ⓓ Ⓔ	12. Ⓐ Ⓑ Ⓒ Ⓓ Ⓔ	19. Ⓐ Ⓑ Ⓒ Ⓓ Ⓔ	26. Ⓐ Ⓑ Ⓒ Ⓓ Ⓔ	33. Ⓐ Ⓑ Ⓒ Ⓓ Ⓔ
6. Ⓐ Ⓑ Ⓒ Ⓓ Ⓔ	13. Ⓐ Ⓑ Ⓒ Ⓓ Ⓔ	20. Ⓐ Ⓑ Ⓒ Ⓓ Ⓔ	27. Ⓐ Ⓑ Ⓒ Ⓓ Ⓔ	34. Ⓐ Ⓑ Ⓒ Ⓓ Ⓔ
7. Ⓐ Ⓑ Ⓒ Ⓓ Ⓔ	14. Ⓐ Ⓑ Ⓒ Ⓓ Ⓔ	21. Ⓐ Ⓑ Ⓒ Ⓓ Ⓔ	28. Ⓐ Ⓑ Ⓒ Ⓓ Ⓔ	35. Ⓐ Ⓑ Ⓒ Ⓓ Ⓔ

Section 9: Multiple-Choice Writing

1. Ⓐ Ⓑ Ⓒ Ⓓ Ⓔ	8. Ⓐ Ⓑ Ⓒ Ⓓ Ⓔ	15. Ⓐ Ⓑ Ⓒ Ⓓ Ⓔ	22. Ⓐ Ⓑ Ⓒ Ⓓ Ⓔ	29. Ⓐ Ⓑ Ⓒ Ⓓ Ⓔ
2. Ⓐ Ⓑ Ⓒ Ⓓ Ⓔ	9. Ⓐ Ⓑ Ⓒ Ⓓ Ⓔ	16. Ⓐ Ⓑ Ⓒ Ⓓ Ⓔ	23. Ⓐ Ⓑ Ⓒ Ⓓ Ⓔ	30. Ⓐ Ⓑ Ⓒ Ⓓ Ⓔ
3. Ⓐ Ⓑ Ⓒ Ⓓ Ⓔ	10. Ⓐ Ⓑ Ⓒ Ⓓ Ⓔ	17. Ⓐ Ⓑ Ⓒ Ⓓ Ⓔ	24. Ⓐ Ⓑ Ⓒ Ⓓ Ⓔ	31. Ⓐ Ⓑ Ⓒ Ⓓ Ⓔ
4. Ⓐ Ⓑ Ⓒ Ⓓ Ⓔ	11. Ⓐ Ⓑ Ⓒ Ⓓ Ⓔ	18. Ⓐ Ⓑ Ⓒ Ⓓ Ⓔ	25. Ⓐ Ⓑ Ⓒ Ⓓ Ⓔ	32. Ⓐ Ⓑ Ⓒ Ⓓ Ⓔ
5. Ⓐ Ⓑ Ⓒ Ⓓ Ⓔ	12. Ⓐ Ⓑ Ⓒ Ⓓ Ⓔ	19. Ⓐ Ⓑ Ⓒ Ⓓ Ⓔ	26. Ⓐ Ⓑ Ⓒ Ⓓ Ⓔ	33. Ⓐ Ⓑ Ⓒ Ⓓ Ⓔ
6. Ⓐ Ⓑ Ⓒ Ⓓ Ⓔ	13. Ⓐ Ⓑ Ⓒ Ⓓ Ⓔ	20. Ⓐ Ⓑ Ⓒ Ⓓ Ⓔ	27. Ⓐ Ⓑ Ⓒ Ⓓ Ⓔ	34. Ⓐ Ⓑ Ⓒ Ⓓ Ⓔ
7. Ⓐ Ⓑ Ⓒ Ⓓ Ⓔ	14. Ⓐ Ⓑ Ⓒ Ⓓ Ⓔ	21. Ⓐ Ⓑ Ⓒ Ⓓ Ⓔ	28. Ⓐ Ⓑ Ⓒ Ⓓ Ⓔ	35. Ⓐ Ⓑ Ⓒ Ⓓ Ⓔ

Section 1

The Essay

Time: 25 minutes

Directions: In response to the following prompt, write an essay on a separate sheet of paper (the answer sheet). You may use extra space in the question booklet to take notes and to organize your thoughts, but only the answer sheet will be graded.

"Once a person's curiosity, on any subject, is aroused it is surprising just how far it may lead him in pursuit of its object, how readily it overcomes every obstacle." — Georges Ifrah

"Curiosity is one of the most permanent and certain characteristics of a vigorous intellect." — Samuel Johnson

Does curiosity help or harm? Discuss the role of curiosity in human life, drawing upon history, literature, current events, or your own experience and observations.

STOP YOU MAY CHECK YOUR WORK ON THIS SECTION ONLY.
DO NOT GO BACK TO ANY PREVIOUS SECTION.

Section 2

Critical Reading

Time: 25 minutes for 25 questions

Directions: Choose the *best* answer to each question. Mark the corresponding oval on the answer sheet.

Directions for Questions 1–8: Select the answer that *best* fits the meaning of the sentence.

Example: After he had broken the dining room window, Hal's mother _____ him.

(A) selected

(B) serenaded

(C) fooled

(D) scolded

(E) rewarded

The answer is (D).

---

1. Helen's response to the flood is not simply intellectual, but _____.

    (A) practical

    (B) theoretical

    (C) philosophical

    (D) ethical

    (E) strident

2. _____ research into the origins of Delkong culture indicates that a hunter-gatherer society was established about 2,000 years earlier than was previously thought.

    (A) Prior

    (B) Contemporary

    (C) Theoretical

    (D) Antiquated

    (E) Discredited

3. It has been suggested that the _____ references to architectural history _____ the paper's focus on engineering concepts.

    (A) documented . . . affect

    (B) sophisticated . . . enhance

    (C) myriad . . . weaken

    (D) impeccable . . . distort

    (E) obscure . . . sharpen

4. Its presence in all languages has led many to the conclusion that grammar is _____.

    (A) innate

    (B) inevitable

    (C) multifaceted

    (D) extraneous

    (E) coincidental

5. By subsidizing small business, the government hopes to _____ the once prosperous area.

    (A) stagnate

    (B) annex

    (C) enervate

    (D) aggrandize

    (E) reinvigorate

6. Although Deeplock has promised to shorten the agenda, the council is _____ about discussing the topic of global warming and will insist that it be included.

    (A) ambivalent

    (B) adamant

    (C) perplexed

    (D) apathetic

    (E) neutral

7. Notwithstanding the _____ effort on the part of the entire team, the championship went to the other division for the first time in ten years.

    (A) herculean

    (B) spontaneous

    (C) gratuitous

    (D) pluralistic

    (E) intermittent

Go on to next page

8. The revolt against Puritanism in the 18th century was perhaps more intense than the author's _____ conveys.

   (A) dissertation

   (B) historiography

   (C) memoir

   (D) polemic

   (E) diatribe

Directions for Questions 9–12: Choose the *best* answer to each question based on what is stated or implied in the passage or in the introductory material.

Questions 9 and 10 are based on the following passage, excerpted from The Transformational Leader *by Noel M. Tichy and Mary Anne Devanna (Wiley).*

Line   Clearly, the ability to decide what the mission and the strategy of the organization will be is a source of significant power. Technically focused textbooks and consulting groups advise
(05) organizations on how to do strategic planning, but they do not shed much light on how to allocate power in the actual strategic decision-making process. What levels of the organization should be involved in the process? Should tech-
(10) nical decisions be made by those with technical expertise or by general managers? Should the chairperson make the decision alone? A set of decisions must be made to determine who will influence the formulation of the mission and
(15) strategy.

9. Which statement is implied in the passage?

   (A) There are many different ways to come to a decision in a large organization.

   (B) The same person should not formulate both mission and strategy for an organization.

   (C) Powerful people are the only ones who should make a decision.

   (D) Textbooks that focus on technical matters are not useful.

   (E) All levels of an organization should be involved in decision making.

10. The author believes that power comes from

    (A) technical expertise

    (B) political connections

    (C) the ability to make decisions about goals and methods

    (D) job titles

    (E) recommendations made by consulting groups

Questions 11 and 12 are based on the following passage, excerpted from Physical Science in the Middle Ages *by Edward Grant (Wiley).*

Line   During the course of the fifth century, the Western half [of the Roman Empire] fell prey to invading Germanic tribes, and by 500 A.D., much of it was in their control. Despite subsequent efforts of the Eastern emperor, Justinian, only
(05) the trappings of Empire remained — the substance was dead, and Western Europe evolved new forms of social and governmental activity to cope with conditions drastically different from those of a few centuries earlier.
(10)

11. According to the passage, the Emperor Justinian

    (A) resigned his post as head of the Eastern half of the Roman Empire

    (B) designed new forms of social and governmental activity

    (C) attempted to maintain the power and organization of the Roman Empire at its height

    (D) was in favor of merging the Western and Eastern halves of the Roman Empire

    (E) fought against the Western half of the Roman Empire

12. What is the meaning of "trappings" in Line 6?

    (A) device to catch enemies

    (B) ornamental factors

    (C) bureaucracy

    (D) spirit

    (E) government

Go on to next page

Directions for Questions 13–25: Choose the *best* answer from among those given, based on what the author states or implies in the passage.

Questions 13 to 24 refer to the following passage, an excerpt from The Knight *by Alan Baker (Wiley), which discusses feudalism.*

Line [M]any attempts . . . have been made to analyze and define it [feudalism], attempts that are far from being closely related to one another. Bearing these caveats in mind, let us attempt a
(05) useful definition of feudalism that will be of some help in our understanding of the society in which the knight lived and operated. The feudal society came into existence in France, Germany, the Kingdom of Burgundy-Aries, and Italy in about
(10) the tenth century. Countries that came under their influence — England, some of the Christian kingdoms of Spain, and the Latin principalities of the Near East — also possessed feudal attributes. Although there are other countries, such
(15) as Egypt and India, that displayed some analogies with feudalism in the distant past, leading some historians to label them (controversially) as feudal, the society that most closely parallels the situation in medieval Europe is Japan.
(20) European feudalism was characterized by obligations of service (especially military service) between the vassal and his lord. In return for the vassal's service, the lord was obliged to offer protection and a livelihood to his vassal,
(25) including the land grant. In Japan the daimyos, bushi, or samurai were comparable to the vassals in Europe, and the land that was granted to them was more or less equivalent to that granted to the vassal by his lord in return for his service.
(30) In addition, an institution very close to vassalage prevailed in Russia between the thirteenth and sixteenth centuries.

In Europe the lord and the vassal were securely locked into a mutually beneficial
(35) arrangement: for the vassal there was protection and land; for the lord, there were days owed in military service, whether in battle or the garrisoning of the castle, plus counsel before embarking on an important course of action. Also among
(40) the vassal's obligations to his lord were the fee known as relief, when he received his land; the obligation to contribute to any ransom that might be demanded should his lord be captured; to contribute to his crusading expenses; and to
(45) help out when the lord's son was knighted or his daughter married. In addition, permission had to be sought if the vassal wished to marry, or to marry off his own daughter. Upon the vassal's death, his widow and children would be pro-
(50) vided for by the lord, who would see to their education and marriage; should he die without a wife or heirs, the land would revert to the lord.

It is easy to see that feudalism was, at its center, defined by the localization of political,
(55) military, and economic power in the hands of lords and their vassals, who exercised that power from their castle headquarters, each of which held complete sway over the district in which it was situated. The resulting hierarchy
(60) resembled a pyramid, with the lowest vassals at the base and the king, of course, at the summit. This was not the case in every nation, however; in Germany, for instance, the summit of the pyramid did not reach the king, being occupied
(65) instead by the great princes.

The results of feudalism were mixed, to say the least. On the negative side, it meant that the state had a relationship with the heads of groups rather than directly with individuals farther down
(70) the social scale. Under a weak king, these men claimed sovereignty for themselves, and fought among themselves rather than allowing the state to judge their claims. This resulted in the private wars that scarred the medieval landscape. The
(75) overlords claimed numerous rights for themselves, including that of issuing private coinage, building private castles, and the power to raise taxes. Each of these manorial groups tried to be self-sufficient and to consolidate its possessions.
(80) Skirmishes and all-out wars were frequent and accounted for much of the violence, precariousness, and unpredictability of medieval life. In addition, the powers possessed by the church meant that in times of disputed succession it
(85) claimed the right not only to defend itself and maintain order, but also to nominate the ruler. This, of course, made it impossible for the church to remain impartial in matters of state, and the cause of the church frequently became identified
(90) with a particular claimant.

This must be balanced against the positive results of feudalism; for instance, the cohesion it supplied to the nations in which it operated. In the absence of any mature concept of nationality
(95) in the centuries following the fall of the Roman Empire, feudalism supplied some measure of territorial organization, linking the Germanic and Roman political systems and providing a pyramidal hierarchy that resulted in at least
(100) a nominal political and economic stability.

Go on to next page

13. In Paragraph 1, the author implies that

    (A) feudalism originated in Japan

    (B) feudalism spread from England to Spain

    (C) it is generally agreed that Egypt and India had feudal societies

    (D) it is impossible to define feudalism

    (E) no single definition of feudalism will be accepted by all historians

14. According to Lines 1–19 (Paragraph 1), the most probable reason a form of feudalism existed in England and Spain is that

    (A) England and Spain were influenced by countries in which feudalism was well established

    (B) the merits of feudalism were overwhelming

    (C) the system was imposed by colonial powers

    (D) the system was spread by traders

    (E) knights traveling from one country to another needed feudalism to survive

15. The author mentions Russia (Lines 30–32)

    (A) as an additional example of a society with a full-fledged feudal system

    (B) to show that the vassal/lord relationship existed in countries without fully feudal societies

    (C) to contrast Russia's system of vassalage with Japan's

    (D) because Russia had no vassals

    (E) to prove that feudalism existed in the modern era

16. Based on this excerpt, what is the best definition of vassal?

    (A) a lord who commanded knights

    (B) a soldier who fought for his country

    (C) a noble who ruled over a substantial area

    (D) someone who served a lord in return for land and other rights

    (E) a tenant farmer who worked but did not own the land

17. Which idea is implied but not stated in the passage?

    (A) Land was the basis of wealth in feudal society.

    (B) Knights were at war more often than not.

    (C) Japanese daimyos were superior to European vassals.

    (D) Feudalism provided benefits only to the wealthy.

    (E) Marriage was a purely private decision.

18. All of the following are obligations owed to feudal lords by their vassals except

    (A) approval of marriage partners

    (B) erection of a castle

    (C) fees in return for land grants

    (D) financial support for important events

    (E) military service

19. According to the passage, feudal lords

    (A) were obliged to accept their vassals' advice

    (B) controlled the peasants

    (C) consulted with other lords before making important decisions

    (D) could seek advice from their vassals

    (E) found marriage partners for the children of their vassals

20. The author of the passage would most likely agree with which statement?

    (A) Feudalism was directly responsible for the instability of the medieval period.

    (B) Feudalism was weak in Germany because princes had too much power.

    (C) Feudalism worked best when religion played no role.

    (D) The feudal system did not work well in the absence of a strong king.

    (E) Feudalism protected the rights of women.

Go on to next page

21. In Line 60, the pyramid analogy implies that

    (A) German feudalism was unstable

    (B) castles were constructed in the same way as pyramids

    (C) the king's power equaled that of the ancient Egyptian pharaohs

    (D) all vassals were equal

    (E) vassals had varying degrees of power

22. The word "this" in Line 91 refers to

    (A) feudalism

    (B) the violence and unpredictability of medieval life

    (C) the impartiality of the church in matters of politics

    (D) the link between the church and a particular claimant of the throne

    (E) all the disadvantages of feudalism described in the preceding paragraph

23. What is the closest meaning of "nominal" (Line 100)?

    (A) alleged to be true

    (B) just enough to deserve the name

    (C) justified under the circumstances

    (D) supposed to be true

    (E) purportedly

24. The author's tone may best be described as

    (A) dispassionate

    (B) strident

    (C) didactic

    (D) satirical

    (E) critical

25. The best title for this passage is

    (A) Feudalism in Europe and Japan

    (B) A Definition of Feudalism

    (C) The Rights of Vassals

    (D) The Disadvantages of Feudalism

    (E) The Pyramid of Power

STOP YOU MAY CHECK YOUR WORK ON THIS SECTION ONLY. DO NOT GO BACK TO ANY PREVIOUS SECTION.

Section 3
Mathematics

Time: 25 minutes for 20 questions

Directions: Choose the *best* answer to each question. Mark the corresponding oval on the answer sheet.

Notes:

✔ You may use a calculator.

✔ All numbers used in this exam are real numbers.

✔ All figures lie in a plane.

✔ All figures may be assumed to be to scale unless the problem specifically indicates otherwise.

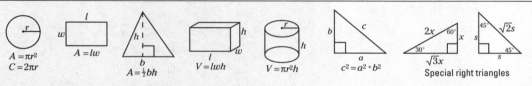

$A = \pi r^2$
$C = 2\pi r$

$A = lw$

$A = \frac{1}{2}bh$

$V = lwh$

$V = \pi r^2 h$

$c^2 = a^2 + b^2$

Special right triangles

There are 360 degrees of arc in a circle.

There are 180 degrees in a straight line.

There are 180 degrees in the sum of the interior angles of a triangle.

1. In a 28-student class, the ratio of boys to girls is 3:4. How many girls are there in the class?

   (A) 4

   (B) 9

   (C) 12

   (D) 16

   (E) 25

2. If $f(x) = 2x^4$, then $f(-2) =$

   (A) −256

   (B) −32

   (C) 0

   (D) 32

   (E) 256

3. In a drawer are seven pairs of white socks, nine pairs of black socks, and six pairs of brown socks. Getting dressed in a hurry, Josh pulls out a pair at a time and tosses them on the floor if they are not the color he wants. Looking for a brown pair, Josh pulls out and discards a white pair, a black pair, a black pair, and a white pair. What is the probability that on his next reach into the drawer he will pull out a brown pair of socks?

   (A) ⅓

   (B) ³⁄₁₁

   (C) ⁶⁄₁₇

   (D) ⁷⁄₁₈

   (E) ⁹⁄₂₂

Go on to next page

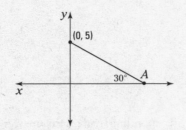

4. What are the coordinates of point A in the diagram above?

    (A) $(0, 10)$

    (B) $(5, 0)$

    (C) $\left(5\sqrt{3}, 0\right)$

    (D) $(10, 0)$

    (E) $\left(10\sqrt{3},\ 0\right)$

5. Evaluate $\left(4^0 + 64^{1/2}\right)^{-2}$.

    (A) -81

    (B) $\frac{1}{81}$

    (C) $\frac{1}{9}$

    (D) 3

    (E) 6

6. The ratio of Dora's money to Lisa's money is 7:5. If Dora has \$24 more than Lisa, how much does Dora have?

    (A) \$10

    (B) \$14

    (C) \$60

    (D) \$84

    (E) \$144

7. In a triangle, the second side is 3 cm longer than the first side. The length of the third side is 5 cm less than twice the length of the first side. If the perimeter is 34 cm, find the length, in centimeters, of the *longest* side.

    (A) 3

    (B) 8

    (C) 9

    (D) 12

    (E) 13

8. On a number line, point A is at -4 and point B is at 8. What point is $\frac{1}{4}$ of the way from A to B?

    (A) -2

    (B) -1

    (C) 0

    (D) 1

    (E) 2

9. If $2y - c = 3c$, then $y =$

    (A) $\frac{c}{2}$

    (B) c

    (C) $\frac{3c}{2}$

    (D) $2c$

    (E) $3c$

10. If $\dfrac{x-1}{x-2} = \dfrac{x+7}{x+2}$, then x equals

    (A) 1

    (B) 2

    (C) 3

    (D) 4

    (E) 5

11. Let $\&x$ be defined as $x + 3$ if x is prime, and as $2x$ if x is composite. Which of the following would produce a result of 18?

    I. $\&15$

    II. $\&9$

    III. $\&36$

    (A) I only

    (B) II only

    (C) III only

    (D) both I and II

    (E) both II and III

Go on to next page

12. The volume of a gas, *V*, in cubic centimeters (cc), is directly proportional to its temperature, *T*, in Kelvins (K). If a gas has a volume of 31.5 cc at 210 K, then its volume at 300 K would be

(A) 121.5 cc

(B) 49 cc

(C) 45 cc

(D) 22.05 cc

(E) 0.805 cc

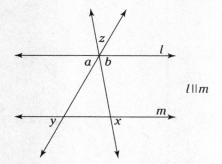

14. In this diagram (not drawn to scale), *x* = 70°, *y* = 30°. The sum *a* + *b* + *z* equals

(A) 40°

(B) 90°

(C) 100°

(D) 120°

(E) 180°

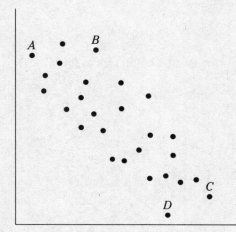

13. If the data in the scatterplot above were approximated by a linear function, the line would come *closest* to which pair of points?

(A) *A* and *B*

(B) *A* and *C*

(C) *A* and *D*

(D) *B* and *C*

(E) *C* and *D*

15. In a sequence of evenly spaced numbers, the first term is 7, and the 20th term is 159. The fourth term of the sequence would be

(A) 32

(B) 31

(C) 30

(D) 29

(E) 28

Go on to next page

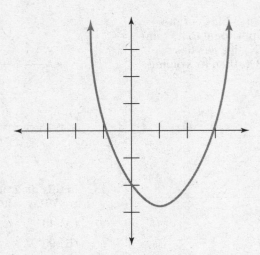

16. This graph represents a function, **f**(x). Which of the following graphs could represent **f**(x + 4)?

(A)

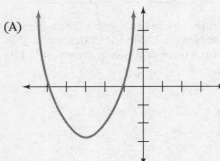

(B)

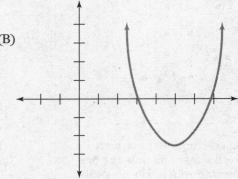

(C)

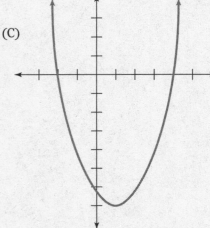

(D)

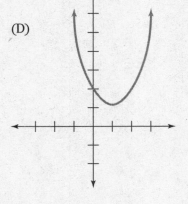

(E)

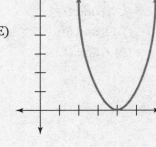

Go on to next page

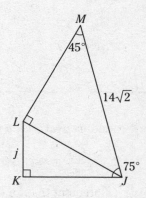

17. In this diagram, the measure of side *j* is

(A) 7

(B) $7\sqrt{2}$

(C) $7\sqrt{3}$

(D) 14

(E) $14\sqrt{2}$

18. In a class of 100 students, 65 take Spanish, 32 take art, and 14 take both Spanish and art. How many students do not take either Spanish or art?

(A) 3

(B) 11

(C) 17

(D) 18

(E) 35

19. Max has 3 hours to study for his tests the next day. He decides to spend *k* percent of this time studying for math. Which of the following represents the number of minutes he will spend studying for math?

(A) $k/300$

(B) $3k/100$

(C) $100k/180$

(D) $180k/100$

(E) $18,000/k$

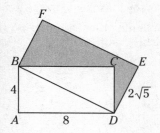

20. Given that *ABCD* and *BDEF* are rectangles, find the shaded area in this diagram.

(A) 24

(B) $16\sqrt{5}$

(C) 20

(D) $8\sqrt{5}$

(E) 16

Section 4
Critical Reading

Time: 25 minutes for 24 questions

Directions: Choose the *best* answer to each question. Mark the corresponding oval on the answer sheet.

Directions for Questions 1–9: Select the answer that *best* fits the meaning of the sentence.

Example: Winning the prize, Harold was _____ in praising his competitors.

(A) negligent

(B) obstinate

(C) ridiculous

(D) gracious

(E) foolish

The answer is (D).

1. Elwood was admired by the citizens of the town who knew him, yet _____ by strangers who had merely read of his actions in the paper.

   (A) ignored

   (B) revered

   (C) esteemed

   (D) condemned

   (E) adored

2. The ambassadors assumed an early end to hostilities, despite _____ from rebel groups.

   (A) resistance

   (B) surrender

   (C) withdrawal

   (D) compromise

   (E) interrogation

3. The mayor's statement that funds for police and firefighters should be _____ was belied by her insistence that taxes be _____.

   (A) enhanced . . . raised

   (B) decreased . . . lowered

   (C) increased . . . slashed

   (D) cut . . . frozen

   (E) expanded . . . suspended

4. The Supreme Court's decision in Brown vs. Board of Education _____ legalized segregation, but more than a half century later, separate schools for black and white children _____.

   (A) sanctioned . . . flourish

   (B) outlawed . . . persist

   (C) permitted . . . lag

   (D) terminated . . . intimidate

   (E) promoted . . . exist

5. Jane Austen wrote many of her novels in a small parlor in the family home in Chawton, relying on a squeaky door to _____ her when visitors approached so that she could hide her manuscript and thus _____ her work.

   (A) entertain . . . publicize

   (B) warn . . . reveal

   (C) surprise . . . disguise

   (D) rationalize . . . preserve

   (E) alert . . . conceal

Go on to next page

6. Although the opposing factions were not able to achieve _____, they left the jury room in _____.

   (A) unity . . . discord
   (B) agreement . . . anger
   (C) leniency . . . silence
   (D) consensus . . . amity
   (E) deliberations . . . disarray

7. After studying cancer for many decades, scientists have come to the conclusion that cancer is not one disease but rather a(n) _____ of conditions with _____ symptoms, ranging from solid tumors to an unchecked proliferation of white blood cells.

   (A) predominance . . . equal
   (B) variety . . . opposing
   (C) array . . . identical
   (D) cluster . . . diverse
   (E) catalog . . . congruent

8. When she won the lottery, her friends expected Eleanor to be _____, but she was surprisingly _____.

   (A) jovial . . . affable
   (B) elated . . . mirthful
   (C) depressed . . . morose
   (D) intimidated . . . confident
   (E) acrimonious . . . cheerful

9. The display of religious artifacts in that store is quite _____, including pieces from many periods and nations.

   (A) ubiquitous
   (B) eclectic
   (C) international
   (D) parochial
   (E) ecclesiastical

Directions for Questions 10–24: Base your answers on information in either or both of the following passages. You may also answer questions on what is implied in the passages or about the relationship between the two passages.

Passages I and II are drawn from Into the House of Ancestors: Inside the New Africa *by Karl Maier (Wiley).*

Passage 1

Joram Mariga never left home without his pocket knife. When he was not working as a government agricultural worker, he could usually be found whittling away on some piece of scrapwood that he picked up while riding his motorcycle along the myriad trails that wind through the majestic mountains of eastern Zimbabwe. He was always cutting, chipping, slicing, and shaping wood, something he and his brothers had been doing since they were teenagers. Enjoyment of crafts, of working with the hands, ran in the family. His mother Edina was particularly gifted at pottery, but it was Mariga's father Sindoga who stirred their interest in carving. "We grew up loving to carve, and I did it just to please myself," Mariga says. He taught his two best friends, Robert and Titus, to carve too.

Mariga was a worker for the Ministry of Agriculture in the mid-1950s in Nyanga, a picturesque region of stunning peaks, forests, lakes, and waterfalls straddling the border with Mozambique, to help small farmers improve their crop production. As he journeyed up and down the hills on his government-issued BSA 350cc motorcycle, it became apparent that what the area and its farmers needed most were roads. "There were only tracks and only a few big enough to be called roads. It was difficult for the small farmers to bring their produce to the markets." Mariga took charge of a work gang of forty men and two tractors to clear a road to the district administrator's office. "The tractors just plowed along, pushing all the stones to one side. I never thought anything about them. They were rocks."

Then, one cool sunny day in August 1958, at the base of a rocky outcrop known as a kopje, the grader blades chipped off a piece of a remarkable stone that caught Mariga's eye. "I admired the color of that small stone. It was greenish, and when you picked it up, you could feel that it was slippery, like soap. I didn't know what it was, and I had never seen anything like it. If you looked through it facing the rays of the sun, it was a little bit translucent." Only later did he learn that he had found a piece of soapstone. Mariga continued with the job of clearing the road that day, but he could not stop fiddling with the stone. As usual, when it was time for a break, out came his knife. "I decided, since it is so slippery, why can't I use my pocket knife on it? And when I did, the knife was able to cut it easily."

From that moment on, Mariga, at the age of 31, became obsessed with stone carving, a fixation that over the next four decades would spawn

Line (05) (10) (15) (20) (25) (30) (35) (40) (45) (50)

Go on to next page

(55) one of the most exciting movements in modern African art. It took years and almost a divine amount of luck and coincidence to develop, but when it did, the sculpture from Zimbabwe would be exhibited all over the world and would fetch (60) tens of thousands of dollars apiece on the international market. The sculptors themselves were transformed from largely illiterate farmers and unemployed workers to ambassadors for their country and their continent.

Passage II

(65)   At the end of the twentieth century, education stands at a crossroads in Africa. While weakening central governments, ever-tightening budgets, and armed conflict have undermined the ambitious plans for training drawn up after independence, (70) everyone agrees that higher educational standards are a prerequisite to economic growth. All the reform programs and much-sought-after foreign investment will make little difference unless Africa's citizens are armed with the necessary intel- (75) lectual firepower to capitalize on them. Building modern economies and establishing democratic political systems without an educated citizenry would be comparable to trying to run a computer without software. Investment in primary education, (80) says the World Bank, is the single biggest factor that sets off the phenomenal growth of the Southeast Asian "tiger" economies from those of the rest of the Third World. John Nkoma, a professor of physics and dean of the Faculty of Science at (85) the University of Botswana, believes homegrown technology must play a role: "Science has been a potent force in driving the technological development of the industrialized countries of Asia. Clearly Africa and the Third World in general cannot be an (90) exception." Unfortunately, right now Africa's drive for knowledge is in reverse gear. Spending on research and development is less than half of 1 percent of the world's total. Roughly half of all grade-school-age children are not enrolled. If atten- (95) dance continues to fall at the current rate, 59 million African children will be out of school by the year 2000. There is only one region in the world where the percentage of children who do not attend school is rising. It is Africa.

(100)   By all accounts, something must be done quickly to reverse the trend. Part of the answer lies in governments allocating more funds to education, spending those resources more efficiently, and placing greater emphasis on educat- (105) ing young girls, who right now are twice as likely to drop out of school as boys. State intervention alone is not enough, especially where governments increasingly lack the economic and political power to effect change.

10. What is the primary purpose of the first paragraph (Lines 1–17) of Passage I?

(A) to explain the importance of artistic expression

(B) to orient the reader to conditions in Africa

(C) to introduce Joram Mariga and his family and friends

(D) to show the geographical setting for the events in the passage

(E) to explain the basis of Mariga's discovery

11. Mariga's journeys into the mountains (Lines 23–29)

(A) were made more difficult by road crews

(B) became impossible because of poor road conditions

(C) enabled him to understand the difficulties farmers faced getting their crops to market

(D) allowed him to carve

(E) were intended to explore local artwork

12. All of the following words may describe the soapstone that Mariga discovered except

(A) slick

(B) smooth

(C) green

(D) opaque

(E) soft

13. The passage implies but does not state that Joram Mariga

(A) could not fully appreciate the potential marketing value of soapstone carvings

(B) had no artistic training

(C) gave up his government job in order to concentrate on art

(D) taught many Africans to carve soapstone

(E) was not interested in his job with the Ministry of Agriculture

Go on to next page

14. The "largely illiterate farmers and unemployed workers" became "ambassadors for their country and their continent" (Lines 62–64) because

    (A) the Ministry of Agriculture deals with many foreign countries

    (B) the government employed them

    (C) their carvings show the creativity and artistry of Africans to all who bought them

    (D) they traveled to other countries to sell their artwork

    (E) they easily moved their product to market once the roads were improved

15. Education in Africa "stands at a crossroads" (Line 66) because

    (A) Africans must choose between technology and traditional education

    (B) the plans for educational advancement have been undermined by political and economic problems

    (C) Africans must develop strong governments before educational improvements can be made

    (D) without changes, education may deteriorate so completely that reform becomes impossible

    (E) governments do not want to educate children

16. The comparison between an uneducated citizenry in a democracy to "a computer without software" (Lines 78–79)

    (A) shows that education is necessary for sound political choices

    (B) highlights the importance of technology

    (C) illustrates that education is a political act

    (D) reveals the way in which education is influenced by politics

    (E) emphasizes that citizens must vote in order for democracy to work

17. In Passage II, the author cites all of the following factors as important to African development except

    (A) technology

    (B) foreign investment

    (C) education

    (D) respect for traditional ways

    (E) women's rights

18. In comparison to the economies of Southeast Asia (Line 82), Africa

    (A) has more foreign aid

    (B) invests less in technology

    (C) invests more money in university education

    (D) invests more money in primary education

    (E) invests less money in primary education

19. John Nkomas (Lines 83–90) is quoted because

    (A) he challenges the importance of education

    (B) "homegrown" technology cannot exist without good education

    (C) he admires the economies of Asia

    (D) he favors economic growth

    (E) physics is a subject taught in schools

20. In the context of Passage II, which best describes the meaning of "tiger" (Line 82)?

    (A) endangered

    (B) predatory

    (C) powerful

    (D) dangerous

    (E) fierce

Go on to next page

21. Which statement would the author be most likely to add to Passage II?

(A) Foreign nations should establish schools in Africa.

(B) Communities and private individuals must support education.

(C) Educational reform is dependent upon good government policy.

(D) Africa should hire teachers from Southeast Asia.

(E) Taxes to support education must be increased.

22. Between Passage I and Passage II, the author's attitude toward Africa changes

(A) from optimism about African development to apathy

(B) from faith in the power of individuals to calls for government and community action

(C) from admiration for traditional crafts to skepticism about their market potential

(D) from respect for government employees to doubts about their dedication

(E) by becoming more feminist

23. Both passages are primarily concerned with

(A) the hardships of African life

(B) the future of Africa

(C) the role of government in Africa

(D) the link between politics and social welfare

(E) the development of the African economy

24. Which statement best compares the two passages?

(A) Passage II is more general than Passage I.

(B) Passage I is less descriptive than Passage II.

(C) Passage I takes a less personal viewpoint than Passage II.

(D) Passage II illustrates the points made in Passage I.

(E) Both passages use narrative to make a point.

STOP DO NOT TURN THE PAGE UNTIL TOLD TO DO SO. DO NOT RETURN TO A PREVIOUS TEST.

Section 5

Mathematics

Time: 25 minutes for 18 questions

Directions: This section contains two different types of questions. For Questions 1–8, choose the *best* answer to each question. Mark the corresponding oval on the answer sheet. For Questions 9–18, follow the separate directions provided before those questions.

Notes:

↙ You may use a calculator.

↙ All numbers used in this exam are real numbers.

↙ All figures lie in a plane.

↙ All figures may be assumed to be to scale unless the problem specifically indicates otherwise.

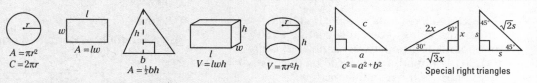

$$A = \pi r^2 \qquad A = lw \qquad A = \tfrac{1}{2}bh \qquad V = lwh \qquad V = \pi r^2 h \qquad c^2 = a^2 + b^2$$
$$C = 2\pi r$$

Special right triangles

There are 360 degrees of arc in a circle.

There are 180 degrees in a straight line.

There are 180 degrees in the sum of the interior angles of a triangle.

1. If the distance from Springfield to Watertown is 13 miles, and the distance from Watertown to Pleasantville is 24 miles, then the distance from Pleasantville to Springfield in miles could not be:

(A) 10

(B) 12

(C) 13

(D) 24

(E) 36

2. In a certain game, there are only two ways to score points; one way is worth 3 points, and the other is worth 5 points. If Tamsin's total score is 61, which of the following could be the number of 3-point scores that Tamsin had?

(A) 10

(B) 11

(C) 12

(D) 13

(E) 14

Go on to next page

3. A number, *n*, is defined as a "tweener" if both $n - 1$ and $n + 1$ are prime. Which of the following numbers is a tweener?

    (A) 2

    (B) 8

    (C) 30

    (D) 36

    (E) 48

4. If the square of *x* is 12 less than the product of *x* and 5, which of the following expressions could be used to solve for *x*?

    (A) $x^2 = 5x - 12$

    (B) $x^2 = 12 - 5x$

    (C) $2x = 12 - 5x$

    (D) $2x = 5x - 12$

    (E) $x^2 = (x + 5) - 12$

5. A batch of mixed nuts was created by adding 5 pounds of peanuts, costing $5.50 per pound, to 2 pounds of cashews, costing $12.50 per pound. What would be the cost, per pound, of the resulting mixture?

    (A) $7.35

    (B) $7.50

    (C) $9.00

    (D) $10.50

    (E) $12.00

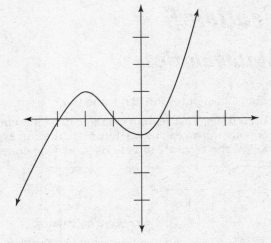

6. If this graph represents *f*(*x*), then the number of solutions to the equation *f*(*x*) = 1 is

    (A) zero

    (B) one

    (C) two

    (D) three

    (E) It cannot be determined from the information given.

7. The solution set to the equation $|3x - 1| = 7$ is

    (A) {2}

    (B) {2⅔}

    (C) {–2}

    (D) {–2, 2⅔}

    (E) {–2, 2}

8. A square is changed into a rectangle by adding 3 meters to one side and subtracting 2 meters from the other side. The new rectangle has an area of 50 square meters. Find the original length of a side of the square.

    (A) 5 meters

    (B) 6 meters

    (C) 7 meters

    (D) 8 meters

    (E) 9 meters

Go on to next page

Directions for student-produced response Questions 9–18: Solve the problem and then write your answer in the boxes on the answer sheet. Then mark the ovals corresponding to your answer, as shown in the following example. Note the fraction line and the decimal points.

Answer: 7/2

Answer: 3.25

Answer: 853

Write your answer in the box. You may start your answer in any column.

Although you do not have to write the solutions in the boxes, you do have to blacken the corresponding ovals. You should fill in the boxes to avoid confusion. Only the blackened ovals will be scored. The numbers in the boxes will not be read.

There are no negative answers.

Mixed numbers, such as 3½, must be gridded in as decimals (3.5) or as fractions (7/2). Do not grid in 3½; it will be read as 31/2.

Grid in a decimal as far as possible. Do not round your answer and leave some boxes empty.

A question may have more than one answer. Grid in only one answer.

9. Lauren took four exams. Her scores on the first three are 89, 85, and 90. If her average (arithmetic mean) on all four exams is 90, what did she get on the fourth exam?

10. In a school survey, 40% of all students chose history as their favorite subject; 25% chose English; and 14 chose some other subject as their favorite. How many students were surveyed?

11. Find the value of x that satisfies $\sqrt{4x-8}+1=7$.

12. For all numbers p and q, where $p \neq 4$, let $p \backslash\backslash q$ be defined as $\dfrac{pq}{p-4}$. For what value of p does $p\backslash\backslash 7 = 21$?

13. The ratio of a rectangle's width to its length is 2:5. If its perimeter is 84 feet, find its width, in feet.

14. Renting a private party room in a restaurant can be modeled as a linear function. If the cost of a party of 8 is $270, and the cost of a party of 10 is $320, find the cost, in dollars, of a party of 18.

Go on to next page

15. Darren receives $9 an hour for his after-school job, but gets paid 1½ times this salary for each hour he works on a week-end. If he worked 18 hours one week and received $189, how many of these hours did he work on weekends?

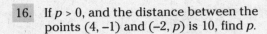

16. If $p > 0$, and the distance between the points $(4, -1)$ and $(-2, p)$ is 10, find p.

17. If $a - b = 8$ and $ab = 10$, then $a^2 + b^2 =$

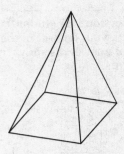

18. The pyramid above has a square base of length 10 cm and a height of 12 cm. Determine the total surface area of all five faces, in square centimeters.

STOP YOU MAY CHECK YOUR WORK ON THIS SECTION ONLY.
DO NOT GO BACK TO ANY PREVIOUS SECTION.

Section 6
Multiple-Choice Writing

Time: 25 minutes for 35 questions

Directions: Choose the *best* answer to each question. Mark the corresponding oval on the answer sheet.

Directions for Questions 1–18: Each sentence is followed by five choices. Choose the answer that *best* improves the sentence. If the underlined portion of the sentence is best left alone, choose (A).

Example: <u>Bert and him went</u> to the store to buy boots in preparation for the approaching storm.

(A) Bert and him went

(B) Bert and he went

(C) Bert and he had gone

(D) Bert and him had gone

(E) Bert and himself went

The correct answer is (B).

1. Jenny finds that she has time only for playing sports and studying, <u>not to audition for the school musical as well</u>.

    (A) not to audition for the school musical as well

    (B) not for auditioning for the school musical as well

    (C) and to audition for the school musical there is not enough time

    (D) and no time to audition for the school musical also

    (E) but also not to audition for the school musical

2. Yesterday the weather forecaster noted a sharp fall in barometric <u>pressure, this is an indication</u> that a storm is coming.

    (A) pressure, this is an indication

    (B) pressure; and this is an indication

    (C) pressure, which is an indication

    (D) pressure, which had indicated

    (E) pressure, and indicates

3. The lion had a thorn <u>in it's paw, but</u> the zookeeper was able to take care of the problem.

    (A) in it's paw, but

    (B) in its paw, but

    (C) in it's paw but

    (D) in its paw but

    (E) in its' paw, but

4. The Native American guides <u>objected to him trespassing</u> on sacred ground.

    (A) objected to him trespassing

    (B) has objected to him trespassing

    (C) objected to him having trespassed

    (D) objected that he trespassed

    (E) objected to his trespassing

Go on to next page

5. <u>Just between you and I, the school board would like</u> to place less emphasis on standardized tests.

(A) Just between you and I, the school board would like

(B) Just between you and I, the school board likes

(C) Just between you and me, the school board would like

(D) Between just you and I, the school board would like

(E) Between just you and I, the school board likes

6. At present, <u>Max's family traveled</u> to California eight years in a row.

(A) Max's family traveled

(B) everyone in Max's family traveled

(C) Max's family has traveled

(D) Max's family had traveled

(E) Max's family will have traveled

7. <u>Impatiently waiting at the curb, the taxi sped past the toddler who was holding his mama's hand.</u>

(A) Impatiently waiting at the curb, the taxi sped past the toddler who was holding his mama's hand.

(B) The taxi sped past the toddler who was holding his mama's hand impatiently waiting at the curb.

(C) Impatiently waiting at the curb, the toddler watched the taxi speed past, holding his mama's hand.

(D) The toddler impatiently waiting at the curb held his mama's hand and watched the taxi speed past.

(E) The toddler impatiently waiting at the curb held his mama's hand, and watched the taxi speed past.

8. Duke's rubber bone is one of those adorable dog <u>toys that are sold in every petshop.</u>

(A) toys that are sold in every petshop.

(B) toys which are sold in every petshop.

(C) toys that is sold in every petshop.

(D) toys, that is sold in every petshop.

(E) toys, that are sold in every petshop.

9. The reason <u>protestors object to the biology curriculum is because</u> they believe that students should not dissect a frog.

(A) protestors object to the biology curriculum is because

(B) protestors object to the biology curriculum is that

(C) protestors, they object to the biology curriculum is because

(D) the biology curriculum was objected to by protestors is because

(E) the biology curriculum had been protested is that

10. Tim can't understand <u>why Olivia doesn't write as well as him.</u>

(A) why Olivia doesn't write as well as him

(B) how Olivia doesn't write as well as him

(C) the reason why Olivia doesn't write as well as him

(D) why Olivia doesn't write as well as he

(E) why Olivia didn't write as well as him

11. The executive chef prepared the delicious and nutritious <u>casserole, however his assistant deserved</u> all the credit for developing the recipe.

(A) casserole, however his assistant deserved

(B) casserole; however his assistant had deserved

(C) casserole, however, his assistant deserved

(D) casserole however his assistant was deserving of

(E) casserole; however, his assistant deserved

Go on to next page →

12. Deborah gave a piece of birthday cake <u>to whomever she thought would eat it</u>.

    (A) to whomever she thought would eat it

    (B) to whomever she thought would like to eat it

    (C) to whoever she thought would eat it

    (D) to whoever she thought would have eaten it

    (E) to whomever she thought would have eaten it

13. The gas station <u>stood where the supermarket was</u>.

    (A) stood where the supermarket was

    (B) stood where the supermarket has been

    (C) had stood where the supermarket had been

    (D) stood, where the supermarket was

    (E) stood where the supermarket had been

14. Neither the teacher nor the students <u>was willing to forgo the class trip and substitute</u> a virtual tour of the museum.

    (A) was willing to forgo the class trip and substitute

    (B) were willing to forgo the class trip and they would substitute

    (C) was willing to forgo the class trip, but substituting

    (D) were willing to forgo the class trip and substitute

    (E) was willing to forgo the class trip, substituting

15. <u>In the newspaper it says that</u> the state colleges are considering a tuition increase to meet rising costs.

    (A) In the newspaper it says that

    (B) In the newspaper the article says that

    (C) The newspaper reports that

    (D) The newspaper, says that

    (E) The newspaper it says that

16. The results of that scientific study are considered suspect because of possible bias on the part of the researchers, <u>who were funded by a pharmaceutical company</u>.

    (A) who were funded by a pharmaceutical company

    (B) and the study was funded by a pharmaceutical company

    (C) because the study, which was funded by a pharmaceutical company

    (D) of pharmaceutical company's funding

    (E) in that the pharmaceutical company funded it

17. The Czech Republic and Slovakia were once united as "Czechoslovakia," <u>and the groups had two different languages and traditions</u>.

    (A) and the groups had two different languages and traditions

    (B) although the groups had two different languages and traditions

    (C) and they had two different languages and traditions

    (D) despite the fact that the groups were those who had two different languages and traditions

    (E) two different languages and traditions were in the country

18. The faulty part may cause the stroller to collapse, <u>and this is why the company has recalled the product</u>.

    (A) and this is why the company has recalled the product

    (B) therefore the company has recalled the product

    (C) so the company has recalled the product

    (D) which is why the company has recalled the product

    (E) and the company recalled the product for this reason

Go on to next page

Directions for Questions 19–29: In each of the following sentences, identify the underlined portion that contains an error. If a sentence contains no errors, choose (E) for "no error."

Example:

    <u>Irregardless</u> of the fact that the National
      A
Weather Service <u>predicted rain,</u> Dexter
             B
<u>resented</u> the <u>students' request</u> to postpone
  C   D
the picnic. <u>No error.</u>
           E

The correct answer is (A).

---

19. Annie <u>announced that</u> everyone
          A
<u>should bring</u> <u>their gym equipment</u> to the
   B   C
<u>track meet</u> so that she can determine the
   D
most marketable sports logo. <u>No error.</u>
                     E

20. The <u>costliest option</u> of the two plans
      A
<u>he offered</u> would have cost <u>us</u> more <u>than</u> a
  B   C   D
million dollars. <u>No error.</u>
         E

21. <u>Because</u> she found the <u>charity's video</u> so
  A   B
<u>inspiring, Kirsten</u> decided to donate
    C
<u>three years'</u> salary to the children's educa-
   D
tion fund. <u>No error.</u>
        E

22. Janine <u>will try</u> <u>and determine</u> the best time
     A   B
to wash the car, <u>but</u> no matter when
          C
<u>we start</u>, we must finish before the rain
  D
begins. <u>No error.</u>
      E

23. Most of <u>his fencing buddies</u> <u>have suffered</u>
       A   B
from <u>the sport</u>; fortunately the padding
    C
<u>nearly prevents every</u> serious wound.
   D
<u>No error.</u>
 E

24. Archie <u>has taught himself</u> to perform
      A
several difficult <u>gymnastic moves,</u> <u>which</u>
        B   C
he does better <u>than anyone on his team</u>.
         D
<u>No error.</u>
 E

25. The janitor <u>generally checked</u> for broken
        A
<u>windows only</u> when an inspector was
  B
<u>due, consequently</u>, a surprise visit from
   C
the superintendent <u>was quite</u> unwelcome.
        D
<u>No error.</u>
 E

26. One of the students in <u>Albert's</u> comedy
          A
class, along with three aspiring screenwrit-
ers, <u>are going</u> to Hollywood <u>to meet</u> with an
   B   C
agent <u>who may be able to sell</u> the script for
     D
a great deal of money. <u>No error.</u>
           E

27. Henry <u>can't remember who</u> he should bill
     A
for the broken <u>window, but</u> he <u>knows that</u>
        B   C
the responsibility belongs to <u>someone</u> on
        D
the baseball team. <u>No error.</u>
       E

28. <u>Marisa told</u> her aunt <u>that she didn't care</u>
  A   B
enough about the <u>environment</u>, which
        C
<u>has become more polluted</u> every year.
    D
<u>No error.</u>
 E

29. <u>Agnes was</u> the only one of those historians
  A
who <u>was</u> shocked by the discoveries of
   B
<u>ours</u> that <u>have been published</u> in the
 C   D
university journal. <u>No error.</u>
        E

Go on to next page →

Directions for Questions 30–35: These questions are based on the following essay. Choose the best answer to each question.

[1] These days it is possible to watch trials on television. [2] Several important trials have been televised for months on end, and a whole TV network shows nothing but this. [3] But you have to wonder whether justice is best served when the camera is rolling. [4] In one big trial a few years ago, the attorneys became television stars and the judge looked at the camera more than at the people in his courtroom. [5] The man on trial got off, perhaps because the jury was influenced by the publicity and glamour surrounding him.

[6] True, the jury cannot see the broadcast. [7] They often must stay in hotels during important trials. [8] However they may still be influenced by the fact that viewers can see the judge and witnesses. [9] Also, attorneys and court employees may play to the camera, acting more dramatic than they should just because the world is watching and they know it.

[10] It is important to have justice open to the public. [11] In a dictatorship, they keep their power partly through secrecy and lies. [12] If you see the judge and understand how the ruling is made, you may be more likely to accept the rule of law. [13] If you hear the verdict and never understand what the witnesses said, you may feel that justice is not really considered.

[14] Every case is different, and the judge ultimately decides whether the television reporters can broadcast live or only comment outside the courtroom. [15] The decision to keep the cameras away, however, should not be taken lightly. [16] The more the public knows about law, the better the law will be served.

30. In the context of this essay, which of the following is the best revision of Sentences 1 and 2?

   (A) These days it is possible to watch trials on television. Several important trials have been televised for months on end, and a whole TV network shows nothing but this. (No change)

   (B) These days it is possible to watch trials on television, and several important trials have been televised for months on end, while a whole TV network shows nothing else.

   (C) These days it is possible to watch an actual, live trial on television, sometimes for months. In fact, an entire television network shows nothing but trials.

   (D) The Justice Network broadcasts nothing but trials, some of which last for months. These trials are not fiction. Viewers see live court proceedings with real defendants.

   (E) One television network shows trials, all day, every day. These trials are real, and some last for months.

31. What is the purpose of Paragraph 2?

   (A) to show why broadcasting trials is acceptable

   (B) to answer objections to trial broadcasting that may arise

   (C) to argue against broadcasting trials

   (D) to continue the example given in Paragraph 1

   (E) to prepare the way for Paragraph 3

Go on to next page

32. How may Sentences 6 and 7 best be combined?

    (A) True, the jury cannot see the broadcast, they often must stay in hotels during important trials.

    (B) True, the jury, that must often stay in hotels during important trials, cannot see the broadcast.

    (C) True, the jury cannot see the broadcast, due to the fact that they often must stay in hotels during important trials.

    (D) True, the jury cannot see the broadcast because of the fact that they often must stay in hotels during important trials.

    (E) True, the jury, which must often stay in hotels overnight during important trials, cannot see the broadcast.

33. Which of the following is the best revision of Sentence 9?

    (A) Also, attorneys and court employees may play to the camera, acting more dramatic than they should just because the world is watching and they know it. (No change)

    (B) Also, attorneys and court employees may behave more dramatically than they should just because they know that the camera allows the world to watch.

    (C) Also, attorneys and court employees may play to the camera, acting more dramatic than they should just because the world is watching and they know they are on television.

    (D) Also, attorneys and court employees may play to the camera, acting more dramatic because the world is watching.

    (E) Also, attorneys and court employees may play to the camera, acting more dramatic than they should just because the world is watching through the camera.

34. How should Sentence 10 be changed?

    (A) It is important to have justice open to the public. (No change)

    (B) Most important is the fact that justice should be open to public view.

    (C) On the other hand, justice should be open to the public.

    (D) Despite what you may say, it is important to have justice open to the public.

    (E) It is important if justice is open to the public.

35. What is the purpose of the last paragraph?

    (A) to come to a firm conclusion about whether trial broadcasting should be allowed

    (B) to let the reader decide whether trial broadcasting should be allowed

    (C) to emphasize the importance of the issue of judicial fairness

    (D) to emphasize the importance of the decision about broadcasting

    (E) to show why only the judge can decide whether broadcasting is justified

STOP YOU MAY CHECK YOUR WORK ON THIS SECTION ONLY. DO NOT GO BACK TO ANY PREVIOUS SECTION.

Section 7
Critical Reading

Time: 20 minutes for 19 questions

Directions: Choose the *best* answer to each question. Mark the corresponding oval on the answer sheet.

Directions for Questions 1–6: Select the answer that *best* fits the meaning of the sentence.

Example: After he had broken the dining room window, Hal's mother _____ him.

(A) selected

(B) serenaded

(C) fooled

(D) scolded

(E) rewarded

The answer is (D).

1. The study of identical twins reared separately has provided evidence that one's genetic makeup is a powerful but not _____ force.

    (A) omnipotent

    (B) distinguishing

    (C) intellectual

    (D) coercive

    (E) understood

2. To reduce _____, the company will no longer mail monthly paper statements to those with _____ to online statements.

    (A) confusion . . . entry

    (B) error . . . tendencies

    (C) conflict . . . admission

    (D) litter . . . admittance

    (E) waste . . . access

3. The _____ author churned out at least one book a year.

    (A) tabloid

    (B) efficient

    (C) outstanding

    (D) prolific

    (E) capable

4. With interest but without _____, the baby examined the new toy from every angle.

    (A) dexterity

    (B) prejudice

    (C) apathy

    (D) enthusiasm

    (E) lethargy

5. The crew quarters on the submarine were so _____ that each sailor was _____ only a tiny locker.

    (A) large . . . given

    (B) capacious . . . assigned

    (C) cramped . . . allotted

    (D) voluminous . . . apportioned

    (E) commodious . . . allocated

6. Glazing his pottery in _____ colors, the artist's display resembled a rainbow.

    (A) pale

    (B) pastel

    (C) myriad

    (D) subdued

    (E) sensible

Go on to next page ⟹

Directions for Questions 7–10: Choose the *best* answer from the information supplied or implied by the passages.

Passage I is drawn from Mary Shelley's famous novel, Frankenstein. *In this excerpt, the narrator describes his scientific studies. Passage II comes from* Basic Statistics: A Primer for the Biomedical Sciences *by Olive Jean Dunn (Wiley) and discusses the role of statistics in medical research.*

Passage I

Line Two years passed in this manner, during which I paid no visit to Geneva, but was engaged, heart and soul, in the pursuit of some discoveries which I hoped to make. None but those who
(05) have experienced them can conceive of the enticements of science. In other studies you go as far as others have gone before you, and there is nothing more to know; but in a scientific pursuit there is continual food for discovery and
(10) wonder. A mind of moderate capacity which closely pursues one study must infallibly arrive at great proficiency in that study; and I, who continually sought the attainment of one object of pursuit and was solely wrapped up in this,
(15) improved so rapidly that at the end of two years I made some discoveries in the improvement of some chemical instruments, which procured me great esteem and admiration at the university.

Passage II

    The use of numerical methods in the field of
(20) medical research creates a problem for the research worker, whose training and interests are often quite nonmathematical. Some look back with longing to the good old days of medical research, when biostatistics was unheard of
(25) and when statistics seemed to have no role to play. The number of research workers who use numerical methods is increasing, however, as is the number of articles in medical journals that involve statistics. Thus the research worker
(30) must make some kind of adjustment to the newer ways in research.

7. In Passage I, "food" (Line 9) can best be defined as
   (A) thirst
   (B) hunger
   (C) recipe
   (D) fuel
   (E) nutrition

8. In Passage II, the author's attitude toward biostatistics may be characterized as
   (A) critical
   (B) nostalgic
   (C) fearful
   (D) favorable
   (E) adverse

9. The author of Passage II would agree with which of the following statements?
   (A) Medicine in times past was more technological than statistical.
   (B) Medical researchers should take a course in statistics.
   (C) Mathematics has no place in medical training.
   (D) The inclusion of statistics makes publication of medical research less likely.
   (E) Old-fashioned doctors were better equipped to treat patients.

10. In contrast to the author of Passage II, the narrator in Passage I
   (A) gives credit to the role of passion in science
   (B) places more emphasis on literature
   (C) is uninterested in mathematics
   (D) publishes in many medical journals
   (E) does not mention research in the context of education

Go on to next page

Directions for Questions 11–19: Choose the *best* answer to each question, based on the information in the passage.

This passage is excerpted from Jane Austen's novel, Northanger Abbey. ***Note:*** *A "living" is an appointment to the post of minister in a particular area. A "living" carries a salary.*

Line No one who had ever seen Catherine Morland in her infancy would have supposed her born to be a heroine. Her situation in life, the character of her father and mother, her own
(05) person and disposition, were all equally against her. Her father was a clergyman, without being neglected, or poor, and a very respectable man, though his name was Richard — and he had never been handsome. He had a considerable
(10) independence besides two good livings — and he was not in the least addicted to locking up his daughters. Her mother was a woman of useful plain sense, with a good temper, and, what is more remarkable, with a good constitution. She
(15) had three sons before Catherine was born; and instead of dying in bringing the latter into the world, as anybody might expect, she still lived on — lived to have six children more — to see them growing up around her, and to enjoy excel-
(20) lent health herself. A family of ten children will be always called a fine family, where there are heads and arms and legs enough for the number; but the Morlands had little other right to the word, for they were in general very plain, and
(25) Catherine, for many years of her life, as plain as any. She had a thin awkward figure, a sallow skin without colour, dark lank hair, and strong features — so much for her person; and not less unpropitious for heroism seemed her mind. She
(30) was fond of all boy's plays, and greatly preferred cricket not merely to dolls, but to the more heroic enjoyments of infancy, nursing a dormouse, feeding a canary-bird, or watering a rose-bush. Indeed she had no taste for a garden; and
(35) if she gathered flowers at all, it was chiefly for the pleasure of mischief — at least so it was conjectured from her always preferring those which she was forbidden to take. Such were her propensities — her abilities were quite as
(40) extraordinary.

She never could learn or understand anything before she was taught; and sometimes not even then, for she was often inattentive, and occasionally stupid. Her mother was three
(45) months in teaching her only to repeat the "Beggar's Petition"; and after all, her next sister, Sally, could say it better than she did. Not that Catherine was always stupid — by no means; she learnt the fable of "The Hare and Many Friends" as quickly as any girl in England. Her mother (50) wished her to learn music; and Catherine was sure she should like it, for she was very fond of tinkling the keys of the old forlorn spinner; so, at eight years old she began. She learnt a year, and could not bear it; and Mrs. Morland, who did not (55) insist on her daughters being accomplished in spite of incapacity or distaste, allowed her to leave off. The day which dismissed the music-master was one of the happiest of Catherine's life. Her taste for drawing was not superior; (60) though whenever she could obtain the outside of a letter from her mother or seize upon any other odd piece of paper, she did what she could in that way, by drawing houses and trees, hens and chickens, all very much like one another. Writing (65) and accounts she was taught by her father; French by her mother: her proficiency in either was not remarkable, and she shirked her lessons in both whenever she could. What a strange, unaccountable character! — for with all these (70) symptoms of profligacy at ten years old, she had neither a bad heart nor a bad temper, was seldom stubborn, scarcely ever quarrelsome, and very kind to the little ones, with few interruptions of tyranny; she was moreover noisy and (75) wild, hated confinement and cleanliness, and loved nothing so well in the world as rolling down the green slope at the back of the house.

Such was Catherine Morland at ten. At fifteen, appearances were mending; she began to (80) curl her hair and long for balls; her complexion improved, her features were softened by plumpness and colour, her eyes gained more animation, and her figure more consequence. Her love of dirt gave way to an inclination for finery, and (85) she grew clean as she grew smart; she had now the pleasure of sometimes hearing her father and mother remark on her personal improvement.

11. According to Paragraph 1 (Lines 1–40), a heroine ordinarily

   (A) takes part in normal family life

   (B) comes from a troubled family

   (C) is wealthy

   (D) has two surviving parents

   (E) must not suffer

Go on to next page

12. What does the author imply about men named Richard (Line 8)?

    (A) They are usually not respectable.

    (B) They are inclined to spiritual pursuits.

    (C) They are seldom rich.

    (D) They suffer from neglect.

    (E) They can be trusted completely.

13. What, according to the passage, is the most surprising fact about Mrs. Morland?

    (A) her love for her daughter

    (B) her lack of particularly good looks

    (C) her lack of sense

    (D) her tendency to nervousness

    (E) her good health

14. What phrase best defines "good constitution" (Line 14)?

    (A) intelligence

    (B) sensible nature

    (C) sturdy body

    (D) respect for the law

    (E) robust health

15. All of the following describe the young Catherine Morland except

    (A) mischievous

    (B) thin

    (C) athletic

    (D) plain

    (E) studious

16. Based on the passage, it is likely that "The Hare and Many Friends," compared to the "Beggar's Petition," (Lines 46–49)

    (A) contains more difficult language

    (B) was required by Mrs. Morland

    (C) is longer

    (D) is easier to memorize

    (E) holds less interest for Catherine

17. What best defines "bear" (Line 55) in the context of this passage?

    (A) stand

    (B) learn

    (C) continue

    (D) excel

    (E) remove

18. Catherine's reaction to the dismissal of the music-master (Lines 58–60) is probably

    (A) the opposite of what her mother expected

    (B) literally true

    (C) exaggerated by the author for comic effect

    (D) typical of a girl of her time

    (E) unexpected by all

19. One can infer from the passage that which of the following subjects was part of the normal instruction of a young girl of Catherine's time?

    (A) sports

    (B) languages

    (C) geography

    (D) dancing

    (E) sculpture

STOP YOU MAY CHECK YOUR WORK ON THIS SECTION ONLY. DO NOT GO BACK TO ANY PREVIOUS SECTION.

Section 8
Mathematics

Time: 20 minutes for 16 questions

Directions: Choose the *best* answer to each question. Mark the corresponding oval on the answer sheet.

Notes:

 ✔ You may use a calculator.

 ✔ All numbers used in this exam are real numbers.

 ✔ All figures lie in a plane.

 ✔ All figures may be assumed to be to scale unless the problem specifically indicates otherwise.

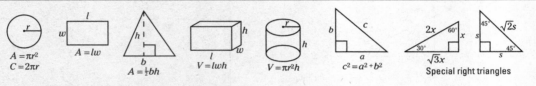

There are 360 degrees of arc in a circle.

There are 180 degrees in a straight line.

There are 180 degrees in the sum of the interior angles of a triangle.

---

1. If an eight-slice pizza has a diameter of 12 inches, what is the area of one slice, in square inches?

   (A) 2.25π

   (B) 4.5π

   (C) 9π

   (D) 18π

   (E) 36π

2. Find x if $2(x + 4) = 6$

   (A) -1

   (B) 0

   (C) 1

   (D) 2

   (E) 3

3. A certain radioactive element has a half-life of 20 years. Thus, a sample of 100 grams deposited in 1980 would have decayed to 50 grams by 2000 and to 25 grams by 2020. How much of this sample would remain in 2100?

   (A) 0 grams

   (B) 1¹⁄₁₆ grams

   (C) 2½ grams

   (D) 3⅛ grams

   (E) 5 grams

4. Set S contains the numbers 20 to 40, inclusive. If a number is chosen at random from S, what is the probability that this number is even?

   (A) ¹⁰⁄₂₀

   (B) ¹¹⁄₂₀

   (C) ¹⁰⁄₂₁

   (D) ¹¹⁄₂₁

   (E) ¹²⁄₂₁

Go on to next page

5. The number *n* satisfies the following properties:

   I.   It has three digits.

   II. Its units digit is the sum of its tens digit and its hundreds digit.

   III. It is a perfect square.

   Which number could be *n?*

   (A) 156

   (B) 400

   (C) 484

   (D) 516

   (E) 729

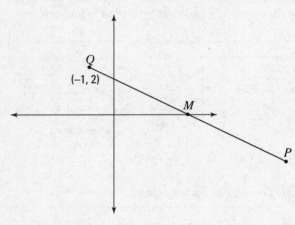

6. In this figure, the slope of line *PQ* is –⅓, and *M* is the midpoint of the line *PQ.* What are the coordinates of point *P?*

   (A) (8, –1)

   (B) (9, –1)

   (C) (10, –2)

   (D) (11, –2)

   (E) (12, –2)

7. If $ab = n$, $b + c = x$, and $n \neq 0$, which of the following must equal *n?*

   (A) $ax + c$

   (B) $ax - c$

   (C) $ax - ac$

   (D) $ax - cx$

   (E) $ac - ax$

8. The number *g* is divisible by 3, but not by 9. Which of the following is a possible remainder when 7*g* is divided by 9?

   (A) 0

   (B) 2

   (C) 4

   (D) 6

   (E) 8

9. If $a > 0$, which of the following statements must be true?

   (A) $a^2 > a$

   (B) $a > \frac{1}{a}$

   (C) $\sqrt{a} < a$

   (D) $2a > a$

   (E) $\frac{1}{a} < 1$

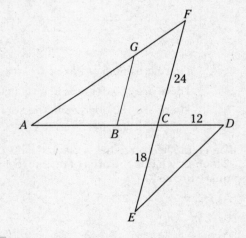

10. In this diagram (not drawn to scale), $AF \parallel ED$, $GB \parallel EF$, and $AG = GF$. The length of *AB* is

    (A) 24

    (B) 18

    (C) 16

    (D) 12

    (E) 8

Go on to next page

11. If $2a + 3b = 17$ and $2a + b = 3$, then $a + b =$

    (A) 1

    (B) 5

    (C) 7

    (D) 7.5

    (E) 10

12. A bicycle has a front wheel radius of 18 inches. If the bicycle wheel travels 50 revolutions, approximately how many feet has the bicycle rolled?

    (A) 2,827

    (B) 471

    (C) 353

    (D) 236

    (E) 235

13. If p and q are positive integers, then $\left(5^{-p}\right)\left(5^{q+1}\right)^{p}$ is equivalent to

    (A) 5

    (B) $5^{pq + p}$

    (C) 5^{pq}

    (D) $5^{pq - p}$

    (E) $5^{q + 1}$

14. In a set of five positive whole numbers, the mode is 90 and the average (arithmetic mean) is 80. Which of the following statements is false?

    (A) The number 90 must appear two, three, or four times in the set.

    (B) The number 240 cannot appear in the set.

    (C) The number 80 must appear exactly once in the set.

    (D) The five numbers must have a sum of 400.

    (E) The median cannot be greater than 90.

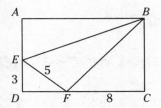

15. Given that $ABCD$ is a rectangle, and triangle BCF is isosceles, find the length of the line segment BE in this diagram.

    (A) $\sqrt{89}$

    (B) $8\sqrt{2}$

    (C) 12

    (D) $\sqrt{153}$

    (E) 13

16. Melvin, Chris, Enoch, Dave, Carey, Mike, Dan, and Peter are choosing dorm rooms for college. Each room holds four people. They have the following requirements:

    I.   Mike and Melvin refuse to live together.

    II. Enoch will live with Chris or Carey (or possibly both).

    III. If Dave and Dan live together, Peter will live with them.

    When rooms are chosen, Melvin, Carey, and Dan live together. Which of the following groups must live in the other room?

    (A) Chris, Dave, and Mike

    (B) Chris, Mike, and Peter

    (C) Dave, Enoch, and Peter

    (D) Dave, Mike, and Peter

    (E) Enoch, Mike, and Peter

STOP YOU MAY CHECK YOUR WORK ON THIS SECTION ONLY. DO NOT GO BACK TO ANY PREVIOUS SECTION.

Section 9

Multiple-Choice Writing

Time: 10 minutes for 14 questions

Directions: Choose the one answer that *best* improves the sentence. Mark the corresponding oval on the answer sheet. If the underlined portion of the sentence is best left alone, choose (A).

Example: <u>Bert and him went</u> to the store to buy boots in preparation for the approaching storm.

(A) Bert and him went

(B) Bert and he went

(C) Bert and he had gone

(D) Bert and him had gone

(E) Bert and himself went

The correct answer is (B).

---

1. The movement of refugees into centralized locations facilitates the delivery of essential services, <u>in order that the refugees should survive until the crisis is over</u>.

    (A) in order that the refugees should survive until the crisis is over

    (B) because the refugees will survive until the crisis is over

    (C) so that the refugees survive until the crisis is over

    (D) and the goal is that the refugees survive until the crisis is over

    (E) with the goal being survival of the refugees until the crisis is over

2. Mr. Berens reported <u>that his parking permit was displayed</u> on the front windshield, although the traffic officer claimed otherwise on the ticket.

    (A) that his parking permit was displayed

    (B) his parking permit it was displayed

    (C) about his parking permit being displayed

    (D) regarding his parking permit, which was displayed

    (E) in reference to his parking permit, he displayed it

3. For centuries, historians have been debating the role of Cleopatra, <u>and the claim that she was as powerful as any Roman ruler is controversial</u>.

    (A) and the claim that she was as powerful as any Roman ruler is controversial

    (B) and they claim that she was as powerful as any Roman ruler, though some disagree

    (C) including the claim that she was as powerful as any Roman ruler

    (D) about whether she was as powerful as any Roman ruler, which is controversial

    (E) claiming controversially that she was as powerful as any Roman ruler

4. <u>Having seen his father's law practice, Joseph was determined to become one himself</u> someday.

    (A) Having seen his father's law practice, Joseph was determined to become one himself

    (B) Having seen his father's law practice, Joseph was determined to enter that field

    (C) Having seen his father's law practice, Joseph was determined about becoming one himself

    (D) Having seen his father's law practice, Joseph was determined to become a lawyer himself

    (E) Joseph, having seen his father's law practice, was determined to become one himself

Go on to next page

5. The French artist Manet <u>identifying with the realism of his predecessors, which</u> in turn grew out of Romanticism.

   (A) identifying with the realism of his predecessors, which

   (B) identifying with the realism of his predecessors, that

   (C) was identifying with the realism of his predecessors, which

   (D) had identified with the realism of his predecessors

   (E) identified with the realism of his predecessors, which

6. For the majority of banks receiving funds from the government in the current economic downturn, <u>salary caps were requirements and they didn't like them.</u>

   (A) salary caps were requirements and they didn't like them

   (B) salary caps were requirements they didn't like

   (C) they disliked required salary caps

   (D) the required salary caps were what they didn't like

   (E) they had to accept salary caps, which they didn't like

7. The ceramics teacher <u>giving his students five possible glazes, there is at least one that suits</u> each vase.

   (A) giving his students five possible glazes, there is at least one that suits

   (B) having given his students five possible glazes, there is at least a suitable one for

   (C) gives his students five possible glazes; at least one glaze is suitable for

   (D) gives his students five possible glazes, at least one of them being suited for

   (E) gives his students five possible glazes, at least one suiting

8. Viruses, <u>when entered in the body</u>, activate the immune system.

   (A) when entered in the body

   (B) having entered the body

   (C) when they had entered the body

   (D) because of entering the body

   (E) entered the body

9. Given the high rate of accidents, the superintendent objects <u>to our organizing</u> a rock-climbing club.

   (A) to our organizing

   (B) to us organizing

   (C) that we would be organizing

   (D) to the organizing by us of

   (E) to organizing

10. After having been told by their leaders that the war would be short and then subsequently disappointed, the citizens <u>rebelled toward the government</u>.

    (A) rebelled toward the government

    (B) were rebels toward the government

    (C) they rebelled in relation to the government

    (D) rebelled against the government

    (E) were rebellious and it was toward the government

11. In the tradition of her ancestors, who carved intricate designs on their houses, Ella <u>will decorate</u> for hours at a time.

    (A) will decorate

    (B) would be decorating

    (C) will have decorated

    (D) was decorating

    (E) decorated

Go on to next page

12. Sent to boarding school at an early age, <u>the curriculum was hard for Sandra</u>.

    (A) the curriculum was hard for Sandra

    (B) the curriculum, it was hard for Sandra

    (C) the curriculum for Sandra was very hard

    (D) Sandra was finding the curriculum hard

    (E) Sandra found the curriculum hard

13. George Washington inspired his soldiers <u>by his heroism and that he was always motivated by patriotism</u>.

    (A) by his heroism and that he was always motivated by patriotism

    (B) because he was heroic and that he was always motivated by patriotism

    (C) that he was heroic and that he was always motivated by patriotism

    (D) by his heroism and patriotism

    (E) in that he had heroism and because he was motivated by patriotism

14. The literary works of ancient Greece <u>are equally as interesting as those</u> of ancient Rome.

    (A) are equally as interesting as those

    (B) are equally interesting as those

    (C) are interesting, equally to those

    (D) is equally interesting as the works

    (E) are equally as interesting as the works

STOP YOU MAY CHECK YOUR WORK ON THIS SECTION ONLY. DO NOT GO BACK TO ANY PREVIOUS SECTION.

Chapter 21

Practice Exam 1: Answers and Explanations

....

After you finish taking Practice Exam 1 in Chapter 20, take some time to go through the answers and explanations in this chapter to find out which questions you missed and why. Even if you answered a question correctly, read the explanation that goes with it because I tuck in some additional information that'll be useful on the real SAT. If you're short on time, turn to the end of this chapter to find an abbreviated answer key.

Note: To determine your score on this practice test, turn to the appendix.

Section 1: The Essay

You can't write a masterpiece about curiosity in 25 minutes, but you should be able to make two or three points on the subject, introduce your thoughts in a brief paragraph, and come to at least some sort of conclusion. Here's one possible outline for an essay addressing the role curiosity plays in human life:

- ✔ **Introductory paragraph:** State your *thesis* (or main argument): Curiosity killed the cat, but it is a quality worth dying for because life without curiosity is not worth living. Then mention the points you use to support that thesis:

  - Curiosity impels the great explorers.

  - Without curiosity there would be no scientific discoveries.

- ✔ **Body paragraphs:** Explore the supporting points, one in each paragraph. Mention a couple of explorers and their discoveries, and explain what would be lost to humanity if not for curiosity. Then go on to talk about research scientists who are driven by the need to know and how their work makes an impact on humanity. Again, use some specific examples.

- ✔ **Concluding paragraph:** State your conclusion: Curiosity drives the human race forward, but this quality is not without drawbacks. Nuclear arms, for example, would not have been developed if humans were satisfied with what was already known. Still, the rich knowledge of the universe and the benefits of modern medicine may be attributed to curiosity, so, overall, humanity benefits from this trait.

Now that you have an idea how a well-organized essay for this test prompt might flow, it's time to score your own essay. Before you get started, turn to Chapter 8 and read the samples there. Then score your essay using the scoring rubric in Chapter 7; be honest with yourself as you determine how your essay rates according to the standards in the rubric.

Section 2: Critical Reading

1. **A.** The clues are *not* and *but,* which set up a contrast. The best contrast to *intellectual* is *practical. Theoretical* (not concrete, existing only in thought) and *philosophical* (relating to a system of thought) are in the land of ideas, as is *intellectual,* so no contrast there. *Ethical* (moral) and *strident* (loud and unpleasant, like the guy who sits next to me at Yankees games) aren't opposites of *intellectual.*

Look for negative words that signal a change of direction in the sentence.

2. **B.** The clue in the sentence is *than was previously thought.* If you were to place your own word in the blank, you might choose *new* or *current. Contemporary* (occurring now) is the only answer that reflects the right time. *Prior* (earlier, happening before) and *antiquated* (old-fashioned) don't make sense. *Theoretical* just doesn't fit the context.

3. **C.** You can crack this sentence by considering the contrasting nature of the two elements — architectural history and engineering. A paper on engineering shouldn't have architectural history in it, so those references would blur or weaken the focus. This concept takes you to Choice (C), where you find *myriad* (countless), which is the correct answer.

   Were you tempted by Choice (D)? Job references often use the term *impeccable* to describe job candidates — or, at least, you hope yours do! — but *impeccable* means "faultless" and doesn't fit the meaning of the sentence.

4. **A.** Choice (B) may tempt you because, if grammar is everywhere, its presence — and your days of fun with nouns and verbs — may seem *inevitable* (unavoidable). But *innate* means "inborn" or "natural." If every language has grammar, it probably comes from within. The sentence makes it clear that grammar can't be *extraneous* (extra, unnecessary) or *coincidental* (just happens to be there). *Multifaceted* (many sided, versatile) could apply to grammar, but the sentence has no hook to attach that meaning.

5. **E.** The clue is the phrase *once prosperous.* The government is adding money to the economy (*subsidize* means "to pay part of the costs") to *reinvigorate* (add life to) the area. Two bad but appealing choices are Choices (C) and (D). *Enervate* resembles *energy,* so you may have thought the word meant "energize." However, it actually means "weaken." *Aggrandize* means "to add power," so it isn't an impossible selection, but Choice (E) is still better. *Stagnate* (to grow stale, to remain without change) and *annex* (to make part of) aren't even close.

6. **B.** The council is clearly insisting that global warming be the subject of Deeplock's meeting. *Adamant* means "uncompromising" or "insistent." *Ambivalent* (having mixed feelings), *apathetic* (not caring), and *neutral* (not taking a position) don't fit. *Perplexed* may be an option because, if the council is confused, it may want to discuss the issue. However, Choice (B) is best because it matches the "won't take no for an answer" tone of the sentence.

7. **A.** Zero in on *notwithstanding,* a nice mouthful that means "despite" or "in spite of." The sentence tells you that despite some kind of effort, the team lost. The best choice has to have something to do with a great or really strong effort. *Herculean* — a word that is derived from the name of the Greek hero Hercules — fits the bill. Hercules was famous for being "great and strong," which is what the adjective derived from his name now means.

   Spontaneous (spur of the moment, unplanned), *gratuitous* (needless, uncalled for), *pluralistic* (reflecting many viewpoints), and *intermittent* (stopping and starting at irregular intervals) don't do the job.

8. **A.** Did Choice (B) fool you? The sentence has to do with history, so you may have been tempted by the resemblance between *historiography* and *history.* But *historiography* is the study of how history is written, not history itself. Because the sentence is referring to history, *dissertation* (a scholarly paper) is appropriate. A *memoir* is made up of personal reminiscences. *Polemic* (a bitter argument, especially about religion) and *diatribe* (a verbal attack) have intense meanings, and the sentence seeks the opposite.

9. **A.** The questions in the middle of the paragraph provide the key to the actual answer to this question. If you ask who should make a decision, you imply that more than one possible path to a decision exists. Hence, Choice (A) is a good option. Choice (B) is out because nothing in the passage separates mission and strategy. Choice (C) is wrong because it's the opposite of Choice (A) and thus the opposite of what the passage implies. Strategic planning is useful, as are some (albeit unbelievably boring) texts that teach this discipline, so Choice (D) is out of the running, too. In my ideal world, Choice (E) would be the correct answer because then even my lowly level (a teacher) would have a role in decision making; however, the passage doesn't clearly imply the statement presented in this choice, so (E) is wrong.

10. **C.** Sentence 1, which deals with the source of *significant power*, is the crucial part here. *Goals* is another word for *mission* and *methods* is another word for *strategy,* so Choice (C) is basically a reworded Sentence 1 — and the correct answer.

11. **C.** According to the passage, Justinian made *efforts* but could salvage only the appearance, not the *substance,* of the Empire. So what kind of efforts did he make? Check out the last sentence of the passage: In Western Europe, new forms of social and governmental activity evolved. The key word here is *new;* thus, Justinian must have been trying to keep the old forms, without success. Choice (C) wins the prize.

12. **B.** In normal everyday English, a *trap* is something that catches you, so you may have zeroed in on Choice (A) when you first read this question. Bad idea. In the context of the passage, the word *trappings* refers to appearance, especially ornamental details — not substance.

 Vocabulary-in-context questions like Question 12 often include a common meaning of the vocabulary word in their answer choices. Be careful when reading these questions and the passages that go with them; make sure you choose the meaning of the word that goes with the passage's context.

13. **E.** The first sentence states that attempts to define feudalism are "far from being closely related to one another," so disagreement exists. You can rule out Choice (A) because the paragraph states that feudalism *came into existence* in France. The paragraph contains no information about feudalism's spreading from England to Spain, the concept that Choice (B) states. The passage uses a form of the word *controversial to* describe the labeling of Egypt and India as feudal. Because *controversial* means "not generally agreed upon," Choice (C) is wrong. Finally, Choice (D) is a dud because the author does define feudalism, which, therefore, isn't impossible to define.

14. **A.** Lines 10–14 state that "countries that came under their influence . . . possessed feudal attributes." Choice (A) is the only answer that refers to that influence.

15. **B.** The author provides only one detail about Russia — that it had a system *very close* to vassalage. Thus, you can dump Choices (A) and (D) right away. Choice (E) also bites the dust because the 16th century is fairly far from modern, as Shakespeare's sometimes-impossible vocabulary shows. Both Choices (B) and (C) are possible answers, but you need more information to contrast Russia and Japan, so Choice (B) is the best answer.

16. **D.** The easy definition of *vassal* — a knight — isn't an option, so you have to look for something that means the same thing as *knight.* The passage makes clear that vassals traded military service and other obligations for land and other rights, such as protection of widows and children, so Choice (D) is correct.

17. **A.** The passage details how land is transferred (Lines 25–29 and 52) but mentions no other economy, so inferring that land was the basis of wealth — the statement in Choice (A) — is a safe bet. Little evidence in the passage supports Choices (B) and (C), and the passage directly contradicts Choices (D) and (E).

18. **B.** The castle had to be *garrisoned* (Lines 37–38), that is, staffed by soldiers (not *erected* by soldiers). The passage says nothing about the people who had to carve and carry all the stones that eventually became the castle. The other choices are all mentioned in the passage as obligations that vassals owed their feudal lords.

19. **D.** As soon as you read this question, you can rule out Choice (B) because the peasants don't play a role in the passage, although in real life they did do all the work. Choice (E) is also wrong because the lord gives permission for marriage but doesn't do matchmaking duty. The other three choices concern advice; the crucial sentence that helps you decide which one is right appears in Lines 38–39. One of the lord's advantages in the lord-vassal relationship was receiving counsel from his vassals. Therefore, Choice (D) is the right one. Forced advice (A) isn't an advantage (imagine your mom advising you to do your home-work), and the passage says nothing about lords seeking advice from their peers, an idea contained in Choice (C).

20. **D.** Choice (A) is appealing at first glance because Lines 80–82 talk about instability. However, Choice (D) is better because the instability is linked to the absence of a strong ruler (sort of like a game of dodgeball when the ref ducks out for a cup of coffee). The pas-sage doesn't support Choices (B), (C), or (E).

21. **E.** A pyramid is narrow at the top and gradually widens as you move toward the base. In the analogy, the king is the top of the pyramid, but those under him (the vassals) are ranked from highest (just under the king) to lowest (the base). Choice (E) is the correct answer.

22. **E.** This question forces you to figure out which word or idea the pronoun *this* replaces. Your clue is the end of the sentence, which mentions *the positive results of feudalism,* which balances *this.* Okay, the balance of something positive is something negative. Because *this* follows a whole list of negatives, you can safely conclude that the whole list is tucked into that one word, making Choice (E) the right answer.

23. **B.** *Nominal* comes from the root word for "name." As the passage makes clear, plenty of in-fighting disturbed the political and economic order. But the passage also states that feudal-ism supported *some measure of territorial organization.* Bingo, Choice (B) is your answer.

24. **A.** The word **dispassionate** means "without emotion, logical, calm." The author is simply dis-cussing feudalism and evaluating it reasonably, without emotion, as Choice (A) states. The other four words don't fit: **strident** — Choice (B) — is the harsh tone employed by talk-show guests who attempt to out-scream each other. Choice (C), **didactic**, refers to educa-tional speech or writing, the kind that aims to improve the morals of the audience. This passage makes no moral judgments, so you can rule out Choice (E), as well. Choice (D) is out because **satirical** means "mocking."

25. **B.** Okay, I confess that I like Choice (E), but the pyramid is just one analogy. It isn't enough to carry the whole piece. Choices (A), (C), and (D) are good for parts of the passage, but the more general Choice (B) is the best answer.

Section 3: Mathematics

1. **D.** If you add the numbers in the ratio, you get 7. There are 28 total students, which is 7×4. Therefore, multiply the original ratio numbers by 4 to get 12 boys and 16 girls. You can double-check your work by doing this equation: $12 + 16 = 28$.

2. **D.** Plugging in the number gives you $2(-2)^4$. Remembering the acronym PEMDAS (see Chapter 12 if you don't remember), you know to do the exponent first: $(-2)^4 = (-2)(-2)(-2)(-2) = +16; 2(16) = 32$.

3. **A.** The drawer contained 22 pairs of socks originally. However, Josh has thrown 4 pairs on the floor, so he now has 18 pairs to choose from, 6 of which are brown. His probability of success is therefore $6/18 = 1/3$.

4. **C.** This question is the first of many appearances of the 30-60-90 triangle on these practice exams. In this type of triangle, the length of the hypotenuse is always twice the length of the shorter leg, while the longer leg's length equals the shorter leg's length times $\sqrt{3}$.

Because you know the shorter leg equals 5, you know that the longer leg is $5\sqrt{3}$, and so the coordinates are $\left(5\sqrt{3},0\right)$.

5. **B.** This question isn't too bad as long as you remember your exponent rules. (Check out Chapter 14 if you need a refresher.) By definition, $4^0 = 1$, and $64^{1/2}$ is the square root of 64, which equals 8. So the expression in parentheses equals $1 + 8 = 9$; 9^{-2} means the reciprocal of 9^2 (or 81), so the answer is $\frac{1}{81}$.

6. **D.** Don't let this one fool you. Thinking that the girls have $24 combined is tempting, but that's not what the problem says. To do this problem, you need to find two numbers in the ratio 7:5 that have a difference of 24. You can work this problem a couple of ways. One is to use algebra: You can call Dora's money $7x$ and Lisa's money $5x$. Then you can say that $7x = 5x + 24$, or $7x - 5x = 24$. Thus, $2x = 24$, and $x = 12$. Plugging 12 back into the original equation (always an important step) tells you that Lisa's money is $5(12) = \$60$, and Dora's is $7(12) = \$84$. The other way to solve this problem is to subtract the numbers in the ratio instead of adding them. Because $7 - 5 = 2$, and 2 goes into 24 12 times, you can multiply the original ratio numbers by 12, giving you the same answers you get using algebra.

7. **E.** Quick quiz: What's the first thing you need to do when you read this problem? If you answered, "Draw the triangle," you win a prize! (The prize, of course, is an improved SAT score.) Drawing the triangle is only half the battle, though; you also have to label the triangle properly. Here you can use a guideline developed by a former colleague of mine: Let your variable stand for the second thing mentioned in the problem. In this case, the second thing mentioned is the first side, so let $x =$ the first side. The second side is then $x + 3$, and the third side is $2x - 5$. (Don't fall into the trap of thinking it's $5 - 2x$.) The finished triangle looks like this:

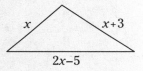

The perimeter, 34, is the sum of all the sides, so $(x) + (x + 3) + (2x - 5) = 34$. Combining the like terms on the left side gives you $4x - 2 = 34$. Adding two to each side gives you $4x = 36$, which leaves you with $x = 9$. Now you need to plug 9 into the original equations: The first side is 9 cm, the second is $9 + 3 = 12$ cm, and the third is $2(9) - 5 = 13$ cm. Because this third side is the longest, 13 cm is the answer.

8. **B.** You can draw the line and count spaces to determine that the points are 12 units apart, or you can simply subtract: $8 - (-4) = 12$. (Distance always involves a difference.) $\frac{1}{4}$ of 12 is 3, so you need to find the point 3 units to the right of -4; $-4 + 3 = -1$.

9. **D.** To solve for y, isolate y on one side of the equation:

$$2y - c = 3c$$
$$+c+c$$
$$\frac{2y}{2} = \frac{4c}{2}$$
$$y = 2c$$

10. **C.** On the real SAT, try all the numbers by plugging them in; doing so is usually faster than working out the problem. I do it the long way here, though, so you can practice your algebra skills. Start by cross-multiplying to get $(x - 1)(x + 2) = (x + 7)(x - 2)$. Now you can use FOIL (a technique I explain in Chapter 14) to get $x^2 + 2x - 1x - 2 = x^2 - 2x + 7x - 14$. Simplifying each side, you get $x^2 + x - 2 = x^2 + 5x - 14$. A neat thing happens when you start to combine the like terms on different sides. You can subtract x^2 from both sides, which means that both x^2 terms just disappear, leaving you with the simple linear equation $x - 2 = 5x - 14$. Subtracting x from both sides yields $-2 = 4x - 14$. Now you add 14 to each side to get $12 = 4x$, and $x = 3$.

11. **B.** Because 15 is composite (it's 3×5), &15 = 2(15) = 30. 9 is also composite, so &9 = 2(9) = 18. 36 is composite, too, and &36 = 2(36) = 72. Only option II works, so Choice (B) is the correct answer.

A *prime* number is divisible only by itself and 1. A *composite* number is anything that isn't prime or special. (Zero and one are considered "special" numbers.) Turn to Chapter 12 for more information on these types of numbers.

12. **C.** Direct variation problems require a ratio — in this case, the ratio of volume to temperature. Thus, you can write $\frac{cc}{K} = \frac{cc}{K}, \frac{31.5}{210} = \frac{x}{300}$. Cross-multiply to get $210x = 9,450$ and divide by 210 to get $x = 45$.

13. **B.** This scatterplot shows a negative trend, so the line of best fit would go roughly from the top left to the bottom right. However, point D is significantly lower than the rest of the points. If you try drawing a line between A and D, or B and D, you see that it's not that close to a lot of the points. However, the line from A to C is a good approximation of the scatterplot as a whole, as you can see in this diagram:

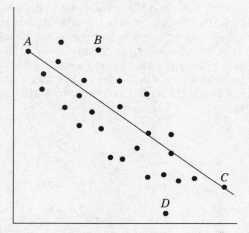

14. **E.** To be honest, you don't even need to know what x and y equal in this problem. Look at the angle marked c in the diagram below (not drawn to scale). Angles c and z are vertical angles, which means that their measures are equal. Also, angles a, c, and b form a straight line, so $a + c + b = 180°$. Therefore, $a + b + z = 180°$. By the way, you can also figure out the actual angle measurements if you want to: $a = 30°$, $b = 70°$, and $z = 80°$.

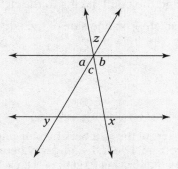

15. **B.** Although there are 18 terms between 7 and 159, the increment must be applied 19 times. Because $159 - 7 = 152$, and $152 \div 19 = 8$, each term must be 8 units greater than the one before it. So the sequence begins 7, 15, 23, 31 . . . (and you have your answer).

16. **A.** The function — $f(x + 4)$ — moves the graph 4 units to the left because you're adding 4 to x. (Chapter 14 gives you more information on functions.)

17. **A.** To answer this question, you must first realize that the triangles here are special; break up the 75° angle at the bottom right into a 45° angle and a 30° angle. The top right triangle is a 45-45-90 triangle, which makes both of its legs equal to 14. The bottom leg is also the hypotenuse of the 30-60-90 triangle at the bottom. In a 30-60-90 triangle, the hypotenuse must be twice the shortest leg, which is j. Therefore, j equals 7.

Don't remember the special triangle ratios you need to know for this problem? Well, don't panic. They're at the top of each mathematics section of the SAT, so take a quick peek at the directions at the beginning of the section to refresh your memory.

18. **C.** You can solve this problem using simple arithmetic. If you add up the 65 Spanish students and the 32 art students, you get a total of 97 students. However, you counted the 14 students who take both subjects twice, so you need to subtract 14, giving you 83 students in either Spanish or art. (This method always works to find the total number of things in two groups combined: Add up the number in each group, and then subtract the overlap.) If 83 students are in Spanish and/or art, you're left with $100 - 83 = 17$ who don't take either subject.

19. **D.** Because the answer should be in minutes, start by turning 3 hours into 180 minutes. You know that k percent of these 180 minutes is going to be used for math. What does k percent mean? Why, it means $k/100$. Taking a percent of a number involves multiplication, so your answer is $180 \times k/100$, or $180k/100$.

20. **A.** ABD is a right triangle, so you can find BD using the Pythagorean Theorem: $(4)^2 + (8)^2 = c^2$; $16 + 64 = c^2$; $80 = c^2$; so $c = \sqrt{80}$. Because $DE = 2\sqrt{5}$, the area of $BDEF$ is $\sqrt{80} \times 2\sqrt{5} = 2\sqrt{400} = 2(20) = 40$. Now, the shaded region's area is the area of the rectangle $BDEF$ minus the area of the triangle CBD, and the area of CBD equals ½ × base × height = ½ × 8 × 4 = 16. Thus, the area of the shaded region is $40 - 16 = 24$.

Section 4: Critical Reading

1. **D.** The word *yet* signals a change in direction for the sentence — a contrast between admired and something else. Choice (D) is the only option that opposes *admired*. Choices (B), (C), and (E) are synonyms of *admired*. And if the strangers are reading about Elwood, they aren't ignoring him, which makes Choice (A) wrong.

2. **A.** The whole sentence revolves around the word *despite*. The ambassadors have made an assumption that is challenged, but not overturned, by the word in the blank. *Resistance* works well here. Choices (B), (C), and (D) don't challenge the ambassadors' views (*withdrawal* means "pulling out" and *compromise* means "giving in a bit"). *Interrogation* (questioning) is in another vocabulary universe entirely.

3. **C.** The choices all contain relatively easy words, but the tricky part of this question is the word *belied,* which means "proved false." After you figure out that definition, you know you're looking for an impossible pair. Increasing services while slashing taxes? Why, yes, that's the answer. (It's also what every politician promises and none can deliver.)

4. **B.** SAT questions don't rely on historical knowledge, but if you know anything about segregation and the courts, you have a leg up on this question. Segregation isn't legal, so you can immediately drop Choices (A), (C), and (E), which allow the practice. When you check out Choices (B) and (D), you see that *persist* (continue) easily beats out *intimidate* (threaten).

5. **E.** The most important clue here is the word *hide.* If Jane Austen is hiding her manuscript, *publicize* and *reveal* are definitely out, so you can eliminate Choices (A) and (B). Check out the three remaining possibilities: *alert* and *conceal* go together nicely.

Don't stop when you find a word that fits the first blank in the sentence. Always check both blanks. Otherwise, you may overlook the better answer (and get the wrong answer).

6. **D.** *Although* is the word to watch here. Check out the first half of the sentence. In general, what are juries trying to achieve? A vote of 12 to 0 on a verdict, right? So the first blank may be filled by Choices (A), (B), or (D) because all imply agreement. The *although* signals that the second blank is a bit of a surprise, so *amity* (friendship) is better than *discord* (disagreement, which you already know) and *anger* (which you may expect when people have differing views).

7. **D.** To answer this question, you need to focus on two important spots in the sentence: *not . . . but*. This pair of words tells you that you're looking for the opposite of one disease. Still in the running at this point are Choices (B), (C), (D), and (E). Now send your eyeball to the end of the sentence, which gives you two very different details — solid tumors and *proliferation* (rapid growth) of white blood cells. With this info in mind, you can determine that the best choice is *diverse*, so Choice (D) is correct.

8. **D.** This question is a particularly difficult one. Filling in the blanks with your own words may lead you to *happy* and *sad,* given that the word *but* signals a contrast. Choices (A) and (B) start you off with happy words and then let you down as far as *sad* goes, because *affable* means "friendly" and *mirthful* means "full of laughter." Choices (C) and (E) also bite the dust because no one expects a lottery winner to be depressed or *acrimonious* (bitter). But you may think a shy person would be *intimidated* (threatened) by wealth and surprised to see her confident, so Choice (D) is your answer.

9. **B.** The second half of the sentence holds the key: The items are of various ages and from lots of countries. *Eclectic* (from different sources) plops into the sentence nicely. The question-writer (okay, me, but I'm just doing what those tricksters at the SAT will do to you) has tucked in Choices (D) and (E), two church references, to distract you. Choice (C), *international,* makes sense with the *many . . . nations* part of the sentence but ignores periods, so it's wrong. *Ubiquitous* (appearing everywhere) doesn't work at all.

10. **E.** Paragraph 1 makes it clear that Mariga carves all the time, and because of his family background and talents, he's open to artistic possibilities. By explaining these background facts, the author paves the way (Get it? The passage is about stone!) for the discovery of soapstone as a carving material.

11. **C.** You can rule out Choices (A), (B), and (E) because they contradict information in the passage. Mariga's trips were easier after the road crew did their work, and the journey was clearly not impossible because he made it. Nor did Mariga travel for artistic purposes; he was sent by the Ministry of Agriculture. Choice (D) is a good (but wrong) answer because Paragraph 1 tells you that he would be carving no matter where he was, because carving was his passion. The best answer is Choice (C) because the paragraph clearly sets up a cause-and-effect relationship; Mariga bumps along and sympathizes with the farmers who have to get their crops over the nonexistent roads.

12. **D.** The passage states that if you hold the stone up to the light, it is translucent. The opposite of *translucent*, which means "letting light pass through," is *opaque*, which means "not letting light pass through."

13. **D.** The last paragraph of Passage I changes focus from Mariga's obsession with soapstone to a small industry based on the creation of soapstone carvings. The author doesn't explain how those two are related, but the passage strongly implies that Mariga was at least partly responsible. Also, the first paragraph of Passage I presents Mariga as a teacher who couldn't resist showing his friends, Titus and Robert, how to carve. The only other *enticing* (tempting) choices are (C) and (E) because Mariga probably had more fun carving than farming. Nonetheless, the passage more strongly supports Choice (D), so it's the *best* answer.

14. **C.** Line 59 explains that the soapstone carvings were "exhibited all over the world." The author clearly admires the artwork, so Choice (C) is the correct answer.

15. **D.** The passage describes the crisis in Africa that has limited educational growth (war, funding, and so on) and also states that "something must be done quickly to reverse the trend" (Lines 100–101). The implication is that if the situation isn't changed now, it may never be.

16. **A.** You can't run a computer without software because the software is the "brain" telling the computer what to do. The same thing goes for voters. If the voters aren't educated, they can't choose good, effective leaders who will make a positive difference during their time in office.

17. **D.** The author doesn't say anything about traditional ways, but each of the other choices pops up somewhere in Passage II, so Choice (D) is the one you want here.

18. **E.** *Investment in primary education* differentiates Southeast Asia from Africa. The whole passage describes the problems of African education, so you can safely bet that Africa invests less, not more, in primary education.

19. **B.** John Nkoma doesn't want Africa to be *the exception* to the rule of technological development stemming from basic science. Basic science is a short hop (just a skip, really) from good education.

20. **C.** The SAT writers describe the economies of Southeast Asia in a positive way, so you can feel confident going with Choice (C).

21. **B.** The passage ends with the idea that governments can't do it all, especially the weak governments that exist in some parts of Africa, so Choice (B) is the next logical statement.

22. **B.** The first passage deals with the discovery and marketing of soapstone carvings, concentrating on the role of one man. The second discusses the need for government investment in education, which is described as only part of the solution, with community action being essential as well. Choice (B) illustrates this change in attitude.

23. **E.** A couple of these choices lose only by a nose because although they fit most of the material in these two passages, they don't fit everything. The key is to look for the best answer. Hardships — Choice (A) — occur in the hilly country of Passage I and are implied by the lack of education in Passage II, but neither passage focuses on that aspect of African life. Choices (B) and (C) fit well with Passage II but not Passage I. Choice (D) is a poor fit all around. Choice (E) is the best answer because the development of the art market dominates Passage I, and Passage II links education to African economic development.

24. **A.** Passage I tells a story of one specific individual and his experience. Passage II contains broader, more general statements about education, the economy, and technology.

Section 5: Mathematics

1. **A.** To help you solve this problem, make a quick drawing of the situation. (Remember, the towns don't have to be in a straight line.)

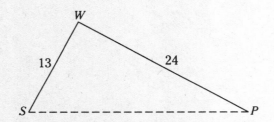

The distance you're interested in is the dotted line. Hey, wait a minute: This diagram is a triangle! Therefore, you can use the triangle inequality, which tells you that the sum of any two sides of a triangle must be greater than the third side. The number 10 doesn't satisfy the inequality because 10 + 13 = 23, which is less than 24, so you have your answer.

2. **C.** If you multiply each of the choices by 3 points, you get 30, 33, 36, 39, and 42. Because all the other scores are worth 5 points, you must be able to add a multiple of 5 to one of these numbers to get 61. The only one that works is 36 because 36 + 25 = 61.

3. **C.** Don't fall into the trap of thinking that 1 is prime. Two numbers, 1 and 0, are called "special." Thus, 2 isn't a tweener because 2 – 1 = 1 and 1 isn't prime. The number 8 isn't a tweener, because 8 + 1 = 9 and 9 isn't prime, either. (It's 3 × 3.) But 30 is a tweener because 30 – 1 = 29, which is prime, and 30 + 1 = 31, which is also prime. After you've found the answer, you can move on to the next question; there's no need to check the last two options, which are wrong.

4. **A.** Don't fall for the old "less than" trick. "Twelve less than something" is the thing minus 12 — not the other way around. So you want an expression that says "x squared is 5 times x minus 12," and (A) is the winner.

5. **B.** Five pounds of peanuts times $5.50 is $27.50, and two pounds of cashews times $12.50 is $25.00, so the total cost is $52.50 for seven pounds. $52.50 divided by 7 is $7.50.

6. **C.** The number of solutions to the equation $f(x) = 1$ is just the number of times that the graph has a height of 1, which you can see in the following diagram:

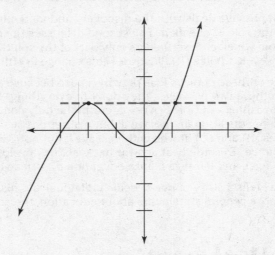

7. **D.** In general, absolute-value equations have two solutions, so even if you don't know how to do this problem, you can confidently guess Choice (B) or (D). To solve this problem the long way, do the following:

$$|3x - 1| = 7$$

$$3x - 1 = 7 \qquad \text{or} \qquad 3x - 1 = -7$$
$$\underline{+1 \quad +1} \qquad\qquad\qquad \underline{+1 \quad +1}$$
$$\frac{3x}{3} = \frac{8}{3} \qquad\qquad\qquad \frac{3x}{3} = \frac{-6}{3}$$
$$x = 2\tfrac{2}{3} \qquad \text{or} \qquad x = -2$$

8. **C.** As is often the case on the SAT, the trial-and-error method works great here. If you don't want to use trial and error, you can call the original side of the square x, making the rectangle's sides $x + 3$ and $x - 2$. Because the area is 50, you write $(x + 3)(x - 2) = 50$. Use the FOIL

method to get $x^2 - 2x + 3x - 6 = 50$, or $x^2 + x - 56 = 0$. (Remember, to solve a quadratic equation, you must make one side equal zero.) You can factor this equation into $(x + 8)(x - 7) = 0$. This equation is true when x equals either –8 or 7, but it doesn't make sense for a square to have a side of –8. Therefore, 7 is your answer. (Turn to Chapter 14 for more info on the FOIL method.)

9. **96.** This problem is simple if you remember an easy trick: total = number × average. In this case, the total must equal $4 \times 90 = 360$. Adding up Lauren's first three scores gives you 264, and $360 - 264 = 96$.

Another good way to solve this problem is to play the over/under game. For each score, figure out how much it is over or under the average. In this case, you get –1, –5, and 0. Adding up these numbers gives you –6, so Lauren is 6 points under average before she takes her last exam. Thus, she needs 6 points over her average, or a 96, on the last exam.

10. **40.** Sixty-five percent chose history or English, leaving 35 percent for other subjects. This 35 percent represents 14 students, so you're basically being asked, "35 percent of what number is 14?" You can use the is/of method to solve this problem: $\frac{14}{x} = \frac{35}{100}$, $35x = 1,400$, $x = 40$.

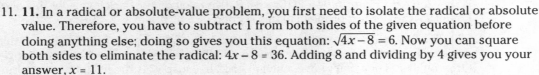

The *is/of method* relies on this formula: $\frac{\text{is}}{\text{of}} = \frac{\%}{100}$. See Chapter 12 for more information.

11. **11.** In a radical or absolute-value problem, you first need to isolate the radical or absolute value. Therefore, you have to subtract 1 from both sides of the given equation before doing anything else; doing so gives you this equation: $\sqrt{4x-8} = 6$. Now you can square both sides to eliminate the radical: $4x - 8 = 36$. Adding 8 and dividing by 4 gives you your answer, $x = 11$.

12. **6.** Using the definition given in the question, $p \backslash\backslash 7 = \frac{p(7)}{p-4}$ or just $\frac{7p}{p-4}$. Because the question says this equation equals 21, write $\frac{7p}{p-4} = 21$.

By cross-multiplying (you can put 21 over 1 if it helps), you get $7p = 21(p - 4)$ or $7p = 21p - 84$. Subtracting $21p$ from both sides gives you $(-14)p = -84$, and dividing both sides by –14 yields $p = 6$. Double-check your answer by doing the following: $6\backslash\backslash 7 = (6)(7)/(6-4) = \frac{42}{2} = 21$.

13. **12.** When a question tells you the ratio of unknown quantities, you can simply tack an x onto the end of each number. Thus, the length of the rectangle is $5x$ and the width is $2x$. Now you may want to draw and label a rectangle to help you solve this problem:

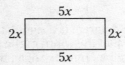

Don't fall into the trap of writing $2x + 5x = 84$; a rectangle has four sides, not two. Write either $2x + 5x + 2x + 5x = 84$ or $2(2x + 5x) = 84$. Either way, the left side is $14x$, so $14x = 84$, and $x = 6$. Another trap lurks here: 6 isn't the answer. You represented the width with $2x$ in your original equation, so the width is $2(6) = 12$ feet.

14. **520.** A linear function has the form $y = mx + b$. In this problem, x is the number of people, while y is the cost. You can choose from several ways to work out this problem, but here I focus on the slope, which is the change in y divided by the change in x. When the number of people increases by 2, the cost increases by $50. Therefore, the slope $m = \frac{50}{2} = 25$. Now, because a party for 10 costs $320, a party of 18 adds 8 people, for $8 \times \$25 = \$200$ more. So a party of 18 costs $520.

15. **6.** Although you can use trial and error to answer this question, I use algebra here to give you a little more practice. Darren makes $9 an hour on weekdays, and $1\frac{1}{2} \times \$9 = \$13.50$ on weekends. If you let d equal his weekday hours and e equal his weekend hours, you know

that \$9(*d*) + \$13.50(*e*) = \$189.00. You also know that *d* + *e* = 18 (his total hours), so you can solve this problem using substitution: *d* = 18 – *e*, so \$9(18 – *e*) + \$13.50*e* = \$189. Distributing: \$162 – \$9*e* + \$13.50*e* = \$189. Combining like terms, you get \$162 + \$4.50*e* = \$189. Now just subtract 162 from both sides and divide by 4.50, to get *e* = 6. Simple, right?

16. **7.** Remember the distance formula? (I hope so because you need it to solve this problem!) It tells you that the distance between two points, (x_1, y_1) and (x_2, y_2), is $\sqrt{(x_2 - x_1)^2 + (y_2 - y_1)^2}$. Substituting the numbers from the question, you get

    $$10 = \sqrt{((-2)-(4))^2 + (p-(-1))^2} = \sqrt{(-6)^2 + (p+1)^2} = \sqrt{36 + (p+1)^2}.$$

    Because this is a radical equation, square both sides, so 100 = 36 + $(p + 1)^2$. Subtract 36 from both sides to get 64 = $(p + 1)^2$. The easiest way to solve this problem is to think about squares. If a quantity (in this case, *p* + 1) squared is 64, then the quantity must equal 8 or –8. But the question tells you that *p* is positive, so *p* + 1 = 8, and *p* = 7.

17. **84.** You can try to figure out what *a* and *b* equal, but doing so isn't worth the energy. The key to getting this question right is remembering the formulas that I discuss in Chapter 14 — specifically, the one that says that $(a - b)^2 = a^2 - 2ab + b^2$. Do you see how this helps? You know that $(a - b) = 8$, so $(a - b)^2 = a^2 - 2ab + b^2 = 64$. This question asks you for $a^2 + b^2$, which is $(a^2 - 2ab + b^2) + 2ab$, or 64 + 2(10) = 84. Pat yourself on the back if you got this one right; I think it's the hardest problem in this section.

18. **360.** The total surface area is the sum of the area of the square and the area of the four triangles. The area of the square is easy to find: It's simply 10 × 10 = 100. The triangles are a little tougher. They don't have a height of 12 because 12 is the height of the pyramid, but the triangles are slanted. However, if you look at the following diagram, you see that you can find the height of the slanted triangles by using the Pythagorean Theorem.

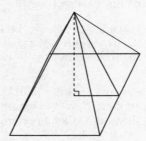

The little triangle in the diagram is a right triangle. One leg is 12 (the height of the pyramid). The second leg is half the width of the square, or 5. This triangle is actually the world's second-most famous right triangle, the 5-12-13 triangle. (If you didn't remember this little tidbit, you could've figured it out with the Pythagorean Theorem.) The hypotenuse, 13, is the altitude of each of the tilted triangles that make up the sides of the pyramid. Because the triangle's area is ½ × base × height, each triangle's area is ½ × 10 × 13 = 65. The four triangles together have an area of 4 × 65 = 260. Adding in the 100 from the base gives you 360, which is the answer.

Section 6: Multiple-Choice Writing

1. **B.** Got a match? No, I'm not talking about smoking or lighting a fire. I'm talking about *playing*, *studying*, and *to audition*, all of which should, but don't, match in structure. (In other words, they should be *parallel*.) Change *to audition* to *for auditioning*. Do you hear how the sentence sounds more balanced now?

2. **C.** Choice (A) is no good because you have two sentences joined by a comma — a big no-no. Choice (B) is overkill: You don't need a semicolon and a joining word *(and)*. Choice (D) drops out because the verb tense is wrong, and Choice (E) makes no sense. Thus, the correct answer is Choice (C).

3. **B.** The SAT writers are testing two different punctuation marks in this question: the apostrophe and the comma. You don't need an apostrophe because the possessive pronoun *(its)* never has one. You do need a comma because when you glue two sentences together with a joining word *(but* in this sentence) you must place a comma before the joining word.

4. **E.** The guides aren't objecting to *him*, just to the *trespassing*. To place the emphasis on *trespassing,* change the *him* to *his*.

5. **C.** *Between* is a preposition and takes an object, not a subject pronoun. Always say, "between you and me," not "between you and I."

6. **C.** This sentence connects the present to the past. The verb *has traveled* (present-perfect tense for you grammar buffs who just have to know) connects those two time periods.

7. **D.** The rule for introductory verb forms is that the next person or thing in the sentence has to be doing the action of the verb. In this sentence, the taxi can't speed and wait at the same time, so the toddler has to be waiting. Thus, you can rule out Choice (A) immediately. Other choices drop away because of misplaced descriptions. Choice (B) is out because the hand is waiting. Choice (C) hits the mat because the taxi is holding hands, and Choice (E) has an unnecessary comma.

   Whenever you see a sentence on the SAT beginning with a verb form, watch out! The SAT makers love to mix up who's doing what in the sentence to make sure you're paying attention.

8. **A.** The rubber bone isn't the only toy sold; it's one of a group of toys. The toys in the group are sold, so you can rule out Choices (C) and (D). *Which* usually comes after a comma, and *that* is generally used without a comma. These two facts allow you to drop Choices (B) and (E).

9. **B.** *The reason is that* is correct; *the reason is because* is never right. Only Choices (B) and (E) use *that,* but Choice (E) has the wrong verb tense.

10. **D.** The missing word in this sentence is *can*, as in "why Olivia doesn't write as well as he *can*." After you add the missing word, you're more likely to hear the correct answer because *him can* sounds strange. The grammar rule behind this question is that *he* may act as a subject of the verb *can*. The pronoun *him* is for objects only.

11. **E.** *However* can't join sentences by itself; it must be accompanied by a semicolon. Both Choices (B) and (E) have semicolons, but Choice (B) adds a *had,* changing the verb to past-perfect tense, which you need only when you're placing one event in the past **prior to** (before) another.

12. **C.** The subjects and verbs pair up this way: *she thought, whoever/whomever would eat.* The pronoun *whoever* is for subjects and *whomever* is for objects. In this sentence, therefore, you need *whoever*. Choice (C) beats out Choice (D) because of verb tense.

13. **E.** Although you may really hate verb tense, the rule on *had* is simple: The helping verb *had* places an action further in the past than the straight, unadorned past tense. So you have a supermarket being torn down and replaced by a gas station. The supermarket is further in the past, so it gets the *had*, or more specifically, the *had been*.

   Be sure you understand the sequence of events when checking verb tense.

14. **D.** With *neither/nor* sentences (and also *either/or*), match the verb to the closest subject. *Students* takes a plural verb, so you need *were* in this sentence. Choice (B) has the correct verb, but it adds an unnecessary *they would,* so Choice (D) is correct.

15. **C.** The *it* of Choices (A) and (E) is unnecessary, as is the article in Choice (B). (Also, articles don't "say" anything because articles can't speak.) Choice (D) has an extra comma.

16. **A.** Sometimes the hardest questions are the ones that are correct as they are. The original sentence pairs a plural pronoun (*who,* which refers to the plural noun *researchers*) with a plural verb *(were).* A-okay for this one!

17. **B.** The word *although* fits the meaning of the sentence better than *and* because *although* introduces a condition, which, in this sentence, is the fact that one country had two different languages and traditions. The other choices introduce unnecessary words.

18. **C.** The word *so* may join one idea to another in the sentence in a cause-and-effect relationship. Were you fooled by Choice (D)? The pronoun *which* may substitute for a noun or pronoun, but not for an entire subject/verb expression.

19. **C.** The key here is *everyone,* a singular word that must be paired with another singular word or phrase, such as *his or her,* but definitely not with the plural word *their.*

 20. **A.** *Costliest* compares one thing to everything else. *Costlier* compares two things.

In general, use *-er* comparisons between two things and *-est* for larger groups.

21. **E.** The answer to this question is *No error.* Did I trip you up with Choice (D)? Perhaps the apostrophe surprised you because apostrophes are usually associated with missing letters or with possession. But whenever you're talking about time and money, you may find an apostrophe, as in *an hour's homework* or *two weeks' pay.*

22. **B.** Janine isn't going to do two separate things — try and determine. She will *try to determine.*

23. **D.** If the padding *nearly prevents,* it doesn't prevent at all. If it prevents *nearly every wound,* one or two stabs slip through. Thus, for the sentence to make sense, the *nearly* has to be moved.

24. **D.** If it's his team, Archie is on it, so he should do better than anyone *else* on his team.

25. **C.** *Consequently* looks like a word that's strong enough to join two sentences, but it's actually a weakling. To join the sentences, you need to add a semicolon before *consequently.*

26. **B.** The *along with* is just camouflage; the real subject of this sentence is *one.* The verb must match the subject, so *are* needs to change to *is.*

27. **A.** *Who* is for subjects and *whom* is for objects. In this sentence, *whom* is the object of *should bill.* Think of the sentence as *he should bill whom,* and the answer becomes obvious.

28. **B.** Who didn't care — Marisa or her aunt? No one knows (at least not from reading this sentence). The pronoun *she* must be clarified.

29. **E.** The SAT often includes sentences that contain this kind of construction: "the only one of the _____ who (or that or which) _____." In this sort of sentence, the pronoun *who* or *that* or *which* refers to the *one* and, therefore, is singular and requires a singular verb. If you picked Choice (B) as the error, you fell into the trap because the verb *was* is singular and totally correct.

30. **D.** In an argumentative essay like the one presented in this test, the more detail you include to support your points, the better. Choice (D) provides the name of the network and delivers the remaining facts concisely and clearly and, thus, improves the original sentence.

31. **B.** A useful technique in essay writing — one you may use when you write your own SAT essay — is called *concession and reply.* With this technique, you anticipate the reader's objections to your argument and answer those objections in advance. The second paragraph of the essay presents some of the arguments in favor of broadcasting trials and responds to those arguments.

32. **E.** Tucking the information about hotel stays into the first sentence is effective. Clauses beginning with *that* are seldom set off by commas.

33. **B.** Sentence 9 in its original version is wordy and contains two grammatical errors — *dramatic* instead of *dramatically* and a vague pronoun *(it).* Choice (B) is clearer and shorter.

34. **C.** When starting a new paragraph, look for a *transition* — a word or phrase that shows the reader the logical connection between the two paragraphs. Choices (C) and (D) are the only two with transitions, but Choice (D) introduces a completely irrelevant *you*.

35. **D.** The writer takes pains to explain that each case is different, so Choices (A) and (B) are definitely wrong. Choice (C) is too broad. Choice (E) is tempting, but the writer hasn't provided evidence to back up the idea that only the judge can decide.

Section 7: Critical Reading

1. **A.** The structure of the sentence points you toward a word that contrasts with *powerful*. Yes, genes are powerful, but they're not _____. (Fill in the blank with something else.) Choice (A), *omnipotent* (all powerful), creates the contrast you're looking for. The only other possibility is Choice (D), but *coercive* (forcing, like a bully after your lunch money) is too strong here.

2. **E.** Dump the mailed paper statement, and what do you achieve? A reduction in *litter* and *waste* — the first words in Choices (D) and (E). Now check the second possibility. You don't have *admittance* to a Web site; you have *access*. There you have it: Choice (E) is the answer you're looking for.

3. **D.** Several answers are possible, namely Choices (B), (D), and (E), but the best one is Choice (E) because *prolific* (productive) best matches the one-book-a-year statement.

4. **A.** Picture a baby with a toy. She attempts to eat it, throw it, sit on it, and otherwise examine it, but her movements lack skill because, well, babies have limited motor control. Choice (A) fits best because *dexterity* means "great control over movement." The other choices aren't even close, but here's a little vocabulary lesson anyway. *Lethargy* means "extreme weariness," as in "I'm holding the remote but am too tired to push the button."

5. **C.** The first thing that should catch your attention in this sentence is *only a tiny locker*. Okay, that phrase rules out any choices referring to large size, including Choices (A), (B), (D), and (E), all of which refer to the opposite of small. What's left? Choice (C), which begins with an antonym of *large* — *cramped*.

6. **C.** Picture a rainbow and you've arrived at the right answer. A rainbow has, by definition, many colors. *Myriad* means "numerous" or "countless."

7. **D.** This one is tricky. Choices (A), (B), (C), and (E) all deal with food or drink, but the author is talking about motivation. *Fuel* comes closest in the sense that you fuel or power *discovery and wonder*.

8. **D.** If the researcher *must make* an adjustment to biostatistics, he or she is the wave of the future. The researcher may be critical, nostalgic, fearful, or adverse (all wrong answers), but the author is favorable.

9. **B.** Medical researchers have to know statistics — no matter how much that subject makes them tear out their hair — as the last two sentences of the passage make clear.

10. **A.** Passage II doesn't mention passion at all, but Passage I's narrator (the mad scientist who creates the "monster," by the way) says that he is into his work *heart and soul*. Choice (B) is a trap because the first passage is from a novel but isn't about literature at all. Choices (C) and (D) are also wrong because the first passage doesn't give any evidence either way. Both passages mention education, so Choice (E) is incorrect as well.

11. **B.** The passage begins with Austen's trademark irony. No one would think of Catherine as a heroine because her parents are alive, they have enough money, and they're sensible people. To answer the question, then, you need to figure out how Catherine differs from a heroine, a situation covered by Choice (B).

12. **A.** Her father was "a very respectable man, though his name was Richard," so you can infer that men named Richard aren't generally respectable.

13. **E.** The passage states that Mrs. Morland, "instead of dying in bringing the latter [Catherine] into the world, as anybody might expect . . . still lived." The passage also mentions her *good constitution* — a reference to good health.

14. **E.** The passage elaborates on Mrs. Morland's survival and the fact that she bore ten children and still enjoyed good health. Those details clue you in to the fact that a *good constitution* is robust, or strong, health.

15. **E.** The passage states that Catherine will do anything rather than study.

16. **D.** The passage makes clear that Catherine isn't a student and her mother doesn't make a big deal out of her daughter's education. So if Catherine can learn a piece, it is probably a no-brainer. Choice (D) is the only option that fits this criteria.

17. **A.** She can't take it anymore and gives up her lessons. Thus, she can't *stand* it.

18. **C.** This passage's tone is humorous exaggeration, and this line is no exception. However much you hate a teacher, you probably wouldn't see his or her dismissal as one of the happiest days of your life.

19. **B.** The passage mentions French, as well as *account* (math), drawing, writing, and music. The other activities aren't part of Catherine's official education.

Section 8: Mathematics

1. **B.** The area of the pizza is πr^2. The radius is 6, because the diameter is 12, and the area is 36π. Dividing by eight slices gives you 4.5π.

2. **A.** As is the case with several math questions on the SAT, the best strategy here is to plug the answer choices into the equation given in the question. Lucky for you, the first answer, Choice (A), works in the equation, so you can stop right there. If you'd rather do algebra to solve this problem, though, start by distributing the 2, to get $2x + 8 = 6$. Subtracting 8 from both sides gives you $2x = -2$, and $x = -1$.

3. **B.** The easiest way to solve this problem is to make a table, dividing by 2 every 20 years:

2000	2020	2040	2060	2080	2100
50	25	12.5	6.25	3.125	1.5625

   The final answer, 1.5625, is the same as $1\frac{9}{16}$.

4. **D.** First off, you must realize that the set contains 21 numbers, not 20. Remember that to find the size of a list of numbers, you subtract the first and last numbers and then add one. (Count them if you don't believe me.) Now, the even numbers are 20, 22, . . . up to 40, which makes five numbers in the 20s, five in the 30s, and 40, which makes 11 numbers out of 21.

5. **E.** All the numbers have three digits. Only Choices (A), (D), and (E) have a units (ones) digit that equals the sum of the other two digits. And, using a calculator, you can see that the square roots of 156 and 516 are decimals, while the square root of 729 is 27, which makes it your answer.

6. **D.** A slope of $-\frac{1}{3}$ means that the line goes down 1 space every time it moves 3 spaces to the right. Because point *M* is on the *x*-axis, the line has gone down 2 spaces by the time it reaches *M*, so it must have moved 6 spaces to the right. In other words, point *M* is at (5, 0). Point *M* is the midpoint of the line, which means that it's halfway to point *P*. So to get to point *P*, you need to move another 2 spaces down and 6 spaces right, which puts you at (11, –2).

7. **C.** Because $b + c = x$, $b = x - c$. So you can substitute $(x - c)$ for b in the first equation, and write $a(x - c) = n$. Because of the parentheses, you have to use the distributive law to get $ax - ac = n$, which is Choice (C).

8. **D.** Possible numbers for g are numbers like 3, 6, 12, 15, 21, and so on. If you try multiplying these numbers by 7 and then dividing by 9, you discover that the remainder is always 3 or 6. Because 3 isn't one of your choices, 6 is the right answer.

9. **D.** A lot of these answers look true. However, if you let a equal 1, or a number less than 1, you realize that most of them become false. This question is an old SAT trap; numbers between zero and one (such as fractions) behave in funny ways. The only statement that is true for all positive numbers is Choice (D): Twice any positive number must be bigger than the original number.

10. **E.** Because this problem involves parallel lines, you need to look for angles that are congruent. You can find them by looking for lines that make a *Z* or a backwards *Z*. Looking first at the bigger triangles, you can mark the diagram as follows:

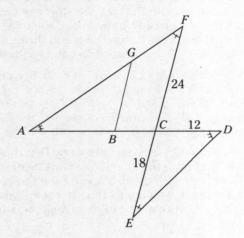

Notice that the two angles in the middle are vertical, so they're also equal. This diagram is a picture of similar triangles: Segment *AC* matches segment *CD*, segment *CF* matches segment *CE*, and segment *AF* matches segment *DE*. Therefore, you can use a ratio to figure out the length of *AC*: $\frac{AC}{CD} = \frac{CF}{CE}$, $\frac{AC}{12} = \frac{24}{18}$.

Cross-multiplying your ratio tells you that $18(AC) = 288$, and $AC = 16$. Now, because $GB \parallel EF$, triangle *ABG* is similar to *ACF*, as well. And because $AG = GF$, the line *GB* cuts triangle *ACF* in half, which means that *AB* is half the length of *AC*, or 8.

Be very careful that you match up the right parts when you write a ratio. Otherwise, you'll undoubtedly get the wrong answer. For example, if you matched line *AC* with line *CE* in the ratio for Question 10 by accident, you'd get the incorrect answer.

11. **B.** By adding the two expressions, you discover that $4a + 4b = 20$, so $a + b = 5$. You can also solve for the variables to get $a = -2$ and $b = 7$, which gives you the same answer.

12. **B.** Ah, yes, an SAT classic. Every time a wheel rotates, it covers the equivalent of one circumference of distance. The circumference equals $2\pi r$, but you have to be careful about units. The wheel has a radius of 18 inches, but your answer needs to be in feet. The circumference is $2 \times 18 \times \pi$ inches $= 36\pi$ inches $= 3\pi$ feet $=$ about 9.4248 feet. Therefore, 50 revolutions covers $50 \times 9.4248 = 471$ feet.

13. **C.** This problem involves exponent laws: When you take a power of a power, such as $\left(5^{q+1}\right)^p$, you multiply the powers. So this expression equals $5^{p(q+1)} = 5^{pq+p}$. Also, when you multiply exponents, you add the powers, so $\left(5^{-p}\right)\left(5^{q+1}\right)^p = \left(5^{-p}\right)5^{pq+p} = 5^{(-p+pq+p)} = 5^{pq}$.

14. **C.** Take each statement one at a time. Choice (A) is true. The mode appears most often, which means the set has to have two, three, or four 90s. Choice (B) requires you to remember this formula: Total = Number × Mean. In this case, the five numbers must add up to $5 \times 80 = 400$. Because you know the set has at least two 90s, which add up to 180, the other three numbers must add up to 220. But because the numbers are all positive, you wouldn't have enough room for the last two numbers if 240 were in the set, which makes Choice (B) true. Choice (C) is false because making a list whose average is 80 without including any 80s in the list is easy. Try it yourself and see.

    You could, of course, stop there (and you probably should, to save time, on the real test). But I want you to give you your money's worth, so I continue through the rest of the answer choices. Choice (D) is definitely true; you used this fact already when you checked Choice (A). In Choice (E), the median of an odd number of numbers is the middle number. So if the median were greater than 90, then three of the five numbers would have to be greater than 90. But you already know from Choice (A) that the set must include at least two 90s. You can't have a list with two 90s and three numbers greater than 90 and still have the average be 80. Thus, the median can't be greater than 90.

15. **E.** Because triangle *BCF* is isosceles, *BC* = *CF* = 8. Because angle *D* is a right angle, triangle *DEF* is the world-famous 3-4-5 right triangle, and *DF* = 4. Because *DC* = 4 + 8 = 12, *AB* is also 12. And, because *AD* = *BC* = 8, *AE* = 8 – 3 = 5. Now you're ready to find *EB*, the hypotenuse of the right triangle *ABE*. You can, of course, use the Pythagorean Theorem, but you'll save time if you realize that you're face to face with a 5-12-13 right triangle, and *BE* = 13.

16. **A.** Call the room shared by Melvin, Carey, and Dan room *X*, and the other room *Y*. Because Mike and Melvin won't live together, Mike must be in room *Y*. Now, if Dave and Dan live together, Peter will live with them, but you can't fit two more people into room *X*, so Dave and Dan must live apart, which puts Dave in room *Y* also. Similarly, because Enoch will live with Chris or Carey, Chris can't be in room *X* either, which puts Chris, Dave, and Mike in room *Y*.

Section 9: Multiple-Choice Writing

1. **C.** Connecting words (*conjunctions*, in grammar lingo) add meaning to the sentence. Using your reading comprehension skills, you know that you're looking for a cause-and-effect relationship between the two parts of the sentence, so you can rule out Choices (D) and (E) right away (the words *and* and *with* don't give you a cause-and-effect relationship). Then consider concise, economical wording, and Choice (C) pops to the top.

2. **A.** One rule to keep in mind is that simplest is often best, at least when it comes to written expression. Every choice except Choice (A) adds unnecessary words, and Choice (E) goes further into no-no land by creating a comma splice; two complete sentences shouldn't be linked only by a comma. For this question, stick with the original!

3. **C.** If historians are debating, you already know that the topic is *controversial* (in dispute), so you can lop off the end of the original sentence. Choice (C) is the only answer that does the job (explaining why Cleopatra's role is controversial) without extra words.

4. **D.** This question tests your knowledge of pronouns. *One* is a pronoun, so it must refer to a particular noun or pronoun. In the original sentence, the most logical meaning of *one* is "lawyer," but *lawyer* doesn't appear in the sentence. Only Choice (D) contains the word *lawyer,* so you know it's the right answer.

5. **E.** The original sentence leaves you hanging because it doesn't complete the thought. (Read it aloud and you'll hear that something's missing.) You need a verb to pair with the subject *Manet*. Choices (C), (D), and (E) all supply verbs, so any of them could be right at this point. Looking at these choices more closely, you can see that Choice (C) isn't right because *was identifying* implies an ongoing situation, as in "Manet was identifying while something else happened." Choice (D) is wrong because *had* places one action before another, and the sentence doesn't justify that sort of timeline. Choice (E) supplies a plain old, past-tense verb, which is just what you need here.

6. **B.** The original sentence tacks on an extra idea — "and they didn't like them." Your task is to tuck that idea into the sentence more neatly, which you can accomplish with Choice (B). Choice (C) may draw your eye because it's short and sweet, and conciseness is often an advantage in this sort of question. However, the sentence begins with *for*, so you're looking at something that was *for the banks. They* doesn't pair well with *for the banks*. What you're looking for is the idea that *salary caps* were unlikable *for the banks*. Choice (B) supplies that meaning.

7. **C.** You can't glue two sentences together with a comma. Well, you can, but then you have to go to Grammar Jail. Choice (C) adds a semicolon, which links the ideas legally.

8. **B.** The subject/verb pair in this sentence is *viruses activate*. In between this pair is a little extra information — what happens to *activate* the body's defenses (the viruses enter the body). Choice (B) is the best answer because it's in *present-perfect tense*, a tense that ties the present (activate the immune system) with the past (when the viruses entered).

9. **A.** *Organizing* is a *gerund*, which is a fancy English-teacher term for the *–ing* form of a verb that acts like a noun. But you don't need special grammar vocabulary to crack this sentence. The superintendent doesn't object to *us*, as Choice (B) states. He objects to the organizing of a dangerous club. The possessive pronoun *our* points the reader toward the key word *organizing*.

10. **D.** If you're rebelling, you go *against*, not *toward* the government. The other choices add unnecessary words.

11. **E.** In a sentence, one verb's tense should match another's, unless you have a good reason to change tenses. *Carved* is past tense, and Choice (E) matches that tense with *decorated*. The sentence would also make sense with a present-tense verb (the ancestors *carved* long ago and Ella *decorates* now), but *decorates* isn't an option.

12. **E.** The introductory phrase *(Sent . . . age)* has to describe the subject of the sentence. The curriculum wasn't sent to boarding school; Sandra was. So you have to find an option that makes Sandra the subject; you can narrow down the answer to Choices (D) and (E). No ongoing action justifies Choice (D), so Choice (E) rules.

13. **D.** Whatever elements of the sentence the conjunction *and* links must have the same grammatical identity. *By his heroism* is a prepositional phrase, but "that he was always motivated by patriotism" has a subject/verb pair. (In case you're desperate to know, a subject/verb pair creates a *clause*.) Even without the official grammar terms, you can hear that the original sentence is unbalanced. Choice (D) restores equilibrium to the sentence and is the right answer.

14. **B.** I hear "equally as" all over the place these days, but sadly, it isn't correct English. Dump the *as* and you're all set.

Answer Key for Practice Exam 1

Section 2

1. A	8. A	15. B	22. E
2. B	9. A	16. D	23. B
3. C	10. C	17. A	24. A
4. A	11. C	18. B	25. B
5. E	12. B	19. D	
6. B	13. E	20. D	
7. A	14. A	21. E	

Section 3

1. D	6. D	11. B	16. A
2. D	7. E	12. C	17. A
3. A	8. B	13. B	18. C
4. C	9. D	14. E	19. D
5. B	10. C	15. B	20. A

Section 4

1. D	7. D	13. D	19. B
2. A	8. D	14. C	20. C
3. C	9. B	15. D	21. B
4. B	10. E	16. A	22. B
5. E	11. C	17. D	23. E
6. D	12. D	18. E	24. A

Section 5

1. A	6. C	11. 11	16. 7
2. C	7. D	12. 6	17. 84
3. C	8. C	13. 12	18. 360
4. A	9. 96	14. 520	
5. B	10. 40	15. 6	

Section 6

1. B	10. D	19. C	28. B
2. C	11. E	20. A	29. E
3. B	12. C	21. E	30. D
4. E	13. E	22. B	31. B
5. C	14. D	23. D	32. E
6. C	15. C	24. D	33. B
7. D	16. A	25. C	34. C
8. A	17. B	26. B	35. D
9. B	18. C	27. A	

Section 7

1. A	6. C	11. B	16. D
2. E	7. D	12. A	17. A
3. D	8. D	13. E	18. C
4. A	9. B	14. E	19. B
5. C	10. A	15. E	

Section 8

1. B	5. E	9. D	13. C
2. A	6. D	10. E	14. C
3. B	7. C	11. B	15. E
4. D	8. D	12. B	16. A

Section 9

1. C	5. E	9. A	13. D
2. A	6. B	10. D	14. B
3. C	7. C	11. E	
4. D	8. B	12. E	

Chapter 22

Practice Exam 2

- -

*1*f you survived Practice Exam 1 in Chapter 20, you may be at the movies right now, throwing popcorn at the latest Hollywood shoot-'em-up. Still here? Okay, I guess that means you want to try again. Follow the procedures described at the beginning of Chapter 20 (the first practice exam): Sit in a quiet room, turn off the phone, and place a timer (an ordinary watch or clock works fine) right in front of your face. Spend no more than the allotted time on each part (I tell you how much at the beginning of each section) and resist the temptation to (a) fold the answer sheet into a paper airplane and fly it out the window (b) peek at Chapter 23, which contains the answers and explanations, or (c) call a friend to set up your weekend party schedule.

Note: The real SAT you take will have ten sections, instead of the nine you see here, because the College Board throws in an "equating section" that doesn't count toward your score but allows the testers to evaluate new questions. The SAT doesn't tell you which section is useless (to you). Because I'm here to help you score high on the SAT, I don't include an equating section in any of the practice tests in this book. Nice of me, huh?

Answer Sheet

For Section 1, use two sheets of loose-leaf or notebook paper to write your essay. (On the real exam, the answer booklet contains two lined sheets.) For Sections 2 through 9, use the ovals and grid-ins to record your answers. Begin with Number 1 for each new section. If any sections have fewer than 35 questions, leave the extra spaces blank.

Section 2: Critical Reading

1. Ⓐ Ⓑ Ⓒ Ⓓ Ⓔ   8. Ⓐ Ⓑ Ⓒ Ⓓ Ⓔ   15. Ⓐ Ⓑ Ⓒ Ⓓ Ⓔ   22. Ⓐ Ⓑ Ⓒ Ⓓ Ⓔ   29. Ⓐ Ⓑ Ⓒ Ⓓ Ⓔ
2. Ⓐ Ⓑ Ⓒ Ⓓ Ⓔ   9. Ⓐ Ⓑ Ⓒ Ⓓ Ⓔ   16. Ⓐ Ⓑ Ⓒ Ⓓ Ⓔ   23. Ⓐ Ⓑ Ⓒ Ⓓ Ⓔ   30. Ⓐ Ⓑ Ⓒ Ⓓ Ⓔ
3. Ⓐ Ⓑ Ⓒ Ⓓ Ⓔ   10. Ⓐ Ⓑ Ⓒ Ⓓ Ⓔ   17. Ⓐ Ⓑ Ⓒ Ⓓ Ⓔ   24. Ⓐ Ⓑ Ⓒ Ⓓ Ⓔ   31. Ⓐ Ⓑ Ⓒ Ⓓ Ⓔ
4. Ⓐ Ⓑ Ⓒ Ⓓ Ⓔ   11. Ⓐ Ⓑ Ⓒ Ⓓ Ⓔ   18. Ⓐ Ⓑ Ⓒ Ⓓ Ⓔ   25. Ⓐ Ⓑ Ⓒ Ⓓ Ⓔ   32. Ⓐ Ⓑ Ⓒ Ⓓ Ⓔ
5. Ⓐ Ⓑ Ⓒ Ⓓ Ⓔ   12. Ⓐ Ⓑ Ⓒ Ⓓ Ⓔ   19. Ⓐ Ⓑ Ⓒ Ⓓ Ⓔ   26. Ⓐ Ⓑ Ⓒ Ⓓ Ⓔ   33. Ⓐ Ⓑ Ⓒ Ⓓ Ⓔ
6. Ⓐ Ⓑ Ⓒ Ⓓ Ⓔ   13. Ⓐ Ⓑ Ⓒ Ⓓ Ⓔ   20. Ⓐ Ⓑ Ⓒ Ⓓ Ⓔ   27. Ⓐ Ⓑ Ⓒ Ⓓ Ⓔ   34. Ⓐ Ⓑ Ⓒ Ⓓ Ⓔ
7. Ⓐ Ⓑ Ⓒ Ⓓ Ⓔ   14. Ⓐ Ⓑ Ⓒ Ⓓ Ⓔ   21. Ⓐ Ⓑ Ⓒ Ⓓ Ⓔ   28. Ⓐ Ⓑ Ⓒ Ⓓ Ⓔ   35. Ⓐ Ⓑ Ⓒ Ⓓ Ⓔ

Section 3: Mathematics

1. Ⓐ Ⓑ Ⓒ Ⓓ Ⓔ   8. Ⓐ Ⓑ Ⓒ Ⓓ Ⓔ   15. Ⓐ Ⓑ Ⓒ Ⓓ Ⓔ   22. Ⓐ Ⓑ Ⓒ Ⓓ Ⓔ   29. Ⓐ Ⓑ Ⓒ Ⓓ Ⓔ
2. Ⓐ Ⓑ Ⓒ Ⓓ Ⓔ   9. Ⓐ Ⓑ Ⓒ Ⓓ Ⓔ   16. Ⓐ Ⓑ Ⓒ Ⓓ Ⓔ   23. Ⓐ Ⓑ Ⓒ Ⓓ Ⓔ   30. Ⓐ Ⓑ Ⓒ Ⓓ Ⓔ
3. Ⓐ Ⓑ Ⓒ Ⓓ Ⓔ   10. Ⓐ Ⓑ Ⓒ Ⓓ Ⓔ   17. Ⓐ Ⓑ Ⓒ Ⓓ Ⓔ   24. Ⓐ Ⓑ Ⓒ Ⓓ Ⓔ   31. Ⓐ Ⓑ Ⓒ Ⓓ Ⓔ
4. Ⓐ Ⓑ Ⓒ Ⓓ Ⓔ   11. Ⓐ Ⓑ Ⓒ Ⓓ Ⓔ   18. Ⓐ Ⓑ Ⓒ Ⓓ Ⓔ   25. Ⓐ Ⓑ Ⓒ Ⓓ Ⓔ   32. Ⓐ Ⓑ Ⓒ Ⓓ Ⓔ
5. Ⓐ Ⓑ Ⓒ Ⓓ Ⓔ   12. Ⓐ Ⓑ Ⓒ Ⓓ Ⓔ   19. Ⓐ Ⓑ Ⓒ Ⓓ Ⓔ   26. Ⓐ Ⓑ Ⓒ Ⓓ Ⓔ   33. Ⓐ Ⓑ Ⓒ Ⓓ Ⓔ
6. Ⓐ Ⓑ Ⓒ Ⓓ Ⓔ   13. Ⓐ Ⓑ Ⓒ Ⓓ Ⓔ   20. Ⓐ Ⓑ Ⓒ Ⓓ Ⓔ   27. Ⓐ Ⓑ Ⓒ Ⓓ Ⓔ   34. Ⓐ Ⓑ Ⓒ Ⓓ Ⓔ
7. Ⓐ Ⓑ Ⓒ Ⓓ Ⓔ   14. Ⓐ Ⓑ Ⓒ Ⓓ Ⓔ   21. Ⓐ Ⓑ Ⓒ Ⓓ Ⓔ   28. Ⓐ Ⓑ Ⓒ Ⓓ Ⓔ   35. Ⓐ Ⓑ Ⓒ Ⓓ Ⓔ

Section 4: Critical Reading

1. Ⓐ Ⓑ Ⓒ Ⓓ Ⓔ   8. Ⓐ Ⓑ Ⓒ Ⓓ Ⓔ   15. Ⓐ Ⓑ Ⓒ Ⓓ Ⓔ   22. Ⓐ Ⓑ Ⓒ Ⓓ Ⓔ   29. Ⓐ Ⓑ Ⓒ Ⓓ Ⓔ
2. Ⓐ Ⓑ Ⓒ Ⓓ Ⓔ   9. Ⓐ Ⓑ Ⓒ Ⓓ Ⓔ   16. Ⓐ Ⓑ Ⓒ Ⓓ Ⓔ   23. Ⓐ Ⓑ Ⓒ Ⓓ Ⓔ   30. Ⓐ Ⓑ Ⓒ Ⓓ Ⓔ
3. Ⓐ Ⓑ Ⓒ Ⓓ Ⓔ   10. Ⓐ Ⓑ Ⓒ Ⓓ Ⓔ   17. Ⓐ Ⓑ Ⓒ Ⓓ Ⓔ   24. Ⓐ Ⓑ Ⓒ Ⓓ Ⓔ   31. Ⓐ Ⓑ Ⓒ Ⓓ Ⓔ
4. Ⓐ Ⓑ Ⓒ Ⓓ Ⓔ   11. Ⓐ Ⓑ Ⓒ Ⓓ Ⓔ   18. Ⓐ Ⓑ Ⓒ Ⓓ Ⓔ   25. Ⓐ Ⓑ Ⓒ Ⓓ Ⓔ   32. Ⓐ Ⓑ Ⓒ Ⓓ Ⓔ
5. Ⓐ Ⓑ Ⓒ Ⓓ Ⓔ   12. Ⓐ Ⓑ Ⓒ Ⓓ Ⓔ   19. Ⓐ Ⓑ Ⓒ Ⓓ Ⓔ   26. Ⓐ Ⓑ Ⓒ Ⓓ Ⓔ   33. Ⓐ Ⓑ Ⓒ Ⓓ Ⓔ
6. Ⓐ Ⓑ Ⓒ Ⓓ Ⓔ   13. Ⓐ Ⓑ Ⓒ Ⓓ Ⓔ   20. Ⓐ Ⓑ Ⓒ Ⓓ Ⓔ   27. Ⓐ Ⓑ Ⓒ Ⓓ Ⓔ   34. Ⓐ Ⓑ Ⓒ Ⓓ Ⓔ
7. Ⓐ Ⓑ Ⓒ Ⓓ Ⓔ   14. Ⓐ Ⓑ Ⓒ Ⓓ Ⓔ   21. Ⓐ Ⓑ Ⓒ Ⓓ Ⓔ   28. Ⓐ Ⓑ Ⓒ Ⓓ Ⓔ   35. Ⓐ Ⓑ Ⓒ Ⓓ Ⓔ

Section 5: Mathematics

1. Ⓐ Ⓑ Ⓒ Ⓓ Ⓔ   8. Ⓐ Ⓑ Ⓒ Ⓓ Ⓔ   15. Ⓐ Ⓑ Ⓒ Ⓓ Ⓔ   22. Ⓐ Ⓑ Ⓒ Ⓓ Ⓔ   29. Ⓐ Ⓑ Ⓒ Ⓓ Ⓔ
2. Ⓐ Ⓑ Ⓒ Ⓓ Ⓔ   9. Ⓐ Ⓑ Ⓒ Ⓓ Ⓔ   16. Ⓐ Ⓑ Ⓒ Ⓓ Ⓔ   23. Ⓐ Ⓑ Ⓒ Ⓓ Ⓔ   30. Ⓐ Ⓑ Ⓒ Ⓓ Ⓔ
3. Ⓐ Ⓑ Ⓒ Ⓓ Ⓔ   10. Ⓐ Ⓑ Ⓒ Ⓓ Ⓔ   17. Ⓐ Ⓑ Ⓒ Ⓓ Ⓔ   24. Ⓐ Ⓑ Ⓒ Ⓓ Ⓔ   31. Ⓐ Ⓑ Ⓒ Ⓓ Ⓔ
4. Ⓐ Ⓑ Ⓒ Ⓓ Ⓔ   11. Ⓐ Ⓑ Ⓒ Ⓓ Ⓔ   18. Ⓐ Ⓑ Ⓒ Ⓓ Ⓔ   25. Ⓐ Ⓑ Ⓒ Ⓓ Ⓔ   32. Ⓐ Ⓑ Ⓒ Ⓓ Ⓔ
5. Ⓐ Ⓑ Ⓒ Ⓓ Ⓔ   12. Ⓐ Ⓑ Ⓒ Ⓓ Ⓔ   19. Ⓐ Ⓑ Ⓒ Ⓓ Ⓔ   26. Ⓐ Ⓑ Ⓒ Ⓓ Ⓔ   33. Ⓐ Ⓑ Ⓒ Ⓓ Ⓔ
6. Ⓐ Ⓑ Ⓒ Ⓓ Ⓔ   13. Ⓐ Ⓑ Ⓒ Ⓓ Ⓔ   20. Ⓐ Ⓑ Ⓒ Ⓓ Ⓔ   27. Ⓐ Ⓑ Ⓒ Ⓓ Ⓔ   34. Ⓐ Ⓑ Ⓒ Ⓓ Ⓔ
7. Ⓐ Ⓑ Ⓒ Ⓓ Ⓔ   14. Ⓐ Ⓑ Ⓒ Ⓓ Ⓔ   21. Ⓐ Ⓑ Ⓒ Ⓓ Ⓔ   28. Ⓐ Ⓑ Ⓒ Ⓓ Ⓔ   35. Ⓐ Ⓑ Ⓒ Ⓓ Ⓔ

9.   10.   11.   12.   13.

14.   15.   16.   17.   18.

Section 6: Multiple-Choice Writing

1. Ⓐ Ⓑ Ⓒ Ⓓ Ⓔ   8. Ⓐ Ⓑ Ⓒ Ⓓ Ⓔ   15. Ⓐ Ⓑ Ⓒ Ⓓ Ⓔ   22. Ⓐ Ⓑ Ⓒ Ⓓ Ⓔ   29. Ⓐ Ⓑ Ⓒ Ⓓ Ⓔ
2. Ⓐ Ⓑ Ⓒ Ⓓ Ⓔ   9. Ⓐ Ⓑ Ⓒ Ⓓ Ⓔ   16. Ⓐ Ⓑ Ⓒ Ⓓ Ⓔ   23. Ⓐ Ⓑ Ⓒ Ⓓ Ⓔ   30. Ⓐ Ⓑ Ⓒ Ⓓ Ⓔ
3. Ⓐ Ⓑ Ⓒ Ⓓ Ⓔ   10. Ⓐ Ⓑ Ⓒ Ⓓ Ⓔ   17. Ⓐ Ⓑ Ⓒ Ⓓ Ⓔ   24. Ⓐ Ⓑ Ⓒ Ⓓ Ⓔ   31. Ⓐ Ⓑ Ⓒ Ⓓ Ⓔ
4. Ⓐ Ⓑ Ⓒ Ⓓ Ⓔ   11. Ⓐ Ⓑ Ⓒ Ⓓ Ⓔ   18. Ⓐ Ⓑ Ⓒ Ⓓ Ⓔ   25. Ⓐ Ⓑ Ⓒ Ⓓ Ⓔ   32. Ⓐ Ⓑ Ⓒ Ⓓ Ⓔ
5. Ⓐ Ⓑ Ⓒ Ⓓ Ⓔ   12. Ⓐ Ⓑ Ⓒ Ⓓ Ⓔ   19. Ⓐ Ⓑ Ⓒ Ⓓ Ⓔ   26. Ⓐ Ⓑ Ⓒ Ⓓ Ⓔ   33. Ⓐ Ⓑ Ⓒ Ⓓ Ⓔ
6. Ⓐ Ⓑ Ⓒ Ⓓ Ⓔ   13. Ⓐ Ⓑ Ⓒ Ⓓ Ⓔ   20. Ⓐ Ⓑ Ⓒ Ⓓ Ⓔ   27. Ⓐ Ⓑ Ⓒ Ⓓ Ⓔ   34. Ⓐ Ⓑ Ⓒ Ⓓ Ⓔ
7. Ⓐ Ⓑ Ⓒ Ⓓ Ⓔ   14. Ⓐ Ⓑ Ⓒ Ⓓ Ⓔ   21. Ⓐ Ⓑ Ⓒ Ⓓ Ⓔ   28. Ⓐ Ⓑ Ⓒ Ⓓ Ⓔ   35. Ⓐ Ⓑ Ⓒ Ⓓ Ⓔ

Section 7: Critical Reading

1. Ⓐ Ⓑ Ⓒ Ⓓ Ⓔ   8. Ⓐ Ⓑ Ⓒ Ⓓ Ⓔ   15. Ⓐ Ⓑ Ⓒ Ⓓ Ⓔ   22. Ⓐ Ⓑ Ⓒ Ⓓ Ⓔ   29. Ⓐ Ⓑ Ⓒ Ⓓ Ⓔ
2. Ⓐ Ⓑ Ⓒ Ⓓ Ⓔ   9. Ⓐ Ⓑ Ⓒ Ⓓ Ⓔ   16. Ⓐ Ⓑ Ⓒ Ⓓ Ⓔ   23. Ⓐ Ⓑ Ⓒ Ⓓ Ⓔ   30. Ⓐ Ⓑ Ⓒ Ⓓ Ⓔ
3. Ⓐ Ⓑ Ⓒ Ⓓ Ⓔ   10. Ⓐ Ⓑ Ⓒ Ⓓ Ⓔ   17. Ⓐ Ⓑ Ⓒ Ⓓ Ⓔ   24. Ⓐ Ⓑ Ⓒ Ⓓ Ⓔ   31. Ⓐ Ⓑ Ⓒ Ⓓ Ⓔ
4. Ⓐ Ⓑ Ⓒ Ⓓ Ⓔ   11. Ⓐ Ⓑ Ⓒ Ⓓ Ⓔ   18. Ⓐ Ⓑ Ⓒ Ⓓ Ⓔ   25. Ⓐ Ⓑ Ⓒ Ⓓ Ⓔ   32. Ⓐ Ⓑ Ⓒ Ⓓ Ⓔ
5. Ⓐ Ⓑ Ⓒ Ⓓ Ⓔ   12. Ⓐ Ⓑ Ⓒ Ⓓ Ⓔ   19. Ⓐ Ⓑ Ⓒ Ⓓ Ⓔ   26. Ⓐ Ⓑ Ⓒ Ⓓ Ⓔ   33. Ⓐ Ⓑ Ⓒ Ⓓ Ⓔ
6. Ⓐ Ⓑ Ⓒ Ⓓ Ⓔ   13. Ⓐ Ⓑ Ⓒ Ⓓ Ⓔ   20. Ⓐ Ⓑ Ⓒ Ⓓ Ⓔ   27. Ⓐ Ⓑ Ⓒ Ⓓ Ⓔ   34. Ⓐ Ⓑ Ⓒ Ⓓ Ⓔ
7. Ⓐ Ⓑ Ⓒ Ⓓ Ⓔ   14. Ⓐ Ⓑ Ⓒ Ⓓ Ⓔ   21. Ⓐ Ⓑ Ⓒ Ⓓ Ⓔ   28. Ⓐ Ⓑ Ⓒ Ⓓ Ⓔ   35. Ⓐ Ⓑ Ⓒ Ⓓ Ⓔ

Section 8: Mathematics

1. Ⓐ Ⓑ Ⓒ Ⓓ Ⓔ   8. Ⓐ Ⓑ Ⓒ Ⓓ Ⓔ   15. Ⓐ Ⓑ Ⓒ Ⓓ Ⓔ   22. Ⓐ Ⓑ Ⓒ Ⓓ Ⓔ   29. Ⓐ Ⓑ Ⓒ Ⓓ Ⓔ
2. Ⓐ Ⓑ Ⓒ Ⓓ Ⓔ   9. Ⓐ Ⓑ Ⓒ Ⓓ Ⓔ   16. Ⓐ Ⓑ Ⓒ Ⓓ Ⓔ   23. Ⓐ Ⓑ Ⓒ Ⓓ Ⓔ   30. Ⓐ Ⓑ Ⓒ Ⓓ Ⓔ
3. Ⓐ Ⓑ Ⓒ Ⓓ Ⓔ   10. Ⓐ Ⓑ Ⓒ Ⓓ Ⓔ   17. Ⓐ Ⓑ Ⓒ Ⓓ Ⓔ   24. Ⓐ Ⓑ Ⓒ Ⓓ Ⓔ   31. Ⓐ Ⓑ Ⓒ Ⓓ Ⓔ
4. Ⓐ Ⓑ Ⓒ Ⓓ Ⓔ   11. Ⓐ Ⓑ Ⓒ Ⓓ Ⓔ   18. Ⓐ Ⓑ Ⓒ Ⓓ Ⓔ   25. Ⓐ Ⓑ Ⓒ Ⓓ Ⓔ   32. Ⓐ Ⓑ Ⓒ Ⓓ Ⓔ
5. Ⓐ Ⓑ Ⓒ Ⓓ Ⓔ   12. Ⓐ Ⓑ Ⓒ Ⓓ Ⓔ   19. Ⓐ Ⓑ Ⓒ Ⓓ Ⓔ   26. Ⓐ Ⓑ Ⓒ Ⓓ Ⓔ   33. Ⓐ Ⓑ Ⓒ Ⓓ Ⓔ
6. Ⓐ Ⓑ Ⓒ Ⓓ Ⓔ   13. Ⓐ Ⓑ Ⓒ Ⓓ Ⓔ   20. Ⓐ Ⓑ Ⓒ Ⓓ Ⓔ   27. Ⓐ Ⓑ Ⓒ Ⓓ Ⓔ   34. Ⓐ Ⓑ Ⓒ Ⓓ Ⓔ
7. Ⓐ Ⓑ Ⓒ Ⓓ Ⓔ   14. Ⓐ Ⓑ Ⓒ Ⓓ Ⓔ   21. Ⓐ Ⓑ Ⓒ Ⓓ Ⓔ   28. Ⓐ Ⓑ Ⓒ Ⓓ Ⓔ   35. Ⓐ Ⓑ Ⓒ Ⓓ Ⓔ

Section 9: Multiple-Choice Writing

1. Ⓐ Ⓑ Ⓒ Ⓓ Ⓔ   8. Ⓐ Ⓑ Ⓒ Ⓓ Ⓔ   15. Ⓐ Ⓑ Ⓒ Ⓓ Ⓔ   22. Ⓐ Ⓑ Ⓒ Ⓓ Ⓔ   29. Ⓐ Ⓑ Ⓒ Ⓓ Ⓔ
2. Ⓐ Ⓑ Ⓒ Ⓓ Ⓔ   9. Ⓐ Ⓑ Ⓒ Ⓓ Ⓔ   16. Ⓐ Ⓑ Ⓒ Ⓓ Ⓔ   23. Ⓐ Ⓑ Ⓒ Ⓓ Ⓔ   30. Ⓐ Ⓑ Ⓒ Ⓓ Ⓔ
3. Ⓐ Ⓑ Ⓒ Ⓓ Ⓔ   10. Ⓐ Ⓑ Ⓒ Ⓓ Ⓔ   17. Ⓐ Ⓑ Ⓒ Ⓓ Ⓔ   24. Ⓐ Ⓑ Ⓒ Ⓓ Ⓔ   31. Ⓐ Ⓑ Ⓒ Ⓓ Ⓔ
4. Ⓐ Ⓑ Ⓒ Ⓓ Ⓔ   11. Ⓐ Ⓑ Ⓒ Ⓓ Ⓔ   18. Ⓐ Ⓑ Ⓒ Ⓓ Ⓔ   25. Ⓐ Ⓑ Ⓒ Ⓓ Ⓔ   32. Ⓐ Ⓑ Ⓒ Ⓓ Ⓔ
5. Ⓐ Ⓑ Ⓒ Ⓓ Ⓔ   12. Ⓐ Ⓑ Ⓒ Ⓓ Ⓔ   19. Ⓐ Ⓑ Ⓒ Ⓓ Ⓔ   26. Ⓐ Ⓑ Ⓒ Ⓓ Ⓔ   33. Ⓐ Ⓑ Ⓒ Ⓓ Ⓔ
6. Ⓐ Ⓑ Ⓒ Ⓓ Ⓔ   13. Ⓐ Ⓑ Ⓒ Ⓓ Ⓔ   20. Ⓐ Ⓑ Ⓒ Ⓓ Ⓔ   27. Ⓐ Ⓑ Ⓒ Ⓓ Ⓔ   34. Ⓐ Ⓑ Ⓒ Ⓓ Ⓔ
7. Ⓐ Ⓑ Ⓒ Ⓓ Ⓔ   14. Ⓐ Ⓑ Ⓒ Ⓓ Ⓔ   21. Ⓐ Ⓑ Ⓒ Ⓓ Ⓔ   28. Ⓐ Ⓑ Ⓒ Ⓓ Ⓔ   35. Ⓐ Ⓑ Ⓒ Ⓓ Ⓔ

Section 1

The Essay

Time: 25 minutes

Directions: In response to the following prompt, write an essay on a separate sheet of paper (the answer sheet). You may use extra space in the question booklet to take notes and to organize your thoughts, but only the answer sheet will be graded.

"Both the man of science and the man of art live always at the edge of mystery, surrounded by it." — J. Robert Oppenheimer, scientist who worked on the atomic bomb

"But the creative person is subject to a different, higher law than mere national law. Whoever has to create a work, whoever has to bring about a discovery or deed which will further the cause of all of humanity, no longer has his home in his native land but rather in his work." — Stephan Zweig, Austrian writer

To what extent should a scientist, an explorer, or a creative artist consider the consequences of his or her work? Drawing upon your own observations and experience or your knowledge of history, current events, and literature, comment on the obligation of an artist, explorer, or scientist to the public good.

STOP YOU MAY CHECK YOUR WORK ON THIS SECTION ONLY. DO NOT GO BACK TO ANY PREVIOUS SECTION.

Section 2
Critical Reading

Time: 25 minutes for 25 questions
Directions: Choose the *best* answer to each question. Mark the corresponding oval on the answer sheet.

Directions for Questions 1–9: Select the answer that *best* fits the meaning of the sentence.

Example: After he had broken the dining room window, Hal's mother _____ him.

(A) selected
(B) serenaded
(C) fooled
(D) scolded
(E) rewarded

The answer is (D).

1. The vice president was _____ by the behavior of the president, who did not even glance at his second-in-command during the inauguration ceremony.
   (A) buoyed
   (B) reassured
   (C) intimidated
   (D) inspired
   (E) affected

2. The _____ of various city states into one nation triggered a period of extraordinary artistic and social growth.
   (A) segregation
   (B) integration
   (C) polarization
   (D) proclamation
   (E) division

3. Angered by the loss of _____ evidence, the detective _____ his subordinates.
   (A) crucial . . . upbraided
   (B) insignificant . . . scolded
   (C) outdated . . . demoted
   (D) compelling . . . promoted
   (E) adverse . . . affronted

4. The _____ corporation took pains to safeguard its _____ production methods.
   (A) deregulated . . . multifaceted
   (B) moribund . . . innovative
   (C) affluent . . . lucrative
   (D) secretive . . . well-publicized
   (E) scrupulous . . . unethical

5. The pragmatic teacher's goal was not to create a test that was particularly easy or hard for her pupils but rather one that _____ their studies.
   (A) discouraged
   (B) heightened
   (C) repressed
   (D) daunted
   (E) motivated

6. The array of characters Shakespeare created makes his plays unique, and actors from every age strive to interpret the _____ roles he created.
   (A) myriad
   (B) convoluted
   (C) versatile
   (D) intuitive
   (E) nebulous

7. Lucy continued her crusade to save the rain forest; furthermore, she strove to _____ the local animal population.
   (A) annihilate
   (B) decimate
   (C) eradicate
   (D) preserve
   (E) proliferate

Go on to next page

8. Dagmar was always _____ in her approach to homework, never completing today what she could postpone until the last possible minute.

   (A) doleful
   (B) doctrinaire
   (C) diffident
   (D) diligent
   (E) dilatory

9. The _____ performance by that actor garnered few _____ from the audience.

   (A) conventional . . . critiques
   (B) effective . . . ovations
   (C) convincing . . . plaudits
   (D) affected . . . kudos
   (E) explicit . . . explanations

Directions for Questions 10–21: Choose the *best* answer to each question based on what is stated or implied in the passage or in the introductory material.

This passage from Freud: Darkness in the Midst of Vision *by Louis Breger (Wiley) discusses the work of Jean-Marie Charcot, a 19th-century pioneer of psychology who studied hysteria.*

Line   By the late 1880s, Charcot had turned his attention to hysteria, and it was here that his need for power and control most interfered with his scientific aims. Hysteria — from the Greek
(05) word for "womb" — was a little understood condition, sometimes believed to be no more than malingering. It was stigmatized by the medical establishment and associated with witchcraft and medieval states of possession. Hysterical
(10) patients displayed a variety of symptoms including amnesias, paralyses, spasms, involuntary movements, and anesthesias. Closely related were cases of so-called neurasthenia, characterized by weakness and lassitude. Unlike the neu-
(15) rological conditions that Charcot had previously studied, no anatomical basis could be found for these syndromes. Looking back from today's vantage point, it is doubtful if there ever was a single entity that could be described as hysteria.
(20) The diagnosis was, rather, a grab bag for a variety of conditions whose common feature was that they were "psychological," that no discernable physical causes could be found for them.

From a modern standpoint, the so-called hyster-
(25) ics comprised a diverse group: some probably had medical conditions that were undiagnosable at the time, others psychotic and borderline disorders, and many — it seems clear from the descriptions — suffered from severe anxiety,
(30) depression, the effects of a variety of traumas, and dissociated states.
   Charcot made crucial contributions to the understanding of hysteria, clarifying the psychological-traumatic nature of symptoms and
(35) conducting convincing hypnotic demonstrations. In addition to the so-called hysterical women on the wards of the [hospital], there were a number of persons of both sexes who had been involved in accidents — for example, train wrecks — who dis-
(40) played symptoms such as paralyses after the accident. Some of them were classified as cases of "railway spine" and "railway brain" because their symptoms mimicked those found after spinal cord or brain injuries. Physicians debated, with much
(45) fervor, whether these conditions had a physical basis. Charcot studied several such patients and was able to demonstrate the absence of damage to the nervous system, hence proving the psychological nature of the symptoms. His most convincing
(50) demonstration relied on the use of hypnosis, a procedure which he had rehabilitated and made scientifically respectable. He was able to hypnotize subjects and suggest that when they awoke from their trances their limbs would be paralyzed.
(55) These hypnotically induced symptoms were exactly the same as those of both hysterical patients and the victims of accidents. He was also able to remove such symptoms with hypnotic suggestion. In a related demonstration, he was able to
(60) distinguish between hysterical and organic amnesia, using hypnosis to help patients recover lost memories, which was not possible, of course, when the amnesia was based on the destruction of brain tissue. While these demonstrations estab-
(65) lished the psychological nature of hysterical symptoms, it was a psychology without awareness. The patients were not conscious, either of the origin and nature of their symptoms — they were not malingering or deliberately faking — or of their
(70) reactions to the hypnotic suggestions. Charcot spoke of a post-traumatic "hypnoid state" — what today would be called dissociation — the blotting out of consciousness of events and emotions associated with traumatic events.
(75) Charcot's genuine contributions were several. He made hysteria a respectable subject of scientific study, described and classified syndromes on the basis of symptoms, and differentiated the condition from known neurological

Go on to next page

(80) diseases. By documenting a number of cases of male hysteria, he disproved the old link between the condition and the organs of female sexuality. He reestablished hypnotism as a research tool and showed how it could be employed to induce

(85) and remove hysterical and post-traumatic symptoms. Finally, and perhaps most significant in terms of its long-range importance for Freud, all these findings and demonstrations gave evidence of an unconscious mind.

10. According to the passage, hysteria was once considered

(A) cause for lifelong hospitalization

(B) treatable only with powerful drugs

(C) fully understood

(D) incurable

(E) possession by an evil spirit

11. The author cites all of the following conditions as hysterical except

(A) lack of feeling

(B) inability to move

(C) uncontrolled bodily activity

(D) wild laughter

(E) memory loss

12. The meaning of "psychological" (Line 22) in this context may best be described as

(A) mentally ill

(B) requiring psychotherapy

(C) not arising from a physical condition

(D) the result of childhood events

(E) unconscious

13. According to the passage, Charcot

(A) linked hysteria to disturbing events in the patient's life

(B) cured hysteria

(C) understood that hysteria was actually a group of illnesses, not one condition

(D) relied primarily on drug therapy for his patients

(E) could not prove the effectiveness of this treatment

14. The author probably mentions patients "of both sexes" (Line 38)

(A) to counter the idea that only females become hysterical

(B) to be fair to both male and female patients

(C) even though Charcot treated only women

(D) to show that Charcot treated everyone who asked

(E) because Charcot believed that hysteria was linked to female anatomy

15. "Railway spine" and "railway brain" (Line 42) are

(A) injuries resulting from train accidents

(B) terms once used for conditions resembling paralysis and head injuries

(C) imaginary ailments intended to deceive insurance companies

(D) physical injuries that take a psychological toll

(E) states displayed only under hypnosis

16. Charcot used hypnosis for all of the following except

(A) to distinguish between physical and psychological symptoms

(B) to enable a patient to move body parts that were previously immobile

(C) to restore memories to some patients

(D) to paralyze a patient

(E) to retrieve memories from brain-damaged patients

17. "Dissociation" (Line 72) results from

(A) a blow to the head

(B) an unconscious process

(C) physical trauma

(D) a desire to deceive the doctor

(E) a deliberate forgetting of disturbing experiences

Go on to next page

18. By inserting the word "genuine" into Line 75, the author implies that
    (A) some of Charcot's work did not advance science
    (B) Charcot was sincere in his belief that hysteria was a real illness
    (C) Charcot should not be overly praised
    (D) Charcot was more important than Freud
    (E) Charcot's work can be duplicated by other scientists

19. Based on information in the passage, the author would probably agree with which of the following statements?
    (A) Hysteria is best treated with hypnosis.
    (B) Hysterics should not be treated medically.
    (C) Hysteria is always linked to severe physical danger, such as a train wreck.
    (D) To scientists today, hysteria is a meaningless term.
    (E) Hysteria is a condition of female patients.

20. The author's tone may best be described as
    (A) nostalgic
    (B) admiring
    (C) biased
    (D) informative
    (E) critical

21. A good title for this passage is
    (A) Charcot's Work on Hysteria
    (B) Charcot and Psychology
    (C) Charcot's Influence on Freud
    (D) The Life of Jean-Marie Charcot
    (E) Hysteria from Ancient through Modern Times

Directions for Questions 22–25: Choose the *best* answer to each question based on what is stated or implied in the passage or in the introductory material.

Questions 22 and 23 are based on the following passage, excerpted from The Hidden Universe *by Roger J. Tayler (Wiley).*

Some direct study of the past is in fact possible because light from distant objects such as galaxies has taken a very long time to reach the Earth. Although light travels 300,000 kilometers in a second, it is possible to observe galaxies (05) which are so distant that light has taken much more than a thousand million years to reach us. We are therefore seeing these galaxies as they were a very long time ago, whereas we are seeing nearby galaxies as they were only a few million (10) years ago and the Sun as it was eight minutes ago.

22. Which statement is supported by the passage?
    (A) Nearby galaxies give off light that is older than light from distant galaxies.
    (B) It is possible to see a current view of distant galaxies.
    (C) Light from the Sun shows that the Sun is farther from the Earth than other stars.
    (D) Light that reaches our eyes may have originated during different time periods.
    (E) Light travels at different speeds depending upon which galaxy it originates from.

23. A good title for this passage would be
    (A) Time Travel
    (B) The Speed of Light
    (C) Direct Study of the Past
    (D) Characteristics of Light
    (E) The Relationship between Light, Time, and Distance

Go on to next page

Questions 24 and 25 are based on the following passage, excerpted from Rogue Asteroids and Doomsday Comets: The Search for the Million Megaton Menace That Threatens Life on Earth by Duncan Steel (Wiley).

If one asks another casual visitor to that megalithic monument [Stonehenge] to define its purpose, the answer will generally be along the lines of, "I think it has something to do with
(05) astronomy and observing the Sun." What I am going to argue is that the first part of that answer is correct — that it does have something to do with astronomy — but that the original construction at Stonehenge was for observing an astro-
(10) nomical phenomenon that as yet has not been recognized. The conundrum of the original motivation of Stonehenge is abstruse and recondite, even profound, and has occupied archaeologists and astronomers alike for decades.

24. According to the passage, Stonehenge

(A) was built to study the position of the Sun

(B) was intended to study another aspect of astronomy

(C) can be understood by archaeologists

(D) has not been studied well

(E) should be considered an unsolvable mystery

25. The words inside the dashes (Lines 7–8) are intended to

(A) give an example of a mistake often made about Stonehenge

(B) explain the author's view of archaeology

(C) show people's misconceptions about Stonehenge

(D) illustrate the "first part of the answer" that the author refers to

(E) specify the monument's purpose

STOP YOU MAY CHECK YOUR WORK ON THIS SECTION ONLY. DO NOT GO BACK TO ANY PREVIOUS SECTION.

Section 3
Mathematics

Time: 25 minutes for 20 questions

Directions: Choose the *best* answer and darken the corresponding oval on the answer sheet.

Notes:

✔ You may use a calculator.

✔ All numbers used in this exam are real numbers.

✔ All figures lie in a plane.

✔ All figures may be assumed to be to scale unless the problem specifically indicates otherwise.

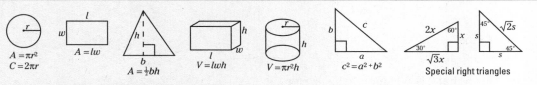

$A = \pi r^2$
$C = 2\pi r$

$A = lw$

$A = \frac{1}{2}bh$

$V = lwh$

$V = \pi r^2 h$

$c^2 = a^2 + b^2$

Special right triangles

There are 360 degrees of arc in a circle.

There are 180 degrees in a straight line.

There are 180 degrees in the sum of the interior angles of a triangle.

---

1. If $p = 5$ and $q = -4$, then $p(p - q) =$

    (A) −45

    (B) −5

    (C) 4

    (D) 5

    (E) 45

2. A coat was on sale for 50% off. Katie bought the coat, using a "$10 off the current price" coupon. If she paid $35 for the coat, what was its original price?

    (A) $45

    (B) $70

    (C) $80

    (D) $90

    (E) $95

3. If the ratio of k to m is the same as the ratio of m to n, then which of the following must be true?

    (A) $kn = m^2$

    (B) $k + m = m + n$

    (C) $kn = 2m$

    (D) $km = mn$

    (E) $k - m = m - n$

Go on to next page

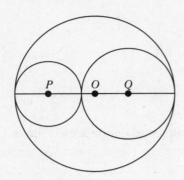

4. In this circle, point O is the center of the large circle, and points P and Q are the centers of the two smaller circles. If the distance $PQ = 6$, then the area of the large circle is

   (A) 144π

   (B) 72π

   (C) 36π

   (D) 12π

   (E) 6π

5. Given that o is odd and that e is even, which of the following must be odd?

   (A) oe

   (B) $(o - e)(o + e)$

   (C) $o(o + 1)$

   (D) $(e + 1)(o - 1)$

   (E) $e(o - e)$

6. A train leaves the station at 10:45 p.m. and arrives at its destination at 2 a.m. the next day (without changing time zones). The train was stopped for ½ hour while it had engine trouble; the rest of the time, its average speed was 80 miles per hour. What total distance did the train travel?

   (A) 120 miles

   (B) 140 miles

   (C) 220 miles

   (D) 240 miles

   (E) 260 miles

7. How many hours are in w weeks and d days?

   (A) $7w + d$

   (B) $168w + 24d$

   (C) $24w + 168d$

   (D) $168w + d$

   (E) $7w + 24d$

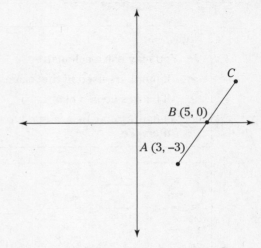

8. Given that B is the midpoint of line segment AC, which of the following is not true?

   (A) The distance from A to C is 5 units.

   (B) Point C has coordinates $(7, 3)$.

   (C) The distance from A to B is equal to the distance from B to C.

   (D) The line segment connecting A to B has the same slope as the line segment connecting B to C.

   (E) The slope of AC is positive.

Go on to next page

9. Getting ready for a party, Nandan expected to set up ⅓ of the tables needed. Unfortunately, one of the people helping him did not show up. As a result, he now had to set up ½ of the tables. If he had to set up 4 more tables than he expected, what was the total number of tables set up for the party?

    (A) 8
    (B) 12
    (C) 20
    (D) 24
    (E) 30

10. Which of the following equations would have a graph that passes through the point (–1, 4)?

    (A) $y = x - 5$
    (B) $x + y = 5$
    (C) $-x + 3 = y$
    (D) $2y - 3x = 5$
    (E) $y = x^2 + 5$

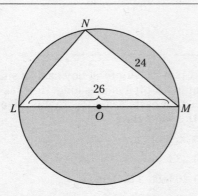

11. Find the shaded area in this figure, where O is the center of the circle.

    (A) $676\pi - 240$
    (B) $676\pi - 120$
    (C) $576\pi - 120$
    (D) $169\pi - 240$
    (E) $169\pi - 120$

12. The three-digit number *ABC* has the following properties:

    The middle digit is the sum of the first and last digits.

    None of the digits repeat.

    ABC is divisible by 5.

    Which of the following could equal *B?*

    (A) 6
    (B) 5
    (C) 4
    (D) 3
    (E) 2

*Questions 13–15 deal with the following graph of **f**(x):*

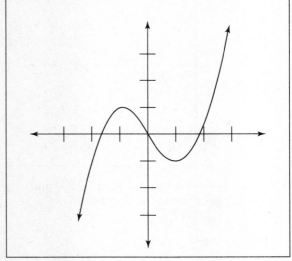

13. The number of solutions to ***f***(x) = 0 is

    (A) 0
    (B) 1
    (C) 2
    (D) 3
    (E) It cannot be determined from the graph alone.

Go on to next page

14.   Which of the following graphs represents $f(x) - 2$?

(A)
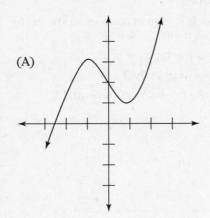

(B)
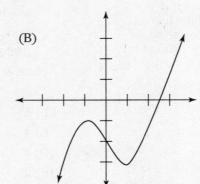

(C)
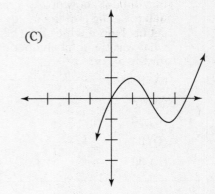

(D)
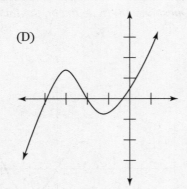

(E)
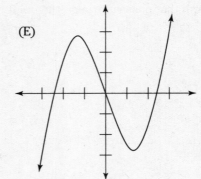

15.   If a line were drawn connecting $f(3)$ and $f(-2)$, the slope of this line would be

(A) positive

(B) negative

(C) zero

(D) not a real number

(E) It cannot be determined from the graph alone.

16.   If $|a - b| < 4$ and $|a| < 3$, then b could be

(A) –8

(B) –7

(C) –6

(D) 7

(E) 8

17.   At 1 p.m., a 5-foot-tall boy casts a shadow that is 1 foot, 3 inches long. How tall is a tree that casts a shadow that is 7 feet long at the same time?

(A) 35 feet

(B) 28 feet

(C) 26 feet, 9 inches

(D) 10 feet, 9 inches

(E) 1 foot, 8 inches

18.   If $vw = x$, $wx = y$, and $xy = z$, which of the following would be equal to yz?

(A) $v^2 w^2$

(B) $v^3 w^5$

(C) $v^4 w^4$

(D) $v^4 w^6$

(E) $v^5 w^8$

Go on to next page

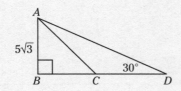

19. In this triangle, *AC* bisects angle *BAD*. Find *AC*. (Figure is not drawn to scale.)

    (A) $5\sqrt{2}$

    (B) $5\sqrt{3}$

    (C) $10\sqrt{3}$

    (D) 5

    (E) 10

20. Rick and Jacob play a game in which each one rolls two six-sided dice (each die is numbered from one to six). Rick's score is the sum of his two rolls. Jacob's score is three times the lower number that he rolls; for example, if he rolls a 2 and a 5, his score is 6. On his first roll, Rick rolls a 4 and a 5. Find the probability that Jacob's rolls will result in his having exactly the same score as Rick.

    (A) $\frac{5}{12}$

    (B) $\frac{7}{12}$

    (C) $\frac{5}{36}$

    (D) $\frac{7}{36}$

    (E) $\frac{9}{36}$

STOP YOU MAY CHECK YOUR WORK ON THIS SECTION ONLY. DO NOT GO BACK TO ANY PREVIOUS SECTION.

Section 4
Critical Reading

Time: 25 minutes for 24 questions

Directions: Choose the *best* answer to each question. Mark the corresponding oval on the answer sheet.

Directions for Questions 1–10: Select the answer that *best* fits the meaning of the sentence.

Example: Fearful of _____ insulting his host, Mike read a book about the etiquette of the country he was visiting.

(A) purposely

(B) politely

(C) happily

(D) accidentally

(E) unconsciously

The answer is (D).

---

1. According to animal behaviorists, all breeds share _____ characteristics, though each dog exhibits _____ traits.

   (A) exceptional . . . extreme

   (B) ordinary . . . everyday

   (C) genetic . . . significant

   (D) common . . . unique

   (E) adverse . . . shared

2. After hours of intense study and with the help of a powerful computer, the detective was able to decipher the meaning of the victim's _____ note.

   (A) cryptic

   (B) unintelligible

   (C) legible

   (D) noxious

   (E) restrained

3. The malfunction of even one connection _____ the entire system.

   (A) surmounts

   (B) nullifies

   (C) consolidates

   (D) jeopardizes

   (E) champions

4. The assortment of dolls in the heir's room was quite _____, ranging from heroic soldiers to delicate infants to exotic fashion figures.

   (A) eclectic

   (B) uniform

   (C) universal

   (D) mundane

   (E) expensive

5. Curiosity about the _____ of life on Mars has resulted in a(n) _____ examination of the Red Planet.

   (A) pestilence . . . cursory

   (B) possibility . . . sustained

   (C) existence . . . advantageous

   (D) eradication . . . scientific

   (E) withdrawal . . . intrusive

6. The establishment of a new broadcast network must be the work of _____ who are _____ as well as businesslike.

   (A) visionaries . . . prosaic

   (B) artists . . . culpable

   (C) innovators . . . creative

   (D) opportunists . . . conservative

   (E) despots . . . collegial

Go on to next page

7. Even more exciting than the final score can be the _____ plays of the tournament.

    (A) generic

    (B) extraneous

    (C) intemperate

    (D) ubiquitous

    (E) critical

8. After so many years of experience, the interviewer couldn't be _____ by any questions the potential employee asked.

    (A) jaded

    (B) bored

    (C) nonplussed

    (D) exhausted

    (E) inspired

9. Their _____ relationship was characterized by _____ arguments.

    (A) affable . . . jocular

    (B) vivacious . . . sententious

    (C) amicable . . . continual

    (D) adversarial . . . infrequent

    (E) malevolent . . . innocuous

10. No one who is _____ will travel abroad _____.

    (A) conscientious . . . extensively

    (B) prescient . . . neutrally

    (C) organized . . . listlessly

    (D) xenophobic . . . willingly

    (E) fatuous . . . foolishly

Directions for Questions 11–24: Base your answers on information in either or both of these passages. You may also answer questions on what is implied in the passages or about the relationship between the two passages.

Passage I is an excerpt from The Big Splat, or How Our Moon Came to Be *by Dana Mackenzie (Wiley). It discusses problems involved in creating an accurate measure of longitude. Passage II, which is taken from* A Brief History of Flight *by T.A. Heppenheimer (Wiley), describes ways in which early aircraft pilots navigated.*

Passage 1

In the 1700s and 1800s, as the world economy became increasingly dependent on long-distance sea voyages and exploration of unknown lands, navigation on the open seas became one of the greatest scientific problems (05) of the day. Even in charted waters, a ship could run aground if its course had been plotted incorrectly. And in uncharted waters, what would be the use of discovering a new island or harbor if you might never find it again? (10)

The position of a ship can be described by its latitude and longitude. Finding the latitude — the ship's distance north or south of the equator, measured in degrees — was a fairly routine matter. In the northern hemisphere, it is especially (15) simple. The higher in the sky the North Star is, the farther you are from the equator; for example, if it is fifty degrees above the horizon, you are at fifty degrees north latitude. If it is just on the horizon, you are on the equator. (20)

Longitude was a whole different matter. Nowadays, longitude is measured in terms of the number of degrees east or west of the prime meridian, which passes through the Royal Observatory in Greenwich, England. However, (25) that has been the custom only since 1884; before then, a captain would measure his position with respect to a port in his home country.

The lack of a standard "starting place" for longitudes was only a minor part of the main prob- (30) lem, which was that no one had a good way of measuring east-to-west distances. Because of Earth's rotation, the longitude difference corresponds to the difference between local time and the time at your port of departure, with each hour (35) of time corresponding to fifteen degrees of longitude. The local time is easy to determine, because the sun is highest in the sky at noon. But it is not so easy to keep track of the time in your port of origin. Until 1761, there were no clocks capable of (40) keeping steady time on board a rocking ship. Even as late as the early 1800s, naval chronometers were still too expensive to be standard equipment. Thus sailors had to look for other ways to keep track of the time back home. (45)

Passage 11

Pilots navigated by following railroad tracks, swooping down to read a town's name from a water tower. When the weather closed in, they came down to low altitudes and continued onward, still following the tracks. This practice developed (50) such nuances as keeping to the right, to avoid

Go on to next page ⇒

Line

collisions with low-flying oncoming planes. Hazards of the business included running into a locomotive, or hitting a hill pierced by a tunnel.

(55)   In 1923 Paul Henderson began lighting airways across the nation. The effort featured lighthouses, 50-foot steel towers supporting revolving beacons of 500,000 candlepower that were fitted with 6-inch reflectors. These marked the main air-
(60) fields and could be seen a hundred miles away. Smaller beacons, visible for sixty miles, marked the emergency fields. Flashing acetylene lamps, spaced every three miles, defined the route.

The first such airway ran between Chicago
(65) and Cheyenne, Wyoming, in flat country where construction was easy. It covered the central one-third of the country. Flights could then take off from either coast at dawn, reach the airway by dusk, then fly through the night along its length
(70) and continue onward the next day. In initial tests, Henderson showed that his aircraft could beat the trains by two or even three days. He spanned the nation by extending his lighted airways across the Appalachians and the Rockies,
(75) and launched a scheduled coast-to-coast service. It began in mid 1924 and soon settled down to definite times of less than thirty hours eastbound and under thirty-six hours westbound.

The Commerce Department extended these
(80) lighted airways during the subsequent decade; its lines of beacons formed an eighteen-thousand-mile network by 1933. Again, though, pilots could see and follow these lights only when visibility was adequate. When this was not the case, they
(85) continued to rely on the time-honored procedure of following the railroad tracks. They even did this at night, turning on landing lights. The steel rails, brightly illuminated, looked like ribbons of silver as they rolled past.

(90)   Radio also became useful for navigation, creating beamlike transmissions that fliers could follow from one transmitter to the next. It was not possible to produce a true beam like that from a searchlight; that would have demanded the use of
(95) microwave frequencies, which were beyond the state of the art. Instead the emphasis was on the clever use of low-frequency methods, with which it proved possible to offer a valuable service.

The key was the loop antenna, a rectangular
(100) circuit of wires rising vertically from the ground. It gave the strongest signal when facing the loop edge-on, as well as for some distance to the left or right. But there was little or no signal at right angles to this direction. German investigators
(105) had learned of this as early as 1908, and the firm Telefunken had introduced a radio navigation system for the wartime dirigibles. It did not work well, particularly at long distances, and after the war the U.S. Army's Signal corps asked the
(110) National Bureau of Standards to come up with something better.

11. Both Passage I and Passage II primarily concern

(A) human ingenuity in the face of difficulty

(B) difficulties in navigation

(C) the importance of determining where you are located

(D) flight navigation

(E) ship navigation

12. The tone of both passages may best be described as

(A) inspirational

(B) critical

(C) entertaining

(D) informational

(E) sentimental

13. In contrast to Passage I, Passage II

(A) concerns a more modern era

(B) is more scientific

(C) gives more detail about navigation

(D) focuses more on the problems of navigation

(E) has a more historical view

14. Passage I implies that "charted waters" (Line 6)

(A) are more shallow than uncharted waters

(B) are not safe if the chart is followed incorrectly

(C) are close to land, not on the open sea

(D) may be charted inaccurately

(E) are more dangerous than open water

15. The words "Longitude was a whole different matter" (Line 21)

(A) emphasize the ease of determining latitude

(B) alert the reader to the fact that different methods were used to calculate longitude

(C) refer to the difficulty in calculating latitude

(D) explain why longitude was easier to calculate than latitude

(E) set up a contrast with latitude

Go on to next page

16. Passage I relates time to distance because

    (A) neither can be measured with complete accuracy
    (B) distance is relative to the time of day
    (C) the distance between two points may be measured by the difference in local time at each point
    (D) time is relative when you are traveling
    (E) it takes time to travel

17. Passage I implies that accurate timepieces

    (A) were invented by the Royal Navy
    (B) were destroyed by the movement of a ship
    (C) were invented in order to facilitate navigation
    (D) did not always work at sea before 1761
    (E) did not exist until 1761

18. According to Passage I, naval chronometers (Line 42) are probably

    (A) clocks especially adapted to tell time at sea
    (B) devices that have been in existence since ancient times
    (C) useful only at sea
    (D) part of the Royal Navy's battle equipment
    (E) difficult to use

19. According to Passage II, early pilots

    (A) could navigate without visual cues
    (B) could not fly too high
    (C) faced danger when flying low
    (D) were required to fly at night
    (E) gained experience on railroads

20. Pilots descended in bad weather (Lines 48–50) in order to

    (A) avoid lightning
    (B) see landmarks more clearly
    (C) be ready for emergency landings
    (D) alert a train conductor to their routes
    (E) save fuel

21. In the context of Passage II, which of the following descriptions do not refer to "lighthouses" (Lines 56–57)?

    (A) navigational aids for planes
    (B) moving displays of lights
    (C) markers at prominent airfields
    (D) towers with reflectors and high-power lamps
    (E) navigational aids for ships

22. Passage II implies that lighted airways

    (A) were bad for the environment
    (B) made air travel competitive with train travel
    (C) crisscrossed hilly areas before they were built on flat surfaces
    (D) made air travel less expensive
    (E) helped train travel compete with air travel

23. The "landing lights" (Line 87) probably

    (A) were better than lightways in clear weather
    (B) could be turned on only when the plane was on land
    (C) could be used only during landing
    (D) illuminated the earth under the plane
    (E) alerted the airport that the plane was about to land

24. The invention of radio (Lines 90–98)

    (A) perfected long distance navigation
    (B) had no effect on aviation
    (C) made air travel easier
    (D) depended upon a loop antenna
    (E) was achieved by a German company

STOP YOU MAY CHECK YOUR WORK ON THIS SECTION ONLY. DO NOT GO BACK TO ANY PREVIOUS SECTION.

Section 5

Mathematics

Time: 25 minutes for 18 questions

Directions: This section contains two different types of questions. For Questions 1–8, choose the *best* answer to each question. Mark the corresponding oval on the answer sheet. For Questions 9–18, follow the separate directions provided before those questions.

Notes:

✔ You may use a calculator.

✔ All numbers used in this exam are real numbers.

✔ All figures lie in a plane.

✔ All figures may be assumed to be to scale unless the problem specifically indicates otherwise.

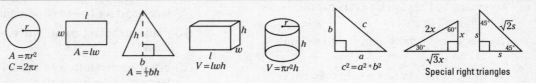

$A = \pi r^2$
$C = 2\pi r$

$A = lw$

$A = \frac{1}{2}bh$

$V = lwh$

$V = \pi r^2 h$

$c^2 = a^2 + b^2$

Special right triangles

There are 360 degrees of arc in a circle.

There are 180 degrees in a straight line.

There are 180 degrees in the sum of the interior angles of a triangle.

1. What is the result when –8 is subtracted from 10?

   (A) 18

   (B) 2

   (C) –2

   (D) –18

   (E) –80

2. A certain shipping company charges $3.99 per pound for packages of 15 pounds or less, and $3.49 per pound for packages weighing more than 15 pounds. If Lyle sends two 10-pound packages, and Gretchen sends one 20-pound package, what is the difference between their total costs?

   (A) $0

   (B) $0.50

   (C) $7.50

   (D) $10

   (E) $69.80

Go on to next page

3. How many degrees of arc does the minute hand of a clock cover in 20 minutes?

   (A) 180

   (B) 120

   (C) 60

   (D) 30

   (E) 20

4. How many total triangles (of any size) are in this drawing?

   (A) 9

   (B) 10

   (C) 11

   (D) 12

   (E) 13

5. Which of the following numbers is the smallest?

   (A) π

   (B) $3\frac{1}{7}$

   (C) 3.14

   (D) $3.1\overline{4}$

   (E) $\sqrt{10}$

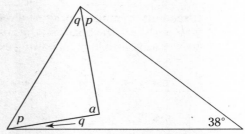

Note: Figure not drawn to scale.

6. What is the value in degrees of a in this diagram?

   (A) 38

   (B) 76

   (C) 90

   (D) 109

   (E) 142

Questions 7 and 8 both deal with the equation $\frac{ax}{x+2} = b$, where $a \neq b$.

---

7. For what value of x does this equation have no solution?

   (A) -2

   (B) -1

   (C) 0

   (D) 1

   (E) 2

8. When the equation has a solution, $x =$

   (A) $\frac{2}{a-b}$

   (B) $\frac{2b}{a-b}$

   (C) $\frac{2b}{a}$

   (D) $b + 2$

   (E) $a - 2b$

Go on to next page

Directions for student-produced response Questions 9–18: Solve the problem and then write your answer in the boxes on the answer sheet. Then mark the ovals corresponding to your answer as shown in the following example. Note the fraction line and the decimal points.

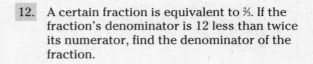

Answer: 7/2   Answer: 3.25   Answer: 853

Write your answer in the box. You may start your answer in any column.

Although you do not have to write the solutions in the boxes, you do have to blacken the corresponding ovals. You should fill in the boxes to avoid confusion. Only the blackened ovals will be scored. The numbers in the boxes will not be read.

There are no negative answers.

Mixed numbers, such as 3½, may be gridded in as a decimal (3.5) or as a fraction (⅞). Do not grid in 3½; it will be read as ³½.

Grid in a decimal as far as possible. Do not round your answer and leave some boxes empty.

A question may have more than one answer. Grid in one answer only.

---

9. If 2½ sticks of butter measure 20 tablespoons, how many tablespoons are in 4 sticks of butter?

10. Find the smallest even number that is divisible by 3, 5, and 7.

11. In this regular pentagon, find the sum, in degrees, of the angles *a, b, c, d,* and *e.*

12. A certain fraction is equivalent to ⅔. If the fraction's denominator is 12 less than twice its numerator, find the denominator of the fraction.

13. Find a solution to the equation $p^2 = 3p + 40$.

14. A sequence of numbers begins 1, 5, 4, 8, 7, 11, 10. What would be the 21st term of this sequence?

Go on to next page

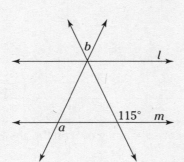

15. In this diagram, lines *l* and *m* are parallel. Find *a* − *b*, in degrees.

16. If all the integers from 1 to 2,010 inclusive were written down, how many total digits would appear?

17. If $xy = 120$, and $\frac{1}{x} + \frac{1}{y} = \frac{1}{4}$, find $x + y$.

18. The shortest side of triangle *T* is 10 cm long, and triangle *T*'s area is 84 cm². Triangle *U* is similar to triangle *T*, and the shortest side of triangle *U* is 15 cm long. Find the area of triangle *U* in cm².

STOP YOU MAY CHECK YOUR WORK ON THIS SECTION ONLY. DO NOT GO BACK TO ANY PREVIOUS SECTION.

Section 6
Multiple-Choice Writing

Time: 25 minutes for 35 questions

Directions: Choose the *best* answer to each question. Mark the corresponding oval on the answer sheet.

Directions for Questions 1–11: Each sentence is followed by five choices. Decide which choice *best* improves the sentence. If the underlined portion of the sentence is best left alone, choose (A).

Example: <u>Bert and him went</u> to the store to buy boots in preparation for the approaching storm.

(A) Bert and him went

(B) Bert and he went

(C) Bert and he had gone

(D) Bert and him had gone

(E) Bert and himself went

The correct answer is (B).

---

1. Watching the whale slide effortlessly through the water, <u>the passengers who had all paid high prices for the voyage applauded</u>.

   (A) the passengers who had all paid high prices for the voyage applauded

   (B) the passengers that had all paid high prices for the voyage applauded

   (C) the passengers, who had all paid high prices for the voyage, applauded

   (D) the passengers, that had all paid high prices for the voyage, applauded

   (E) the passengers all paid high prices for the voyage and applauded

2. The star shortstop was <u>more skillful at fielding ground balls than anyone</u> on her team.

   (A) more skillful at fielding ground balls than anyone

   (B) more skillful at fielding ground balls than anyone else

   (C) the most skilled at fielding ground balls than anyone

   (D) skillful at fielding ground balls more than anyone

   (E) more skilled at fielding ground balls, than anyone

3. Not only sipping extremely hot coffee <u>but also if you pick up a heated plate</u> without an oven mitt can be dangerous.

   (A) but also if you pick up a heated plate

   (B) but also, if you pick up a heated plate

   (C) but also to pick up a heated plate

   (D) but also picking up a heated plate

   (E) but also if you were picking up a heated plate

4. <u>When the supermarket chain added a prepared foods section, it</u> was clearly a wise move.

   (A) When the supermarket chain added a prepared foods section, it

   (B) The supermarket chain added a prepared foods section, and it

   (C) The supermarket chain having added a prepared foods section, it

   (D) The supermarket chain's adding a prepared foods section

   (E) The supermarket chain adding a prepared foods section

Go on to next page

5. Everyone in <u>the chorus, except Tomas and I, is going</u> to wear a black robe for tonight's concert.

   (A) the chorus, except Tomas and I, is going

   (B) the chorus except Tomas and I is going

   (C) the chorus, except Tomas and I, are going

   (D) the chorus, except Tomas and me, is going

   (E) the chorus, accept Tomas and I, is going

6. The photograph that everyone is searching for, which <u>was taken last July, has been sitting</u> in my album for three weeks and is still there.

   (A) was taken last July, has been sitting

   (B) had been taken last July, has been sitting

   (C) has taken last July, has been sitting

   (D) was taken last July, have been sitting

   (E) was taken last July, will have been sitting

7. The huge slate of candidates means that the voters may select <u>whoever they like the best</u> for the post of vice-president.

   (A) whoever they like the best

   (B) whoever they like best

   (C) whoever they like better

   (D) who they like the best

   (E) whomever they like the best

8. By the time students from low-income families graduate from college, they <u>will have acquired a substantial debt</u>.

   (A) they will have acquired a substantial debt

   (B) they has acquired a substantial debt

   (C) they acquired a substantial debt

   (D) they would have acquired a substantial debt

   (E) a substantial debt will be acquired by them

9. <u>To write a good essay, a dictionary and a word-processing program are helpful.</u>

   (A) To write a good essay, a dictionary and a word-processing program are helpful.

   (B) A dictionary and a word-processing program are helpful to write a good essay.

   (C) To write a good essay, a dictionary and a word-processing program is helpful.

   (D) Writing a good essay, a dictionary and a word-processing program are helpful.

   (E) To write a good essay, you may find that a dictionary and a word-processing program are helpful.

10. <u>She feels very bad about having forgotten</u> the little boy's name, but she plans to apologize for the lapse.

    (A) She feels very bad about having forgotten

    (B) She feels very badly about having forgotten

    (C) She feels very badly about forgetting

    (D) She feels very badly that she forgot

    (E) Having forgotten, she feels bad about

11. <u>There's three pencils and a stack of paper</u> on the editor's desk, supplies for the busy reporters of a major newspaper.

    (A) There's three pencils and a stack of paper

    (B) There are three pencils and a stack of paper

    (C) There is three pencils and a stack of paper

    (D) They're three pencils and a stack of paper

    (E) There is a stack of paper and three pencils

Go on to next page ➡

Directions for Questions 12–29: In each of the following sentences, identify the underlined portion that contains an error. If a sentence contains no errors, choose (E) for "no error."

Example:

Irregardless of the fact that the National
   A
Weather Service predicted rain, Dexter
                     B
resented the students' request to postpone
   C   D
the picnic. No error.
               E

The correct answer is (A).

---

12. Interested in family history, Lucy is
    A   B
searching for information about her

father's mother, her grandmother, in
         C

order to construct a complete family tree.
        D

No error.
   E

13. One glance at the curator's notes
                       A
reveals that the ceramic pot, which is a
   B   C
valuable antique, should of been repaired
                     D
during the night. No error.
                     E

14. Gazing up at the stars, the telescope was
    A   B
not strong enough to please my uncle, who
                               C
is an ardent amateur astronomer. No error.
   D   E

15. For Mortimer's plan to be successful, several
        A   B
factors must fall into place immediately, and
        C
I don't believe they will. No error.
                   D   E

16. The mayor, who we all know is a great cham-
        A   B
pion of the poor, has asked the city council
                  C
to repeal the tax for any family whose income
           D
is below the poverty line. No error.
                           E

17. If the street would have been less congested,
                A
traffic would have flowed more quickly, and
          B   C
we would have arrived at the meeting on
       D
time. No error.
       E

18. The class trip to the museum was a great
                              A
success, however, the students missed a
   B   C
great deal of normal class work because of
                              D
their outing. No error.
               E

19. His work in advanced mathematics is
    A
equally as important as her work in physics,
   B   C
but he is paid less because his employer is
                D
nearly bankrupt. No error.
                  E

20. Because of its fragile condition, the director
    A   B
of the nation's archives objected to
                        C
the document being handled. No error.
   D   E

21. The affect of the newest forms of technol-
    A   B
ogy cannot be exaggerated; the entertain-
              C
ment industry must undergo a radical
                D
change in order to survive. No error.
                             E

22. With ten seconds to go, the students in
    A
the packed stadium are clapping in the
                   B
belief that either Marshall or his teammates
   C
has the ability to save the game. No error.
D   E

Go on to next page

23. When the scholar <u>read</u> the newest transla-
    _A
    tion of Homer's famous <u>epic, The Odyssey,</u>
    _B
    he <u>returned</u> the book to the library and
    _C
    reviewed <u>a number of other</u> translations of
    _D
    this epic poem. <u>No error.</u>
    _E

24. The candidates <u>waiting to be interviewed</u>
    _A
    <u>could not help but wonder</u> <u>whether</u> their
    _B   _C
    qualifications <u>would please</u> the managing
    _D
    director. <u>No error.</u>
    _E

25. <u>The further you travel,</u> <u>the more you long</u>
    _A   _B
    for the <u>comfortable</u> environment of home
    _C
    and <u>its daily routine.</u> <u>No error.</u>
    _D   _E

26. <u>Influenced by his experiences</u> <u>observing</u>
    _A   _B
    <u>inmates</u> in a <u>women's</u> prison, Picasso
    _C
    painted several pictures of emaciated
    women during <u>his so-called "blue period."</u>
    _D
    <u>No error.</u>
    _E

27. <u>The executive committee</u> debated <u>as to</u>
    _A   _B
    <u>whether</u> the exhibit <u>should be</u> <u>subject to</u>
    _C   _D
    <u>prior approval</u> by all the members. <u>No error.</u>
    _E

28. The researchers <u>working with cancer cells,</u>
    _A
    <u>but not those studying</u> genetics, <u>designed</u>
    _B   _C
    <u>several experiments</u> to determine <u>the affect</u>
    _D
    <u>of the surrounding normal cells.</u> <u>No error.</u>
    _E

29. <u>The publisher selected</u> one of the few
    _A
    books <u>that has</u> a <u>comprehensive table of</u>
    _B   _C
    <u>contents</u> and <u>attractive, colorful</u> illustra-
                      _D
    tions. <u>No error.</u>
    _E

Directions for Questions 30–35: These questions are based on the following essay. Choose the *best* answer to each question.

[1] In choosing a college the possibility of studying in a foreign country should be considered. [2] Whether saying guten tag or buenos dias or bon jour, the chance to learn about another culture cannot be duplicated. [3] Personally, in my opinion I think that no true education is complete without at least one semester abroad.

[4] I studied in Spain. [5] I learned about Spanish history from people who lived it. [6] My art lessons in the United States were only taught from slides and reproductions, but in Spain I studied in the Prado, the most famous art museum in the country. [7] This is a great advantage to students because the paintings are very vivid when seen personally. [8] I attended a bullfight twice, consequently I understood that this ancient ritual is not just about the animal being killed but rather about a struggle against death that must be lost by everyone some day.

[9] Students go to many countries for this sort of education, and they return better than when they went. [10] Their language skills are not the only improvement. [11] In a recent study by psychologists it says that students who have lived in more than one country show more

Go on to next page ➡

tolerance of the different customs they may encounter in their daily life. 12 This reason, along with many others, justifies the time and expense of foreign study. 13 In conclusion, I think that everyone should study outside of their own country at least once in their lives.

30. The best revision for Sentence 1 is

   (A) In choosing a college the possibility of studying in a foreign country should be considered. (no change)

   (B) Everyone should consider the possibility of studying in a foreign country when they are choosing a college.

   (C) To choose a college, consider the possibility that you may study abroad.

   (D) In choosing a college, consider the possibility of foreign study.

   (E) Everyone, in choosing a college, should consider whether they can study abroad.

31. A good revision for Sentence 2 is

   (A) Whether saying guten tag or buenos dias or bon jour, the chance to learn about another culture cannot be duplicated. (no change)

   (B) Whether you say guten tag or buenos dias or bon jour, the chance to learn about another culture is unique and can't be duplicated.

   (C) Whether you say guten tag or buenos dias or bon jour, the chance to learn about another culture is unique.

   (D) The chance to learn about another culture can't be duplicated according to whether one says guten tag or buenos dias or bon jour.

   (E) It doesn't matter whether you say guten tag or buenos dias or bon jour, the chance to learn about another culture can't be duplicated.

32. The best way to combine Sentences 4 and 5 is

   (A) I studied in Spain, I learned about Spanish history from people who lived it.

   (B) Studied in Spain, I learned about Spanish history from people who lived it.

   (C) I studied in Spain, and I learned about Spanish history from people who lived it.

   (D) When I studied in Spain, I learned about Spanish history from people who lived it.

   (E) Given that I studied in Spain, I learned about Spanish history from people who lived it.

33. The main purpose of Paragraph 2 is to

   (A) explain that foreign schools are superior to American universities

   (B) argue with the reader who sees disadvantages to foreign study

   (C) support the idea that studying abroad gives insight into culture

   (D) give the reader an impression of life in Spain

   (E) introduce the narrator of the piece on a personal level

34. How should Sentences 9 and 10 be combined?

   (A) Students go to many countries for this sort of education, and they return better than when they went because not only are their language skills improved.

   (B) Students return better than when they went from many countries, in more than language skills.

   (C) Not only language skills improve when students studying in foreign countries.

   (D) Students' language skills are not the only improvement.

   (E) Students better their language skills and other things.

Go on to next page →

35. What is the best revision of Sentence 11?

(A) In a recent study by psychologists it says that students who have lived in more than one country show more tolerance of the different customs they may encounter in their daily life. (no change)

(B) A recent psychological study reported that students who have lived in more than one country show more tolerance of different customs encountered in daily life.

(C) A recent study by psychologists says that students who have lived in more than one country show more tolerance of the different customs they may encounter in their daily life.

(D) In a recent study by psychologists it says that students who have lived in more than one country are more tolerant of different customs in their daily life.

(E) More tolerance of different customs they may encounter in daily life is the result of living abroad, according to a recent psychology study.

Section 7
Critical Reading

> **Time:** 20 minutes for 22 questions
>
> **Direction:** Choose the *best* answer to each question. Mark the corresponding oval on the answer sheet.

Directions for Questions 1–6: Select the answer that *best* fits the meaning of the sentence.

Example: Fearful of _____ insulting his host, Mike read a book about the etiquette of the country he was visiting.

(A) purposely

(B) politely

(C) happily

(D) accidentally

(E) unconsciously

The answer is (D).

1. Once dozens of tailors created traditional bull-fighting suits, but a sharp _____ in the popularity of the sport has reduced that number to five.

    (A) expansion

    (B) regression

    (C) decline

    (D) escalation

    (E) limit

2. Because the child was _____ and the parents were unwilling to _____ her, the tour's progress through the museum was halted.

    (A) intractable . . . force

    (B) eager . . . urge

    (C) confused . . . instruct

    (D) recalcitrant . . . indulge

    (E) enthusiastic . . . coax

3. The _____ student painstakingly checked and rechecked every answer to eliminate any careless mistakes.

    (A) indolent

    (B) vigorous

    (C) imprudent

    (D) diligent

    (E) lackadaisical

4. True _____ do not waver even when confronted by overwhelming obstacles.

    (A) cynics

    (B) idealists

    (C) realists

    (D) pessimists

    (E) skeptics

5. The proposed development project was vetoed by the mayor, who cited environmental _____, including air pollution resulting from an expanded population.

    (A) growth

    (B) renumeration

    (C) complications

    (D) benefits

    (E) concerns

6. The star's _____ image, presented in countless photos, belied her _____ past.

    (A) simplistic . . . complicated

    (B) ordinary . . . aristocratic

    (C) wholesome . . . notorious

    (D) omnipresent . . . missing

    (E) imperfect . . . restricted

Go on to next page

Directions for Questions 7–18: Choose the *best* answer from information supplied or implied by the passages.

This passage from Ice Blink *by Scott Cookman (Wiley) discusses early 19th-century explorer John Franklin's search for a northwest passage, a shorter, safer, Arctic route to the Far East.*

Line   [John Franklin's] plan was to ascend today's Snare River, cross over to the headwaters of the Coppermine River, descend to its mouth on the shores of the Arctic Ocean, follow the coastline
(05) eastward in search of the Northwest Passage, and return. The fact that this involved paddling and portaging over 1,200 miles through some of the most unforgiving wilderness in the world did not seem to trouble him much. He had been
(10) given his chance.

Governor Sir George Simpson, head of the Hudson's Bay Company, who had agreed to support the expedition, didn't think much of it. No light judge of character, he was blunt in his estima-
(15) tion of Franklin: "Lieut. Franklin, the Officer who commands the party, has not the physical powers required for the labor of moderate Voyaging in this country; he must have three meals per diem, Tea is indispensible, and with the utmost exertion he
(20) cannot walk Eight miles on one day."

Indeed, Franklin set out like an unprepared summer camper. By his own admission, he embarked with only ". . . two casks of flour, 200 dried reindeer [caribou] tongues, some dried
(25) moosemeat, portable [dried] soup and arrow-root, sufficient in the whole for ten days' consumption [for his entire party]." He naively presumed that a band of Chippewyan natives hired at Fort Providence (a chief named
(30) Akaitcho, two guides, and seven hunters) could feed them all. Ten days later, the hunters having found no game, the food was gone. Franklin's fishing nets produced only "4 carp." The hungry voyageurs "broke into open discontent" and
(35) refused to continue unless they were fed.

Franklin threatened to ". . . inflict the heaviest punishment on any who should persist in their refusal to go on." He was saved making good on this completely hollow threat (his
(40) Englishmen were out-numbered five to one, after all, and couldn't go anywhere without the voyageurs) only when the Chippewyan hunters providentially arrived with the flesh of two caribou. Hunger, which was to stalk the expedition all of
(45) its days, was momentarily kept at bay. But it was, to say the least, an inauspicious beginning.

Less than three weeks out of Fort Providence, at a lake above the headwaters of the Snare River, even this shaky beginning came to an end. By Franklin's calendar it was only August 19th and, in (50) his mind, the height of the summer voyaging season. Despite the scarcity of food, he was determined to press ahead, straight across the height of land and down the Coppermine to the frozen ocean. Akaitcho, the Chippewyan chief, was oper- (55) ating on an entirely different calendar. He pointed out the falling leaves and told Franklin winter was near and it was too late in the season to proceed. He said that eleven days' travel would put them north of the tree line, out in the "barren lands," (60) with no protection from the weather or wood for fires. He said descending the Coppermine would consume forty days more, that the caribou had already left the river for the winter, and food would be impossible to find in the "barren lands." (65) Akaitcho concluded that if Franklin wanted to go on, he was a dead man. Franklin replied the Englishmen had "instruments by which we could tell the state of the air and water" and that winter was not "so near as he [Akaitcho] supposed." The (70) chief threw up his hands and said that "as his advice was neglected, his presence was useless, and he would therefore return to Fort Providence with his hunters." Franklin, as completely dependent upon the Chippewyans for food as he was (75) upon the voyageurs for transport, had no choice but to "reluctantly" halt for the winter. He had not reached the Coppermine, much less descended it. In fact, he had traveled only seventeen days from Fort Providence and had already exhausted all his (80) provisions and experienced two near mutinies.

Eleven days later, true to Akaitcho's prediction, the temperatures turned freezing. Franklin put his voyageurs to work building a "dwelling house" for the Englishmen. By December (about (85) the time he would have been returning from the Arctic Ocean, if Akaitcho hadn't stopped him from going) the outside temperature plummeted to 57 degrees below zero.

7. The first paragraph (Lines 1–10) implies that Franklin's plan

    (A) relied on established routes

    (B) would be difficult if not impossible

    (C) depended upon chance

    (D) was well thought out

    (E) could be accomplished easily by anyone brave enough to try

Go on to next page ⟶

8. In the context of this passage, light (Line 14) may best be defined as

   (A) illuminating

   (B) insignificant

   (C) spiritual

   (D) all-knowing

   (E) perceptive

9. Governor Simpson's comment (Lines 18–19) that "Tea is indispensable" shows

   (A) the need for hot beverages in a cold climate

   (B) the universal appeal of tea

   (C) that Simpson judged Franklin fit to lead the expedition

   (D) that Franklin intended to maintain high standards during his trip

   (E) Simpson's poor opinion of Franklin's ability to adapt to the wilderness

10. The author's comment that "Franklin set out like an unprepared summer camper" (Lines 21–22) is intended to

    (A) contrast with Governor Simpson's point of view

    (B) relate Franklin's journey to the reader's personal experience

    (C) stress that the voyage took place during warm weather

    (D) emphasize how greatly Franklin underestimated the difficulty of the expedition

    (E) elicit sympathy for Franklin

11. The material in quotation marks in Paragraph 3 (Lines 23–27) is most likely drawn from

    (A) a biography of Franklin

    (B) a diary kept by Franklin during the expedition

    (C) an account by the Native American guides

    (D) Governor Simpson's records

    (E) a scholarly book on the Franklin expedition

12. Franklin's leadership, according to the passage,

    (A) relied on threats

    (B) took into account the needs of the expedition members

    (C) did not take into account the abilities of the Native Americans

    (D) was based on meticulous planning

    (E) changed in a wilderness setting

13. August 19th (Line 50) is cited because

    (A) the author had good records of the events of that date

    (B) Franklin made a crucial mistake on that date

    (C) the Native Americans saw that date as the midpoint of summer

    (D) it was a turning point of the expedition

    (E) it was a rare point of agreement between the Native Americans and Franklin

14. The argument about weather between Franklin and Akaitcho

    (A) emphasizes Franklin's incompetence

    (B) shows that Franklin's confidence is justified

    (C) is never resolved

    (D) reveals the prejudices of both Franklin and Akaitcho

    (E) illustrates the superiority of scientific instruments

15. The mutinies are described as "near" (Line 81) because

    (A) they rose above the level of threats

    (B) they did not break out into open fighting

    (C) they were led by people close to Franklin

    (D) they occurred close together in time

    (E) they took place within the expedition itself

Go on to next page

16. The author would most likely disagree with which statement?

    (A) Franklin's travel plan was too ambitious.

    (B) Governor Simpson should not have approved Franklin's expedition.

    (C) Native American ability to predict the weather is overrated.

    (D) Arctic travel should not be attempted without adequate preparation.

    (E) Franklin's arrogance was a factor in the failure of his expedition.

17. By mentioning the temperature in December (Line 89) the author implies that

    (A) Franklin was correct in his estimation of the weather

    (B) Akaitcho was wrong

    (C) the temperature was severe but not life-threatening

    (D) Franklin's expedition could not have survived such a temperature

    (E) the cold weather was far off

18. A good title for this passage is

    (A) Foolish Expeditions

    (B) Early Explorers

    (C) The Franklin Expedition

    (D) Akaitcho and Franklin: A Cultural Clash

    (E) The Northwest Passage

Directions for Questions 19–22: Choose the *best* answer from the information supplied or implied by the passages.

Passage I is an excerpt from The House of Science *by Philip R. Holzinger (Wiley). It discusses the origins of the earth. Passage II is an excerpt from* The Big Splat, or How Our Moon Came to Be *by Dana Mackenzie (Wiley). In Passage II the author discusses Immanuel Kant's theories on the origin and nature of the solar system.*

Passage 1

The story of our earth begins about 4.6 billion years ago — a time when the rest of the planets in our solar system were also forming. Early in its history, our planet was made up of a hodgepodge of materials, some of which were radioactive. These radioactive materials generated great quantities of heat, as did the large number of meteors that struck the earth at this time. The heat generated was sufficient to melt most of the planet, making our early earth a forbidding molten world!

Passage II

Kant's model of the solar system began with an initial, formless cloud of gas or smoke, which contracts under the force of gravity. One might expect the cloud to simply collapse to a point, end of story. But Kant assumed that the "fine particles" in the cloud would also repel each other. (He made an incorrect analogy to the diffusion of smoke, which he thought was due to a repulsive force.) This repulsion would give them a sideways motion and allow them to take up circular orbits around the growing Sun. After many collisions between these orbiting particles [Kant thought], an overall direction of rotation would be established.

19. The exclamation point at the end of Passage I

    (A) emphasizes the great contrast between the earth we know today and the earth when it was formed

    (B) reveals that the molten earth was hotter than the earth today

    (C) shows that the author disapproves of this theory of the earth's formation

    (D) stresses the dangers of radioactive material

    (E) underlines the danger of molten minerals

20. In the context of Passage I, "forbidding" (Lines 10–11) means

    (A) hindering

    (B) denying

    (C) not allowing

    (D) possessing difficult characteristics

    (E) hot

Go on to next page

21. In Passage II, the best interpretation of "end of story" (Line 16) is that

    (A) the solar system would end after a complete collapse

    (B) there is no more to say about Kant's theory

    (C) Kant's theory is completely incorrect

    (D) Kant could not reason further than this point

    (E) a point, like a period, ends a story

22. Both passages primarily concern

    (A) astronomy

    (B) astrology

    (C) theories later proved wrong

    (D) the beginnings of planets and other heavenly bodies

    (E) science

STOP YOU MAY CHECK YOUR WORK ON THIS SECTION ONLY. DO NOT GO BACK TO ANY PREVIOUS SECTION.

Section 8
Mathematics

Time: 15 minutes for 16 questions

Directions: Choose the *best* answer to each question. Mark the corresponding oval on the answer sheet.

Notes:

✔ You may use a calculator.

✔ All numbers used in this exam are real numbers.

✔ All figures lie in a plane.

✔ All figures may be assumed to be to scale unless the problem specifically indicates otherwise.

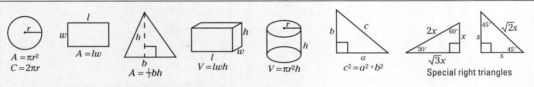

$A = \pi r^2$
$C = 2\pi r$

$A = lw$

$A = \frac{1}{2}bh$

$V = lwh$

$V = \pi r^2 h$

$c^2 = a^2 + b^2$

Special right triangles

There are 360 degrees of arc in a circle.

There are 180 degrees in a straight line.

There are 180 degrees in the sum of the interior angles of a triangle.

1. In football, a touchdown is worth 6 points, a field goal is worth 3 points, and an extra point is worth 1 point. Which formula represents the total number of points scored by a team if they scored t touchdowns, f field goals, and e extra points?

   (A) $6t + 3f + e$

   (B) $t^6 + f^3 + e$

   (C) $6(t + 3f + e)$

   (D) $3t + 6f + e$

   (E) $(6 + t) + (3 + f) + (1 + e)$

2. Sean claims that every number is either prime or the product of two primes. Which number could Vickie use to disprove Sean's statement?

   (A) 2

   (B) 10

   (C) 15

   (D) 18

   (E) 57

3. On a number line, four evenly spaced marks are placed between –2 and 13. What is the coordinate of the second such mark?

   (A) 1

   (B) 4

   (C) 5.5

   (D) 7

   (E) 7.5

4. What is the length of a rectangle whose perimeter is 40 inches and whose width is 8 inches?

   (A) 2½ inches

   (B) 5 inches

   (C) 12 inches

   (D) 16 inches

   (E) 32 inches

Go on to next page

5. Owen needs to travel 400 miles in 8 hours. If he averages m miles per hour for the first three hours, what does his average speed need to be for the remaining 5 hours?

   (A) $\dfrac{400 - 3m}{5}$

   (B) $\dfrac{400 - 3m}{8}$

   (C) $\dfrac{400 - m}{5}$

   (D) $50 - {}^{m}\!/_{3}$

   (E) $80 - 3m$

6. Which point is not 5 units from the origin?

   (A) $(-5, 0)$

   (B) $(5, 5)$

   (C) $(3, -4)$

   (D) $(0, 5)$

   (E) $(0, -5)$

7. Find the perimeter of a square whose diagonal has length $6\sqrt{2}$ m.

   (A) 6 m

   (B) $12\sqrt{2}$ m

   (C) 24 m

   (D) $24\sqrt{2}$ m

   (E) 48 m

8. How many two-digit numbers contain one even digit and one odd digit?

   (A) 20

   (B) 25

   (C) 45

   (D) 50

   (E) 55

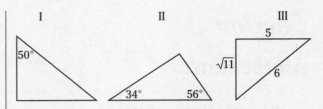

9. Which of these three triangles must be a right triangle? (Figures are not drawn to scale.)

   (A) I only

   (B) II only

   (C) I and III

   (D) II and III

   (E) I, II, and III

10. If $d^{1/2} + 5 = 9$, then $d^{-1} =$

   (A) -16

   (B) -4

   (C) -2

   (D) ½

   (E) ¹⁄₁₆

Go on to next page

Questions 11 and 12 use the following graphs.

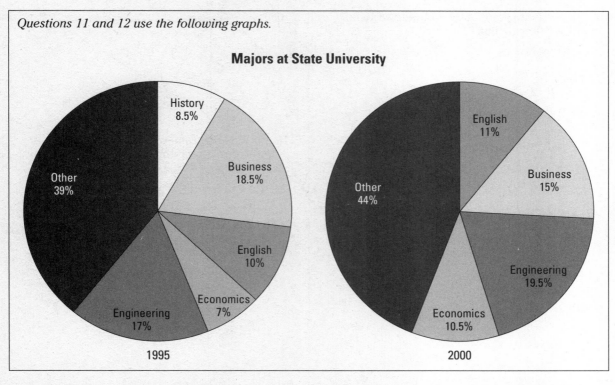

Majors at State University

1995

2000

---

11. If 5,000 students attended State U in 1995, how many majored in history or English?

    (A) 185

    (B) 425

    (C) 500

    (D) 925

    (E) 1,850

---

12. Which is a valid conclusion, based on the graphs alone?

    (A) More students majored in English in 2000 than in 1995.

    (B) More students majored in business in 1995 than in 2000.

    (C) History was the most popular major in 1995.

    (D) Fewer students majored in economics in 1995 than in 2000.

    (E) In 2000, more students majored in engineering than in English.

---

13. Four consecutive even integers are written down. Which of the following statements *must* be true?

    (A) The average (arithmetic mean) of the numbers is even.

    (B) The median of the numbers is even.

    (C) The sum of the numbers is 2½ times the largest number.

    (D) The median is not one of the numbers on the list.

    (E) The largest number on the list is more than twice as large as the smallest.

---

14. Let >n be defined as the smallest perfect square greater than *n*. For example, >3 = 4 and >4 = 9. Which of the following is equal to >5 + >9?

    (A) >10

    (B) >14

    (C) >20

    (D) >25

    (E) >45

Go on to next page

15. If $j^2 > j$, and $j^3 > j$, but $j^2 > j^3$, then which of the following must be true?

    (A) $j < -1$

    (B) $-1 < j < 0$

    (C) $0 < j < 1$

    (D) $1 < j < 2$

    (E) $j > 2$

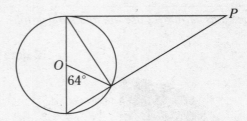

16. In this diagram, where O is the center of the circle, find the measure of angle P, in degrees.

    (A) 32

    (B) 36

    (C) 45

    (D) 58

    (E) 64

STOP YOU MAY CHECK YOUR WORK ON THIS SECTION ONLY.
DO NOT GO BACK TO ANY PREVIOUS SECTION.

Section 9

Multiple-Choice Writing

Time: 10 minutes for 14 questions

Directions: Each sentence is followed by five choices. Decide which choice *best* improves the sentence, and darken the corresponding oval on the answer sheet. If the underlined portion of the sentence is best left alone, choose (A).

Example: <u>Bert and him went</u> to the store to buy boots in preparation for the approaching storm.

(A) Bert and him went

(B) Bert and he went

(C) Bert and he had gone

(D) Bert and him had gone

(E) Bert and himself went

The correct answer is (B).

1. <u>Either windmills or solar power are planned for that building's heating system</u> in order to comply with the highest environmental standards.

   (A) Either wind mills or solar power are planned for that building's heating system

   (B) Either wind mills or solar power is planned for that building's heating system

   (C) Either wind mills or solar power are in the plan for that building's heating system

   (D) Wind mills or solar power, being planned for that building's heating system

   (E) Planned for that building's heating system are either wind mills or solar power

2. Before e-mail is delivered to your inbox, <u>every message goes through</u> a filter that weeds out junk mail.

   (A) every message goes through

   (B) every message goes by

   (C) every one of your messages go through

   (D) it goes through

   (E) it will go through

3. <u>If a person naps for just a short time every day, they will be more relaxed and efficient.</u>

   (A) If a person naps for just a short time every day, they will be more relaxed and efficient.

   (B) If a person naps for just a short time every day, you will be more relaxed and efficient.

   (C) If a person naps for just a short time every day, they will be more relaxed and work more efficiently.

   (D) If a person naps for just a short time every day, he or she will be more relaxed and efficient.

   (E) Napping for just a short time every day, they will be more relaxed and efficient.

4. The level of skill needed to create stained glass <u>are the same as metalwork.</u>

   (A) are the same as metalwork

   (B) are the same as metalwork's

   (C) are the same as the level of skill needed for metalwork

   (D) and metalwork's are the same

   (E) and metalwork is the same

Go on to next page

5. Hampered by injury, the sprinter took <u>as long as ten minutes or many more minutes</u> to cover the same distance he had once run in 5.5 minutes.

    (A) as long as ten minutes or many more minutes

    (B) ten minutes, or even more,

    (C) at least ten minutes

    (D) ten minutes, which is more than ever before

    (E) more than ten minutes, and some minutes in addition,

6. Elaborate <u>costumes, being part of the Halloween parade, which</u> gives enjoyment to both spectators and participants.

    (A) costumes, being part of the Halloween parade, which

    (B) costumes are part of the Halloween parade, which

    (C) costumes, being part of the Halloween parade, that

    (D) costumes, as part of the Halloween parade, which

    (E) costumes, which are part of the Halloween parade and they

7. San Francisco is famous for its cable cars, <u>and they climb the steep hills of that city, and they attract</u> many tourists.

    (A) and they climb the steep hills of that city, and they attract

    (B) and they climb the steep hills of that city, they attract

    (C) which climb the steep hills of that city and attract

    (D) that, as they climb the steep hills of that city, they attract

    (E) climbing the steep hills of that city, and attracting

8. <u>The longer that actor plays a role, the more he understands his character.</u>

    (A) The longer that actor plays a role, the more he understands his character.

    (B) The longer that actor plays a role, and the more he understands his character.

    (C) The longer that actor plays a role; the more he understands his character.

    (D) If that actor plays a role longer, he understands his character more and more.

    (E) That actor, playing a role for more time, understands his character more.

9. Some gardeners prefer to start seedlings indoors during the last weeks of winter, <u>so they will have</u> a head start when the weather warms in the spring.

    (A) so they will have

    (B) in order that they will have

    (C) so the plants, they will have

    (D) so the plants will have

    (E) although they will have

10. Colors affect you in subtle, <u>unconscious ways, having meaning that you are not aware of but it's in your mind.</u>

    (A) unconscious ways, having meaning that you are not aware of but it's in your mind

    (B) unconscious ways

    (C) unconsciously, having meaning that you are not aware of

    (D) unconscious ways, but they're in your mind

    (E) unconscious ways you are not aware of

11. Being on deadline and hoping to impress the boss, the stock analyst <u>prepared the report really quick</u>.

    (A) prepared the report really quick

    (B) had prepared the report really quick

    (C) prepared the report really quickly

    (D) prepared the report real quickly

    (E) preparing the report really quick

Go on to next page

12. The Board of Directors <u>appointed an inves-tigator for to discover</u> why profits plum-meted in the last year.

    (A) appointed an investigator for to discover

    (B) had appointed an investigator for to discover

    (C) appointed an investigator with the intention of discovering

    (D) appointed an investigator to discover

    (E) appointed an investigator who has a job to discover

13. The orchid is one of the many plants in his greenhouse <u>that has not flourished</u>.

    (A) that has not flourished

    (B) which it not having flourished

    (C) that was not flourishing

    (D) which has not flourished

    (E) that have not flourished

14. Colleges now offer students many more electives, <u>and it has sometimes confused</u> freshmen trying to decide which courses to take.

    (A) and it has sometimes confused

    (B) which has sometimes confused

    (C) and the choices have sometimes confused

    (D) sometimes confused

    (E) and sometimes confused

STOP YOU MAY CHECK YOUR WORK ON THIS SECTION ONLY. DO NOT GO BACK TO ANY PREVIOUS SECTION.

Chapter 23

Practice Exam 2: Answers and Explanations

● ●

After you finish taking Practice Exam 2 in Chapter 22, spend some time going through the answers and explanations I offer you in this chapter to find out which questions you missed and why. Even if you answered every question correctly, read the explanations in this chapter because I sneak some tips and warnings into the explanations to be sure you're ready-set-go for the actual SAT. If you're short on time, you can quickly check your answers with the abbreviated answer key I provide at the end of the chapter.

Note: To determine your score on this practice test, turn to the appendix.

Section 1: The Essay

You can handle this essay question in a couple of ways, but the first quotation gives you a huge hint about the SAT graders' expectations. As you know, the atomic bomb exists, and not everyone is happy about it. J. Robert Oppenheimer, the author of the first quotation, helped create the bomb (a fact you get from the test question). He later had second thoughts about his work, but you don't have to know this fact to write a good essay. What you do have to know — and reflect in your essay — is the complexity of the situation. Because the SAT graders don't quote the inventor of, say, cancer-fighting drugs, they expect you to say something about the drawbacks of the human urge to discover and invent (such as the fact that people can now blow up the entire planet). At the same time, though, the test graders are unlikely to smile upon an essay that declares that the human race should be content with couch-potatohood.

Your best bet as you write your essay is to come up with one or two examples of human discoveries or creations and then talk about the pros (in one paragraph) and the cons (in another paragraph). Introduce the essay with a paragraph about consequences and your view on how well an inventor/artist/scientist can foresee them and how much the inventor/ artist/scientist should worry about them. Then add two body paragraphs (the pros and cons) and a conclusion (your final opinion on responsibility). Here are two possible outlines, one for a scientist and one for an artist:

Scientific View

✔ **Introduction:** State your thesis: Human beings need to stretch the body of knowledge. Without human restlessness, everyone would still be living in caves eating uncooked twigs. However, scientists must consider the probable uses of their discoveries.

✔ **Body Paragraph 1:** Describe some of the wonders created by science, including advances in medicine and technology.

Avoid the essay trap of example overkill. You have literally millions of examples at your disposal for this topic. Be careful not to turn your essay into a giant list. Choose one or two strong examples and explain how they support your thesis.

✔ **Body Paragraph 2:** Discuss some drawbacks of the examples from the preceding paragraph. Modern medicine, for instance, can prolong life way past the point when it's worth living. Technology has not saved human beings from pollution and has taken away some of the personal interactions that raise the quality of life.

✔ **Conclusion:** No one can foresee everything, but scientists should take reasonable precautions to control the results of their work because they have the power to affect millions of people for good or evil.

Artistic view

✔ **Introduction:** State your thesis: Although artists create in order to express themselves, they should consider other factors, such as the effect of their work on society, when they make art.

✔ **Body Paragraph 1:** Explain the benefits to an artist of self-expression. Discuss the way in which new artistic movements — cubism, for example — often shock audiences when they first appear. If artists create only works that please the audience, the artists sacrifice too much.

✔ **Body Paragraph 2:** Concede the fact that artists don't work in a vacuum. If artists' work supports stereotypes or hateful ideas, they can harm real people with their creations. The art of the Nazi era or the racial stereotypes in early 20th-century American films, for example, fueled and justified prejudice and discrimination.

✔ **Conclusion:** Conclude with the idea that artists must balance their personal need to express themselves freely with their obligation not to harm society. Freedom and responsibility go hand in hand.

Now that you've seen a couple of different options for how to organize an essay addressing the obligation an artist/scientist should have to the public good, it's time to score your own essay. Before you get started, turn to Chapter 8 and read the samples there. Then score your essay using the scoring rubric in Chapter 7; be honest with yourself as you determine how your essay matches up against the rubric.

Section 2: Critical Reading

1. **C.** Process of elimination (and perhaps some life experience in being ignored by a boss or teacher) gets you through this question with ease. How would you feel if you were the vice president in the question? Not *buoyed* (spirits lifted), *reassured* (calmed, given confidence), or *inspired* (stimulated, stirred by ideas), I'm sure. *Intimidated* (threatened) is a good match — far better than the overly general *affected* (influenced).

2. **B.** The word that probably pops into your head as you read this question (and I don't mean "lunchtime!") is *unification*. But that's not an option. The closest choice is *integration,* which is more or less the opposite of Choices (A), (C), and (E), so, if you're stuck on this question, you can guess using process of elimination. Choice (D) is somewhere on Mars because you can't make a proclamation into something (a *proclamation* is an official declaration).

3. **A.** Okay, you can dump Choice (D) immediately because real-world knowledge tells you that angry people don't hand out promotions. Choices (B) and (C) are also wrong because losing insignificant or outdated material won't send any detective for ulcer medicine. Choice (E) isn't bad because *affront* means "to insult," but Choice (A) is better because *crucial* fits the sentence better than *adverse*. (*Crucial* means "essential" and *adverse* means "unfavorable" or "harmful.") In case you were wondering, to *upbraid* is basically to yell like a drill sergeant during basic training.

4. **C.** If the corporation is *affluent*, it's making lots of money, and *lucrative* means "profitable," so Choice (C) fits the context of the sentence. On the other hand, Choice (A) doesn't make

much sense in terms of context, although the SAT writers want you to relate *deregulated* (removing or without rules) to *multifaceted* (lots of variety). Choices (B), (D), and (E) are non-starters because their word pairs are opposites, and the sentence calls for similar words.

To help you understand why Choices (B), (D), and (E) are wrong, consider their definitions. *Mor-* or *mort-* relates to death. (Think *mortuary, morbid, mortal.*) In the context of the sentence, *moribund* means that the corporation is so stale that it may as well be dead. *Innovative* contains the root *nov*, or new. *Scrupulous* applies to the kind of person who follows every rule and considers every aspect of morality, no matter how tiny — not a good pair for *unethical*, which means disregarding *ethics* (principles of right and wrong).

5. **E.** If the teacher is *pragmatic*, she's practical. She wants to get the job done (to increase her students' knowledge and understanding). So *motivated* (giving reason to act) fits this sentence best. A close second is Choice (B), but *heighten* intensifies feelings, so it's a poor fit for studies. Choices (A), (C), and (D) are the opposite of what you want.

6. **A.** Notice the *and* in the sentence? That word tells you to look for a continuation of meaning, not a change in direction. The first half of the sentence talks about variety, and *myriad* means "various, diverse." *Convoluted* (complicated or elaborate) and *versatile* (multitalented, adaptable) are there to lead you astray because both contain an element of variety, but *myriad* is the best answer. *Intuitive* (relying on instinct or gut feeling) and *nebulous* (cloudy, vague) aren't in the running.

7. **D.** The clue here is *furthermore,* which tells you that the two halves of the sentence more or less match. If Lucy is *saving* the rain forest, she isn't trying to wipe out (*annihilate, decimate,* and *eradicate*) Bambi and friends. *Proliferate* sounds good, but you can't proliferate something else. The animals can *proliferate* (reproduce) all by themselves, but Lucy can only *preserve* them.

8. **E.** You can crack this sentence by filling in your own word. *Irresponsible* comes to mind, at least to teachers like me. You may say *slow* or *reluctant.* Of all the D words in the choices, only *dilatory* (tending to delay) fits the why-should-I-do-it-now-when-it-isn't-due-for-two-whole-hours attitude portrayed in the sentence. *Diligent* (responsible, hard-working) travels in the opposite direction. *Doleful* (sad), *doctrinaire* (rigid in belief), and *diffident* (shy) don't make sense in the sentence.

9. **D.** An audience doesn't give *kudos* (praise) to an *affected* performance, which is unreal or phony. (At least not in theory; boy bands continue to earn lots of cash.)

The key to Question 9 is to think of the real world. What does the audience give to a good or bad performance? After you answer that question, look for pairs that fit. A *conventional* performance is stale and boring, so it will gather a lot of *critiques* (detailed criticism), not a few. An *effective* performance (one that does the job — that is, entertains the audience) receives many, not few, *ovations* (rounds of applause). The same goes for Choice (C).

10. **E.** You find the answer to this question in Lines 8–9, which tell you that hysteria used to be "associated with witchcraft and medieval states of possession."

Because this question is the first one after the passage, the odds are that the answer is in the first few lines of the passage. As you've probably guessed, questions toward the end may refer to the end of the passage. However, this general guideline goes out the window for questions that take into account the entire reading selection.

11. **D.** Did the SAT writers trip you up on this one? When you think of *hysteria,* you probably picture out-of-control laughter that brings forth a slap ("for his own good"). But Lines 11–12 mention Choice (E) *amnesias,* Choice (B) *paralyses,* Choice (C) *spasms* or *involuntary movements,* and Choice (A) *anesthesias.* Only laughter is missing from the passage, so Choice (D) is your answer.

Real-world knowledge helps on the SAT, but the final answer must always make sense in the context of the reading material provided.

12. **C.** The passage defines *psychological* as a state with "no discernable physical causes." Choice (C) comes the closest to this definition.

13. **A.** Paragraph 2 says that Charcot clarified the *psychological-traumatic nature of symptoms* and mentions survivors of train wrecks, so you can choose Choice (A) with confidence.

    Choice (C) is a favorite SAT trap: It contains a statement that actually appears in the passage but doesn't fit the question. Beware of such traps!

14. **A.** The term **hysteria** comes from the Greek word for "womb," and the passage implies that it was once thought to be only a female disease. Hence, *of both sexes* counters that idea. Choice (A) is the right one. Also, Line 81 mentions *the old link* between hysteria and women.

15. **B.** According to Lines 42–44, Charcot says the *railway spine* and *railway brain* were cases in which "symptoms mimicked those found after spinal cord or brain injuries." This question is chock-full of little traps. Choice (A) tempts you because it mentions trains, and Choice (E) may grab your attention because Charcot did use hypnosis. But Choice (B) fits best.

16. **E.** Lines 62–64 tell you that memories blotted out by physical injuries to the brain couldn't be retrieved by hypnosis, so you know Choice (E) is the right answer.

17. **B.** Charcot's *hypnoid state* is linked to the term **dissociation**, which is clearly defined as a *blotting out* of certain memories. Line 67 says that patients aren't aware of what they're doing, so Choices (D) and (E) aren't acceptable.

18. **A.** The last paragraph lists several of Charcot's accomplishments, but the word *genuine* immediately sets up a comparison. If the accomplishments discussed in the passage are his genuine ones, Charcot must have made some unsupported claims or performed some doubtful research.

19. **D.** The runner-up is Choice (A) because Charcot did treat hysteria with hypnosis. But Charcot worked in the late 19th century, and Choice (A) contains a present-tense verb *(is)*. Medicine has certainly changed in the last hundred years or so, and for this reason, Choice (A) doesn't measure up. Choice (D), on the other hand, is supported by Lines 24–25, which refers to *so-called hysterics.*

20. **D.** The author presents just the facts in the passage, and thus the tone is best described as informative.

21. **A.** Choices (B) and (E) are too broad, and Choice (C) is too narrow. Choice (D) doesn't make the grade because the passage doesn't tell you anything about Charcot's life. Only Choice (A) remains.

22. **D.** The light isn't new or old, according to the passage. It just travels different distances. So depending on what you're looking at, you're seeing different times.

23. **E.** The first four choices are too general. *Direct Study of the Past,* Choice (C), may be what I do when I clean out my pockets after a night out with friends, but it doesn't explain what the passage is about. Choice (E) is the best option because it tells readers what to expect from the passage.

24. **B.** The passage states that the monument wasn't built to study the sun because only "the first part of the answer is correct." The author also explains that no one yet knows what *astronomical phenomenon* Stonehenge was built to observe, so Choice (B) is the best answer.

25. **D.** Choice (E) is the runner-up because the author is attempting to explain Stonehenge's purpose. However, the comment inside the dashes is simply clarifying the meaning of *the first part of the answer,* not giving a theory all by itself. Therefore, Choice (D) wins the prize.

Section 3: Mathematics

1. **E.** Plugging 5 and –4 into the equation $p(p - q)$ gives you $(5)(5 - -4) = (5)(5 + 4) = (5)(9) = 45$.

2. **D.** The easiest approach to this problem is to start at the end: Katie used her $10 coupon and paid $35, so the price was $45 without the coupon. Because this price was 50% off the original price, it originally cost twice as much, or $90.

3. **A.** *Ratio* is just a fancy name for fraction, so this problem says that $^k\!/_m = {}^m\!/_n$. Cross-multiplying gives you $kn = m^2$, or Choice (A).

4. **C.** The key to figuring out this problem is noticing that the line containing points O, P, and Q is a diameter of the large circle and that it also contains the diameters of the two smaller circles. So the diameter of circle O equals the sum of the diameters of circles P and Q. Meanwhile, the line segment PQ is composed of the *radii* (plural of *radius*) of the two small circles. Because these two radii add up to 6, the diameters of the small circles add up to 12. The diameter of circle O is 12 and its radius is 6. Finally, because the circle's area is πr^2, the large circle's area is $\pi(6)^2 = 36\pi$.

5. **B.** All the answer choices involve multiplication, and the only way to get an odd number as the answer to a multiplication problem is to multiply two odd numbers. Thus, you can throw out Choices (A) and (E) right away because you multiply by e in both of them. Choices (C) and (D) are also no good: If o is odd, $o - 1$ and $o + 1$ are both even. These calculations leave you with Choice (B). As always, check to make sure that your answer really does work. An odd plus or minus an even is always odd, so both $o - e$ and $o + e$ are odd, and the product must also be odd.

6. **C.** From 10:45 p.m. to midnight is 1 hour 15 minutes, and from midnight to 2 a.m. is another 2 hours. Thus, the train was moving for 3 hours 15 minutes minus the 30 minutes (½ hour) it was stopped, for a total of 2 hours 45 minutes. Two hours × 80 miles per hour is 160 miles. Because 45 minutes is ¾ of an hour, you need to add another ¾ × 80 = 60 miles, giving you 220 miles.

7. **B.** You know there are 24 hours in a day, so to find the number of hours in a week, calculate 24 hours × 7 days = 168 hours. Now you have $168w$ hours. Add $24d$ for the leftover days. Another approach: In w weeks and d days, there are $7w + d$ total days. Multiplying by 24 hours in a day gives you $24(7w + d)$, and distributing gives you $168w + 24d$.

8. **A.** As always with this type of problem, go through each answer choice one at a time. Choice (A) requires the distance formula, but first you need to find the coordinates of point C. You could use a formula, but common sense works best. To get from A to B, move 2 spaces to the right and 3 spaces up. Because Choice (B) is the midpoint of AC, do the same thing to get from B to C. Starting from $(5, 0)$, moving 2 spaces to the right and 3 spaces up puts you at $(7, 3)$. To find the distance from A to C, use the formula for the distance between two points (distance $= \sqrt{(x_2 - x_1)^2 + (y_2 - y_1)^2}$). Plug in the numbers for points A and C:

$$\sqrt{((7) - (3))^2 + ((3) - (-3))^2} = \sqrt{(4)^2 + (6)^2} = \sqrt{16 + 36} = \sqrt{52},$$ which doesn't equal 5. Because the question asks you for the statement that *isn't* true, you have your answer — Choice (A).

When you take the real SAT, you don't have to check every possibility if you're pretty sure about your answer. If you finish early, you can always go back and double-check.

Those of you who want to see why the other choices are wrong (and therefore true), keep reading. You discovered that Choice (B) is true as you worked through Choice (A). You may think you need to use the distance formula again to check Choice (C), but this answer is really just the definition of the midpoint; if B is the midpoint of AC, this statement must be true. If you really want to do the math, both distances are $\sqrt{13}$. Choice (D) sure looks like it should be true, but it's a good excuse to haul the slope formula out of storage. Slope $= \dfrac{y_2 - y_1}{x_2 - x_1}$. Using points A and B gives you $m = \dfrac{(0)-(-3)}{(5)-(3)} = \dfrac{3}{2}$; using B and C gives you $m = \dfrac{(3)-(0)}{(7)-(5)} = \dfrac{3}{2}$. As you can see, they're equal. Choice (E) follows logically from the answers you got as you worked through Choice (D). If both pieces of the line have a slope of ³⁄₂, then so does the whole line AC. Notice, by the way, that you don't add slopes as you would distances.

9. **D.** You could write an algebra equation for this problem, but reasoning it out works fine, too. The fraction of the tables that Nandan had to set up changed from ⅓ to ½. In math, *change* is always a cue to subtract, and ½ – ⅓ = ⅙. (Solve this without a calculator just for the practice.) So Nandan had to set up ⅙ more tables than he expected — 4 tables, according to the problem. If 4 is ⅙ of the total, then the total number of tables is $4 \times 6 = 24$.

10. **C.** Don't waste your time trying to draw graphs to solve this problem. If the graph of an equation passes through a point, then the coordinates of the point are a solution to the equation. So you need to plug in –1 for x and 4 for y in each of the equations given in the answer choices. Solve the equations. In the equation in Choice (C), the key is that $-(-1) = 1$, so the equation becomes $1 + 3 = 4$, which is a correct equation.

Make sure you don't mix up the numbers. For example, if you carelessly put –1 in for y and 4 in for x in the equation $y = x - 5$ in Choice (A), you'd end up choosing Choice (A) as the correct answer — and you'd be wrong!

11. **E.** LM is a diameter, which means it divides the circle into two 180° arcs. Because N is an inscribed angle (it's on the edge of the circle), its measure is half of the lower 180° arc, or 90°. Yep, it's a right triangle! Because you know the lengths of two sides of the triangle, you can find the third. Remember that 26 is the hypotenuse, so your equation should be $x^2 + 24^2 = 26^2$, which gives you $x^2 + 576 = 676$, $x^2 = 100$, and $x = 10$. Now for the real problem — finding the area of the shaded portion of the circle, which equals the area of the circle minus the area of the triangle. The circle's diameter is 26, so its radius is 13, and the area of a circle = $\pi r^2 = \pi(13)^2 = 169\pi$. The triangle's area is ½ × base × height, but you need to be careful. Twenty-six isn't the base because you don't have a height to go with it. Instead, you need to use the two legs of the right triangle as the base and height. (It may help to rotate the book if you have trouble visualizing this concept.) So the triangle's area is ½(10)(24) = 120, and the answer is $169\pi - 120$.

12. **A.** Start with the last fact given in the question, that the three-digit number ABC is divisible by 5. Every number that's divisible by 5 ends in either 0 or 5, so C must be one of those numbers. The first and second facts make it impossible for C to be zero, because, if C were zero, A and B would be equal to each other, which is illegal. Therefore, C must be 5. Because $B = A + C$, and A must be at least 1, B must be at least 6.

13. **D.** When $f(x) = 0$, the graph has a height of 0; in other words, it crosses the x-axis. As you can see from the graph, it crosses the x-axis in three places. Notice that you don't actually need to know where it crosses the x-axis. You just need to count the number of times it does so.

14. **B.** Here you just need to move the graph down 2 spaces.

15. **A.** The first step in answering this problem is drawing the line in question:

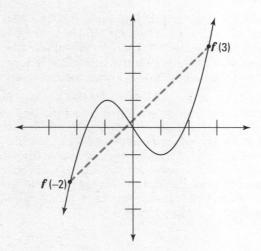

After you draw the line, don't jump the gun and start calculating the slope. Doing so is a waste of time because the question doesn't ask for the slope. All you have to do is look at the graph to determine that the slope is positive and then mark Choice (A).

To figure out what kind of slope a line has, imagine an ant walking on the line from left to right. If it's going uphill, the slope is positive. If it's going downhill, the slope is negative. The ant isn't going up or down when the line is horizontal (flat), so a horizontal line has a slope of zero. And, finally, the ant could be going up or down on a vertical line, so a vertical line has no slope.

16. **C.** In case you didn't already know, this question is tough. When a problem looks complicated, start with the simplest part you can see. In this case, the simplest part is $|a| < 3$. If you make a positive, the result must be less than 3. So a could be a number like 1, 2, 2.3, or ⅛, or it could be the negative versions of any of these numbers. So what can't a be? It can't be 3 or bigger than 3, and it can't be –3 or less than –3.

Okay, now it's time to tackle $|a - b| < 4$. Start by plugging Choice (A), $b = -8$, into the equation. Then $|a - b| = |a - (-8)| = |a + 8|$. If you try some possible a values, you see that you can't make this equation equal less than 4. The same thing happens when you plug in Choices (B), (D), and (E). But if you try Choice (C), you get $|a - b| = |a - (-6)| = |a + 6|$. Now if you let $a = -2.5$, or any number between –2 and –3, the answer is less than 4.

Question 16 is a lot of work. On the real SAT, you probably want to skip a problem if it looks this time-consuming. Save your energy for easier problems, and go back to the really complex ones if you have time after you answer all the other questions.

17. **B.** This is a classic ratio problem, made more complicated by the presence of both feet and inches. You could convert everything to inches, but because I like fractions (a sad but true statement about my life), I'm going to change 1 foot 3 inches to 1¼ feet. So the ratio says that $\frac{1\frac{1}{4}}{5} = \frac{7}{x}$. Notice that the top numbers stand for the shadows, while the bottom ones stand for the heights of the objects in question. Doing that crazy cross-multiplication thing gives you $(1\frac{1}{4})(x) = (5)(7)$ or $1\frac{1}{4}x = 35$. Now don't be scared: You have to divide both sides by 1¼, or ⁵⁄₄. To divide 35 by ⁵⁄₄, multiply by the reciprocal, or ⅘: $35 \times \frac{4}{5} = \frac{140}{5} = 28$.

18. **B.** The answer choices have only v and w in them, so you need to start this problem by turning everything into those letters. You already know that $x = vw$, so $y = wx = w(vw) = vw^2$. To continue, you need to remember two things: First, the ws both have an "invisible 1" as their exponents, and second, you need to add exponents when you multiply powers of the same bases. Because $z = xy$, $z = (vw)(vw^2) = v^2w^3$. You're looking for yz, which your work tells you equals $(vw^2)(v^2w^3) = v^3w^5$.

19. **E.** What a surprise: a special right triangle! *ABD* is a 30-60-90 right triangle, with ∠*BAD* measuring 60 degrees. Because *AC* bisects ∠*BAD*, both ∠*CAD* and ∠*BAC* measure 30 degrees. Hey! That makes *ABC* a 30-60-90 triangle, too! In triangle *ABC*, line *AB* is opposite the 60° angle, which means that it equals the shortest side times $\sqrt{3}$. The shortest side, *BC*, is therefore 5. And the longest side is always twice as long as the shortest side, so *AC* = 10.

20. **D.** Rick's score was 9 (because it's 4 + 5). For Jacob to have the same score, three times his lowest roll must also be 9, so his lowest roll must be 3. So he could roll a 3 and a 3, a 3 and a 4, a 3 and a 5, or a 3 and a 6. Ah, but be careful. To roll a 3 and a 4, for example, he could roll 3 then 4 or 4 then 3. Jacob can really roll 7 possible combinations: (3, 3); (3, 4); (4, 3); (3, 5); (5, 3); (3, 6); or (6, 3). So 7 is the *numerator* (the top half of the fraction). Now what? You have to find the *denominator* (the bottom half of the fraction), which counts the total number of possibilities. Using the counting principle, you multiply the number of possibilities for each action. In this case, there are 6 possibilities for each die, so there are 6 × 6 = 36 total possibilities, and your answer is $\frac{7}{36}$.

Section 4: Critical Reading

1. **D.** The signal word here — the one that should light up in neon in your head — is *though*. *Though* (like its cousin, *although*) tells you that the sentence is changing direction. So right away you can rule out Choices (A) and (B) because their pairs are synonyms. Your next task is to decode the sentence. The first blank is about sharing — think *common* — and the second blank is about what isn't shared — think *unique*.

2. **A.** If the note is *clear*, you don't need hours of intense study and a computer to figure it out. Therefore, you need the opposite of clear for this sentence. Choices (A) and (B) are both possible, but Choice (A) is better because the note was deciphered eventually, making unintelligible too strong. (***Cryptic*** means "puzzling.")

3. **D.** Placing your own word in the sentence may lead you to *crashes*, especially if you're thinking about computer systems. The closest answer then is Choice (D) because ***jeopardize*** means "to place in danger."

   In case you were wondering, ***surmount*** means "to overcome," and ***nullify*** means "to counteract" or "to undo the effect of," as in this sentence: One burp was enough to nullify the impression of courtesy that Flink had been laboring to create. As you can see, neither of those terms fits the context of the sentence.

4. **A.** The sentence emphasizes variety, listing three separate types of dolls, so Choice (B) bites the dust instantly. Choice (C) is tempting, but ***universal*** (true throughout the universe) has to come in second to ***eclectic***, which means "from varied sources or origins."

   Don't be swayed the wrong way by one word in a sentence. In Question 4, *heir* may lead you to consider Choice (E) because you associate inheriting with money. But the rest of the sentence doesn't support that choice.

5. **B.** Before you even looked at the choices, you probably thought of *possibility* or *existence* for the first blank because in the real world, not the SAT, people are always wondering about whether little green guys are wandering around the Red Planet. Keeping this fact in mind, you just need to decide between Choices (B) and (C). Choice (B) triumphs over Choice (C) because ***sustained*** (constant, unceasing) is better than ***advantageous*** (giving an advantage) in the context of the sentence.

6. **C.** Who makes a new broadcast network? Checking only the first blank, you can rule out only Choice (E) because ***despots*** are tyrants. Okay, maybe you've read about some of the media moguls and kept Choice (E). No matter. You still need to narrow down the field, and the second blank is where all the action is. The sentence tells you that the people who establish a new network must be businesslike and have one other quality. Chances are

that other quality contrasts with *businesslike* or at least complements it. What's a good pair for businesslike? *Creative* — which, by the way, is the opposite of *prosaic* (commonplace, dull).

7. **E.** This question relies on your vocabulary more than anything else. If a play is *generic*, it's common, or not special in any way. *Extraneous* (extra, not essential) is way off base, as are *intemperate* (lacking self-control) and *ubiquitous* (appearing everywhere). The best choice here is *critical,* which describes the kind of play (homerun, double play, spectacular catch) that the Yankees always make when I duck into the kitchen for a snack.

8. **C.** With so much experience, the interviewer has probably seen it all and then some, so seeing him or her *nonplussed* (rattled, shaken up) isn't going to happen.

9. **A.** This question is a no-go for anyone who hasn't swallowed a dictionary. For the rest of you out there: *affable* and *amicable* mean "friendly," *vivacious* means "lively," and *malevolent* means "evil." If you crack the vocabulary code for the first blank, you're still stuck for the second, which needs to match the first one in tone. Choice (A) fits because *jocular* is a fancy way for saying joking. If you're friendly, you can still have mock arguments (during which you throw rubber frying pans at each other). Just to finish the word-building exercise: *Sententious* refers to arguments with a moral tone and *innocuous* means innocent.

10. **D.** *Xenophobia* is the Greek word for "fear of foreigners," and if you're afraid of foreigners, you don't go *abroad* (out of the country). If you answered this one correctly, you're definitely Ivy League material, whether the admissions officers realize it or not.

11. **B.** Choice (A) is too general, and Choices (D) and (E) are too limited because each applies to only one passage. The runner-up is Choice (C), but the passages say much less about why you want to know where you are and much more about how hard it was for early seafarers and pilots to navigate. For this reason, Choice (B) is your winner.

12. **D.** These two passages do in fact contain some inspirational material — the ability of human beings to rise to a challenge — so you may be tempted by Choice (A). But overall, they sound more like something a competent, somewhat-interesting science or social studies teacher would say while instructing you about longitude and navigation.

13. **A.** Passage I discusses the 18th-century problem of determining longitude, while Passage II deals with the early part of the 20th century.

14. **B.** This one contains a few sandbars that can run your SAT ship aground if you're not careful. Choices (A) and (C) seem to be good options in terms of real-life experience because it makes sense that the water nearest land would be mapped, or charted, first. But the passage doesn't give you much to go on, and the SAT doesn't rely on real life, so you need to eliminate both options. Choice (D) doesn't jibe with the passage, which refers to a course being plotted incorrectly, and Choice (E) has no basis in the passage at all. Thus, by process of elimination (and by looking at the passage), you know that Choice (B) is the best answer.

15. **E.** The paragraph preceding the sentence quoted in this question (Lines 11–20) discusses how easy figuring out latitude is. The lines after this sentence (Lines 25–45) explain why longitude is tough to calculate. This sentence, therefore, sets up the comparison.

16. **C.** Check out the fourth paragraph of Passage I, which explains the fact that 15 degrees equals one hour and the problem of keeping time after you've left your home port. These details point you to Choice (C).

17. **D.** Lines 40–41 explain that until 1761, "there were no clocks capable of keeping steady time on board a rocking ship." Thus, you know that Choice (D) is the right answer.

18. **A.** The sentence about naval chronometers follows one that discusses telling time on board a rocking ship, strongly implying that these two topics are one and the same.

19. **C.** Crashing into locomotives and hills (Lines 52–54) certainly fits my definition of *danger on the ground,* so Choice (C) is the best answer.

20. **B.** According to Line 50, pilots descended in bad weather to continue *following the tracks*. In this context, *landmarks* is another word for *tracks*.

21. **E.** In the real world (not on MTV and not on the SAT), lighthouses are those cute little towers on seacoasts. According to Passage II, they light the way for planes, not ships.

A typical SAT ploy is to lead you to the wrong answer by providing a logical (but wrong) real-world answer. Always choose your answer based on the information in the passage. The real world can help you, but the passage is always the final authority.

22. **B.** The third paragraph of Passage II goes into a lot of detail about the aircraft that "could beat the trains by two or even three days" (Lines 71–72) after lightways were constructed. So assuming that lightways made planes an acceptable alternative to trains is reasonable — unlike the present day, when you're in the security line for three hours, only to find that your flight was canceled.

23. **D.** When the lightways weren't visible, the pilots followed the tracks, which they illuminated with the landing lights at night, according to Lines 84–87.

24. **C.** Radio assisted, but didn't perfect, navigation and thus made air travel easier — until someone invented those annoying background music systems that play in grounded airplanes (and elevators).

Section 5: Mathematics

1. **A.** The tricky part here is the phrase "subtracted from." "Two subtracted from five," for example, means 5 – 2, not 2 – 5. Take care not to write (–8) – 10 for this problem. Instead, do 10 – (–8) = 10 + 8 = 18.

A bunch of phrases signal subtraction — "subtracted from," "less than," and "fewer than" are the most common — and they all require you to switch the order of the quantities being subtracted.

2. **D.** Lyle's cost is 2 packages × 10 pounds × $3.99 = $79.80. Gretchen's cost is 20 pounds × $3.49 = $69.80, and the difference between them is $79.80 – $69.80 = $10.

3. **B.** Twenty minutes is one-third of an hour, so the minute hand covers one-third of a circle. Because a full circle has 360°, one-third of a circle is ⅓ × 360° = 120°.

4. **E.** Seeing that the drawing contains nine little triangles is fairly easy. Adding the big triangle gives you ten, but you can't forget to count the three "mama bear" triangles, which you can see here:

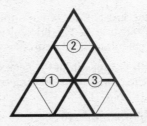

Adding in these three triangles gives you 13 total.

5. **C.** To solve this problem, you need to do a little estimating: π is about 3.1415; 3½ is 3.142857; 3.14 is just 3.14; $3.1\overline{4}$ = 3.14444..., and $\sqrt{10}$ is about 3.16. Thus, 3.14 is the smallest.

6. **D.** Look first at the large triangle. You know one angle, 38°, and the other two angles are both equal to $p + q$. Thus, you can write $(p + q) + (p + q) + 38 = 180$, which gives you $2p + 2q + 38 = 180$, and, finally, $2p + 2q = 142$. At this point, some people frustrate themselves by trying to figure out what p and q equal. Unfortunately, you don't have enough information to do that calculation; however, if $2p + 2q = 142$, you can divide both sides by 2 to get $p + q = 71$. If you look at the little triangle, you realize that you now have all the information you need. Because the angles of the little triangle are a, p, and q, you can write $a + p + q = 180$; because $p + q = 71$, $a + 71 = 180$, and $a = 109$.

7. **A.** Two big things are illegal in algebra: You can't take the square root of a negative number, and you can't divide by zero. The denominator here is $x + 2$, which would equal zero when $x = -2$, so -2 is your forbidden value.

8. **B.** When solving an equation like this one, some people are more comfortable making both sides into fractions. So you can write $\frac{ax}{x+2} = \frac{b}{1}$ and then cross-multiply to get $ax = b(x + 2)$, or $ax = bx + 2b$. To solve for x, you need all the xs on one side, so subtract bx from both sides to get $ax - bx = 2b$. Now, because x is in both terms on the left side, you can factor it out: $x(a - b) = 2b$. And, finally, dividing by $a - b$ gives you $\frac{2b}{a-b}$, which is Choice (B).

9. **32.** This question is best done as a proportion problem: $\frac{2\frac{1}{2}}{20} = \frac{4}{x}$. So $2\frac{1}{2}x = 80$. Dividing by $2\frac{1}{2}$ gives you $x = 80 \div 2\frac{1}{2} = 80 \div \frac{5}{2} = 80 \times \frac{2}{5} = \frac{160}{5} = 32$.

10. **210.** Every even number must be divisible by 2, so $2 \times 3 \times 5 \times 7 = 210$.

11. **360.** This is an old semi-trick question: In any shape, the sum of the exterior angles is always 360 degrees. As long as you remember what an exterior angle looks like, you should ace this type of question if it shows up on the SAT.

12. **36.** This problem employs the same subtraction trick as Question 1 in this section: If you let the numerator equal n, then the denominator is $2n - 12$, not $12 - 2n$. Thus, $\frac{2}{3} = \frac{n}{2n-12}$. So, $2(2n - 12) = 3n$, or $4n - 24 = 3n$. Subtracting $4n$ from both sides gives you $-24 = -n$, and dividing by -1 gives you $n = 24$. But wait! That's not the answer: n is the numerator, but the problem asks for the denominator. So plug 24 into $2n - 12$: $2(24) - 12 = 36$. If you have time, take a minute to check that $\frac{24}{36}$ really does equal $\frac{2}{3}$.

13. **8.** Although you may be able to get the answer by trial and error, this problem is really begging to be factored. To factor a *quadratic equation* (that is, an equation with something "squared" in it), you must first set the equation equal to zero. Making the squared term negative is never a good idea, so you should solve as follows:

$$p^2 = 3p + 40$$
$$\underline{-3p \quad -3p}$$
$$p^2 - 3p = 40$$
$$\underline{-40 \quad -40}$$
$$p^2 - 3p - 40 = 0$$

This equation factors out to $(p - 8)(p + 5) = 0$. It has two solutions: $p = 8$ and $p = -5$. Because you can't grid a negative answer, you have to go with 8.

14. **31.** This problem is an example of an alternating sequence; it alternates between adding 4 and subtracting 1 from each term. You could just follow the pattern out to the 21st term, but there's an easier way. Look at all the odd terms: 1, 4, 7, 10. Each term is 3 more than the previous term. So, the 21st term must follow this pattern. You can solve this problem by making a list of only the odd terms, like this:

1st	3rd	5th	7th	9th	11th	13th	15th	17th	19th	21st
1	4	7	10	13	16	19	22	25	28	31

15. **65.** In this problem, you can't actually figure out a and b. Because the problem asks for $a - b$, one good way to start is to look for an angle that would be equal to $a - b$. First off, look at the angle marked p in the diagram below, in which p and b are vertical angles. Hence $p = b$. Now check out the (unnamed) angle where I've drawn a curve in the following diagram. Because this drawing contains parallel lines, this unnamed angle is equal to a; these angles are called *corresponding angles*.

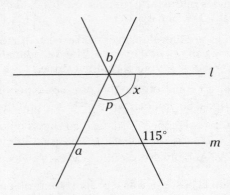

The angle marked x is equal to $a - b$. Again, you can use the properties of parallel lines: x corresponds to the (unmarked) angle right below 115°. Because this angle and 115° make a straight line, it must equal $180° - 115° = 65°$. So $x = 65$, and $a - b = 65$.

16. **6933.** Wow, that's a lot of numbers. They come in the following four groups:

    One-digit numbers: 1 to 9, for $9 \times 1 = 9$ digits

    Two-digit numbers: 10 to 99, for $90 \times 2 = 180$ digits (Did you remember the formula to count the numbers? It's $99 - 10 + 1 = 90$.)

    Three-digit numbers: 100 to 999, for $900 \times 3 = 2,700$ digits

    Four-digit numbers: 1,000 to 2,010, for $1,011 \times 4 = 4,044$ digits

    Your total is $9 + 180 + 2,700 + 4,044 = 6,933$.

17. **30.** This question is all about working with fractions. Consider $\frac{1}{x} + \frac{1}{y} = \frac{1}{4}$. When you're working with fractions, getting a common denominator on each side is a good idea. Do the following to get a common denominator:

$$\left(\frac{y}{y}\right)\frac{1}{x} + \left(\frac{1}{y}\right)\frac{x}{x} = \frac{1}{4}$$

$$\frac{y}{xy} + \frac{x}{xy} = \frac{1}{4}$$

$$\frac{x+y}{xy} = \frac{1}{4}$$

Notice how I always put the letters in alphabetical order; that's standard practice in algebra. Does anything about the fraction on the left side look familiar? It should: The numerator is $x + y$, which is what you're looking for; the denominator is xy, which equals 120. Now you can write $\frac{x+y}{120} = \frac{1}{4}$, so $4(x + y) = 120$, and $x + y = 30$.

18. **189.** You don't really need a diagram to solve this one, but I include one out of habit, anyway:

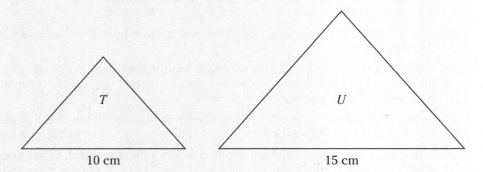

10 cm   15 cm

The sides of triangle *U* are 1½ times bigger than the sides of triangle *T* (because 15 ÷ 10 = 1½). Now you need to remember an obscure (but important-on-the-SAT) fact: The ratio of the areas of similar figures is the square of the ratio of their sides because the area of a triangle is ½ × base × height, and both the base and the height are 1½ times bigger. So the area is 1½ × 1½ = 2¼ times bigger. And 84 cm² × 2¼ = 189 cm².

Section 6: Multiple-Choice Writing

1. **C.** The expression "who had all paid high prices for the voyage" isn't essential to the meaning of the sentence, so it's considered to be extra. The rules of grammar tell you to set off extra information with commas. Choice (D) isn't acceptable because *that* usually signals essential or identifying information, which appears in the sentence without commas.

2. **B.** The sentence indicates that the shortstop is on the team, so you must add *else* to the sentence.

Are you confused about *more* and *most* comparisons? *More* does the job for comparisons between two elements; *most* describes the extreme in a group of three or more. In this sentence, the shortstop is compared to every other player on the team, but — and here's the catch — she's compared to the other players one by one. Therefore, *more* is the word you want.

3. **D.** The pair *not only . . . but also* needs to link two similar grammatical structures. In other words, the pair links expressions that match. *Sipping* doesn't match *if you pick,* but *sipping* is a good mate for *picking.*

4. **D.** You need to delete the pronoun *it* from the sentence because, according to the grammar police, a pronoun may replace one and only one word (a noun). Choice (D) is better than Choice (E) because the *adding* was the wise move, not the *chain.* The possessive form (*chain's*) correctly places the attention on *adding.*

5. **D.** *Except* is a preposition, so the expression is *except Tomas and me.* The pronoun *I* is only for subjects and subject complements. The pronoun *me* is the one you want for objects.

6. **A.** When you read this sentence, think tense (but don't be nervous). The first verb, *was,* is okay because you're just expressing an action in the past. The second verb, *has been sitting,* connects past (the last three weeks) and present (still there). Adding *has* to a verb connects present and past.

7. **E.** *Who* and *whoever* are for subjects and *whom* and *whomever* are for objects. In Question 7, all the verbs have subjects: *slate means, voters may select,* and *they like.* Because you don't need a subject for any of the verbs in the sentence, you must need an object, or *whomever* (which is, in fact, the object of *like*).

8. **A.** *Will have acquired* implies a deadline, and the first part of the sentence supplies one: college graduation.

9. **E.** Who's writing that *good essay* mentioned in the sentence? In Choices (A) through (D), the answer is no one, which, of course, can't be correct. Choice (E) is the only one to include a writer — *you* — in the sentence.

10. **A.** Surprised by this answer? If you feel *badly,* your sense of touch is damaged in some way, or maybe you're wearing mittens. If your mood is sad or upset, you feel *bad.*

11. **B.** The pencils and paper, added together, make a plural subject. (They also make great missiles when the editor is angry.) A plural subject needs a plural verb, so Choices (A), (C), and (E) (all of which use the singular verb *is*) don't make the cut. Choice (D) is out because *they're* means "they are," not "there are."

12. **C.** *Her father's mother* and *her grandmother* are the same person, so Choice (C) is repetitive.

13. **D.** The following expressions don't exist in proper English: *must of, should of, could of,* and *would of.* You need to change the *of* to *have.* The confusion arises when you shorten the expressions, as in *should've,* which sounds like *should of.*

14. **A.** When a sentence begins with a verb form, the subject needs to be performing that action. In this sentence, the telescope is the thing doing the gazing. Nope! You need a person. Because telescope isn't underlined, you need to choose the introductory verb phrase, *gazing up at the stars.*

15. **E.** Sometimes the hardest questions are the ones that have no errors because after a couple of SAT sentences, you tend to find mistakes everywhere. This one, however, is fine as is.

16. **E.** Another correct sentence. Yikes! Two in a row! Actually, I put these together to illustrate a point. Don't try to find a pattern of letter choices; instead, look for grammar errors. By the way, if you chose Choice (A), you fell into a common trap. Take your finger and cover up *we all know.* Now read the sentence. Can you "hear" that "who is a great champion of the poor" sounds better than "whom is a great champion of the poor"?

 Whenever you see a self-contained expression, such as *we know, I believe,* or *everyone thinks,* cover it up with your fingers and see how the sentence reads without those words. Chances are you'll find the real error, if one is present, when the distraction is removed.

17. **A.** This sentence states a "condition contrary to fact," as grammarians say, because the street *was* congested. The *if* portion of this kind of sentence never has *would* in it. Instead, the sentence needs to read, "If the street were . . . ."

18. **B.** *However* can't join two sentences. You need to insert a semicolon before *however* or serve time for creating a run-on sentence.

19. **B.** Dump the word *equally.* The expression *equally as* is improper, according to the grammar police. *As* gets the comparison job done; you don't need *equally.*

20. **D.** The director doesn't object to the *document* but rather to the *document's being handled.* The possessive — see that little apostrophe? — places the emphasis on *being handled,* where it belongs.

21. **A.** In almost every sentence (and in every sentence on the SAT), *affect* is a verb, as in ten days without sleep can *affect* your SAT score. The word you need in Sentence 21 is *effect,* which in SAT-land is usually a noun but sometimes a verb, as in "to effect (or bring about) a change."

22. **D.** With *either . . . or* and *neither . . . nor* sentences, the verb must match the subject that's closer to it. In Sentence 22, *teammates* is closer and must match *have* because both *teammates* and *have* are plural.

23. **A.** You can't read and return at the same time, so the sentence should say, *When the scholar had read. . . .* The *had* places the action of reading before the action of returning.

24. **B.** The expression *could not help* is negative, and so is *but*. In Standard English, two negatives equal one positive. The correct way to say this thought is *could not help wondering*.

25. **A.** *Farther* and *further* look similar, but they have two distinct roles. *Farther* is for distance — and is, therefore, the correct word to use in Sentence 25. *Further* is for extra intensity.

26. **E.** Yes, this one is perfect, just like me, and, of course, you.

27. **B.** The committee *debated whether,* not *as to whether.* The *as to* here is unnecessary.

28. **D.** Here's an *affect* that needs to be an *effect.* Check out the explanation for Question 21 for more information.

29. **B.** How many books have an informative table of contents and gorgeous pictures? According to the sentence, *a few* do, which means the *that* in the sentence is plural and takes a plural verb.

When you see *the only one that* or *the only one who,* go for a singular verb after *that* or *who.* In sentences stating *one of the* ____ *that* or *one of the* ____ *who,* you probably need a plural verb.

30. **D.** Short but sweet gets the job done here, which is why Choice (D) is the right answer. The original sentence is wordy and relies on passive voice *(should be considered)* — never a good choice. Also, Choices (B) and (E) are wrong for this reason: *Everyone* can't be paired with *they* because *everyone* is singular and *they* is plural.

31. **C.** The original sentence is missing a subject, and Choices (B) through (E) supply one. Choice (B) is repetitive (*unique* means "can't be duplicated"), and Choice (D) is wordy. Choice (C) is the most concise option, so it's the best.

32. **D.** Choice (A) is a run-on sentence, and Choice (B) has a tense problem. Choice (C) makes sense grammatically, but *and* is the most basic joiner and can be improved using the structure in Choice (D). Choice (E) is wordy.

33. **C.** Each detail shows why foreign study adds to one's education.

34. **C.** Choices (A) and (B) are too wordy, while Choices (D) and (E) are too minimal. Choice (C) hits the target right on the nose: It's concise but complete.

35. **B.** The pronoun *it* is flapping around unnecessarily in Choices (A) and (D). Choice (C) is wordy, and Choice (E) provides no clear meaning for *they*.

Section 7: Critical Reading

1. **C.** If the number of tailors has gone from *dozens* to *five,* you're looking for a word that means "decrease." Naturally, the SAT writers have complicated the situation by including two choices, (B) and (C), that express a downward trend. Choice (B), however, refers to a decrease in age, as in a *regression* (movement backward) from adulthood to infancy. Choice (C) is the answer you seek.

2. **A.** The tour's not moving, and the kid's to blame. You've been there, right? You've seen the toddler with her heels dug into the ground, shouting, "Make me!" or something similar. So the first blank has to describe a child who won't move. Choice (A), *intractable* (not budging), and Choice (D), *recalcitrant* (stubborn), both work. Now picture the parents in this situation. What are they *unwilling* to do? *Indulge* (give in) is the opposite of what you need, so Choice (D) is out. Choice (A), *force,* fits perfectly.

3. **D.** If the student is *painstakingly* going over every answer, he's careful and working hard. Choice (D) — *diligent* — means exactly that. Even though you now know the answer, take a moment to build up your vocabulary: *indolent* means "lazy," *vigorous* means "energetic,"

imprudent means "foolish," and *lackadaisical* means "having no daisies." Just kidding — scratch that last one. A *lackadaisical* person is careless.

4. **B.** Which word describes people who won't quit, no matter how tough things are? Choice (B) because *idealists* go to extremes.

5. **E.** This one contains a typical SAT trap. The sentence mentions an *expanded population,* so you may be drawn to Choice (A) because *growth* and *expanded* seem to go together. However, the sentence (and apparently *the mayor*) deals with environmental problems, or *concerns,* as expressed by Choice (E).

6. **C.** The important word in this short sentence is *belied*. If you know the meaning — to contradict — you immediately search for two words that are opposites. Two choices express opposites — (C) and (D) — but Choice (D) makes little sense when applied to a person, even though the sentence mentions *countless photos.* The blanks are talking about the star's image, not where or how often the image is seen.

7. **B.** Line 8 mentions the "most unforgiving wilderness in the world." As the rest of the passage makes clear, the fact that the difficulty "did not seem to trouble him much" says more about Franklin's ego than the possibility of success.

8. **B.** The negative may have tripped you up here. Simpson is *no light judge* of character and reads Franklin accurately. In other words, he's a good judge, not an insignificant one.

9. **E.** According to Simpson, Franklin wasn't the sort to rough it. Though he was set to travel 1,200 miles, he couldn't walk more than 8 miles on a good day. The tea example shows just how much Franklin needed to survive — the equivalent of requiring a whirlpool bathtub on a camping trip.

10. **D.** Choices (A) and (C) conflict with the content of the passage; Simpson thought Franklin was extremely unprepared, and the weather during the planned trip would be far from summery. Choices (B) and (E) are interesting but not really appropriate. How many SAT takers can relate to an Arctic voyage? And why should the reader sympathize with someone who set off without supplies? Thus, through the process of elimination, you know that Choice (D) is the right one.

11. **B.** The language of the quotation is appropriate for the early 19th century, but the passage begins by stating that it is Franklin's *admission* (Line 22). This fact probably rules out Choices (C) and (D). Because no other author is cited, the most likely source of the quotation is Choice (B).

12. **A.** Franklin "threatened to '. . . inflict the heaviest punishment on any who should persist in their refusal to go on'" (Lines 36–38), but his threat was *completely hollow* (Line 39) because he was outnumbered. Because his men were hungry, you can rule out Choices (B) and (D). Choice (E) isn't supported by any evidence. Choice (C) is tempting because Franklin didn't take into account the Native Americans' ability to predict the weather. However, he did consider their hunting skills, so Choice (A) is best overall.

13. **D.** That date is when the expedition came to an end (Line 77).

14. **A.** Franklin thinks, just like those guys on the radio (not to mention the Internet), that he can predict the weather with scientific instruments. Ha! Franklin ignores the experienced traveler (Akaitcho), who is proved correct by the cold temperatures.

15. **B.** The mutinies of the expedition were averted by the killing of a caribou (providing food) and Franklin's decision to halt. Open fighting never took place.

16. **C.** The passage makes clear that Akaitcho was correct in his weather forecast.

Not wanting to offend anyone, the SAT writers are extremely unlikely to place a negative comment about an ethnic group in the test unless that comment is proved wrong.

17. **D.** This one's easy, unless you know something about weatherproofing that has escaped the rest of the human race (in which case you should drop the SAT prep and apply for a patent). If it's 57 below, you're in trouble — big trouble.

18. **C.** Choices (A), (B), and (E) are too general. Choice (D) is too narrow. Choice (C) is, in the immortal words of Goldilocks, *just right*.

Title questions usually follow the pattern illustrated in Question 18. A couple of choices will be too narrow and a couple will be too broad. Look for something that covers all the information in the passage but not the entire universe.

19. **A.** Walked over any liquid rocks, lately? The world in Passage I resembles that of a sci-fi special. The exclamation point is supposed to underline the contrast between the real (non-molten) earth and the image of a melting planet presented in the passage.

20. **D.** Okay, melted rock is certainly hot, but Choice (E) doesn't cut it because the word *forbidding* describes the world, which certainly sounds as if it possessed *difficult characteristics*.

21. **A.** Kant's view is that the *formless cloud* would draw in on itself more and more until it would *collapse to a point,* an event that would end the solar system before it even began, certainly signaling the *end of story* for everyone and everything else.

22. **D.** A couple of the other choices are close, but Choice (D) fits best. Passage I talks about the early (very early) earth. Passage II hits the solar system at its beginning.

Section 8: Mathematics

1. **A.** This one is pretty simple. Just multiply each way to score by the number of points it's worth and add the three ways together.

2. **D.** The number 2 is prime, and $10 = 2 \times 5$, $15 = 3 \times 5$, and $57 = 3 \times 19$. Each of these numbers is the product of two primes. But $18 = 2 \times 9$ or 3×6, and neither 9 nor 6 is prime.

3. **B.** Here's the number line for you:

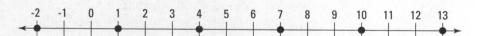

Notice that you have four marks but five spaces (one between each pair of marks, including 13 and –2). The distance between the endpoints is $13 - (-2) = 15$. Thus, each of the five spaces is three units wide. So from left to right, the four marks are at 1, 4, 7, and 10.

4. **C.** As always, using a drawing to help you visualize a problem can't hurt:

8 in.   8 in.

Notice that I put 8 inches on two sides. Don't write something like $x + 8 = 40$; a rectangle has four sides, not two. If you call the two missing sides in the diagram x, the equation is $x + x + 8 + 8 = 40$, or $2x + 16 = 40$. Then $2x = 24$, and $x = 12$.

5. **A.** You know that distance = speed × time, so Owen has traveled $3m$ miles so far. That journey leaves him with $400 - 3m$ miles still to go in 5 hours. Because distance = speed × time, speed = $\text{distance}/\text{time}$, and Choice (A) is your answer.

6. **B.** Don't pick Choice (C) just because it doesn't have any 5s in it. Instead, do a quick drawing of Choice (C). There's your old friend, the 3-4-5 triangle:

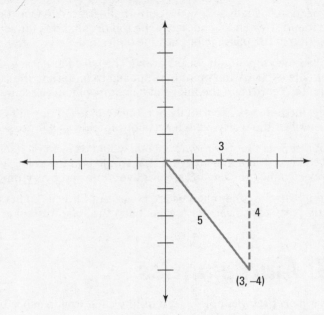

You can also use the distance formula to check whether the distance from each point to the origin is 5. Choices (A), (D), and (E) are all five units from the origin — left, up, and down, respectively. But Choice (B) is more than 5 units away from the origin. You can figure this out by making a drawing or by using the distance formula: $\sqrt{(5-0)^2 + (5-0)^2} = \sqrt{5^2 + 5^2} = \sqrt{25+25} = \sqrt{50}$, which is not 5.

7. **C.** Here's the square with the diagonal drawn:

Hopefully, you recognize that the triangles in this drawing are both 45-45-90 triangles. So the hypotenuse — which is also the diagonal of the square — equals a leg times $\sqrt{2}$. Because the legs are just the sides of the square, each leg equals 6 m, and the perimeter is 4×6 m = 24 m.

8. **C.** First, realize that this problem has two possibilities: an even number followed by an odd, or an odd followed by an even. If the first number is even, it could be 2, 4, 6, or 8 (four possibilities). The second number must then be 1, 3, 5, 7, or 9 (five possibilities). Using the counting principle, $4 \times 5 = 20$ possible numbers. If the first number is odd, it could be 1, 3, 5, 7, or 9 (five possibilities). The second number must then be 0, 2, 4, 6, or 8 (five possibilities); don't forget about zero! So you have $5 \times 5 = 25$ more possibilities, for a total of $20 + 25 = 45$ possible two-digit numbers.

9. **D.** Triangle I looks like a right triangle, but the diagram doesn't provide any actual evidence that it is. Triangle II, on the other hand, has two angles that add up to 90°, so the third angle must be 90°. Triangle III has sides of 5, $\sqrt{11}$, and 6. You can test whether this triangle is right by using the Pythagorean Theorem: $(5)^2 + \left(\sqrt{11}\right)^2 = 25 + 11 = 36$, which is 6^2, so Triangle III is a right triangle, too.

10. **E.** $d^{1/2}$ is the same as $\sqrt{d}$, so $\sqrt{d} + 5 = 9$ and $\sqrt{d} = 4$. This fact doesn't mean that $d = \sqrt{4} = 2$, but it does mean that $d = 4^2 = 16$. So $d^{-1} = (16)^{-1} = \frac{1}{16}$.

11. **D.** For history and English combined, 8.5% + 10% = 18.5%. Next, 18.5% of 5,000 = 0.185 × 5,000 = 925.

12. **E.** Well, Choice (C) is obviously false, judging by the first graph. Choices (A), (B), and (D) all suffer from the same problem: You have no idea how many students attended State U in 2000. Comparing the number of people in each major in the two different years is impossible. The second graph shows that Choice (E) is true.

13. **D.** To begin this problem, I'll try using 2, 4, 6, and 8 as my numbers to see what happens. Their average is (2 + 4 + 6 + 8) ÷ 4 = 20 ÷ 4 = 5, which isn't even, so Choice (A) is false. The median is the middle number, but because there are four numbers in the list, you have to average the two numbers closest to the middle. Here, those numbers are 4 and 6, so the median is also 5, which makes Choice (B) false, too. Now, I'm going to skip to Choice (D) for a moment because it also deals with the median. Notice that whatever four numbers I use for my list, I'll always have to do the same thing as I just did before: average the two middle numbers, which will give me a number that isn't on the list. Therefore, Choice (D) is the answer because it's always true. You may be wondering about Choices (C) and (E). They're true for the list 2, 4, 6, 8, but they aren't *always* true. For example, if you choose 10, 12, 14, and 16 as your numbers, Choices (C) and (E) are false.

When you try to solve a problem with an example, as you did in Question 13, there's always a danger that what works for your example won't work for someone else's. Be on the lookout! If you have time, try out two examples to make sure your answer works for all examples — and isn't specific to yours.

14. **C.** Following the definition given in the question, >5 = 9, and >9 = 16, so 9 + 16 = 25. Now don't go for the "obvious" answer, Choice (D), because >25 must be greater than 25. The correct answer is Choice (C) because 25 is the smallest perfect square greater than 20.

15. **B.** The first two statements aren't unusual, but the third is a little weird. If you try a "normal" number, like 4, for j, then $4^2 = 16$ and $4^3 = 64$; notice that j^2 isn't greater than j^3, so you know j isn't a positive number greater than 2. What about a fraction, like ½? Then $(\frac{1}{2})^2 = \frac{1}{4}$, and $(\frac{1}{2})^3 = \frac{1}{8}$, and $j^2 > j^3$. But wait a minute: Now j^2 and j^3 are both smaller than j, which contradicts the first two statements. So how about a negative number, like –2? Well, $(-2)^2 = 4$, which is greater than –2, but $(-2)^3 = -8$, which isn't. So you're left with a negative fraction. Try –½: $(-\frac{1}{2})^2 = \frac{1}{4}$, which is greater than –½; $(-\frac{1}{2})^3 = -\frac{1}{8}$, which is also greater than –½ because it's farther to the right on a number line. And, finally, $\frac{1}{4} > -\frac{1}{8}$, so the third condition is satisfied, too. Thus, you have your answer: j is any number between 0 and –1.

16. **A.** I take the liberty of naming the three unnamed points in my diagram (and you should, too):

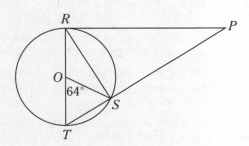

The one angle that you know, 64°, is a central angle. Arc *ST* must also be 64°. Because arc *RST* is a semicircle, arc *RS* must measure 180° – 64° = 116°. Now you can look at some angles. ∠*PRT* is the meeting of a *tangent line* (a line that touches the circle at exactly one point) and a diameter, so it must be 90°. (This fact is worth memorizing.) ∠*T* is *inscribed* (having both its endpoints and its center on the circumference of the circle), so it must be half of its arc, 116°, and ½ × 116° = 58°. Finally, because triangle *PRT* must contain 180°, that leaves 180° – (90° + 58°) = 180° – 148° = 32° for ∠*P*. (For more on tangents and inscribed angles, turn to Chapter 16.)

Section 9: Multiple-Choice Writing

1. **B.** When you run across a *neither . . . nor* or *either . . . or* sentence, look for the subject that's physically closer to the verb. That subject rules: If the subject is singular, the verb has to be singular also. If the subject is plural, you need a plural verb. In Question 1, *solar power* is closer than *windmills. Solar power* is singular, so it requires the singular verb *is.*

2. **A.** *Every message* is singular, so it pairs nicely with the singular verb *goes.* Therefore, Choice (C) is wrong because it contains the plural verb *go.* Choice (B) messes up the preposition because material passes *through* a filter, not *by* one. Choices (D) and (E) fail because the pronoun *it* may refer to either *e-mail* or *inbox,* and all pronoun references should be absolutely clear.

3. **D.** *A person* is a singular, third-person noun. (*Third-person* is the English teacher's term for talking *about,* not *to* or *as,* somebody.) Any pronoun referring to *a person* must also be singular and third person. *He or she* (or *it,* which doesn't fit the meaning of the sentence) are your pronoun choices, so Choice (D) is the best answer.

4. **E.** In the original sentence, the *level of skill* is wrongly compared to *metalwork.* Choices (C) and (E) express the intended meaning of the sentence, but Choice (C) repeats words unnecessarily. Choice (E) gets the job done without repetition.

5. **C.** Why complicate life? He's hobbling along, but he arrives at his destination. How long did it take him? *At least ten minutes,* otherwise known as Choice (C).

6. **B.** An English sentence is a reasonable thing. All it wants is a complete thought expressed partly through a matching subject/verb pair. (Okay, it also wants punctuation, good spelling, and a time-share in Miami, but work with me here.) Choice (A) has two dependent ideas — "being part of the Halloween parade" and "which gives enjoyment to both spectators and participants." Those dependent ideas can't stand alone and be considered a grammatically correct sentence. Choice (B) creates a complete thought by changing *being* to *are.*

7. **C.** The original sentence isn't wrong grammatically; it's just clunky. (Don't you love my technical term?) Choice (C) pulls the ideas together without fuss.

8. **A.** Yes, I actually threw in a correct sentence, as the SAT also does occasionally. The comparison — and the sentence — is complete in Choice (A).

9. **D.** What does the pronoun *they* refer to? The *gardeners* or the *seedlings*? As the sentence is written, *they* is *ambiguous* (having two possible meanings). Choice (D) clarifies the situation: The plants, not the gardeners, get a head start.

10. **B.** The words *unconscious ways* imply everything else that's underlined in the sentence. Drop the unnecessary words and go with Choice (B).

11. **C.** When you're describing an action, you need an adverb *(quickly),* not an adjective *(quick).* Anything that intensifies a description should also be an adverb, so *really* (an adverb) is appropriate, and *real* (an adjective) isn't.

12. **D.** The expression *for to* isn't Standard English, so you can rule out Choices (A) and (B). Choices (C) and (E) aren't grammatically incorrect, but Choice (D) does the job more efficiently.

13. **E.** Use your reading comprehension skills to decide how many plants are in the category expressed by the underlined words — one or more than one? Logic tells you that more than one plant didn't *flourish* (grow well). Because the underlined expression refers to many plants, *that* is plural and requires the plural verb *have*.

14. **C.** What does the pronoun *it* mean? In general, a pronoun may refer to only one word. In Choice (A), *it* refers to an entire statement — "Colleges now offer students many more electives." Incorrect! Choice (B) has the same problem as Choice (A) because *which* is also a pronoun and is governed by the same pronoun rules. Choice (C) clarifies the meaning of *it* by substituting the noun *choices*. Choices (D) and (E) are just plain wrong.

Answer Key for Practice Exam 2

Section 2

1. C	8. E	15. B	22. D
2. B	9. D	16. E	23. E
3. A	10. E	17. B	24. B
4. C	11. D	18. A	25. D
5. E	12. C	19. D	
6. A	13. A	20. D	
7. D	14. A	21. A	

Section 3

1. E	6. C	11. E	16. C
2. D	7. B	12. A	17. B
3. A	8. A	13. D	18. B
4. C	9. D	14. B	19. E
5. B	10. C	15. A	20. D

Section 4

1. D	7. E	13. A	19. C
2. A	8. C	14. B	20. B
3. D	9. A	15. E	21. E
4. A	10. D	16. C	22. B
5. B	11. B	17. D	23. D
6. C	12. D	18. A	24. C

Section 5

1. A	6. D	11. 360	16. 6933
2. D	7. A	12. 36	17. 30
3. B	8. B	13. 8	18. 189
4. E	9. 32	14. 31	
5. C	10. 210	15. 65	

Section 6

1. C	10. A	19. B	28. D
2. B	11. B	20. D	29. B
3. D	12. C	21. A	30. D
4. D	13. D	22. D	31. C
5. D	14. A	23. A	32. D
6. A	15. E	24. B	33. C
7. E	16. E	25. A	34. C
8. A	17. A	26. E	35. B
9. E	18. B	27. B	

Section 7

1. C	7. B	13. D	19. A
2. A	8. B	14. A	20. D
3. D	9. E	15. B	21. A
4. B	10. D	16. C	22. D
5. E	11. B	17. D	
6. C	12. A	18. C	

Section 8

1. A	5. A	9. D	13. D
2. D	6. B	10. E	14. C
3. B	7. C	11. D	15. B
4. C	8. C	12. E	16. A

Section 9

1. B	5. C	9. D	13. E
2. A	6. B	10. B	14. C
3. D	7. C	11. C	
4. E	8. A	12. D	

Chapter 24

Practice Exam 3

● ●

You don't have to do the practice exams in order, but most people tend to start at one and move forward in the number line. So I'm assuming that you've already bolted yourself to a chair for seven hours of testing — not all at one time, I hope. (If this is your first practice exam, turn to Practice Exam 1 in Chapter 20 and read the introduction for a few general guidelines.) After you have two exams in the rearview mirror, you probably know which areas are your strengths and which areas call for extra attention. Apply that knowledge to this practice test. Go a little faster through your best sections, and turn your concentration dial up to maximum when you hit the hard spots.

When you complete this exam, dance or snowboard or tweet or do something nonacademic. Then check your work in Chapter 25 and use the scoring guidelines in the appendix to determine your SAT score.

Note: The real SAT you take will have ten sections, instead of the nine you see here, because the College Board throws in an "equating section" that doesn't count toward your score but allows the testers to evaluate new questions. The SAT doesn't tell you which section is useless (to you). Because I'm here to help you score high on the SAT, I don't include an equating section in any of the practice tests in this book. Nice of me, huh?

Answer Sheet

For Section 1, use two sheets of loose-leaf or notebook paper to write your essay. For the questions in Sections 2 through 9, use the ovals and grid-ins to record your answers. Begin with Number 1 for each new section. If any sections have fewer than 35 questions, leave the extra spaces blank.

Section 2: Critical Reading

1. Ⓐ Ⓑ Ⓒ Ⓓ Ⓔ   8. Ⓐ Ⓑ Ⓒ Ⓓ Ⓔ   15. Ⓐ Ⓑ Ⓒ Ⓓ Ⓔ   22. Ⓐ Ⓑ Ⓒ Ⓓ Ⓔ   29. Ⓐ Ⓑ Ⓒ Ⓓ Ⓔ
2. Ⓐ Ⓑ Ⓒ Ⓓ Ⓔ   9. Ⓐ Ⓑ Ⓒ Ⓓ Ⓔ   16. Ⓐ Ⓑ Ⓒ Ⓓ Ⓔ   23. Ⓐ Ⓑ Ⓒ Ⓓ Ⓔ   30. Ⓐ Ⓑ Ⓒ Ⓓ Ⓔ
3. Ⓐ Ⓑ Ⓒ Ⓓ Ⓔ   10. Ⓐ Ⓑ Ⓒ Ⓓ Ⓔ   17. Ⓐ Ⓑ Ⓒ Ⓓ Ⓔ   24. Ⓐ Ⓑ Ⓒ Ⓓ Ⓔ   31. Ⓐ Ⓑ Ⓒ Ⓓ Ⓔ
4. Ⓐ Ⓑ Ⓒ Ⓓ Ⓔ   11. Ⓐ Ⓑ Ⓒ Ⓓ Ⓔ   18. Ⓐ Ⓑ Ⓒ Ⓓ Ⓔ   25. Ⓐ Ⓑ Ⓒ Ⓓ Ⓔ   32. Ⓐ Ⓑ Ⓒ Ⓓ Ⓔ
5. Ⓐ Ⓑ Ⓒ Ⓓ Ⓔ   12. Ⓐ Ⓑ Ⓒ Ⓓ Ⓔ   19. Ⓐ Ⓑ Ⓒ Ⓓ Ⓔ   26. Ⓐ Ⓑ Ⓒ Ⓓ Ⓔ   33. Ⓐ Ⓑ Ⓒ Ⓓ Ⓔ
6. Ⓐ Ⓑ Ⓒ Ⓓ Ⓔ   13. Ⓐ Ⓑ Ⓒ Ⓓ Ⓔ   20. Ⓐ Ⓑ Ⓒ Ⓓ Ⓔ   27. Ⓐ Ⓑ Ⓒ Ⓓ Ⓔ   34. Ⓐ Ⓑ Ⓒ Ⓓ Ⓔ
7. Ⓐ Ⓑ Ⓒ Ⓓ Ⓔ   14. Ⓐ Ⓑ Ⓒ Ⓓ Ⓔ   21. Ⓐ Ⓑ Ⓒ Ⓓ Ⓔ   28. Ⓐ Ⓑ Ⓒ Ⓓ Ⓔ   35. Ⓐ Ⓑ Ⓒ Ⓓ Ⓔ

Section 3: Mathematics

1. Ⓐ Ⓑ Ⓒ Ⓓ Ⓔ   8. Ⓐ Ⓑ Ⓒ Ⓓ Ⓔ   15. Ⓐ Ⓑ Ⓒ Ⓓ Ⓔ   22. Ⓐ Ⓑ Ⓒ Ⓓ Ⓔ   29. Ⓐ Ⓑ Ⓒ Ⓓ Ⓔ
2. Ⓐ Ⓑ Ⓒ Ⓓ Ⓔ   9. Ⓐ Ⓑ Ⓒ Ⓓ Ⓔ   16. Ⓐ Ⓑ Ⓒ Ⓓ Ⓔ   23. Ⓐ Ⓑ Ⓒ Ⓓ Ⓔ   30. Ⓐ Ⓑ Ⓒ Ⓓ Ⓔ
3. Ⓐ Ⓑ Ⓒ Ⓓ Ⓔ   10. Ⓐ Ⓑ Ⓒ Ⓓ Ⓔ   17. Ⓐ Ⓑ Ⓒ Ⓓ Ⓔ   24. Ⓐ Ⓑ Ⓒ Ⓓ Ⓔ   31. Ⓐ Ⓑ Ⓒ Ⓓ Ⓔ
4. Ⓐ Ⓑ Ⓒ Ⓓ Ⓔ   11. Ⓐ Ⓑ Ⓒ Ⓓ Ⓔ   18. Ⓐ Ⓑ Ⓒ Ⓓ Ⓔ   25. Ⓐ Ⓑ Ⓒ Ⓓ Ⓔ   32. Ⓐ Ⓑ Ⓒ Ⓓ Ⓔ
5. Ⓐ Ⓑ Ⓒ Ⓓ Ⓔ   12. Ⓐ Ⓑ Ⓒ Ⓓ Ⓔ   19. Ⓐ Ⓑ Ⓒ Ⓓ Ⓔ   26. Ⓐ Ⓑ Ⓒ Ⓓ Ⓔ   33. Ⓐ Ⓑ Ⓒ Ⓓ Ⓔ
6. Ⓐ Ⓑ Ⓒ Ⓓ Ⓔ   13. Ⓐ Ⓑ Ⓒ Ⓓ Ⓔ   20. Ⓐ Ⓑ Ⓒ Ⓓ Ⓔ   27. Ⓐ Ⓑ Ⓒ Ⓓ Ⓔ   34. Ⓐ Ⓑ Ⓒ Ⓓ Ⓔ
7. Ⓐ Ⓑ Ⓒ Ⓓ Ⓔ   14. Ⓐ Ⓑ Ⓒ Ⓓ Ⓔ   21. Ⓐ Ⓑ Ⓒ Ⓓ Ⓔ   28. Ⓐ Ⓑ Ⓒ Ⓓ Ⓔ   35. Ⓐ Ⓑ Ⓒ Ⓓ Ⓔ

Section 4: Critical Reading

1. Ⓐ Ⓑ Ⓒ Ⓓ Ⓔ   8. Ⓐ Ⓑ Ⓒ Ⓓ Ⓔ   15. Ⓐ Ⓑ Ⓒ Ⓓ Ⓔ   22. Ⓐ Ⓑ Ⓒ Ⓓ Ⓔ   29. Ⓐ Ⓑ Ⓒ Ⓓ Ⓔ
2. Ⓐ Ⓑ Ⓒ Ⓓ Ⓔ   9. Ⓐ Ⓑ Ⓒ Ⓓ Ⓔ   16. Ⓐ Ⓑ Ⓒ Ⓓ Ⓔ   23. Ⓐ Ⓑ Ⓒ Ⓓ Ⓔ   30. Ⓐ Ⓑ Ⓒ Ⓓ Ⓔ
3. Ⓐ Ⓑ Ⓒ Ⓓ Ⓔ   10. Ⓐ Ⓑ Ⓒ Ⓓ Ⓔ   17. Ⓐ Ⓑ Ⓒ Ⓓ Ⓔ   24. Ⓐ Ⓑ Ⓒ Ⓓ Ⓔ   31. Ⓐ Ⓑ Ⓒ Ⓓ Ⓔ
4. Ⓐ Ⓑ Ⓒ Ⓓ Ⓔ   11. Ⓐ Ⓑ Ⓒ Ⓓ Ⓔ   18. Ⓐ Ⓑ Ⓒ Ⓓ Ⓔ   25. Ⓐ Ⓑ Ⓒ Ⓓ Ⓔ   32. Ⓐ Ⓑ Ⓒ Ⓓ Ⓔ
5. Ⓐ Ⓑ Ⓒ Ⓓ Ⓔ   12. Ⓐ Ⓑ Ⓒ Ⓓ Ⓔ   19. Ⓐ Ⓑ Ⓒ Ⓓ Ⓔ   26. Ⓐ Ⓑ Ⓒ Ⓓ Ⓔ   33. Ⓐ Ⓑ Ⓒ Ⓓ Ⓔ
6. Ⓐ Ⓑ Ⓒ Ⓓ Ⓔ   13. Ⓐ Ⓑ Ⓒ Ⓓ Ⓔ   20. Ⓐ Ⓑ Ⓒ Ⓓ Ⓔ   27. Ⓐ Ⓑ Ⓒ Ⓓ Ⓔ   34. Ⓐ Ⓑ Ⓒ Ⓓ Ⓔ
7. Ⓐ Ⓑ Ⓒ Ⓓ Ⓔ   14. Ⓐ Ⓑ Ⓒ Ⓓ Ⓔ   21. Ⓐ Ⓑ Ⓒ Ⓓ Ⓔ   28. Ⓐ Ⓑ Ⓒ Ⓓ Ⓔ   35. Ⓐ Ⓑ Ⓒ Ⓓ Ⓔ

Section 5: Mathematics

1. Ⓐ Ⓑ Ⓒ Ⓓ Ⓔ   8. Ⓐ Ⓑ Ⓒ Ⓓ Ⓔ   15. Ⓐ Ⓑ Ⓒ Ⓓ Ⓔ   22. Ⓐ Ⓑ Ⓒ Ⓓ Ⓔ   29. Ⓐ Ⓑ Ⓒ Ⓓ Ⓔ
2. Ⓐ Ⓑ Ⓒ Ⓓ Ⓔ   9. Ⓐ Ⓑ Ⓒ Ⓓ Ⓔ   16. Ⓐ Ⓑ Ⓒ Ⓓ Ⓔ   23. Ⓐ Ⓑ Ⓒ Ⓓ Ⓔ   30. Ⓐ Ⓑ Ⓒ Ⓓ Ⓔ
3. Ⓐ Ⓑ Ⓒ Ⓓ Ⓔ   10. Ⓐ Ⓑ Ⓒ Ⓓ Ⓔ   17. Ⓐ Ⓑ Ⓒ Ⓓ Ⓔ   24. Ⓐ Ⓑ Ⓒ Ⓓ Ⓔ   31. Ⓐ Ⓑ Ⓒ Ⓓ Ⓔ
4. Ⓐ Ⓑ Ⓒ Ⓓ Ⓔ   11. Ⓐ Ⓑ Ⓒ Ⓓ Ⓔ   18. Ⓐ Ⓑ Ⓒ Ⓓ Ⓔ   25. Ⓐ Ⓑ Ⓒ Ⓓ Ⓔ   32. Ⓐ Ⓑ Ⓒ Ⓓ Ⓔ
5. Ⓐ Ⓑ Ⓒ Ⓓ Ⓔ   12. Ⓐ Ⓑ Ⓒ Ⓓ Ⓔ   19. Ⓐ Ⓑ Ⓒ Ⓓ Ⓔ   26. Ⓐ Ⓑ Ⓒ Ⓓ Ⓔ   33. Ⓐ Ⓑ Ⓒ Ⓓ Ⓔ
6. Ⓐ Ⓑ Ⓒ Ⓓ Ⓔ   13. Ⓐ Ⓑ Ⓒ Ⓓ Ⓔ   20. Ⓐ Ⓑ Ⓒ Ⓓ Ⓔ   27. Ⓐ Ⓑ Ⓒ Ⓓ Ⓔ   34. Ⓐ Ⓑ Ⓒ Ⓓ Ⓔ
7. Ⓐ Ⓑ Ⓒ Ⓓ Ⓔ   14. Ⓐ Ⓑ Ⓒ Ⓓ Ⓔ   21. Ⓐ Ⓑ Ⓒ Ⓓ Ⓔ   28. Ⓐ Ⓑ Ⓒ Ⓓ Ⓔ   35. Ⓐ Ⓑ Ⓒ Ⓓ Ⓔ

9.   10.   11.   12.   13.

14.   15.   16.   17.   18.

Section 6: Multiple-Choice Writing

1. Ⓐ Ⓑ Ⓒ Ⓓ Ⓔ   8. Ⓐ Ⓑ Ⓒ Ⓓ Ⓔ   15. Ⓐ Ⓑ Ⓒ Ⓓ Ⓔ   22. Ⓐ Ⓑ Ⓒ Ⓓ Ⓔ   29. Ⓐ Ⓑ Ⓒ Ⓓ Ⓔ
2. Ⓐ Ⓑ Ⓒ Ⓓ Ⓔ   9. Ⓐ Ⓑ Ⓒ Ⓓ Ⓔ   16. Ⓐ Ⓑ Ⓒ Ⓓ Ⓔ   23. Ⓐ Ⓑ Ⓒ Ⓓ Ⓔ   30. Ⓐ Ⓑ Ⓒ Ⓓ Ⓔ
3. Ⓐ Ⓑ Ⓒ Ⓓ Ⓔ   10. Ⓐ Ⓑ Ⓒ Ⓓ Ⓔ   17. Ⓐ Ⓑ Ⓒ Ⓓ Ⓔ   24. Ⓐ Ⓑ Ⓒ Ⓓ Ⓔ   31. Ⓐ Ⓑ Ⓒ Ⓓ Ⓔ
4. Ⓐ Ⓑ Ⓒ Ⓓ Ⓔ   11. Ⓐ Ⓑ Ⓒ Ⓓ Ⓔ   18. Ⓐ Ⓑ Ⓒ Ⓓ Ⓔ   25. Ⓐ Ⓑ Ⓒ Ⓓ Ⓔ   32. Ⓐ Ⓑ Ⓒ Ⓓ Ⓔ
5. Ⓐ Ⓑ Ⓒ Ⓓ Ⓔ   12. Ⓐ Ⓑ Ⓒ Ⓓ Ⓔ   19. Ⓐ Ⓑ Ⓒ Ⓓ Ⓔ   26. Ⓐ Ⓑ Ⓒ Ⓓ Ⓔ   33. Ⓐ Ⓑ Ⓒ Ⓓ Ⓔ
6. Ⓐ Ⓑ Ⓒ Ⓓ Ⓔ   13. Ⓐ Ⓑ Ⓒ Ⓓ Ⓔ   20. Ⓐ Ⓑ Ⓒ Ⓓ Ⓔ   27. Ⓐ Ⓑ Ⓒ Ⓓ Ⓔ   34. Ⓐ Ⓑ Ⓒ Ⓓ Ⓔ
7. Ⓐ Ⓑ Ⓒ Ⓓ Ⓔ   14. Ⓐ Ⓑ Ⓒ Ⓓ Ⓔ   21. Ⓐ Ⓑ Ⓒ Ⓓ Ⓔ   28. Ⓐ Ⓑ Ⓒ Ⓓ Ⓔ   35. Ⓐ Ⓑ Ⓒ Ⓓ Ⓔ

Section 7: Critical Reading

1. Ⓐ Ⓑ Ⓒ Ⓓ Ⓔ   8. Ⓐ Ⓑ Ⓒ Ⓓ Ⓔ   15. Ⓐ Ⓑ Ⓒ Ⓓ Ⓔ   22. Ⓐ Ⓑ Ⓒ Ⓓ Ⓔ   29. Ⓐ Ⓑ Ⓒ Ⓓ Ⓔ
2. Ⓐ Ⓑ Ⓒ Ⓓ Ⓔ   9. Ⓐ Ⓑ Ⓒ Ⓓ Ⓔ   16. Ⓐ Ⓑ Ⓒ Ⓓ Ⓔ   23. Ⓐ Ⓑ Ⓒ Ⓓ Ⓔ   30. Ⓐ Ⓑ Ⓒ Ⓓ Ⓔ
3. Ⓐ Ⓑ Ⓒ Ⓓ Ⓔ   10. Ⓐ Ⓑ Ⓒ Ⓓ Ⓔ   17. Ⓐ Ⓑ Ⓒ Ⓓ Ⓔ   24. Ⓐ Ⓑ Ⓒ Ⓓ Ⓔ   31. Ⓐ Ⓑ Ⓒ Ⓓ Ⓔ
4. Ⓐ Ⓑ Ⓒ Ⓓ Ⓔ   11. Ⓐ Ⓑ Ⓒ Ⓓ Ⓔ   18. Ⓐ Ⓑ Ⓒ Ⓓ Ⓔ   25. Ⓐ Ⓑ Ⓒ Ⓓ Ⓔ   32. Ⓐ Ⓑ Ⓒ Ⓓ Ⓔ
5. Ⓐ Ⓑ Ⓒ Ⓓ Ⓔ   12. Ⓐ Ⓑ Ⓒ Ⓓ Ⓔ   19. Ⓐ Ⓑ Ⓒ Ⓓ Ⓔ   26. Ⓐ Ⓑ Ⓒ Ⓓ Ⓔ   33. Ⓐ Ⓑ Ⓒ Ⓓ Ⓔ
6. Ⓐ Ⓑ Ⓒ Ⓓ Ⓔ   13. Ⓐ Ⓑ Ⓒ Ⓓ Ⓔ   20. Ⓐ Ⓑ Ⓒ Ⓓ Ⓔ   27. Ⓐ Ⓑ Ⓒ Ⓓ Ⓔ   34. Ⓐ Ⓑ Ⓒ Ⓓ Ⓔ
7. Ⓐ Ⓑ Ⓒ Ⓓ Ⓔ   14. Ⓐ Ⓑ Ⓒ Ⓓ Ⓔ   21. Ⓐ Ⓑ Ⓒ Ⓓ Ⓔ   28. Ⓐ Ⓑ Ⓒ Ⓓ Ⓔ   35. Ⓐ Ⓑ Ⓒ Ⓓ Ⓔ

Section 8: Mathematics

1. Ⓐ Ⓑ Ⓒ Ⓓ Ⓔ   8. Ⓐ Ⓑ Ⓒ Ⓓ Ⓔ   15. Ⓐ Ⓑ Ⓒ Ⓓ Ⓔ   22. Ⓐ Ⓑ Ⓒ Ⓓ Ⓔ   29. Ⓐ Ⓑ Ⓒ Ⓓ Ⓔ
2. Ⓐ Ⓑ Ⓒ Ⓓ Ⓔ   9. Ⓐ Ⓑ Ⓒ Ⓓ Ⓔ   16. Ⓐ Ⓑ Ⓒ Ⓓ Ⓔ   23. Ⓐ Ⓑ Ⓒ Ⓓ Ⓔ   30. Ⓐ Ⓑ Ⓒ Ⓓ Ⓔ
3. Ⓐ Ⓑ Ⓒ Ⓓ Ⓔ   10. Ⓐ Ⓑ Ⓒ Ⓓ Ⓔ   17. Ⓐ Ⓑ Ⓒ Ⓓ Ⓔ   24. Ⓐ Ⓑ Ⓒ Ⓓ Ⓔ   31. Ⓐ Ⓑ Ⓒ Ⓓ Ⓔ
4. Ⓐ Ⓑ Ⓒ Ⓓ Ⓔ   11. Ⓐ Ⓑ Ⓒ Ⓓ Ⓔ   18. Ⓐ Ⓑ Ⓒ Ⓓ Ⓔ   25. Ⓐ Ⓑ Ⓒ Ⓓ Ⓔ   32. Ⓐ Ⓑ Ⓒ Ⓓ Ⓔ
5. Ⓐ Ⓑ Ⓒ Ⓓ Ⓔ   12. Ⓐ Ⓑ Ⓒ Ⓓ Ⓔ   19. Ⓐ Ⓑ Ⓒ Ⓓ Ⓔ   26. Ⓐ Ⓑ Ⓒ Ⓓ Ⓔ   33. Ⓐ Ⓑ Ⓒ Ⓓ Ⓔ
6. Ⓐ Ⓑ Ⓒ Ⓓ Ⓔ   13. Ⓐ Ⓑ Ⓒ Ⓓ Ⓔ   20. Ⓐ Ⓑ Ⓒ Ⓓ Ⓔ   27. Ⓐ Ⓑ Ⓒ Ⓓ Ⓔ   34. Ⓐ Ⓑ Ⓒ Ⓓ Ⓔ
7. Ⓐ Ⓑ Ⓒ Ⓓ Ⓔ   14. Ⓐ Ⓑ Ⓒ Ⓓ Ⓔ   21. Ⓐ Ⓑ Ⓒ Ⓓ Ⓔ   28. Ⓐ Ⓑ Ⓒ Ⓓ Ⓔ   35. Ⓐ Ⓑ Ⓒ Ⓓ Ⓔ

Section 9: Multiple-Choice Writing

1. Ⓐ Ⓑ Ⓒ Ⓓ Ⓔ   8. Ⓐ Ⓑ Ⓒ Ⓓ Ⓔ   15. Ⓐ Ⓑ Ⓒ Ⓓ Ⓔ   22. Ⓐ Ⓑ Ⓒ Ⓓ Ⓔ   29. Ⓐ Ⓑ Ⓒ Ⓓ Ⓔ
2. Ⓐ Ⓑ Ⓒ Ⓓ Ⓔ   9. Ⓐ Ⓑ Ⓒ Ⓓ Ⓔ   16. Ⓐ Ⓑ Ⓒ Ⓓ Ⓔ   23. Ⓐ Ⓑ Ⓒ Ⓓ Ⓔ   30. Ⓐ Ⓑ Ⓒ Ⓓ Ⓔ
3. Ⓐ Ⓑ Ⓒ Ⓓ Ⓔ   10. Ⓐ Ⓑ Ⓒ Ⓓ Ⓔ   17. Ⓐ Ⓑ Ⓒ Ⓓ Ⓔ   24. Ⓐ Ⓑ Ⓒ Ⓓ Ⓔ   31. Ⓐ Ⓑ Ⓒ Ⓓ Ⓔ
4. Ⓐ Ⓑ Ⓒ Ⓓ Ⓔ   11. Ⓐ Ⓑ Ⓒ Ⓓ Ⓔ   18. Ⓐ Ⓑ Ⓒ Ⓓ Ⓔ   25. Ⓐ Ⓑ Ⓒ Ⓓ Ⓔ   32. Ⓐ Ⓑ Ⓒ Ⓓ Ⓔ
5. Ⓐ Ⓑ Ⓒ Ⓓ Ⓔ   12. Ⓐ Ⓑ Ⓒ Ⓓ Ⓔ   19. Ⓐ Ⓑ Ⓒ Ⓓ Ⓔ   26. Ⓐ Ⓑ Ⓒ Ⓓ Ⓔ   33. Ⓐ Ⓑ Ⓒ Ⓓ Ⓔ
6. Ⓐ Ⓑ Ⓒ Ⓓ Ⓔ   13. Ⓐ Ⓑ Ⓒ Ⓓ Ⓔ   20. Ⓐ Ⓑ Ⓒ Ⓓ Ⓔ   27. Ⓐ Ⓑ Ⓒ Ⓓ Ⓔ   34. Ⓐ Ⓑ Ⓒ Ⓓ Ⓔ
7. Ⓐ Ⓑ Ⓒ Ⓓ Ⓔ   14. Ⓐ Ⓑ Ⓒ Ⓓ Ⓔ   21. Ⓐ Ⓑ Ⓒ Ⓓ Ⓔ   28. Ⓐ Ⓑ Ⓒ Ⓓ Ⓔ   35. Ⓐ Ⓑ Ⓒ Ⓓ Ⓔ

Section 1

The Essay

Time: 25 minutes

Directions: In response to the following prompt, write an essay on a separate sheet of paper (the answer sheet). You may use extra space in the question booklet to take notes and to organize your thoughts, but only the answer sheet will be graded.

"They that soar too high, often fall hard; which makes a low and level Dwelling preferable."
— William Penn

"The credit belongs to the man who . . . at the best knows in the end the triumph of high achievement and who at the worst, if he fails, at least he fails while daring greatly. . . . his place shall never be with those cold and timid souls who know neither victory nor defeat."
— Theodore Roosevelt

Does ambition help or harm? Should one attempt something that seems impossible, or is it better to create goals that are clearly achievable? In a well-organized essay, address these questions, developing and supporting your point of view by drawing upon history, literature, current events, or your own experience and observations.

STOP YOU MAY CHECK YOUR WORK ON THIS SECTION ONLY. DO NOT GO BACK TO ANY PREVIOUS SECTION.

Section 2
Critical Reading

Time: 25 minutes for 24 questions

Directions: Choose the *best* answer to each question. Mark the corresponding oval on the answer sheet.

Directions for Questions 1–8: Select the answer that *best* fits the meaning of the sentence.

Example: After he had broken the dining room window, Hal's mother _____ him.

(A) selected

(B) serenaded

(C) fooled

(D) scolded

(E) rewarded

The answer is (D).

1. Because filmmaker James Woody is so identified with New York City, the announcement that his next film would be set in rural Oregon _____ critics.

    (A) mystified

    (B) attracted

    (C) confused

    (D) delighted

    (E) surprised

2. The shy smiles of the celebrity _____ fans who believed that she was _____.

    (A) amused . . . outgoing

    (B) amazed . . . diffident

    (C) reassured . . . depressed

    (D) antagonized . . . talented

    (E) appalled . . . celebrated

3. The resort's marketing campaign was so _____ that it attracted not only the wealthy but also those of limited means.

    (A) broad

    (B) narrow

    (C) effective

    (D) imaginative

    (E) innovative

4. The _____ of the cellphone means that workers required to carry them are never out of reach of their employers.

    (A) divisiveness

    (B) insignificance

    (C) versatility

    (D) tyranny

    (E) proliferation

5. Ultimately the complexity of the subject demands a _____ approach instead of the generalizations _____ by that commentator.

    (A) heavy-handed . . . envisioned

    (B) nuanced . . . spouted

    (C) confrontational . . . presented

    (D) problematic . . . championed

    (E) basic . . . rejected

6. It is essential, when new technology becomes _____, to examine its impact on society and culture.

    (A) innovative

    (B) redundant

    (C) lucrative

    (D) versatile

    (E) pervasive

Go on to next page

7. He was a _____ reader, seldom without his nose in a book.

   (A) voracious

   (B) competitive

   (C) instinctive

   (D) implausible

   (E) sporadic

8. Success didn't come to that executive _____ but rather as a result of years of _____.

   (A) suddenly . . . education

   (B) unexpectedly . . . effort

   (C) haphazardly . . . planning

   (D) undeservedly . . . infighting

   (E) randomly . . . experimentation

Directions for Questions 9–20: Choose the *best* answer to each question based on what is stated or implied in the passages or in the introductory material.

These two passages, from different authors, refer to events that took place during World War I.

Passage I

Line

Today the papers announce the stunning news that Germany has declared war against Russia. The report must be sufficiently authen-
(05) tic, for, as if by magic, the Belgian army is already gathering itself together with an almost superhuman rapidity, proof of which we have had in the masses of troops that have been pass-ing the house all day. Yesterday, trouble was a newspaper rumor; today, deadly earnestness.
(10) And what excitement all about! The air is posi-tively charged and the whole community is agog; people with anxious faces accost each other in the street; farmers neglect their crops to come into town, bank clerks lay down their pens and
(15) shop doors are beginning to close.

Hundreds of soldiers and cannon have been passing all night, and this morning routes in every direction are blockaded by detachments from different regiments. There are uniforms of
(20) all types and colors, the ensemble looking like a variegated bouquet snatched hurriedly by the wayside; the sorting will come later, one doesn't ask how. The old farm at the end of the garden

has been turned into a barracks, and recruits are being drilled among the apple trees in the
(25) orchard. The excitement is intense.

A detachment of Belgian soldier boys slept in the stables last night. Monsieur X. sent them his best cigars, and this morning, as soon as they tumbled out, they made a straight line for the
(30) kitchen whence they scented hot coffee. The good heart of the old, fat cook, who is a native of Amsterdam, was melted at once and she gave unsparingly until they flattered and coaxed her into such a state of bewilderment that even
(35) Dutch patience was at last exhausted when she saw them pouring in and pouring in and boldly attacking her sumptuous pantries en masse.

Preparations for war are going on rapidly; scores of automobiles are racing past like mad
(40) things, carrying Governmental messages no doubt and the Government itself, by its eternal prerogative, is commandeering for its use every-body's private property — horses, cows, auto-mobiles, pigs, merchandise, provisions, etc. And
(45) how one gives for one's country! The men, their goods; the women, their sons. The spirit of the people is magnificent. Huge loads of hay in long processions like caravans are coming in from the country along with immense droves of cattle. In
(50) the orchard adjoining the château[1] are already domiciled two hundred or more cows and the discordant melody from this hoarse-throated chorus, uninterrupted day or night, is driving us to madness. Indoors, we ourselves are laying in a
(55) supply of things in case of necessity and the kitchen is piled high with bags of flour, coffee, beans, tinned goods, etc., and in the pasture is a new cow. Beef will probably be the *pièce de resis-tance*[2] for many a day.
(60)

   1. House. 2. Main dish.

Passage II

The sudden seizure of railroads for war pur-poses in Germany, France, Austria and Russia, cut off thousands of travelers in villages that were almost inaccessible. Europeans being com-paratively close to their homes, were not in
(65) straits as severe as the Americans whose only hope for aid lay in the speedy arrival of American gold. Prices of food soared beyond all precedent and many of these hapless strangers went under.
(70)

Seaports, and especially the pleasure resorts in France, Belgium and England, were placed under a military supervision. Visitors were ordered to return to their homes and every resort was shrouded with darkness at night.
(75)

Go on to next page

Stock exchanges throughout the United States were closed, following the example of European stock exchanges. Ship insurance soared to prohibitive figures. Reservists of the French and
(80) German armies living outside of their native land were called to the colors and their homeward rush still further complicated transportation for civilians. All the countries of Europe clamored for gold. North and South America complied with
(85) the demand by sending cargoes of the precious metal overseas. The German ship Kron Prinzessin with a cargo of gold, attempted to make the voyage to Hamburg, but a wireless warning that Allied cruisers were waiting for it
(90) off the Grand Banks of Newfoundland, compelled the big ship to turn back to safety in America.

Channel boats bearing American refugees from the Continent to London were described as floating hells. London was excited over the war
(95) and holiday spirit, and overrun with five thousand citizens of the United States tearfully pleading with the American Ambassador for money for transportation home or assurances of personal safety.

(100) The condition of the terror-stricken tourists fleeing to the friendly shores of England from Continental countries crowded with soldiers dragging in their wake heavy guns, resulted in an extraordinary gathering of two thousand
(105) Americans at a hotel one afternoon and the formation of a preliminary organization to afford relief. Some people who attended the meeting were already beginning to feel the pinch of want with little prospects of immediate help.

9. The phrase "as if by magic" (Line 4) implies that the author

(A) believes the Belgian army is ill-prepared for battle

(B) is unaware that the Belgian army is on the move

(C) did not see the preparations of the Belgian army

(D) hopes for a miraculous victory for the Belgian army

(E) did not realize that Belgian troops were capable of swift movement

10. The "deadly earnestness" mentioned in Line 9 is illustrated by which of the following selections from Passage I?

(A) "the whole community is agog" (Line 11)

(B) "recruits are being drilled among the apple trees in the orchard" (Lines 24–26)

(C) "Dutch patience was at last exhausted" (Line 36)

(D) "scores of automobiles are racing past like mad things" (Lines 40–41)

(E) "The men, their goods; the women, their sons" (Lines 46–47)

11. In the context of Lines 10–11, "positively charged" may best be defined as

(A) filled with excitement

(B) polluted

(C) disrupted by static

(D) confused

(E) optimistic

12. The third paragraph of Passage I (Lines 27–38)

(A) shows how patriotic citizens should react to the war

(B) criticizes "Monsieur X." for withholding supplies

(C) reveals the stinginess of the cook

(D) portrays the soldiers as hungry boys

(E) indicts the government for failing to supply adequate rations to the troops

13. Lines 39–48 imply that

(A) the Government seizes private property for no reason

(B) men and women are equally involved in the war

(C) women's most important concern is their families

(D) the population makes sacrifices willingly

(E) war is frightening

Go on to next page

14. Based on the comment, "We ourselves are laying in a supply of things in case of necessity" (Lines 55–56), with which statement would the author agree?

    (A) Food supplies may be erratic in wartime.

    (B) In a farming community, food is a major source of income.

    (C) Food supplies should be stored in the kitchen.

    (D) The Government must stockpile sufficient food to feed the populace.

    (E) Every family is an independent entity.

15. The author's tone in Passage I may be characterized as

    (A) regretful

    (B) nostalgic

    (C) excited

    (D) amazed

    (E) antagonistic

16. According to Lines 64–70, American travelers in war-stricken countries were worse off than Europeans because the Americans were

    (A) considered enemy combatants

    (B) short of food

    (C) unable to exchange gold for food

    (D) too poor to buy food

    (E) farther from home

17. The purpose of Lines 92–99 is to

    (A) contrast the dire situation of American tourists with the mood of Londoners

    (B) show how Britain helped America during the war

    (C) describe the plight of Londoners

    (D) criticize Americans who fled to London

    (E) explain the role of the American Ambassador

18. What is the best definition of "want" in the context of Line 108?

    (A) desire

    (B) need

    (C) discomfort

    (D) wish

    (E) absence

19. The main idea of Passage II is

    (A) the situation of Americans in Europe when war broke out

    (B) changes in the money supply during World War I

    (C) the dangers of tourism

    (D) the horrors of war

    (E) American self-sufficiency

20. Which statement about these two passages is correct?

    (A) Passage I is more general than Passage II.

    (B) Passage I provides an overview, while Passage II is an eyewitness account.

    (C) Passage I is more personal than Passage II.

    (D) Passage II is narrower in focus than Passage I.

    (E) Passage I was written later than Passage II.

Directions for Questions 21–24: Two questions follow each of the passages below. Choose the *best* answer to each question based on what is stated or implied in the passages.

The water question is one of real interest to both city and country dwellers, although the chances are that the country dweller knows less about his source of supply than the city dweller can know if he chooses to investigate. The city dweller should know whence and by what means the water flows from his faucet, if for no other reason than that he may do his part in seeing that the money spent by his city or town brings adequate return to the taxpayer. For the rural homemaker, of course, the problem usually becomes an individual one. . . . Is the water supply adequate? Are we obtaining the water for household and farm purposes without more labor than is compatible with good management? (Line) (05) (10) (15)

Go on to next page ⟶

21. According to the passage, in what way do people who live in the country differ from those who reside in the city?

    (A) Country people need more water.

    (B) City residents are more concerned about the cost of water.

    (C) Adequate water supply is not a problem for country people.

    (D) Country dwellers may recognize a problem only if their own water supply is affected.

    (E) City and country residents compete for water.

22. The main idea of the article from which this passage is excerpted most likely concerns

    (A) water allocation and safety

    (B) tax policy

    (C) the benefits of rural life

    (D) the availability of information to residents of rural areas

    (E) the rivalry between country and city dwellers

In the light of day their breath of vague terror was dissipated. There was no place for mystery nor dread under this floor of brilliant sunshine. The smiling sapphire floor rolled ever on before us. . . . I had proven, almost to my own (05) satisfaction, that what we had beheld had been a creation of the extraordinary atmospheric attributes of these highlands, an atmosphere so unique as to make almost anything of the kind possible. But Drake was not convinced. (10)

Line

23. The "extraordinary atmospheric attributes" refers to

    (A) the scenic vista

    (B) air quality

    (C) air pressure

    (D) the weather

    (E) mysterious visions

24. Based on the information in the passage, which statement might Drake make to the narrator?

    (A) The mystery is solved.

    (B) A new day improves every situation.

    (C) The unique weather of the highlands does not explain what we saw.

    (D) Sunshine has calmed my fears.

    (E) You and I agree about what we witnessed.

STOP YOU MAY CHECK YOUR WORK ON THIS SECTION ONLY. DO NOT GO BACK TO ANY PREVIOUS SECTION.

Section 3

Mathematics

Time: 25 minutes for 18 questions

Directions: This section contains two different types of questions. For Questions 1–8, choose the *best* answer to each question. Mark the corresponding oval on the answer sheet. For Questions 9–18, follow the separate directions provided before those questions.

Notes:

✔ You may use a calculator.

✔ All numbers used in this exam are real numbers.

✔ All figures lie in a plane.

✔ All figures may be assumed to be to scale unless the problem specifically indicates otherwise.

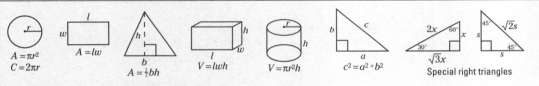

There are 360 degrees of arc in a circle.

There are 180 degrees in a straight line.

There are 180 degrees in the sum of the interior angles of a triangle.

---

1. A student walked at a rate of 10 feet per second for 2 seconds, then at 15 feet per second for 3 seconds. Her average speed, in feet per second, was

    (A) 12

    (B) 12.5

    (C) 13

    (D) 13.5

    (E) 14

---

2. If $a = \frac{1}{2}$, $b = \frac{2}{3}$, and $c = \frac{5}{8}$, which of the following is true?

    (A) $c < b < a$

    (B) $c < a < b$

    (C) $b < c < a$

    (D) $a < b < c$

    (E) $a < c < b$

---

3. Given that $f(x) = x^3$, for which number is $f(x) < x$?

    (A) –2

    (B) –1

    (C) 0

    (D) 1

    (E) 2

Go on to next page

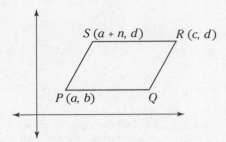

4. *PQRS* is a parallelogram, three of whose coordinates are shown. The coordinates of point *Q* must be

    (A) $(a + n, b)$

    (B) $(a + 2n, b)$

    (C) $(c + n, b)$

    (D) $(c - n, b)$

    (E) $(c - 2n, b)$

5. In a list of consecutive odd integers, the second number can be represented by x. The first number in the list could be represented by

    (A) $x - 3$

    (B) $x - 2$

    (C) $x - 1$

    (D) $x + 1$

    (E) $x + 2$

6. If p is divisible by 12, and q is divisible by 20, then $p + q$ must be divisible by

    I.   2

    II. 4

    III. 32

    (A) I only

    (B) II only

    (C) III only

    (D) I and II only

    (E) I, II, and III

7. Two lines in the coordinate plane, l and m, pass through the point (3, 4). Line l also passes through (5, 8). If line m is perpendicular to line l, then line m also passes through

    (A) (0, 0)

    (B) (1, 5)

    (C) (1, 8)

    (D) (5, 0)

    (E) (8, 5)

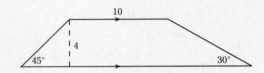

8. What is the total area of the trapezoid pictured above?

    (A) $32 + 4\sqrt{2} + 4\sqrt{3}$

    (B) $48 + 8\sqrt{3}$

    (C) 64

    (D) $56 + 16\sqrt{3}$

    (E) $96 + 16\sqrt{3}$

Go on to next page

Directions for student-produced response Questions 9–18: Solve the problem and then write your answer in the boxes on the answer sheet. Mark the ovals corresponding to the answer, as shown in the following example. Note the fraction line and the decimal points.

Answer: $^7/_2$ Answer: 3.25   Answer: 853

Write your answer in the box. You may start your answer in any column.

Although you do not have to write the solutions in the boxes, you do have to blacken the corresponding ovals. You should fill in the boxes to avoid confusion. Only the blackened ovals will be scored. The numbers in the boxes will not be read.

There are no negative answers.

Mixed numbers, such as 3½, may be gridded in as a decimal (3.5) or as a fraction (⁷/₂). Do not grid in 3½; it will be read as ³¹/₂.

Grid in a decimal as far as possible. Do not round your answer and leave some boxes empty.

A question may have more than one answer. Grid in one answer only.

9. If $x + 100 = 2x$, what is the value of x?

10. A rectangle's length is twice its width. If its area is 32 square inches, find its width, in inches.

11. The height of an object thrown in the air with an initial velocity of 96 feet per second can be modeled by the function $h(t) = -16t^2 + 96t$, where h is in feet and t is in seconds. What would be the ball's maximum height, in feet?

12. If 20 percent of half a number is 17, what was the original number?

Go on to next page

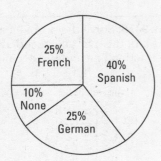

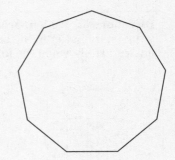

13. The pie graph above shows the percentage of students who take each foreign language at a certain high school. If 260 students take either French or Spanish, how many students go to the school?

14. If the area of an equilateral triangle is $64\sqrt{3}$, find the length of one of its sides.

15. If $w^2 - v^2 = 54$ and $w - v = 9$, find the value of $2w + 2v$.

16. What is the value of the *smallest* number that is divisible by 2, 3, 4, 5, and 6?

17. The polygon shown has nine sides. How many additional lines must be drawn in order to make sure that every vertex (corner) is connected to every other vertex?

18. Car rental company *A* charges $80 per day, plus 25 cents per mile driven. Car rental company *B* charges $100 per day, plus 10 cents per mile driven. If you plan on renting a car for 3 days, for what number of miles would the costs of the two cars be equivalent?

STOP   YOU MAY CHECK YOUR WORK ON THIS SECTION ONLY. DO NOT GO BACK TO ANY PREVIOUS SECTION.

Section 4
Critical Reading

Time: 25 minutes for 24 questions

Directions: Choose the *best* answer to each question. Mark the corresponding oval on the answer sheet.

Directions for Questions 1–5: Select the answer that *best* fits the meaning of the sentence.

Example: After he had broken the dining room window, Hal's mother _____ him.

(A) selected

(B) serenaded

(C) fooled

(D) scolded

(E) rewarded

The answer is (D).

---

1. In everyday conversation and in the media, the new constitution was debated, though no _____ emerged.

   (A) discord

   (B) dissent

   (C) discrepancy

   (D) consensus

   (E) plan

2. The goal of the seminar was not only to share information but also to build a(n) _____ group that would trust and depend upon each other.

   (A) intellectual

   (B) cohesive

   (C) adhesive

   (D) communicative

   (E) hard-working

3. The executive is known for his _____ style of leadership; his subordinates know that he wants to hear their opinions and ideas, however contrary to the executive's own views.

   (A) pragmatic

   (B) idealistic

   (C) aggressive

   (D) hierarchical

   (E) inclusive

4. Compared with negotiations for other properties, which ended in lawsuits and ill will, working out the lease for that office building was a relatively _____ process.

   (A) complicated

   (B) swift

   (C) harmonious

   (D) difficult

   (E) secretive

5. Her daily strolls gave her insight into the _____ rhythms of the neighborhood.

   (A) quotidian

   (B) exemplary

   (C) inexplicable

   (D) tenacious

   (E) estranged

Go on to next page

Directions for Questions 6–9: Choose the *best* answer to each question based on what is stated or implied in the passages or in the introductory material.

The first passage is excerpted from a 1919 book titled Vocational Guidance for Girls *by Marguerite Stockman Dickson. The second is drawn from* Small Loans, Big Dreams *by Alex Counts (Wiley) and describes part of the screening process of a bank that awards small loans to poor women in Bangladesh and other countries.*

Passage 1

Line   The radicals would have us believe that the question of woman's status in the world requires an upheaval of society for its settlement. Says one, the "man's world" must be transformed into
(05) a human world, with no baleful insistence on the femininity of women and that it is the human qualities, shared by both man and woman, which must be emphasized. The work of the world — with the single exception of childbearing — is
(10) not man's work nor woman's work, but the work of the race, they say.

Passage 11

Can a woman speak loudly and clearly while looking an area manager in the eye? When pushed, does she stand up for herself? In short,
(15) the bank wants to know whether a lifetime of oppression by the dominant gender has left a prospective member so compliant that she would turn over money she had received from the bank to her husband without raising a fuss.
(20) The bank leaders want to have some confidence that in such a case, the woman would alert her group members [other loan recipients] and center chief and ask them to intervene.

6. With which statement is the author of Passage I likely to agree?

   (A) Behavior is individual, not related to one's gender.

   (B) Women and men can do the same work.

   (C) Society is properly organized with regard to gender.

   (D) Men should share in the work of child-rearing.

   (E) More women should work outside the home.

7. The author of Passage II would probably endorse

   (A) financial independence for women

   (B) loyalty to family over her own self-interest

   (C) a husband's leadership within the family

   (D) passive acceptance of life's circumstances

   (E) unlimited loans for poor women

8. The "race" referred to in Line 11 is most likely

   (A) a competition

   (B) one's ethnic background

   (C) one's skin color

   (D) all of humanity

   (E) the nation

9. The author of Passage II favors which of the following as a support system for borrowers?

   (A) her family

   (B) other women who have received loans

   (C) the government

   (D) the men of her village

   (E) business advisors

Go on to next page

Directions for Questions 10–15: Choose the *best* answer to each question based on what is stated or implied in the passage or in the introductory material.

The passage is excerpted from a 19th-century novel.

Line It was Miss Murdstone who was arrived, and a gloomy-looking lady she was; dark, like her brother, whom she greatly resembled in face and voice; and with very heavy eyebrows, nearly
(05) meeting over her large nose, as if, being disabled by the wrongs of her sex from wearing whiskers, she had carried them to that account. She brought with her two uncompromising hard black boxes, with her initials on the lids in hard
(10) brass nails. When she paid the coachman she took her money out of a hard steel purse, and she kept the purse in a very jail of a bag which hung upon her arm by a heavy chain, and shut up like a bite. I had never, at that time, seen such a
(15) metallic lady altogether as Miss Murdstone was.

She was brought into the parlour with many tokens of welcome, and there formally recognized my mother as a new and near relation. Then she looked at me, and said, "Is that your boy, sister-in-
(20) law?" My mother acknowledged me. "Generally speaking," said Miss Murdstone, "I don't like boys. How d'ye[1] do, boy?" Under these encouraging circumstances, I replied that I was very well, and that I hoped she was the same; with such an indif-
(25) ferent grace, that Miss Murdstone disposed of me in two words: "Wants manners!"

Having uttered which, with great distinctness, she begged the favour of being shown to her room, which became to me from that time
(30) forth a place of awe and dread, wherein the two black boxes were never seen open or known to be left unlocked, and where (for I peeped in once or twice when she was out) numerous little steel fetters and rivets, with which Miss Murdstone
(35) embellished herself when she was dressed, generally hung upon the looking-glass in formidable array.

As well as I could make out, she had come for good, and had no intention of ever going
(40) again. She began to "help" my mother next morning, and was in and out of the store-closet all day, putting things to rights, and making havoc in the old arrangements. Almost the first remarkable thing I observed in Miss Murdstone was, her
(45) being constantly haunted by a suspicion that the servants had a man secreted somewhere on the premises. Under the influence of this delusion,

she dived into the coal-cellar at the most untimely hours, and scarcely ever opened the door of a dark cupboard without clapping it to (50) again, in the belief that she had got him. Though there was nothing very airy about Miss Murdstone, she was a perfect Lark in point of getting up. She was up (and, as I believe to this hour, looking for that man) before anybody in (55) the house was stirring. Peggotty gave it as her opinion that she even slept with one eye open; but I could not concur in this idea; for I tried it myself after hearing the suggestion thrown out, and found it couldn't be done. (60)

1. *A shortened form of "How do you do?"*

10. The narrator compares Miss Murdstone's eyebrows to
    (A) her brother
    (B) overweight people
    (C) boxes
    (D) men's whiskers
    (E) a bite

11. In Lines 1–15, Miss Murdstone is "a metallic lady" in the narrator's view for all of the following reasons EXCEPT
    (A) her nasty disposition
    (B) her boxes
    (C) her purse
    (D) her handbag
    (E) the chain of her bag

12. In the context of Lines 24–25, "indifferent" may best be defined as
    (A) uncaring
    (B) mediocre
    (C) exceptional
    (D) unconventional
    (E) fair

13. The narrator implies that in the future his relationship with Miss Murdstone
    (A) becomes more loving
    (B) is that of mentor and student
    (C) revolves around her search for a hidden man
    (D) is characterized by fear
    (E) is helpful to his mother

Go on to next page

14. The word "help" is in quotation marks in Line 40 because

    (A) the author wishes to add emphasis to the word

    (B) the word is a direct quotation from the narrator's mother

    (C) the word is a direct quotation from the narrator

    (D) the word is a direct quotation from Miss Murdstone

    (E) Miss Murdstone's actions aren't helpful

15. The interaction between the narrator and Peggotty in Lines 56–60

    (A) shows the ignorance of the narrator

    (B) characterizes Peggotty as ignorant

    (C) reveals antagonism between the narrator and Peggotty

    (D) illustrates Peggotty's admiration for Miss Murdstone

    (E) exemplifies the narrator's inquisitive nature

Directions for Questions 16–24: Choose the *best* answer to each question based on what is stated or implied in the passage or in the introductory material.

The passage is excerpted from Rice: Origin, History, Technology, and Production *(Wiley).*

Line   Rice cultivation, milling, and marketing is one of America's oldest agribusinesses. Indeed, rice is one of humankind's most ancient and most universally consumed foods. It is the one
(05) grain crop grown almost exclusively for human food. The advent of cultivated grains in human society is closely associated with the inception of the city and civilization. Sometime around 10,000 B.C. grain began to be cultivated. Many
(10) believe that the earliest cultivation was along the Yellow River of China or in similar aquatic and tropical terrain in Asia. Cultivation eventually extended from the Yellow River of China to the Amur River on the border between the Soviet
(15) Union and China. Because of its unique adaptability to diverse growing conditions, its ease of preparation and palatability, and its durability in storage, rice cultivation spread rapidly to the

cool climates and high mountains of Nepal and India, to the hot deserts of Pakistan, Iran, and (20) Egypt, and into the tropical and desert regions of Southeast Asia and Africa. The inception of agriculture came with the cultivation of rice and other wild grains. After thousands of years of sameness and virtual stagnation, with the advent (25) of agriculture human development suddenly accelerated.

   Agriculture brought an abundance of food that humankind previously had not experienced. Cultivation, rather than hunting and gathering, (30) became the primary economic endeavor and prescribed a revolutionary new social order — the city. The city's primary economic function was as that of a granary. Its major social function was as a nursery for the young, and a safe and defensible (35) refuge for its inhabitants. Cities organized existing human life into a new state of dynamic tension and interaction intrinsic to civilization, and civilization brought with it the need to administer the land and the water used to irrigate the land. (40) Agriculture imposed civilization upon humans, and rice early became the most widely cultivated and universally consumed grain.

   The necessity for agriculture generally is associated with the receding glaciers of the last (45) ice age more than 10,000 years ago, the subsequent moderation of climate, and the demise and retreat of large animal species to more northern regions. The scarcity of game forced humans into more intensive reliance on wild and then on (50) domesticated grains and foodstuffs. The diversion of human energies from hunting to agriculture and to a state of civilization occupied thousands of years, during which time regional and cultural distinctions arose, differentiating (55) one civilization from another. Societies often were distinguished by the food they ate and the manner in which they produced or obtained their food. Assuming that the search, production, and their consumption are major components of (60) human endeavor through the years, the most widely consumed of all human foods — rice — deserves a prominent place in history.

   In the second and third millennium B.C., the tribes of central Asia and India offered milk and (65) rice in the ceremonial fires to Agni, the god of fire and witness to all creation. They offered rice because rice was their choicest food. Rice in India continues to be used in rituals and prayer. It is the first food offered the infant, and the first (70) mouthful offered by a new bride to her husband. In the Western world and the United States, rice is thrown on the bride and groom at weddings as

Go on to next page ⟶

a symbol of abundance and fertility. The *Susruta*
(75) *Samhita*, compiled in India in about 1000 B.C.,
classifies rice by varieties based on duration,
water requirements, and nutritional values. Rice
was cultivated during the dynastic period in
Egypt. Carbonized grains have been found in the
(80) pyramids. Rice entered into trade between Rome
and Egypt and between Egypt, India, and China.
Rice is mentioned in Chinese records of 2800
B.C. In Chinese, the spoken word and the written
character for cooked rice is *fan*, which is also the
(85) word for food, and when pronounced with a different intonation is the verb *to eat*.

16. The "inception of the city and civilization"
(Lines 7–8) most likely occurred

    (A) before grain was cultivated

    (B) around 10,000 B.C.

    (C) after China began to trade with neigh-
    boring countries

    (D) when wild grains died out

    (E) around 2800 B.C.

17. Examples of the "unique adaptability"
(Lines 15–16) of rice include all of the
following EXCEPT

    (A) its cultivation along the Yellow River of
    China

    (B) rice plants in the mountains of India

    (C) rice crops in the deserts of Pakistan

    (D) the cultivation of rice along with other
    wild grains

    (E) rice plants in tropical Africa

18. In the context of Line 17, "durability" may
be defined as

    (A) sturdiness

    (B) permanence

    (C) stability

    (D) strength

    (E) hardiness

19. In the context of this passage, the "stagnation" referred to in Line 25 was probably a
long period in which human beings

    (A) lived in the same place

    (B) had the same traditions

    (C) lived by hunting and gathering

    (D) ate cultivated foods

    (E) changed their diet frequently

20. The purpose of Paragraph 2 (Lines 28–43)
is to

    (A) show how cities resulted from the
    invention of agriculture

    (B) relate cities to their food sources

    (C) praise cities for providing grain to
    citizens

    (D) criticize cities for the tension they
    cause between citizens

    (E) connect agriculture to the raising of
    children

21. Which statement from Paragraph 3 (Lines
44–63) justifies the "prominent place in history" that rice "deserves" (Line 63)?

    (A) "the necessity for agriculture generally
    is associated with the receding glaciers
    of the last ice age" (Lines 44–46)

    (B) "the demise and retreat of large animal
    species" (Lines 47–48)

    (C) "[t]he diversion of human energies
    from hunting to agriculture occupied
    thousands of years" (Lines 51–54)

    (D) "regional and cultural distinctions
    arose, differentiating one civilization
    from another" (Lines 54–56)

    (E) "the search, production, and [food]
    consumption are major components of
    human endeavor" (Lines 59–61)

Go on to next page

22. Which title best expresses the main idea of paragraph four?

    (A) Rice through the Ages

    (B) The Importance of Rice

    (C) Rice in Many Cultures

    (D) The Rice Trade

    (E) Rice in Asia

23. The fact that in India rice is "the first food offered the infant" and given "by a new bride to her husband" (Lines 70–71) suggests that rice

    (A) is easily digestible

    (B) symbolizes new life

    (C) is available to all

    (D) can be obtained without difficulty

    (E) may be enjoyed by everyone

24. The best evidence that rice is an important part of the Chinese diet is that rice

    (A) was traded between Egypt, India, and China

    (B) was mentioned in Chinese records of 2800 B.C.

    (C) has its own written character

    (D) is a synonym for the Chinese word for food

    (E) may be pronounced with more than one intonation

STOP YOU MAY CHECK YOUR WORK ON THIS SECTION ONLY. DO NOT GO BACK TO ANY PREVIOUS SECTION.

Section 5
Mathematics

Time: 25 minutes for 20 questions

Directions: Choose the *best* answer and darken the corresponding oval on the answer sheet.

Notes:

✔ You may use a calculator.

✔ All numbers used in this exam are real numbers.

✔ All figures lie in a plane.

✔ All figures may be assumed to be to scale unless the problem specifically indicates otherwise.

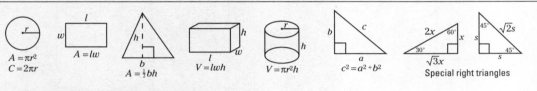

$A = \pi r^2$
$C = 2\pi r$

$A = lw$

$A = \frac{1}{2}bh$

$V = lwh$

$V = \pi r^2 h$

$c^2 = a^2 + b^2$

Special right triangles

There are 360 degrees of arc in a circle.

There are 180 degrees in a straight line.

There are 180 degrees in the sum of the interior angles of a triangle.

1. If $4n + 6 = 34$, then n equals

   (A) 7

   (B) 8

   (C) 9

   (D) 10

   (E) 11

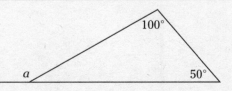

2. The angle marked "a" in the drawing above measures

   (A) 30°

   (B) 100°

   (C) 130°

   (D) 140°

   (E) 150°

3. Doug is thinking of an even number that is bigger than zero but less than 10. The probability that his number is 8 is

   (A) ⅛

   (B) ⅙

   (C) ⅕

   (D) ¼

   (E) ⁸⁄₁₀

4. In an 11th-grade math class, five students have no pets, eight students have one pet, four students have two pets, two students have three pets, and one student has four pets. What is the average number of pets per student in this class?

   (A) about 1.16

   (B) 1.3

   (C) 1.55

   (D) about 1.73

   (E) none of the above

Go on to next page

5. Which expression represents the number of cents, c, that a customer received from a one-dollar bill after buying n candies each costing 5 cents?

(A) $c = 1 - 5n$

(B) $c = 100 - 5n$

(C) $c = 95n$

(D) $c = 100 - 0.05n$

(E) $c = 1.00 - 0.05n$

6. At a certain high school, the ratio of boys to girls is 4:5. Which number could *not* represent the total number of students in the school?

(A) 360

(B) 400

(C) 450

(D) 540

(E) 999

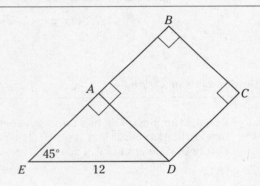

7. Given that $ACBD$ is a square, its area is

(A) 12

(B) 36

(C) 72

(D) 144

(E) 288

8. Given that x and y are positive integers, and that $(xy) - (x + y)$ is even, which of the following must be true?

(A) Both x and y must be even.

(B) Both x and y must be odd.

(C) Either x or y must be even.

(D) Either x or y must be odd.

(E) One of the two numbers must be even, and the other one must be odd.

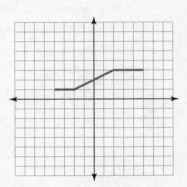

9. Given the graph of $f(x)$ above, $f(1)$ would equal

(A) –2

(B) 0

(C) 2

(D) 2.5

(E) 3

Go on to next page

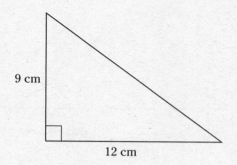

9 cm

12 cm

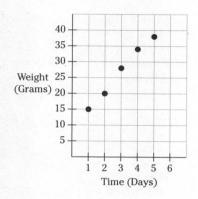

Weight (Grams)

Time (Days)

10. The perimeter of the right triangle pictured above is

(A) 21 cm

(B) 36 cm

(C) 42 cm

(D) 54 cm

(E) 108 cm

11. The factors of a positive number n are all the positive numbers that n can be divided by without leaving a remainder; this includes 1 and n itself. For example, the factors of 10 are 1, 2, 5, and 10. How many positive numbers less than 50 have an *odd* number of factors?

(A) 0

(B) 1

(C) 7

(D) 16

(E) 49

12. To go on a certain amusement-park ride, you must be at least 50 inches tall, but not taller than 70 inches. Which of the following is an inequality that represents h, the height of people allowed to go on this ride?

(A) $|h - 60| \le 10$

(B) $|h - 10| \le 60$

(C) $|h - 50| \le 20$

(D) $|70 - h| \le 20$

(E) $|h - 60| \ge 10$

13. The graph above shows the weight of a hamster, in grams, over a period of several days. The linear function that best models the hamster's weight, w, as a function of its age in days, a, is which of the following?

(A) $w = 6a$

(B) $w = 10a$

(C) $w = 6a + 10$

(D) $w = 10a + 6$

(E) $w = 8a + 8$

14. If $x^{3/4} = 64^{1/2}$, what does x equal?

(A) 2

(B) 6

(C) 8

(D) 16

(E) $42^{2/3}$

15. Which of the following equations has 3 as a solution?

I. $x^2 - 9x = 0$

II. $x^2 + x - 12 = 0$

III. $x^2 + 6x + 9 = 0$

(A) I only

(B) II only

(C) III only

(D) I and II

(E) II and III

Go on to next page

16. A sequence of numbers is created by starting with k, and then adding 3 to the previous number to create each new number. If the 20th number in this sequence is 55, then k equals

    (A) –5

    (B) –2

    (C) 1

    (D) 5

    (E) 35

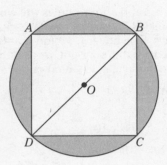

17. If the diameter of circle O is 10 cm, and $ABCD$ is a square, then the area of the shaded region in cm^2 is which of the following?

    (A) $25\pi - 50$

    (B) $25\pi - 25$

    (C) $50\pi - 50$

    (D) $50\pi - 100$

    (E) $100\pi - 100$

18. If $3a + 2b = -4$, and $2a + 3b = -11$, then $5a - 5b =$

    (A) –15

    (B) 5

    (C) 7

    (D) 15

    (E) 35

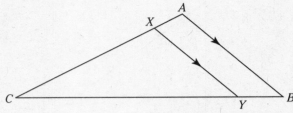

Note: Figure not drawn to scale.

19. In the drawing above, line segment XY is parallel to line segment AB. If $AB = 10$, $XY = 6$, and the area of triangle ABC is 50, then the area of triangle XYC is

    (A) 18

    (B) 24

    (C) 30

    (D) 36

    (E) 44

20. Biking with the wind, a cyclist took 40 minutes to complete a ride. Biking against the wind, the cyclist took 60 minutes to complete the same ride. Assuming that the cyclist bikes 30 miles per hour without any wind, and that the wind's speed was constant, the speed of the wind, in miles per hour, was

    (A) 5

    (B) 6

    (C) 8

    (D) 10

    (E) There is not enough information given.

STOP YOU MAY CHECK YOUR WORK ON THIS SECTION ONLY.
DO NOT GO BACK TO ANY PREVIOUS SECTION.

Section 6
Multiple-Choice Writing

Time: 25 minutes for 35 questions

Directions: Choose the *best* answer to each question. Mark the corresponding oval on the answer sheet.

Directions for Questions 1–11: Each sentence is followed by five choices. Decide which choice *best* improves the sentence. If the underlined portion of the sentence is best left alone, choose (A).

Example: <u>Bert and him went</u> to the store to buy boots in preparation for the approaching storm.

(A) Bert and him went

(B) Bert and he went

(C) Bert and he had gone

(D) Bert and him had gone

(E) Bert and himself went

The correct answer is (B).

---

1. After the fight, Justin's new coat was <u>equally as ripped as Anthony's</u>.

   (A) equally as ripped as Anthony's

   (B) as ripped as Anthony

   (C) as ripped as Anthony's

   (D) equal in rips to Anthony

   (E) equally ripped as Anthony

2. The municipal government, concerned about the number of traffic accidents involving bicycles, has passed a law requiring <u>registration of every vehicle, it takes effect</u> on January 1.

   (A) registration of every vehicle, it takes effect

   (B) registration of every vehicle which it takes effect

   (C) all vehicles to be registered, it takes effect

   (D) that every vehicle be registered, and the registration law becomes effective

   (E) registration of every vehicle; the law takes effect

3. Libby's grandfather, who carries several sets of keys, sets off the metal detector at airports <u>more often than her relatives</u>.

   (A) more often than her relatives

   (B) more often than her relatives do

   (C) oftener than her relatives

   (D) more often than her other relatives

   (E) more often than her relatives'

4. During the first act of the play, the spotlights wobbled <u>a little, and it had destroyed the actors' concentration</u>.

   (A) a little, and it had destroyed the actors' concentration

   (B) a little, which was destroying the actors' concentration

   (C) a little, and the actors' concentration, it was destroyed

   (D) a little and destroyed the actors' concentration

   (E) a little because it destroyed the actors' concentration

5. Selecting a new chief executive, <u>the problems facing the company seemed more manageable to the trustees</u>.

   (A) the problems facing the company seemed more manageable to the trustees

   (B) the trustees saw the problems facing the company as more manageable

   (C) the problems were more manageable that were facing the company according to the trustees

   (D) the trustees saw problems that were more manageable as they faced the company

   (E) the trustees saw more manageable problems which were facing the company

Go on to next page

6. The most common reason for computer crashes is <u>that the operating system code contains an error</u>.

   (A) that the operating system code contains an error

   (B) because the operating system code contains an error

   (C) the operating system code containing an error

   (D) the operating system code, that it contains an error

   (E) the operating system code, that contains an error

7. The unclaimed package, <u>which was wrapped in brown paper and which was tied with string</u>, attracted a great deal of attention.

   (A) which was wrapped in brown paper and which was tied with string

   (B) wrapped in brown paper and which was tied with string

   (C) that was wrapped in brown paper and that was tied with string

   (D) wrapped in brown paper and tied with string

   (E) which was wrapped in brown paper, and which was also tied with string

8. Rushing to the meeting before the comfortable blue chair was taken, <u>the seat was discovered to be occupied already by Alex</u>.

   (A) the seat was discovered to be occupied already by Alex

   (B) the seat was already occupied by Alex, it was discovered

   (C) Alex discovered the seat was already occupied

   (D) Alex discovered the seat, and it was already occupied

   (E) Alex, discovering that the seat was occupied already

9. <u>The ability to ski, ice-skate, and knowing karate</u> were all skills Darian worked hard to perfect.

   (A) The ability to ski, ice-skate, and knowing karate

   (B) The ability to ski, ice-skate, and karate

   (C) The ability to ski, to ice-skate, and knowing karate

   (D) The ability to ski, ice-skate, and do karate

   (E) Skiing, ice-skating, and to know karate

10. British writer Jane Austen lived <u>in small towns most of her life, living in rural areas</u> except for a short period when she lived in the city of Bath.

   (A) in small towns most of her life, living in rural areas

   (B) in small, rural towns most of her life

   (C) in small towns most of her life, and she was living in rural areas

   (D) in small towns, she lived in rural areas for most of her life

   (E) in rural areas, in small towns, in which she lived for most of her life

11. The reporter for that metropolitan paper, as well as many other representatives of the <u>media, has been pressured to identify</u> confidential sources.

   (A) media, has been pressured to identify

   (B) media, have been pressured to identify

   (C) media, has been pressured in that they should identify

   (D) media; has been pressured to identify

   (E) media, which has been pressured to identify

Go on to next page

Directions for Questions 12–29: In each of the following sentences, identify the underlined portion that contains an error. If a sentence contains no errors, choose (E) for "no error." *Note:* No sentence contains more than one error.

Example:

    <u>Irregardless</u> of the fact that the National
          A
Weather Service <u>predicted rain,</u> Dexter <u>resented</u>
             B   C
the <u>students' request</u> to postpone the picnic.
        D

<u>No error.</u>
 E

The correct answer is (A).

12. When negotiations <u>began, the</u> ambassador
               A
and her <u>assistants entered</u> the room
         B
<u>quietly, and</u> then the ambassador <u>repeats</u>
    C   D
her demand for trade concessions.
<u>No error.</u>
 E

13. Pablo Picasso <u>often changed his style</u>
                A
of <u>painting, not to please</u> a patron or
      B
<u>to conform</u> to the expectations of his
  C
<u>teachers, but to create art</u> that matched
       D
his inner vision. <u>No error.</u>
            E

14. The animal shelter <u>receives funding</u> neither
            A
<u>from the state government or from local</u>
          B
<u>officials</u> and <u>is</u> entirely supported
          C
<u>by charitable donations.</u> <u>No error.</u>
      D   E

15. Although the <u>intricately carved</u> box and
            A
chest of drawers <u>are</u> on display <u>as beautiful</u>
           B   C
art <u>objects, its</u> roomy interior provides
      D
convenient storage space. <u>No error.</u>
                  E

16. Milo <u>said that he was</u> going <u>to try and</u>
       A   B
<u>arrive</u> earlier <u>for his English class</u> in order
                C
<u>not to miss</u> the beginning of the lesson.
    D
<u>No error.</u>
 E

17. Langston <u>Hughes, who's</u> poems <u>are read</u>
          A   B
throughout the world, <u>is one</u> of the premier
               C
writers of the period <u>known as the Harlem</u>
               D
Renaissance. <u>No error.</u>
         E

18. The fact that Samuel Johnson <u>is incarcerated</u>
                A
when the crime <u>was committed</u> <u>convinced</u>
         B   C
Detective Amos that Johnson <u>was innocent</u>.
                 D
<u>No error.</u>
 E

19. According to the manual <u>that bus drivers</u>
                A
<u>must study</u>, accidents <u>to</u> which the tailpipe
               B
<u>is damaged</u> <u>are classified</u> as serious events.
  C   D
<u>No error.</u>
 E

20. <u>Either the sewing machine is defective</u> or
           A
<u>cleaned improperly</u> with an <u>oil-based</u> solu-
    B   C
tion instead <u>of soap and water.</u> <u>No error.</u>
       D   E

21. The gardener's <u>request,</u> given to Will and <u>I</u>,
          A   B
will be honored <u>if</u> funds <u>become</u> available
           C   D
in the new budget. <u>No error.</u>
            E

22. <u>Chester commented</u> that <u>George's</u> voice
     A   B
sounded <u>odd</u> because <u>he had not yet</u>
      C   D
recovered from a cold. <u>No error.</u>
              E

Go on to next page

23. The chief executive <u>editor, not</u> the writers,
    A
    <u>has been</u> under pressure <u>to complete</u> the
    B C
    <u>latest</u> issue. <u>No error.</u>
    D E

24. <u>That flowering plant</u>, which <u>needs</u> more
    A B
    care than others in the <u>greenhouse is</u> very
    C
    precious to Marie <u>because her mother</u>
    D
    <u>planted it</u>. <u>No error.</u>
    E

25. Pleased by his success <u>in expanding</u> the
    A
    business, the designer took a <u>long-postponed</u>
    B
    vacation <u>and returned</u> ready to work <u>hardest</u>.
    C D
    <u>No error.</u>
    E

26. The teacher will share the <u>leftover candy,</u>
    A
    <u>which</u> she <u>purchased</u> <u>for Halloween,</u>
    B C
    <u>between you and I</u>. <u>No error.</u>
    D E

27. The bandage <u>on one</u> of the <u>dog's paws</u>
    A B
    <u>were designed</u> to prevent infection or
    C
    <u>further</u> injury. <u>No error.</u>
    D E

28. <u>Disputed by the defense</u> attorney <u>was</u> the
    A B
    eyewitness <u>testimony and the fingerprints</u>
    C
    <u>found</u> at the crime scene. <u>No error.</u>
    D E

29. The television <u>ratings are</u> <u>real important</u> in
    A B
    <u>determining the advertising rates</u> for com-
    C
    mercials <u>aired</u> during each show. <u>No error.</u>
    D E

Directions for Questions 30–35: These questions are based on the following essay. Choose the *best* answer to each question.

☐1 Teenagers, like everyone, make many choices every day. ☐2 In some high school cafeterias, the food, including pizza and fried food, isn't healthy enough for growing young people. ☐3 The teenagers don't always like to eat good food, but if they have good food available, they may make better selections.

☐4 Some cafeteria food comes from surplus crops. ☐5 The government supports American farmers by buying surplus food and distributing it to school children through cafeteria lunches. ☐6 Economics, not nutrition, are the goal. ☐7 Also, school officials try to appeal to students' appetites because they know that students who don't like the choices offered may waste food. ☐8 A student will put good food on their plate, but if they don't like the taste, they will throw it out.

☐9 School cafeterias are part of education. ☐10 What can be more important than eating properly and promoting health? ☐11 If junk food would not be offered and healthy food prepared, students would eventually learn a valuable life lesson. ☐12 The American farmer grows healthy crops or produces meat and milk products. ☐13 The problem isn't the food, but its preparation. ☐14 Given delicious, nutritious food, teens will eat well and society will benefit.

Go on to next page ➡

30. Which sentence would be a good first sentence for Paragraph 1?

    (A) Teenagers should be taught about nutrition.

    (B) Making good choices is something that should be taught in school.

    (C) School cafeterias should serve nutritious food, but many do not.

    (D) It is a problem when you consider the kind of food served in school.

    (E) Eating properly is important.

31. Which sentence, inserted before Sentence 4, would be a good introduction to Paragraph 2?

    (A) The selection of food offered in a high school cafeteria is not based on health.

    (B) Economics and taste are important.

    (C) Neither economics nor taste matters in the cafeteria.

    (D) American farmers grow too much food.

    (E) Some farmers sell their crops to the government.

32. Which sentence below represents the best combination of Sentences 4 and 5?

    (A) Some cafeteria food is bought by the government from surplus food grown by farmers.

    (B) Cafeteria lunches are made of government surplus food.

    (C) Bought from farmers, the government distributes surplus food to children as school lunches.

    (D) Some cafeteria food comes from surplus crops, and the government buys the food from farmers and gives it to school children.

    (E) Some cafeteria food comes from surplus crops, which the government buys from farmers and distributes in the form of school lunches.

33. Which sentence represents the best revision of Sentence 8?

    (A) A student will put good food on his or her plate, but if you don't like the taste, you'll throw out the food.

    (B) Students put good food on their plates, but if they don't like the taste, they'll throw out the food.

    (C) Students, who put good food on their plates, throw it out if the taste isn't liked.

    (D) Even though a student selects good food, they may not eat it and instead throw it out.

    (E) Students who select good food for their plates and don't like it, throw it out.

34. The best revision of the portion of Sentence 11 shown below is which of the following?

    If junk food would not be offered

    (A) If junk food would not be offered (no change)

    (B) If junk food would have been offered

    (C) If junk food were offered

    (D) If junk food are

    (E) If junk food would be offered

35. Which sentence(s) should be removed from the last paragraph of the essay?

    (A) Sentence 9

    (B) Sentences 9 and 10

    (C) Sentence 11

    (D) Sentences 12 and 13

    (E) Sentence 14

STOP YOU MAY CHECK YOUR WORK ON THIS SECTION ONLY. DO NOT GO BACK TO ANY PREVIOUS SECTION.

Section 7
Critical Reading

Time: 20 minutes for 19 questions

Directions: Choose the *best* answer to each question. Mark the corresponding oval on the answer sheet.

Directions for Questions 1–6: Select the answer that *best* fits the meaning of the sentence.

Example: After he had broken the dining room window, Hal's mother _____ him.

(A) selected

(B) serenaded

(C) fooled

(D) scolded

(E) rewarded

The answer is (D).

---

1. George pretends that his talent is _____, but he has practiced many hours each day for years to perfect his skills.

    (A) innate

    (B) instinctive

    (C) acquired

    (D) important

    (E) intuitive

2. "Walking on eggshells" and other common expressions create _____ images.

    (A) confusing

    (B) fearful

    (C) vivid

    (D) unimaginable

    (E) tentative

3. The boxer hopped from foot to foot in an effort to _____ his opponent's punches.

    (A) confound

    (B) evade

    (C) counter

    (D) resist

    (E) distract

4. The tiny cottage filled with old-fashioned furniture and devoid of modern appliances struck the visitor as _____.

    (A) conventional

    (B) convenient

    (C) simplistic

    (D) artificial

    (E) quaint

5. The artist, early in her career, was not just _____ but actually _____.

    (A) precocious . . . terrible

    (B) assertive . . . aggressive

    (C) talented . . . unskilled

    (D) naive . . . proficient

    (E) immature . . . seasoned

6. Despite the drop in temperature, patches of ice _____.

    (A) persisted

    (B) melted

    (C) widened

    (D) cracked

    (E) persevered

Go on to next page

Directions for Questions 7–19: Choose the *best* answer to each question based on what is stated or implied in the passage or in the introductory material.

The passage is an excerpt from a memoir of a young woman setting off for a year of study abroad.

Line   It's August, 1968, and the Democratic National Convention has just begun. I'm sitting on the floor in the middle of the living room, my spine stiff with grief and fear and determination.
(05) Though a sofa and easy chairs surround me, I choose this uncomfortable spot and stare at the television screen. As the morning hours give way to afternoon, images of demonstrators and police flicker by, to be replaced by politicians
(10) and confetti and balloons.

I see but do not comprehend. I'm not there, really. I'm in another place already. My plane leaves in the evening. By this time tomorrow I'll be in Spain for the start of a twelve-month stay.
(15) My family is in the house, though it's a Thursday and therefore a workday. As I sit like a statue in the living room, Bobby and Mom and Dad enter and leave for various reasons. I pay little attention to them, though at least for my mother, my
(20) leaving is a very big deal.

Since the previous spring when I got permission to go, Mom's been shopping for things she assumes I can't buy abroad. Four weeks earlier Alla, a college friend, helped me paint the out-
(25) side of an oversize black trunk that I shipped air freight. It's supposed to be (and indeed it is) waiting for me in the Spanish airport. Inside the trunk are cold-weather clothing and dozens of bottles of shampoo, tubes of toothpaste, and
(30) other products. "You don't know what you can buy there," she says, as she squeezes stuff into every bit of space, "and these things are from home."

Painted on the trunk are cartoonish daisies
(35) and something that resembles a field of green grass. (Neither Alla nor I have any artistic talent whatsoever.) I'm twenty, but I've never been in a plane, never gone to a restaurant alone — or even that often with company — never stayed
(40) alone in a hotel. I'm twenty, a child more than a woman, and the trunk reflects my status. Nevertheless, I'm getting out.

My campaign for Spain started long ago. In the summer between sixth and seventh grades
(45) (seventh and eighth for Bobby), Mom took a

full-time job in the local grocery. We were to enroll in summer school. Both Bobby and I were good students, so summer school was enrich-ment, not remedial. I wanted to learn a language. From an early age I'd fantasized that I could speak (50) and communicate with others in a way that no one else in my family understood. My solitary walks to school were filled with imaginary words and long conversations I could hear in my head — long, rhythmic syllables from a land that didn't (55) exist, one where I wasn't the youngest, weakest link.

Mom said French was "the language of cul-tured people." Automatically I enrolled in Spanish. The class was filled with high-school- (60) age kids who'd failed Introduction to Spanish, and I didn't exactly fit in. But I was used to not fitting in, and from the very first moment I took the textbook and devoured it. I was going to speak Spanish if it was the last thing I did. Later I (65) signed up for Spanish in high school, where I was offered the chance to study for a few months in South America. (Mom said no.) I chose Spanish as my college major, and from sophomore year onward, I lobbied for the chance to have a year (70) abroad. The professor called home, pleading my case, and this time I got a yes.

Now it's time to leave. Dad's only comment on the situation came a few weeks before when he and Mom had to sign a permission form. Was (75) I allowed to travel on school holidays? Could I leave the dorm on weekends? What were my per-sonal, parent-applied rules? Holding the paper and frowning, he said, "I'm signing my name in the 'no restrictions' box. But stay off motorcy- (80) cles. They're dangerous." I tearfully nodded, though I'd never actually met anyone with a motorcycle. I didn't mind giving in. He hardly ever asked me for anything, I thought then.

At 6 p.m. Dad backs out of the driveway. On (85) Darson Avenue — fortunately there are no cars around — he jams on the brakes. "You don't have to go. And if you're unhappy, you can come home." I shake my head. I won't be unhappy. I won't.

We get to the terminal and check in. I'm (90) popcorn ready to pop. The plane, just my luck, is delayed. We're a little island of discomfort, goodbyes said too soon. I want them to go away so I can begin. When my flight is called, I hug everyone and walk into the curving tunnel that (95) leads to the plane. It's the opposite of birth; I'm laboring to *leave*, not *enter* the family. I feel the contractions squeezing me out. I don't turn around, but I know that Mom and Dad and Bobby get smaller and smaller as I walk. (100)

Go on to next page

7. The image of the narrator sitting on the floor (Lines 2–3) represents

    (A) isolation

    (B) political unrest

    (C) subservience

    (D) confusion

    (E) guilt

8. All of these statements express similar ideas EXCEPT

    (A) "I see but do not comprehend" (Line 11)

    (B) "I'm not there" (Line 11)

    (C) "I'm in another place already" (Line 12)

    (D) "Now it's time to leave" (Line 73)

    (E) "I want them to go away so I can begin" (Lines 93–94)

9. The statement that "at least for my mother, my leaving is a very big deal" (Lines 19–20) implies that

    (A) the rest of the family wants the narrator to leave

    (B) the rest of the family wants the narrator to stay

    (C) the narrator doesn't understand her mother's feelings

    (D) the mother exaggerates the dangers of the trip

    (E) the narrator comprehends her mother's emotions

10. The mother's words, "You don't know what you can buy there" (Lines 30–31) imply that in the mother's view

    (A) American products are essential for the daughter's well-being

    (B) European products are inferior

    (C) the daughter is moving beyond the mother's knowledge and experience

    (D) the mother is a more experienced traveler than her daughter

    (E) the mother is worried about money

11. The narrator most likely says that "the trunk reflects [her] status" (Lines 41) because the trunk

    (A) is about to be sent abroad

    (B) shows the narrator's youth through its "cartoonish" drawings (Line 34)

    (C) is filled with the narrator's belongings

    (D) will be sent ahead by air

    (E) is leaving the United States

12. The narrator's fantasy about an ability to "speak and communicate with others in a way no one else in my family understood" (Lines 50–52) reveals her

    (A) need for privacy

    (B) belief that foreign-language learning is valuable

    (C) desire to separate herself from her family

    (D) confusion between reality and illusion

    (E) creative ability

13. The narrator's choice of Spanish may be attributed to

    (A) her rebellion against her mother's wishes

    (B) a love of Spain

    (C) the desire to be considered "cultured" (Lines 58–59)

    (D) a remedial summer course in that language

    (E) her experiences in South America

14. "I thought then" (Line 84) suggests that the narrator

    (A) wants the reader to understand her thought process

    (B) feels obligated to her father

    (C) later reevaluated her view of her father

    (D) wants to follow her father's rules

    (E) never understood her father's request

Go on to next page

15. The narrator repeats "I won't" (Line 89) because she

    (A) wants to reassure her family

    (B) is reassuring herself

    (C) fears that her family will not believe her

    (D) always presents herself emphatically

    (E) firmly believes the statement is true

16. Which of the following best expresses the meaning of "I'm popcorn ready to pop" (Lines 90–91) in the context of this passage?

    (A) The situation is stressful.

    (B) I am patient.

    (C) I am angry.

    (D) I am ready to start a new life.

    (E) It is hard to say goodbye.

17. The "little island of discomfort" (Line 92) is equivalent to

    (A) "sitting on the floor in the middle of the living room" (Lines 2–3)

    (B) the trunk with "cartoonish daisies" (Line 34)

    (C) "solitary walks to school" (Lines 52–53)

    (D) "I didn't exactly fit in" (Line 62)

    (E) the "curving tunnel" (Line 95)

18. The fact that "Mom and Dad and Bobby get smaller and smaller" (Lines 99–100) shows that

    (A) the narrator understands artistic perspective

    (B) the family isn't an important part of the narrator's identity

    (C) the narrator has already forgotten about her family

    (D) the narrator carries an image of her family with her on the trip

    (E) the family will be less influential in the narrator's life after she leaves

19. The passage suggests that the narrator's relationship with her family is

    (A) affectionate

    (B) conflicted

    (C) antagonistic

    (D) sympathetic

    (E) hostile

STOP YOU MAY CHECK YOUR WORK ON THIS SECTION ONLY. DO NOT GO BACK TO ANY PREVIOUS SECTION.

Section 8

Mathematics

Time: 20 minutes for 16 questions

Directions: Choose the *best* answer and darken the corresponding oval on the answer sheet.

Notes:

✔ You may use a calculator.

✔ All numbers used in this exam are real numbers.

✔ All figures lie in a plane.

✔ All figures may be assumed to be to scale unless the problem specifically indicates otherwise.

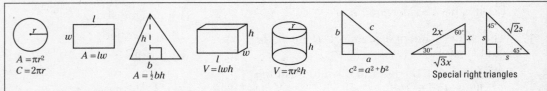

$A = \pi r^2$
$C = 2\pi r$

$A = lw$

$A = \frac{1}{2}bh$

$V = lwh$

$V = \pi r^2 h$

$c^2 = a^2 + b^2$

Special right triangles

There are 360 degrees of arc in a circle.

There are 180 degrees in a straight line.

There are 180 degrees in the sum of the interior angles of a triangle.

1. If k is an integer less than 8, then the greatest possible value of $2k - 1$ is

    (A) 6
    (B) 7
    (C) 13
    (D) 14
    (E) 15

2. The sum of the odd numbers from 3 to 11, including both 3 and 11, is

    (A) 24
    (B) 32
    (C) 35
    (D) 45
    (E) 63

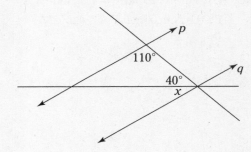

3. In the diagram above, lines p and q are parallel. The measure of the angle marked x is

    (A) 30°
    (B) 40°
    (C) 50°
    (D) 60°
    (E) 70°

Go on to next page

4. The price of a certain train ticket is directly proportional to the number of miles traveled. If a ten-mile trip costs $3.75, then a 24-mile trip would cost

   (A) $6.15

   (B) $9.00

   (C) $10.50

   (D) $15.00

   (E) $17.75

5. If $a \Delta b = b^2 - 3a$, then $-4 \Delta -2 =$

   (A) −22

   (B) −16

   (C) −8

   (D) 16

   (E) 22

6. A function is defined by $f(x) = \dfrac{100}{13 - \sqrt{x}}$. For what value(s) of x would the function equal 25?

   (A) 12.5 only

   (B) 12.5 or $5.\overline{5}$

   (C) 81 only

   (D) 81 or −81

   (E) none of the above

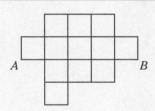

7. Each box in the shape above is a square. If the total area of the shape is 48 square units, then the length of AB is

   (A) 5 units

   (B) 10 units

   (C) 20 units

   (D) 40 units

   (E) 80 units

8. A bag of candy was divided among four children. The first child got exactly one-fourth of the candy. Then, the second child got one-third of the candy that was left. Next, the third child got one-half of the candy remaining. Finally, the fourth child got everything left over. Which child now has the *least* candy?

   (A) The first child got the least.

   (B) The second child got the least.

   (C) The third child got the least.

   (D) The third and fourth children are tied for the least.

   (E) All four children got the same amount of candy.

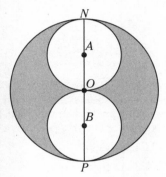

9. In the diagram above, O is the center of the large circle, and A and B are the centers of the two smaller circles. If the length of NP is 8, then the area of the shaded region is

   (A) 4π

   (B) 8π

   (C) 16π

   (D) 32π

   (E) 48π

Go on to next page

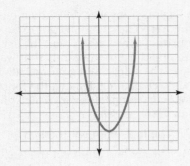

10. The graph above shows $y = f(x)$. Which point would have to appear on the graph of $y = 2f(x) + 4$?

(A) $(-1, 0)$

(B) $(0, 1)$

(C) $(1, 0)$

(D) $(2, -2)$

(E) $(10, 0)$

11. On a hike, a student walked 10 kilometers due north, 5 kilometers due east, and 2 kilometers due south. Her distance, in a straight line, from her starting point is now closest to

(A) 2.6 kilometers

(B) 8 kilometers

(C) 9.4 kilometers

(D) 12.1 kilometers

(E) 17 kilometers

12. The expression $(x - 5)^2$ is equivalent to

(A) $x^2 - 10x + 25$

(B) $x^2 + 25$

(C) $x^2 - 10$

(D) $x^2 - 5x + 25$

(E) $x^2 - 25$

13. Let $a \sim b$ equal:

    $2a$, if $a > b$

    $b + 3$, if $b > a$

    5, if $a = b$

Which of the following would equal 14?

(A) $5 \sim 7$

(B) $7 \sim 8$

(C) $7 \sim 7$

(D) $7 \sim 5$

(E) $11 \sim 7$

14. If it takes x widgets to make one thingumajig, and one thingumajig can produce y whatchamacallits, then the number of widgets needed to produce n whatchamacallits is

(A) $\dfrac{nx}{y}$

(B) nxy

(C) $\dfrac{ny}{x}$

(D) $\dfrac{xy}{n}$

(E) $\dfrac{x}{ny}$

Go on to next page

15. In a deck of 12 cards, each card has one of the symbols below on each side. Some cards have the same symbols on both sides; some cards have different symbols. If every symbol appears on at least two different cards, and Symbols A and B together appear on a total of 13 sides, what is the *maximum* number of cards that could have Symbol D on both sides?

Symbol A   Symbol B   Symbol C   Symbol D

(A) One

(B) Two

(C) Three

(D) Four

(E) Five

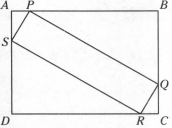

16. The diagram above shows two rectangles, *ABCD* and *PQRS*. If *AP* = 4, *QR* = 7, and $RD = 3\sqrt{33}$, then the area of *PQRS* is

(A) 84

(B) $21\sqrt{33}$

(C) 147

(D) 231

(E) $\left(4 + 3\sqrt{33}\right)\left(12 + \sqrt{33}\right)$

STOP YOU MAY CHECK YOUR WORK ON THIS SECTION ONLY.
DO NOT GO BACK TO ANY PREVIOUS SECTION.

Section 9
Multiple-Choice Writing

Time: 10 minutes for 14 questions

Directions: Each sentence is followed by five choices. Decide which choice *best* improves the sentence and darken the corresponding oval on the answer sheet. If the underlined portion of the sentence is best left alone, choose (A).

Example: <u>Bert and him went</u> to the store to buy boots in preparation for the approaching storm.

(A) Bert and him went

(B) Bert and he went

(C) Bert and he had gone

(D) Bert and him had gone

(E) Bert and himself went

The correct answer is (B).

1. <u>When they had heard</u> about an Etruscan chariot on display at the Metropolitan Museum of Art, the citizens of the Italian town where the chariot was unearthed immediately claimed ownership.

   (A) When they had heard

   (B) When heard

   (C) Hearing

   (D) To hear

   (E) With hearing

2. Amy Tan, whose novels <u>explore the lives of Asian Americans, included</u> elements of Chinese culture and history in her work.

   (A) explore the lives of Asian Americans, included

   (B) explore the lives of Asian Americans, had included

   (C) explore the lives of Asian Americans, including

   (D) exploring the lives of Asian Americans, included

   (E) explore the lives of Asian Americans, includes

3. No one disputes his <u>patriotism, nor can anyone</u> challenge his integrity.

   (A) patriotism, nor can anyone

   (B) patriotism; nor can anyone

   (C) patriotism, also no one can

   (D) patriotism, and can anyone

   (E) patriotism, with anyone can

4. Many public works programs of the Depression era <u>were intended in creating</u> jobs for the unemployed.

   (A) were intended in creating

   (B) were intended to create

   (C) intended in creating

   (D) with the intention of creating

   (E) they were intended to create

5. Ancient Egyptian scribes sat cross-legged and wrote on "desks," <u>with them being their</u> cloth kilts stretched tightly across their knees.

   (A) with them being their

   (B) their

   (C) with their being their

   (D) they were their

   (E) which were their being

Go on to next page

6. Construction projects <u>which appear to start slowly, with months of work going</u> into preparation of the site and foundation, before the skeleton of the building rises quickly.

   (A) which appear to start slowly, with months of work going

   (B) which appear to start slowly, have months of work going

   (C) appear to start slowly, with months of work going

   (D) that appear to start slowly, with months of work going

   (E) which appear to start slowly, and months of work go

7. The best applicant for a position in technical services <u>is good at detail, calm during interactions with customers, and knows</u> about the devices a company sells.

   (A) is good at detail, calm during interactions with customers, and knows

   (B) is good at detail and calm during interactions with customers, while also knowing

   (C) is good at detail, calming customers when they interact, and knows

   (D) is good at detail, remains calm during interactions with customers, and knows

   (E) is good at detail, calm during interactions with customers, and they know

8. <u>Whether genetically engineered crops are a benefit or a danger, it is a matter of controversy.</u>

   (A) Whether genetically engineered crops are a benefit or a danger, it is a matter of controversy.

   (B) Whether genetically engineered crops are a benefit or a danger is a matter of controversy.

   (C) If genetically engineered crops are a benefit or a danger, is a matter of controversy.

   (D) Genetically engineered crops are a benefit or a danger, and people think it is a matter of controversy.

   (E) Controversially, genetically engineered crops are a benefit or a danger to many people.

9. <u>Having learned Spanish and English as a child</u>, Eleanor is fluent in both languages.

   (A) Having learned Spanish and English as a child

   (B) Learning Spanish and English as a child

   (C) As a child, she learned Spanish and English

   (D) Learned as a child, Spanish and English are languages and

   (E) While she was learning Spanish and English as a child

10. The philosopher was so intent on making her <u>argument, and she was walking</u> into a wall of the coffee shop.

    (A) argument, and she was walking

    (B) argument, and walked

    (C) argument, and she walked

    (D) argument, walking

    (E) argument that she walked

11. Seattle's Space Needle is not only <u>a symbol of the city but it also attracts tourists</u> because of its unparalleled view.

    (A) a symbol of the city but it also attracts tourists

    (B) a symbol of the city attracting tourists

    (C) a symbol of the city but also a tourist attraction

    (D) a symbol of the city and it also attracts tourists

    (E) a symbol of the city that also attracts tourists

12. <u>After viewing the elephants, lions, and tigers, the sea lions are a real treat.</u>

    (A) After viewing the elephants, lions, and tigers, the sea lions are a real treat.

    (B) After having viewed the elephants, lions, and tigers, the sea lions are a real treat.

    (C) The elephants, lions, and tigers having viewed, the sea lions are real treat.

    (D) If a person views the elephants, lions, and tigers, the sea lions are a real treat to them.

    (E) After viewing the elephants, lions, and tigers, you'll find that the sea lions are a real treat.

Go on to next page

13. All over the park are thousands of trees, <u>the variety including exotic species and the more common domestic oaks and maples</u>.

    (A) the variety including exotic species and the more common domestic oaks and maples

    (B) and the variety includes exotic species and the more common domestic oaks and maples

    (C) including exotic species and the more common domestic oaks and maples

    (D) which has variety that includes exotic species and the more common domestic oaks and maples

    (E) exotic species and the more common domestic oaks and maples are the variety there

14. <u>Although painted wooden statues are popular with tourists,</u> most artists in that area have long since moved on to other media.

    (A) Although painted wooden statues are popular with tourists,

    (B) Painted wooden statues are popular with tourists, and

    (C) Although painted wooden statues are popular with tourists, but

    (D) Painted wooden statues are popular with tourists, where

    (E) Although painted wooden statues being popular with tourists,

STOP YOU MAY CHECK YOUR WORK ON THIS SECTION ONLY.
DO NOT GO BACK TO ANY PREVIOUS SECTION.

Chapter 25

Practice Exam 3:
Answers and Explanations

. . . .

After you finish taking Practice Exam 3 in Chapter 24, spend some time checking your work by reading over the answers and explanations I provide in this chapter. Prop your eyelids open with toothpicks long enough to read every explanation — particularly for the questions you skipped or answered incorrectly but also for the questions you got right. You never know when I'll include something that will help you increase your score on the real SAT! If you're short on time, check out the abbreviated answer key I provide at the end of this chapter.

Note: To determine your score on this practice test, turn to the appendix.

Section 1: The Essay

This essay prompt asks you to think about ambition, effort, and goals. Is it better to aim high and risk falling flat on your face, or should you take a safer, surer shot? In horse-racing terms, should you bet your bank account on a long shot that *might* have a big payoff but also *might* put you in the poorhouse? Or should you select the favorite and limit your bet so you can't win a fortune but can't lose one either?

As always, you have 25 minutes to decide which position to take on this issue and to dig up some good historical, literary, or personal evidence to back up what you say. Here's a sturdy outline that you can adapt to a variety of ideas:

- **Introduction:** State your thesis, quoting from Penn or Roosevelt if you wish. (You have two options: "Go for it!" or "Play it safe.") Then plop in a couple of briefly stated supporting points. For example, in the go-for-it essay, you might explain how you took an honors course that no one thought you could handle, yet you succeeded. On the other hand, if you're taking the play-it-safe position, you might write about the Greek myth of Icarus, a character who soared too close to the sun on wax wings, which melted, sending him plunging to his death. Two, maybe three, supporting examples are enough to get your point across to your audience.

- **Body paragraphs:** Expand on the supporting points you briefly mentioned in the introduction — one in each paragraph. Be as specific as possible. Continuing with one of the examples from the preceding paragraph, if you're explaining your success in a tough honors course, don't just say that you studied hard. Explain how you left swimming practice every day at 4 p.m. and read your textbook under a plastic bag in the shower. Mention that you taped flash cards to the back of your sister's head so you could study while she drove you to school. You get the idea: Provide plenty of details.

- **Conclusion:** Here's where you very slightly stretch the ideas you've covered thus far. In the play-it-safe essay, you may conclude that realistic, practical goals accomplish more for the world and society than flashier, reach-for-the-moon aspirations. In the go-for-it version, you may consider the world without daring visionaries; perhaps the human race would still be living in caves.

After you have a good idea of what a solid outline looks like for the ambition debate addressed in Practice Exam 3's essay prompt, it's time to score your own essay. Before you get started, turn to Chapter 8 and read the samples there. Then score your essay using the scoring rubric in Chapter 7; be honest with yourself as you determine how your essay measures up to the rubric.

Section 2: Critical Reading

1. **E.** The key word in this sentence is *because,* which tells you that you're looking for cause and effect. The sentence reveals that Woody has established a pattern: always filming movies in New York City. What happens when someone breaks a pattern? Everyone is *surprised* — also known as Choice (E).

2. **C.** Go through the word pairs in order. The celebrity is *shy,* so if the fans believed she was *outgoing* (the opposite of *shy*), the verb you insert in the first blank must have an element of surprise in it. *Amused* doesn't fill the bill, so Choice (A) is wrong. Choice (B) has the opposite problem. The verb *amazed* expresses extreme surprise, but *diffident* is a synonym for *shy.* Choices (D) and (E) make no sense. Why would fans be *antagonized* (irritated) or *appalled* (disgusted) by a celebrity who's *talented* or *celebrated?* Choice (C), on the other hand, is a perfect match. The celebrity was smiling, which *reassured* worried fans who imagined that their star was *depressed.*

3. **A.** The sentence tells you that the resort's advertisements hit both mega-millionaires and people who have to count every penny. That's a *broad* range, making (A) the answer you're looking for. The only other possibility is (C) because a good ad campaign is, by definition, *effective.* However, Choice (A) fits the sentence more specifically because it takes into account the wide span between *the wealthy* and *those of limited means.*

4. **D.** Think you're on a lunch break? Think again, according to the sentence. Your boss can get you even as you munch on a double cheeseburger. Real-life experience helps here because I bet you see a phone call from the boss as a kind of *tyranny,* not *divisiveness* (causing separation), *insignificance* (unimportance), *versatility* (having many uses), or *proliferation* (expansion).

5. **B.** The subject is complex, and generalizations simplify. Hence, you need a verb that condemns generalizations. Okay, Choices (B) and (E) fill that bill because *rejected* means "not accepted," and the word *spouted* has a negative connotation. (A *connotation* is a feeling associated with a word.) What sort of approach is favored *instead of* generalizations? A *nuance* is a "shade of meaning" or a "fine distinction." Thus, Choice (B) works better than (E) because the subject is complex, not basic.

6. **E.** If technology is *pervasive* (all over the place), it's bound to have an effect on just about everything, including *society and culture.* Choice (A) doesn't work because *innovative* means "new," and you don't want to say that *new technology is new.* The other choices, *redundant,* (repetitive), *lucrative* (profitable), and *versatile* (useful in many ways) don't fit the sentence because they don't imply an essential study.

7. **A.** If your nose is always in a book, you have a fierce appetite for reading — in other words, a *voracious* appetite. (Good thing books aren't fattening.) I don't know of any reading competitions, so Choice (B) isn't a good answer. The sentence doesn't tell you anything about the subject's approach to reading, so you have no way of knowing whether he was taught to enjoy reading or whether his habit was *instinctive* — Choice (C). Choices (D) and (E) — *implausible* (unbelievable) and *sporadic* (occurring from time to time) — just don't fit the context of the sentence.

8. **C.** The *but* in this sentence tells you that you need opposites. At first glance, Choice (A) seems like a good candidate because education doesn't happen *suddenly.* (Trust me. I'm a teacher and I know.) But the two words aren't really opposites, so Choice (A) isn't the best answer. Choice (C), on the other hand, has exactly what you're looking for: *Haphazardly* is the term for things that are done without *planning.*

9. **C.** The author of this passage is shocked by the rapid mobilization of Belgian forces. One day they're nowhere (at least in the author's universe), and the next, they're "passing the house all day" (Lines 7–8). Therefore, it's reasonable to assume that the author didn't see the army's preparations for the march. Choice (A) doesn't work because the author makes no comment on the quality of the troops in the passage. The passage flatly contradicts (B), as the author sees the troops on the road. You can dump Choice (D), too, because when you say *as if by magic,* you're actually ruling out magic. Choice (E) is a close second to the correct answer, because *as if by magic* includes an element of surprise. However, (C) is better because it refers to the sudden appearance of the army, not the army's general ability to mobilize.

10. **E.** *Agog* (Line 11) is a word that describes the mouth-open, I-can't-believe-what-is-happening state of mind. The community may be agog for many reasons, including non-deadly ones, so you know Choice (A) is wrong. Choices (B), (C), and (D) are observations of relatively innocent activities, so you can drop them from consideration, too. Choice (E), on the other hand, hits the "deadly" button right on the mark because the line preceding *deadly earnestness* says "how one gives for one's country" (Line 46). What do women give? According to the passage, their sons, who may die in defense of Belgium.

11. **A.** Just past the phrase "positively charged" (Lines 10–11) is a reference to the community as "agog" (Line 11), which means "filled with excitement." Hence, *positively charged* is a metaphor for that human emotion. Choices (B), (C), and (D) are too negative. Choice (E) may have tempted you because of the word *positively;* however, *optimistic* doesn't convey the feeling of anticipation so intense that it resembles an electric current. No doubt remains: Choice (A) is your answer.

12. **D.** The soldiers in the third paragraph (Lines 27–38) aren't serious figures in a fight to the death with the enemy. In this paragraph, they're "boys" (Line 27) who have just awakened and are hungry, so Choice (D) is the answer you seek. Although "Monsieur X" (Line 28) helps out, he's not presented as a model to others, so (A) is wrong. The passage doesn't criticize him and the Government when the soldiers overrun his ability to provide food, so you can also eliminate (B) and (E). True, the cook's patience does give out, but the author writes that "even Dutch patience was at last exhausted" (Lines 35–36), implying that most people would have balked sooner than the cook. Hence, (C) doesn't fit either.

13. **D.** The selected lines explain that the Government has taken what it needs for the war, including livestock and personal possessions. Yet the writer doesn't hint that these seizures are in any way unjustified. On the contrary, the writer lists them as examples of "how one gives for one's country" (Line 46). Thus, you can drop (A) from your list of possible answers. Because the writer says that "men [give] their goods; the women [give] their sons" (Lines 46–47), you may have considered Choice (B) or (C). However, *goods* and *sons* aren't equal, and, by giving their sons to the war effort, the women place patriotism above family. The declaration that the "spirit of the people is magnificent" (Lines 47–48) seals the deal, because all the sacrifices listed in the paragraph are, according to the writer, done in the right spirit — in other words, *willingly,* making (D) the answer you seek. You can reject (E) because these lines don't express fear at all.

14. **A.** Passage I describes events in Belgium following Germany's declaration of war on Russia. The "supply of things" (Line 56) and the fact that troops have already eaten some of the family's food supply (Lines 37–38) suggest that strolling to the local supermarket to restock might not be possible. From this statement you can infer that the author of Passage I would endorse Choice (A). The only other answer that comes close is (E) because the family is preparing for "necessity" (Line 56). Nevertheless, the author doesn't protest the fact that the "Government . . . is commandeering" (Lines 42–43) various items. Therefore, no family is independent but rather potentially part of the war effort.

15. **C.** Though the author mentions some deadly realities of war (the sacrifice of sons to the war effort), the overall tone is that of an excited observer, relating what occurred after war was declared. Her comment "what excitement all about" (Line 10) points you to Choice (C). Although (D) is a close second because the author seems a little dazzled by what she sees, the word *amazed* requires more of an I-can't-believe-what-happened attitude than you see in the passage.

16. **E.** Here's a straight factual question, checking to see whether you were paying attention at the beginning of Passage II. Lines 64–66 specifically state that "Europeans being comparatively close to their homes, were not in straits as severe as the Americans." Bingo! Choice (E) rules.

17. **A.** This paragraph refers to "American refugees" who were traveling to London in "floating hells" (Lines 92–94). Anything that resembles hell may be described as *dire*, which means "in serious or desperate circumstances." Londoners, on the other hand, were "excited over the war and holiday spirit" (Lines 94–95). Hence, Choice (A) is the best answer.

18. **B.** As always with vocabulary-in-context questions, turn to the sentence and plug in a word that makes sense to you. You already know that Americans were "pleading" for transportation home (Lines 95–98) and that they formed a "preliminary organization to afford relief" (Lines 106–107). What can "pinch" (Line 108) and require "relief" (Line 107)? Choices (B) and (C) are good candidates, but *pinch* already expresses discomfort, so (B) is the best answer.

19. **A.** Every paragraph of Passage II talks about Americans in Europe at the outbreak of World War I, so Choice (A) works perfectly here. True, money is mentioned frequently in Passage II and the Americans certainly weren't having a good vacation, but Choices (B) and (C) are too general, as is (D). Choice (E) is too narrow; the formation of a self-help society is mentioned only in passing (Line 106).

20. **C.** Passage I is an account of an eyewitness, a Belgian, who describes the immediate neighborhood in the wake of Germany's declaration of war. Passage II steps back a little, recounting the plight of Americans stranded in Europe during the same time period and providing an overview of their plight. Choice (C) is clearly your answer because eyewitness accounts are always personal.

21. **D.** Lines 3–12 state that "the problem" with water "usually becomes an individual one" and that the "country dweller knows less about his source" than a city dweller who "chooses to investigate." The implication is that the country dweller faces a water problem alone, in a practical way, as illustrated in the last two questions in the passage (Lines 12–15). Thus, Choice (D) is the answer you seek.

22. **A.** Just about every line deals with water, and the passage begins with "The water question" — a sure sign that the writer is going to answer that question. Hence, Choice (A) makes the most sense.

23. **D.** You know something mysterious showed up because "what we had beheld" (Line 6) filled the observers with "mystery dread." However, the narrator cites the "extraordinary atmospheric attributes" (Lines 7–8) as a probable cause of the mystery, not as the mystery itself. So you're left with a vocabulary-in-context question. In this case, Choices (B) and (C) are probably too narrow, and (A) isn't a quality of the atmosphere. Hence, Choice (D), the weather, is the answer you want.

24. **C.** This short passage hints that something (think a Halloween-scary sort of something) showed up one night, but the next day the narrator proved "almost" (Line 9) that whatever they "had beheld" (Line 6) was a trick of the "extraordinary atmospheric attributes of these highlands" (Lines 7–8). In other words, the weather in the highlands scared the pants off the narrator and Drake. Because Drake "was not convinced" (Line 10), you have to look for an opposing view, which is expressed only by Choice (C).

Section 3: Mathematics

1. **C.** Average speed equals total distance divided by total time, *not* just the average of the two speeds. The student traveled 20 feet over the first 2 seconds and 45 feet over the next 3, which makes 65 feet ÷ 5 seconds, or 13 feet per second.

2. **E.** Probably the easiest way to do this problem is to change the numbers to decimals: $a = \frac{1}{2} = 0.5$, $b = \frac{2}{3} = 0.666\ldots$, and $c = \frac{5}{8} = 0.625$. Now that you have decimals, you can see that $a < c < b$.

3. **A.** The best way to solve this problem is to substitute each answer choice into the given equation. Lucky for you, $(-2)^3 = -8$, which is less than -2, so you can stop checking the possibilities right there.

4. **D.** To get from point S to point P, you have to move n spaces to the left, so the same must be true to get from R to Q. That fact tells you that the x-coordinate of Q must be $c - n$.

5. **B.** Don't fall into the old "odd-integers trap!" Even though the numbers are odd, they still must differ by 2. (If you don't believe me, think of 3, 5, 7 . . . .) Because the question tells you that the second number is x, the first one must be 2 less than x, or $x - 2$.

6. **D.** The easiest approach to this question is to pick numbers. Remember: When you take this approach, don't pick numbers that are too simple. Here, for example, you shouldn't pick 12 and 20 themselves, nor should you just multiply each one by the same number. Instead, try doubling 12 to get 24 and tripling 20 to get 60. If you add them together, you get 84, which is divisible by 2 and 4, but not 32. This result makes sense because both 12 and 20 are divisible by 4. Therefore, you can expect your answer to be divisible by 4, too (and, thus, also by 2).

7. **B.** I'd start by making a quick sketch:

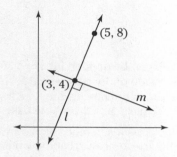

   Perpendicular lines have slopes that are negative reciprocals, so first find the slope of l: $\frac{8-4}{5-3} = 2$. That means line m has a slope of $-\frac{1}{2}$. Now you can just put some of the given points on the line by counting spaces on improvised graph paper (draw your own lines), or you can try plugging the answer choices into the slope formula, in which case plugging in Choice (B) gives you $\frac{5-4}{1-3} = -\frac{1}{2}$.

8. **B.** This trapezoid has a rectangle in the middle, a 45-45-90 triangle on the left, and a 30-60-90 triangle on the right, so I suggest dividing it up into its three pieces. The rectangle's area is just $4 \times 10 = 40$. The left triangle is isosceles, so its base and height are both 4, and its area is $(4 \times 4) \div 2 = 8$. In the triangle on the right, 4 is the shortest side, which makes the hypotenuse 8 and the base $4\sqrt{3}$. Thus, its area is $(4 \times 4\sqrt{3}) \div 2 = 8\sqrt{3}$. Putting them all together gives you Choice (B).

9. **100.** Just subtracting x from each side gives you the answer here.

10. **4.** You can solve this problem by using trial and error or by letting $l = 2w$, writing $(2w)(w) = 32$, and then solving for w.

11. **144.** When I took the SAT, graphing calculators weren't in existence, so I had to work this one out by hand. Luckily, times have changed, and you can just plug the numbers into your calculator to find the answer. If you don't have such a magical device, rely on the formula that says the vertex of a parabola occurs at $x = \frac{-b}{2a}$, where b is the x-coefficient and a is the x^2-coefficient (although here you're using t, not x). Plugging in here tells you that the vertex occurs when $t = \frac{-(96)}{2(-16)} = 3$, and plugging this result into the original equation gives you $h = 144$.

12. **170.** 20 percent is one-fifth, and one-fifth of one-half is one-tenth, so the original number was $10 \times 17 = 170$.

13. **400.** The graph tells you that 65% of the students take either French or Spanish, so you can use the old *is-of* formula: $\frac{\text{is}}{\text{of}} = \frac{\%}{100}$. Here, the number you know, 260, *is* 65% *of* the number you're looking for, so you can write $\frac{260}{x} = \frac{65}{100}$. Cross-multiplying gives you $65x = 26,000$, and, thankfully, 65 goes into 26,000 a nice, even 400 times.

14. **16.** To solve this problem, I recommend creating a simple sketch:

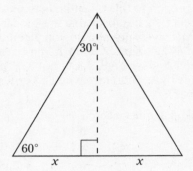

An equilateral triangle can be divided into two 30-60-90 triangles, as you can see in my sketch. If you let each side of the base equal x, then the height equals $x\sqrt{3}$. Because the area is half the base times the height, the area is $x^2\sqrt{3}$, which means that $x^2 = 64$, and $x = 8$. But wait! x was half the base, not the whole base, so your answer is 16.

15. **12.** The expression $w^2 - v^2$ is a difference of two squares, which factors into $(w - v)(w + v) = 54$. Because you know that $w - v = 9$ and that the whole thing equals 54, you can say that $w + v = 6$, so $2w + 2v = 12$. Notice that you don't know what w and v are individually but that you don't really care, either. This reminds me of a story about a student who was both ignorant and apathetic . . . oh, never mind. (For more information on finding the difference of two squares, turn to Chapter 14.)

16. **60.** You can actually ignore the 2 and 3 here because every number that's divisible by both of them is also divisible by 6. Now, because the number is divisible by 4 and 5, it must also be divisible by 20 (because 4 and 5 have no common factors). If you try out multiples of 20, you see that 20 and 40 aren't divisible by 6, but that 60 is divisible by 6, so 60 is your answer.

17. **27.** Imagine that you have only the 9 vertices, and none of them are connected yet. Pick a vertex and connect it to each of the others, drawing 8 lines. Now pick another vertex and connect it to all the vertices. It was already connected to the first vertex, so you draw 7 new lines. The third vertex will already be connected to the first and third, so it needs only 6 new lines. After all the vertices are completely connected, you will have $8 + 7 + 6 + 5 + 4 + 3 + 2 + 1 = 36$ lines. The original drawing already has 9 of those lines drawn in, so you need $36 - 9 = 27$ more lines.

18. **400.** Car A costs $80d + 0.25m$, where d is days and m is miles. Car B costs $100d + 0.10m$. If you plug in 3 for d and make the equations equal, you get $240 + 0.25m = 300 + 0.10m$. Combining like terms gives you $0.15m = 60$, and dividing gives you $m = 400$.

Section 4: Critical Reading

1. **D.** If people are debating, they don't agree. So what hasn't emerged? An agreement, otherwise known as a *consensus*. Therefore, Choices (A), (B), and (C) are out because they imply disagreement — the reverse of what you need in this sentence. Choice (E) seems possible at first, but *plan* implies action, and nothing in the sentence refers to action. In fact, a constitution is more of a theoretical structure by which actions are measured. Thus, (D) is the answer you're looking for.

2. **B.** To "trust and depend upon each other" is another way of saying that the group will stick together and work as a team, a quality best expressed by Choice (B) — *cohesive*. Choice (C) may have fooled you, but an *adhesive* is the glue or substance that sticks one thing to another, a meaning that doesn't fit with *depend upon each other*. Choice (D) is tempting, too, because groups should communicate. However, communication isn't enough to justify *trust and depend,* especially when the communication runs along the lines of "You're fired!" or "Don't look for a raise during this century."

3. **E.** If your boss wants to know what you think, he's *inclusive*. In other words, he pulls everyone into the inner circle. A close second, but *not* the correct answer, is (B), because the "let's all sit and talk as equals" sort of boss is probably idealistic. However, the sentence specifically mentions that *subordinates* are supposed to share their thoughts with the *boss,* a statement that tips the scale toward *inclusive*. *Hierarchical*, by the way, is a system characterized by levels of power — the type of system in which subordinates' ideas are generally *not* welcome.

4. **C.** The very first word of the sentence sets up a comparison between negotiations resembling war *(lawsuits and ill will)* and something else. So you're looking for a contrast, and Choice (C) fills the bill. The only other possibility is (B) because law suits take forever, and *swift* expresses the opposite. However, *harmonious* works as a contrast to both *lawsuits* and *ill will,* making (C) the best answer.

5. **A.** This one is pure vocabulary. If you know the answer choices, you're in. If they puzzle you, you're better off skipping this question. *Quotidian* means "everyday" and refers to the day-to-day activities that fill your time. The question mentions *daily strolls,* so this answer fits perfectly. The other choices simply don't work; *exemplary* is "ideal; the standard model," *inexplicable* is "unexplainable," as in all those strangely plotted TV shows involving flying islands and time travel, *tenacious* is a fancy way of saying "stubborn," and *estranged* is "separated; not speaking," as in an estranged spouse who is headed for divorce court.

6. **C.** When an author says that "the radicals would have us believe," you know that the author *doesn't* believe whatever comes next in the sentence or paragraph. The rest of the excerpt is devoted to explaining the position of "the radicals" (Line 1), which is that the "man's world" (Line 4) should become "a human world" (Line 5) and, "with the single exception of childbearing" (Line 9), all work should be open to the "[human] race" (Line 11), instead of to only one gender. After you decode the paragraph, all you need to do is find a statement that contradicts the radicals' position, which is (C).

7. **A.** The introduction to these passages (the text in italics that appears before the passages) helps you out with this question. The bank makes loans to poor *women,* not to poor people. Clearly, this bank supports female financial independence. Even if you skipped the introduction — something you should *never* do — you still see evidence in the passage that supports Choice (A). The bank wants to know whether a woman can stand up for herself and not "turn over money" (Line 18) "to her husband" (Line 19) as a "lifetime of oppression" (Lines 15–16) may have taught her to do.

8. **D.** Though several answers here are synonyms for *race,* only Choice (D) fits the sentence, which emphasizes neither man's work nor woman's work (Line 10) but the work of the human race.

9. **B.** Lines 21–23 state that the screening process checks whether a woman, faced with a demand from her husband for money, would "alert her group members and center chief and ask them to intervene." Thus, Choice (B) is the answer you're looking for.

10. **D.** This passage, an excerpt from *David Copperfield* by Charles Dickens, displays Dickens's famous ability to create a character with just a few words. Miss Murdstone's "very heavy eyebrows" (Line 4) are described as the whiskers (facial hair) she would have on her chin and cheeks if she were a man. The wording is a little confusing, so this question is really testing whether or not you can decode old-fashioned and complicated expressions. Here's the translation: Miss Murdstone is "disabled by the wrongs of her sex" (Lines 5–6) (women don't, in general, have whiskers!), and she "carried" (Line 7), or wore, the eyebrows "to that account," which in modern terms would be *on account of that fact* or *because of that fact.*

11. **A.** Miss Murdstone is literally covered with metal. Choice (B) is wrong because her "hard black boxes" (Lines 8–9) have "her initials on the lids in hard brass nails" (Lines 9–10). Choice (C) is out because her purse is made of "hard steel" (Line 11). You can eliminate (D) and (E) because the purse is kept in a "jail of a bag" (Line 12) and suspended by a "chain" (Line 13). Jails are characterized by metal bars, and chains are usually made of metal. All that's left is her *disposition,* or tendency, which is certainly nasty but not made of metal.

12. **B.** The narrator has just heard Miss Murdstone say, "Generally speaking . . . I don't like boys" (Lines 20–21), followed by the social formula, "How d'ye do" (Line 22), which is "How do you do?" in modern terms. It's not surprising that the narrator's response, hoping that Miss Murdstone is well, doesn't have a lot of sincerity in it. She starts the social formality of asking how you're doing, and he finishes it in a *mediocre* (so-so or unexceptional) way.

13. **D.** According to the narrator, Miss Murdstone's room is "from that time forth a place of awe and dread" (Lines 29–30). *Dread* is another word for extreme fear, so (D) wins the gold medal for this question. Did (E) catch your eye? The SAT-makers like to throw in an answer that appears in the passage but doesn't answer the question they're asking. Miss Murdstone is supposed to "help" (Line 40) the narrator's mother, but the narrator's relationship with Miss Murdstone isn't included in that statement. Besides, as the next question points out, "help" isn't exactly what Miss Murdstone supplies.

14. **E.** Most of the time, quotation marks signal that you're reading the exact words of a character (or, in nonfiction, of a real person). However, quotation marks can also indicate a gap between intention and reality. Miss Murdstone is supposed to be helping, and she may even have used that word in describing her own actions. But later in the sentence, the narrator says that she made "havoc in the old arrangements" (Lines 42–43) by moving things around. *Havoc* means "chaos," and creating chaos doesn't help anyone. Thus, Choice (E) is the best answer.

15. **A.** When Peggotty says that Miss Murdstone "slept with one eye open" (Line 57), Peggotty is describing Murdstone's *vigilance,* or watchfulness, in fanciful terms (with a figure of speech). The narrator says that he "tried it" (Line 58) and "found it couldn't be done" (Line 60) because he accepted Peggotty's words as the *literal,* or actual, truth. His confusion comes from his ignorance; he's just too young to separate a figure of speech from reality. The only other possibility is Choice (E) because the narrator does experiment with his own sleep. However, (A) is better because the narrator isn't questioning Peggotty's comment (and *inquisitive* means "tending to ask questions"). Instead, he's trying to duplicate what he believes is Miss Murdstone's habit.

16. **B.** If you know that *advent* means "arrival or beginning" and *inception* means "a start or foundation," you're all set for this one. The passage states that "the advent of cultivated grains in human society is closely associated with the inception of the city and civilization" (Lines 6–8). The very next sentence tells you that "around 10,000 B.C. grain began to be cultivated" (Lines 8–9). Put those two thoughts together, and you see that Choice (B) is correct.

17. **D.** Lines 11–22 list the many places that rice grows, and a quick glance reveals that rice plants may be found along rivers (A), in the mountains (B), in the desert (C), and in the tropics (E). What's left? A statement about rice and other grains, (D), which tells you nothing about the *adaptability*, or flexibility, of the plant.

18. **E.** The passage refers to the "durability in storage" (Lines 17–18) of rice. So if you dump a ton of rice into your kitchen closet, it's not likely to spoil because of its *hardiness* (ability to endure and survive). The other choices, all synonyms of *durability,* are best used in other situations. If you're purchasing a chair for your three-ton elephant to sit on, go for (A), (C), or (D). When you buy an engagement ring, you hope that the relationship has the sort of durability expressed by (B).

19. **C.** Even if the word *stagnation* is unfamiliar to you, you can still answer this question by putting on your detective hat and searching for clues. The last sentence of Paragraph 1 mentions "thousands of years of sameness and virtual stagnation" (Lines 24–25). Right away you know that Choice (E) is out because you're looking for something related to *sameness*. What didn't change? Check out the next paragraph, which begins by explaining that

"agriculture" (Line 28) replaced "hunting and gathering" (Line 30) — hello, Choice (C)! Did Choice (D) trick you? Because stagnation came *before* the cultivation of other food sources, (D) is a no-go.

20. **A.** According to Paragraph 2, "the primary economic endeavor" (Line 31) is cultivation, which "prescribed a revolutionary new social order — the city" (Lines 31–33). When *cultivation* (another word for agriculture) was invented, cities arose. The other choices illustrate a favorite SAT torture — sorry, I mean trick. Everything listed in Choices (B) through (E) appears in Paragraph 2, but all those facts serve to explain the cause-and-effect statement given in Choice (A).

21. **E.** This passage talks about rice, and rice is food. (Yup. There's some in my refrigerator right now.) Because Choice (E) asserts that getting and eating food is a big part of human *endeavor*, or effort, rice is important and, therefore, has a *prominent* (important) place in history. Choices (A), (B), and (C) all discuss the rise of agriculture, but they provide reasons or time spans and don't deal with the significance of rice. Choice (D) is close, but not correct, because "differentiating one civilization from another" (Lines 55–56) is less directly related to the importance of rice than (E).

22. **C.** A paragraph's title is an umbrella that covers all the ideas in the paragraph but nothing beyond the paragraph. Using that standard, Choices (A) and (B) are too wide, and (D) and (E) are too narrow. Choice (C) covers all the areas mentioned in the paragraph — from Asia to Africa to Europe — and all the time periods (2800 B.C., 1000 B.C., and right now, when Americans pelt newly married couples with the uncooked grain).

23. **B.** What do an infant and a man who has been married for only a few minutes have in common? Both are beginning a new life, as Choice (B) states.

24. **D.** According to Lines 83–85, the "written character for cooked rice is . . . also the word for food" — pretty good evidence that eating rice is as basic as, well, eating.

Section 5: Mathematics

1. **A.** This question relies on old-fashioned algebra: subtracting 6 from both sides gives you $4n = 28$, and dividing both sides by 4 gives you $n = 7$.

2. **E.** The missing angle in the triangle must be $30°$. And because a and this angle make a straight line ($180°$), a must be $150°$ (the difference of $180 - 30$). In case you're interested, the great world of geometry has also come up with a rule for this sort of problem: The exterior angle of a triangle is always equal to the sum of the two remote interior angles.

3. **D.** Four even numbers are possible (2, 4, 6, and 8), so his chance of choosing 8 is just ¼.

4. **B.** The total number of pets is $5 \times 0 + 8 \times 1 + 4 \times 2 + 2 \times 3 + 1 \times 4 = 26$. The total number of students is $5 + 8 + 4 + 2 + 1 = 20$. There you have it: $26 \div 20 = 1.3$.

5. **B.** The key here is being able to tell your dollars from your sense (sorry, I mean *cents*). You want an expression in cents, and a dollar is 100 cents, so your answer is $100 - 5n$.

6. **B.** In a ratio problem, the total number of things involved (in this case, people) must always be divisible by the sum of the ratios. Here, $4 + 5 = 9$, and all the numbers except 400, are divisible by 9.

7. **C.** This question is a tricky case of the 45-45-90 triangle. The 12 on the triangle's base is actually its hypotenuse, and the helpful formula list at the start of each math section tells you that the hypotenuse of this special type of triangle is $x\sqrt{2}$, where x is the length of a leg. That means each leg must be $\frac{12}{\sqrt{2}}$, which is just an annoying number. But no fear! The leg of the triangle is also the side of the square, which means that the square's area is $\left(\frac{12}{\sqrt{2}}\right)^2 = \frac{144}{2} = 72$.

8. **A.** You can do this one by picking numbers, but you can also reason it out: If both numbers are odd, then xy is odd, but $x + y$ is even, so $(xy) - (x + y)$ is odd. But if one is even and one is odd, then the opposite happens, so the result is still odd. Only if both numbers are even will the result be even.

9. **D.** On a graph, $f(x)$ just means the y-value for a given x. Looking at the graph, you can see that $y = 2.5$ when $x = 1$.

10. **B.** According to the Pythagorean Theorem, the hypotenuse equals $\sqrt{9^2 + 12^2} = \sqrt{81 + 144} = \sqrt{225} = 15$. To find the perimeter, just add up the sides: $9 + 12 + 15 = 36$. By the way, if you answered 54, you found the triangle's *area*, not its perimeter.

11. **C.** Usually, factors come in pairs. For example, in the case of 10 you have 1×10 and 2×5. The only way to end up without a pair is if one of the factors involves the same number twice. You have the same number twice only if the number is a perfect square. Take 16, for example. You have 1×16, 2×8, and 4×4, which makes only 5 factors, an odd number. So how many positive perfect squares are less than 50? There are 7 such numbers: 49, 36, 25, 16, 9, 4, and 1.

12. **A.** The expression $|x - a|$ means "the distance between x and a." In this case, you must be no more than 10 inches from a height of 60 inches. Another way to see that this is the right answer is to plug in 70 and 50 for h. Doing so eliminates all choices except for (A) and (E). Choice (E), however, gives you numbers on the "outside" of 50 and 70, but (A) gives you numbers on the "inside," so (A) is right.

13. **C.** The hamster seems to grow between 4 and 8 grams per day, which means that 6 is a reasonable slope for the function. Because it weighed 15 grams after 1 day, it's also reasonable for it to have weighed 10 grams or so at 0 days (although I have to admit that's a pretty big hamster).

14. **D.** Here's the deal: $64^{1/2} = \sqrt{64} = 8$ and $x^{3/4} = \left(\sqrt[4]{x}\right)^3$, so $\left(\sqrt[4]{x}\right)^3 = 8$. Taking the cube root of both sides gives you $\sqrt[4]{x} = 2$, and taking both sides to the fourth power gives you $x = 2^4 = 16$.

15. **B.** The first equation factors to $x(x - 9) = 0$, the second to $(x + 4)(x - 3) = 0$, and the third to $(x + 3)(x + 3) = 0$. Therefore, the first has solutions of 0 and 9, the second of -4 and 3, and the third of -3 and -3. Two traps await you here. First, lots of people accidentally factor the first equation into $(x + 3)(x - 3)$, but that's $x^2 - 9$, not $x^2 - 9x$. The second trap is forgetting that the roots are the *opposite* of the factors, so 3 isn't a solution to the third equation.

16. **B.** By the time you get to the 20th number, you've added three 19 times (not 20). Thus, you've added $19 \times 3 = 57$. Because you're now at 55, you must have started at $55 - 57 = -2$.

17. **A.** Because the circle's diameter is 10, its radius is 5, and its area is $\pi r^2 = 25\pi$. The square's diagonal cuts it into two 45-45-90 triangles, so just like in Question 7, one side of the square must measure $\frac{10}{\sqrt{2}}$, and its area must be $\left(\frac{10}{\sqrt{2}}\right)^2 = \frac{100}{2} = 50$. The shaded area just equals the circle's area minus the square's.

18. **E.** You can choose from a bunch of ways to do this problem, but the best is to notice that you can subtract the two given equations like so:

$$3a + 2b = -4$$
$$-(2a + 3b = -11)$$
$$a - b = 7$$

So $5a - 5b = 35$.

19. **A.** The rule in this case says that if two figures are similar, the ratio of their areas is the *square* of the ratios of their sides. This rule holds true for any two-dimensional figure, whether it's a triangle, a circle, or whatever. Because the ratio of the sides is 6:10, the ratio of the areas must be 36:100, and $^{36}\!/_{100} \times 50 = 18$.

20. **B.** Let the wind's speed equal x. Because the cyclist bikes 30 miles per hour without any wind, his speed was $30 + x$ with the wind, and $30 - x$ against the wind. With the wind, the trip took 40 minutes, but you have to convert this to $\frac{2}{3}$ of an hour because you're measuring speed in miles per hour. Similarly, against the wind, the trip took one hour exactly. The distance was the same both times, and distance equals speed times time. Bingo: $\frac{2}{3}(30 + x) = 1(30 - x)$. Distributing gives you $20 + (\frac{2}{3})x = 30 - x$, and regrouping gives you $(\frac{5}{3})x = 10$. Finally, you can multiply both sides by $\frac{3}{5}$, and $x = 6$. As befits the last problem in the section, this one is pretty hard!

Section 6: Multiple-Choice Writing

1. **C.** In grammar world, using the phrase *equally as* equals a felony. Justin's coat may be *equally ripped,* but it can't be *equally as ripped.* Therefore, Choice (A) is wrong. The second issue in this sentence is what you're comparing. Choices (B), (D), and (E) compare *Justin's coat* — an item of clothing — to *Anthony,* a person. You know that's not the intended meaning. You can rip a coat but not a person. You're left with Choice (C), the right answer.

2. **E.** The original, as well as Choice (C), joins two complete sentences with a comma. Uh oh — no can do! Commas are very useful punctuation marks, but they're not strong enough to link sentences. Choice (B) avoids the comma problem by throwing in a pronoun (which). However, the combination of the two pronouns together *(which it)* isn't Standard English. Choice (D) isn't wrong grammatically, but it's wordy and thus not as good as (E).

3. **D.** By definition, a grandfather is a relative. All the answer choices, except for (D), exclude Libby's grandfather from the category of relative. The crucial word *other* keeps Grandpa in the family, though it doesn't help him with the metal detector.

4. **D.** You don't need *had* unless you're placing one event before another in the past. In this question, the wobbling and the destroying are simultaneous, so (A) is wrong. Choice (B) solves the tense problem but creates a pronoun error. *Which* may not refer to a subject/verb combo. In Choice (B), *which* refers to "the spotlights wobbled a little." Penalty box! Choice (C) adds an unnecessary *it,* and (E) distorts the meaning with *because.* Choice (D) correctly pairs the subject *spotlight* with two verbs, *wobbled* and *destroyed.*

5. **B.** When a sentence begins with a descriptive verb form, the verb form has to describe the subject of the sentence. In the original sentence, "selecting a new chief executive" describes *problems.* But the problems aren't selecting anything; the *trustees* are the ones selecting. Now that you've dumped (A) and (C), go for the shortest and most fluid expression, which is (B).

6. **A.** The verb *is* functions as an equal sign in this sentence, so whatever is in front of the equal sign must have more or less the same grammatical identity as what follows it. *Reason* is a noun, and "that the operating system code contains an error" is a noun clause. Don't worry about the English-teacher lingo. Just flip the sentence to see if it still makes sense. If it does, chances are it's correct.

The reason is because or *the problem is because* or just about any noun followed by *is because* is all wrong, all the time.

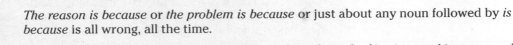

7. **D.** SAT questions are created by teachers, and teachers don't enjoy marking papers. The faster we finish, the happier we are. If you plop unnecessary words into your sentences, we mark them out with a red pencil. Choice (D) does the same basic job as (A), but (D) is shorter; therefore, it's the answer the SAT writers want.

8. **C.** This sentence begins with a descriptive verb form *(rushing),* which must describe the subject of the sentence. The seat can't be rushing, so Choices (A) and (B) are nonstarters. Of the other three choices, only (C) and (D) make a complete sentence. Because (C) is more concise, it edges out (D).

9. **D.** Parallel lines look the same, and so should elements of the sentence that do the same job. This principle of grammar is called *parallelism*, which is often a hot topic on the SAT. Choice (A) isn't correct because *to ski* doesn't match *knowing karate*. (You absolutely *have* to know the grammar terms? Fine: *To ski* is an infinitive and *knowing karate* is a gerund. Happy now?) Choice (B) looks okay at first because the *to* may be understood. However, you can't say *to karate*. Thus, (D) is the only answer with three matching items.

10. **B.** Why repeat *lived* and *living?* Go for Choice (B), which expresses everything you need to know without adding any extra words.

11. **A.** This sentence — along with, come to think of it, all English sentences — requires *agreement.* Singular subjects have to pair with singular verbs, and plural subjects with plural verbs. The subject of the sentence is *reporter,* which is a singular word, so the singular verb *has* is correct. The long interrupter ("as well as many other representatives of the media") appears to add people and, therefore, to create a plural subject. But appearances, as Internet daters know, may be deceiving. Grammatically, *as well as* doesn't have anything to do with *reporter.* Thus, Choice (B), the plural verb *have,* is a trap the SAT makers set up to make sure you're paying attention.

12. **D.** *Tense* is the quality of the verb that expresses time. You can't switch tenses without a reason, just as you can't set your teacher's clock two hours ahead in order to get out of school early. The sentence begins in past tense (with *began* and *entered*) and then switches to present tense (with *repeats*). Penalty box!

13. **E.** Yup. This one has no error. Did (B) or (D) trick you? The commas are correct because they set off the false statements from the true ones.

14. **B.** *Neither* pairs with *nor* and *either* with *or.* Don't mix and match!

15. **D.** Which object has a roomy interior — the box or the chest? The pronoun *its* doesn't tell you, and the first goal of writing is communication. Change the pronoun to a noun (either *the box's* or *the chest's*) and the meaning is unmistakable.

16. **B.** Milo isn't attempting two separate actions: trying and arriving. Instead, he's going to *try to arrive* — one action.

17. **A.** The contraction *who's* means *who is.* The word needed in this sentence is the possessive *whose.*

18. **A.** The first verb in the sentence *(is)* is in present tense, but the rest of the sentence employs past-tense verbs *(was committed, convinced,* and *was).* Grammar rules prohibit littering, talking in class . . . sorry, wrong list. Grammar rules prohibit unnecessary shifts in tense, so Choice (A) contains the error.

19. **B.** The SAT sometimes checks basic knowledge — whether you know some common expressions that are correct simply because they're the way people speak and write. Question 19 falls into this category. Standard English calls for *accidents in which,* not *accidents to which.*

20. **B.** *Either* and *or* are a pair. Whatever elements of the sentence they join must have the same grammatical identity. In the original sentence, a complete sentence ("the sewing machine is defective") comes after the *either,* but only a partial sentence ("cleaned . . . water") follows the *or.* The correct version, by the way, is "Either the sewing machine is defective or it was cleaned improperly with an oil-based solution instead of soap and water."

21. **B.** The pronoun *I* works for subjects, not objects. In this sentence, you need an object because you have a preposition, *to,* and all prepositions require objects.

When you have a combination of a noun and a pronoun, take your finger and cover the noun. Read the sentence again. Often the right answer becomes obvious. For example, in Question 21, you'd hear "given to I." It sounds wrong, doesn't it? That's because it *is* wrong.

22. **D.** Who hadn't yet recovered from a cold? George or Chester? It might be George because George had laryngitis and, therefore, sounded odd. Or it might be Chester, whose ears were stuffed. The pronoun *he* is the issue here. Insert a name, and you know what's going on. Without a name, you're lost.

23. **E.** Ignore the interruption between the commas, and you see that the singular verb *has been* matches the singular subject *editor*.

24. **C.** Some descriptions — those that aren't essential to the meaning of the sentence — are set off by commas. To set off a description that lies in the middle of the sentence, you need two commas, and in Question 24, one comma is missing. You need to insert a second comma after *greenhouse*.

25. **D.** This sentence presents a comparison problem. *Hardest* compared to what? Hardest of all the designers? Hardest in the company? The sentence doesn't say, so the comparison is incomplete. You may be wondering about the hyphen in Choice (B). When two words combine to form one description, they're joined by a hyphen.

26. **D.** I have no idea why *between you and I* is such a popular (but incorrect) expression. The preposition *between* calls for an object, and *I* can serve as a subject, not an object.

27. **C.** The subject of the sentence is *bandage,* a singular noun, so you have to pair it with the singular verb *was*. In case you're wondering, *further* means "more intense or additionally." *Farther* refers to distance.

28. **B.** In 99 percent of all English sentences, the subject comes before the verb. (Okay, I made the number up. I have no idea what the percentage is; I just know that most of the time, you see the subject and the verb in that order.) In Question 28, the usual pattern is reversed, and the subject of the sentence follows the verb. The compound subject ("the eyewitness testimony and the fingerprints") is plural, so you need the plural verb *were*, not the singular *was*.

29. **B.** The expression *real important* is fine for conversation, but in Standard English, you need *really important*. Why? Because *real* is an adjective and may describe a noun, as it does in phrases like *the real reason* or *a real test*. *Really,* on the other hand, is an adverb, and its job is to describe a verb or a descriptive word, such as *important*.

30. **C.** All three sentences in Paragraph 1 deal with the type of food served in school cafeterias and the way in which teenagers relate to that food (although if this were a realistic essay, food fights would be in there somewhere). The first sentence of that paragraph needs to establish the author's point of view. Of the five given answers, Choice (C) best expresses that point of view: Give teens more appropriate choices, and they'll eat in a healthier way.

31. **A.** In Paragraph 2, the author explains how both economics and taste matter when cafeteria menus are created. Paragraph 1 asserts that school lunches aren't always healthful. The goal of Question 31 is to join these two ideas with a transition. Choice (A) refers to the ideas in Paragraph 1 *and* the ideas in Paragraph 2, making it a fine transitional sentence. Although Choice (B) is attractive at first glance, it's too general to be an effective transition. Economics and taste where? In what context? Choice (B) doesn't say. Choices (C) and (D) are just plain wrong, and (E), although true, isn't the topic of this essay.

32. **E.** When you combine sentences, your goal is a smooth, concise result. Of course, you also need to include all the relevant ideas. The two best candidates here are (A) and (E). Choice (A) loses out to (E) because (A) uses passive voice — *is bought, grown by*. Choice (E), which employs active verbs — *comes, buys, distributes* — is your winner.

33. **B.** The original version of Sentence 8 matches the noun *student* (which is singular) with the plural pronouns *their* and *they*. Penalty box. In the world of grammar, you must pair singular with singular and plural with plural. Also illegal is a shift in person. Choice (A) starts out in third person, talking about the student, and then shifts to second person (you). Choice (B) is consistent: the third-person plural *students* matches third-person plural pronouns.

34. **C.** Subjunctive voice, a grammar term you don't have to know, is what they're testing in this question. I won't go into technical detail; all you have to know is that when you have an *if* sentence that expresses something untrue, you don't want to insert a *would* into the *if* portion of the sentence. Instead, go for *were*, as in "if I were the Queen of Grammar." Choice (C) acknowledges that junk food is offered, so subjunctive is appropriate.

35. **D.** The last paragraph is the author's recommendation for change. Sentences 12 and 13 talk about crops and taste — topics covered in Paragraph 2. Repeating them in the third paragraph serves no purpose.

Section 7: Critical Reading

1. **A.** The sentence hinges on the word *but,* which signals a change in direction. The verb *pretends* is another clue; George creates an appearance, but the reality doesn't match it. Okay, what's the reality? He practices *many hours each day.* The appearance must be different from this reality, so you're looking for a talent that just shows up and doesn't have to be learned (in other words, an *innate* talent). Choices (B) and (E) also refer to qualities that are hard-wired, not taught. However, *instinctive* usually refers to actions that have to do with survival (eating, running from danger, and the like), and *intuitive* describes information, not talent.

2. **C.** When you read the sentence, did a little picture pop up in your mind? Probably, which is why *vivid,* a word meaning "producing strong or clear mental images," is right on target.

3. **B.** The key to this sentence lies at the end — the possessive phrase *his opponent's punches.* The boxer's hopping isn't aimed at the opponent; it's aimed at the punches. You can't *confound,* or confuse, a punch. Nor can you distract one. Therefore, cross out Choices (A) and (E). The hopping doesn't *counter* (oppose) or resist the punches either, so (C) and (D) are also out. The act of hopping simply moves the boxer around so he can *evade,* or avoid, getting a broken nose from the opponent's punches.

4. **E.** The word *quaint* refers to something charming and a little out-of-date, as in the sentence I hear all the time: "You don't have a cellphone? How quaint!" The cottage falls into that category easily. Did Choice (C) fool you? *Simplistic* doesn't mean "simple." It means something that's overly simplified — a quick and easy route that can't substitute for something more complex.

5. **B.** Because of the pairing of the words *not just* and *but,* the sentence implies a progression or an intensification. The only answer that falls into this category is (B). If you're *assertive,* you don't hesitate to put yourself forward, as in "You should listen to what I have to say." If you're *aggressive,* you approach violence, as in "Listen to what I have to say or you'll regret it!"

6. **B.** When the temperature drops, ice generally forms or, if it's already there, continues to exist. The word *despite* in the sentence alerts you to the need for an unusual occurrence — a break in the pattern. Choice (B) is the only answer that moves away from existence toward nonexistence.

7. **A.** The narrator says that she's "not there" (Line 11) and that she pays *little* "attention" (Lines 18–19) to family members as they walk in and out of the room. Choice (A) expresses the sense of solitude that the narrator implies when she says she sits "on the floor in the middle of the living room" (Line 3), almost like an island. True, Choice (B) expresses the events that are on the television screen — "demonstrators and police" (Lines 8–9) — but those events don't capture the narrator's attention; she's disconnected. Hence, Choice (A) works better. Choice (C) fails because the narrator seems in control at this point. The decision to leave has been made, and any alterations are up to her, as confirmed in the father's statement, "You don't have to go" (Lines 87–88). Choices (D) and (E) aren't even in the running.

8. **D.** Choice (D) is a statement of fact, an observation. The other choices all revolve around the narrator's feelings of detachment or *alienation* from the family. Choice (E) is a runner-up because the narrator comments on her family ("I want them to go away"), but (D) is more impersonal and, therefore, the better choice.

9. **E.** You can use the process of elimination to find this answer. Choice (A) can't be correct because the father's statement in Lines 87–88 ("You don't have to go") shows that at least one other family member doesn't want the narrator to leave. However, you don't know anything about Bobby's opinion, so you can't select (B) either. Choice (D) doesn't work because, although the mother is worried about toothpaste and shampoo (Lines 28–30), a lack of toiletries hardly qualifies as danger. Choices (C) and (E) are opposites. The mother's preparations and her statement that "these things are from home" (Lines 32–33) show that the narrator's interpretation is correct, making (E) the right answer.

10. **C.** The full statement from the mother concludes with "these things are from home" (Lines 32–33). Taken together, you have a comment on the unknown ("you don't know what you can buy there" — Lines 30–31) and a tie to familiar places (home). So Choice (C) makes a lot of sense. Any of the other responses might be true, but the passage gives you no evidence to support them. The passage doesn't mention either money or the quality of European shampoo and toothpaste. Because the reader has no way to figure out how much the mother has traveled, (D) isn't correct.

11. **B.** The information about the trunk's drawings is the key here. They appear "cartoonish" (Line 34), similar to a child's drawings. The trunk description is tucked into a paragraph listing what the narrator hasn't done – flown on a plane, eaten alone in a restaurant, and so forth. Lack of experience is associated with youth (yes, I know, sometimes this association is unfair or just plain wrong), so Choice (B) is bubble-worthy.

12. **C.** Throughout the passage, the narrator scatters some clues about her alienation from her family, and this phrase — as well as the paragraph it appears in — is a big one. The narrator wants to be in a land where she isn't "the youngest, weakest link" (Lines 56–57). In the real world, therefore, she *is* the youngest and weakest. The language no one else understands is a way to be different, to have her own place separate from her family, an idea expressed in Choice (C).

13. **A.** This one is easy. Some of the answers are just plain wrong because information in the passage clearly contradicts them. You can drop (C) because French, not Spanish, is cited by the narrator's mother as being "cultured" (Lines 58–59). Lines 48–49 tell you that the summer course was not remedial; thus, (D) is also incorrect. The narrator didn't make it to South America because "Mom said no" (Line 68), so (E) is wrong, too. The only choices left are (A) and (B). Because this is the narrator's first trip to Spain and she says nothing about the country itself, (B) isn't a good option. Bingo: One order of teen rebellion coming right up.

14. **C.** "Then" (Line 84) is the key to this question. First, the narrator tells you what she thought at the time: "He hardly ever asked me for anything" (Lines 83–84). Next, the narrator qualifies this statement with a time clue, "I thought then" (Line 84). Clearly, the narrator's idea of her father changed, which leads you to Choice (C). Choice (A) is too general; the whole passage explains how the narrator thinks. Choice (B) is tricky: Yes, the narrator implies that she feels obligated, but the words implying this idea come from the part of the sentence preceding the phrase in Question 14.

15. **B.** The words that the narrator says aloud are placed in quotation marks and the given phrase isn't punctuated that way, so Choice (A) can't be correct. After all, you can't reassure someone without words. Choices (C), (D), and (E) aren't even in the running, as the passage supplies no evidence for these answers. Choice (B) draws upon a childlike habit: You tell yourself that everything will be okay, and then you tell yourself again (and maybe again!) to convince yourself that everything will be okay. So repeat after me: I will ace the SAT. I will.

16. **D.** Lines 90–100 describe the time period just before the narrator leaves for Spain. Most of the paragraph focuses on the future ("I want them to go away so I can begin" — Lines 93–94). When popcorn pops, a hard kernel changes into a tasty snack. The narrator is ready to change — to go abroad — and to start a new life; Choice (D) expresses this message.

17. **A.** By definition, islands are cut off from the mainland. The narrator's "in the middle of the living room" (the island) and sitting "on the floor" (Line 3) instead of on the sofa or a chair (the discomfort).

18. **E.** The narrator doesn't "turn around" (Lines 98–99), but she knows that her family is shrinking. She's not talking about art lessons — Choice (A). Instead, she's describing her relationship to her family. She says that she's "laboring to *leave*, not *enter*, the family" (Line 97). Leaving the family diminishes their influence over her, an idea expressed in Choice (E).

19. **B.** Throughout the passage, the narrator sprinkles little hints that all is not well. Her leaving "at least for [her] mother" (Line 19) is difficult, but what about the other two family members mentioned? The narrator says, "I'm getting out" (Line 42), the sort of comment you'd expect from a prisoner. Her rebellion when her mother suggests French also displays conflict. Choice (B) fits this level of unease better than either (C) or (E), which are more extreme choices. After all, the narrator cries (Line 81) and hugs (Line 94).

Section 8: Mathematics

1. **C.** The largest that k could be is 7, and $2(7) - 1 = 13$.

2. **C.** Yes, you could just add up all the odd numbers from 3 to 11, but it's easier to take them in pairs: 3 plus 11 is 14, and so is $5 + 9$. That's two 14s, which is 28; now you just have to include 7, which makes a total of 35.

3. **A.** Because 110° and 40° are two angles of a triangle, the sum of the three angles has to be 180°, which means the third angle must be 30°. The third angle makes a Z with x, and, because the original lines are parallel, these angles are congruent. (Officially, the 30° angle in the triangle and x are *alternate interior angles*.)

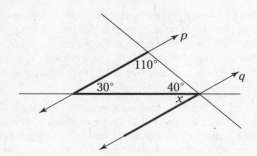

4. **B.** Because the two numbers are directly proportional, you can set up a proportion: $\frac{10}{3.75} = \frac{24}{x}$. Doing that wacky cross-multiplying thing gives you $10x = 90$, so $x = \$9.00$. (For more information on proportions, check out Chapter 12.)

5. **D.** This one isn't too tough if you're careful with the negative signs: $(-2)^2 - 3(-4) = 4 + 12 = 16$.

6. **C.** Don't plug in 25 for x; you want the whole function to equal 25. So, $25 = \frac{100}{13 - \sqrt{x}}$, and $13 - \sqrt{x}$ must equal 4. Therefore, $\sqrt{x}$ equals 9, which is true when $x = 81$.

7. **B.** The figure contains 12 squares, so each one has an area of $48 \div 12 = 4$ and, thus, each side has a length of 2. Because AB covers 5 sides, its length is 10.

8. **E.** Yes, this one is a trick question. If (like me) you think fractions are cool, you solved this question this way: ¼ goes to the first child, which leaves ¾. One-third of that equals ⅓ × ¾ = ¼, so ¼ goes to the second child, too, with ½ of the candy still left. Because the third child takes half of the half that's left, that's another ¼, and the fourth child gets the ¼ that remains. Of course, you can also do this problem by picking a nice number (say, 100) and working it out that way, a method you might like better.

9. **B.** Because the whole circle has a diameter of 8, its radius is 4 and its area is πr^2, or 16π. (Don't fall into the common trap of squaring the diameter by accident.) Each smaller circle has half the radius of the large one, which is 2, so each one has an area of 4π. There you go: The shaded area is $16\pi - (2 \times 4\pi) = 16\pi - 8\pi = 8\pi$.

10. **D.** Performing this transformation doubles all the y-coordinates and then adds 4 to them, without changing the x-coordinates. Doing so with each of the five points on the original graph gives you $(-1, 4)$, $(0, -2)$, $(1, -4)$, $(2, -2)$, and $(3, 4)$. Only Choice (D) is in the list.

11. **C.** As is often the case, drawing a diagram like this one can help you solve this problem:

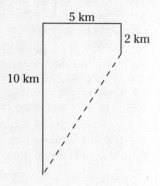

The dotted line shows the student's distance from home, which is the hypotenuse of a right <u>triangle</u> with legs 5 and 8 (from 10 − 2). That ol' Pythagorean Theorem tells you that $d = \sqrt{8^2 + 5^2} = \sqrt{89} \approx 9.43$.

12. **A.** Ah, yes, an old trap from my algebra classes. To solve this problem, you can use a formula I explain in Chapter 14: $(a + b)^2 = (a + b)(a + b) = a^2 + 2ab + b^2$. I'd memorize that formula, if I were you. But, if your memory freezes, just use the FOIL method by writing $(x − 5)(x − 5)$. Now follow the FOIL steps. Multiply the first terms $(x \cdot x = x^2)$. Now multiply the outer terms $(x \cdot −5 = −5x)$. Next, multiply the inner terms $(−5 \cdot x = −5x)$. Now multiply the last terms $(−5 \times −5 = 25)$. Combine the results, and you end up with Choice (A).

Check out Chapter 14 for more details about factoring and using the FOIL method.

13. **D.** You know that 5~7 equals 10 because $b > a$, and you're told to add 3 to b when that happens. Also, 7~8 equals 11 for the same reason. Moving on, 7~7 equals 5 because $a = b$. And 7~5 equals 2×7, which is 14, because $a > b$. You have your answer, but checking the last one just for safety tells you that 11~7 equals 2×11, which is 22.

14. **A.** To solve this problem, I'll pick pretty numbers and say that 10 widgets makes a thingumajig and that a thingumajig can produce 2 whatchamacallits. So it takes 5 widgets, or ⅖, to make one whatchamacallit. To make n whatchamacallits, you have to multiply by n, which is what Choice (A) tells you to do.

15. **D.** The 12 cards have a total of 24 sides, and symbols A and B represent 13 of them. Because you want C to show up as much as possible, the easiest way to do so is to have only As and Bs on 6 cards (12 sides), with one more on a side of another card. Now you can put a C on the other side of that card and another C on some other card. You've taken care of the rule that each symbol must appear on at least two cards, and you've used a total of 8 cards. Thus, you're left with a maximum of 4 cards that could be all Ds.

16. **C.** Because you know QR, your goal is to find either RS or PQ. Now, PS must be the same as QR, so $PS = 7$ and the Pythagorean Theorem tells you that $AS = \sqrt{7^2 − 4^2} = \sqrt{33}$. The next key step is to realize that triangles APS and DSR are similar, because angles A and D are both right angles, while APS and DSP are also congruent. Thus, triangle DSR is exactly three times as big as triangle APS, so SR is just three times bigger than PS, and $SR = 21$. Finally, the area of $PQRS$ is $7 \times 21 = 147$.

Section 9: Multiple-Choice Writing

1. **C.** Got a watch? This sentence is mostly about timing. Only two choices, (A) and (C), are serious contenders. The word *immediately* tells you that the two actions in the sentence (hearing about the chariot and claiming ownership) took place more or less at the same time. Choice (A) is wrong because it places the hearing before the unearthing. Choice (C), on the other hand, expresses a simultaneous situation. Therefore, (C) is the right answer.

2. **E.** In the question's original sentence, *explore* is in present tense and the second verb, *included,* shifts to past tense. As you may recall from past grammar lessons, you should never change tense unnecessarily in a sentence. Thus, you know Choice (E) is the winner because it aligns the second verb with the first by changing *included* to *includes.*

3. **A.** Sometimes I feel sorry for *nor.* It's a perfectly respectable *conjunction* (a word that joins equal elements of a sentence), but people tend to ignore it in favor of *and, but,* and *or* — also conjunctions. The sentence is correct as written because *nor* links two complete thoughts. Did Choice (B) fool you? It's wrong because you don't need a semicolon to join the sentences because *nor* has already done the job.

4. **B.** *Were intended* is the main verb in the sentence, but if you stop there, the thought is incomplete. An *infinitive,* the to-plus-a-verb form, generally follows the main verb. Two choices, (B) and (E), supply an infinitive, but (E) throws in the unnecessary pronoun *they.*

5. **B.** Short and sweet works here. The underlined portion of the sentence is the definition of *desks.* "Their cloth kilts stretched tightly across their knees" is all you need for that definition. Case closed.

6. **C.** About a gazillion years ago, English teachers decided that every sentence must express a complete thought. The original sentence in Question 6 doesn't, because *which appear to start slowly* leaves you hanging. The pronoun *which* generally begins a description, and when a *which* statement follows a subject, it usually interrupts the subject/verb pair. In the original sentence, you have no subject/verb pair. Choice (C) creates a subject/verb pair, *projects appear,* and turns a fragment into a complete thought.

7. **D.** When you see a list in a sentence, everything in it should have the same grammatical identity. The original sentence lists three things: "is good at detail," "calm during interactions with customers," and "knows about the devices the company sells." The first and third items begin with verbs, but the second item begins with an adjective. Choice (D) adds a verb, so you're all set.

8. **B.** In the original sentence, the pronoun *it* refers to a whole bunch of words — everything that precedes the comma. Problem! A pronoun can't substitute for any expression containing a subject/verb combo. Choice (B) takes care of the problem by dumping the pronoun. Choice (C) is close but has two flaws: When you're presenting two alternatives, *whether* is better than *if.* Also, you don't need a comma after the word *danger.* Choice (D) is clumsy, and (E) is illogical because *controversially,* a description, has nothing to describe.

9. **A.** Logic tells you that *Eleanor is fluent* now because of something that happened before now. *Having learned,* the descriptive verb form in Choice (A), places the learning before the fluency — exactly what you want. Choice (D) begins with a descriptive verb form, too, and the past tense places it before the fluency. However, (D) is wordy, and (A) is concise. No doubt about it: (A) is better.

10. **E.** The sentence (which, by the way, describes a scene I actually witnessed), implies cause and effect. The philosopher is discussing lofty ideas and ignoring little details like walls. Choice (E) has cause and effect built into it with the *so . . . that* pair, making (E) the right answer.

11. **C.** *Not only* pairs with *but also* to join together similar things. In the original sentence, you have the noun *symbol* right after *not only.* But after the conjunction *but,* you have the subject/verb pair *it also attracts.* Choice (C) solves the problem by placing the noun *tourist attraction* after the second conjunction. Now the conjunction pair links nouns and their descriptors.

12. **E.** The answer choices fiddle with several verb tenses, but this question actually presents a description problem. Who's viewing the *elephants, lions, and tigers?* In the original sentence, the sea lions are viewing them, because a verb statement at the beginning of a sentence automatically attaches itself to the subject of the sentence. Only Choices (D) and (E) insert viewers. Choice (D) doesn't make the grade because *person* is singular and *them* is plural. Choice (E) solves the description problem nicely.

13. **C.** Sometimes simplest is best, and this sentence is one of those times. If you've got *exotic* and *common,* the reader already knows that the park has *variety.*

14. **A.** This sentence contrasts what tourists like and what artists do. *Although* generally presents a condition and explains what happened *despite* that condition. The original sentence expresses that idea perfectly.

Answer Key for Practice Exam 3

Section 2

1. E	7. A	13. D	19. A
2. C	8. C	14. A	20. C
3. A	9. C	15. C	21. D
4. D	10. E	16. E	22. A
5. B	11. A	17. A	23. D
6. E	12. D	18. B	24. C

Section 3

1. C	6. D	11. 144	16. 60
2. E	7. B	12. 170	17. 27
3. A	8. B	13. 400	18. 400
4. D	9. 100	14. 16	
5. B	10. 4	15. 12	

Section 4

1. D	7. A	13. D	19. C
2. B	8. D	14. E	20. A
3. E	9. B	15. A	21. E
4. C	10. D	16. B	22. C
5. A	11. A	17. D	23. B
6. C	12. B	18. E	24. D

Section 5

1. A	6. B	11. C	16. B
2. E	7. C	12. A	17. A
3. D	8. A	13. C	18. E
4. B	9. D	14. D	19. A
5. B	10. B	15. B	20. B

Section 6

1. C	10. B	19. B	28. B
2. E	11. A	20. B	29. B
3. D	12. D	21. B	30. C
4. D	13. E	22. D	31. A
5. B	14. B	23. E	32. E
6. A	15. D	24. C	33. B
7. D	16. B	25. D	34. C
8. C	17. A	26. D	35. D
9. D	18. A	27. C	

Section 7

1. A	6. B	11. B	16. D
2. C	7. A	12. C	17. A
3. B	8. D	13. A	18. E
4. E	9. E	14. C	19. B
5. B	10. C	15. B	

Section 8

1. C	5. D	9. B	13. D
2. C	6. C	10. D	14. A
3. A	7. B	11. C	15. D
4. B	8. E	12. A	16. C

Section 9

1. C	5. B	9. A	13. C
2. E	6. C	10. E	14. A
3. A	7. D	11. C	
4. B	8. B	12. E	

Chapter 26

Practice Exam 4

● ●

*T*aking an SAT exam is a little like banging your head against the wall: You feel good when you stop! If you've been working your way through the five practice tests in this book in order (although you don't have to do so), this test is almost the last bit of wall. So reread the general SAT directions at the beginning of Chapter 20 and get ready to smash any possible barrier between you and a higher score. Answers and explanations for this exam appear in Chapter 27, but don't peek ahead until after you finish going through this test!

Note: The real SAT you take will have ten sections, instead of the nine you see here, because the College Board throws in an "equating section" that doesn't count toward your score but allows the testers to evaluate new questions. The SAT doesn't tell you which section is useless (to you). Because I'm here to help you score high on the SAT, I don't include an equating section in any of the practice tests in this book. Nice of me, huh?

Answer Sheet

For Section 1, use two sheets of loose-leaf or notebook paper to write your essay. For the questions in Sections 2 through 9, use the ovals and grid-ins to record your answers. Begin with Number 1 for each new section. If any sections have fewer than 35 questions, leave the extra spaces blank.

Section 2: Critical Reading

1. Ⓐ Ⓑ Ⓒ Ⓓ Ⓔ   8. Ⓐ Ⓑ Ⓒ Ⓓ Ⓔ   15. Ⓐ Ⓑ Ⓒ Ⓓ Ⓔ   22. Ⓐ Ⓑ Ⓒ Ⓓ Ⓔ   29. Ⓐ Ⓑ Ⓒ Ⓓ Ⓔ
2. Ⓐ Ⓑ Ⓒ Ⓓ Ⓔ   9. Ⓐ Ⓑ Ⓒ Ⓓ Ⓔ   16. Ⓐ Ⓑ Ⓒ Ⓓ Ⓔ   23. Ⓐ Ⓑ Ⓒ Ⓓ Ⓔ   30. Ⓐ Ⓑ Ⓒ Ⓓ Ⓔ
3. Ⓐ Ⓑ Ⓒ Ⓓ Ⓔ   10. Ⓐ Ⓑ Ⓒ Ⓓ Ⓔ   17. Ⓐ Ⓑ Ⓒ Ⓓ Ⓔ   24. Ⓐ Ⓑ Ⓒ Ⓓ Ⓔ   31. Ⓐ Ⓑ Ⓒ Ⓓ Ⓔ
4. Ⓐ Ⓑ Ⓒ Ⓓ Ⓔ   11. Ⓐ Ⓑ Ⓒ Ⓓ Ⓔ   18. Ⓐ Ⓑ Ⓒ Ⓓ Ⓔ   25. Ⓐ Ⓑ Ⓒ Ⓓ Ⓔ   32. Ⓐ Ⓑ Ⓒ Ⓓ Ⓔ
5. Ⓐ Ⓑ Ⓒ Ⓓ Ⓔ   12. Ⓐ Ⓑ Ⓒ Ⓓ Ⓔ   19. Ⓐ Ⓑ Ⓒ Ⓓ Ⓔ   26. Ⓐ Ⓑ Ⓒ Ⓓ Ⓔ   33. Ⓐ Ⓑ Ⓒ Ⓓ Ⓔ
6. Ⓐ Ⓑ Ⓒ Ⓓ Ⓔ   13. Ⓐ Ⓑ Ⓒ Ⓓ Ⓔ   20. Ⓐ Ⓑ Ⓒ Ⓓ Ⓔ   27. Ⓐ Ⓑ Ⓒ Ⓓ Ⓔ   34. Ⓐ Ⓑ Ⓒ Ⓓ Ⓔ
7. Ⓐ Ⓑ Ⓒ Ⓓ Ⓔ   14. Ⓐ Ⓑ Ⓒ Ⓓ Ⓔ   21. Ⓐ Ⓑ Ⓒ Ⓓ Ⓔ   28. Ⓐ Ⓑ Ⓒ Ⓓ Ⓔ   35. Ⓐ Ⓑ Ⓒ Ⓓ Ⓔ

Section 3: Mathematics

1. Ⓐ Ⓑ Ⓒ Ⓓ Ⓔ   8. Ⓐ Ⓑ Ⓒ Ⓓ Ⓔ   15. Ⓐ Ⓑ Ⓒ Ⓓ Ⓔ   22. Ⓐ Ⓑ Ⓒ Ⓓ Ⓔ   29. Ⓐ Ⓑ Ⓒ Ⓓ Ⓔ
2. Ⓐ Ⓑ Ⓒ Ⓓ Ⓔ   9. Ⓐ Ⓑ Ⓒ Ⓓ Ⓔ   16. Ⓐ Ⓑ Ⓒ Ⓓ Ⓔ   23. Ⓐ Ⓑ Ⓒ Ⓓ Ⓔ   30. Ⓐ Ⓑ Ⓒ Ⓓ Ⓔ
3. Ⓐ Ⓑ Ⓒ Ⓓ Ⓔ   10. Ⓐ Ⓑ Ⓒ Ⓓ Ⓔ   17. Ⓐ Ⓑ Ⓒ Ⓓ Ⓔ   24. Ⓐ Ⓑ Ⓒ Ⓓ Ⓔ   31. Ⓐ Ⓑ Ⓒ Ⓓ Ⓔ
4. Ⓐ Ⓑ Ⓒ Ⓓ Ⓔ   11. Ⓐ Ⓑ Ⓒ Ⓓ Ⓔ   18. Ⓐ Ⓑ Ⓒ Ⓓ Ⓔ   25. Ⓐ Ⓑ Ⓒ Ⓓ Ⓔ   32. Ⓐ Ⓑ Ⓒ Ⓓ Ⓔ
5. Ⓐ Ⓑ Ⓒ Ⓓ Ⓔ   12. Ⓐ Ⓑ Ⓒ Ⓓ Ⓔ   19. Ⓐ Ⓑ Ⓒ Ⓓ Ⓔ   26. Ⓐ Ⓑ Ⓒ Ⓓ Ⓔ   33. Ⓐ Ⓑ Ⓒ Ⓓ Ⓔ
6. Ⓐ Ⓑ Ⓒ Ⓓ Ⓔ   13. Ⓐ Ⓑ Ⓒ Ⓓ Ⓔ   20. Ⓐ Ⓑ Ⓒ Ⓓ Ⓔ   27. Ⓐ Ⓑ Ⓒ Ⓓ Ⓔ   34. Ⓐ Ⓑ Ⓒ Ⓓ Ⓔ
7. Ⓐ Ⓑ Ⓒ Ⓓ Ⓔ   14. Ⓐ Ⓑ Ⓒ Ⓓ Ⓔ   21. Ⓐ Ⓑ Ⓒ Ⓓ Ⓔ   28. Ⓐ Ⓑ Ⓒ Ⓓ Ⓔ   35. Ⓐ Ⓑ Ⓒ Ⓓ Ⓔ

Section 4: Critical Reading

1. Ⓐ Ⓑ Ⓒ Ⓓ Ⓔ   8. Ⓐ Ⓑ Ⓒ Ⓓ Ⓔ   15. Ⓐ Ⓑ Ⓒ Ⓓ Ⓔ   22. Ⓐ Ⓑ Ⓒ Ⓓ Ⓔ   29. Ⓐ Ⓑ Ⓒ Ⓓ Ⓔ
2. Ⓐ Ⓑ Ⓒ Ⓓ Ⓔ   9. Ⓐ Ⓑ Ⓒ Ⓓ Ⓔ   16. Ⓐ Ⓑ Ⓒ Ⓓ Ⓔ   23. Ⓐ Ⓑ Ⓒ Ⓓ Ⓔ   30. Ⓐ Ⓑ Ⓒ Ⓓ Ⓔ
3. Ⓐ Ⓑ Ⓒ Ⓓ Ⓔ   10. Ⓐ Ⓑ Ⓒ Ⓓ Ⓔ   17. Ⓐ Ⓑ Ⓒ Ⓓ Ⓔ   24. Ⓐ Ⓑ Ⓒ Ⓓ Ⓔ   31. Ⓐ Ⓑ Ⓒ Ⓓ Ⓔ
4. Ⓐ Ⓑ Ⓒ Ⓓ Ⓔ   11. Ⓐ Ⓑ Ⓒ Ⓓ Ⓔ   18. Ⓐ Ⓑ Ⓒ Ⓓ Ⓔ   25. Ⓐ Ⓑ Ⓒ Ⓓ Ⓔ   32. Ⓐ Ⓑ Ⓒ Ⓓ Ⓔ
5. Ⓐ Ⓑ Ⓒ Ⓓ Ⓔ   12. Ⓐ Ⓑ Ⓒ Ⓓ Ⓔ   19. Ⓐ Ⓑ Ⓒ Ⓓ Ⓔ   26. Ⓐ Ⓑ Ⓒ Ⓓ Ⓔ   33. Ⓐ Ⓑ Ⓒ Ⓓ Ⓔ
6. Ⓐ Ⓑ Ⓒ Ⓓ Ⓔ   13. Ⓐ Ⓑ Ⓒ Ⓓ Ⓔ   20. Ⓐ Ⓑ Ⓒ Ⓓ Ⓔ   27. Ⓐ Ⓑ Ⓒ Ⓓ Ⓔ   34. Ⓐ Ⓑ Ⓒ Ⓓ Ⓔ
7. Ⓐ Ⓑ Ⓒ Ⓓ Ⓔ   14. Ⓐ Ⓑ Ⓒ Ⓓ Ⓔ   21. Ⓐ Ⓑ Ⓒ Ⓓ Ⓔ   28. Ⓐ Ⓑ Ⓒ Ⓓ Ⓔ   35. Ⓐ Ⓑ Ⓒ Ⓓ Ⓔ

Section 5: Mathematics

1. Ⓐ Ⓑ Ⓒ Ⓓ Ⓔ 8. Ⓐ Ⓑ Ⓒ Ⓓ Ⓔ 15. Ⓐ Ⓑ Ⓒ Ⓓ Ⓔ 22. Ⓐ Ⓑ Ⓒ Ⓓ Ⓔ 29. Ⓐ Ⓑ Ⓒ Ⓓ Ⓔ
2. Ⓐ Ⓑ Ⓒ Ⓓ Ⓔ 9. Ⓐ Ⓑ Ⓒ Ⓓ Ⓔ 16. Ⓐ Ⓑ Ⓒ Ⓓ Ⓔ 23. Ⓐ Ⓑ Ⓒ Ⓓ Ⓔ 30. Ⓐ Ⓑ Ⓒ Ⓓ Ⓔ
3. Ⓐ Ⓑ Ⓒ Ⓓ Ⓔ 10. Ⓐ Ⓑ Ⓒ Ⓓ Ⓔ 17. Ⓐ Ⓑ Ⓒ Ⓓ Ⓔ 24. Ⓐ Ⓑ Ⓒ Ⓓ Ⓔ 31. Ⓐ Ⓑ Ⓒ Ⓓ Ⓔ
4. Ⓐ Ⓑ Ⓒ Ⓓ Ⓔ 11. Ⓐ Ⓑ Ⓒ Ⓓ Ⓔ 18. Ⓐ Ⓑ Ⓒ Ⓓ Ⓔ 25. Ⓐ Ⓑ Ⓒ Ⓓ Ⓔ 32. Ⓐ Ⓑ Ⓒ Ⓓ Ⓔ
5. Ⓐ Ⓑ Ⓒ Ⓓ Ⓔ 12. Ⓐ Ⓑ Ⓒ Ⓓ Ⓔ 19. Ⓐ Ⓑ Ⓒ Ⓓ Ⓔ 26. Ⓐ Ⓑ Ⓒ Ⓓ Ⓔ 33. Ⓐ Ⓑ Ⓒ Ⓓ Ⓔ
6. Ⓐ Ⓑ Ⓒ Ⓓ Ⓔ 13. Ⓐ Ⓑ Ⓒ Ⓓ Ⓔ 20. Ⓐ Ⓑ Ⓒ Ⓓ Ⓔ 27. Ⓐ Ⓑ Ⓒ Ⓓ Ⓔ 34. Ⓐ Ⓑ Ⓒ Ⓓ Ⓔ
7. Ⓐ Ⓑ Ⓒ Ⓓ Ⓔ 14. Ⓐ Ⓑ Ⓒ Ⓓ Ⓔ 21. Ⓐ Ⓑ Ⓒ Ⓓ Ⓔ 28. Ⓐ Ⓑ Ⓒ Ⓓ Ⓔ 35. Ⓐ Ⓑ Ⓒ Ⓓ Ⓔ

9. 10. 11. 12. 13.
14. 15. 16. 17. 18.

Section 6: Multiple-Choice Writing

1. Ⓐ Ⓑ Ⓒ Ⓓ Ⓔ 8. Ⓐ Ⓑ Ⓒ Ⓓ Ⓔ 15. Ⓐ Ⓑ Ⓒ Ⓓ Ⓔ 22. Ⓐ Ⓑ Ⓒ Ⓓ Ⓔ 29. Ⓐ Ⓑ Ⓒ Ⓓ Ⓔ
2. Ⓐ Ⓑ Ⓒ Ⓓ Ⓔ 9. Ⓐ Ⓑ Ⓒ Ⓓ Ⓔ 16. Ⓐ Ⓑ Ⓒ Ⓓ Ⓔ 23. Ⓐ Ⓑ Ⓒ Ⓓ Ⓔ 30. Ⓐ Ⓑ Ⓒ Ⓓ Ⓔ
3. Ⓐ Ⓑ Ⓒ Ⓓ Ⓔ 10. Ⓐ Ⓑ Ⓒ Ⓓ Ⓔ 17. Ⓐ Ⓑ Ⓒ Ⓓ Ⓔ 24. Ⓐ Ⓑ Ⓒ Ⓓ Ⓔ 31. Ⓐ Ⓑ Ⓒ Ⓓ Ⓔ
4. Ⓐ Ⓑ Ⓒ Ⓓ Ⓔ 11. Ⓐ Ⓑ Ⓒ Ⓓ Ⓔ 18. Ⓐ Ⓑ Ⓒ Ⓓ Ⓔ 25. Ⓐ Ⓑ Ⓒ Ⓓ Ⓔ 32. Ⓐ Ⓑ Ⓒ Ⓓ Ⓔ
5. Ⓐ Ⓑ Ⓒ Ⓓ Ⓔ 12. Ⓐ Ⓑ Ⓒ Ⓓ Ⓔ 19. Ⓐ Ⓑ Ⓒ Ⓓ Ⓔ 26. Ⓐ Ⓑ Ⓒ Ⓓ Ⓔ 33. Ⓐ Ⓑ Ⓒ Ⓓ Ⓔ
6. Ⓐ Ⓑ Ⓒ Ⓓ Ⓔ 13. Ⓐ Ⓑ Ⓒ Ⓓ Ⓔ 20. Ⓐ Ⓑ Ⓒ Ⓓ Ⓔ 27. Ⓐ Ⓑ Ⓒ Ⓓ Ⓔ 34. Ⓐ Ⓑ Ⓒ Ⓓ Ⓔ
7. Ⓐ Ⓑ Ⓒ Ⓓ Ⓔ 14. Ⓐ Ⓑ Ⓒ Ⓓ Ⓔ 21. Ⓐ Ⓑ Ⓒ Ⓓ Ⓔ 28. Ⓐ Ⓑ Ⓒ Ⓓ Ⓔ 35. Ⓐ Ⓑ Ⓒ Ⓓ Ⓔ

Section 7: Critical Reading

1. Ⓐ Ⓑ Ⓒ Ⓓ Ⓔ   8. Ⓐ Ⓑ Ⓒ Ⓓ Ⓔ   15. Ⓐ Ⓑ Ⓒ Ⓓ Ⓔ   22. Ⓐ Ⓑ Ⓒ Ⓓ Ⓔ   29. Ⓐ Ⓑ Ⓒ Ⓓ Ⓔ
2. Ⓐ Ⓑ Ⓒ Ⓓ Ⓔ   9. Ⓐ Ⓑ Ⓒ Ⓓ Ⓔ   16. Ⓐ Ⓑ Ⓒ Ⓓ Ⓔ   23. Ⓐ Ⓑ Ⓒ Ⓓ Ⓔ   30. Ⓐ Ⓑ Ⓒ Ⓓ Ⓔ
3. Ⓐ Ⓑ Ⓒ Ⓓ Ⓔ   10. Ⓐ Ⓑ Ⓒ Ⓓ Ⓔ   17. Ⓐ Ⓑ Ⓒ Ⓓ Ⓔ   24. Ⓐ Ⓑ Ⓒ Ⓓ Ⓔ   31. Ⓐ Ⓑ Ⓒ Ⓓ Ⓔ
4. Ⓐ Ⓑ Ⓒ Ⓓ Ⓔ   11. Ⓐ Ⓑ Ⓒ Ⓓ Ⓔ   18. Ⓐ Ⓑ Ⓒ Ⓓ Ⓔ   25. Ⓐ Ⓑ Ⓒ Ⓓ Ⓔ   32. Ⓐ Ⓑ Ⓒ Ⓓ Ⓔ
5. Ⓐ Ⓑ Ⓒ Ⓓ Ⓔ   12. Ⓐ Ⓑ Ⓒ Ⓓ Ⓔ   19. Ⓐ Ⓑ Ⓒ Ⓓ Ⓔ   26. Ⓐ Ⓑ Ⓒ Ⓓ Ⓔ   33. Ⓐ Ⓑ Ⓒ Ⓓ Ⓔ
6. Ⓐ Ⓑ Ⓒ Ⓓ Ⓔ   13. Ⓐ Ⓑ Ⓒ Ⓓ Ⓔ   20. Ⓐ Ⓑ Ⓒ Ⓓ Ⓔ   27. Ⓐ Ⓑ Ⓒ Ⓓ Ⓔ   34. Ⓐ Ⓑ Ⓒ Ⓓ Ⓔ
7. Ⓐ Ⓑ Ⓒ Ⓓ Ⓔ   14. Ⓐ Ⓑ Ⓒ Ⓓ Ⓔ   21. Ⓐ Ⓑ Ⓒ Ⓓ Ⓔ   28. Ⓐ Ⓑ Ⓒ Ⓓ Ⓔ   35. Ⓐ Ⓑ Ⓒ Ⓓ Ⓔ

Section 8: Mathematics

1. Ⓐ Ⓑ Ⓒ Ⓓ Ⓔ   8. Ⓐ Ⓑ Ⓒ Ⓓ Ⓔ   15. Ⓐ Ⓑ Ⓒ Ⓓ Ⓔ   22. Ⓐ Ⓑ Ⓒ Ⓓ Ⓔ   29. Ⓐ Ⓑ Ⓒ Ⓓ Ⓔ
2. Ⓐ Ⓑ Ⓒ Ⓓ Ⓔ   9. Ⓐ Ⓑ Ⓒ Ⓓ Ⓔ   16. Ⓐ Ⓑ Ⓒ Ⓓ Ⓔ   23. Ⓐ Ⓑ Ⓒ Ⓓ Ⓔ   30. Ⓐ Ⓑ Ⓒ Ⓓ Ⓔ
3. Ⓐ Ⓑ Ⓒ Ⓓ Ⓔ   10. Ⓐ Ⓑ Ⓒ Ⓓ Ⓔ   17. Ⓐ Ⓑ Ⓒ Ⓓ Ⓔ   24. Ⓐ Ⓑ Ⓒ Ⓓ Ⓔ   31. Ⓐ Ⓑ Ⓒ Ⓓ Ⓔ
4. Ⓐ Ⓑ Ⓒ Ⓓ Ⓔ   11. Ⓐ Ⓑ Ⓒ Ⓓ Ⓔ   18. Ⓐ Ⓑ Ⓒ Ⓓ Ⓔ   25. Ⓐ Ⓑ Ⓒ Ⓓ Ⓔ   32. Ⓐ Ⓑ Ⓒ Ⓓ Ⓔ
5. Ⓐ Ⓑ Ⓒ Ⓓ Ⓔ   12. Ⓐ Ⓑ Ⓒ Ⓓ Ⓔ   19. Ⓐ Ⓑ Ⓒ Ⓓ Ⓔ   26. Ⓐ Ⓑ Ⓒ Ⓓ Ⓔ   33. Ⓐ Ⓑ Ⓒ Ⓓ Ⓔ
6. Ⓐ Ⓑ Ⓒ Ⓓ Ⓔ   13. Ⓐ Ⓑ Ⓒ Ⓓ Ⓔ   20. Ⓐ Ⓑ Ⓒ Ⓓ Ⓔ   27. Ⓐ Ⓑ Ⓒ Ⓓ Ⓔ   34. Ⓐ Ⓑ Ⓒ Ⓓ Ⓔ
7. Ⓐ Ⓑ Ⓒ Ⓓ Ⓔ   14. Ⓐ Ⓑ Ⓒ Ⓓ Ⓔ   21. Ⓐ Ⓑ Ⓒ Ⓓ Ⓔ   28. Ⓐ Ⓑ Ⓒ Ⓓ Ⓔ   35. Ⓐ Ⓑ Ⓒ Ⓓ Ⓔ

Section 9: Multiple-Choice Writing

1. Ⓐ Ⓑ Ⓒ Ⓓ Ⓔ   8. Ⓐ Ⓑ Ⓒ Ⓓ Ⓔ   15. Ⓐ Ⓑ Ⓒ Ⓓ Ⓔ   22. Ⓐ Ⓑ Ⓒ Ⓓ Ⓔ   29. Ⓐ Ⓑ Ⓒ Ⓓ Ⓔ
2. Ⓐ Ⓑ Ⓒ Ⓓ Ⓔ   9. Ⓐ Ⓑ Ⓒ Ⓓ Ⓔ   16. Ⓐ Ⓑ Ⓒ Ⓓ Ⓔ   23. Ⓐ Ⓑ Ⓒ Ⓓ Ⓔ   30. Ⓐ Ⓑ Ⓒ Ⓓ Ⓔ
3. Ⓐ Ⓑ Ⓒ Ⓓ Ⓔ   10. Ⓐ Ⓑ Ⓒ Ⓓ Ⓔ   17. Ⓐ Ⓑ Ⓒ Ⓓ Ⓔ   24. Ⓐ Ⓑ Ⓒ Ⓓ Ⓔ   31. Ⓐ Ⓑ Ⓒ Ⓓ Ⓔ
4. Ⓐ Ⓑ Ⓒ Ⓓ Ⓔ   11. Ⓐ Ⓑ Ⓒ Ⓓ Ⓔ   18. Ⓐ Ⓑ Ⓒ Ⓓ Ⓔ   25. Ⓐ Ⓑ Ⓒ Ⓓ Ⓔ   32. Ⓐ Ⓑ Ⓒ Ⓓ Ⓔ
5. Ⓐ Ⓑ Ⓒ Ⓓ Ⓔ   12. Ⓐ Ⓑ Ⓒ Ⓓ Ⓔ   19. Ⓐ Ⓑ Ⓒ Ⓓ Ⓔ   26. Ⓐ Ⓑ Ⓒ Ⓓ Ⓔ   33. Ⓐ Ⓑ Ⓒ Ⓓ Ⓔ
6. Ⓐ Ⓑ Ⓒ Ⓓ Ⓔ   13. Ⓐ Ⓑ Ⓒ Ⓓ Ⓔ   20. Ⓐ Ⓑ Ⓒ Ⓓ Ⓔ   27. Ⓐ Ⓑ Ⓒ Ⓓ Ⓔ   34. Ⓐ Ⓑ Ⓒ Ⓓ Ⓔ
7. Ⓐ Ⓑ Ⓒ Ⓓ Ⓔ   14. Ⓐ Ⓑ Ⓒ Ⓓ Ⓔ   21. Ⓐ Ⓑ Ⓒ Ⓓ Ⓔ   28. Ⓐ Ⓑ Ⓒ Ⓓ Ⓔ   35. Ⓐ Ⓑ Ⓒ Ⓓ Ⓔ

Section 1

The Essay

Time: 25 minutes

Directions: In response to the following prompt, write an essay on a separate sheet of paper (the answer sheet). You may use extra space in the question booklet to take notes and to organize your thoughts, but only the answer sheet will be graded.

"We learn wisdom from failure much more than from success. We often discover what will do by finding out what will not do; and probably he who never made a mistake never made a discovery." —Samuel Smiles

What does one learn, if anything, from failure? Can failure be a benefit or must it be harmful? In a well-organized essay, address these questions, developing and supporting your point of view by drawing upon history, literature, current events, or your own experience and observations.

STOP YOU MAY CHECK YOUR WORK ON THIS SECTION ONLY. DO NOT GO BACK TO ANY PREVIOUS SECTION.

Section 2
Critical Reading

Time: 25 minutes for 24 questions

Directions: Choose the *best* answer to each question. Mark the corresponding oval on the answer sheet.

Directions for Questions 1–8: Select the answer that *best* fits the meaning of the sentence.

Example: After he had broken the dining room window, Hal's mother _____ him.

(A) selected

(B) serenaded

(C) fooled

(D) scolded

(E) rewarded

The answer is (D).

---

1. Achieving a vaccination rate of 25 percent, said health officials, gives "herd _____" and prevents a serious outbreak of the disease.

    (A) mentality

    (B) immunity

    (C) contagion

    (D) conviviality

    (E) vulnerability

2. After his novel had been rejected by several publishers, the critic wrote _____ and inappropriately about every work of fiction that crossed his desk.

    (A) mercilessly

    (B) disinterestedly

    (C) justifiably

    (D) dispassionately

    (E) impartially

3. The audience, initially _____, soon listened with _____ attention to the spellbinding orator.

    (A) frustrated . . . objective

    (B) restive . . . sporadic

    (C) skeptical . . . periodic

    (D) indifferent . . . rapt

    (E) aggressive . . . erratic

4. Ms. Benning graciously chose to _____ the election to her opponent once it was clear that the voters had rejected her bid for office.

    (A) supersede

    (B) concede

    (C) transmit

    (D) transfer

    (E) supplant

5. Having chosen a _____ dessert, the diner _____ for the increased caloric intake by eating very little of the main course.

    (A) tiny . . . strove

    (B) light . . . reached

    (C) minimal . . . argued

    (D) low-calorie . . . opted

    (E) rich . . . compensated

6. Despite _____ planning, the team was surprised by the strength of its opponents.

    (A) incomplete

    (B) oppressive

    (C) meticulous

    (D) premature

    (E) untimely

Go on to next page

7. Over the course of several tours of duty, the _____ recruit became a battle-tested soldier.

   (A) raw

   (B) enlisted

   (C) veteran

   (D) patriotic

   (E) loyal

8. May, known for her _____ nature, should look for a telephone plan that allows an unlimited number of minutes.

   (A) taciturn

   (B) reserved

   (C) loquacious

   (D) diffident

   (E) combative

Directions for Questions 9–12: Choose the *best* answer to each question based on what is stated or implied in the passages or in the introductory material.

These two passages focus on scientific discovery. They are excerpted from Scientific American Inventions and Discoveries *by Rodney Carlisle (Wiley).*

Passage 1

Line   There are many devices, appliances, and simple machines so common in our everyday life that we rarely think of them as having been invented. The crank and the compound crank
(05) are such items. They did not exist in the ancient world but were common by the 1600s, employed in various practical applications such as pulling a bucket from a well on a turned shaft, and a wide variety of situations in which it was neces-
(10) sary to transform continuous rotary motion into reciprocating motion, or to transform reciprocating motion into rotary motion. The first established use of a crank was in a water-powered bellows dated to A.D. 31 in China.

Passage 11

(15)   The fact that matter is composed of discrete elements had been supposed since antiquity, with accepted science, derived from the ancient

philosopher Empedocles (493–433 B.C.), holding that all matter was composed of four essences or elements: earth, air, fire, and water. The search (20) for the magical fifth essence, or *quintessence,* was a quest of medieval alchemists. They believed that the stars, planets, and other heavenly bodies were composed of the quintessence, and that it was present on Earth but difficult to (25) extract. In their pursuit of the quintessence . . . alchemists and metallurgists identified 13 elements, mostly metals.

9. According to Passage I, the crank was

   (A) always a part of everyday life

   (B) invented in a laboratory

   (C) discovered in China in A.D. 31

   (D) created to fulfill everyday needs

   (E) overlooked until the 1600s

10. Passage I discusses "rotary motion" and "reciprocating motion" (Lines 10–12) as

    (A) types of motion transformed by cranks

    (B) necessary processes of extracting water from a well

    (C) inventions popular in the 1600s

    (D) types of motion with limited applications

    (E) incompatible with cranks

11. In the context of Line 18, "holding" may best be defined as

    (A) gripping

    (B) embracing

    (C) believing

    (D) storing

    (E) grasping

12. In contrast to the process of invention described in Passage I, the discovery of elements recounted in Passage II

    (A) is practical rather than theoretical

    (B) begins with a theory, not with an everyday need

    (C) is more modern

    (D) takes place over a longer span of time

    (E) contains a magical element

Go on to next page

This passage focuses on the work of Muhammed Yunus, an economist and banker from Bangladesh who created the Grameen Bank to give small loans to those too poor to qualify for traditional loans. The passage is excerpted from Small Loans, Big Dreams *by Alex Counts (Wiley).*

Line   The genius of Muhammed Yunus's work is not that he figured out how to empower poor people with loans, but that he was able to develop a model that he could replicate more than a thou-
(05)   sand times while maintaining control over the quality of the enterprise. The difference is critical to understanding the implications of what he has accomplished. One branch can serve 2,000 people, whereas a thousand branches can serve 2
(10)   million. It takes an entirely different set of skills to start a pilot project than it does to successfully franchise it. Pilot projects reach hundreds of poor people; franchises can touch millions.

In circles where poverty and environmental
(15)   issues are discussed, one often hears the comment "Small is beautiful." Tiny programs tailored to local needs are romanticized, while anything big — governments, corporations, even large non-profit organizations — is distrusted. Rarely is it
(20)   considered that while small may often be beautiful, small is, after all, still small. A world in which thousands of successful pilot projects reach a tiny percentage of the world's poor, and leave the vast majority untouched, is a world where mass pov-
(25)   erty is destined to persist and deepen.

It is hardly an exaggeration to say that nearly every major problem facing the world has several solutions that have been proven effective on a small scale. But only if the best of those projects
(30)   can be replicated or franchised, and expanded while maintaining reasonably high quality, will there be hope for resolving the interconnected mesh of social, environmental, and economic injustices that are tearing at the insides of humanity.

(35)   Muhammed Yunus has demonstrated that large-scale replication of an effective antipoverty strategy can be both successful and profitable. He resisted the temptation to keep Grameen small (and easily controlled by him), and in the process
(40)   reached two million borrowers, created a decentralized management structure, and trained a workforce of 11,000 people. Doing so has not always been easy. Striking the right balance

between keeping all Grameen branches similar while allowing for innovation and experimentation
(45)   came after years of trial and error. The conditions that gave rise to widespread employee discontent in 1991 were a result of bigness, and so was the gradual decline in the zealousness with which some employees carried out their duties.
(50)

Fueling the aggressive expansion program was the managing director's faith in the ability of people to use credit well even when they were not directly supervised by him. Many Grameen critics predicted disaster when Yunus was not there to
(55)   monitor everything, but their fears have proven largely unfounded. Bangladeshis, long portrayed as lacking the skills for middle management and business ownership, have demonstrated those abilities as Grameen staff and borrowers.
(60)

Other poverty-focused credit programs in Bangladesh, many of them Grameen imitators, now reach 2.5 million *additional* families. Furthermore, Grameen replication programs in other Third World countries now reach tens of
(65)   thousands of people, and many projects are growing rapidly. Each month, dozens of people from other developing countries come to Bangladesh to learn how Grameen works so that they can start similar projects after returning home.
(70)

For many years, one of the most serious criticisms of Grameen was that credit was not the magic bullet that some accused Yunus as touting it to be. The problem of poverty, critics argued, was complex, and needed a solution that took
(75)   into account not only its financial dimensions, but also things like ignorance, political power-lessness, and ill health. Other programs that provided credit, for example, required that borrowers undergo a six-month course on liter-
(80)   acy and political organizing before they were allowed to take a loan. Experts scoffed at Grameen's requiring as little as seven hours of training before releasing loans to borrowers. The conventional wisdom questioned whether poor,
(85)   uneducated people knew what to do with small loans without more guidance from above.

Yunus rejected these ideas. He admitted that poverty was a multifaceted problem, but he did not believe it necessarily needed a multifaceted solu-
(90)   tion. The poor, he argued, already had skills, were already politically conscious, and were already aware of the need for schooling and taking care of their health. It was first and foremost their lack of income that made using their skills impossible.
(95)   Providing investment capital for additional income generation, he asserted, would unlock the capacity of poor people to solve many, if not all, of the manifestations of poverty that affected their lives.

Go on to next page

13. As used in Line 11, "pilot project" is best defined by which other phrase from the passage?

    (A) "a model that he could replicate more than a thousand times" (Lines 4–5)

    (B) "circles where poverty and environmental issues are discussed" (Lines 14–15)

    (C) "Tiny programs tailored to local needs" (Lines 16–17)

    (D) "a tiny percentage of the world's poor" (Lines 22–23)

    (E) "solutions that have been proven effective on a small scale" (Lines 28–29)

14. The author's objections to pilot projects include all of the following EXCEPT that they

    (A) involve too few people

    (B) often apply only to a specific situation

    (C) can't be reproduced

    (D) are too expensive

    (E) operate on a small scale

15. The comment that "Tiny programs . . . are romanticized" implies that such programs

    (A) aren't evaluated fairly

    (B) bring people together

    (C) are seen as impractical

    (D) can accomplish more than programs with more limited goals

    (E) contrast unfavorably with government efforts

16. Lines 32–34, which reference "the interconnected mesh of social, environmental, and economic injustices that are tearing at the insides of humanity," imply that

    (A) poverty causes environmental problems

    (B) poor people are unjustly deprived in several different ways

    (C) wealthy people look down upon the poor

    (D) economic troubles should be solved through the justice system

    (E) wealthy and poor people have much in common

17. From the information given in the fourth paragraph (Lines 35–50), the reader understands that the Grameen Bank

    (A) was never controlled by Muhammed Yunus

    (B) became successful almost immediately

    (C) relies on a uniform business strategy

    (D) gives its employees too little power

    (E) allows its managers a great deal of autonomy

18. Lines 46–50 ("the conditions that gave rise to . . . their duties")

    (A) indicate that Yunus's critics were correct when they "predicted disaster" (Line 55)

    (B) are an example of the "trial and error" mentioned in Line 46

    (C) show that the "managing director's faith in the ability of people to use credit well" (Lines 52–53) was misplaced

    (D) reveal the need for Yunus "to monitor everything" (Lines 55–56)

    (E) contradict the claim that Bangladeshis were "lacking the skills for middle management and business ownership" (Lines 58–59)

19. The purpose of the sixth paragraph (Lines 61–70) is to

    (A) urge support for international relief efforts

    (B) exaggerate the magnitude of the problems faced by the Grameen Bank

    (C) indicate the scope of poverty in Bangladesh

    (D) explain that the Grameen Bank has competitors

    (E) show that the achievements of the Grameen Bank are not unique

Go on to next page

20. The critics of the Grameen Bank most likely favor programs that focus on which of the following?

    I.   Better education
    II.   Universal health care
    III. Political power for the poor

    (A) I only
    (B) II only
    (C) III only
    (D) all of the above
    (E) none of the above

21. The author refers to the "magic bullet that some accused Yunus as touting" to show that

    (A) Yunus's critics accurately represented his beliefs
    (B) Yunus's critics misinterpreted his beliefs
    (C) more than the efforts of one man are necessary to reduce poverty
    (D) Yunus boasted of his success
    (E) Yunus himself did not believe that his efforts would be successful

22. In the context of Line 92, what is the best definition of "conscious"?

    (A) aware
    (B) alert
    (C) awake
    (D) deliberate
    (E) intentional

23. With which saying would Muhammed Yunus be most likely to agree?

    (A) Small is beautiful.
    (B) Imitation is the highest form of flattery.
    (C) The love of money is the root of all evil.
    (D) A penny saved is a penny earned.
    (E) A fool and his money are soon parted.

24. The author's attitude toward Muhammed Yunus may be characterized as

    (A) skeptical
    (B) admiring
    (C) congratulatory
    (D) sympathetic
    (E) dispassionate

STOP YOU MAY CHECK YOUR WORK ON THIS SECTION ONLY. DO NOT GO BACK TO ANY PREVIOUS SECTION.

Section 3

Mathematics

Time: 25 minutes for 20 questions

Directions: Choose the *best* answer to each question. Mark the corresponding oval on the answer sheet.

Notes:

- ✔ You may use a calculator.

- ✔ All numbers used in this exam are real numbers.

- ✔ All figures lie in a plane.

- ✔ All figures may be assumed to be to scale unless the problem specifically indicates otherwise.

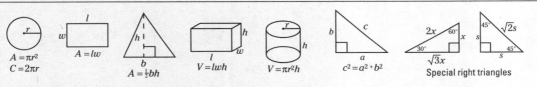

$A = \pi r^2$
$C = 2\pi r$

$A = lw$

$A = \tfrac{1}{2}bh$

$V = lwh$

$V = \pi r^2 h$

$c^2 = a^2 + b^2$

Special right triangles

There are 360 degrees of arc in a circle.

There are 180 degrees in a straight line.

There are 180 degrees in the sum of the interior angles of a triangle.

1. If four more than a number is the same as three times the number, the number must be

   (A) 1
   (B) 2
   (C) 3
   (D) 4
   (E) 5

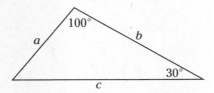

2. Based on the triangle above, which statement is true?

   (A) $a > b > c$
   (B) $a > c > b$
   (C) $b > c > a$
   (D) $b > a > c$
   (E) $c > b > a$

Go on to next page

3. Which of the following number lines represents the solution to the inequality $|x+3| < 5$?

    (A)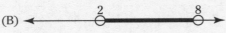

    (B) ![number line from 2 to 8 open circles]

    (C) ![number line rays beyond -8 and 2]

    (D) ![number line from -8 to 2 open circles]

    (E) ![number line solution with 2]

4. A store sign advertised, "All Coats _____% Off," but someone had forgotten to write in the correct percentage. If a coat that usually costs $75 was on sale for $60, what was the missing percentage?

    (A) 15

    (B) 20

    (C) 25

    (D) 40

    (E) 80

5. Given that $a + c = 7$ and $b - c = 4$, $a + b$ must equal

    (A) –11

    (B) –3

    (C) 3

    (D) 7

    (E) 11

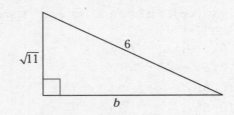

6. What is the length of side b in the triangle above?

    (A) $6 - \sqrt{11}$

    (B) 5

    (C) $\sqrt{47}$

    (D) $\sqrt{157}$

    (E) 25

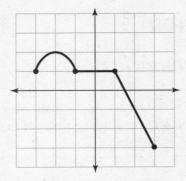

7. The graph above represents $f(x)$. If $g(x) = 2f(x) - 3$, then $g(2) =$

    (A) –5

    (B) –2

    (C) –1

    (D) 1

    (E) 5

8. If $(x + y)^2 = 53$ and $(x - y)^2 = 37$, then $xy =$

    (A) 4

    (B) 16

    (C) 45

    (D) 90

    (E) It cannot be determined from the information given.

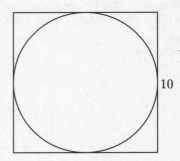

9. If a dart is thrown at the dartboard above, the probability that the dart lands in the square but *not* in the circle is closest to

    (A) 10%

    (B) 20%

    (C) 25%

    (D) 50%

    (E) 80%

Go on to next page

10. Let $x \sim y$ be defined as $\dfrac{x+y}{y-1}$. For what value of x does $x \sim 3 = x$?

    (A) 0

    (B) 1

    (C) 2

    (D) 3

    (E) 4

11. Which of the following must be true for x, given that x is a negative integer?

    (A) $x \geq -x$

    (B) $x \geq x^2$

    (C) $x \geq x^3$

    (D) $x \geq \frac{1}{x}$

    (E) $x \geq \frac{x}{2}$

12. If three consecutive odd integers have a sum of -15, the smallest of the three integers equals

    (A) -7

    (B) -6

    (C) -5

    (D) -4

    (E) -3

13. 25% of the marbles in a jar are red. After 20 red marbles are added to the jar, 50% of the marbles are now red. How many total marbles were originally in the jar?

    (A) 12

    (B) 16

    (C) 20

    (D) 40

    (E) 80

14. If $a^{-2/3} = 9$, then $a =$

    (A) $-\dfrac{27}{2}$

    (B) -6

    (C) $\dfrac{1}{27}$

    (D) $\sqrt[3]{81}$

    (E) 27

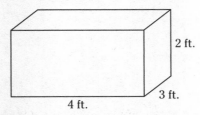

2 ft.

3 ft.

4 ft.

15. Gasoline is being poured into a cylindrical container with a radius of 5 feet and a height of 6 feet. Originally, the gasoline was stored in the box-shaped container shown here. Roughly how many of these containers would be needed to fill the tank completely?

    (A) 8

    (B) 10

    (C) 12

    (D) 15

    (E) 20

16. Line l passes through the origin and has a slope of $\frac{3}{2}$. Line m is perpendicular to line l and intersects it at the point $(-6, -4)$. Where does line m cross the y-axis?

    (A) $(0, -18)$

    (B) $(0, -13)$

    (C) $(0, -8)$

    (D) $(0, 5)$

    (E) $(-8\frac{2}{3}, 0)$

Go on to next page

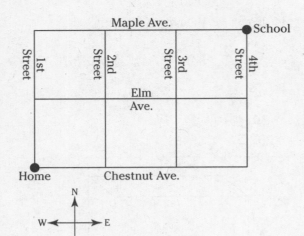

17. The diagram above shows the possible routes from Benjamin's home to his school. He always walks only north and east, and he makes sure to always walk at least one block on Elm Avenue. How many different routes can he take to get to school?

(A) Three

(B) Four

(C) Five

(D) Six

(E) Seven

18. Two circles lie in a plane and share the same center but have different radii. A line is drawn such that the line never enters the smaller circle. What is the maximum number of total points at which the line could touch the circles?

(A) 1

(B) 2

(C) 3

(D) 4

(E) 5

19. A list of three integers has an average (arithmetic mean) of 6. If the median of the numbers is −1, what is the smallest positive number that could appear in the list?

(A) 1

(B) 6

(C) 18

(D) 20

(E) 21

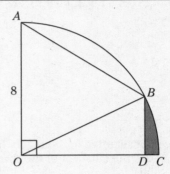

20. In the figure above, OAC is one quarter of a circle with a radius of 8. If $AB = OC$, then the area of the shaded region is

(A) $\frac{16}{3}\pi - 8\sqrt{3}$

(B) $\frac{64}{3}\pi - 16\sqrt{3}$

(C) $\frac{16}{3}\pi - 8$

(D) $16\pi - 16\sqrt{3}$

(E) $\frac{32}{3}\pi - 16$

STOP YOU MAY CHECK YOUR WORK ON THIS SECTION ONLY. DO NOT GO BACK TO ANY PREVIOUS SECTION.

Section 4
Critical Reading

Time: 25 minutes for 24 questions

Directions: Choose the *best* answer to each question. Mark the corresponding oval on the answer sheet.

Directions for Questions 1–5: Select the answer that *best* fits the meaning of the sentence.

Example: After he had broken the dining room window, Hal's mother _____ him.

(A) selected

(B) serenaded

(C) fooled

(D) scolded

(E) rewarded

The answer is (D).

---

1. Artists, however realistic their styles, are not content merely to record a scene but rather strive to _____ it.

    (A) document

    (B) beautify

    (C) symbolize

    (D) interpret

    (E) represent

2. The outcasts searched for a path out of the _____ and into the fertile _____ of acceptance.

    (A) wilderness . . . fields

    (B) cities . . . streets

    (C) towns . . . heavens

    (D) wasteland . . . void

    (E) desert . . . marsh

3. The shopper _____ through the stores in a leisurely way, more interested in passing time than acquiring items.

    (A) plodded

    (B) strolled

    (C) stomped

    (D) strutted

    (E) charged

4. Their _____ romantic bliss soon gave way to boredom, interspersed with the usual tensions of everyday life.

    (A) core

    (B) leading

    (C) initial

    (D) final

    (E) foremost

5. Antiquated handwriting is characterized by fancy _____, quite alien to the clean, modern lines favored today.

    (A) austerity

    (B) rigor

    (C) flexibility

    (D) flourishes

    (E) simplicity

Go on to next page

Directions for Questions 6–9: Read the following passages, and choose the *best* answer to each question based on what is stated or implied in the passages.

The first passage is an excerpt from Jean Jacques Rousseau's Emile. *The second is an excerpt from an autobiographical novel written by James Weldon Johnson in the early 20th century.*

Line   The newborn child needs to stretch and to move his limbs so as to draw them out of the torpor in which, rolled into a ball, they have so long remained. We do stretch his limbs, it is true,
(05) but we prevent him from moving them. We even constrain his head into a baby's cap. It seems as if we were afraid he might appear to be alive. The inaction, the constraint in which we keep his limbs, cannot fail to interfere with the circulation
(10) of the blood and of the secretions, to prevent the child from growing strong and sturdy, and to change his constitution.

6. The author probably wrote the above passage after observing babies who were

   (A) playing in a playpen

   (B) nursing from a bottle

   (C) wrapped in a blanket

   (D) bareheaded

   (E) ill

7. Which of the following best expresses the meaning of "constitution" (Line 12) in the context of this passage?

   (A) government

   (B) establishment

   (C) organization

   (D) official document

   (E) health

Line   I stood there feeling embarrassed and foolish, not knowing what to say or do. I am not sure but that he felt pretty much the same. My mother stood at my side with one hand on my shoulder,
(05) almost pushing me forward, but I did not move. I can well remember the look of disappointment, even pain, on her face; and I can now understand that she could expect nothing else but that at the name "father" I should throw myself into his arms.
(10) But I could not rise to this dramatic, or, better, melodramatic, climax. Somehow I could not arouse any considerable feeling of need for a father.

8. The narrator's attitude toward his father may best be described as

   (A) hostility

   (B) anger

   (C) antagonism

   (D) indifference

   (E) concealed joy

9. The narrator's comment that he couldn't "rise to this dramatic, or, better, melodramatic, climax" (Lines 10–11) implies that he

   (A) believes that he is in a theater

   (B) thinks his mother's expectations are unrealistic

   (C) fears that he will disappoint his father

   (D) understands the importance of the moment

   (E) dislikes any show of emotion

Directions for Questions 10–18: Read the following passage, and choose the *best* answer to each question based on what is stated or implied in the passage.

Line   I remember some bad times, most of them back home on Excenus 23; the worst was when Dad fell under the reaping machine but there was also the one when I got lost twenty miles from home with a dud radio, at the age of twelve; and
(05) the one when Uncle Charlie caught me practicing emergency turns in a helicar round the main weather-maker; and the one on Figuerra being chased by a cyber-crane; and the time when Dad decided to send me to Earth to do my Education.
(10)   This time is bad in a different way, with no sharp edges but a kind of desolation. Most people I know are feeling bad just now, because at Russett College we finished our Final Examination five days ago and Results are not
(15) due for a two weeks.
    My friend B Laydon says this is yet another Test; anyone still sane at the end being proved tough enough to break a molar on; she says also. The worst part is in bed remembering all the things
(20) she could have written and did not; the second worst is also in bed picturing how to explain to her parents when they get back to Earth that *someone* has to come bottom and in a group as brilliant as Russett College Cultural Engineering Class this is
(25) really no disgrace. I am not worried that way so

Go on to next page ➡

much, I cannot remember what I wrote anyway and I can think of one or two people I am pretty sure will come bottomer than me.

(30)   I would prefer to think it is just Finals cause me to feel miserable but it is not. In Psychology they taught us The mind has the faculty of concealing any motive it is ashamed of, especially from itself; seems unfortunately mine does not
(35) have this gadget supplied. I never wanted to come to Earth. I was sent to Russett against my will and counting the days till I could get back to Home, to Father and Excenus 23, but the sad truth is that now the longed-for moment is nearly
(40) on top of me I do not want to go.

       Dad's farm was a fine place to grow up, but now I had four years on Earth the thought of going back there makes me feel like a three-weeks' chicken got to get back in its shell. B and I are on
(45) an island in the Pacific. Her parents are on Caratacus researching on local art forms, so she and I came here to be miserable in company and away from the rest. It took me years on Earth to get used to all this water around, it seemed unnat-
(50) ural and dangerous to have it all lying loose that way, but now I shall miss even the Sea.

       The reason we have this long suspense over Finals is that they will not use Reading Machines to mark the papers for fear of cutting down criti-
(55) cal judgment; so each paper has to be read word by word by three Examiners and there are forty-three of us and we wrote six papers each. What I think is I am sorry for the Examiners, but B says they were the ones who set the papers and it
(60) serves them perfectly right.

       One of the main attractions on this Island is swimming under water, especially by moonlight. Dad sent me a fish-boat as a birthday present two years back, but I never used it yet on
(65) account of my above-mentioned attitude to water. Now I got this feeling of Carpe Diem[1], make the most of Earth while I am on it because probably I shall not pass this way again.

       1. A Latin phrase usually translated as "seize the day."

10. Based on evidence from the passage, which of the following is probably true about "Excenus 23" (Line 2)?

    I.   It is an area of Earth.

    II. It has a dry climate.

    III. It is a fantasy world created by the narrator.

    (A) I only

    (B) II only

    (C) III only

    (D) II and III only

    (E) none of the above

11. The narrator's statement that "This time is bad in a different way, with no sharp edges" (Lines 11–12) indicates that the narrator

    (A) has adapted to the situation

    (B) is upset about final examinations

    (C) feels a general depression

    (D) is extremely upset but reluctant to admit it

    (E) hides his or her feelings

12. The "Test" referred to in Line 18 is

    (A) waiting for exam results

    (B) grades on the Finals

    (C) pleasing one's parents

    (D) a dental exam

    (E) competition for top grades

13. Which of the following best expresses the meaning of "tough enough to break a molar on" (Line 19)?

    (A) a common, painful situation

    (B) containing an obstacle that must be avoided

    (C) tough, but a natural part of life

    (D) so difficult that one falls apart

    (E) hard enough to damage a sturdy body part

14. The narrator's reference to "a three-weeks' chicken got to get back in its shell" (Lines 43–44) implies that

    (A) the narrator has outgrown her home

    (B) the narrator can't wait to leave Earth

    (C) the narrator feels stranded

    (D) returning home is desirable

    (E) the narrator must struggle to break free of her father

15. The narrator and B Laydon differ in that B

    (A) generally gets better grades than the narrator

    (B) wants to return to her parents

    (C) is more likely to criticize adults

    (D) is interested in art

    (E) likes the water

Go on to next page ➡

16. The narrator and B Laydon want to be "away from the rest" (Line 48) probably because the other students

    (A) did worse on their exams
    (B) didn't like B Laydon and the narrator
    (C) were more willing to leave Earth
    (D) were afraid of being so close to water
    (E) had additional exams

17. The declaration that "I shall miss even the Sea" reveals the narrator's

    (A) hatred of water
    (B) plans to avoid the Island
    (C) attachment to her life on the Island
    (D) regret at losing other aspects of life on Earth
    (E) commitment to sailing

18. Given the narrator's reference to "Carpe Diem," which of the following actions is likely?

    (A) B and the narrator will stay on the island.
    (B) The narrator will find a way to return to Earth.
    (C) The father will visit the narrator.
    (D) The narrator will sail in a boat.
    (E) The narrator will refuse to leave Earth.

Directions for Questions 19–24: Read the following passage, which is from *The Universal Book of Astronomy from the Andromeda Galaxy to the Zone of Avoidance* by David J. Darling (Wiley). Answer the questions following the passage by choosing the *best* answer.

Line   Mars has a varied and interesting surface. The southern hemisphere is dominated by ancient cratered highlands similar to those of the Moon. In contrast, most of the northern hemisphere con-
(05) sists of plains that are much younger, lower in elevation, and have a more complex history. An abrupt elevation change of several kilometers seems to occur at the boundary. The origin of this global dichotomy and sharp boundary are
(10) unknown; one theory invokes a massive impact shortly after Mars was formed.

Mars has an important place in human imagination due to long-standing speculation that it harbors, or has harbored, life. This idea was encouraged, in the last quarter of the nineteenth (15) century, by reported observations of linear features on the surface, argued by Percival Lowell and some others to be artificial, and of seasonal changes in the brightness of some areas that were thought to be caused by vegetation growth. (20) The linear features are now known to be nonexistent or in some cases, ancient dry water-courses. The color changes have been ascribed to dust storms. However, interest has been rekindled in the possibility of Martian life by several factors. (25) These include controversial remains contained in meteorites that have come from Mars, mounting evidence that water has played — and may continue to play — a decisive role in the Martian surface and subsurface environment, and the (30) discovery of hardy microbes on Earth (known as extremophiles) that would probably be capable of surviving on Mars. The Viking landers[1] carried out a series of life-seeking experiments but produced either negative or ambiguous results. (35) Further investigations are planned.

Much of the renewed optimism for life on Mars comes from a wealth of data suggesting that, up to about 3.5 billion years ago, Mars was much more like Earth, with large amounts of surface (40) water — a key ingredient to life as we know it. Some images, showing what appear to be recently formed gullies and debris flow features, even hint at the continued presence of liquid water, possibly in subsurface aquifers. Especially intriguing (45) are dark stains that have appeared in a period of less than a year in certain regions, such as around Olympus Mons. Measurements strongly indicate that vast amounts of water, most of it probably frozen, lie at shallow depths over much of the (50) planet's surface.

1. Unmanned vehicles sent to the surface of Mars to gather information.

19. The "global dichotomy" (Line 9) is

    (A) an impact of massive proportions
    (B) a split between those who believe that life exists on Mars and those who don't
    (C) a border
    (D) two different surface textures and ages
    (E) linear features

Go on to next page

20. In the context of Line 14, which of the following best expresses the meaning of "harbors"?

    (A) ports

    (B) anchorages

    (C) shelters

    (D) refuges

    (E) embraces

21. Percival Lowell's observations of Mars (Lines 16–17) led him to conclude that

    (A) living beings constructed highways or canals on Mars

    (B) Mars changes color because of disturbances in its dust

    (C) meteorites struck Mars

    (D) microbes lived on Mars

    (E) Mars was lifeless

22. According to the passage, all of the following statements about Mars are true EXCEPT

    (A) Mars has enough water to sustain life.

    (B) Some microbes on Earth could survive on Mars.

    (C) Human beings have been fascinated by the possibility of life on Mars.

    (D) Mars expeditions have discovered evidence of extinct life forms.

    (E) Mars expeditions have not found evidence of living beings.

23. The statement that "interest has been rekindled" (Line 24) implies which of the following?

    (A) Scientists never give up.

    (B) For a period of time, people discounted the possibility of life on Mars.

    (C) Funding for Mars expeditions is dependent upon scientists' interests.

    (D) Scientific experiments are variable.

    (E) Evidence of life on Mars is difficult to obtain.

24. In the context of Line 31, "hardy" may best be defined as

    (A) enduring

    (B) difficult

    (C) tiny

    (D) extreme

    (E) independent

STOP YOU MAY CHECK YOUR WORK ON THIS SECTION ONLY. DO NOT GO BACK TO ANY PREVIOUS SECTION.

Section 5

Mathematics

Time: 25 minutes for 18 questions

Directions: This section contains two different types of questions. For Questions 1–8, choose the *best* answer to each question. Mark the corresponding oval on the answer sheet. For Questions 9–18, follow the separate directions provided before those questions.

Notes:

- ✔ You may use a calculator.
- ✔ All numbers used in this exam are real numbers.
- ✔ All figures lie in a plane.
- ✔ All figures may be assumed to be to scale unless the problem specifically indicates otherwise.

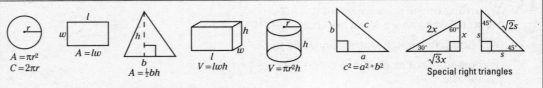

$A = \pi r^2$
$C = 2\pi r$

$A = lw$

$A = \frac{1}{2}bh$

$V = lwh$

$V = \pi r^2 h$

$c^2 = a^2 + b^2$

Special right triangles

There are 360 degrees of arc in a circle.

There are 180 degrees in a straight line.

There are 180 degrees in the sum of the interior angles of a triangle.

1. Which of the following points is farthest from 2 on a number line?

    (A) −2

    (B) ½

    (C) $\sqrt{2}$

    (D) 2.2

    (E) $2\sqrt{2}$

2. The chart shows the profit a company made on two products over a five-year period. During what year was the company's total profit the greatest?

    (A) 2000

    (B) 2001

    (C) 2002

    (D) 2003

    (E) 2004

3. Between which two years did Product X have the largest *percent* increase in profit?

    (A) 2000 and 2001

    (B) 2001 and 2002

    (C) 2002 and 2003

    (D) 2003 and 2004

    (E) 2004 and 2005

Questions 2 and 3 refer to the following chart.

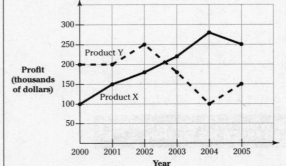

Go on to next page

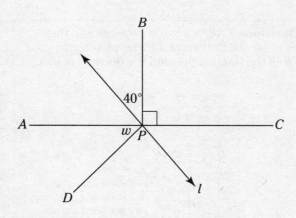

Note: Figure not to scale

4. In the figure above, if *APC* is a straight line and line *l* bisects angle *DPC,* what is the measure of the angle marked *w?*

    (A) 40°

    (B) 50°

    (C) 60°

    (D) 70°

    (E) 80°

5. A store sells T-shirts for $15.00 each. If you buy 2, 3, or 4 shirts, every shirt after the first is 20% off. After this, every shirt after the fourth is 50% off the original price. An expression that represents the total cost, *C*, of buying *n* shirts, where *n* > 4, would be

    (A) $C = 15n$

    (B) $C = 15 + 12(n - 1) + 7.50(n - 4)$

    (C) $C = 15 + 12(n - 4) + 7.5n$

    (D) $C = 51 + 7.5(n - 4)$

    (E) $C = 51 + 7.5n$

6. If *j* is positive and *k* is negative, which of the following is the greatest?

    (A) $j + k$

    (B) $j - k$

    (C) jk

    (D) $k - j$

    (E) $k \div j$

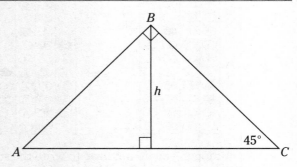

7. If the line segment marked *h* in the figure above is 5 cm long, then the perimeter of triangle *ABC* equals

    (A) 10

    (B) $10 + 10\sqrt{2}$

    (C) 20

    (D) $20 + 20\sqrt{2}$

    (E) 30

$$1\ 1\ 2\ 1\ 2\ 3\ 1\ 2\ 3\ 4\ 1\ 2\ 3\ 4\ 5\ldots$$

8. The number above begins with a "1", then continues "12," "123," "1234," and so on until the number "9" is reached. How many digits are in the final number?

    (A) 36

    (B) 40

    (C) 45

    (D) 54

    (E) 81

Go on to next page

Directions for student-produced response Questions 9–18: Solve the problem and then write your answer in the boxes on the answer sheet. Mark the ovals corresponding to your answer, as shown in the following example. Note the fraction line and the decimal points.

Answer: $^7/_2$ Answer: 3.25   Answer: 853

Write your answer in the box. You may start your answer in any column.

Although you do not have to write the solutions in the boxes, you do have to blacken the corresponding ovals. You should fill in the boxes to avoid confusion. Only the blackened ovals will be scored. The numbers in the boxes will not be read.

There are no negative answers.

Mixed numbers, such as 3½, must be gridded in as decimals (3.5) or as fractions (⅞). Do not grid in 3½; it will be read as ³½.

Grid in a decimal as far as possible. Do not round your answer and leave some boxes empty.

A question may have more than one answer. Grid in only one answer.

9. At a certain school, each student has an ID number containing three digits. The number may not begin with a zero, and may not end with a 7, 8, or 9. How many possible ID numbers are there?

10. Lorraine jogged for 8 minutes at a rate of 400 feet per minute, then walked for 2 minutes at a rate of 200 feet per minute. What was her average speed during this time, in feet per minute?

11. Find n if $32^n = 2^{2n+33}$.

12. Let a number be "pretty" if it is divisible by 5. Let a number be "friendly" if it only contains even digits (42, for example). Let a number be "happy" if its digits add up to 10 (523, for example). Find the *smallest* number that is pretty, friendly, and happy.

13. At South Side High School, one-half of the juniors have English class second period, one-third of the juniors have English class fifth period, and 12 students have English class sixth period. If every student has exactly one English class, how many students are in the junior class?

Go on to next page

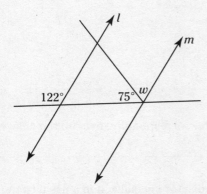

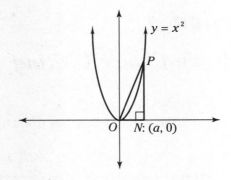

14. In the drawing above, $l \parallel m$. Find the value of w in degrees.

15. Find a value of x which satisfies $x^2 + x = 72$.

16. If $x + 11 = 5y$ and $3x - 11 = 9y$, find the value of $\frac{x}{y}$.

17. Given that point P in the drawing above lies on the graph of $y = x^2$, and that the area of triangle NOP is 108, find a.

18. Given $f(x) = \sqrt{164 + 5x}$ and $g(x) = x - 8$, find the value of x for which $f(x) = g(x)$.

Section 6
Multiple-Choice Writing

Time: 25 minutes for 35 questions

Directions: Choose the *best* answer to each question. Mark the corresponding oval on the answer sheet.

Directions for Questions 1–11: Each sentence is followed by five choices. Choose the answer that *best* improves the sentence. If the underlined portion of the sentence is best left alone, choose (A).

Example: <u>Bert and him went</u> to the store to buy boots in preparation for the approaching storm.

(A) Bert and him went

(B) Bert and he went

(C) Bert and he had gone

(D) Bert and him had gone

(E) Bert and himself went

The correct answer is (B).

1. <u>The building inspector arriving</u> in ten minutes, the construction manager instructed the brick layers to complete the wall quickly.

   (A) The building inspector arriving

   (B) The building inspector will be arriving

   (C) Because of the building inspector arriving

   (D) Since the building inspector would have arrived

   (E) Because the building inspector would arrive

2. The actor specialized in a nasal twang, <u>sounding as if he swallowed a balloon</u>.

   (A) sounding as if he swallowed a balloon

   (B) sounding as if he had swallowed a balloon

   (C) sounding like a balloon he swallowed

   (D) and he sounded as if he swallowed a balloon

   (E) and he sounded as if he would have swallowed a balloon

3. The fierce gusts of wind from this storm, now approaching the coast, <u>breaks previous records for that area</u>.

   (A) breaks previous records for that area

   (B) breaks records for that area that were made previously

   (C) break previous records for that area

   (D) previously breaks records for that area

   (E) breaks the area's previous records

4. The plane, which was flying low over the city, <u>and which was equipped with special lenses to capture night images</u>, despite the low levels of light.

   (A) and which was equipped with special lenses to capture night images

   (B) was equipped with special lenses to capture night images

   (C) equipped as it was with special lenses to capture night images

   (D) being equipped with special lenses to capture night images

   (E) because it was equipped with special lenses capturing night images

Go on to next page

5. The jury discussed the matter whether the defendant should be found guilty, considering the fact that the defense attorney presented compelling reasons for acquittal.

   (A) the matter whether the defendant should be found guilty

   (B) the matter as to whether the defendant should be found guilty

   (C) the defendant's being found guilty, if it was right

   (D) whether the defendant should be found guilty

   (E) either finding the defendant guilty or not

6. The passengers waited five hours to be evacuated from the derailed train, fortunately no one was injured.

   (A) the derailed train, fortunately no one was injured

   (B) the derailed train, fortunately, no one was injured

   (C) the derailed train; fortunately no one was injured

   (D) the derailed train although fortunately no one was injured

   (E) the derailed train, it was fortunate that no one was injured

7. Being as it was suspicious, the old bones the janitor found were preserved for inspection by police officers.

   (A) Being as it was suspicious, the old bones the janitor found were preserved

   (B) Suspiciously, the janitor's discovery of old bones was preserved for inspection

   (C) Being that it was suspicious, the old bones the janitor found were preserved

   (D) The janitor preserved the old bones found suspiciously

   (E) Because the old bones were suspicious, the janitor preserved them

8. The chalk dust and mold in that classroom may cause health problems for those who spend time there.

   (A) may cause health problems for those who spend time there

   (B) may be causing people, spending time there, health problems

   (C) may cause one who spends time there health problems

   (D) may cause health problems for the ones spending time there

   (E) perhaps causing health problems for those spending time there

9. The new electronic reading device, capable of containing hundreds of books and lightweight as well for easy travel.

   (A) device, capable of containing

   (B) device, and it is capable of containing

   (C) device, capable to contain

   (D) device is capable of containing

   (E) device, being capable of containing

10. Because of the slow economy, the luxury department store is selling their merchandise at bargain-basement prices.

    (A) is selling their merchandise

    (B) are selling their merchandise

    (C) sells their merchandise

    (D) is selling its merchandise

    (E) having sold their merchandise

11. One factor matters more than deficit spending, depletion of the Federal Reserve funds, and a high unemployment rate: that consumers are confident.

    (A) rate: that consumers are confident

    (B) rate: consumer confidence

    (C) rate; how confident consumers are

    (D) rate, how confident consumers are

    (E) rate; consumers being confident

Go on to next page

Directions for Questions 12–29: In each of the following sentences, identify the underlined portion that contains an error. If a sentence contains no errors, choose (E) for "no error."

Example:

<u>Irregardless</u> of the fact that the National
        A
Weather Service <u>predicted rain,</u> Dexter <u>resented</u>
                        B   C
the <u>students' request</u> to postpone the picnic.
        D

<u>No error.</u>
        E

The correct answer is (A).

12. <u>Eaten by koala bears</u>, eucalyptus <u>leaves</u> are
        A   B
    tender <u>when young,</u> and <u>they are prized</u>
                C   D
    by people who appreciate the species.
    <u>No error.</u>
        E

13. The stuffed monkey, <u>along with</u> several
                            A
    <u>other</u> toys, <u>sits</u> on the shelf, ready and will-
        B   C
    ing to comfort any sick <u>child, who wants</u> to
                                D
    play. <u>No error.</u>
            E

14. <u>The title of Blue Highways</u>, an account of a
        A
    trip author William Least Heat Moon <u>took</u>
                                            B
    on back roads, <u>coming</u> from the blue lines
                        C
    <u>that show the location</u> of these roads on
        D
    standard maps. <u>No error.</u>
                        E

15. The <u>reason</u> the physician <u>has recom-</u>
            A   B
    <u>mended</u> that test is <u>because</u> the patient's
                                C
    blood pressure drops at <u>seemingly random</u>
                                D
    intervals. <u>No error.</u>
                    E

16. If <u>you subscribe</u> <u>to premium cable television</u>
        A   B   C
    channels, a viewer may <u>nearly double</u> the
                                D
    monthly charges. <u>No error.</u>
                        E

17. <u>It has become</u> <u>more clearer</u> in recent years
        A   B
    exactly why standardized tests <u>have become</u>
                                        C
    the <u>criteria</u> for college entrance. <u>No error.</u>
            D   E

18. <u>Although the refrigerator was operating</u>
        A
    <u>continuously</u>, the ice cream <u>had melted</u>
        B   C
    before <u>we removed it</u> from the freezer.
                D
    <u>No error.</u>
        E

19. Many artists <u>are not appreciated</u> during
                        A
    <u>his or her lifetime</u>, but after death some
        B
    unknown painters <u>go on</u> to achieve fame
                        C
    and <u>to earn</u> a fortune for their heirs.
            D
    <u>No error.</u>
        E

20. Each of the editors <u>agree</u> <u>that the article</u>
                            A   B
    <u>should be published</u>, but <u>neither is</u> sure
                                        C
    that the author will accept minimal pay-
    ment for <u>his efforts</u>. <u>No error.</u>
                D   E

21. <u>The white whale</u> in the classic <u>American</u>
        A   B
    novel <u>Moby Dick</u> <u>is</u> probably more famous
                        C
    than <u>any animal</u> in fiction. <u>No error.</u>
            D   E

22. A number of letters <u>has been addressed</u>
                            A
    <u>incorrectly</u>, but the post office <u>will return</u>
        B   C
    them <u>to us</u> in time to reprint the labels.
            D
    <u>No error.</u>
        E

Go on to next page

23. That gossipy crowd <u>loves</u> to spread the
    _A
    latest scandal<u>, true or not,</u> but <u>they</u> seldom
    _B _C
    talk <u>to you and I</u> because we know the
    _D
    truth. <u>No error.</u>
    _E

24. <u>Every</u> smile <u>from</u> a baby <u>is</u> delightful, but
    _A _B _C
    the first smile is <u>most</u> special than any
    _D
    other. <u>No error.</u>
    _E

25. One difficulty <u>facing</u> the principal is
    _A
    <u>how to improve</u> attendance <u>while he</u>
    _B _C
    <u>has to avoid</u> overcrowded classrooms
    <u>in an era when constructing</u> a new facility
    _D
    isn't possible. <u>No error.</u>
    _E

26. The actors <u>which</u> <u>need</u> more time to learn
    _A _B
    <u>their</u> lines <u>are required</u> to attend extra
    _C _D
    rehearsals every evening this week. <u>No error.</u>
    _E

27. President Abraham Lincoln<u>,</u> <u>whose</u>
    _A _B
    Emancipation Proclamation <u>is</u> a key
    _C
    moment in American history<u>,</u> <u>being often</u>
    _A _D
    studied in school. <u>No error.</u>
    _E

28. <u>Traditional</u> Spanish statues <u>may be</u>
    _A _B
    identified <u>easy</u> by <u>their</u> painted and carved
    _C _C
    wood surfaces. <u>No error.</u>
    _E

29. <u>Living in a large metropolitan area</u>, the
    _A
    sidewalks <u>are</u> always <u>crowded, and</u> the
    _B _C
    streets are clogged <u>with cars.</u> <u>No error.</u>
    _D _E

Directions for Questions 30–35: These questions are based on the following essay. Choose the best answer to each question.

[1] The ladder I bought last week has a sticker on it. [2] The sticker tells me that I "could be injured" if I fall off the ladder. [3] I guess the ladder company is afraid that I will sue them if I lose my balance and am injured. [4] Recently, a student's family sued a school district because their daughter broke her ankle sliding into a base. [5] She was playing softball, and the family said they didn't teach her how to slide well enough!

[6] It seems that common sense isn't assumed anymore. [7] People sue because their coffee is hot or because they take the wrong dose of medicine. [8] Matches are labeled saying that they can start fires! [9] The buyer of a product should have some responsibility. [10] Of course, sometimes a product is defective. [11] When a person get hurt from a product that isn't designed properly, they should be able to sue and get their medical bills paid. [12] However, the general public and companies are important. [13] Consumers should be protected, but manufacturers should also be protected from irresponsible consumers.

Go on to next page

30. Which of the following would be the best revision, if any, of Sentences 1 and 2?

    (A) The ladder I bought last week has a sticker on it. The sticker tells me that I "could be injured" if I fall off the ladder. (no change)

    (B) The ladder I bought last week has a sticker on it; it tells me that I "could be injured" if I fall off.

    (C) The ladder I bought last week has a sticker on it, which tells me that I "could be injured" if I fall off.

    (D) According to the sticker, I "could be injured" by me falling off the ladder I bought last week.

    (E) The ladder I bought last week has a sticker warning me that I "could be injured" if I fall off.

31. Which of these sentences, if any, should be inserted between Sentences 3 and 4?

    (A) Leave unchanged.

    (B) I understand the ladder manufacturer's fear, because some people sue for injuries they themselves should have prevented.

    (C) I am not the only one who could sue; others do too.

    (D) Lawsuits, which worry the ladder company, happen at times, even when they should not.

    (E) I won't sue because I won't fall off the ladder, but sometimes people do get hurt.

32. To improve the logical structure of this essay, which change should the writer make?

    (A) Leave unchanged.

    (B) Move Sentence 6 to the end of the first paragraph. Begin the second paragraph with Sentence 7.

    (C) Move Sentences 7 and 8 to the end of the first paragraph.

    (D) Delete Sentence 6.

    (E) Begin the essay with Sentence 6.

33. How should Sentence 11 be revised?

    (A) When a person get hurt from a product that isn't designed properly, they should be able to sue and get their medical bills paid. (no change)

    (B) When a person gets hurt from a product that isn't designed properly, you should be able to sue and get your medical bills paid.

    (C) When people get hurt from a product that isn't designed properly, they should be able to sue and get their medical bills paid.

    (D) People can be injured by their products, that aren't designed properly, and they should sue for medical expenses.

    (E) Injured by a product that isn't designed properly, they should be able to sue and get their medical bills paid.

34. Which of the following is the best revision of Sentence 12?

    (A) Leave unchanged.

    (B) Omit.

    (C) Combine it with Sentence 13.

    (D) Move it to the end of the essay.

    (E) Insert it before Sentence 1.

35. Which is the primary strategy used in this essay?

    (A) narration

    (B) description

    (C) examples

    (D) quotations

    (E) symbolism

STOP YOU MAY CHECK YOUR WORK ON THIS SECTION ONLY. DO NOT GO BACK TO ANY PREVIOUS SECTION.

Section 7
Critical Reading

> **Time:** 20 minutes for 19 questions
>
> **Directions:** Choose the *best* answer to each question. Mark the corresponding oval on the answer sheet.

> **Directions for Questions 1–6:** Select the answer that *best* fits the meaning of the sentence.
>
> Example: After he had broken the dining room window, Hal's mother _____ him.
>
> (A) selected
>
> (B) serenaded
>
> (C) fooled
>
> (D) scolded
>
> (E) rewarded
>
> The answer is (D).

1. Studies show that teenagers often _____ parental advice and turn instead to _____.

    (A) accept . . . friends

    (B) reject . . . peers

    (C) consider . . . experts

    (D) ponder . . . relatives

    (E) respect . . . grandparents

2. "I am not _____," declared the host. "I am open to all opinions, if they are supported by evidence and logic."

    (A) dogmatic

    (B) flexible

    (C) dictatorial

    (D) assertive

    (E) repressive

3. In addition to capturing vast amounts of data, the newest scientific instruments also _____ the information.

    (A) survey

    (B) gather

    (C) probe

    (D) analyze

    (E) appraise

4. The cause of vertigo, or dizziness, may not always be _____ unless other physical symptoms are present.

    (A) examined

    (B) investigated

    (C) ascertained

    (D) theorized

    (E) instituted

5. The grueling ordeal that marathon runners undergo may take a toll, but _____ athletes minimize the chances of injury.

    (A) motivated

    (B) physical

    (C) optimistic

    (D) recreational

    (E) fit

6. To make the bill more _____ to voters, the senator added an amendment that phased in the tax increase.

    (A) palatable

    (B) abhorrent

    (C) interesting

    (D) diverting

    (E) onerous

Go on to next page

Directions for Questions 7–19: Choose the *best* answer to each question based on what is stated or implied in the passages or in the introductory material.

Both passages discuss Death Valley, an area in the western United States.

Passage 1

Line The moon gave us so much light that we decided we would start on our course, and get as far as we could before the hot sun came out, and so we went on slowly and carefully in the partial
(05) darkness, the only hope left to us being that our strength would hold out till we could get to the shining snow on the great mountain before us. We reached the foot of the range we were descending about sunrise. There was here a wide wash from
(10) the snow mountain, down which some water had sometime run after a big storm, and had divided into little rivulets only reaching out a little way before they had sunk into the sand.

We had no idea we could now find any water
(15) till we at least got very near the snow, and as the best way to reach it we turned up the wash although the course was nearly to the north. The course was up a gentle grade and seemed quite sandy and not easy to travel. It looked as if there
(20) was an all day walk before us, and it was quite a question if we could live long enough to make the distance. There were quite strong indications that the water had run here not so very long ago, and we could trace the course of the little
(25) streams round among little sandy islands. A little stunted brush grew here, but it was so brittle that the stems would break as easy as an icicle.

In order to not miss a possible bit of water we separated and agreed upon a general course,
(30) and that if either one found water he should fire his gun as a signal. After about a mile or so had been gone over I heard Roger's gun and went in his direction. He had found a little ice that had frozen under the clear sky. It was not thicker
(35) than window glass. After putting a piece in our mouths we gathered all we could and put it into the little quart camp kettle to melt. We gathered just a kettle full, besides what we ate as we were gathering, and kindled a little fire and melted it.
(40) I can but think how providential it was that we started in the night, for in an hour after the sun had risen that little sheet of ice would have melted and the water sank into the sand. Having quenched our thirst we could now eat, and found
(45) that we were nearly starved also. In making this meal we used up all our little store of water, but we felt refreshed and our lives renewed so that we had better courage to go on.

Passage 11

The desert floras shame us with their cheerful adaptations to the seasonal limitations. Their
(50) whole duty is to flower and fruit, and they do it hardly, or with tropical luxuriance, as the rain admits. It is recorded in the report of the Death Valley expedition that after a year of abundant rains, on the Colorado Desert was found a speci-
(55) men of Amaranthus ten feet high. A year later the same species in the same place matured in the drought at four inches. One hopes the land may breed like qualities in her human offspring, not tritely to "try," but to do. Seldom does the desert
(60) herb attain the full stature of the type. Extreme aridity and extreme altitude have the same dwarfing effect, so that we find in the high Sierras and in Death Valley related species in miniature that reach a comely growth in mean temperatures.
(65) Very fertile are the desert plants in expedients to prevent evaporation, turning their foliage edgewise toward the sun, growing silky hairs, exuding gum. The wind, which has a long sweep, harries and helps them. It rolls up dunes about the stocky
(70) stems, encompassing and protective, and above the dunes, which may be, as with the mesquite, three times as high as a man, the blossoming twigs flourish and bear fruit.

There are many areas in the desert where
(75) drinkable water lies within a few feet of the surface, indicated by the mesquite and the bunch grass (Sporobolus airoides). It is this nearness of unimagined help that makes the tragedy of desert deaths. It is related that the final break-
(80) down of that hapless party that gave Death Valley its forbidding name occurred in a locality where shallow wells would have saved them. But how were they to know that? Properly equipped it is possible to go safely across that ghastly
(85) sink, yet every year it takes its toll of death, and yet men find there sun-dried mummies, of whom no trace or recollection is preserved. To underestimate one's thirst, to pass a given landmark to the right or left, to find a dry spring where one
(90) looked for running water — there is no help for any of these things.

7. In the context of Line 9, "wash" may best be defined as

(A) clean snow

(B) bathing in water

(C) a coating of snow

(D) area eroded by water

(E) a surge of water

Go on to next page

8. Which statement about the narrator and his fellow traveler in Passage I is true?

    (A) They are tired from hiking all day.

    (B) The narrator and his fellow traveler cannot agree on a course of action.

    (C) They are in danger of death.

    (D) Their advance planning saves their lives.

    (E) They compete for food and water.

9. Which statement most likely reflects the views of the travelers in Passage I?

    (A) One for all and all for one.

    (B) Every man for himself.

    (C) Absence makes the heart grow fonder.

    (D) You don't know what you have until you lose it.

    (E) No news is good news.

10. The author of Passage II would probably see the "brush" referred to in Line 26 as evidence of

    (A) "cheerful adaptations" (Lines 49–50)

    (B) "tropical luxuriance" (Line 52)

    (C) "full stature" (Line 61)

    (D) "stocky stems" (Lines 70–71)

    (E) "blossoming twigs" (Lines 73–74)

11. The narrator in Passage I sees their early start as "providential" (Line 40) for which of the following reasons?

    I. The travelers knew that ice would melt in the heat of the day.

    II. The travelers started early to avoid the heat of the day.

    III. The travelers found the ice by chance.

    (A) I only

    (B) II only

    (C) III only

    (D) I and II

    (E) II and III

12. Why do desert plants "shame us" (Line 49)?

    (A) Plants are more adaptable than people.

    (B) Plants provide flowers and fruit.

    (C) Human actions harm the environment.

    (D) Humans use plants without thinking.

    (E) Some plant species attain greater height than is possible for human beings.

13. Which of the statements below best expresses the meaning of "One hopes the land may breed like qualities in her human offspring" (Lines 58–59)?

    (A) Human beings, like plants, should conserve energy.

    (B) Human beings should cultivate the same survival skills seen in desert plants.

    (C) Human beings should be more in tune with nature.

    (D) A natural habitat should be respected.

    (E) Trying isn't good enough.

14. The author of Passage II cites all of the following as factors influencing the survival of desert plants EXCEPT

    (A) size

    (B) shape

    (C) age

    (D) foliage

    (E) dunes

15. According to Passage II, why is desert death a "tragedy" (Line 79)?

    (A) Travelers don't understand how difficult it is to cross the desert.

    (B) Most deaths are preventable.

    (C) Help is not available when travelers need it.

    (D) Many die because they are not aware of nearby water sources.

    (E) Desert maps are unreliable.

Go on to next page

16. Which of the following best defines "sink" in the context of Line 86?

    (A) basin

    (B) submerge

    (C) desert

    (D) subsurface

    (E) water source

17. The "mummies" (Line 87) are

    (A) artifacts of an ancient civilization

    (B) animals preserved by the dry climate

    (C) the remains of travelers

    (D) the bodies of desert dwellers

    (E) museum exhibits

18. Which comment would the author of Passage II be most likely to make to the travelers described in Passage I?

    (A) You should have stayed away from the desert.

    (B) It was your responsibility to be aware of all water sources.

    (C) You must prepare well in order to have a safe journey.

    (D) You should have looked for landmarks.

    (E) On arrival, adapt yourself to the desert environment.

19. In comparison with Passage I, Passage II is

    (A) more creative

    (B) more specific

    (C) more personal

    (D) more scientific

    (E) less idealistic

STOP YOU MAY CHECK YOUR WORK ON THIS SECTION ONLY. DO NOT GO BACK TO ANY PREVIOUS SECTION.

Section 8

Mathematics

Time: 20 minutes for 16 questions
Directions: Choose the *best* answer to each question. Mark the corresponding oval on the answer sheet.

Notes:

✔ You may use a calculator.

✔ All numbers used in this exam are real numbers.

✔ All figures lie in a plane.

✔ All figures may be assumed to be to scale unless the problem specifically indicates otherwise.

       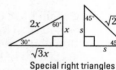

$A = \pi r^2$
$C = 2\pi r$

$A = lw$

$A = \frac{1}{2}bh$

$V = lwh$

$V = \pi r^2 h$

$c^2 = a^2 + b^2$

Special right triangles

There are 360 degrees of arc in a circle.

There are 180 degrees in a straight line.

There are 180 degrees in the sum of the interior angles of a triangle.

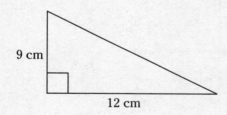

1. The area of the right triangle pictured above is

    (A) 21 cm^2

    (B) 36 cm^2

    (C) 42 cm^2

    (D) 54 cm^2

    (E) 108 cm^2

2. The solution set to the equation $x^2 = x$ is

    (A) {0}

    (B) {1}

    (C) {0, 1}

    (D) {–1, 0}

    (E) {–1, 1}

3. The ratio of seniors to juniors in a certain club is 5:3. If there are 40 students in the club, then the number of juniors is

    (A) 3

    (B) 15

    (C) 23

    (D) 24

    (E) 25

Go on to next page

4. Which of the following patterns could be folded up into a six-sided rectangular box, without making any cuts?

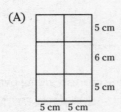

(A)

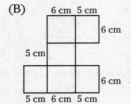

(B)

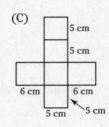

(C)

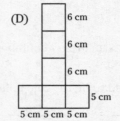

(D)

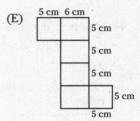

(E)

---

5. In a certain board game, the number of points you earn in each round is a linear function of the number of spaces you control at the end of the round. If you control 3 spaces, you win 10 points. If you control 5 spaces, you win 16 points. If you control 8 spaces, the number of points you win would be

    (A) 6
    (B) 22
    (C) 25
    (D) 26
    (E) 160

6. Regular pentagon *ABCDE* has sides of length *x*. Regular pentagon *FGHIJ* has sides of length 2*x*. If the area of pentagon *ABCDE* is 20, then the area of pentagon *FGHIJ* is

    (A) 40
    (B) 80
    (C) 100
    (D) 200
    (E) 400

7. Find *n* if $\sqrt{n+5} - 3 = 4$

    (A) 2
    (B) 14
    (C) 20
    (D) 44
    (E) 620

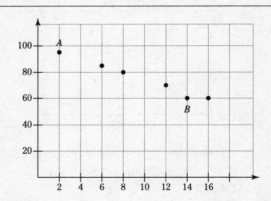

8. Asked to estimate an equation for the data pictured above, a student drew a line connecting points *A* and *B*. The equation that would most closely fit this line would be

    (A) $y = -3x + 100$
    (B) $y = 3x + 100$
    (C) $y = -\frac{1}{3}x + 100$
    (D) $y = -3x + 95$
    (E) $y = -\frac{1}{3}x + 95$

Go on to next page

9. Sergei decided to give everyone else in his study group 3 candies each, planning to have 2 left over for himself. However, one member of the group was sick; as a result, he gave 4 candies to everyone who showed up, and there was only one left over for him. How many candies were originally in the bag?

    (A) 5

    (B) 13

    (C) 17

    (D) 29

    (E) 34

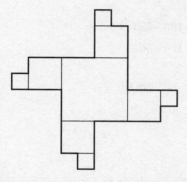

10. In this figure, each side of the large center square is twice as long as each side of the four medium-sized squares. Each side of the medium-sized squares is twice as long as each side of the four small squares. If the small squares have sides of length 1 cm, find the perimeter of the entire figure.

    (A) 40 cm

    (B) 52 cm

    (C) 60 cm

    (D) 64 cm

    (E) 80 cm

11. At a family reunion, 4 men have a grandson present, 12 have a son present, and 21 have a father present. What is the minimum number of men that could be at the reunion?

    (A) 21

    (B) 25

    (C) 29

    (D) 33

    (E) 37

12. In a certain triangle, angle X is twice the size of angle Y, and angle Z is 45 degrees smaller than angle X. Triangle XYZ must be

    I.   A right triangle

    II.   An isosceles triangle

    III. An equilateral triangle

    (A) I only

    (B) II only

    (C) III only

    (D) I and II

    (E) I and III

13. Points E, F, G, and H lie on a number line, but not in that order (in either direction). If the distance EG = 23, GH = 11, and F is the midpoint of EH, then the distance FH must equal

    (A) 6

    (B) 11

    (C) 12

    (D) 17

    (E) 34

Go on to next page ⟹

14. *a* and *b* are both positive integers greater than one. If *a* is a factor of both $b + 2$ and $b - 3$, then *b* could equal

(A) 21

(B) 25

(C) 29

(D) 33

(E) 37

15. Ms. Belton's class and Ms. Jimenez's class have no students in common. If 45 percent of Ms. Belton's students play a sport, 30 percent of Ms. Jimenez's students play a sport, and 40 percent of the students in the two classes combined play a sport, which statement must be true?

(A) The two classes have the same number of students.

(B) The two classes have 30 students total.

(C) Ms. Belton's class has exactly 20 students.

(D) Ms. Jimenez's class has twice as many students as Ms. Belton's.

(E) Ms. Belton's class has twice as many students as Ms. Jimenez's.

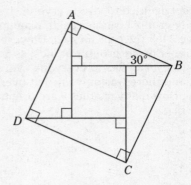

16. The drawing above shows four identical triangles surrounding a smaller square. Given that $AB = 10$, find the area of the square.

(A) $100 - 100\sqrt{3}$

(B) $100 - 50\sqrt{3}$

(C) 25

(D) $100 - 50\sqrt{2}$

(E) 50

STOP YOU MAY CHECK YOUR WORK ON THIS SECTION ONLY. DO NOT GO BACK TO ANY PREVIOUS SECTION.

Section 9
Multiple-Choice Writing

Time: 10 minutes for 14 questions

Directions: Choose the one answer that *best* improves the sentence. Mark the corresponding oval on the answer sheet. If the underlined portion of the sentence is best left alone, choose (A).

Example: <u>Bert and him went</u> to the store to buy boots in preparation for the approaching storm.

(A) Bert and him went

(B) Bert and he went

(C) Bert and he had gone

(D) Bert and him had gone

(E) Bert and himself went

The correct answer is (B).

1. <u>Both jumping off the sofa,</u> a flash of lightning exploded over our heads and thunder echoed in our ears.

   (A) Both jumping off the sofa,

   (B) Both of us jumping off the sofa,

   (C) We jumped off the sofa because

   (D) We had jumped off the sofa because

   (E) Jumping off the sofa,

2. The theater company applied for a variety of grants, <u>but only was given funds by the National Endowment for the Arts</u>.

   (A) but only was given funds by the National Endowment for the Arts

   (B) but the National Endowment for the Arts only gave them funds

   (C) but it only was given funds by the National Endowment for the Arts

   (D) but only the National Endowment for the Arts gave them funds

   (E) but it was only from the National Endowment for the arts that they were given funds

3. Parents objected to the fact that in this term's exercise classes, students studied <u>neither good nutrition nor how exercise is beneficial</u> for health.

   (A) neither good nutrition nor how regular exercise is beneficial

   (B) neither how good nutrition nor regular exercise is beneficial

   (C) neither the benefits of good nutrition nor regular exercise

   (D) the benefits of neither good nutrition nor regular exercise

   (E) no good nutrition, and they didn't learn about regular exercise

4. Skidding across the icy road and fighting to control the car, <u>the winter storm frightened the driver</u>.

   (A) the winter storm frightened the driver

   (B) the driver was frightened by the winter storm

   (C) the winter storm, it frightened the driver

   (D) the driver, who was frightened, in the winter storm

   (E) the driver that was frightened by the winter storm

Go on to next page

5. <u>In a recent scientific survey, it showed that a simple checklist of safety precautions</u> can reduce post-operative complications by 50%.

   (A) In a recent scientific survey, it showed that a simple checklist of safety precautions

   (B) In a recent scientific survey, it had showed that a simple checklist of safety precautions

   (C) According to a recent scientific survey, a simple checklist of safety precautions

   (D) In a recent scientific survey, showing that a simple checklist of safety precautions

   (E) A simple checklist of safety precautions in a recent scientific survey, it

6. <u>Prized for its ability to mimic human speech</u>, mynah birds are popular pets in many parts of the world.

   (A) Prized for its ability to mimic human speech

   (B) Being prized for its ability to mimic human speech

   (C) Prized for their ability to mimic human speech

   (D) Because it is prized for its ability to mimic human speech

   (E) Having been prized for their ability to mimic human speech

7. Director Alfred Hitchcock is <u>equally as renowned for his suspense films as for his comedies</u>.

   (A) equally as renowned for his suspense films as for his comedies

   (B) equally renowned for his suspense films as his comedies

   (C) renowned in an equal way for his suspense films as for his comedies

   (D) renowned equally as for his suspense films and for his comedies

   (E) equally renowned for his suspense films and his comedies

8. In 1981, Sandra Day O'Connor <u>became a Justice of the Supreme Court, she was</u> the first female to hold that position.

   (A) became a Justice of the Supreme Court, she was

   (B) became a Justice of the Supreme Court and

   (C) became a Justice of the Supreme Court, Justice O'Connor was

   (D) had become a Justice of the Supreme Court, and she was

   (E) by becoming a Justice of the Supreme Court, she was

9. The foundation <u>moved its headquarters to New York ten years ago and was located</u> on that city's most elegant street, Park Avenue, until recently.

   (A) moved its headquarters to New York ten years ago and was located

   (B) moved its headquarters to New York ten years ago and has been located

   (C) moved its headquarters to New York ten years ago, it being located

   (D) moved its headquarters to New York ten years ago, being located

   (E) moved its headquarters to New York ten years ago, located

10. The architects' job <u>is to try and design</u> an energy-efficient, cost-effective structure.

   (A) is to try and design

   (B) is to try by designing

   (C) is to try and to also design

   (D) is to try and to design

   (E) is to try to design

Go on to next page ⟩

11. The ancient <u>Mayans, performing human sacrifices in religious rituals, they understood</u> the human circulatory system.

    (A) Mayans, performing human sacrifices in religious rituals, they understood

    (B) Mayans, performing human sacrifices in religious rituals, understood

    (C) Mayans were performing human sacrifices in religious rituals, and they understood

    (D) Mayans, who performed human sacrifices in religious rituals, they understood

    (E) Mayans, performing human sacrifices in religious rituals, they were understanding

12. If I <u>would have known about your allergy, I wouldn't have served</u> peanut-butter cookies.

    (A) would have known about your allergy, I wouldn't have served

    (B) would know about your allergy, I wouldn't have served

    (C) knew about your allergy, I wouldn't have served

    (D) had known about your allergy, I wouldn't have served

    (E) would have known about your allergy, I wouldn't serve

13. The park ranger spoke at length <u>to the campers, Roger and he, who attempted</u> to feed the animals.

    (A) to the campers, Roger and he, who attempted

    (B) to Roger and he, who were campers that had attempted

    (C) to the campers, Roger and him, who attempted

    (D) to the campers, Roger and him, they attempted

    (E) to Roger and him, who attempted as campers

14. This is the only one of the books in that chef's <u>immense library that has</u> a recipe for salt codfish.

    (A) immense library that has

    (B) immense library that have

    (C) immense library, which has

    (D) immense library, which have

    (E) immense library, and it has

STOP YOU MAY CHECK YOUR WORK ON THIS SECTION ONLY. DO NOT GO BACK TO ANY PREVIOUS SECTION.

Chapter 27

Practice Exam 4: Answers and Explanations

• •

Have you ever looked at your face through a magnifying glass? Gross, right? You can see every little blemish and speck of dirt. But that examination helps you clean up your act. Think of this chapter as a magnifying glass for your brain — well, the portions of your brain that face the SAT. (The normal spots, those that help you download music or grab the best seat in the cafeteria, aren't important right now.)

After you complete Practice Exam 4, check your work by reading the answers and explanations I provide in this chapter. Don't skimp on this task. Read the explanations even for correct answers, but spend an extra minute or two on any questions you got wrong. If you're short on time, you can quickly check your answers with the abbreviated answer key I provide at the end of the chapter.

Note: To determine your score on this practice test, turn to the appendix.

Section 1: The Essay

Don't you love that a man named *Smiles* made a statement about failure? Also, don't you adore being asked to think about failure while you're taking a test you definitely want to ace? No worries. This question is actually a softball. (For the athletically challenged, a softball is relatively easy to hit.) All you need to do is come up with a few rain clouds that turned out to have silver linings. Then you just have to develop your position — the only reasonable one, really — that people can often learn from their mistakes. Notice the word *often* in that last sentence. You *could* write that failure is always terrible and then pen a few hundred words about the spelling bee you lost in second grade, explaining how it crushed your academic career. You *could* also say that failure is always wonderful, explaining that your ten-years-to-life sentence gave you plenty of time to practice taking SAT tests. But I expect that the nuanced view will appeal to your readers more.

So use your 25 minutes to come up with historical, literary, or personal evidence supporting the argument that failure isn't always bad. Then organize your thoughts into a concise, cohesive essay. Here's one way to organize your essay:

> ✔ **Introduction:** State your thesis, quoting from Mr. Smiles (I love writing that name!) if you wish. Briefly mention the supporting points you plan to expand on in the body of the essay. For example, you may describe a NASA failure that led to improved safety standards or better equipment. You can include that spelling bee (or some other academic fiasco), too. Don't ignore literature, which is littered with epic failures. Look for one that has redeeming values. After you have two or three solid examples, you're all set to start the body of your essay.

- ✔ **Body paragraphs:** Flesh out the supporting points, one in each paragraph. Be as specific as possible. Continuing the example from the preceding paragraph, you may describe the embarrassment you felt at being the first contestant eliminated in the spelling bee and then show the reader how you buckled down and memorized the dictionary, eventually winning a gold medal in the Spelling Olympics. (Yes, I know that spelling isn't an Olympic sport. I'm just making up an example.)

- ✔ **Conclusion:** Instead of restating your introduction in different terms, use your conclusion to move ahead. What sort of failure is helpful? What kind of failure is a disaster with no redeeming features? Answer these questions (and more) in this paragraph.

Now that you've seen one way to organize your thoughts effectively to address the failure-related essay prompt, it's time to score your essay. Before you get started, turn to Chapter 8 and read the samples there. Then turn a magnifying glass on your own work, and score your essay using the scoring rubric I provide in Chapter 7; be honest with yourself as you critique your essay. Otherwise, your score won't help you determine what you still need to work on before you take the real SAT.

Section 2: Critical Reading

1. **B.** The key word in this sentence is *prevents,* which means that the disease won't reach epidemic proportions. What stops disease? Not a state of mind — Choice (A) — or a willingness to take part in social gatherings — Choice (D). Choices (C) and (E) imply that the population may become ill, the opposite of what the sentence says. Thus, you're left with (B), *immunity,* or "resistance to disease."

2. **A.** A critic with a grudge is a writer's worst nightmare! All writers hope their reviewers will write favorably, or at least fairly, about their creations. With this fact in mind, you can quickly cross off Choices (B), (D), and (E) because they all mean "without bias." (Yes, I know that *disinterestedly* looks as if it means "without interest," but it doesn't. It means "without bias.") Choice (C) is a nonstarter because *justifiably* and *inappropriately* are opposites. Go for Choice (A), which expresses the type of attack that fits the sentence's intended meaning.

3. **D.** This sentence sets up a contrast between the audience's first and later reactions, so you know you're searching for a pair that expresses a progression. The best choice is (D) because the initial *indifference,* or lack of interest, turns to total concentration, and *rapt* means "completely absorbed."

4. **B.** Ms. Benning gave up, an action expressed by the word *concede,* which is why Choice (B) is the right way to go here. In case you're interested, *supersede* means "to follow or take over from," and *transmit* means "to spread or to pass on a message." You can "pass on" an opinion, but not an election. One more vocabulary word: *supplant,* which means "to displace" or "to replace."

5. **E.** All the action in this sentence is at the end (just like the meal the sentence describes). The diner chose a dessert that resembles Mount Everest (in other words, a rich dish) and merely picked at the main course to *compensate,* or "make up for," the dessert's high calorie count. The other four choices involve desserts that *don't* increase the total number of calories, being "tiny" (A), "light" (B), "minimal" (C), or "low-calorie" (D).

6. **C.** What sort of planning surprises the Yankees? (I couldn't resist throwing in a reference to my favorite ballplayers.) Planning that doesn't work or that is *incomplete.* However, if you chose Choice (A), you fell into the SAT makers' trap because *despite* tells you that the planning should've worked. What kind of planning should do the job? *Meticulous* planning (the kind that covers every little detail). Bingo: (C) is the answer you seek.

7. **A.** This sentence describes a process, a change from some sort of *recruit*, or beginner, to a soldier who has seen and survived some action. Choices (B), (C), (D), and (E) are tempting because all refer to qualities that a soldier has. However, only (A) contrasts the newness of the recruit with the maturity of the older warrior.

8. **C.** To crack this one, you need a good vocabulary, one especially rich in words that describe how much a person talks. Choice (C), *loquacious*, means "talkative" and fits nicely in the sentence. Choices (A), (B), and (D) are *antonyms*, or opposites, of loquacious. Steer clear of those because if May isn't opening her mouth, she doesn't need a lot of time on the phone. Did Choice (E) catch your eye? A combative caller may use a lot of minutes, but not necessarily. Haven't you ever fought with someone who yells briefly and then hangs up? I have! Hence, the best answer is (C).

9. **D.** The passage specifically refers to a crank as having "practical applications such as pulling a bucket from a well" (Lines 7–8). Because cranks "did not exist in the ancient world" (Lines 5–6), Choice (A) is wrong. The "first established use" (Lines 12–13) was in China in A.D. 31, but *established* doesn't necessarily mean *discovered*, and no information about the actual invention of the crank is supplied. Therefore, you can eliminate Choices (B) and (C). The fact that the crank was "common by the 1600s" (Line 6) doesn't mean that the device was *overlooked* until that era. In fact, to become common implies that cranks were around earlier and grew in popularity over time. You're left with Choice (D), which just happens to be the best answer.

10. **A.** Line 8 contains the word *and*, which adds a practical use of cranks to the example already given, that of drawing water from a well. Because you're adding another use of cranks, you're moving away from wells and also from Choice (B). What's added is "a wide variety of situations" (Line 9) in which cranks are helpful, a statement that rules out (D). The passage tells you that cranks change "rotary motion into reciprocating motion" (Lines 10–11) and vice versa, simultaneously eliminating (E) and pointing you toward (A). The remaining possibility, (C), bites the dust because nothing in the passage tells you when rotary and reciprocating motion was invented.

11. **C.** Empedocles had a theory about the "four essences or elements" (Lines 19–20). He is described as "holding" that theory — in other words, "believing in it." The other choices are all definitions of *holding*, but none fit the context of Line 18.

12. **B.** Line 16 tells you that the existence of elements "had been supposed since antiquity," so elements began as an idea, or theory, long before they were proved real — hello, Choice (B)! Choice (A) is wrong because it states the opposite, and (C) drops out because the only date in Passage I is A.D. 31, and the only dates in Passage II are B.C. dates — from an even earlier time period. Choice (D) may be true in the real world, but the passage doesn't tell you how long scientists worked. As for (E) — the SAT isn't Harry Potter's world, and discoveries may be considered magical without actually being magical.

13. **C.** A pilot project leads the way, much as the pilot of a plane leads the passengers to their destination. (Their luggage, however, is another story entirely, at least when I fly.) The passage tells you that not all pilot projects can be replicated (Lines 29–30), so (A) can't be correct. Choices (B) and (D) are random lines drawn from the passage, so you're left with (C) and (E). Of the two, (C) is better because the passage refers to "successful" pilot projects (Line 22), implying that not all succeed, and (E) assumes that the projects have been "proven effective" (Line 28).

14. **D.** The passage concerns what the author sees as the best quality of the Grameen Bank — that its model can be replicated and adapted easily, thus reaching many more poor people. The author contrasts this success with pilot projects, which, as he explains in Line 12, reach "hundreds of people" instead of the millions affected by the Grameen Bank. Choices (A), (B), (C), and (E) deal with this limitation. Nowhere does the passage address funding, so (D) is clearly the best answer.

15. **A.** How do you feel when romance hits? Happy and optimistic, I bet. Your newly beloved can do no wrong. But romance doesn't last. Either your relationship deepens into love, when you see and accept your beloved's faults, or it crashes and burns. This real-life experience helps you decode the statement that in the do-good crowd — "circles where poverty and environmental issues are discussed" (Lines 14–15) — small projects are seen with a romantic eye and thus aren't evaluated fairly, as Choice (A) states. Choice (B) bets that you'll go for the hug-kiss sort of romance (which, I might add, is wrong); (C) and (E) are the opposite of what the author says in the passage. Choice (D) doesn't cut it because tiny programs have limited goals, and you can't compare something to itself.

16. **B.** A "mesh" (Line 33) is a net, woven from threads. Lines 33–34 cite three types of problems — "social, environmental, and economic" — that are all "injustices." Thus, poverty, which is the topic discussed in the passage as a whole and in this paragraph in particular, affects its victims in several ways, as Choice (B) states.

17. **E.** *Autonomy* means "independence," and Lines 40–41 explain that Grameen Bank has a "decentralized management structure." Without a center, power is spread out — precisely the concept that Choice (E) states. Choice (A) isn't right because Yunus has always had some control; after all, he founded the bank! Choices (B), (C), and (D) are contradicted by the paragraph, so they're all wrong, too.

18. **B.** The lines cited in the question show that Grameen Bank had some growing pains. The right formula wasn't immediately present, though the passage as a whole makes clear that the Bank has succeeded. In 1991, some employees experienced "discontent" (Line 47) and some "carried out their duties" badly (Lines 49–50). These troubles fall into the category of "trial and error" (Line 46) because when you try things, you fail until you happen upon the road to success. Thus, Choice (B) is the one you seek. Choice (A) may have tempted you, but the eventual success of the Grameen Bank shows that the critics were wrong. Choice (C) flops because Bangladeshis "demonstrated those abilities as Grameen staff and borrowers" (Lines 59–60). The successful "decentralized management structure" (Lines 40–41) contradicts Choice (D), and Lines 57–60 kick (E) out of the running.

19. **E.** Representatives of other developing countries come to Bangladesh "to learn how Grameen works" (Line 69). They, and other organizations within Bangladesh, have used Grameen Bank as a model. Hence, Grameen's achievements aren't unique, and Choice (E) belongs in the winner's circle.

20. **D.** Lines 74–75 tell you that critics see "the problem of poverty" as "complex," one needing "a solution that [takes] into account . . . ignorance, political powerlessness, and ill health" (Lines 75–78). Ignorance is cured by *better education,* ill health is alleviated by *universal health care,* and political powerlessness is reduced by giving *political power to the poor.* Therefore, all three options are correct, and the right answer is (D).

21. **A.** To *tout* is to "publicize and support" an idea. Line 73 states that Yunus was accused of touting his approach as a "magic bullet" that would end poverty. The last paragraph of the passage explains that although Yunus admitted that the problem of poverty was complex, he still favored a simple solution — "investment capital" (Line 96) to "unlock the capacity of poor people to solve many, if not all, of the manifestations of poverty" (Lines 97–99). Therefore, the critics did, in fact, explain Yunus's ideas accurately.

22. **A.** Everything in the answer list is a possible meaning of the word *conscious,* but the poor are *aware* of politics, not *alert* or *awake* or any of the other choices.

23. **B.** The entire passage praises Yunus for creating a business model that can be re-created over and over again. Yunus, therefore, wasn't interested in being the *only* banker for the poor. Instead, he wanted to be a model that others could imitate. Did the quotations about money — Choices (C), (D), and (E) — tempt you? The test makers often try to fool you by placing obvious but wrong answers in the mix. Yunus wasn't against money (C), and he wanted people to invest, not save (D). Nor did he see his borrowers as foolish. And as Lines 19–25 show, Yunus favored large-scale efforts, not small ones, as (A) states.

24. **B.** Except for a hint of criticism in Lines 54–57, everything in the passage supports Muhammed Yunus (who, by the way, is one of my own heroes!) and praises his efforts. The only other answers in the running are (C) and (D). However, *congratulatory* implies that the author is writing *to* Yunus instead of *about* him. *Sympathetic* is a weaker term than *admiring*, and, because this author goes all out, *admiring* is the better fit.

Section 3: Mathematics

1. **B.** You can do this one as an algebra problem by writing $n + 4 = 3n$ and solving to get $n = 2$. Or, you can just try plugging in all the possibilities until one works.

2. **E.** Because the angles of a triangle must add up to 180°, the angle in the bottom-left corner must equal 50°. Remember the useful fact that the largest angle is across from the largest side. (The same is true for the smallest angle and the smallest side.)

3. **D.** Solving absolute-value equations or inequalities requires solving two related problems. In this case, you need to take $|x + 3| < 5$ and create two inequalities: $x + 3 < 5$ and $x + 3 > -5$. Solving each of these inequalities gives you $x < 2$ and $x > -8$, so Graph (D) is your answer.

4. **B.** The amount saved on the coat is $75 - $60 = $15. To turn this savings amount into a percentage, calculate $\frac{15}{75} \times 100 = 20\%$.

5. **E.** Don't waste your time trying to figure out what a, b, and c equal. The key here is noticing what happens when you add the first two equations together:

$$\begin{array}{r} a + c = 7 \\ + \ b - c = 4 \\ \hline a + b = 11 \end{array}$$

6. **B.** This question is a straightforward, Pythagorean Theorem problem. Just make sure you set it up correctly: $\left(\sqrt{11}\right)^2 + b^2 = 6^2$ (6 is the hypotenuse). Working out this problem gives you $11 + b^2 = 36$, $b^2 = 25$, and $b = 5$.

7. **A.** Looking at the graph tells you that $f(2) = -1$. So, by rule, $g(2) = 2f(2) - 3 = 2(-1) - 3 = -5$.

8. **A.** This problem is a lot like Question 5 in that you can (and should) solve it without bothering to figure out what x and y equal. The key is remembering to use the super-useful formula I discuss in Chapter 14, the one that says $(a + b)^2 = a^2 + 2ab + b^2$. Applying this formula to the information you're given in Question 8 tells you that $x^2 + 2xy + y^2 = 53$ and $x^2 - 2xy + y^2 = 37$. If you subtract the second equation from the first, the x^2 and y^2 terms cancel themselves out, leaving you with $2xy - (-2xy) = 53 - 37$, which becomes $4xy = 16$, so $xy = 4$.

9. **B.** The area of the square is just $10 \times 10 = 100$. The area of the circle is πr^2, which is $\pi(5)^2 = 25\pi$, or about 78.5. So the probability that the dart lands in the square but *not* in the circle is $\frac{100 - 78.5}{100} \approx 21.5\%$, which is closest to 20%.

10. **D.** Substituting 3 for y gives you $x - 3 = \frac{x+3}{3-1} = \frac{x+3}{2}$. You want this equation to equal x, so $\frac{x+3}{2} = x$. Multiplying both sides by 2 gives you $x + 3 = 2x$, and subtracting x from each side gives you $x = 3$. As always, if you aren't in the mood to do algebra, you can find this answer by plugging in answer choices until you find one that works.

11. **C.** If x is negative, then $-x$ and x^2 are both positive. Therefore, both Choice (A) and Choice (B) are false. Choice (C) looks true: For example, $(-1)^3 = -1$, and $-1 \geq -1$, while $(-2)^3 = -8$, and $-2 \geq -8$. As usual, you should stop right there on the real test, but I'll check the last two choices just for fun. (D) doesn't work: For example, -2 isn't greater than or equal to $-\frac{1}{2}$. (E) is true for positive numbers, but not for negative numbers: 6 is greater than 3, but -6 is smaller than -3. Choice (C) it is.

12. **A.** If you solve this problem using algebra, you need to let the integers equal x, $x + 2$, and $x + 4$. (Do you remember this from Chapter 14?) Adding these expressions gives you $3x + 6 = -15$, or $x = -7$. This answer makes the other numbers -5 and -3, and -7 is the smallest. You can also use reason to figure out this problem: Because the numbers add up to -15, the middle number must be one-third of -15, or -5, and, thus, the other numbers are -7 and -3.

13. **D.** This question is an algebra problem. Let n equal the number of marbles in the jar. Therefore, originally $0.25n$ (or $\frac{n}{4}$) of the marbles are red. When you add 20 red marbles, $0.25n + 20$ are now red, out of $n + 20$ total. Because that's 50%, you can write $0.25n + 20 = 0.50(n + 20)$, which gives you $0.25n + 20 = 0.50n + 10$. Combining like terms gives you $10 = 0.25n$, and multiplying both sides by 4 (or dividing by 0.25) gives you $n = 40$.

14. **C.** To solve an equation like this one, you need to use the reciprocal of the exponent: $\left(a^{\frac{-2}{3}}\right)^{\frac{-3}{2}} = (9)^{\frac{-3}{2}}$. The exponents cancel each other out on the left side, leaving you with just a. On the right side, use a calculator if you want; if you do, make sure to put the exponent in parentheses when you type it in. To solve this problem the old-fashioned way, write $9^{\frac{-3}{2}} = \dfrac{1}{\left(\sqrt[2]{9}\right)^3} = \dfrac{1}{3^3} = \dfrac{1}{27}$.

15. **E.** The original containers have a volume of $2 \times 3 \times 4 = 24$ cubic feet. If you don't remember the volume of a cylinder, check out the reference table at the top of the Math section: $V = \pi r^2 h = \pi(5)^2(6) = 150\pi =$ about 471. Next, you just have to divide: $471 \div 24 = 19.6$, or roughly 20.

16. **B.** Perpendicular lines have slopes that are negative reciprocals, so line m has a slope of $-\frac{3}{2}$. Because m passes through $(-6, -4)$, you can write it in point-slope form as $y - (-4) = -\frac{3}{2}(x - -6)$. Distributing gives you $y + 4 = (-\frac{3}{2})x - 9$, and subtracting 4 gives you $y = (-\frac{3}{2})x - 13$. That calculation makes -13 the y-intercept, which is what the problem asks for.

17. **D.** If Benjamin starts out walking north, he has to turn east on Elm Avenue (because he must walk at least one block on it). From there, he has three possible routes to school. If he starts walking east, he has three more possible routes, as the diagram below shows:

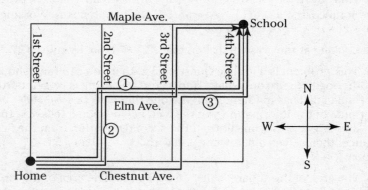

All together, Benjamin has six possible routes.

18. **C.** Drawing time! Here are the circles:

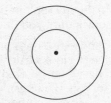

By the way, circles sharing the same center are called *concentric*. The problem says that the line can't enter the small circle, but it doesn't say that the line can't touch the circle. The SAT makers keep you on your toes with these little details. You can draw your line like this:

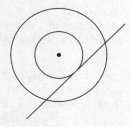

The line touches the circles at three points.

19. **D.** The *median* is the middle number when the three numbers are listed in order. So you can list the numbers as a, -1, b. Also, you know that the mean is 6, and therefore the total of the three numbers is 18. (Do you remember why? The total = the average × the number of things, or $18 = 6 \times 3$. This formula is really worth knowing.)

   Now comes the tricky part: a can't be greater than -1, but nothing prevents it from *equaling* -1. It's tempting to make $a = -2$, which makes $b = 21$. But if you let $a = -1$, then b can equal 20. Because -1 is the biggest you can possibly make a, 20 must be the smallest that b can ever be.

20. **A.** Because $AB = OC$, it's also true that $AB = OA$ and $AB = OB$ (because OA and OB are also radii, and all radii are equal). That makes OAB an equilateral triangle, so all of its angles equal 60°. Therefore, angle BOD must be 30°, which makes triangle BOD a 30-60-90 triangle. Using the 30-60-90 pattern (which is at the top of the math section, if you forget it), you know that $BD = 4$ and $OD = 4\sqrt{3}$ and that the area of triangle BOD is $\dfrac{4\left(4\sqrt{3}\right)}{2} = 8\sqrt{3}$. Now the shaded region equals the circular sector BOC minus triangle BOD, and sector BOC is one-twelfth of a circle (because it has 30° out of the 360° in a circle). So the area of BOC is $\dfrac{\pi(8)^2}{12} = \dfrac{64\pi}{12} = \dfrac{16\pi}{3}$. After all that work, you discover the right answer is Choice (A).

Section 4: Critical Reading

1. **D.** The *not . . . but* structure of the sentence tells you that you need an opposite for *record*. Immediately, you can rule out Choices (A) and (E) because they're synonyms. Choices (B) and (C) are too narrow; some artists make a scene more beautiful, and some don't. Some go for symbolism, and others shy away from that technique. But all artists *add* something to a scene (by interpreting it). Therefore, Choice (D) is the best answer.

2. **A.** You're in metaphor-land here, though even without knowing that literary term for a comparison, you probably detected the need for opposites. After all, *outcasts* are searching for a path from one thing to another. Clearly they want a change. Only Choices (A) and (E) are opposites, but (A) wins because *fertile fields* are generally viewed as good, while *marshes,* which are swampy, mosquito-filled areas, aren't.

3. **B.** All the answer choices refer to movement, but only (B) fits the *leisurely way* cited in the sentence. If you're just killing time, you probably aren't plodding (A), which has an air of duty and burden attached to it. Choice (C) suggests anger, (D) pride, and (E) haste — none of which fit the feeling in the sentence.

4. **C.** The clue here is the expression *gave way,* which implies the passage of time. Choices (C) and (D) address time, but (C) is the better answer because it suggests a move from the beginning to something later. (D) travels in the opposite direction, from the end *(final)* to, well, even more of an end!

5. **D.** This question about handwriting tests your vocabulary. A *flourish* is an extra decoration, perhaps a little squiggle at the end of a word or an extra curve on a capital letter. If you know that definition, this one's easy to answer because it asks you to contrast *fancy* somethings with *clean, modern lines.*

6. **C.** Line 5 says that *we prevent* newborns from moving their *limbs* (arms and legs), so (C) makes sense here. The only other possibility is (E) because the author worries that preventing movement may "interfere with the circulation of the blood" (Lines 9–10) and "prevent the child from growing strong and sturdy" (Lines 10–11). However, because the problems the author mentions are in the future, (E) isn't a good fit.

7. **E.** As is often the case with vocabulary-in-context questions, all the answers are definitions of the given word. However, only one makes sense in the context of the passage — *health,* also known as (E).

8. **D.** The narrator says that he wasn't able to "arouse any considerable feeling of need for a father" (Lines 11–12). He isn't for or against the man; he just doesn't see any purpose to the meeting or to this presence in his life. (In other words, he's *indifferent* toward his father.)

9. **B.** The mother is *almost pushing* (Line 5) the son toward the father, but the boy and his father are *feeling embarrassed and foolish* (Line 1). *Melodrama* features exaggerated emotions and expression of those emotions. The mother expects the son to throw himself *into his [father's] arms* (Line 9), but the boy doesn't feel anything. Hence, his mother's expectations are unrealistic, as (B) states.

10. **B.** The narrator's home is *Excenus 23* (Line 2) and he or she is being sent to Earth "to do [his or her] Education" (Line 10). Therefore, Statement I is false because you can't be sent to Earth if you're already on Earth. The narrator's comment that it took "years on Earth to get used to all this water around" (Lines 48–49) indicates that Statement II is correct. Statement III is tricky. Of course no one's traveled to inhabited planets and returned to Earth, so Excenus 23 *is* a fantasy — but it's a fantasy created by the author, not by the narrator of the story. Because only II is correct, (B) is your answer.

11. **C.** The clue to the answer lies after the quotation, when the narrator admits to feeling *a kind of desolation* (Line 12). Anyone feeling desolation hasn't adapted, so you can rule out (A). The narrator mentions that "[m]ost people . . . are feeling bad" because of exams (Lines 12–13) but later comments, "I would prefer to think that it is just Finals . . . but it is not" (Lines 30–31), so (B) doesn't work either. Because the narrator is open about his or her feelings, (D) and (E) are wrong. You're left with (C), which is perfect because *desolation* is sadness with a hint of isolation — ingredients of depression.

12. **A.** According to Lines 18–19, if you're still sane after going through the two-week period between exams and receiving the results of those exams, you pass the Test. Thus, Choice (A) is your answer.

13. **E.** Your molars, which you are probably grinding every time you think about the SAT, are the wide teeth in the back of your jaw. They don't break easily, so (E) fits nicely. Choice (D) is a close second, but broken teeth, though unpleasant, don't cause their owners to fall apart. Choice (E) is definitely better.

14. **A.** Once a chick breaks out of its shell, it can't go back in — particularly after three weeks' growth. The chick won't fit, and the shell isn't the cozy home it was before the chick left it. Move these ideas from chicks to humans, and you see that (A) is your answer.

15. **C.** The narrator feels sorry for the Examiners who have to read a ton of examinations (an appropriate response, in my experience!), but the narrator's friend B says that "it serves them perfectly right" (Line 60) because the Examiners assigned the work. Add in B's comment

about the waiting period between exams and grades being *yet another Test* and you see B's harsh attitude toward adults.

16. **C.** Lines 46–48 tell you that "she and I came here to be miserable in company and away from the rest." The implication is that the others aren't miserable. Because the narrator's distress comes from the realization that he or she doesn't want to leave Earth, the others may be more willing to do so.

17. **D.** Only two answers — (C) and (D) — are serious contenders. (C) looks promising — at first glance — because the narrator *is* attached. However, that attachment isn't to the Island, which is just a place to spend time until the grades come out. Instead, the narrator is attached to life on Earth, even to the Sea, which was frightening at first. Thus, (D) is your answer.

18. **D.** The narrator's father sent a *fish-boat* (Line 63), but the narrator was too afraid of water to use it. Now the narrator realizes that the time on Earth is limited and has decided to "make the most of Earth while [he or she is] on it" (Line 67). Bingo: Out comes the fish-boat and Choice (D).

19. **D.** To crack this question, you need to understand the meaning of **dichotomy**, which is "a split into two contrasting parts." Paragraph one (Lines 1–11) reveals that Mars has distinct halves: *ancient cratered highlands* in the South and *plains that are much younger* in the North. Hello, Choice (D)!

20. **C.** In a typical SAT trap, every answer choice to a vocabulary-in-context question like this one is a definition of *harbors,* but only (C) makes sense in this sentence. Mars may give or may have given shelter to life, at least according to *human imagination* (Lines 12–13) and some recent scientific findings.

21. **A.** Untangling a complicated sentence is your first job here. Percival Lowell shows up in the middle of the second sentence of Paragraph 2 (Line 17). Move him to the beginning of the sentence, delete some extra material, and the meaning becomes clearer: Percival Lowell and some others argued that the linear features observed on Mars were artificial. *Artificial* is the opposite of *natural* and is created by some sort of living being. Choice (A) mentions *living beings,* and the *linear features* referred to in the passage (Lines 16–17, 21) could be highways or canals.

22. **D.** Sharpen your cross-out pencil and eliminate all the answers that *do* appear in the passage. Delete (A) after reading Line 44, which explains the evidence pointing to water on Mars. Scratch out (B) when you hit the discussion of *extremophiles* in Line 32. (C) is a dud, according to Lines 13–14 ("long-standing speculation that it harbors, or has harbored, life"). Because Lines 34–35 tell you that expeditions "produced either negative or ambiguous results," (E) isn't the answer you seek either. What's left? Choice (D).

23. **B.** The first half of Paragraph 2 (Lines 12–24) describes speculation in the 19th century and provides details about some scientists' reasons for believing that life exists on Mars. The second half of the paragraph (Lines 24–36) explains modern theories on the same topic. Somewhere in the middle must have been a period of disbelief, because to **rekindle** is "to reignite or to reawaken."

24. **A.** If you're *hardy,* you can take it — regardless of what "it" is: very hot or very cold temperatures, little water, SAT exams, whatever. Line 32 talks about *extremophiles,* small life forms that can live no matter what you throw at them. (By the way, the suffix *phile* means "lover of." Thus, an *extremophile* loves extreme circumstances — sort of like New Yorkers.)

Section 5: Mathematics

1. **A.** –2 is four units from 2; all the others are significantly closer.

2. **C.** In 2002, the *y*-values of the two lines add up to $430,000, which is larger than the amount in any other year.

3. **A.** From 2000 to 2001, Product X had an increase of $50,000 in profit, from an original $100,000. That's a 50-percent increase. It had a greater dollar increase ($60,000) from 2003 to 2004, but that was from a start of $220,000, and $60,000 is much less than 50 percent of $220,000.

4. **E.** You know that line l in the given figure is a straight line and that all straight lines contain 180°. Thus, you also know that the angle marked x must equal 50° because $40° + 90° + 50° = 180°$. But then angle y must also equal 50° because line l bisects angle DPC, cutting the angle into two equal parts. Because angles x, y, and w make a straight line, the only measurement left for angle w is 80°.

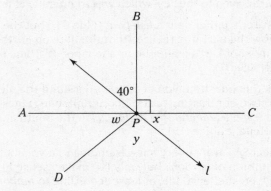

5. **D.** The question tells you that $n > 4$, so start by finding the price of the first four shirts. The first shirt costs $15. The next three are 20% off, so they each cost 80% of $15, which is $12. Thus, the total cost of the first four shirts is $15 + 3 × $12 = $51. All subsequent shirts are 50% off $15, or $7.50. But you've already paid for the first four shirts in your formula, so they cost not $7.5n$, but $7.5(n - 4)$. Combining results gives you Choice (D).

6. **B.** Choices (C), (D), and (E) would be negative. (A) might be negative, if k is something like –10 and j is, for example, 4. But (B) must be positive because subtracting k, a negative number, is the same as adding a positive number. Bingo: (B) is your winner.

7. **B.** You have to admit, this problem is pretty cool: It's a 45-45-90 triangle cut into two smaller ones. If you call the midpoint of the base point D (as you see in the diagram that follows), you can use your 45-45-90 triangle formulas to determine that AD and CD are both 5 and AB and CB are both $5\sqrt{2}$. As a result, the total perimeter of ABC is $10 + 10\sqrt{2}$.

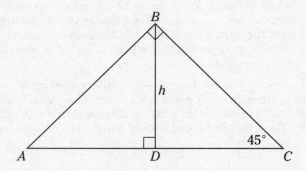

8. **C.** You probably noticed that the length of each string of numbers is the same as the last number: For example, the string ending in 4 is four numbers long. That means the final number will have $1 + 2 + 3 + \ldots + 9$, or 45, digits.

9. **630.** There are 9 possible first digits, 10 possible second digits, and 7 possible third digits. The counting principle tells you to multiply, and $9 × 10 × 7 = 630$.

10. **360.** $8 \times 400 = 3{,}200$ feet, and $2 \times 200 = 400$ feet. That makes 3,600 feet in 10 minutes, or 360 feet per minute.

11. **11.** The key here is to recognize that 32 is 2 to the fifth power. Having done so, you can rewrite the equation as $\left(2^5\right)^n = 2^{2n+33}$. For this to work, it must be true that $5n = 2n + 33$, which makes n equal 11.

12. **280.** For a number to be divisible by 5 and have only even digits, it must end in a zero. Then it would need at least three digits for the digits to add up to ten, and 280 is the smallest three-digit number that fills the bill.

13. **72.** The 12 students represent the whole class minus one-half plus one-third of the class. Because $\frac{1}{2} + \frac{1}{3} = \frac{3}{6} + \frac{2}{6} = \frac{5}{6}$ and $1 - \frac{5}{6} = \frac{1}{6}$, 12 students are one-sixth of the class, and $12 \times 6 = 72$ students are in the whole class.

14. **47.** Because lines l and m are parallel, $w + 75$ must be equal to 122. Straightforward subtraction gives you $w = 47$.

15. **8.** Question 15 is a quadratic equation, so to solve it, you have to make it equal to zero. Doing so gives you $x^2 + x - 72 = 0$, which factors to $(x + 9)(x - 8) = 0$; this equation is true when x is either -9 or 8. You can't grid a negative answer, so go with 8.

16. **3.5 or ⅞.** The $+11$ and -11 in the two equations should tempt you to add them and see what happens. If you do, the 11s cancel out, and you get $4x = 14y$. Dividing both sides by 4 gives you $x = \frac{14y}{4} = \frac{7y}{2}$, and dividing by y gives you $\frac{x}{y} = \frac{7}{2}$.

17. **6.** NOP is a triangle, so its area is one-half its base times its height. You know from the diagram that its base has a length of a; because P is on $y = x^2$, its height must be a^2. Using those numbers, you get $\frac{a\left(a^2\right)}{2} = 108$, so $a^3 = 216$, and $a = 6$.

18. **25.** When $f(x) = g(x)$, $\sqrt{164 + 5x} = x - 8$. To solve this equation, you need to square both sides, which gives you $164 + 5x = x^2 - 16x + 64$. (Notice that I'm using the same cool formula from Question 8 of Section 3.) To solve the equation, you need it to equal zero, which you get by subtracting 164 and $5x$ from both sides. That gives you $x^2 - 21x - 100 = 0$, which factors to $(x - 25)(x + 4) = 0$, which makes x either 25 or -4; go for 25 because you can't grid a negative answer.

Section 6: Multiple-Choice Writing

1. **E.** This cause-and-effect sentence needs a word to connect the cause (the inspector's arrival) to the effect (the crew's doing actual work rather than chomping doughnuts). Choices (C), (D), and (E) add that connecting word, but only (E) has the right verb tense.

2. **B.** Deep in the forests of grammar lies the *subjunctive*, a term that refers to a verb's mood. (I'm not kidding. Verbs have moods, and I'm not talking about cranky or rebellious.) But forget the terminology. What you really need to know to answer this question is that the underlined section of the sentence never happened. When you state a condition that doesn't exist, use *were* or *had*, as in "If I *were* a rich man" or "If I *had* known." The actor didn't swallow a balloon, and the only *had* around is in Choice (B).

3. **C.** The answer choices play around with *previously,* moving it and changing its form. Don't be fooled; *previously* or *previous* isn't the issue here. Take a look at the subject/verb pair: *gusts* (the plural subject) and *breaks* (the original, singular verb). In the grammar world, singular and plural don't get along. Change the verb to plural, as in Choice (C), and you're back on track.

4. **B.** Sentences aren't sentences unless they express at least one complete thought and contain a subject/verb pair. The original sentence leaves you hanging because you have two descriptions but no verb that matches the obvious subject, *plane.* The only choice that supplies the missing verb is (B). If you chose (E), you fell into a typical SAT trap. The *because* statement doesn't count as a complete thought when you're writing or speaking formal English — the type of English tested by the SAT.

5. **D.** Keep it simple and you're home free here. *The matter* isn't necessary because all the reader needs is the topic ("whether the defendant should be found guilty"), so Choice (D) is the answer you seek. Also unnecessary is *if it was right* — Choice (C) — because what else would the discussion be about? Choice (E) is wordy and has a grammatical error tucked into it. The *either. . . or* pair has to link elements with the same grammatical identity. In Choice (E), *finding the defendant guilty* is linked to *not* — clearly a mismatch!

6. **C.** When you stick two complete thoughts together in one sentence, you need the right kind of glue. Legal grammatical "glues" include semicolons; therefore, Choice (C) is the winner here.

7. **E.** First of all, *being as* and *being that* aren't Standard English expressions, so you can cross off Choices (A) and (C). Secondly, the *bones* were suspicious, not the janitor's discovery, so Choices (B) and (D) are gone, too. You're left with (E), which places *suspicious* with *bones* and employs *because,* the proper substitute for *being as.*

8. **A.** The original sentence gets the job done without wasting words. The other choices make unnecessary changes in tense *(may be causing)* or number *(one* or *ones).* Choice (E) is just plain wrong because it doesn't contain a subject/verb pair.

9. **D.** Recite this rule every day when you brush your teeth (okay, *after* you brush your teeth so you don't spit toothpaste all over the mirror): Every sentence needs at least one subject/verb pair that expresses a complete thought. Only Choice (D) meets this standard, pairing *device* (the subject) with *is* (the verb).

10. **D.** The subject of the sentence, *luxury department store,* is singular, and so is the verb paired with it *(is).* As a result, the pronoun referring to the store must also be singular. You need the singular *its* rather than the plural *their.*

11. **B.** When you see a list in a sentence, act like Santa and check it twice. The items in the list must have the same grammatical identity. Even if you can't stick a label on the items, listen to them in your head. Does everything match? In the original sentence, you have a bunch of nouns *(spending, depletion,* and *rate).* The last item should be a noun also, and, in Choice (B), it is. If you wanted to change the colon (:) to a semicolon (;), remember that a semicolon tacks on a complete sentence. In Choices (C) and (E), the semicolon isn't followed by a complete sentence, so those answers are wrong.

12. **D.** People probably prize cute little koala bears, with their oval ears and button noses, but they also likely prize eucalyptus leaves, which provide a key ingredient in cough drops. What's the author of the original sentence trying to say with the pronoun *they?* You don't know because the pronoun is unclear and, therefore, wrong.

13. **D.** In general, when a comma separates a description from the word it describes, the description is extra — not essential to the meaning of the sentence. When the description provides necessary identification, no comma should separate it from the word it describes. In Question 13, you don't know which child the monkey is intended for until you read the phrase "any sick child who wants to play." Every part of that description is essential, so the comma is inappropriate.

14. **C.** The subject of this sentence is *title,* but no verb pairs with it. The closest verb is *coming,* but you can't say, "The title coming." You have to say, "The title comes."

15. **C.** Repeat after me: "The reason is *that.* . . ." Got it? *The reason is because* is common in everyday speech but incorrect in Standard English. In case you're curious about the underlying grammatical logic (and if you are, you seriously need to get a life), *reason* is a noun

and must be balanced in the sentence by another noun or an adjective. (The word *that* introduces a noun or adjective clause.) The word *because,* on the other hand, starts an adverb clause.

16. **B.** *Person* (as in first, second, or third person) is the grammatical term that tells you whether you're talking *to* (the *you* form), *about* (the *he, she, they,* or other noun form), or *as* someone (the *I* form). Grammarians adore consistency, and they don't allow you to switch from one person to another without a very good reason. In Question 16, the sentence begins in second person *(you subscribe)* and then morphs into third person *(a viewer).* Penalty box! To correct the sentence, change *you subscribe* to *one subscribes* or *a person subscribes.* You could also change *a viewer* to *you,* but *a viewer* isn't underlined, so it's not an option.

17. **B.** The *–er* in the word *clearer* creates a comparison; so does the word *more.* You don't need to double dip here. Drop the *more* and the sentence is fine.

18. **E.** I finally threw in a correct sentence. (I bet you thought I couldn't write one!) I'm guessing that you paused over the word **continuously.** It means "without stopping," but it's commonly confused with **continually,** which means "recurring at intervals."

19. **B.** The expression *his or her* is singular and may not refer to *artists,* a plural noun. Also, the word *lifetime* must be made into the plural word *lifetimes.*

20. **A.** The pronoun *each* has only four little letters, but it's incredibly powerful. No matter what you place after the word *each,* the pronoun remains singular and takes a singular verb. In this sentence, however, the verb *agree* is plural.

21. **D.** Logic rules here. The whale is in a novel, which is by definition a work of fiction. Therefore, you can't compare the whale to *any animal in fiction* without removing the whale from that group. Instead, you have to compare the whale to *any other animal* in fiction.

22. **A.** The expression *a number of* really means "some," so the subject of this sentence is actually *some letters.* You can't match that plural subject to the singular verb *has,* so Choice (A) is the answer you seek.

23. **D.** *To* is a preposition and, therefore, needs an object. The pronoun *I,* however, can't be an object. Hence, Choice (D) is the one you want. In case you were wondering, the correct expression is *to you and me.*

24. **D.** *More* is what you use when you're comparing two items; *most* is what you want when you're choosing the extreme from more than two items. The given sentence compares one smile — the baby's first — to *any other,* not to *all others.* The expression *any other* sets up a comparison between two, so *more* is appropriate and *most* is wrong.

25. **C.** The smooth — and correct — version of this sentence includes the expression "how to improve attendance while avoiding overcrowded classrooms." As you see, Choice (C) is where you need to make the change.

26. **A.** Actors are people, and people are generally referred to with the pronoun *who.*

27. **D.** *Being* isn't a verb, or at least it isn't a complete verb. Read the sentence aloud and you can probably hear that the sentence doesn't make sense as written. Change *being* to *is* and you're home free.

28. **C.** How may the statues be identified? *Easily* — an adverb. Not *easy* — an adjective.

29. **A.** The SAT makers love to hit you with sentences that begin with descriptive verb forms (in this case, *living*) to determine whether you know that an introductory verb form must describe the subject. So who's living in a large metropolitan area? The way the sentence is worded, the *sidewalks* are living in the metro area. Nope. To fix this sentence, change Choice (A). If you were rewriting this sentence, you might say something like "In a large metropolitan area, . . ."

30. **E.** Both sentences are short, so combining them is a good idea. The key is to glue the sentences together smoothly without adding any grammatical errors. Choice (B) doesn't do much beyond joining the sentences with a semicolon. Also, the second pronoun *it* in

Choice (B) technically could refer to either *ladder* or *sticker*. (Yes, I know. Logic tells you which noun *it* replaces, but grammarians, including those who write SAT questions, prefer sentences that follow even the pickiest rules.) Choice (C) doesn't make the cut because *which* describes *it,* the stand-in for "ladder," and the ladder doesn't tell anything. The sticker does! Choice (D) starts off well, but *me falling* isn't Standard English. The correct version is *my falling* or just *falling*.

31. **B.** The first paragraph contains two examples of *frivolous* (not serious, silly) lawsuits — one potential and one actual. Yet the writer hasn't provided a transition sentence to guide the reader from the warning label to the ankle injury. Choice (B) does the best job of explaining how the ladder is connected to the ankle.

32. **C.** Choice (C) groups all the examples together and paves the way for Paragraph 2, which asserts that common sense has evaporated in the world of lawsuits and product *liability* (legal responsibility).

33. **C.** *People* is plural, and so are the pronouns *they* and *their*. Choice (C) matches plurals with plurals. The original mixes singular *(person)* with plural pronouns. Choice (B) unnecessarily (and incorrectly) shifts from talking about *a person* to *you,* a pronoun that addresses the reader directly. Choice (D) introduces a set of unnecessary commas, and (E) provides no context for the pronouns *they* and *their*.

34. **B.** Sentence 13 says more or less the same thing as Sentence 12, but 13 is more specific. Dump Sentence 12 and let Sentence 13 make the point.

35. **C.** The writer supplies several examples to make the point: the ladder, the ankle, the coffee, the medicine, and the matches.

Section 7: Critical Reading

1. **B.** The most important word in this sentence is *instead* because it signals a change in direction. Choice (B) explains — accurately, in my experience — that *peers*, or equals, seem more reliable to teens than their parents do. Choice (C) is close because you can imagine a teen considering parental advice and then checking with experts. However, (B) is a better fit because it expresses a sharper change in direction.

2. **A.** This question is easy to answer if you know that *dogmatic* has nothing to do with little furry tail-waggers and actually refers to people who hold onto a position no matter how strong the opposing arguments are. The noun, by the way, is *dogma*, a fancy word for a set of beliefs.

3. **D.** What do you do with information (*data*) once you have it? You analyze it, as Choice (D) says. Choices (A), (C), and (E) are close, but each is more specialized. *Survey* means "to get an overview," *probe* means "to dig deeply, usually with a narrow focus," and *appraise* generally refers to an evaluation of a specific situation or object.

4. **C.** To answer this question, put on your stethoscope and think like a doctor. What do doctors do when someone is dizzy? They try to determine *the cause*. Thus, you need a synonym for determine, and *ascertain*, which means "to become certain of," is just the answer you're looking for.

5. **E.** If you're physically fit, you probably won't get hurt, according to this sentence. (Real life is a different story. There was this pothole . . . but back to the SAT.) Another answer that may have tempted you is (A) because motivated athletes tend to work out a lot and become physically fit and less vulnerable to injury. Wait a sec! *Fit* is Choice (E), so you can skip the middle step expressed in Choice (A) and go directly to the best answer.

6. **A.** The answer choices are obvious if you know what the words mean. *Palatable* means "agreeable," and *abhorrent* means "hateful." *Diverting* means "entertaining"; *onerous* means "burdensome." (*Interesting* you already know. It explains what SAT questions are not.) Okay, why would a senator phase in a tax increase? To make the voters squawk less. Bingo: Choice (A) is what you're looking for.

7. **D.** The "wash from the snow mountain" (Lines 9–10) is described as something "down which some water had run after a big storm" (Lines 10–11). Plus, the narrator and his friend walk *up the wash* (Line 16). Choice (D) fits both of these descriptions. Because the narrator and his friend are trying to reach the snow and because water is scarce, the other choices don't fit the passage's context at all.

8. **C.** Lines 20–21 state that "it was quite a question if we could live long enough" to reach the snowy mountaintops and obtain water. Because Choice (C) deals with death, it's the best one here. True, the travelers are probably tired, but the passage doesn't provide direct evidence to support that idea, so (A) is out. The passage directly contradicts the other answers.

9. **A.** Only two choices, (A) and (D), are serious contenders for "proverb of the year" — or at least "proverb of Passage I." The travelers work together, each agreeing to summon the other when one finds water and then sharing water and food. Therefore, (A) describes their communal values perfectly. (D) has a lot going for it because the lack of water has brought them close to death, but the passage doesn't reveal anything about their attitude toward water *before* it was scarce. Okay, (A) is the better choice.

10. **A.** The *brush* survives with very little water and is *stunted*. Passage II begins with a discussion of a plant that's very tall when rain is abundant but tiny during dry spells. Thus, the *brush* has adapted to the dry environment described in Passage I.

11. **E.** The travelers set out early because they wanted to "get as far as [they] could before the hot sun came out" (Lines 2–3). They searched for water, not ice, and, therefore, found the ice by chance. Had they begun their search a little later, the narrator says, the ice would have melted into the sand. *Providential* means "lucky," and that's what the travelers were because of the facts stated in reasons II and III.

12. **A.** All the answer choices are true, at least in my opinion and, in some cases, in the directly stated opinion of the author of Passage II. However, Lines 49–50 deal with the ability of plants to adapt to extreme conditions, an idea directly expressed in Choice (A).

13. **B.** The quoted lines refer to the adaptation skills that allow a species to grow tall when it rains and to remain short when it doesn't. The *like qualities* mentioned are survival skills because a tall plant in drought conditions would quickly die from lack of water. Did Choice (C) trap you? Nature writing often advocates a back-to-the-land mentality because people who write about nature tend to love it, regardless of the number of flea bites or twisted ankles they endure while exploring it. However, this question isn't about the writer's attitude but rather about a specific statement.

14. **C.** To answer this question, try knocking off the wrong answers one by one. Choice (A) fails because Lines 61–65 make a big deal out of the relationship between size and rainfall amounts. The *stocky stems* (Lines 70–71) help the plants survive, so you can eliminate (B). Lines 67–69 discuss leaf characteristics; therefore, (D) doesn't work either. Choice (E) doesn't cut it because the dunes are *protective* (Line 71). Nowhere does the passage mention age, probably because the author is concerned with the survival of species, not that of an individual plant. Choice (C) is the right answer.

15. **D.** Lines 81–83 explain that a *hapless party* died "where shallow wells would have saved them." (Time to strengthen your vocabulary muscles: *Hapless* means "unlucky" or "miserable.") The travelers didn't know where or how to find those wells. As the passage says, "It is this nearness of unimagined help that makes the tragedy" (Lines 78–79).

16. **A.** Death Valley is the *sink* (Line 86). Picture the shape of a valley and the shape of a sink, and you see that Choice (A) is the answer you seek.

17. **C.** The second paragraph of Passage II discusses the hazards of desert travel and refers to the *toll of death* (Line 86). Put those two ideas together, and Choice (C) emerges as the correct answer.

18. **C.** As Lines 84–85 explain, "Properly equipped, it is possible to go safely across that [desert]." The travelers in Passage I survived, but only by chance. They arose early to beat the heat and thus found unmelted ice to **sustain** them (keep them alive).

19. **D.** Passage I takes you across Death Valley with one party of travelers. Passage II discusses how desert plants survive and how human travelers can minimize risk. In other words, Passage II is more scientific than Passage I.

Section 8: Mathematics

1. **D.** Don't waste your time finding the hypotenuse of the triangle here because you know the triangle's base and height, which are all you need to know to determine the area: $\frac{9(12)}{2} = 54$.

2. **C.** If you plug in the given numbers, you see that 0 and 1 both work, but –1 doesn't.

3. **B.** As I'm sure you remember, in ratio problems the total number of objects (students, in this case) must be divisible by the sum of the numbers in the ratio (5 + 3 = 8). Specifically, you can call the number of seniors $5x$ and the number of juniors $3x$, and write $5x + 3x = 40$, which gives you $x = 5$. Plugging that number back in to the equation gives you 25 seniors and 15 juniors.

4. **E.** Choices (A) and (B) aren't the right shapes to be folded up into boxes, so you can eliminate them right away. Choices (C) and (D) are the right shapes, but you'd have to match a 6-cm side with a 5-cm side, and doing so would leave gaps in the box. Only Choice (E) fully closes up the box.

5. **C.** A linear function has the form $y = mx + b$, where m is the slope and b is the y-intercept. Using x for spaces and y for points, you can find the slope by using the slope formula: $\frac{16-10}{5-3} = \frac{6}{2} = 3$. Using this slope and the fact that moving three spaces gives you 10 points, you can write $10 = 3(3) + b$, so $b = 1$. That makes the equation $y = 3x + 1$, and plugging in 8 gives you 25.

6. **B.** Nothing fancy here: When you double all the sides of any shape, you quadruple its area. In general, if you multiply all the sides by n, you multiply the area by n^2, so you multiply the area of the original pentagon (20) by n^2 (2^2).

7. **D.** You probably realized that you need to square both sides, but did you remember to isolate the radical first? You need to add 3 to both sides before squaring, giving you $\sqrt{n+5} = 7$. Now when you square both sides, you get $n + 5 = 49$, so $n = 44$.

8. **A.** Point A is at (2, 95); point B is at (14, 60). The slope of the line connecting them is $\frac{95-60}{2-14}$, which is very close to –3. Because this line slopes downward, it would rise about 6 units as you moved left from 2 to 0, which means the y-intercept would be around 95 + 6 = 101. Thus, (A) is your best choice.

9. **C.** Let n stand for the number of people in the study group, aside from Sergei. So Sergei had $3n + 2$ candies. When one person didn't show up, he had $4(n - 1) + 1$ candies, which is still the same number of candies. So $3n + 2 = 4(n - 1) + 1$, and the right side simplifies to $4n - 3$. Solving $3n + 2 = 4n - 3$ gives you $n = 5$, but be careful! The problem doesn't ask for the number of *people*, but for the number of *candies*. So plug 5 back in to the equation $3n + 2$ to get 17.

10. **A.** Because the small squares have side lengths of 1 cm, the medium squares' sides are 2 cm each, and the big square's sides are 4 cm each. Label the diagram as I do here:

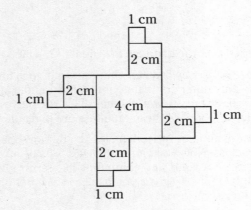

The key is to count only the sides on the outside of the figure, which I conveniently darken in my drawing. Because the figure is symmetrical, focus on just one side. Here's the right side of the drawing:

Three little sides equal 3 cm. The medium square has two full sides and one half-side contributing to the perimeter, for $2 \times 2 + 1 = 4 + 1 = 5$ cm more. And the big square gives a half-side to the perimeter, for another 2 cm. Add them all together and you get 3 cm + 5 cm + 2 cm = 10 cm. Because the figure has four sides just like this one, the answer is 10 cm $\times$ 4 = 40 cm.

11. **B.** Four grandfathers are at the reunion. Because every one of them is also a father, include them in the 12 men who have a son present. That leaves $12 - 4 = 8$ other men who have a son present. These 8 men could all be the grandfathers' children, so they can be counted in the 21 men who have fathers present. That leaves $21 - 8 = 13$ men in the youngest generation. In total, you have $13 + 8 + 4 = 25$ men.

12. **D.** From the instructions, you can write $x = 2y$ and $z = x - 45$. Because the angles must add up to 180°, you have $x + y + z = 180$. Substituting gives you $2y + y + x - 45 = 180$, and substituting $2y$ for x again gives you $2y + y + 2y - 45 = 180$, which becomes $5y = 225$, and $y = 45$. Therefore, $x = 90$ and $z = 45$, which makes the triangle a 45-45-90 triangle — in other words, an isosceles right triangle.

13. **A.** Imagine that you started drawing the number line like this:

If you then tried to put *F* in as *EH*'s midpoint, you'd be forced to put the letters in the order *EFGH,* which the question tells you isn't the case. Drawing the line backward doesn't solve your problem either, so you need to try drawing the line like this:

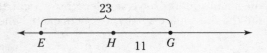

You can now see that the distance *EH* equals 12, which means *F* is 6 units from *H*.

14. **D.** $b + 2$ and $b - 3$ differ by 5, so any number that goes into both of them must also go into 5. But the only numbers that go into 5 are 1 and 5, and you know that *a* is bigger than 1, so $a = 5$. On the list of answer choices, 33 is the only possibility for *b* because $33 + 2 = 35$ and $33 - 3 = 30$, and both of these numbers are divisible by 5.

15. **E.** Let *b* equal the number of students in Ms. Belton's class and *j* equal the number in Ms. Jimenez's class. Now you can write $0.45b + 0.30j = 0.40(b + j)$. Distributing gives you $0.45b + 0.30j = 0.40b + 0.40j$, and combining like terms gives you $0.05b = 0.10j$. Dividing by 0.05 (or multiplying by 20) gives you $b = 2j$, so Ms. Belton's class has twice as many students as Ms. Jimenez's.

16. **B.** The four triangles themselves must form a square, and the area of this square is just $10 \times 10 = 100$. The triangle at the top is a 30-60-90 triangle, and the pattern for these triangles tells you that the missing sides must be 5 and $5\sqrt{3}$, which makes the area of this triangle $\frac{(5)5\sqrt{3}}{2}$. Because the drawing includes four copies of this triangle, the four together have an area of $4 \times \frac{(5)5\sqrt{3}}{2} = 50\sqrt{3}$. After all that work, all that's left is subtraction, and you end up with Choice (B).

Section 9: Multiple-Choice Writing

1. **C.** The verb form that begins the sentence has to apply to the subject. In the original sentence, the lightning is jumping off the sofa. Unlikely! The only two choices that provide the right subject/verb pair are (C) and (D). Choice (C) is better than (D) because in Choice (D) the verb emphasizes that an action *(jumped)* took place before another action *(exploded)*. Logically, the frightening weather took place more or less at the same time as the jumping, so *had* isn't appropriate here.

2. **D.** The original sentence has two problems. First, the sentence begins with *active voice*, the grammar term for a sentence in which the subject *(the theater company)* is performing the action *(applied)*. The second part of the sentence shifts to *passive voice*; now the subject (still *the theater company*) is being acted upon. Because you shouldn't shift from active to passive voice for no reason, you can cross off Choices (A), (C), and (E) right away. The second problem is the placement of *only*. This descriptive word should precede the part of the sentence it describes. The sentence compares funding sources. The company asked for money from many sources, but *only* one — the National Endowment for the Arts — came through. You're not comparing actions *(only gave*, didn't *audit* or *give a part to the director's pal* or something else), so the *only* shouldn't precede *gave*. Choice (D) gets rid of the passive voice and places the *only* where it belongs.

3. **D.** Paired *conjunctions* (words that join) must link similar grammatical elements. In other words, whatever follows *neither* must match whatever follows *nor*. In the original sentence, *good nutrition* and *how regular exercise is beneficial* aren't the same grammatically. The second has a verb, and the first doesn't. Only Choice (D) links a matching pair: *good nutrition* and *regular exercise*.

4. **B.** When a sentence begins with a descriptive verb form, the description must apply to the subject of the sentence. The storm can't skid or drive. Clearly the subject has to be *driver*. Choices (B), (D), and (E) put the driver in the driver's seat, so to speak, but (D) and (E) aren't complete sentences. There you go: (B) is your answer.

5. **C.** The checklist is simple and so is the answer. The *it* isn't necessary, so (A), (B), and (E) are out. Choice (D) creates a fragment, not a complete sentence. Choice (C) gets the job done nicely.

6. **C.** The subject of the sentence is *mynah birds,* which is plural. Therefore, any pronouns referring to *mynah birds* must also be plural. Cross off everything with *its* instead of *their,* and you're left with Choices (C) and (E). The verb tense in (E) is wrong, so (C) is the answer you seek.

7. **E.** The expression *equally as* has caught on in everyday speech, but it's not Standard English. Drop the *as* and you arrive at Choice (E) easily.

8. **B.** A weak little punctuation mark, the comma, isn't allowed to join two complete sentences, as it does in Choice (A). Omit "she was" and add the conjunction *and;* now the second half of the sentence adds more information about Sandra Day O'Connor without creating a run-on sentence.

9. **A.** The sentence mentions two actions, *moved* and *was located.* Both took place at the same time — in the past. Therefore, you need two past-tense verbs, which the original sentence supplies. Did Choice (B) fool you? *Has been located* is in *present-perfect tense*, which connects past and present. But the phrase *until recently* tells you that the *present* isn't present in the sentence, so (B) doesn't work.

10. **E.** The architects have one job: to design. They're making an attempt at that task. The *and* in the original sentence incorrectly creates two separate jobs — to try and to design. Choice (E) fixes the problem.

11. **B.** Pretend that the commas around "performing human sacrifices in religious rituals" are little handles. Lift that description out of the sentence, and you immediately hear a double subject, "The ancient Mayans they understood." You don't need a second subject! Choices (B) and (C) fix that problem, but Choice (C) adds an extra verb to pair with *they.* Why complicate the issue? Choice (B) does the job without adding unnecessary words.

12. **D.** The speaker in the sentence didn't know this equation: one peanut-butter cookie = one trip to the emergency room. To express what grammarians call "condition contrary to fact," you need to use *had* (for action verbs, as in this sentence) or *were* (for states of being) in the portion of the sentence that isn't true (called the *if statement*). Choice (D) is correct.

13. **C.** An *appositive* is a fancy English-teacher term for an equivalent. An appositive should match the term it's paired with in all things grammatical. *Roger and him* is the appositive of *campers.* Why *him* and not *he?* Because *campers* is the object of the preposition *to,* and *him* is the pronoun you want for objects.

14. **A.** The sentence tells you that one — and only one — book in the library contains a recipe for salted codfish (possibly because salted codfish tastes like used shoes). Back to the SAT: The statement beginning with *that* has to be singular because logically *that* refers to *only one,* not to *books.*

Answer Key for Practice Exam 4

Section 2

1. B	7. A	13. C	19. E
2. A	8. C	14. D	20. D
3. D	9. D	15. A	21. A
4. B	10. A	16. B	22. A
5. E	11. C	17. E	23. B
6. C	12. B	18. B	24. B

Section 3

1. B	6. B	11. C	16. B
2. E	7. A	12. A	17. D
3. D	8. A	13. D	18. C
4. B	9. B	14. C	19. D
5. E	10. D	15. E	20. A

Section 4

1. D	7. E	13. E	19. D
2. A	8. D	14. A	20. C
3. B	9. B	15. C	21. A
4. C	10. B	16. C	22. D
5. D	11. C	17. D	23. B
6. C	12. A	18. D	24. A

Section 5

1. A	6. B	11. 11	16. 3.5 or $\frac{7}{2}$
2. C	7. B	12. 280	17. 6
3. A	8. C	13. 72	18. 25
4. E	9. 630	14. 47	
5. D	10. 360	15. 8	

Section 6

1. E	10. D	19. B	28. C
2. B	11. B	20. A	29. A
3. C	12. D	21. D	30. E
4. B	13. D	22. A	31. B
5. D	14. C	23. D	32. C
6. C	15. C	24. D	33. C
7. E	16. B	25. C	34. B
8. A	17. B	26. A	35. C
9. D	18. E	27. D	

Section 7

1. B	6. A	11. E	16. A
2. A	7. D	12. A	17. C
3. D	8. C	13. B	18. C
4. C	9. A	14. C	19. D
5. E	10. A	15. D	

Section 8

1. D	5. C	9. C	13. A
2. C	6. B	10. A	14. D
3. B	7. D	11. B	15. E
4. E	8. A	12. D	16. B

Section 9

1. C	5. C	9. A	13. C
2. D	6. C	10. E	14. A
3. D	7. E	11. B	
4. B	8. B	12. D	

Chapter 28

Practice Exam 5

• •

*G*luttons for punishment (big-time overindulgers who actually like difficult experiences) will find a lot to enjoy in this chapter — one complete SAT exam. If you've worked through these chapters in order, you already know the drill. If you like to skip around and this is your first practice exam, turn to Chapter 20 for general directions. When you finish with Practice Exam 5, do yourself a favor and take your parrot for a walk, watch a trashy television show, or otherwise amuse yourself. Then open up Chapter 29 to score your exam. Good luck!

Note: The real SAT you take will have ten sections instead of the nine you see here because the College Board throws in an "equating section" that doesn't count toward your score but allows the testers to evaluate new questions. The SAT doesn't tell you which section is useless (to you). Because I'm a nice person, I don't include an equating section in any of the practice tests in this book.

Answer Sheet

For Section 1, use two sheets of loose-leaf or notebook paper to write your essay. For the questions in Sections 2 through 9, use the ovals and grid-ins to record your answers. Begin with Number 1 for each new section. If any sections have fewer than 35 questions, leave the extra spaces blank.

Section 2: Critical Reading

1. Ⓐ Ⓑ Ⓒ Ⓓ Ⓔ   8. Ⓐ Ⓑ Ⓒ Ⓓ Ⓔ   15. Ⓐ Ⓑ Ⓒ Ⓓ Ⓔ   22. Ⓐ Ⓑ Ⓒ Ⓓ Ⓔ   29. Ⓐ Ⓑ Ⓒ Ⓓ Ⓔ
2. Ⓐ Ⓑ Ⓒ Ⓓ Ⓔ   9. Ⓐ Ⓑ Ⓒ Ⓓ Ⓔ   16. Ⓐ Ⓑ Ⓒ Ⓓ Ⓔ   23. Ⓐ Ⓑ Ⓒ Ⓓ Ⓔ   30. Ⓐ Ⓑ Ⓒ Ⓓ Ⓔ
3. Ⓐ Ⓑ Ⓒ Ⓓ Ⓔ   10. Ⓐ Ⓑ Ⓒ Ⓓ Ⓔ   17. Ⓐ Ⓑ Ⓒ Ⓓ Ⓔ   24. Ⓐ Ⓑ Ⓒ Ⓓ Ⓔ   31. Ⓐ Ⓑ Ⓒ Ⓓ Ⓔ
4. Ⓐ Ⓑ Ⓒ Ⓓ Ⓔ   11. Ⓐ Ⓑ Ⓒ Ⓓ Ⓔ   18. Ⓐ Ⓑ Ⓒ Ⓓ Ⓔ   25. Ⓐ Ⓑ Ⓒ Ⓓ Ⓔ   32. Ⓐ Ⓑ Ⓒ Ⓓ Ⓔ
5. Ⓐ Ⓑ Ⓒ Ⓓ Ⓔ   12. Ⓐ Ⓑ Ⓒ Ⓓ Ⓔ   19. Ⓐ Ⓑ Ⓒ Ⓓ Ⓔ   26. Ⓐ Ⓑ Ⓒ Ⓓ Ⓔ   33. Ⓐ Ⓑ Ⓒ Ⓓ Ⓔ
6. Ⓐ Ⓑ Ⓒ Ⓓ Ⓔ   13. Ⓐ Ⓑ Ⓒ Ⓓ Ⓔ   20. Ⓐ Ⓑ Ⓒ Ⓓ Ⓔ   27. Ⓐ Ⓑ Ⓒ Ⓓ Ⓔ   34. Ⓐ Ⓑ Ⓒ Ⓓ Ⓔ
7. Ⓐ Ⓑ Ⓒ Ⓓ Ⓔ   14. Ⓐ Ⓑ Ⓒ Ⓓ Ⓔ   21. Ⓐ Ⓑ Ⓒ Ⓓ Ⓔ   28. Ⓐ Ⓑ Ⓒ Ⓓ Ⓔ   35. Ⓐ Ⓑ Ⓒ Ⓓ Ⓔ

Section 3: Mathematics

1. Ⓐ Ⓑ Ⓒ Ⓓ Ⓔ   8. Ⓐ Ⓑ Ⓒ Ⓓ Ⓔ   15. Ⓐ Ⓑ Ⓒ Ⓓ Ⓔ   22. Ⓐ Ⓑ Ⓒ Ⓓ Ⓔ   29. Ⓐ Ⓑ Ⓒ Ⓓ Ⓔ
2. Ⓐ Ⓑ Ⓒ Ⓓ Ⓔ   9. Ⓐ Ⓑ Ⓒ Ⓓ Ⓔ   16. Ⓐ Ⓑ Ⓒ Ⓓ Ⓔ   23. Ⓐ Ⓑ Ⓒ Ⓓ Ⓔ   30. Ⓐ Ⓑ Ⓒ Ⓓ Ⓔ
3. Ⓐ Ⓑ Ⓒ Ⓓ Ⓔ   10. Ⓐ Ⓑ Ⓒ Ⓓ Ⓔ   17. Ⓐ Ⓑ Ⓒ Ⓓ Ⓔ   24. Ⓐ Ⓑ Ⓒ Ⓓ Ⓔ   31. Ⓐ Ⓑ Ⓒ Ⓓ Ⓔ
4. Ⓐ Ⓑ Ⓒ Ⓓ Ⓔ   11. Ⓐ Ⓑ Ⓒ Ⓓ Ⓔ   18. Ⓐ Ⓑ Ⓒ Ⓓ Ⓔ   25. Ⓐ Ⓑ Ⓒ Ⓓ Ⓔ   32. Ⓐ Ⓑ Ⓒ Ⓓ Ⓔ
5. Ⓐ Ⓑ Ⓒ Ⓓ Ⓔ   12. Ⓐ Ⓑ Ⓒ Ⓓ Ⓔ   19. Ⓐ Ⓑ Ⓒ Ⓓ Ⓔ   26. Ⓐ Ⓑ Ⓒ Ⓓ Ⓔ   33. Ⓐ Ⓑ Ⓒ Ⓓ Ⓔ
6. Ⓐ Ⓑ Ⓒ Ⓓ Ⓔ   13. Ⓐ Ⓑ Ⓒ Ⓓ Ⓔ   20. Ⓐ Ⓑ Ⓒ Ⓓ Ⓔ   27. Ⓐ Ⓑ Ⓒ Ⓓ Ⓔ   34. Ⓐ Ⓑ Ⓒ Ⓓ Ⓔ
7. Ⓐ Ⓑ Ⓒ Ⓓ Ⓔ   14. Ⓐ Ⓑ Ⓒ Ⓓ Ⓔ   21. Ⓐ Ⓑ Ⓒ Ⓓ Ⓔ   28. Ⓐ Ⓑ Ⓒ Ⓓ Ⓔ   35. Ⓐ Ⓑ Ⓒ Ⓓ Ⓔ

Section 4: Critical Reading

1. Ⓐ Ⓑ Ⓒ Ⓓ Ⓔ   8. Ⓐ Ⓑ Ⓒ Ⓓ Ⓔ   15. Ⓐ Ⓑ Ⓒ Ⓓ Ⓔ   22. Ⓐ Ⓑ Ⓒ Ⓓ Ⓔ   29. Ⓐ Ⓑ Ⓒ Ⓓ Ⓔ
2. Ⓐ Ⓑ Ⓒ Ⓓ Ⓔ   9. Ⓐ Ⓑ Ⓒ Ⓓ Ⓔ   16. Ⓐ Ⓑ Ⓒ Ⓓ Ⓔ   23. Ⓐ Ⓑ Ⓒ Ⓓ Ⓔ   30. Ⓐ Ⓑ Ⓒ Ⓓ Ⓔ
3. Ⓐ Ⓑ Ⓒ Ⓓ Ⓔ   10. Ⓐ Ⓑ Ⓒ Ⓓ Ⓔ   17. Ⓐ Ⓑ Ⓒ Ⓓ Ⓔ   24. Ⓐ Ⓑ Ⓒ Ⓓ Ⓔ   31. Ⓐ Ⓑ Ⓒ Ⓓ Ⓔ
4. Ⓐ Ⓑ Ⓒ Ⓓ Ⓔ   11. Ⓐ Ⓑ Ⓒ Ⓓ Ⓔ   18. Ⓐ Ⓑ Ⓒ Ⓓ Ⓔ   25. Ⓐ Ⓑ Ⓒ Ⓓ Ⓔ   32. Ⓐ Ⓑ Ⓒ Ⓓ Ⓔ
5. Ⓐ Ⓑ Ⓒ Ⓓ Ⓔ   12. Ⓐ Ⓑ Ⓒ Ⓓ Ⓔ   19. Ⓐ Ⓑ Ⓒ Ⓓ Ⓔ   26. Ⓐ Ⓑ Ⓒ Ⓓ Ⓔ   33. Ⓐ Ⓑ Ⓒ Ⓓ Ⓔ
6. Ⓐ Ⓑ Ⓒ Ⓓ Ⓔ   13. Ⓐ Ⓑ Ⓒ Ⓓ Ⓔ   20. Ⓐ Ⓑ Ⓒ Ⓓ Ⓔ   27. Ⓐ Ⓑ Ⓒ Ⓓ Ⓔ   34. Ⓐ Ⓑ Ⓒ Ⓓ Ⓔ
7. Ⓐ Ⓑ Ⓒ Ⓓ Ⓔ   14. Ⓐ Ⓑ Ⓒ Ⓓ Ⓔ   21. Ⓐ Ⓑ Ⓒ Ⓓ Ⓔ   28. Ⓐ Ⓑ Ⓒ Ⓓ Ⓔ   35. Ⓐ Ⓑ Ⓒ Ⓓ Ⓔ

Section 5: Mathematics

1. Ⓐ Ⓑ Ⓒ Ⓓ Ⓔ   8. Ⓐ Ⓑ Ⓒ Ⓓ Ⓔ   15. Ⓐ Ⓑ Ⓒ Ⓓ Ⓔ   22. Ⓐ Ⓑ Ⓒ Ⓓ Ⓔ   29. Ⓐ Ⓑ Ⓒ Ⓓ Ⓔ
2. Ⓐ Ⓑ Ⓒ Ⓓ Ⓔ   9. Ⓐ Ⓑ Ⓒ Ⓓ Ⓔ   16. Ⓐ Ⓑ Ⓒ Ⓓ Ⓔ   23. Ⓐ Ⓑ Ⓒ Ⓓ Ⓔ   30. Ⓐ Ⓑ Ⓒ Ⓓ Ⓔ
3. Ⓐ Ⓑ Ⓒ Ⓓ Ⓔ   10. Ⓐ Ⓑ Ⓒ Ⓓ Ⓔ   17. Ⓐ Ⓑ Ⓒ Ⓓ Ⓔ   24. Ⓐ Ⓑ Ⓒ Ⓓ Ⓔ   31. Ⓐ Ⓑ Ⓒ Ⓓ Ⓔ
4. Ⓐ Ⓑ Ⓒ Ⓓ Ⓔ   11. Ⓐ Ⓑ Ⓒ Ⓓ Ⓔ   18. Ⓐ Ⓑ Ⓒ Ⓓ Ⓔ   25. Ⓐ Ⓑ Ⓒ Ⓓ Ⓔ   32. Ⓐ Ⓑ Ⓒ Ⓓ Ⓔ
5. Ⓐ Ⓑ Ⓒ Ⓓ Ⓔ   12. Ⓐ Ⓑ Ⓒ Ⓓ Ⓔ   19. Ⓐ Ⓑ Ⓒ Ⓓ Ⓔ   26. Ⓐ Ⓑ Ⓒ Ⓓ Ⓔ   33. Ⓐ Ⓑ Ⓒ Ⓓ Ⓔ
6. Ⓐ Ⓑ Ⓒ Ⓓ Ⓔ   13. Ⓐ Ⓑ Ⓒ Ⓓ Ⓔ   20. Ⓐ Ⓑ Ⓒ Ⓓ Ⓔ   27. Ⓐ Ⓑ Ⓒ Ⓓ Ⓔ   34. Ⓐ Ⓑ Ⓒ Ⓓ Ⓔ
7. Ⓐ Ⓑ Ⓒ Ⓓ Ⓔ   14. Ⓐ Ⓑ Ⓒ Ⓓ Ⓔ   21. Ⓐ Ⓑ Ⓒ Ⓓ Ⓔ   28. Ⓐ Ⓑ Ⓒ Ⓓ Ⓔ   35. Ⓐ Ⓑ Ⓒ Ⓓ Ⓔ

9.   10.   11.   12.   13.

14.   15.   16.   17.   18.

Section 6: Multiple-Choice Writing

1. Ⓐ Ⓑ Ⓒ Ⓓ Ⓔ   8. Ⓐ Ⓑ Ⓒ Ⓓ Ⓔ   15. Ⓐ Ⓑ Ⓒ Ⓓ Ⓔ   22. Ⓐ Ⓑ Ⓒ Ⓓ Ⓔ   29. Ⓐ Ⓑ Ⓒ Ⓓ Ⓔ
2. Ⓐ Ⓑ Ⓒ Ⓓ Ⓔ   9. Ⓐ Ⓑ Ⓒ Ⓓ Ⓔ   16. Ⓐ Ⓑ Ⓒ Ⓓ Ⓔ   23. Ⓐ Ⓑ Ⓒ Ⓓ Ⓔ   30. Ⓐ Ⓑ Ⓒ Ⓓ Ⓔ
3. Ⓐ Ⓑ Ⓒ Ⓓ Ⓔ   10. Ⓐ Ⓑ Ⓒ Ⓓ Ⓔ   17. Ⓐ Ⓑ Ⓒ Ⓓ Ⓔ   24. Ⓐ Ⓑ Ⓒ Ⓓ Ⓔ   31. Ⓐ Ⓑ Ⓒ Ⓓ Ⓔ
4. Ⓐ Ⓑ Ⓒ Ⓓ Ⓔ   11. Ⓐ Ⓑ Ⓒ Ⓓ Ⓔ   18. Ⓐ Ⓑ Ⓒ Ⓓ Ⓔ   25. Ⓐ Ⓑ Ⓒ Ⓓ Ⓔ   32. Ⓐ Ⓑ Ⓒ Ⓓ Ⓔ
5. Ⓐ Ⓑ Ⓒ Ⓓ Ⓔ   12. Ⓐ Ⓑ Ⓒ Ⓓ Ⓔ   19. Ⓐ Ⓑ Ⓒ Ⓓ Ⓔ   26. Ⓐ Ⓑ Ⓒ Ⓓ Ⓔ   33. Ⓐ Ⓑ Ⓒ Ⓓ Ⓔ
6. Ⓐ Ⓑ Ⓒ Ⓓ Ⓔ   13. Ⓐ Ⓑ Ⓒ Ⓓ Ⓔ   20. Ⓐ Ⓑ Ⓒ Ⓓ Ⓔ   27. Ⓐ Ⓑ Ⓒ Ⓓ Ⓔ   34. Ⓐ Ⓑ Ⓒ Ⓓ Ⓔ
7. Ⓐ Ⓑ Ⓒ Ⓓ Ⓔ   14. Ⓐ Ⓑ Ⓒ Ⓓ Ⓔ   21. Ⓐ Ⓑ Ⓒ Ⓓ Ⓔ   28. Ⓐ Ⓑ Ⓒ Ⓓ Ⓔ   35. Ⓐ Ⓑ Ⓒ Ⓓ Ⓔ

Section 7: Critical Reading

1. Ⓐ Ⓑ Ⓒ Ⓓ Ⓔ 8. Ⓐ Ⓑ Ⓒ Ⓓ Ⓔ 15. Ⓐ Ⓑ Ⓒ Ⓓ Ⓔ 22. Ⓐ Ⓑ Ⓒ Ⓓ Ⓔ 29. Ⓐ Ⓑ Ⓒ Ⓓ Ⓔ
2. Ⓐ Ⓑ Ⓒ Ⓓ Ⓔ 9. Ⓐ Ⓑ Ⓒ Ⓓ Ⓔ 16. Ⓐ Ⓑ Ⓒ Ⓓ Ⓔ 23. Ⓐ Ⓑ Ⓒ Ⓓ Ⓔ 30. Ⓐ Ⓑ Ⓒ Ⓓ Ⓔ
3. Ⓐ Ⓑ Ⓒ Ⓓ Ⓔ 10. Ⓐ Ⓑ Ⓒ Ⓓ Ⓔ 17. Ⓐ Ⓑ Ⓒ Ⓓ Ⓔ 24. Ⓐ Ⓑ Ⓒ Ⓓ Ⓔ 31. Ⓐ Ⓑ Ⓒ Ⓓ Ⓔ
4. Ⓐ Ⓑ Ⓒ Ⓓ Ⓔ 11. Ⓐ Ⓑ Ⓒ Ⓓ Ⓔ 18. Ⓐ Ⓑ Ⓒ Ⓓ Ⓔ 25. Ⓐ Ⓑ Ⓒ Ⓓ Ⓔ 32. Ⓐ Ⓑ Ⓒ Ⓓ Ⓔ
5. Ⓐ Ⓑ Ⓒ Ⓓ Ⓔ 12. Ⓐ Ⓑ Ⓒ Ⓓ Ⓔ 19. Ⓐ Ⓑ Ⓒ Ⓓ Ⓔ 26. Ⓐ Ⓑ Ⓒ Ⓓ Ⓔ 33. Ⓐ Ⓑ Ⓒ Ⓓ Ⓔ
6. Ⓐ Ⓑ Ⓒ Ⓓ Ⓔ 13. Ⓐ Ⓑ Ⓒ Ⓓ Ⓔ 20. Ⓐ Ⓑ Ⓒ Ⓓ Ⓔ 27. Ⓐ Ⓑ Ⓒ Ⓓ Ⓔ 34. Ⓐ Ⓑ Ⓒ Ⓓ Ⓔ
7. Ⓐ Ⓑ Ⓒ Ⓓ Ⓔ 14. Ⓐ Ⓑ Ⓒ Ⓓ Ⓔ 21. Ⓐ Ⓑ Ⓒ Ⓓ Ⓔ 28. Ⓐ Ⓑ Ⓒ Ⓓ Ⓔ 35. Ⓐ Ⓑ Ⓒ Ⓓ Ⓔ

Section 8: Mathematics

1. Ⓐ Ⓑ Ⓒ Ⓓ Ⓔ 8. Ⓐ Ⓑ Ⓒ Ⓓ Ⓔ 15. Ⓐ Ⓑ Ⓒ Ⓓ Ⓔ 22. Ⓐ Ⓑ Ⓒ Ⓓ Ⓔ 29. Ⓐ Ⓑ Ⓒ Ⓓ Ⓔ
2. Ⓐ Ⓑ Ⓒ Ⓓ Ⓔ 9. Ⓐ Ⓑ Ⓒ Ⓓ Ⓔ 16. Ⓐ Ⓑ Ⓒ Ⓓ Ⓔ 23. Ⓐ Ⓑ Ⓒ Ⓓ Ⓔ 30. Ⓐ Ⓑ Ⓒ Ⓓ Ⓔ
3. Ⓐ Ⓑ Ⓒ Ⓓ Ⓔ 10. Ⓐ Ⓑ Ⓒ Ⓓ Ⓔ 17. Ⓐ Ⓑ Ⓒ Ⓓ Ⓔ 24. Ⓐ Ⓑ Ⓒ Ⓓ Ⓔ 31. Ⓐ Ⓑ Ⓒ Ⓓ Ⓔ
4. Ⓐ Ⓑ Ⓒ Ⓓ Ⓔ 11. Ⓐ Ⓑ Ⓒ Ⓓ Ⓔ 18. Ⓐ Ⓑ Ⓒ Ⓓ Ⓔ 25. Ⓐ Ⓑ Ⓒ Ⓓ Ⓔ 32. Ⓐ Ⓑ Ⓒ Ⓓ Ⓔ
5. Ⓐ Ⓑ Ⓒ Ⓓ Ⓔ 12. Ⓐ Ⓑ Ⓒ Ⓓ Ⓔ 19. Ⓐ Ⓑ Ⓒ Ⓓ Ⓔ 26. Ⓐ Ⓑ Ⓒ Ⓓ Ⓔ 33. Ⓐ Ⓑ Ⓒ Ⓓ Ⓔ
6. Ⓐ Ⓑ Ⓒ Ⓓ Ⓔ 13. Ⓐ Ⓑ Ⓒ Ⓓ Ⓔ 20. Ⓐ Ⓑ Ⓒ Ⓓ Ⓔ 27. Ⓐ Ⓑ Ⓒ Ⓓ Ⓔ 34. Ⓐ Ⓑ Ⓒ Ⓓ Ⓔ
7. Ⓐ Ⓑ Ⓒ Ⓓ Ⓔ 14. Ⓐ Ⓑ Ⓒ Ⓓ Ⓔ 21. Ⓐ Ⓑ Ⓒ Ⓓ Ⓔ 28. Ⓐ Ⓑ Ⓒ Ⓓ Ⓔ 35. Ⓐ Ⓑ Ⓒ Ⓓ Ⓔ

Section 9: Multiple-Choice Writing

1. Ⓐ Ⓑ Ⓒ Ⓓ Ⓔ 8. Ⓐ Ⓑ Ⓒ Ⓓ Ⓔ 15. Ⓐ Ⓑ Ⓒ Ⓓ Ⓔ 22. Ⓐ Ⓑ Ⓒ Ⓓ Ⓔ 29. Ⓐ Ⓑ Ⓒ Ⓓ Ⓔ
2. Ⓐ Ⓑ Ⓒ Ⓓ Ⓔ 9. Ⓐ Ⓑ Ⓒ Ⓓ Ⓔ 16. Ⓐ Ⓑ Ⓒ Ⓓ Ⓔ 23. Ⓐ Ⓑ Ⓒ Ⓓ Ⓔ 30. Ⓐ Ⓑ Ⓒ Ⓓ Ⓔ
3. Ⓐ Ⓑ Ⓒ Ⓓ Ⓔ 10. Ⓐ Ⓑ Ⓒ Ⓓ Ⓔ 17. Ⓐ Ⓑ Ⓒ Ⓓ Ⓔ 24. Ⓐ Ⓑ Ⓒ Ⓓ Ⓔ 31. Ⓐ Ⓑ Ⓒ Ⓓ Ⓔ
4. Ⓐ Ⓑ Ⓒ Ⓓ Ⓔ 11. Ⓐ Ⓑ Ⓒ Ⓓ Ⓔ 18. Ⓐ Ⓑ Ⓒ Ⓓ Ⓔ 25. Ⓐ Ⓑ Ⓒ Ⓓ Ⓔ 32. Ⓐ Ⓑ Ⓒ Ⓓ Ⓔ
5. Ⓐ Ⓑ Ⓒ Ⓓ Ⓔ 12. Ⓐ Ⓑ Ⓒ Ⓓ Ⓔ 19. Ⓐ Ⓑ Ⓒ Ⓓ Ⓔ 26. Ⓐ Ⓑ Ⓒ Ⓓ Ⓔ 33. Ⓐ Ⓑ Ⓒ Ⓓ Ⓔ
6. Ⓐ Ⓑ Ⓒ Ⓓ Ⓔ 13. Ⓐ Ⓑ Ⓒ Ⓓ Ⓔ 20. Ⓐ Ⓑ Ⓒ Ⓓ Ⓔ 27. Ⓐ Ⓑ Ⓒ Ⓓ Ⓔ 34. Ⓐ Ⓑ Ⓒ Ⓓ Ⓔ
7. Ⓐ Ⓑ Ⓒ Ⓓ Ⓔ 14. Ⓐ Ⓑ Ⓒ Ⓓ Ⓔ 21. Ⓐ Ⓑ Ⓒ Ⓓ Ⓔ 28. Ⓐ Ⓑ Ⓒ Ⓓ Ⓔ 35. Ⓐ Ⓑ Ⓒ Ⓓ Ⓔ

Section 1

The Essay

Time: 25 minutes

Directions: In response to the following prompt, write an essay on a separate sheet of paper (the answer sheet). You may use extra space in the question booklet to take notes and to organize your thoughts, but only the answer sheet will be graded.

"The illiterate of the 21st century will not be those who cannot read and write, but those who cannot learn, unlearn, and relearn." — Alvin Toffler

Must a well-educated person "unlearn" and then "relearn" what he or she has already mastered? Or is knowledge or a skill, once acquired, always an asset? Using examples from literature, history, current events, or your own experience and observations, explain your position on Alvin Toffler's statement.

STOP YOU MAY CHECK YOUR WORK ON THIS SECTION ONLY.
DO NOT GO BACK TO ANY PREVIOUS SECTION.

Section 2

Critical Reading

Time: 25 minutes for 24 questions

Directions: Choose the *best* answer to each question. Mark the corresponding oval on the answer sheet.

Directions for Questions 1–5: Select the answer that *best* fits the meaning of the sentence.

Example: After he had broken the dining room window, Hal's mother _____ him.

(A) selected

(B) serenaded

(C) fooled

(D) scolded

(E) rewarded

The correct answer is (D).

---

1. Refusing aid to a beggar does not always indicate a lack of _____, for many people prefer to donate to charitable organizations.

   (A) feeling

   (B) interest

   (C) compassion

   (D) planning

   (E) individuality

2. In vain, the clerk squinted at his supervisor's _____ handwriting, unable to _____ it.

   (A) sensible . . . evaluate

   (B) illegible . . . decipher

   (C) confusing . . . alleviate

   (D) obtuse . . . normalize

   (E) convoluted . . . scrutinize

3. The _____ method of preserving food, though inefficient, was _____.

   (A) antiquated . . . effective

   (B) modern . . . streamlined

   (C) official . . . healthful

   (D) banal . . . adamant

   (E) compliant . . . rapid

4. The _____ truck driver easily lifted the heavy container.

   (A) brawny

   (B) scrawny

   (C) emaciated

   (D) ardent

   (E) salubrious

5. How can the principal meet the students' expectations if they do not _____ what they want?

   (A) disperse

   (B) articulate

   (C) promulgate

   (D) exemplify

   (E) conceal

Directions for Questions 6–9: Read the following two passages and answer the accompanying questions. Choose the *best* answer to each question based on what is stated or implied in the passages.

Both passages discuss letters: Passage I concerns letters written by Abigail Alcott, mother of writer Louisa May Alcott. Passage II refers to letters from Abigail Adams to her husband John Adams, the second President of the United States.

Passage 1

With Mrs. Alcott, hardship, poverty, the grief of seeing her husband misunderstood and often scoffed at, never lessened her love for him, or her contentment in the marriage relation. The year following her marriage in a letter to her brother she wrote: "My father has never married a daughter or son more completely happy than I

Line

(05)

Go on to next page

am. I have cares, and soon they will be arduous ones, but with the mild, constant, and affection-
(10) ate sympathy and aid of my husband, with the increasing health and loveliness of my quiet and bright little Anna, with good health, clear head, grateful heart and ready hand,—what can I not do when surrounded by influences like this?"

Passage II

(15)   The depreciation of the Continental paper money, the difficulties in the way of managing the property of her husband, her own isolation, and the course of public events in distant parts of the country, form her constant topics. Her let-
(20) ters are remarkable, because they display the readiness with which she could devote herself to the most opposite duties, and the cheerful manner in which she could accommodate herself to the difficulties of the times. She is a farmer
(25) cultivating the land, and discussing the weather and the crops; a merchant reporting prices-current and the rates of exchange, and directing the making up of invoices; a politician speculat-ing upon the probabilities of peace or war; and a
(30) mother writing the most exalted sentiments to her son.

6. In contrast to Passage I, the author of Passage II

    (A) is more critical of the letter writer

    (B) values cheerfulness

    (C) reveals the harsh conditions faced by the letter writer

    (D) explains the letter writer's situation more specifically

    (E) disapproves of the letter writer's actions

7. The "influences" (Line 14) that Abigail Alcott mentions in Passage I are most likely to be

    (A) her brother

    (B) her father

    (C) her husband and daughter

    (D) poverty

    (E) good health

8. In Passage II, Adams is described as "a farmer" (Line 24), a "merchant" (Line 26), a "politician" (Line 28) and a "mother" (Line 30) because

    (A) at various points in her life she filled all these roles

    (B) she aspired to each of these careers

    (C) she read widely on all these subjects

    (D) her husband was not able to fill these roles

    (E) her letters included information on all these topics

9. In the context of Line 22 in Passage II, "opposite" may best be defined as

    (A) contrary

    (B) parallel

    (C) inappropriate

    (D) varied

    (E) clashing

Directions for Questions 10–15: Read the fol-lowing passage and answer the accompanying questions. Choose the *best* answer to each question based on what is stated or implied in the passage.

This passage is an excerpt from 200% of Nothing *by A. K. Dewdney (Wiley).*

Suppose you grant that we are all mathema-   Line
ticians in some sense of that, at a very minimum, we all have this innate, largely unconscious logi-cal ability. Why, then, do we continue to exhibit such awful innumeracy and why, for that matter,   (05)
is mathematics education in such a crisis? The answer is already implicit in what I have said about mathematics in life. Mathematics itself is too simple!

By this I don't mean that the subject is   (10)
simple. Far from it! No subject of human thought has anything like the stunning depth and com-plexity of mathematics. But the elements of mathematics, primary concepts like numbers, sets, relations, and even functions, are really   (15)
quite simple. Paradoxically, it is only this sim-plicity (and clarity) that makes the complexity of mathematics possible.

Those of us with little or no familiarity with formal mathematics are nevertheless used to   (20)

Go on to next page

thinking complex thoughts about complex subjects, namely other people. When we come to study mathematics, we find it hard, perhaps, because we cannot get used to thinking about (25) such simple subjects. It's much harder, for a mind that readily analyzes Aunt Mary's strange behavior at the reception, to realize that A, B, and C have no character or personality whatever.

In mathematical concepts, all unnecessary (30) details have been stripped away by the process of abstraction. The naked idea stands before you and your first temptation is to clothe it with some detail, even if it means missing the whole point of the concept. Deep down you want A, B, (35) and C to have human dimensions. Instead, they simply stand for numbers, sets, or some other apparently barren concept. . . .

As Sheila Tobias, author of *Overcoming Math Anxiety,* has pointed out, people who are intro-(40) duced to mathematical problem solving for the first time routinely try to add dimensions to the problem that simply aren't there. Used to bringing an enormous array of data to the mental table, they simply aren't ready for the utter simplicity of (45) it all. They may attempt to fill in enough lifelike elements to make the characters real and, therefore, manageable by a mind used to more complex situations. Otherwise, the terrain is all too alien.

If mathematics is so hard for people, it may (50) not be due to a lack of innate ability at all, but rather to a cognitive style that demands a certain level of complexity that just isn't there! If this idea holds any truth at all, it may help people learn mathematics better by inspiring them with a (55) sense of confidence. Sometimes expectation paves the way to a completely new learning experience. If the theory holds water, it suggests that the best way to teach mathematics, at least to students encountering it for the first time, is to (60) move gradually toward simple, abstract situations from complicated, real-life ones. Not apples and oranges at the supermarket shelf nor transactions at the cash register, but the shoppers themselves, and the logic of their social interactions.

Reprinted with permission of John Wiley & Sons, Inc.

10. What is the most likely definition of "innumeracy" (Line 5) in the context of this passage?

(A) an inability to count

(B) difficulty understanding sets and functions

(C) confusion about the complexity of mathematics

(D) a failure to understand mathematical concepts

(E) ignorance of higher-level mathematics

11. The author refers to both the "depth and complexity of mathematics" (Lines 12–13) and "primary concepts" (Line 14) in order to

(A) show that mathematical thinking is innate

(B) explain that mathematics is abstract

(C) reveal the contradictions faced by mathematicians

(D) describe how mathematical study should proceed

(E) advocate for increased study of mathematics

12. Which of the following, if any, are true statements about the identity of the letters "A, B, and C" (Lines 27 and 34–35)?

I. They're characters in a math word-problem.

II. They have human characteristics.

III. They're mathematical elements.

(A) I only

(B) II only

(C) III only

(D) all of the above

(E) none of the above

13. With which statement would the author of this passage most likely agree?

(A) Mathematics is accessible to everyone.

(B) Students generally do better than they think they will.

(C) Psychological counseling helps mathematicians.

(D) Many people see mathematics as more complicated than it is.

(E) Anyone who lacks confidence should avoid advanced mathematics courses.

14. In the context of Line 48, the best definition of "alien" is

(A) immigrant

(B) extraterrestrial

(C) unfamiliar

(D) confusing

(E) invasive

Go on to next page

15. According to this passage, how should math instruction be organized?

    (A) Basic concepts should be presented first.

    (B) Students should memorize mathematical rules.

    (C) Students should study abstract concepts before attempting complicated problems.

    (D) Students should be told to concentrate on the human aspect of math problems.

    (E) Teachers should begin with problems based on real situations.

Directions for Questions 16–24: Read the following passage and answer the accompanying questions. Choose the *best* answer to each question based on what is stated or implied in the passage.

This passage is an excerpt from Walden *by Henry David Thoreau.*

Line   Let us spend one day as deliberately as Nature, and not be thrown off the track by every nutshell and mosquito's wing that falls on the rails. Let us rise early and fast, or break fast,
(05) gently and without perturbation; let company come and let company go, let the bells ring and the children cry — determined to make a day of it. Why should we go with the stream? Let us not be upset and overwhelmed in that terrible rapid
(10) and whirlpool called a dinner, situated in the meridian shallows. Weather this danger and you are safe, for the rest of the way is down hill. With unrelaxed nerves, with morning vigor, sail by it, looking another way, tied to the mast like
(15) Ulysses.[1] If the engine whistles, let it whistle till it is hoarse for its pains. If the bell rings, why should we run? We will consider what kind of music they are like. Let us settle ourselves, and work and wedge our feet downward through the
(20) mud and slush of opinion, and prejudice, and tradition, and delusion, and appearance, that alluvion[2] which covers the globe, through Paris and London, through New York and Boston and Concord, through Church and State, through
(25) poetry and philosophy and religion, till we come to a hard bottom and rocks in place, which we can call reality, and say, This is, and no mistake; and then begin, below freshet[3] and frost and fire, a place where you might found a wall or a state,
(30) or set a lamp-post safely, or perhaps a gauge, not

a Nilometer, but a Realometer, that future ages might know how deep a freshet of shams and appearances had gathered from time to time. If you stand right fronting and face to face to a fact,
(35) you will see the sun glimmer on both its surfaces, as if it were a cimeter,[4] and feel its sweet edge dividing you through the heart and marrow, and so you will happily conclude your mortal career. Be it life or death, we crave only reality. If
(40) we are really dying, let us hear the rattle in our throats and feel cold in the extremities; if we are alive, let us go about our business.
    Time is but the stream I go a-fishing in. I drink at it; but while I drink I see the sandy
(45) bottom and detect how shallow it is. Its thin current slides away, but eternity remains. I would drink deeper; fish in the sky, whose bottom is pebbly with stars. I cannot count one. I know not the first letter of the alphabet. I have always
(50) been regretting that I was not as wise as the day I was born. The intellect is a cleaver; it discerns and rifts its way into the secret of things. I do not wish to be any more busy with my hands than is necessary. My head is hands and feet. I feel all
(55) my best faculties concentrated in it. My instinct tells me that my head is an organ for burrowing, as some creatures use their snout and fore paws, and with it I would mine and burrow my way through these hills.

1. Ulysses, a hero of ancient Greek mythology, asked to be tied to the mast of his ship so that he could listen to the enticing songs of sirens without giving in to their enchantment. 2. Flow of water against the shoreline. 3. A stream. 4. A curved knife.

16. The author's attitude toward Nature may be characterized as

    (A) apprehensive

    (B) antagonistic

    (C) idealistic

    (D) uneasy

    (E) hostile

17. In the context of Line 1, what is the best definition of "deliberately"?

    (A) single-mindedly

    (B) respectfully

    (C) slowly

    (D) rationally

    (E) purposefully

Go on to next page

18. What do the "nutshell and mosquito's wing" (Line 3) probably represent?

    (A) trivialities

    (B) natural enemies

    (C) misleading clues

    (D) natural barriers

    (E) elements of sabotage

19. The whistle of an engine (Line 15) and the ringing of a bell (Line 16) serve as

    (A) examples of human achievement

    (B) metaphors for an artificial view of time

    (C) warnings of danger

    (D) aids to those who hear them

    (E) temptations to avoid work

20. The author of this passage advocates all of the following EXCEPT

    (A) facing death realistically

    (B) keeping small events in perspective

    (C) living every day to the fullest

    (D) avoiding formal education

    (E) staying as close to nature as possible

21. What is the "Realometer" (Line 31) supposed to measure?

    (A) water level

    (B) pretense

    (C) time

    (D) fire

    (E) frost

22. Which statements express the author's beliefs about time?

    I.   The time span of each human life is short.

    II. Time itself is eternal.

    III. There is never enough time to accomplish your goals.

    (A) I only

    (B) II only

    (C) I and II

    (D) II and III

    (E) all of the above

23. The statement that "my head is hands and feet" (Line 54) means that the author

    (A) is clumsy

    (B) values manual labor

    (C) learns through travel

    (D) primarily does intellectual work

    (E) is uneducated

24. What is the dominant technique that the author of this passage uses to make his point?

    (A) personal stories

    (B) examples from history

    (C) metaphors and similes

    (D) realistic details

    (E) denunciation of opposing views

STOP YOU MAY CHECK YOUR WORK ON THIS SECTION ONLY. DO NOT GO BACK TO ANY PREVIOUS SECTION.

Section 3

Mathematics

Time: 25 minutes for 20 questions

Directions: Choose the *best* answer to each question. Mark the corresponding oval on the answer sheet.

Notes:

- ✔ You may use a calculator.
- ✔ All numbers used in this exam are real numbers.
- ✔ All figures lie in a plane.
- ✔ All figures may be assumed to be to scale unless the problem specifically indicates otherwise.

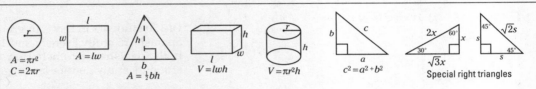

There are 360 degrees of arc in a circle.

There are 180 degrees in a straight line.

There are 180 degrees in the sum of the interior angles of a triangle.

---

1. Evaluate $3(4-2)^2 - 2$.

    (A) -2

    (B) 10

    (C) 20

    (D) 34

    (E) 98

---

2. Which of the following is true for the set of numbers 13, 19, 20, 20, 22, 29, 42, 63?

    I.   median = mode

    II. mean > median

    III. mode < mean

    (A) I only

    (B) II only

    (C) I and III

    (D) II and III

    (E) none of the above

---

3. Line j intersects line k at a 90° angle. If the equation of line j is $y = -\frac{2}{3}x + 7$, which of the following could be the equation of line k?

    (A) $y = \frac{2}{3}x + 7$

    (B) $y = -\frac{2}{3}x + 4$

    (C) $y = \frac{3}{2}x + 4$

    (D) $y = -\frac{3}{2}x + 7$

    (E) $y = 3x + 4$

---

4. If $f(x) = x^2 + 2x + 1$, then $f(-2) =$

    (A) 1

    (B) 3

    (C) 5

    (D) 7

    (E) 9

Go on to next page

5. If $\frac{x}{3}$ is 5 less than 7, what is the value of $3x$?

   (A) 2

   (B) 3

   (C) 6

   (D) 12

   (E) 18

6. In triangle *ABC*, side *AB* is 12 units long and side *BC* is 15 units long. The length of side *AC* may not equal

   (A) 23

   (B) 24

   (C) 25

   (D) 26

   (E) 27

7. If $|x + 2| = 3$, then x is equal to

   (A) –5 only

   (B) 1 only

   (C) 1 and 5

   (D) 1 and –5

   (E) 5 and –5

8. Twenty-one percent of the students enrolled in Algebra II earned As for the year, 33 percent earned Bs, 27 percent earned Cs, and 76 students earned Ds. If all Algebra II students earned either an A, B, C, or D for the year, how many students earned Bs?

   (A) 33

   (B) 100

   (C) 108

   (D) 132

   (E) 400

9. A sports team has four times as many girls as boys. Which of the following can be the number of people on the team?

   (A) 15

   (B) 17

   (C) 19

   (D) 21

   (E) 23

10. If $x^2 + 2ax + a^2 = 16$, which of the following could be the value of $x + a$?

    (A) –8

    (B) –4

    (C) –2

    (D) 2

    (E) 8

11. Of 150 students in the 11th grade, 82 study Spanish, 75 study French, and 15 study both Spanish and French. How many students study neither language?

    (A) 7

    (B) 8

    (C) 9

    (D) 21

    (E) 23

12. For all numbers a and b, let $a \# b$ be defined as a^b. Which of the following is equal to $(3 \# 2) - (2 \# 3)$?

    I. $4 \# 0$

    II. $1 \# 3$

    III. $2 \# 1$

    (A) I only

    (B) II only

    (C) III only

    (D) I and II

    (E) I and III

Go on to next page

13. The diagonal of a rectangle is twice as long as its width. If the width of the rectangle is represented as x, what is the area of the rectangle, in terms of x?

(A) $x\sqrt{3}$

(B) x^2

(C) $x^2\sqrt{2}$

(D) $x^2\sqrt{3}$

(E) $2x^2$

14. A sequence has 9 as its second term and 17 as its fourth term. If each term is a constant amount greater than the previous term, determine the 13th term of the sequence.

(A) 48

(B) 52

(C) 53

(D) 57

(E) 60

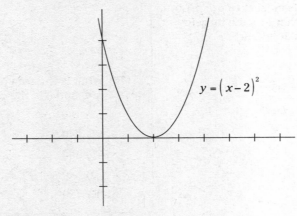

$$y = (x-2)^2$$

15. The graph shown here is of $f(x) = (x-2)^2$.

Which of the following choices represents the graph of $y = f(x) + 3$?

(A)

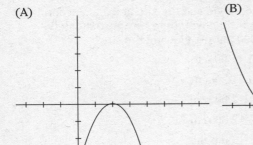

(B)

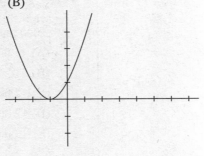

(C)

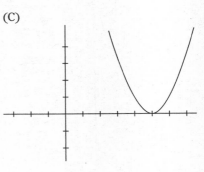

(D)

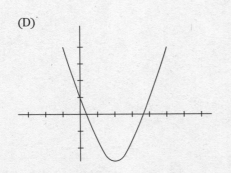

(E)

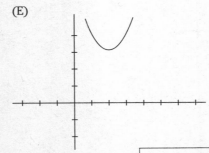

Go on to next page

16. The preceding diagram shows a target made up of two circles inscribed in a rectangle. Which answer is closest to the probability that an arrow that hits the target shown lands on the shaded part?

    (A) 10%

    (B) 20%

    (C) 30%

    (D) 40%

    (E) 50%

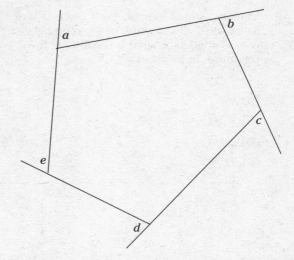

17. What is the sum of the angles marked *a, b, c, d,* and *e* in the preceding diagram?

    (A) 180°

    (B) 270°

    (C) 360°

    (D) 540°

    (E) 720°

18. Jose started a new website and it is quite successful. Every 30 minutes, the number of people viewing the site triples. If 7 people viewed the site at 9 a.m., around what time will there be approximately 2,000 people viewing the site?

    (A) 11:00 a.m.

    (B) 11:30 a.m.

    (C) 12:00 p.m.

    (D) 12:30 p.m.

    (E) 1:00 p.m.

Go on to next page

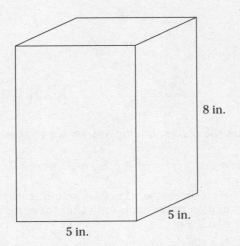

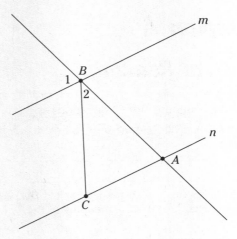

Note: Figure not drawn to scale.

19. This rectangular box, which is empty, has a square base with a length of 5 inches and a height of 8 inches. Beginning at 3 p.m., sand is poured into it at a rate of 5 cubic inches per minute. At what time will the box be exactly three-quarters full?

    (A) 3:06 p.m.

    (B) 3:25 p.m.

    (C) 3:30 p.m.

    (D) 3:35 p.m.

    (E) 3:42 p.m.

20. In the figure shown, $m \parallel n$. If the measure of angle 1 = 35° and $\overline{AB} \cong \overline{CB}$, find the measure of angle 2.

    (A) 35°

    (B) 55°

    (C) 70°

    (D) 110°

    (E) 145°

STOP YOU MAY CHECK YOUR WORK ON THIS SECTION ONLY. DO NOT GO BACK TO ANY PREVIOUS SECTION.

Section 4
Critical Reading

Time: 25 minutes for 24 questions

Directions: Choose the *best* answer to each question. Mark the corresponding oval on the answer sheet.

Directions for Questions 1–8: Select the answer that *best* fits the meaning of the sentence.

Example: After he had broken the dining room window, Hal's mother _____ him.

(A) selected

(B) serenaded

(C) fooled

(D) scolded

(E) rewarded

The correct answer is Choice (D).

---

1. After reviewing her business plan, I _____ her proposal and concentrated on those that had a better chance of success.

   (A) acclaimed

   (B) appreciated

   (C) adopted

   (D) accepted

   (E) discounted

2. Anyone _____ this art form for the first time may be puzzled, but those who have studied abstract painting _____ its complexity.

   (A) encountering . . . grasp

   (B) practicing . . . lose

   (C) collecting . . . overstate

   (D) viewing . . . dismiss

   (E) creating . . . abolish

3. The elderly man's _____ financial habits resulted in a comfortable retirement.

   (A) spendthrift

   (B) prudent

   (C) wasteful

   (D) dissolute

   (E) irresponsible

4. Widespread belief in laws guaranteeing human rights came only after these rights had been _____.

   (A) alleviated

   (B) violated

   (C) elevated

   (D) trespassed

   (E) confused

5. Instead of reviewing the show, the critic wrote about the actor's _____, such as eating green candy before each performance and refusing to say any word containing the letter "e."

   (A) demands

   (B) weaknesses

   (C) talents

   (D) habits

   (E) quirks

6. By _____ the opposing point of view, the politician showed that he had carefully considered his rival's ideas.

   (A) snubbing

   (B) overlooking

   (C) ignoring

   (D) acknowledging

   (E) praising

7. Normally a model of _____, Gary was filled with _____ after the accident.

   (A) restraint . . . confusion

   (B) joviality . . . elation

   (C) equanimity . . . rage

   (D) amiability . . . friendliness

   (E) courtesy . . . anger

Go on to next page

8. Because she had correctly predicted the winner of the election, Sarah gained a reputation for _____.

    (A) retrospection

    (B) introspection

    (C) hindsight

    (D) fortune-telling

    (E) prescience

Directions for Questions 9–12: Each of the following two passages is followed by two questions. Choose the *best* answer to each question based on what is stated or implied in the passages.

The first passage is an excerpt from The Contemporary Encyclopedia of Herbs & Spices *by Tony Hill (Wiley). The second passage is excerpted from* Sacred Fire: The QBR 100 Essential Black Books *by QBR: The Black Review, Max Rodriguez, Angeli Rasbury, and Carol Taylor (Wiley).*

Line   In the wine trade, the different characteristics of each region, each field, and even each row of grapes are embraced and celebrated as part of the beauty of a natural product. The same idea
(05) applies to all sorts of foods, not the least of which are herbs and spices. Growing conditions affect any crop, and since herbs and spices are typically intense versions of plants, they reflect trends and changes in climate and become
(10) potent distillations of variations in any particular region. Spring crops may have more new growth character; fall crops may be more fully developed. Herbs grown in an irrigated desert will taste different from those cultivated on a rainy
(15) coast. These are the differences the cook should want to understand.

Reprinted with permission of John Wiley & Sons, Inc.

9. According to the author, "the beauty of a natural product" (Line 4) is based on

    (A) its purity

    (B) the lack of contaminating factors such as pesticides

    (C) variations between one batch and another

    (D) its ability to grow in many different climates

    (E) the way in which people use the product

10. Compared to other crops, herbs and spices are

    (A) less variable

    (B) more flavorful

    (C) grown in fewer areas

    (D) less concentrated

    (E) more natural

Works of struggle have pride of place in black   Line
literature. A culture's literature is that culture's
communal voice. As such, the literature inevitably
reflects the traumas that culture is going through
at any given time, its burning survival issues.   (05)
Since the beginning of our journey in the West, it
can be argued that the Struggle has been a primary trope of black people in America and
around the modern world. Which way freedom?
Black literature has consistently reflected the   (10)
ongoing struggle for survival and empowerment
waged by the black people of America and the
world. It would be difficult to overestimate the
revolutionary impulse in black literature.

Reprinted with permission of John Wiley & Sons, Inc.

11. With which statement would the author of this passage most likely agree?

    (A) Literature can be appreciated only by understanding its historical context.

    (B) All literature contains an element of conflict.

    (C) Writers cannot express universal truths, only those of a particular culture.

    (D) All literature has in it an element of sadness.

    (E) Without literature, a community cannot express itself fully.

12. The question, "Which way freedom?" (Line 9), serves to

    (A) represent the "Struggle" (Line 7) that black literature addresses

    (B) illustrate a universal sentiment

    (C) quote from a work of literature

    (D) direct the reader's attention to history

    (E) explain why empowerment is necessary

Go on to next page

Directions for Questions 13–24: Read the following two passages and answer the accompanying questions. Choose the *best* answer to each question based on what is stated or implied in the passages.

Passage I is an excerpt from philosopher John Locke's "Essay Concerning Human Understanding." *Passage II is adapted from Plato's* Republic.

Passage 1

Line   We shall not have much reason to complain
of the narrowness of our minds, if we will but
employ them about what may be of use to us; for
of that they are very capable. And it will be an
(05) unpardonable, as well as childish peevishness, if
we undervalue the advantages of our knowledge,
and neglect to improve it to the ends for which it
was given us, because there are some things that
are set out of the reach of it. It will be no excuse
(10) to an idle and untoward servant, who would not
attend his business by candle light, to plead that
he had not broad sunshine. The Candle that is
set up in us shines bright enough for all our purposes. The discoveries we can make with this
(15) ought to satisfy us; and we shall then use our
understandings right, when we entertain all
objects in that way and proportion that they are
suited to our faculties, and upon those grounds
they are capable of being proposed to us; and
(20) not require demonstration, and demand cer-
tainty, where probability only is to be had. If we
will disbelieve everything, because we cannot
certainly know all things, we shall be no better
than he who would not use his legs, but sit still
(25) and perish, because he had no wings to fly.
      When we know our own strength, we shall
the better know what to undertake with hopes of
success; and when we have well surveyed the
POWERS of our own minds, and made some esti-
(30) mate what we may expect from them, we shall
not be inclined either to sit still, and not set our
thoughts on work at all, in despair of knowing
anything; nor on the other side, question everything, and disclaim all knowledge, because some
(35) things are not to be understood. It is of great use
to the sailor to know the length of his line,
though he cannot with it fathom all the depths of
the ocean. It is well he knows that it is long
enough to reach the bottom, at such places as
(40) are necessary to direct his voyage, and caution
him against running upon shoals that may ruin

him. Our business here is not to know all things,
but those which concern our conduct. If we can
find out those measures, whereby a rational
creature, put in that state in which man is in this   (45)
world, may and ought to govern his opinions,
and actions depending thereon, we need not to
be troubled that some other things escape our
knowledge.

Passage II

      Behold! human beings living in a under-   (50)
ground den, which has a mouth open towards
the light and reaching all along the den; here
they have been from their childhood, and have
their legs and necks chained so that they cannot
move, and can only see before them, being pre-   (55)
vented by the chains from turning round their
heads. Above and behind them a fire is blazing at
a distance, and between the fire and the prisoners there is a raised way; and you will see, if you
look, a low wall built along the way, like the   (60)
screen which marionette players have in front
of them, over which they show the puppets.
      And do you see, I said, men passing along
the wall carrying all sorts of vessels, and statues
and figures of animals made of wood and stone   (65)
and various materials, which appear over the
wall? Some of them are talking, others silent.
They see only their own shadows, or the shadows of one another, which the fire throws on the
opposite wall of the cave.   (70)
      And if they were able to converse with one
another, would they not suppose that they were
naming what was actually before them? To them,
I said, the truth would be literally nothing but
the shadows of the images.   (75)
      And now look again, and see what will natu-
rally follow if the prisoners are released. At first,
when any of them is liberated and compelled
suddenly to stand up and turn his neck round
and walk and look towards the light, he will   (80)
suffer sharp pains; the glare will distress him,
and he will be unable to see the realities of
which in his former state he had seen the shadows; and then conceive some one saying to him,
that what he saw before was an illusion, but that   (85)
now, when he is approaching nearer to being
and his eye is turned towards more real existence, he has a clearer vision, what will be his
reply? And you may further imagine that his
instructor is pointing to the objects as they pass   (90)
and requiring him to name them—will he not be
perplexed? Will he not fancy that the shadows
which he formerly saw are truer than the objects
which are now shown to him?

Go on to next page

13. Which of the following best expresses the meaning of the statement in Passage I "for of that they are very capable" (Lines 3–4)?

    (A) No one truly understands the limitations of the mind.

    (B) The power of the mind is unlimited.

    (C) Our minds are able to accomplish many useful things.

    (D) We should use our minds to express justified complaints.

    (E) No complaint about the mind's power is justified.

14. In Passage I, the story about the servant who wouldn't work without sunlight is intended to

    (A) convince the reader that limitations cannot be overcome

    (B) explain that we should learn to work within our limits

    (C) compare the weak light of a candle to the strength of sunlight

    (D) express a complaint about a servant

    (E) illustrate the power of the mind

15. The best definition of "ends" (Line 7) in the context of Passage I is

    (A) completions

    (B) limits

    (C) conclusions

    (D) goals

    (E) edges

16. The statement that the "Candle that is set up in us shines bright enough for all our purposes" (Lines 12–14) implies that

    (A) a small amount of intelligence is all anyone needs

    (B) everyone is equally intelligent

    (C) people have unequal levels of intelligence

    (D) what is beyond human intelligence isn't necessary

    (E) the purpose of the human mind is unknown

17. What may the reader conclude from the story about the sailor and his line in Passage I (Lines 35–42)?

    (A) If you know what your brain is capable of, you will use it well.

    (B) A line should be as long as possible in order to survey the ocean's depths.

    (C) The brain's purpose is to foresee danger.

    (D) Everyone's intelligence should be measured by the same standard.

    (E) The line and the brain are both limited, so neither is helpful.

18. Unlike Passage I, Passage II

    (A) includes the literal truth

    (B) employs one comparison only

    (C) assumes that human intelligence is unlimited

    (D) relies on common experiences to make a point

    (E) comes to no conclusion about human intelligence

19. The author of Passage II would most likely agree with which of the following statements?

    (A) Trust your instincts.

    (B) The truth is always obvious.

    (C) Perspective influences what we believe is true.

    (D) Life experience has no bearing on our understanding of reality.

    (E) The ability to discern the truth is universal.

20. What is the best definition of "conceive" in the context of Line 84 in Passage II?

    (A) imagine

    (B) create

    (C) perceive

    (D) hear

    (E) pay attention to

Go on to next page

21. The "illusion" referred to in Line 85 of Passage II is

    (A) objects outside the cave

    (B) objects that cast shadows

    (C) shadows in the cave

    (D) the men in the cave

    (E) the instructor

22. Both Passage I and Passage II

    (A) urge readers to explore and learn

    (B) caution readers to distrust their perceptions

    (C) advocate for greater education

    (D) see human knowledge as limited

    (E) deal with skewed perceptions of reality

23. Which literary technique appears in both passages?

    (A) personification

    (B) metaphor

    (C) concession and reply

    (D) understatement

    (E) hyperbole

24. How would the question in Lines 88–89 of Passage II, "What will be his reply?" most likely be answered?

    (A) You're wrong.

    (B) You're right.

    (C) Both are real.

    (D) Neither is real.

    (E) Being in the light is always better.

Section 5

Mathematics

Time: 25 minutes for 18 questions

Directions: This section contains two different types of questions. For Questions 1–8, choose the *best* answer to each question. Mark the corresponding oval on your answer sheet. For Questions 9–18, follow the separate directions provided before those questions.

Notes:

- ✔ You may use a calculator.
- ✔ All numbers used in this exam are real numbers.
- ✔ All figures lie in a plane.
- ✔ All figures may be assumed to be to scale unless the problem specifically indicates otherwise.

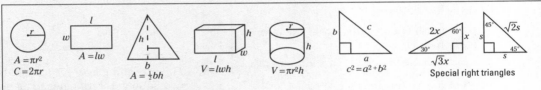

There are 360 degrees of arc in a circle.

There are 180 degrees in a straight line.

There are 180 degrees in the sum of the interior angles of a triangle.

---

1. If $(x + 1)^2 = 64$, then x could be

    (A) –8

    (B) –7

    (C) 7

    (D) 8

    (E) 9

2. Set S contains the numbers $\{1, 2, 3, \ldots, 15\}$. If a number is chosen at random from the set, what is the probability that the number is prime?

    (A) ⅕

    (B) ⁴⁄₁₅

    (C) ⅓

    (D) ⅖

    (E) ⁷⁄₁₅

3. When getting ready in the morning, Marc selects his outfit from among four pairs of pants, six shirts, and two pairs of shoes. If each outfit includes one pair of pants, one shirt, and one pair of shoes, how many different outfits can Marc make?

    (A) 12

    (B) 20

    (C) 27

    (D) 48

    (E) 54

Go on to next page

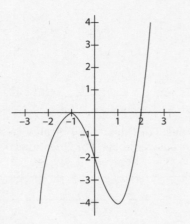

4. The preceding graph represents $f(x)$. How many solutions does the equation $f(x) = -1$ have?

    (A) zero

    (B) one

    (C) two

    (D) three

    (E) It cannot be determined from the information given.

5. Which of the following is equal to $x \cdot (3x^{100})^3$?

    (A) $3x^{104}$

    (B) $27x^{104}$

    (C) $9x^{104}$

    (D) $3x^{301}$

    (E) $27x^{301}$

6. A pitcher of lemonade is created using 5 cups of lemon juice, which cost 85 cents per cup, and 7 cups of sugar water, which cost 25 cents per cup. What is the cost, per cup, of the resulting lemonade?

    (A) $0.30

    (B) $0.50

    (C) $0.80

    (D) $4.25

    (E) $6.00

7. Five students, Johnny, Karen, Lucas, Mario, and Natalia, are comparing the number of articles they have written for the school newspaper. Johnny wrote four articles, the most among the group. Natalia and Mario wrote the same number of articles. Karen wrote one article less than Natalia. Lucas wrote the fewest articles among the boys. What must be true?

    (A) Natalia wrote at most three articles.

    (B) Karen and Lucas wrote the same number of articles.

    (C) Mario wrote four articles.

    (D) Lucas wrote more articles than Natalia.

    (E) Johnny wrote fewer articles than Mario.

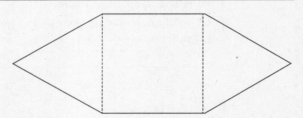

8. The preceding figure is formed by attaching two equilateral triangles to a square with a side length of 4. What is the area of the figure?

    (A) 16

    (B) 24

    (C) $4\sqrt{3} + 16$

    (D) $8\sqrt{3} + 16$

    (E) $16\sqrt{3} + 8$

Go on to next page

Directions for student-produced response Questions 9–18: Solve the problem and then write your answer in the corresponding box on the answer sheet. Mark the ovals corresponding to your answer, as shown in the following example. Note the fraction line and the decimal points.

Answer: $^7/_2$

Answer: 3.25

Answer: 853

Write your answer in the box. You may start your answer in any column.

Although you do not have to write the solutions in the boxes, you do have to blacken the corresponding ovals. You should fill in the boxes to avoid confusion. Only the blackened ovals will be scored. The numbers in the boxes will not be read.

There are no negative answers.

Mixed numbers, such as 3½, must be gridded in as decimals (3.5) or as fractions (⁷/₂). Do not grid in 3½; it will be read as ³¹/₂.

Grid in a decimal as far as possible. Do not round your answer and leave some boxes empty.

A question may have more than one answer. Grid in only one answer.

9. Julie ran the 100-yard dash four times. Her times for the first three dashes were 16 seconds, 18 seconds, and 15 seconds. If her average time on all four dashes was 15.5 seconds, what was her time, in seconds, on the fourth dash?

10. Find a value of x that satisfies $x^2 = 3x + 10$.

11. The line $y = mx + b$ passes through the points (0, 7) and (–2, 3). Determine the value of $m + b$.

12. The ratio of a rectangle's length to its width is 5:3. If its area is 60 square inches, find its width, in inches.

13. When a certain number is divided by 5, the remainder is 2. When the number is divided by 7, the remainder is 6. If you know that the number is positive and less than 50, what is one possible value for the number?

14. If $ab = 4$ and $a + b = 5$, what is the value of $a^2 + b^2$?

15. Hiring a band for a party involves a flat fee and an hourly fee. If it costs $525 to hire a band for 3 hours, and $765 to hire them for 5 hours, what is the flat fee, in dollars?

Go on to next page

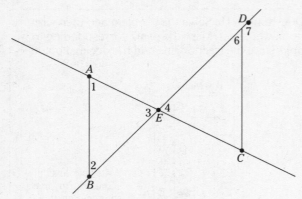

Note: Figure not drawn to scale.

16. Consider the preceding diagram. If $\overline{AB}//\overline{CD}$, the measure of angle 7 is 130°, and the measure of angle 1 is 50°, determine the measure, in degrees, of angle 4.

17. For all numbers g and h, let $g \& h$ be defined as $\dfrac{g^2 + h^2}{2}$. For what value of h does $4 \& h = 26$?

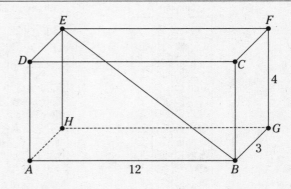

18. Determine the length of segment $\overline{BE}$.

Section 6
Multiple-Choice Writing

Time: 25 minutes for 35 questions

Directions: Choose the *best* answer to each question. Mark the corresponding oval on the answer sheet.

Directions for Questions 1–11: Each sentence is followed by five choices. Choose the answer that *best* improves the sentence. If the underlined portion of the sentence is best left alone, choose (A).

Example: Bert and him went to the store to buy boots in preparation for the approaching storm.

(A) Bert and him went

(B) Bert and he went

(C) Bert and he had gone

(D) Bert and him had gone

(E) Bert and himself went

The correct answer is Choice (B).

1. Margaret, who became a teacher shortly after finishing college, was better than any educator at her job.

   (A) was better than any educator at her job

   (B) did her job better than any educator

   (C) did her job best in comparison to any educator

   (D) was better than any other educator at her job

   (E) had been better than any other educator at her job

2. The real estate broker, correctly predicting a downturn in the market advised his client to sell this year, not next year.

   (A) broker, correctly predicting a downturn in the market advised

   (B) broker, correctly predicting a downturn in the market, advised

   (C) broker, correctly predicting a downturn in the market, he advised

   (D) broker, correctly predicting a downturn in the market, had advised

   (E) broker, he correctly predicted a downturn in the market and advised

3. Some cultures forbid a man from speaking to their mother-in-law on the theory that such a practice forestalls conflict.

   (A) a man from speaking to their mother-in-law

   (B) a man that he not speak to their mother-in-law

   (C) men not to speak to their mothers-in-law

   (D) a man from speaking to his mother-in-law

   (E) men, who should not speak to their mothers-in-law,

4. The gardener watered the plant yesterday and added fertilizer, and it helped the plant grow more quickly.

   (A) The gardener watered the plant yesterday and added fertilizer, and it helped the plant grow more quickly.

   (B) Watering the plant yesterday and adding fertilizer, the plant was helped to grow more quickly by the gardener.

   (C) The gardener watered the plant yesterday and added fertilizer, which helped the plant to grow more quickly.

   (D) Watering the plant and adding fertilizer yesterday, the gardener helped the plant to grow more quickly.

   (E) The watering and fertilizing, by the gardener, yesterday helped the plant grow more quickly.

Go on to next page

5. Placing an order for groceries over the Internet <u>is convenient, however, the buyer doesn't have</u> a chance to see the food and judge its quality firsthand.

   (A) is convenient, however, the buyer doesn't have

   (B) is convenient, and however, the buyer doesn't have

   (C) is convenient; however, the buyer doesn't have

   (D) is convenient, but however, the buyer doesn't have

   (E) is convenient, however; the buyer doesn't have

6. The reason Dansworth <u>was given two additional responsibilities is that</u> his salesmanship is exemplary.

   (A) was given two additional responsibilities is that

   (B) was given two additional responsibilities is because

   (C) has been given two additional responsibilities is because

   (D) was given two additional responsibilities are that

   (E) was given two additional responsibilities are because

7. <u>Although struggling with the most complicated figure-skating moves and falling twice, the judges awarded</u> Sarah high scores.

   (A) Although struggling with the most complicated figure-skating moves and falling twice, the judges awarded

   (B) Although she struggled with the most complicated figure-skating moves and fell twice, the judges awarded

   (C) Although she was struggling with the most complicated figure-skating moves and having fallen twice, the judges awarded

   (D) Although Sarah struggling with the most complicated figure-skating moves and falling twice, the judges awarded

   (E) Although struggling with the most complicated figure-skating moves and falling twice, Sarah was awarded by the judges

8. <u>Whether the mayor authorizes the new zoning laws, which promote environmentally friendly practices, or not</u> remains to be seen.

   (A) Whether the mayor authorizes the new zoning laws, which promote environmentally friendly practices, or not

   (B) Whether the mayor authorizes the new zoning laws, which promote environmentally friendly practices, or whether he does not

   (C) If the mayor authorizes the new zoning laws, which promote environmentally friendly practices,

   (D) If the mayor authorizes the new zoning laws or not, which promote environmentally friendly practices,

   (E) Whether or not the mayor authorizes the new zoning laws, which promote environmentally friendly practices,

9. <u>Given new information, the astronomer revised</u> her theory before submitting her article to that journal.

   (A) Given new information, the astronomer revised

   (B) Her having been given new information, the astronomer revised

   (C) Given new information, the astronomer had revised

   (D) Because of the new information that had been given to her, the astronomer revised

   (E) With her new information having been given, the astronomer revised

10. The wedding <u>that had been scheduled to take place in August, having been postponed</u> because of the bride's illness and rescheduled for November.

   (A) that had been scheduled to take place in August, having been postponed

   (B) , which had been scheduled to take place in August, having been postponed

   (C) had been scheduled to take place in August but was postponed

   (D) had been scheduled to take place in August it was postponed

   (E) that was scheduled to take place in August, it was postponed

Go on to next page

11. Strong winds and hail <u>ripped through the area last night, and tree branches were broken</u> off, crushing cars.

    (A) ripped through the area last night, and tree branches were broken

    (B) ripped through the area last night, and tree branches broke

    (C) had ripped through the area last night, and tree branches were broken

    (D) had ripped through the area last night, and tree branches broke

    (E) ripped through the area last night, and tree branches had broken

Directions for Questions 12–29: In each of the following sentences, identify the underlined portion that contains an error. If the sentence contains no errors, choose (E) for "no error." *Note:* No sentence contains more than one error.

Example: <u>Irregardless</u> of the fact that the
            A
National Weather Service <u>predicted rain</u>,
                                    B
Dexter <u>resented</u> the <u>students' request</u> to
        C   D
postpone the picnic. <u>No error</u>.
                        E

The correct answer is Choice (A).

12. The <u>newspaper, it reported</u> that the popu-
           A
    lation of the town <u>has been increasing</u> for
                          B
    the last ten years, <u>primarily because of</u> new
                          C
    industries <u>that have relocated</u> to the area.
                  D
    <u>No error.</u>
      E

13. The petite gymnast <u>was sure quick</u>
                          A
    <u>to adjust her routine</u> to take <u>into account</u>
      B   C
    new standards <u>announced by</u> the judges.
                     D
    <u>No error.</u>
      E

14. Either of the postcards <u>pinned</u> to that
                              A
    bulletin board <u>are certain to attract</u> the atten-
                     B
    tion of <u>everyone who</u> <u>attends parent-teacher</u>
              C   D
    night. <u>No error.</u>
             E

15. <u>While trick-or-treating</u> yesterday, I <u>received</u>
      A   B
    two entire bags of <u>candy, which</u> I will share
                          C
    <u>between you and I</u>. <u>No error.</u>
      D   E

16. <u>Impressed by his achievements</u>, the univer-
      A
    sity <u>offered</u> the Nobel Prize <u>winner, whose</u>
           B   C
    work on cancer was very promising, the
    chance to have his own lab, unlimited
    funding, and <u>he could hire</u> three assistants.
                    D
    <u>No error.</u>
      E

17. When someone gives a <u>presentation, how-</u>
                              A
    <u>ever</u> complex the information <u>may be</u>,
                                      B
    <u>they must be sure</u> <u>to take the audience</u>
      C   D
    step-by-step through the process. <u>No error.</u>
                                          E

18. The artist Louise Nevelson<u>, whose</u> sculptures
                                    A
    contain vertical columns <u>of wood that reveal</u>
                                 B
    subtle differences, <u>preferred</u> <u>her viewers to</u>
                          C   D
    <u>spend</u> a long period of time contemplating
    her art. <u>No error.</u>
               E

19. <u>Because the drought has been</u> longer
      A
    <u>than</u> <u>anticipated, water</u> restrictions
      B   C
    <u>have been tightened</u> in many areas. <u>No error.</u>
      D   E

20. The <u>large number of police procedural shows</u>
           A
    on television <u>have made</u> the work of a pros-
                     B
    ecutor very <u>difficult, for</u> juries often expect
                   C
    to see <u>the sort of evidence</u> that fiction
              D
    writers routinely insert into their scripts.
    <u>No error.</u>
      E

Go on to next page

21. The fact that the patient's muscles were
    —————   ——————————————
    A   B
    becoming more weaker troubled the
             —————————
                C
    physician, who immediately ordered physi-
    ——————————
         D
    cal therapy. No error.
                 ————————
                    E

22. The marketing team reported that every
    ————————————————————   ————
             A   B
    potential customer and client in the area
    were open to the new product, provided it
    ——————   —
       C   D
    was properly advertised. No error.
                             ————————
                                E

23. My cousins have been living in Spain in
    ————————————————————————
              A
    1982, but they moved to Argentina in 1983,
    —————————   ——————————
        B   C
    when they built a successful business.
    ————
      D
    No error.
    ————————
       E

24. The issue of computer use during school
                             ——————————————
                                  A
    examinations is controversial, some teach-
    ——————————————————————————————
                      B
    ers object to their students' typing essays
        ——————   ————————————————————
         C   D
    in class. No error.
              ————————
                 E

25. Relations between these former allies are
    ——————————————   ————
          A   B
    only complicated by a dispute over water
    ————
     C
    rights, which seemed unimportant during
    ——————————————
         D
    wartime. No error.
             ————————
                E

26. There's three photos of Elizabeth on the
    ——————
      A
    desk, but they are nearly obscured by piles
    ——————————————   ————————————————
          B   C
    of paper, books, and writing material.
              ——————————————
                    D
    No error.
    ————————
       E

27. Having gone on vacation for three years,
                          ————————————————
                                A
    the hotel was fully booked, and only a
    ——————————   ——————————————————
        B   C
    cabin was available. No error.
          ————   ————————
           D   E

28. I can't help but object to your request
      ——————————————————
             A
    to change from one word-processing pro-
    ——————————   ————————————————————
        B   C
    gram to another; what we're using now is
    ——————————————————————
             D
    perfectly acceptable. No error.
                          ————————
                             E

29. The license plate was extremely dented,
                     —————————————— ——————————
                           A   B
    consequently, the owner had to request a
    ——————————————   ——————————————
         B   C
    new one from the Motor Vehicle Bureau.
        ————
         D
    No error.
    ————————
       E

Directions for Questions 30–35: These
questions are based on the following essay.
Choose the *best* answer to each question.

⟦1⟧ Should bullying be a crime? ⟦2⟧ At present, physical intimidation like hitting and threats of bodily harm are prohibited by law. ⟦3⟧ You are also not allowed to blackmail someone by saying that you will reveal secrets. ⟦4⟧ But what about mean comments?

⟦5⟧ Many users of social networking sites have seen nasty comments posted about themselves or others, nothing comes of this but hurt feelings most of the time. ⟦6⟧ Recently, however, these comments, also known as "cyberbullying," have been taken more seriously as the victims have begun to explain their feelings. ⟦7⟧ In extreme cases, victims have even harmed themselves. ⟦8⟧ Making cyberbullying a crime has been proposed in several states. ⟦9⟧ The constitution guarantees freedom of speech. ⟦10⟧ The Supreme Court, nevertheless, stated that shouting "Fire!" in a crowded movie theater was not protected speech. ⟦11⟧ On the other hand, cyberbullying is a real and growing problem.

Go on to next page ⟹

[12] I favor educating, not criminalizing, those who engage in cyberbullying. [13] The Supreme Court may someday hear a case in which cyberbullying is decided as to whether it can be outlawed. [14] I hope that the Justices will see that freedom to express oneself is more important than an artificial restriction.

30. What is the best change to Sentence 2?
    (A) Delete "like hitting and threats of bodily harm."
    (B) Change "are prohibited" to "is prohibited."
    (C) Move "at present" to the end of the sentence.
    (D) Add examples of "bodily harm."
    (E) Place Sentence 2 after Sentence 3.

31. How should Sentence 3 be changed, if at all?
    (A) No change.
    (B) Insert a comma after "someone."
    (C) Change from second person (*you are, you will*) to third person (*people are, they will*).
    (D) Insert "their" before "secrets."
    (E) Add examples of secrets that may be used in blackmail.

32. What is the best revision of the underlined portion of Sentence 5, reproduced here:
    Many users of social networking sites have seen nasty comments posted <u>about themselves or others, nothing comes of this but</u> hurt feelings most of the time.
    (A) No change.
    (B) Change the comma after "others" to a semicolon.
    (C) End the sentence after "others." Begin a new sentence with "Nothing comes from these comments but."
    (D) Insert a comma after "this."
    (E) Change "themselves" to "himself or herself."

33. Which revision, if any, would most improve Paragraph 1?
    (A) No change.
    (B) Delete Sentence 4.
    (C) Move Sentence 12 to Paragraph 1.
    (D) Define "cyberbullying" in Paragraph 1 and delete the phrase, "also known as cyberbullying" from Sentence 6.
    (E) Explain that bullying may take place in person, not just through electronic media.

34. How may Paragraph 2 be improved?
    (A) No change.
    (B) Add more statements on the importance of freedom of speech.
    (C) Explain both positions, for and against the law, more fully.
    (D) Delete Sentence 8.
    (E) Move Sentence 8 to Paragraph 1.

35. How should Sentence 13 be revised, if revision is necessary?
    (A) No change.
    (B) Someday, the Supreme Court may hear a case, and cyberbullying will be outlawed or not.
    (C) Someday, the Supreme Court may hear a case that will decide whether cyberbullying may be outlawed.
    (D) The Supreme Court, someday, may decide a case that means cyberbullying is outlawed, or it is not.
    (E) The Supreme Court may decide a case, and someday cyberbullying will or will not be outlawed.

Section 7
Critical Reading

Time: 20 minutes for 19 questions

Directions: Choose the *best* answer to each question. Mark the corresponding oval on the answer sheet.

Directions for Questions 1–6: Select the answer that *best* fits the meaning of the sentence.

Example: After he had broken the dining room window, Hal's mother _____ him.

(A) selected

(B) serenaded

(C) fooled

(D) scolded

(E) rewarded

The correct answer is Choice (D).

1. The _____ meeting hall provided _____ room for all the delegates.

   (A) capacious . . . ample

   (B) minuscule . . . sufficient

   (C) cramped . . . abundant

   (D) choleric . . . excessive

   (E) gargantuan . . . ineffective

2. Red silk shades _____ the luxurious furniture of the room.

   (A) complimented

   (B) complemented

   (C) insinuated

   (D) belied

   (E) resolved

3. _____ is the enemy of productivity.

   (A) indolence

   (B) ingenuity

   (C) resourcefulness

   (D) motivation

   (E) compensation

4. "I won't make any _____ comments about my opponent," declared the politician, as she vowed to run a positive campaign.

   (A) laudatory

   (B) derogatory

   (C) congratulatory

   (D) deferential

   (E) obsequious

5. The _____ refused to pay for anything beyond the basics, carefully accounting for every dollar.

   (A) spendthrift

   (B) wastrel

   (C) miser

   (D) cutpurse

   (E) philanthropist

6. Because she was late for school so often, the principal _____ the little girl's recess time.

   (A) abridged

   (B) enriched

   (C) expanded

   (D) curtailed

   (E) excerpted

Go on to next page

The passage is an excerpt from The Calling of Katie Makanya *by Margaret McCord (Wiley), a biography of a young girl growing up in South Africa in the late 19th century.*

Line   The town around the railroad station was ugly but the location was worse than any place Katie had ever known. Here the iron houses, streaked with rust, seemed to push their way
(05)   into the road. Broken windows were patched with scraps of wood and stuffed with rags. Few people wandered about in the heat of the day, though Katie heard a mumble of voices behind the walls, the whimpering of children, a quick
(10)   burst of laughter. Occasionally from an open door a shrill voice called out a greeting to Charlotte, who waved and hurried on as if she did not notice the stink of urine, garbage, and stale smoke.
(15)   "Is this where we live?" Katie gasped. "Everything's so — I want to vomit."
       Charlotte stopped suddenly, turning to face her. "Who do you think you are, to come here and criticize? Are you too big for the rest of us?
(20)   Ma doesn't complain. She says we're lucky to find a house with a real chimney and an inside stove. Are you better than Ma?"
       Perhaps she had worked too long for Mrs. Hutchinson, for after the first happiness of
(25)   seeing Ma and Charlotte, Katie began to miss some of the luxuries she had taken for granted in Port Elizabeth — the long bars of yellow soap, the soft sea mist, the endless supply of water.
       It was the dry season in Kimberley when she
(30)   arrived. The water tank was empty. There were rivers in the distance, but it was a long way for the girls to carry water, and Ma doled it out sparingly — so much set aside for tea and coffee, a cupful each morning for their body-washing,
(35)   and all the rest saved for the laundry. There was never enough water to grow vegetables except during the rainy season when the trash overflowed and the roads became rivers of slippery clay.
       Ma never complained. One afternoon a boy
(40)   fell on the road and cut his leg on some broken glass. Ma hurried out to him with bandages and a pan of salt water. Soon the neighbors were calling on her whenever anyone was sick or wounded. Once, when Mrs. Cele fell sick with the
(45)   fever, Ma sent Katie over to her house several times a day to wipe her body down with a wet towel until her fever broke.

       "You're a very good nurse," Mrs. Cele told Katie.
       "That's what I want to be — a nurse," Katie   (50)
told Ma when she got home.
       Ma hesitated and then spoke slowly. "It takes much study to be a proper nurse. You have to know all about medicines —"
       "You can teach me."   (55)
       Mama shook her head. "All I know is how to wash out wounds and bandage them up. This I learned when I was a girl and watched your grandfather caring for his workers on the farm in Blinkwater. But I know nothing about sickness or   (60)
medicine —"
       "You can't be a proper nurse," Charlotte interrupted scornfully. "The nursing schools here are only for white girls. If you go to work in a hospital, you will just be a servant, mopping   (65)
floors and cleaning up after the Europeans. If you really want to do important work, then you must study hard and become a teacher."
       "I don't want to be a teacher," Katie said, feeling discouraged. She too wanted to make Pa   (70)
proud, but she was having as much difficulty at her school in Kimberley as she had had in Port Elizabeth. Her headaches were more frequent now, and by afternoon her eyes were red and swollen.   (75)
       Ma took her to see a white doctor who gave her some medicine — it cost seven and sixpence — and told her not to use her eyes so much. But how could she stop using her eyes when she had to read her books?   (80)
       With Charlotte's help Katie managed to pass her Standard Six examination but she did not win a scholarship to any high school. Although Pa could not hide his disappointment, Katie was secretly relieved. She knew she was not clever in   (85)
her head like Charlotte. All her cleverness was in her hands. Already Ma had taught her how to use the sewing machine, and she was making Charlotte's clothes as well as her own.
       "How is it you don't get headaches when you   (90)
sew, only when you read?" Charlotte asked. When Katie did not answer, she added, "I think you're just lazy."
       To make matters worse, Pa would not allow her to go anywhere without Charlotte. And   (95)
Charlotte gave her no peace. If Katie wanted to stay home and sleep, Charlotte called her a know-nothing. If she wanted to visit her friend Martha, Charlotte would not leave them alone but listened to everything they said.   (100)
       "Am I a baby to be carried around on my sister's back?" Katie grumbled.

Go on to next page ➡

(105) "No," Pa said. "But you are the junior sister. Among my people the eldest girl is always in charge of the younger ones. That is the custom."

"But we don't live among your people. We live here in Kimberley."

"Nevertheless, until Charlotte marries, she will be in charge of you," Pa said firmly.

(110) So the girls did everything together. They went to concerts or meetings at the church. On Saturday afternoons before choir practice they stopped to watch a football game or cricket match, and every Saturday night there was a

(115) party somewhere, sometimes to honor a visiting soccer team, more often to greet a returning traveler or to say goodbye to another.

Reprinted with permission of John Wiley & Sons, Inc.

7. The details included in Paragraph 1 (Lines 1–14) serve to

(A) establish how Katie will face these hardships

(B) explain why Katie is there

(C) reveal Katie's snobbery

(D) show that Katie doesn't belong

(E) illustrate the poverty of the neighborhood

8. How may the relationship between Katie and Charlotte be characterized?

(A) mentor to student

(B) affectionate equals

(C) vicious opponents

(D) fractious relatives

(E) jealous peers

9. What is implied by Charlotte's question (Line 22), "Are you better than Ma?"

(A) Ma is too poor.

(B) Ma complains too much.

(C) Katie complains too much.

(D) Charlotte hopes that Katie will be more capable than Ma.

(E) Katie doesn't understand life in Kimberley.

10. The passage contrasts Port Elizabeth with Kimberley in all these respects EXCEPT

(A) poverty

(B) climate

(C) access to family

(D) availability of water

(E) politics

11. Ma's rationing of water implies which of the following?

(A) The town needs a better well system.

(B) Kimberley is located in a desert.

(C) Ma goes to extremes.

(D) Ma is tyrannical in her demands.

(E) Charlotte and Katie are wasteful.

12. In the context of Line 53, how may "proper" best be defined?

(A) professional

(B) educated

(C) recognized

(D) well-mannered

(E) suitable

13. Charlotte's reaction to Katie's goal may be characterized as

(A) approving

(B) disapproving

(C) appreciative

(D) reflective

(E) unrealistic

14. The author implies that Ma takes Katie to a "white doctor" (Line 76) because

(A) Ma has little money

(B) Katie is white

(C) Ma thinks that Katie needs medicine

(D) Katie's illness is too serious for Ma to treat

(E) Charlotte thinks that Katie will be treated poorly in a hospital

Go on to next page

15. Which of the following statements is true, according to the passage?

    I.   Katie is not a good student.

    II. The family believes in traditional customs.

    III. Katie is lazy.

    (A) I only

    (B) II only

    (C) III only

    (D) all of the above

    (E) none of the above

16. This passage may best be described as

    (A) nostalgic

    (B) realistic

    (C) confrontational

    (D) argumentative

    (E) reflective

17. Judging by the evidence in the passage, with which statement would Katie most likely agree?

    (A) Life in Kimberley is better than life in Port Elizabeth.

    (B) Achieving one's goal is more important than family ties.

    (C) People should be well-educated.

    (D) Conflict can arise even in loving families.

    (E) Society should be more just.

18. The author probably includes the list of activities in the last paragraph (Lines 110–117) in order to

    (A) illustrate the life of a young girl in South Africa

    (B) reveal the happier aspects of the sisters' relationships

    (C) showcase the activities available in Kimberley

    (D) compare it unfavorably to life in Port Elizabeth

    (E) explain why Katie doesn't receive a scholarship

19. The fact that parties are often held "to greet a returning traveler or to say good-bye to another" (Lines 116–117) shows that

    (A) Kimberley is a close-knit community

    (B) people wish to leave Kimberley

    (C) Katie's journey to Port Elizabeth was not unusual

    (D) Kimberley was somewhat isolated from the outside world

    (E) Katie had many opportunities to travel

STOP YOU MAY CHECK YOUR WORK ON THIS SECTION ONLY.
DO NOT GO BACK TO ANY PREVIOUS SECTION.

Section 8

Mathematics

Time: 20 minutes for 16 questions

Directions: Choose the *best* answer and darken the corresponding oval on the answer sheet.

Notes:

- You may use a calculator.
- All numbers used in this exam are real numbers.
- All figures lie in a plane.
- All figures may be assumed to be to scale unless the problem specifically indicates otherwise.

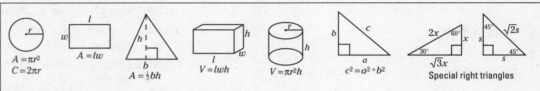

There are 360 degrees of arc in a circle.

There are 180 degrees in a straight line.

There are 180 degrees in the sum of the interior angles of a triangle.

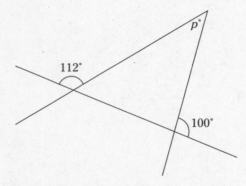

1. What is the value of p in the preceding figure?

   (A) 32

   (B) 68

   (C) 80

   (D) 122

   (E) 148

Note: Questions 2 and 3 refer to the following chart, which represents the money that Sita has in her bank accounts during the years 2008, 2009, and 2010.

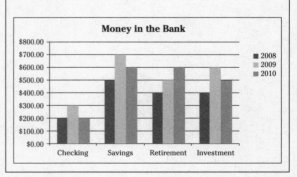

Go on to next page

2. How much money does Sita have, in total, in all of her bank accounts in 2009?

   (A) $1,500
   (B) $2,000
   (C) $2,100
   (D) $2,200
   (E) $2,300

3. If Sita's money in her retirement account in 2008 represents 0.1% of the bank's money, how much money is in the bank?

   (A) $400
   (B) $4,000
   (C) $40,000
   (D) $400,000
   (E) $4,000,000

4. Which linear equation best models the following data?

x	y
–3	8
–1	2
0	–1
2	–7
4	–13

   (A) $y = -\frac{1}{3}x - 1$
   (B) $y = -\frac{1}{3}x + 2$
   (C) $y = -3x - 1$
   (D) $y = 3x - 1$
   (E) $y = 3x + 2$

5. If $f(x) = x^2 - 3x + 1$, then $f(2x) = ?$

   (A) $2x^2 - 3x + 1$
   (B) $2x^2 - 6x + 2$
   (C) $4x^2 - 3x + 1$
   (D) $4x^2 - 6x + 1$
   (E) $2x^3 - 6x^2 + 2x$

6. Given that the following statement is true, which statement is necessarily also true?

   If Mary is at work, then Pierre is having lunch.

   (A) Mary is at work.
   (B) If Pierre is having lunch, then Mary is at work.
   (C) If Mary is not at work, then Pierre is not having lunch.
   (D) If Pierre is not having lunch, then Mary is at work.
   (E) If Pierre is not having lunch, then Mary is not at work.

7. On the xy-coordinate plane, what is the area of the circle centered at (–2, 4) with a point on the circle at (1, 0)?

   (A) 4π
   (B) 9π
   (C) 16π
   (D) 25π
   (E) 36π

Go on to next page

8. Which of the following is true for all values of *a* and *b*?

    I. $ab \le |ab|$

    II. $|a + b| = |a| + |b|$

    III. $|a - b| = |b - a|$

    (A) I only

    (B) III only

    (C) I and III

    (D) II and III

    (E) none of the above

9. The arithmetic mean of four positive integers, *a*, *b*, *c*, and *d*, is 15. When the largest number is subtracted from the product of the smallest three numbers, the result is 34. If $a < b < c < d$, which of the following pairs of equations could correctly express the information given?

    (A) $a + b + c + d = 15$
        $bcd - a = 34$

    (B) $a + b + c + d = 15$
        $abc - d = 34$

    (C) $a + b + c + d = 30$
        $abc - d = 34$

    (D) $a + b + c + d = 60$
        $bcd - a = 34$

    (E) $a + b + c + d = 60$
        $abc - d = 34$

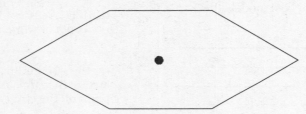

10. If this page were rotated 180° around the dot, the preceding image would match up with itself. Which of the following images, as shown, CANNOT be rotated 180° and match up with itself?

(A)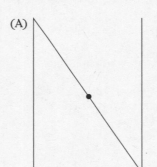

(B)

(C)

(D)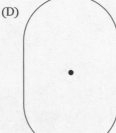

(E)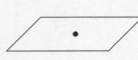

Go on to next page

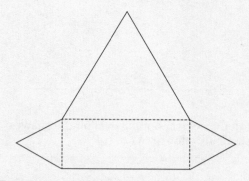

11. The preceding figure is constructed by appending equilateral triangles to three sides of a rectangle. If the rectangle is 6 inches long and 2 inches wide, what is the area of the figure, in square inches?

   (A) 18

   (B) $12 + 10\sqrt{3}$

   (C) $12 + 11\sqrt{3}$

   (D) 32

   (E) $12 + 12\sqrt{3}$

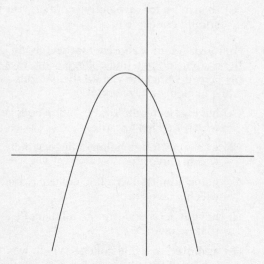

12. The graph shown here is of $y = ax^2 + bx + c$. Which of the following is a true statement?

   (A) $a > 0$ and $c > 0$

   (B) $a < 0$ and $c < 0$

   (C) $a > 0$ and $c < 0$

   (D) $a < 0$ and $c > 0$

   (E) $a < 0$ and $c = 0$

13. Anise has seven necklaces; two of them are identical. If she selects two necklaces without looking, what is the probability that she will select the identical necklaces?

   (A) $\frac{1}{49}$

   (B) $\frac{1}{42}$

   (C) $\frac{2}{49}$

   (D) $\frac{1}{21}$

   (E) $\frac{1}{7}$

14. A wheel with a diameter of 24 inches rolls along the ground. If it rotates 150 times, approximately how far will the wheel travel, in feet?

   (A) 150π

   (B) 240π

   (C) 300π

   (D) 360π

   (E) 480π

15. A sequence begins $\frac{1}{2}$, 2, 8, 32, . . . If $\frac{1}{2}$ is the first term, 2 is the second term, and 8 is the third term, which of the following expressions represents the nth term?

   (A) $\frac{1}{2}(2)^{n-1}$

   (B) $\frac{1}{2}(4)^{n-1}$

   (C) $\frac{1}{2}(4)^{n}$

   (D) 2^{-n}

   (E) 4^{n}

16. For any two real numbers p and q, define $p \square q$ as follows: $p \square q = p + q - 3$. Which of the following equations are true?

   I. $p \square q = q \square p$

   II. $3 \square q = q$

   III. $(p \square q) \square r = p \square (q \square r)$

   (A) I only

   (B) I and II

   (C) I and III

   (D) I, II, and III

   (E) none of the above

STOP YOU MAY CHECK YOUR WORK ON THIS SECTION ONLY. DO NOT GO BACK TO ANY PREVIOUS SECTION.

Section 9

Multiple-Choice Writing

Time: 10 minutes for 14 questions

Directions: Choose the *best* answer to each question. Mark the corresponding oval on the answer sheet. If the underlined portion of the sentence is best left alone, choose (A).

Example: <u>Bert and him went</u> to the store to buy boots in preparation for the approaching storm.

(A) Bert and him went

(B) Bert and he went

(C) Bert and he had gone

(D) Bert and him had gone

(E) Bert and himself went

The correct answer is Choice (B).

1. <u>The musical is nevertheless blessed with an enthusiastic audience, which lasts for several hours.</u>

   (A) The musical is nevertheless blessed with an enthusiastic audience, which lasts for several hours.

   (B) Having lasted for several hours, the musical is nevertheless blessed with an enthusiastic audience.

   (C) Nevertheless, the musical is often blessed with an enthusiastic audience, which lasts for several hours.

   (D) The musical, which lasts for several hours, is often blessed with an enthusiastic audience.

   (E) The musical is nevertheless blessed with an enthusiastic audience, that lasts for several hours.

2. Most educators believe that <u>before a student signs up for an elective course, you should check</u> the requirements and subject matter.

   (A) before a student signs up for an elective course, you should check

   (B) before students sign up for an elective course, you should check

   (C) before a student signs up for an elective course, he or she should check

   (D) signing up for an elective course, you should check

   (E) to sign up for an elective course, you should check

3. Last year's senior representative <u>having been admitted to a fine college, which was his favorite</u> since he visited the campus while in elementary school.

   (A) having been admitted to a fine college, which was his favorite

   (B) was admitted to a fine college, which was his favorite

   (C) being admitted to a fine college, which was his favorite

   (D) having been admitted to a fine college that he favored

   (E) admitted to a fine college, which was his favorite

Go on to next page

4. Comics featuring superheroes often reflect <u>current events; for example, one superhero was shown</u> fighting the Nazis during World War II.

   (A) current events; for example, one superhero was shown

   (B) current events; such as one superhero was shown

   (C) current events, and one superhero was shown

   (D) current events like one superhero was shown

   (E) current events, for example, one superhero showing

5. <u>The Flatiron Building in New York City is shaped like a narrow triangle,</u> it is a historic building that cannot be altered without permission from the Landmarks Preservation Committee.

   (A) The Flatiron Building in New York City is shaped like a narrow triangle,

   (B) The Flatiron Building in New York City, shaped like a narrow triangle,

   (C) Shaped like a narrow triangle, the Flatiron Building in New York City,

   (D) The Flatiron Building in New York City is shaped like a narrow triangle, subsequently

   (E) The Flatiron Building in New York City is shaped like a narrow triangle, and

6. There have been important court decisions <u>that alter society, and the course of history,</u> so the legal system plays a major role in the life of every citizen.

   (A) that alter society, and the course of history,

   (B) which, while they alter society, and the course of history,

   (C) alter society and the course of history,

   (D) that alter society and change history,

   (E) that, while altering society, they change the course of history,

7. <u>If I would have known about</u> the low level of ink in the printer, I would have purchased a new supply.

   (A) If I would have known about

   (B) If I were to have known about

   (C) Would I have known about

   (D) If I had been in the know about

   (E) If I had known about

8. Encouraged by her father to become an artist, <u>many portraits of the Spanish royal family were painted by Sofonisba Anguissola</u> in the 16th century, when nearly all professional artists were male.

   (A) many portraits of the Spanish royal family were painted by Sofonisba Anguissola

   (B) Sofonisba Anguissola painted many portraits of the Spanish royal family

   (C) Sofonisba Anguissola had painted many portraits of the Spanish royal family

   (D) many portraits of the Spanish royal family, they were painted by Sofonisba Anguissola

   (E) many portraits of the Spanish royal family Sofonisba Anguissola painted

9. A psychological experiment determined an important fact <u>about music, and it was learned that pauses</u> in the flow of sound capture the listener's attention most strongly.

   (A) about music, and it was learned that pauses

   (B) about music, pauses

   (C) about music, that pauses

   (D) about music, where it was learned that pauses

   (E) about music, being that pauses

Go on to next page

10. The island nation of Tuvalu, <u>which occupies nine islands in the South Pacific, and they have</u> little land for farming and few industries, earns a significant amount of money licensing its web address, "TV."

    (A) which occupies nine islands in the South Pacific, and they have little

    (B) which occupying nine islands in the South Pacific, and it has little

    (C) which occupies nine islands in the South Pacific and has

    (D) occupying nine islands in the South Pacific, having

    (E) which occupies nine islands in the South Pacific, and it's got little land for farming and few industries,

11. The "Black Sox" baseball scandal of 1919 discovered that some players <u>received money from gangsters, and so they were punished</u>.

    (A) received money from gangsters, and so they were punished

    (B) receiving money from gangsters, they were punished

    (C) were paid by gangsters, who punished

    (D) paid by gangsters, and who were punished

    (E) received money from gangsters and were punished

12. Biology, which is the study of all living things, <u>is more difficult to learn than any subject</u>.

    (A) is more difficult to learn than any subject

    (B) is more difficult to learn than any other subject

    (C) is found by students to be more difficult to learn than any subject

    (D) most students find more difficult to learn than any other subject

    (E) makes learning it more difficult than other subjects

13. When Ellen changed jobs, she had to decide <u>what it was she should do</u> about her health insurance.

    (A) what it was she should do

    (B) what she should be doing

    (C) her actions regarding what she should do

    (D) what she should do

    (E) how she should, with respect to health insurance, do

14. <u>In the grocery store on 12th Street,</u> melons and peaches are prominently featured in a display near the front door.

    (A) In the grocery store on 12th Street,

    (B) On 12th Street, it is in a grocery store that

    (C) Going into a grocery store on 12th Street,

    (D) It is in a grocery store on 12th Street that

    (E) In the grocery that is located on 12th Street,

STOP YOU MAY CHECK YOUR WORK ON THIS SECTION ONLY. DO NOT GO BACK TO ANY PREVIOUS SECTION.

Chapter 29

Practice Exam 5: Answers and Explanations

. . . .

After sweating (or shivering, depending upon your reaction to stress) through an entire SAT exam, you have one last task to perform. Go through your responses, marking them correct or (sigh) incorrect according to the key in this chapter. Then read the explanations for any wrong answers, plus any answers that you guessed correctly.

Note: To determine your score on this practice test, turn to the appendix.

Section 1: The Essay

Alvin Toffler, the author of the quotation in the prompt, is known as a *futurist,* someone who analyzes trends in society in order to determine how things will change in the decades to come. He has often written about technology and the need to adapt, both on the individual and the corporate or governmental levels. You don't need any of the preceding information to write a good essay, however. You just have to zero in on the key words in this quotation, which are *illiterate* (a term traditionally used for someone who cannot read or write) and "unlearn." Toffler's quotation changes the definition of "illiterate" in a surprising way because "unlearn" isn't on most people's list of great activities (particularly teachers' lists!).

Before you write your essay, you have to decide whether or not you agree with Toffler. If you do, your essay may focus on what must be "unlearned." For example, you can mention something — quill pens, for example — that has been *supplanted* (replaced) by better technology, such as the computer I used to write this book. Then you can talk about the "relearn" portion of the quotation, in which the former quill-pen user has to learn to write with a word-processing program.

Teachers (the people who will score your essay) appreciate thoughtfulness. In the preceding quill pen/computer example, don't stop at the easy point: the convenience of changing a word or phrase without rewriting the entire paper. Go deeper. How do computers change the way people write and think? Does the ease of revision make better writers? Or does the machine give the writer the impression that no draft ever has to be completed, given that a keystroke or two can change anything?

A pro-Toffler essay may be structured in several ways. Here's one possibility:

- ✔ **Introduction:** Refer to Toffler's quotation and your support of his ideas. (For example, you may write, "Those who cling to old, outmoded knowledge are losing ground in our changing-every-nanosecond society.") Mention two or three supporting ideas.

- ✔ **Body paragraphs:** Elaborate on one example in each body paragraph. The pen/computer example would be one paragraph, the change to social networking might be another, and so forth.

- ✔ **Conclusion:** Consider the implications of Toffler's ideas. Here's one: People inclined to rigid, structured ideas might be left behind and become bitter as the world moves on without them.

If you don't agree with Toffler, your essay should also include examples. In this case, your examples should illustrate the value of retaining important ideas. Here's a possible structure:

- ✔ **Introduction:** State your objections to Toffler's quotation. (With this approach, you may say something like "Tradition and a knowledge of history are important in order to place new ideas or skills in perspective.") Mention two or three supporting points; one might concern the need to know what the law *was* in order to understand why it has been changed.

- ✔ **Body paragraphs:** Devote one body paragraph to each example. Be sure to include enough detail to make the case that "unlearning" is a dangerous practice.

- ✔ **Conclusion:** Discuss any other objections you have to Toffler's ideas — the disadvantages of a society that changes too quickly or the disorienting effect of living too intensely "in the moment."

TIP

You can organize your essay in other ways, too, and still end up with a fine score. Measure your work using the rubric (scoring guide) in Chapter 7.

Section 2: Critical Reading

1. **C.** The only two answers in the running here are Choices (A) and (C) because the assumption is that giving to those who are less fortunate is a positive quality. Therefore, you're looking for a positive word. Because (C) is more specific than (A), (C) wins. People who have *compassion* express sympathy and concern for others.

2. **B.** This one is easier than it first appears, given that you know the meaning of *decipher,* which is what you do when you stare at a code — or bad handwriting — until you figure out what the letters are. None of the other second choices make sense. You don't *evaluate* (assign worth to), *alleviate* (ease), or *normalize* (make normal) handwriting. You may *scrutinize* (study carefully) it, but because the first part of the sentence already has the clerk squinting at his supervisor's scribble, you don't need to say it again. There you go: Choice (B), which states that the handwriting is *illegible* (unreadable) and something to *decipher,* is your answer.

3. **A.** The key word in this sentence is *though,* which tells you that you're switching from a positive to a negative or vice versa. Look for opposites and Choice (A) pops up. The method was *antiquated* (outdated) but it got the job done, being *effective.*

4. **A.** If you were filling in the blank with your own word, you'd probably choose "muscled" or "strong." Okay, all you need is a synonym for "strong" — which is Choice (A), *brawny.* Choices (B) and (C) are opposites because both imply a lack of muscle, with *emaciated* adding a touch of illness. Choices (D) *ardent* (passionate) and (E) *salubrious* (promoting health) aren't even close.

5. **B.** You probably guessed that the word for this blank must be a synonym of "say." Only Choices (B) and (C) fall into that category, but *promulgate* has a public element to it, implying a cable news report or passionate speeches to crowds. The more neutral *articulate* (explain clearly) is a better fit here because the implied audience for the students' speech is one person, the principal.

6. **D.** Both Abigails had a tough time, but you know more about Abigail Adams (the subject of Passage II) because the author explains that she faced the "depreciation of Continental paper money, the difficulties in the way of managing the property of her husband, [and] her own isolation" (Lines 15–17). All you know about Alcott is that her life included "hardship, poverty, [and] the grief of seeing her husband misunderstood" (Lines 1–2). Because Passage II includes more detail, Choice (D) is the best answer.

7. **C.** To answer this question, untangle the long sentence quoted from Alcott's letter. She mentions the "affectionate sympathy and aid of my husband" (Lines 9–10) and the "increasing health and loveliness of my . . . little Anna" (Lines 11–12). Although the passage doesn't explicitly state that Anna is Alcott's daughter, the *my* implies a parental relationship. No doubt about it: Choice (C) is the answer you seek.

8. **E.** The passage states that Adams's letters are "remarkable" (Line 20) because they reveal how she "could devote herself to the most opposite duties" (Lines 21–22), including those mentioned in the question. This fact may have tempted you to choose (A). However, the passage doesn't tell you that she held public office. Instead, she was "speculating upon the probabilities of peace or war" (Lines 28–29). The clincher is that as a mother she was "writing the most exalted sentiments to her son" (Lines 30–31). The reference to *writing* makes (E) the best choice.

9. **D.** The roles listed in the lines following "opposite" include farmer, merchant, politician, and mother. A varied selection, don't you think? You've got it: Choice (D) works here.

10. **D.** Several definitions of *innumeracy* are possible, and many of the concepts named in the answer choices appear in the passage. However, the passage as a whole addresses more than counting, sets, functions, higher-level math, or the complexity of math. Instead the passage attempts to explain why people can't understand mathematical concepts — Choice (D).

11. **B.** A key idea in this passage is that in math, "all unnecessary details have been stripped away by the process of abstraction" (Lines 29–31). These lines point you to Choice (B), which states that math is *abstract* (theoretical).

12. **C.** Lines 34–35 state that "you want A , B, and C to have human dimensions," but they don't. Or, as Lines 35–37 put it, "they simply stand for numbers, sets, or some other apparently barren concept." Choice (C) is the answer.

13. **D.** The passage states that people are "used to thinking complex thoughts about complex subjects, namely other people" (Lines 20–22) and that "we cannot get used to thinking about such simple subjects" (Lines 24–25) as math. In this question, Choice (D) stands for "definitely the answer"!

14. **C.** People *ascribe* (attribute, assign) human characteristics to abstract mathematical concepts "to make the characters real" (Line 46) because their minds are "used to more complex situations" (Lines 47–48). So when you're solving a math problem, you're trying to make it more familiar, more comfortable. If you don't, the problem is "alien" (Line 48) — unfamiliar — also known as Choice (C).

15. **E.** The passage firmly states that "the best way" (Line 58) to teach math is "to move gradually toward simple, abstract situations from complicated, real-life ones" (Lines 60–61). Yup, Choice (E) is the answer you want!

16. **C.** The passage as a whole urges the reader to "work . . . downward through the mud and slush of opinion, and prejudice, and tradition . . . through poetry and philosophy and religion" (Lines 19–25). Instead of these human traits and accomplishments, the author urges the reader to "spend one day as deliberately as Nature" (Lines 1–2). In other words, the narrator sees Nature idealistically — Choice (C).

17. **E.** In the passage, "deliberately" (Line 1) is followed by the wish "not to be thrown off the track" (Line 2). In other words, the author calls upon the reader to avoid distraction. That request takes you to either Choice (A) or Choice (E), two answers that indicate focus. However, *single-mindedly* introduces an element of obsession or fanaticism, and "deliberately" works better with the less emotional "purposely," which is Choice (E).

18. **A.** Thoreau lists all the things that should happen "without perturbation" (Line 5). *Perturbation* (worry or trouble), includes "company" (Line 6), bells' ringing, and children's crying. In other words, small stuff! A nutshell and a mosquito's wing are also small, so Choice (A) is the best answer, because *trivialities* are unimportant things.

19. **B.** When "the engine whistles" (Line 15) and "the bell rings" (Line 16), the author asks, "Why should we run?" (Lines 16–17). His alternative is to "settle . . . and work" (Lines 18–19). Therefore, you can easily rule out Choices (A) and (E). The passage contains no hint of danger or helpfulness, making (C) and (D) nonstarters too. You're left with Choice (B), which fits with the wish, expressed throughout this passage, to live in accordance with Nature.

20. **D.** Although the author says that he has "been regretting that I was not as wise as the day I was born" (Lines 50–51), he isn't discussing education but rather the way in which human beings tend to move away from a natural rhythm and wisdom toward a more artificial way of life. Choice (D) wins the prize.

21. **B.** The "Realometer" is a play on words. Just as a "Nilometer" (Line 31) measures the water level of the Nile, a "Realometer" measures a "freshet of shams and appearances" (Lines 32–33). The footnote tells you that a "freshet" is "a flow of water," though in this passage the word is used metaphorically to indicate a flow of pretense — Choice (B).

22. **C.** The second paragraph begins with a *metaphor* (an imaginative comparison) — time is "but the stream I go a-fishing in" (Line 43). The passage also says, "While I drink" (Line 44) — during the author's lifetime — the bottom, or death, is visible through the shallow waters. Yet the author states that "eternity remains" (Line 46). You can see that I and II are true, but what about III? Nothing in the passage discusses goals, so III doesn't make the cut. Yup, Choice (C) is the best answer.

23. **D.** The sentence after the comment cited in the question says, "I feel all my best faculties [abilities] concentrated in it" (Lines 54–55), with "it" referring to his head. Thoreau goes on to compare his head to the "snout and fore paws" (Line 57) of an animal that uses these body parts to burrow. Therefore, the author's "head" is his means of work, steering you to Choice (D).

24. **C.** When dinner is a "terrible rapid and whirlpool" (Lines 9–10) and reality is a "hard bottom and rocks in place" (Line 26) and his intellect is a "cleaver" (Line 51), you know that you've left reality and entered the land of imagination, which is where *metaphors* and *similes* — literary devices that compare one thing to another — reside. Yup, Choice (C) is the best answer.

Section 3: Mathematics

1. **B.** Use the acronym PEMDAS (see Chapter 12 if you don't remember what it means) to know that you need to deal with the parentheses first, and then the exponent. So, $3(4-2)^2 - 2 = 3(2)^2 - 2 = 3 \times 4 - 2$. Again, using PEMDAS, you need to do the multiplication before the subtraction: $3 \times 4 - 2 = 12 - 2 = 10$.

2. **D.** The mode, if you remember, is the number that shows up most often, so in this case the mode is 20. The median is the middle number. Because there are two numbers in the middle, 20 and 22, the median is their average, or 21. Already you know that I is not true, so you can eliminate Choices (A) and (C). Now you need to determine the mean, also known as the average. To find the mean, add all the numbers together and divide by the number of numbers: $(13 + 19 + 20 + 20 + 22 + 29 + 42 + 63) \div 8 = 228 \div 8 = 28.5$. Now you know that II and III are both true, so the answer must be Choice D.

3. **C.** If j and k intersect at a 90-degree angle, then they are perpendicular. You may remember that perpendicular lines have slopes that are opposite reciprocals. (See Chapter 14 to brush up on reciprocals.) The slope of j is $-\frac{2}{3}$, and the opposite reciprocal of $-\frac{2}{3}$ is $\frac{3}{2}$. So for line k, you're looking for a line with a slope of $\frac{3}{2}$, and Choice (C) is the only option with that slope.

4. **A.** Plugging in −2 gives you $f(-2) = (-2)^2 + 2(-2) + 1 = 4 + (-4) + 1 = 1$, so Choice (A) is your answer.

5. **E.** Because 5 less than 7 is 2, you know that $\frac{x}{3} = 2$. You can multiply both sides of the equation by 3, getting $x = 6$. Now that you know what x is, $3x$ will be $3(6) = 18$.

6. **E.** Triangle inequality! Remember that in any triangle, the sum of any two sides must be greater than the length of the third side. (See Chapter 16 to review this idea.) So, adding sides AB and BC, you get 27 units. The third side must be shorter than 27, so Choice (E) is the only answer that's impossible.

7. **D.** Remember that the absolute value symbol turns everything inside into a positive number, so you know that $x + 2$ equals 3 or −3. Now you can solve both equations. The first equation, $x + 2 = 3$, results in $x = 1$, and the second, $x + 2 = -3$, results in $x = -5$. Choice (D) is the only option that includes both of these answers.

8. **D.** You can determine what percent of the Algebra II students earned Ds by subtracting all the other percentages from 100%: 100% – 21% – 33% – 27% = 19% of Algebra II students earned Ds. You know that 76 students earned Ds, so 19% = 76 students. You can divide both sides by 19 to find that 1% represents 4 students. To determine how many students earned Bs, simply multiply the percent of students who earned Bs, 33%, by 4: 33 × 4 = 132 students.

9. **A.** If a team has four times as many girls as boys, then out of every five players, four must be girls. So you're looking for an answer that's a multiple of 5. Choice (A) is the only option that works.

10. **B.** The trick to this problem is to see that $x^2 + 2ax + a^2$ can be factored into $(x + a)^2$. Now you can rewrite the equation as $(x + a)^2 = 16$, so you know that $x + a$ has to equal 4 or –4. Choice (B) is the right answer.

11. **B.** Set up a Venn diagram to solve this problem.

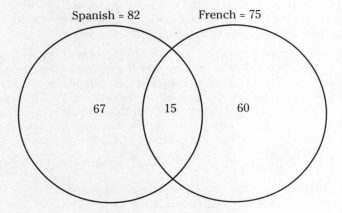

Now you can see that there must be 82 – 15 = 67 students who take only Spanish, and 75 – 15 = 60 students who take only French. Now you can add up the students in each section: 67 + 15 + 60 = 142 students studying Spanish, French, or both. Because there are 150 students in the 11th grade and you just determined that 142 of them are studying French and/or Spanish, that leaves 150 – 142 = 8 students who are not taking either class.

12. **D.** Break this problem into a few different parts: $a \# b = a^b$, $3 \# 2 = 3^2 = 9$, and $2 \# 3 = 2^3 = (2)(2)(2) = 8$. So, $(3 \# 2) - (2 \# 3) = 9 - 8 = 1$. Now you need to check I, II, and III to see which, if any, of them are equal to 1. Because any number raised to the 0 power equals 1, $4 \# 0 = 4^0 = 1$, making Option I true. Therefore, Choices (A), (D), or (E) may be the answer. Option II is true because $1 \# 3 = 1^3 = 1$, so Choice (D) must be the answer. You can check Option III just to be sure: $2 \# 1 = 2^1 = 2$.

13. **D.** Drawing a picture for this problem is a good idea.

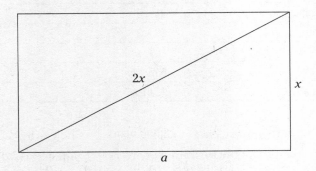

If you don't immediately recognize this as a 30°-60°-90° triangle, you can use the Pythagorean Theorem to find the third side of the right triangle formed by the diagonal (which will be the length of the rectangle). For the moment, call the length of the rectangle a. Plugging into the Pythagorean Theorem, $a^2 + x^2 = (2x)^2$ simplifies to $a^2 + x^2 = 4x^2$, or $a^2 = 3x^2$. You take the square root of both sides and get $a = x\sqrt{3}$. Now that you know the length of the rectangle, you can find the area by multiplying the length by the width: $x \cdot x\sqrt{3} = x^2\sqrt{3}$, Choice (D).

14. **C.** The key to this problem is determining what the constant difference between the terms is. You know the second and fourth terms, so the difference between them ($17 - 9 = 8$) is twice the value of the constant difference, meaning that the constant difference is 4. From here, you can either make a list of the terms until you get to the 13th term (remember that 9 is the second term, not the first!), or you can use the formula you know from Chapter 12: The nth term = the first term + $(n - 1)d$, where d is the difference between the terms in the sequence. For this question, n is 13, d is 4, and you can get the first term by subtracting the constant difference, 4, from the second term: $9 - 4 = 5$. Using the equation, the 13th term is $5 + (13 - 1)4 = 5 + (12)4 = 5 + 48 = 53$.

15. **E.** Adding 3 to a function adds 3 to the y-value of each coordinate on the graph. Therefore, $f(x) + 3$ will look like $f(x)$ shifted vertically upwards by 3 units. Choice (E) is the only option that shows the original graph shifted upwards.

16. **B.** For this problem you want to compare the area of the rectangle to the area of the circles. It would be easiest to assume that the radius of the circle is 1, so that the diameter of the circle is 2. That means the height of the rectangle is 2, and the width of the rectangle is 4. Now you know that the area of the rectangle is $2 \times 4 = 8$, and the area of each circle is $\pi r^2 = \pi(1)^2 = \pi$. Therefore, the area of the shaded part is the area of the rectangle minus twice the area of one circle, or $8 - 2\pi$. You can plug that into your calculator to see that the area of the shaded part is approximately 1.72. The probability of hitting the shaded area will be $\dfrac{\text{Area of shaded part}}{\text{Area of rectangle}} = \dfrac{1.72}{8}$, which is about 21%. Choice (B) is the closest to 21%.

17. **C.** To solve this problem, you have to remember that the sum of the exterior angles of any shape is always 360 degrees. (See Chapter 16 to review this idea.) If you don't remember that handy tip, you can also calculate the sum of the exterior angles for this pentagon. First, you determine what the sum of the interior angles is. Pick one vertex and draw straight lines to each of the other vertices, creating three triangles. You know that each triangle contains 180 degrees, so the pentagon, with three triangles, has $3 \times 180° = 540°$. You also know that each straight line has 180°, so each exterior angle plus its interior angle has 180°. There are five exterior angles, so the sum of all the interior and exterior angles is $5 \times 180° = 900°$. Now all you need to do is subtract: The sum of all the interior and exterior angles minus the sum of the interior angles gives you the sum of the exterior angles: $900° - 540° = 360°$.

18. **B.** For this problem, it's probably easiest just to calculate the numbers.

Time	Calculation	Visits
9:00 a.m.	7	7
9:30 a.m.	7×3	21
10:00 a.m.	21×3	63
10:30 a.m.	63×3	189
11:00 a.m.	189×3	567
11:30 a.m.	567×3	1,701
12:00 p.m.	$1,701 \times 3$	5,103

11:30 a.m. is the time closest to 2,000 visits, so Choice (B) is the best option.

19. **C.** If you want to fill the box three-quarters full, you need to determine what three quarters of the volume of the box is: $\frac{3}{4}(5 \times 5 \times 8) = \frac{3}{4}(200) = 150 \text{ in}^3$. If 5 cubic inches of the box are filled per minute, it will take $\frac{150}{5} = 30$ minutes for the box to fill three quarters of the way from empty. If it starts to fill at 3 p.m., then at 3:30 p.m., it will be three-quarters full. Choice (C) is the right time.

20. **D.** Because line *m* is parallel to line *n*, angle *BAC* equals angle 1 because they are corresponding angles. Because *AB* is congruent to *CB*, triangle *ABC* is an isosceles triangle. Therefore, angle *BCA* is the same as angle *BAC*, so both are 35 degrees. The angles of the triangle must total 180 degrees, so $\angle 2 + \angle BAC + \angle BCA = 180°$, or $\angle 2 + 35° + 35° = 180$. Subtracting, you find that angle 2 is 110 degrees.

Section 4: Critical Reading

1. **E.** If the speaker in the sentence turned to other, more-likely-to-succeed proposals, the speaker rejected *her proposal.* Though "to discount" usually means that you've scored a sale price, it may also mean "to ignore" or "to abandon" — the definition called for here. The other four choices imply the opposite. *Acclaimed,* by the way, is a fancy word for "praised."

2. **A.** So you see a canvas that's red with one little black line. You may say, "I don't get it!" or something similar. But if you've struggled to find exactly the right red and the perfect line length, you know the process of creation is difficult. Therefore, you're searching for a pair that expresses a meeting (*encounter* is "to come upon" or "to meet") and an understanding (*grasp* is "to understand"). This pair appears in Choice (A).

3. **B.** What makes you *comfortable,* financially? A big fat bank account, which you get by saving as much money as possible. All the choices refer to the party-like-there's-no-tomorrow school of financial planning, except for Choice (B). If you're *prudent,* you're careful and sensible — all the way to the bank!

4. **B.** You need a law most when someone has gone against, or *violated,* the principle established by the law — a concept expressed by Choice (B). Did I catch you with Choice (D)? To *trespass* is to go where you don't belong, and you can't travel into (or on or over) a right.

5. **E.** A *quirk* is an odd little habit. (I won't tell you about my quirks if you don't tell me about yours.) Eating green candy and avoiding a vowel are definitely quirks, not just neutral *habits,* also known as Choice (D). Because the actor isn't asking someone else to eat the candy or talk without the letter *e,* Choice (A) doesn't fit. The other answers aren't even close.

6. **D.** How do you know that a politician has *carefully considered* ideas that disagree with his or her own views? Well, you listen for arguments that weigh the pros and cons, statements that *acknowledge,* or recognize, the advantages and disadvantages of a position. No doubt about it: Choice (D) is the one you want. Choices (A), (B), and (C) rule out careful consideration. Choice (E) is tempting, but praise isn't necessarily based on thoughtfulness, so (D) is a better answer.

7. **C.** This sentence calls for opposites — how Gary *normally* behaved and how he behaved *after the accident.* The only answer expressing opposites is Choice (C). For vocabulary builders: *equanimity* means calmness, *restraint* implies that you're holding your feelings in, *joviality* is cheerfulness, and *amiability* is the SAT's way of expressing *friendliness.*

8. **E.** This one is easier than it looks. If she made a prediction that came true, Sarah sees into the future. Immediately you can eliminate Choices (A) and (C), which look to the past. (Words with *retro-* and *hind-* deal with what's behind.) Choice (B), *introspection,* refers to the process of looking inward. Choices (D) and (E) both deal with predictions, but (D) suggests magic, and it's more likely that Sarah relied on polls than potions.

9. **C.** This question contains a familiar trap. Your real-world knowledge may steer you to Choice (A) or (B) because "natural" products are often advertised as free from additives and pesticide residue. However, in the context of the passage — the only context that matters — the author discusses the "trends and changes in climate" (Line 9) that affect taste. The comment about wine's differing characteristics being "embraced and celebrated" (Line 3) reveals that the natural variations are, in the author's view, their beauty.

10. **B.** Lines 7–8 tell you that "herbs and spices are typically intense versions of plants," directing you to Choice (B).

11 **E.** The author states that a "culture's literature is that culture's communal voice" (Lines 2–3). Choice (E) follows logically from that statement, because without "a communal voice," (Line 3) "a community cannot express itself fully," as (E) states.

12. **A.** The lines immediately preceding the question, "Which way freedom?" (Line 9) state that "Struggle has been a primary trope of black people in America" (Lines 7–8) and beyond. Therefore, the question serves as a representation of "Struggle" in this passage. Vocabulary builder: A *trope* is a figure of speech, such as a metaphor.

13. **C.** The key to this question is the pronoun "that" (Line 4). Once you determine the meaning of "that," you know what Locke is talking about. Just before this pronoun is a statement about the mind's powers: "We shall not have much reason to complain" (Line 1) about the mind's limitations ("narrowness" — Line 2) if we "employ" (Line 3) the mind "about what may be of use to us" (Line 3). The last quotation is another way of saying that "our minds are able to accomplish many useful things," also known as Choice (C).

14. **B.** Some work is better than none, according to this passage. The servant isn't excused from chores because the house is lit only by a candle, not by daylight — a concept expressed by Choice (B).

15. **D.** The tricky part of this question is the answer selection. Each answer could be a good definition of "ends," in the correct context. However, the question directs you to the context of Passage I, where "ends" clearly means "goals."

16. **D.** You've probably figured out that the Candle is a symbol of human intelligence. The expression "bright enough" (Line 13) is key, because the statement means that we human beings have enough candle-power (intelligence) for our "purposes" (Lines 13–14). Therefore, the only real contenders are Choices (A) and (D). Choice (D) is better than (A) because the statement you're being questioned about doesn't address the amount of intelligence. The statement simply explains that intelligence is in proportion to human needs.

17. **A.** The line doesn't always reach the bottom of the ocean, but it does warn of shallow water ("caution him against running upon shoals that may ruin him" — Lines 40–42). The line and the brain are *analogous* (similar); if you know what you don't know (the very deep parts of the ocean, in the sailor story), you'll use your brain where it can actually help you (near "shoals," or shallow water — Line 41). No doubt about it: Choice (A) fits perfectly.

18. **B.** Passage I moves from candles to sailors to make a point, but Passage II stays with one comparison, that of the cave. True, Plato goes into detail about the cave, but he never strays from that single comparison. Because human beings aren't stuck in caves, Choices (A) and (D) are out. (Yes, I know that Lines 74–75 state that "the truth would be literally nothing but the shadows of the images," but the literal truth here is in the context of a fantasy about humans who are chained in caves.) Choices (C) and (E) don't make sense in the context of the passage.

19. **C.** Plato, in Passage II, imagines human beings chained in a cave with no chance of perceiving anything but shadows. Because these shadows are all that they see, the shadows seem real. When the chains are off, a former prisoner will see reality, which at first he will reject ("he will be unable to see the realities of which in his former state he had seen the shadows" — Lines 82–84). Therefore, perspective matters, and (C) is your answer.

20. **A.** Passage II is an exercise in visualization. The speaker asks the reader to *imagine* a cave, prisoners, shadows, and finally exposure to objects outside the cave. There you go: Choice (A) is the answer you seek.

21. **C.** This question tests your ability to untangle complicated syntax. (*Syntax* is the way words are put together grammatically to form a sentence.) In Line 76, the very long sentence in which "illusion" (Line 85) appears begins with released prisoners turning toward "the light" (Line 80) and hearing someone say that "what he saw before was an illusion" (Line 85). Well, what the prisoners saw before were shadows — the answer in Choice (C).

22. **D.** When you run across a "both" question in a paired-passage exercise, beware. You often find an answer that's true for *one* of the passages, but not for the other. Here, the only answer that applies to both is Choice (D). In Passage I, the assumption is that no human being can know everything. In Passage II, only some human beings recognize the truth when it's presented to them.

23. **B.** Time to dust off your old English notebooks. A *metaphor* is an implied comparison, such as the candle and the sailor's line in Passage I and the cave in Passage II. Just to build your vocabulary a bit: *personification* occurs when you give human qualities to a nonhuman element. *Concession and reply* (a great tactic for arguing with Authority Figures, by the way) is the acknowledgement of the opposing side's position, just before you demolish that position. *Hyperbole* and *understatement* are opposites; the first term applies when you exaggerate and the second when you minimize a situation.

24. **A.** Plato's whole point is that given only reflections ("shadows" — Line 92) to see, the true object will appear to be an illusion. Therefore, "you're wrong" — Choice (A) — is probably the "reply" to anyone's first view of reality.

Section 5: Mathematics

1. **C.** You know that when you square $x + 1$, you get 64, so $x + 1$ must equal 8 or −8. Set up two equations: $x + 1 = 8$ and $x + 1 = -8$. Solving those equations for x, you get $x = 7$ and $x = -9$. Because −9 is not one of the solutions offered, (C) must be the right choice.

   If you're totally stumped by a problem like this one, you can always plug in the answer choices to see which one works!

2. **D.** Recall that prime numbers are numbers that are only divisible by themselves and 1. Also recall that 1 is not prime (it's "special"), and that 2 is the only even prime. Therefore, the primes that are less than 16 are 2, 3, 5, 7, 11, and 13. Each of the other numbers in the set is divisible by a number besides 1 and itself (15, for example, is divisible by 1, 3, 5, and 15). So you have 6 prime numbers, and there are 15 numbers in the set. Now you see that the probability of picking a prime number is $\frac{6}{15} = \frac{2}{5}$. Choice (D) is the correct answer.

3. **D.** You want to use the counting principle to solve this question. (See Chapter 18 for a refresher on probability.) The counting principle tells you that when multiple events appear in a problem, the total number of possibilities is the product of the number of possibilities for each event. In this problem, you have three events: choosing a pair of pants (four possibilities), choosing a shirt (six possibilities), and choosing a pair of shoes (two possibilities). Therefore, you know that $4 \times 6 \times 2 = 48$ different outfits you can make.

4. **D.** When the test writers (and math teachers in general) talk about $f(x)$, they're really talking about the y-values on the graph. In this question, where you're asked about $f(x) = -1$, you really want to focus on when the y-value is −1. As you can see in the following graph, this happens three times, so $f(x) = -1$ has three solutions.

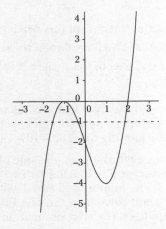

5. **E.** PEMDAS (covered in Chapter 12) reminds you that you need to deal with exponents before multiplication, so you should concern yourself with the $(3x^{100})^3$ first. Recall that exponents distribute inside of the parentheses, and that when you have an exponent

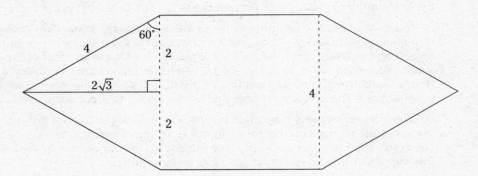

raised to an exponent, you multiply them. Therefore, $(3x^{100})^3 = 3^3 \cdot (x^{100})^3 = 3^3 x^{300} = 27x^{300}$. Now you can deal with the x. You know that $x = x^1$, so $x \cdot x^{300} = x^1 x^{300} = x^{301}$. In the end, you have $27x^{301}$, Choice (E).

6. **B.** If the lemon juice costs 85 cents per cup and you're using 5 cups, you're spending $0.85 \times 5 = \$4.25$ on lemon juice. If the sugar water costs 25 cents per cup and you're using 7 cups of sugar water, you're spending $0.25 \times 7 = \$1.75$ on sugar water. That makes 12 cups of liquid, costing $\$4.25 + \$1.75 = \$6.00$. To determine how much one cup of lemonade costs, divide $6.00 by 12 cups, getting $0.50 per cup, Choice (B).

7. **A.** You know that Johnny wrote four articles and that amount was the largest, so you can eliminate Choice (C), because if Mario had written four articles, Johnny would not have written the most. You can eliminate Choice (E) for the same reason. You know that Lucas wrote the fewest articles among the boys and that Natalia and Mario wrote the same number of articles. Therefore, Lucas wrote fewer articles than Natalia, so Choice (D) is out. You're left with Choices (A) and (B). Karen and Lucas may have written the same number of articles; they both wrote fewer than Johnny, Natalia, and Mario, but it's possible that they wrote different numbers of articles. There's no way to know for sure that Choice (B) is true with the given information. Choice (A), however, must be true. Natalia could not have written four articles because Johnny wrote four and was the most prolific writer; therefore, she wrote three or fewer articles. Choice (A) is the best option.

8. **D.** All the lines in the drawing must be 4 units long. You know this fact because the square's sides all have a length of 4, so the side of the equilateral triangle touching the square is 4 units long. Because the triangles are equilateral, all sides are the same length. The area of the square is $4 \times 4 = 16$ square units. The equilateral triangles have $30°$-$60°$-$90°$ triangles inside of them; you can use your knowledge of special triangles to determine the area of these triangles.

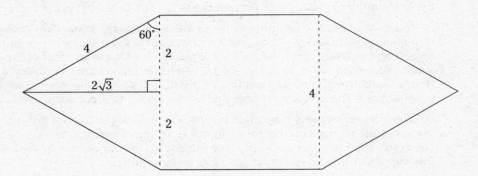

Now you can see that the "height" of this triangle is $2\sqrt{3}$, so the area of the triangle is $\frac{1}{2}bh = \frac{1}{2}(2\sqrt{3})(4) = 4\sqrt{3}$. You have two of these triangles in the figure, so the area of the entire figure is the area of the square plus twice the area of each triangle = $16 + 2(4\sqrt{3}) = 16 + 8\sqrt{3}$.

9. **13.** Because the average time over four dashes was 15.5, the total time for all four races is $4 \times 15.5 = 62$ seconds. You can now subtract each of the three dash times that you know in order to determine the missing time: $62 - 16 - 18 - 15 = 13$ seconds for the final dash.

10. **5.** You first want to put everything on one side of the equation, so that you can factor: $x^2 - 3x - 10 = 0$. To factor, you're looking for two numbers that multiply to -10 that also have a difference of 3. The numbers -5 and 2 will do the trick: $(x - 5)(x + 2) = 0$. Now set each factor equal to 0 and solve for x. You find that x is 5 or -2. Because it's impossible to grid in negative numbers, the answer must be 5.

11. **9.** Hopefully you remember that in $y = mx + b$, m represents the slope of the line, and b represents the y-intercept of the line. (If you don't remember, check out Chapter 14). Question 11 gives you the y-intercept: $(0, 7)$, so you know that $b = 7$. To find the slope, remember that slope $= \dfrac{rise}{run} = \dfrac{y_2 - y_1}{x_2 - x_1} = \dfrac{7-3}{0-(-2)} = \dfrac{4}{2} = 2$, so $m = 2$. With some simple addition, you find that $m + b = 2 + 7 = 9$.

12. **6.** Because the ratio of length to width is 5:3, you can represent the length as $5x$ and the width as $3x$. You know that area equals length $\times$ width, so the area $= (3x)(5x)$, which equals 60. Simplifying, you get that $15x^2 = 60$, and then $x^2 = 4$. Mathematically, this result means that x is either 2 or -2. It doesn't make sense for a rectangle to have a negative dimension, so x is 2. You're looking for the width of the rectangle, which you called $3x$ and which you now know is $3(2) = 6$.

13. **27.** A chart is probably the easiest way to solve this problem. If you know that when you divide a number by 5 you get a remainder of 2, then you know that the number is two more than a multiple of 5. Similarly, the number can be represented as six more than a multiple of 7. Because you know the number is less than 50, you know where to stop your chart.

2 More than Multiples of 5	6 More than Multiples of 7
2	6
7	13
12	20
17	27
22	34
27	41
32	48
37	
42	
47	

Because the number 27 shows up in both columns of the chart, that must be the answer! You can double check: 27 divided by 5 is 5 with a remainder of 2 (check!), and 27 divided by 7 is 3 with a remainder of 6 (check!).

14. **17.** Watch out! Make sure you don't fall into the trap where you think that $(a + b)^2 = a^2 + b^2$. You need to FOIL in order to square $a + b$. (Check out Chapter 14 if you need to brush up on FOIL.) If $a + b = 5$, you can solve for a, and determine that $a = 5 - b$. Using substitution, you can determine that $ab = (5 - b)b = 5b - b^2 = 4$. Set this equal to 0: $b^2 - 5b + 4 = 0$, and then factor: $(b - 1)(b - 4) = 0$. That means b is 1 or 4. If b is 1 then a is 4, and if b is 4 then a is 1. Either way, $a^2 + b^2 = 1^2 + 4^2 = 1 + 16 = 17$.

    Here's another way to think about this problem: Hopefully you remember that $(a + b)^2 = a^2 + 2ab + b^2$, which seems to have all the necessary elements. That means that $(5)^2 = 25 = a^2 + 2ab + b^2$ by substituting $a + b = 5$ into $(a + b)^2 = a^2 + 2ab + b^2$. To get the right side of the equation to equal $a^2 + b^2$, you want to subtract $2ab$, so $25 - 2ab = a^2 + b^2$. You already know that $ab = 4$, so $2ab = 2(4) = 8$, so $a^2 + b^2 = 25 - 2ab = 25 - 8 = 17$.

15. **165.** It costs \$525 to hire the band for 3 hours, and it costs \$765 to hire the band for 5 hours. You can see that 2 extra hours of music costs an additional \$765 $-$ \$525 = \$240, so each hour of music costs \$120. The \$525 is three times the hourly rate plus the flat fee (call the flat fee x), which can be represented as $525 = 3(120) + x$. Solve for x, and you learn that the flat fee is \$165. You can double-check your answer by checking that the flat fee plus 5 hours of music costs \$765: $165 + 5(120) = 165 + 600 = 765$.

16. **80.** For problems like this one, marking up your test booklet is always a great idea. Remember that the drawing isn't to scale. Draw in the values for angles 1 and 7. You can immediately see that angle 6 must have a measure of 180° – 130° = 50°. Then, because you know that $\overline{AB}$ is parallel to $\overline{CD}$, $\overline{BD}$ is a transversal, meaning that angle 2 is equal to angle 6 because they're alternate interior angles. Now you know the measures of two of the angles in the triangle *ABE*, so you know that angle *AEB* = 180° – 50° – 50° = 80°. Angle 4 and angle 3 are vertical angles and, therefore, equal, so the measure of angle 4 is 80 degrees.

17. **6.** Following the pattern given in the definition of & in the problem, you know that $4\,\&\,h = \dfrac{4^2 + h^2}{2} = \dfrac{16 + h^2}{2}$, which you want to set equal to 26. Multiplying both sides of the equation by 2, you get that $16 + h^2 = 52$, so $h^2 = 36$. This result means that *h* equals 6 or –6. The answer must be 6 because you can't grid in negative numbers. If you need to brush up on problems in which the SAT makers create new symbols, check out Chapter 14.

18. **13.** It would be great if you happened to know the three-dimensional version of the distance formula: $d = \sqrt{x^2 + y^2 + z^2}$, but just in case you don't, you can solve this another way. If you can find the distance from point *B* to point *H* using the two-dimensional distance formula $(d = \sqrt{x^2 + y^2})$, which is based on the Pythagorean Theorem, then you can use right triangle *BHE* to find the length of $\overline{BE}$. Check out the following diagram for clarification.

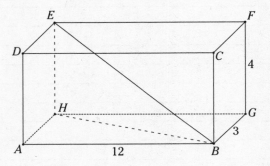

The length of $\overline{BH} = \sqrt{3^2 + 12^2} = \sqrt{9 + 144} = \sqrt{153}$. Using the distance formula again, the length of $\overline{BE}$ is $\sqrt{\left(\sqrt{153}\right)^2 + 4^2} = \sqrt{153 + 16} = \sqrt{169} = 13$.

Section 6: Multiple-Choice Writing

1. **D.** Because Margaret is a teacher, she's an educator, and the original sentence, as well as Choices (B) and (C), removes her from the group of educators. You need "any other" in order to compare Margaret to the group. Choice (D) is a better answer than (E) because *had* places an action in the past *prior to* (before) another action in the past. Logically, Margaret has to do her job after she becomes a teacher, not before. Therefore you can rule out Choice (E) and opt for (D), the correct answer.

2. **B.** The expression *correctly predicting a downturn in the market* is extra, not essential to the meaning of the sentence. Nonessential descriptions are enclosed in commas. The original sentence has the first comma, but not the second (after *market*). Choices (C) and (E) add the pronoun *he,* but because you have a noun *(broker)* doing the job, you don't need a pronoun also. Choice (D) adds an unnecessary *had*.

The helping verb *had* places an action or state of being before another past-tense event.

3. **D.** The noun *man* is singular, so *their* (a plural pronoun) is a mismatch. In Choice (D), the singular noun *man* is correctly matched with *his,* a singular possessive pronoun. Were you tempted by Choices (C) and (E)? In those answers, the plural noun *men* matches the plural pronoun *their.* However, Choice (C) contains a double negative. The word *forbid* tells you what the men can't do, so *not* is **superfluous** (extra, unnecessary). Choice (E) tries to insert a clause *(who should not speak to their mothers-in-law)* in an illogical way.

4. **D.** In sentence improvement (and in all sorts of writing), opt for the concise but complete wording. Choice (D) gets the job done, quickly and cleanly. The original — Choice (A) — is incorrect because the pronoun *it* has no clear meaning. *It* may be the watering, the fertilizer, or the fact that the gardener added these things. Nope! Pronouns must refer **unambiguously** (without a vague or double meaning) to a noun or pronoun (or a couple nouns and/or pronouns). Choice (C) has the same problem, only this time the ambiguous pronoun is *which.* Choices (B) and (E) are passive, which is never a good choice when active voice is available. Choice (B) also has a dangling modifier — the introductory verb form that *must* describe the subject. As Choice (B) is written, *the plant* is watering and fertilizing itself. No doubt about it: Choice (D) is the answer you seek.

5. **C.** The word *however* sounds great, doesn't it? Important and strong! However, *however* isn't allowed to join two complete sentences, which you have in Question 5. Add a semicolon before *however,* and you're all set. If you set your sights on Choice (C), you found the correct answer.

6. **A.** Yes, I actually threw in a correct sentence. I was testing your knowledge (as the SAT makers will) of two basic ideas. *The reason is because* is never correct; always go for *the reason is that.* Also, the subject of the sentence is *reason* (a singular noun), which must be paired with the singular verb *is,* not the plural verb *are.*

7. **B.** In the original sentence — Choice (A) — no person is named as *struggling* and *falling.* By the rules of grammar, therefore, the subject that is named in the sentence (in this case, *judges*) must be performing the actions in the rest of the sentence. But the judges aren't falling, though they may be struggling to decide an appropriate score. Bingo: Choice (A) is out. Choice (C) improperly pairs *was struggling* with *having fallen.* Choice (D) needs a helping verb for *struggling,* such as *was.* Choice (E) slips into passive voice, never a good move. Plus, when you insert the text from Choice (E) into the rest of the sentence, the result doesn't make sense. Yup, Choice (B) is the answer.

8. **E.** The word *whether* is generally paired with *or not* and applies to two alternatives. The elements of this pair shouldn't be too far apart, as they are in Choices (A) and (B). *If* applies to a condition: Something will happen *if* the condition is met. In Question 8, *whether* makes more sense, and Choice (E) places the alternatives near each other, making it the correct answer.

9. **A.** Introductory verb forms without helping verbs (in this sentence, *Given new information*) take on the tense of the main verb in the sentence. In the original sentence, the new information and the revising are more or less simultaneous. This is a **plausible** (believable) meaning, so the sentence is correct as written, and your answer is Choice (A). Choices (B) and (E) don't need the *her,* and (C) has a **superfluous** (extra) *had.* Choice (D) is wordy. The correct answer is (A).

10. **C.** The original "sentence" isn't a complete sentence because it doesn't contain a statement that can stand alone and make sense — an independent clause, in grammar lingo. Choice (C) **rectifies** (corrects) this problem. If you're nuts about understanding the grammatical reasoning, read on. In (C), the subject is *wedding.* The subject is paired with three verbs *(had been scheduled, was postponed, rescheduled),* each of which is linked by a conjunction *(but, and).*

11. **B.** The problem with the original wording, Choice (A), is the switch from active voice *(ripped)* to passive *(were broken)* for no good reason. Choice (B) makes both words active. The other choices complicate the issue unnecessarily by plopping *had* where it doesn't belong.

12. **A.** Why repeat yourself? The *newspaper* and *it* are doing the same job. The correct sentence would read, "The newspaper reported that. . . ."

13. **A.** *Quick* is a description, and the adjective *sure* can't intensify another description. For that job, you need the adverb *surely*.

14. **B.** The pronoun *either* (along with its close relative, *neither*) is singular and should be paired with a singular verb. In this sentence, *are,* a plural verb, doesn't work, so Choice (B) is the answer you seek.

15. **D.** The word *between* is a preposition and should be followed by objective pronouns, not subject pronouns (such as *I*). The correct expression is *between you and me.*

16. **D.** The elements of the list should match grammatically. In Question 16, *chance* and *funding* are nouns, but *he could hire* is a subject-verb combination. Because *could hire* is a mismatch, it's wrong, and Choice (D) is the correct answer.

17. **C.** The pronoun *someone* is singular, but the pronoun *they,* which refers to *someone,* is plural. Mismatch! The correct version is *he or she.*

18. **D.** The expression, *her viewers to spend,* isn't Standard English. The correction would be *that her viewers spend.*

19. **E.** Yes, I finally gave you a correct sentence. Wasn't that nice of me? I did, however, throw in a distraction. Some people worry about beginning a sentence with *because.* Actually, *because* isn't a problem as long as the statement it begins is attached to a complete thought, as it is here.

20. **B.** The subject of this sentence is *number,* a singular noun, which should be paired with a singular verb such as *has made.* Choice (B) is *have made,* a plural verb, and the error you're looking for.

21. **C.** *Weaker* is a comparison already, so *more* isn't needed — or wanted! — here.

22. **C.** The word *every* is extremely strong. Put *every* in front of a subject that appears to be plural (*customer and client,* in this sentence), and the subject becomes singular. Why? I'm so glad you asked. *Every* changes the meaning of the sentence so that the customers and clients are considered individually, one by one. Therefore, *were open* should be *was open,* and Choice (C) is the answer.

23. **A.** The present perfect tense talks about something that began in the past and continues in the present. In Question 23, the cousins no longer live in Spain. Therefore, the present-perfect verb form, *have been living,* is wrong. The correct verb is *lived.*

24. **B.** The comma in Choice (B) joins two complete sentences. Penalty box! You need a semicolon or a conjunction such as *and, because,* or something similar to link these two ideas. Were you fooled by Choice (D)? The teachers don't object to the students. They object to the students' typing. The apostrophe correctly shifts the emphasis from the people to the action.

25. **C.** The *only* should precede the idea to which it refers. The sentence should read *are complicated only by a dispute.*

26. **A.** *Here* and *there* can't be subjects, so the true subject of this sentence is *photos,* a plural noun. *There's* is a contraction of *there is,* but the proper verb is *are.*

27. **B.** The way the sentence now reads, the *hotel* has gone on vacation for three years. Nope. An introductory verb form must refer to the subject of the sentence. Thus, your error is Choice (B). To correct this sort of sentence, you'd need to say something like *Having gone on vacation for three years, the family was disappointed . . .* you get the idea!

28. **A.** Double negatives are a no-no (pun intended). *Can't help* is a negative, as is the *but.* The correct expression is *can't help objecting.*

29. **B.** *Consequently* is a long word, but even so it's not strong enough to link two complete sentences, which you have in Question 29. The comma after *dented* should be a semicolon.

30. **B.** The subject of Sentence 2 is *intimidation*, a singular noun, which requires the singular verb *is prohibited*. The correct answer is Choice (B).

31. **C.** The entire essay is in third person, except for Sentence 3 and a final statement of opinion in the conclusion. The conclusion may be personal, so first person is justified there. However, Sentence 3 sounds awkward — one second-person sentence in the midst of many third-person statements. Take it from me: Choice (C) is best.

32. **C.** Sentence 5 is a run-on — a grammatical felony. You can't glue two complete sentences together with a comma. Choices (B) and (C) both address this issue, but (C) does more. It changes "this" to "these comments," a more specific and therefore better expression.

33. **D.** The topic of this essay is cyberbullying, but that term doesn't appear until the second paragraph. By defining the term in the first paragraph, the reader is alerted to the content of the essay right away — a good strategy! Once the definition is inserted into Paragraph 1, the statement in Sentence 6 isn't necessary.

34. **B.** The paragraph gives some indication why some people want to criminalize cyberbullying, but it doesn't truly explain the importance of free speech — the position the writer *advocates* (argues for) in the last paragraph. To balance the statements about limits on free speech, the writer should address the benefits also.

35. **C.** The original sentence is wordy and awkward. Choice (C) is simpler and more concise. No question, (C) is your answer.

Section 7: Critical Reading

1. **A.** Logic tells you that this sentence can go one of two ways. Either the room was huge and everyone had a ton of space, or the room was tiny and people were stacked to the ceiling like firewood. Choice (A) fits the first scenario, because *capacious* means "roomy," and *ample* means "more than enough." No pair fits the second scenario. Continuing the vocabulary-building exercise, *minuscule* = tiny, *choleric* = angry, and *gargantuan* = huge. Of those three, you may have jumped at "gargantuan." However, the other half of Choice (E) — "ineffective" — doesn't fit the sentence.

2. **B.** To *complement* is "to harmonize with." I don't know about you, but red silk shouts "luxurious" at me (from a distance — I don't live in the lap of luxury!). Choice (A), by the way, differs in just one letter, but the meaning is totally different. To *compliment* is to offer praise. While I'm in vocabulary-building mode, *insinuated* means "hinted" and *belied* means "to show that something is false."

3. **A.** What makes you accomplish 1 percent of your homework? *Indolence,* also known as "laziness," which is choice (A).

4. **B.** The politician in the sentence (unlike some politicians in real life) has chosen the "high road" and "vowed to run a positive campaign." So what would the politician rule out? Anything negative, such as *derogatory* (critical or belittling) comments, which is Choice (B). Vocabulary time: *Laudatory* means "praising or admiring." A *deferential* person treats others as if they were of higher rank. An *obsequious* person flatters or caters to someone else in an extreme manner.

5. **C.** If you pinch every penny twice, you're a *miser,* Choice (C). Choices (A) and (B) waste money, Choice (D) steals it, and Choice (E) gives it to charity. Go for Choice (C) and you're right!

6. **D.** You're looking for a word that means to cut down, because no principal I've ever met (and I've met many) rewards lateness. Therefore, you can dump Choices (B) and (C) immediately. Choice (A), *abridged,* generally refers to written matter, as does Choice (E). You're left with Choice (D), which is the correct answer.

7. **E.** This is a trick question, because Charlotte, Katie's sister, thinks that Katie *is* somewhat snobby — Choice (C). However, that's Charlotte's view, not necessarily the reader's opinion of Katie. Plus, the "snob" issue doesn't emerge until after the lines cited in the question. The other answers, except for Choice (E), have similar problems. Katie's response comes later in the passage, as does her feeling of *alienation* (not belonging) — Choice (D). Nor does the reader ever find out why Katie is there, Choice (B). You're left with Choice (E), a straightforward description of a poor neighborhood.

8. **D.** If you know the meaning of *fractious* (irritated, peevish), this question is easy. Katie and Charlotte annoy each other. ("Who do you think you are, to come here and criticize? — Lines 18–19 — and "Am I a baby, to be carried around on my sister's back?" — Lines 101–102 — are two examples.) You see an element of jealousy — Choice (E) — in Charlotte's comment, "to come here and criticize," but you don't see jealousy in Katie. Choice (C) is too extreme, as *vicious* means "brutal or cruel."

9. **C.** Just before the line cited in Question 9, Charlotte states, "Ma doesn't complain" (Line 20). She also challenges Katie by asking, "Are you too big for the rest of us?" (Line 19). All of these comments are in response to Katie's statement, "I want to vomit" (Line 16). Clearly, Charlotte believes that if their living conditions are adequate for Ma, they're fine for Katie, who shouldn't complain. Choice (C) is the best fit here.

10. **E.** When you encounter a "rule-out" question, cross off everything you find in the passage. Whatever's left is the answer. Choice (A) drops out because Katie thinks about "some of the luxuries" (Line 26) of Port Elizabeth, and the passage opens with a description of poverty (Lines 1–14). Choices (B) and (D) are also nonstarters, given that Katie thinks about "the soft sea mist, the endless supply of water" (Line 28) and then describes the "dry season in Kimberley" (Line 29). Lines 24–25 mention "the first happiness of seeing Ma and Charlotte," ruling out Choice (C). The sole survivor is Choice (E), which is your answer.

11. **A.** Because the passage references "the dry season" (Line 29) and "the rainy season" (Line 37), you know that Kimberley, where the family resides, isn't in a desert. Down goes Choice (B). Choices (C), (D), and (E) aren't supported by the passage, so you're left with Choice (A). True, the passage doesn't talk about the plumbing of Kimberley as a whole, but the reader does hear that "it was a long way for the girls to carry water" (Lines 31–32).

12. **A.** Ma knows only the basics, such as "how to wash out wounds" (Lines 56–57), which she learned by watching Katie's grandfather "caring for his workers" (Line 59). Ma contrasts this informal medical training with the "much study" (Line 53) that Katie would need "to be a proper nurse" (Line 53). These lines lead you to Choice (A) or (B). Of the two, (A) is better because otherwise Ma is saying, in Lines 52–53, that "It takes much study to be an educated nurse" — a repetitive statement. Choice (A) is the correct answer.

13. **B.** Charlotte tells Katie that she "can't be a proper nurse" (Line 62) because the nursing schools are reserved for whites. Charlotte believes that only "mopping floors and cleaning up after the Europeans" (Lines 65–66) is possible for Katie. These comments direct you to Choice (B). Did I catch you with Choice (E)? Charlotte thinks that Katie's plans are "unrealistic," but Charlotte's reaction isn't unrealistic.

14. **D.** Ma is the informal, only partially-trained doctor in the neighborhood. The fact that the author mentions the cost of the doctor visit ("seven and sixpence" — Lines 77–78) implies that this sum is significant to the family. The fact that Ma takes Katie to the doctor anyway tells you that Ma believes the illness is too serious to treat herself, a conclusion that leads you right to Choice (D), the correct answer.

15. **A.** Katie "knew she was not clever in her head like Charlotte" (Lines 85–86), so the first statement is true. Katie's father believes in tradition ("That is the custom" — Line 105), but Katie clearly doesn't, so II isn't true because Katie is in the family. Katie held a job in Port Elizabeth ("she had worked too long" — Line 23) and sews "Charlotte's clothes as well as her own" (Lines 88–89), so III isn't true. There you go: Choice (A) is your answer.

16. **B.** You probably ruled out Choices (C) and (D) immediately, because while the characters may not always get along (Katie and Charlotte especially), the passage itself doesn't *confront* (challenge) the reader. Of the other three choices, Choice (B) is best. *Nostalgic* implies a rosy, those-were-the-days sort of writing, and *reflective* has an element of putting everything in perspective that isn't present in this passage. The facts are there, just as they happened, so Choice (B), "realistic," makes sense.

17. **D.** The key phrase in this question is "the evidence in the passage." Because Kimberley is poor and Katie misses the "luxuries" (Line 26) of Port Elizabeth, Choice (A) doesn't work. Katie is in conflict with her family about careers and her relationship to Charlotte, but the passage shows her accepting, not rebelling against, her parents' wishes, so Choices (B) and (C) don't work. The passage hints at injustices, such as Charlotte's comment that "nursing schools here are only for white girls" (Lines 63–64). However, Katie herself says nothing about justice, eliminating Choice (E). You're left with Choice (D), which makes sense because Katie clearly loves her family, as the passage mentions "happiness of seeing Ma and Charlotte" (Lines 24–25).

18. **B.** Just before the last paragraph, Katie questions why she must stay with her sister. Then comes a list of enjoyable activities that Katie shares with Charlotte. Yup, Choice (B) stands for "best answer."

19. **A.** I live in New York City, and if we had a party for everyone leaving or arriving, partying would be the sole activity in my hometown. But Kimberley is different; a departure or return is an event celebrated by the community — a conclusion that leads you directly to Choice (A).

Section 8: Mathematics

1. **A.** For this problem, the angles given are supplementary to the angles inside of the triangle, so you can find the measure of two of the interior angles of the triangle. You calculate that $180° - 112° = 68°$, and $180° - 100° = 80°$. Now that you know two of the angles inside of the triangle, you can find p, the third angle, because you know that the angles in a triangle must add up to 180 degrees, and $180° - 68° - 80° = 32°$.

2. **C.** You want to find out how much money Sita has in each type of account in 2009. To do so, determine the height of the middle, lightest colored bar in each section of the chart. You'll see that she has $300 in checking, $700 in savings, $500 in retirement, and $600 in investment. Adding those values together, Sita has $2,100 in all her bank accounts in 2009.

3. **D.** To solve this, first determine how much money Sita has in her retirement account in 2008. She has $400. If $400 represents 0.1% of the bank's money, you can set up a proportion with x as the total money in the bank: $\frac{400}{x} = \frac{0.1}{100}$. Cross-multiplying yields $40,000 = 0.1x$, so $x = \$400,000$.

4. **C.** All the equations shown are in slope-intercept ($y = mx + b$) form, so you need to determine the slope and the y-intercept of this line. The y-intercept happens when x is 0, so you already know that the y-intercept is -1. With this knowledge, you can eliminate Choices (B) and (E). Finding the slope is easiest if you can find two x values that are only one apart; -1 and 0 will work in this case. From the chart you can see that when x increases by 1 (from -1 to 0), the y value decreases by 3 (from 2 to -1). This allows you to determine the slope of the line: $m = \frac{\Delta y}{\Delta x} = \frac{-3}{1} = -3$. Choice (C) is the only option with a slope (m) of -3 and a y-intercept (b) of -1. If you prefer, you can solve this problem by choosing an x-value from the chart and plugging it into each of the equations to see which ones give you the correct y-value. Make sure to check all the choices, because you may have picked an x-value that works in more than one of the choices. If that happens, all you have to do is test each of the remaining choices with a new x-value from the chart.

5. **D.** When you see function notation, the first thought that pops into your head should be about substitution. In other words, $f(x)$ tells you the rule to follow, no matter what's put inside of those parentheses. So, $f(2x)$ tells you to replace every x in the original equation with $2x$: $f(2x) = (2x)^2 - 3(2x) + 1$. You can simplify this to Choice (D) if you use PEMDAS (covered in Chapter 12)!

6. **E.** The thing you need to know to solve problems like this is that if you're given an if-then statement, the only other thing that you know is true is the contrapositive of that statement. Say you have the statement "If I study with *SAT For Dummies*, then I ace the SAT." The contrapositive of that statement is "If I don't ace the SAT, then I didn't study with *SAT For Dummies*." The contrapositive switches the order of the original if-then statement and makes the individual parts of the statement have the opposite meaning. If an if-then statement is true, then its contrapositive is automatically also true. So, the contrapositive of "If Mary is at work, then Pierre is having lunch" is "If Pierre is not having lunch, then Mary is not at work."

7. **D.** You need to figure out what the radius of this circle is. You can use the distance formula on those two points if you can draw a quick sketch of where the points are on the xy-coordinate plane, like this:

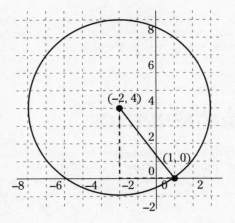

Now you can see that you have a right triangle whose legs are 3 and 4 units long, so the hypotenuse must be 5 units long — it's a 3-4-5 Pythagorean triple! Now that you know that the radius is 5, recall that the formula for the area of a circle is $A = \pi r^2$, so in this case, the area is $\pi 5^2 = 25\pi$.

8. **C.** When in doubt, plug in numbers! For absolute value problems, you probably want to mix up positive and negative numbers so that you know you aren't missing any obvious special cases. To test Option I, use $a = 3$ and $b = -4$. That seems to be true because $-12 \leq 12$. You can also plug in a pair of positive numbers and a pair of negative numbers to double-check. Onwards to Option II! Check out $a = -2$ and $b = 5$. $|-2 + 5| = |3| = 3$, and $|-2| + |5| = 2 + 5 = 7$, so Option II doesn't work. You already know that Choices (B) and (D) won't work. Testing Option III, try out $a = 3$ and $b = -4$. $|3 - (-4)| = |3 + 4| = 7$, and $|-4 - 3| = |-7| = 7$, so Option III works! Choice (C) is the right answer.

9. **E.** The arithmetic mean, also known as the average, is when you add up a bunch of numbers and divide by the number of numbers. So, the arithmetic mean of a, b, c, and d would be $\frac{a+b+c+d}{4} = 15$. None of the answer choices have fractions like this, so multiply both sides by 4 to get $a + b + c + d = 60$. The correct answer must be Choice (D) or (E). Next, you want to subtract the largest number from the product of the smallest three numbers. The problem tells you that $a < b < c < d$, so a is the smallest number and d is the biggest. Therefore, the product of the smallest three numbers is abc, and when you subtract the largest, you get $abc - d = 34$, Choice (E).

10. **B.** In this problem the test actually tells you to turn the paper upside down (rotate it 180 degrees), so go for it! Make sure that each symbol looks the same upside down as it does right side up; the symbol that doesn't work is your answer. When you turn the second symbol (that looks like an E) upside down, it no longer looks like an E, so Choice (B) must be the right answer.

11. **C.** Get the easy part out of the way first: Figure out the area of the rectangle. Area for rectangles is length × width, so the area is $6 \times 2 = 12$ square inches. Next, work on the biggest triangle. It's an equilateral triangle, so you can divide it in half and have two 30°-60°-90° triangles. You may recall that the side opposite the 60° angle is equal to $\sqrt{3}$ times the side opposite the 30° angle. Because the base of the equilateral triangle is 6, the side opposite the 30° angle is half of that, or 3 inches, making the height of the triangle $3\sqrt{3}$. The area of a triangle is $\frac{1}{2}bh$, so in this case, $A = \frac{1}{2}(6)(3\sqrt{3}) = 9\sqrt{3}$. Determining the area of the smaller triangles is similar. Cut them up into 30°-60°-90° triangles. You can now determine that the height is $1\sqrt{3}$; therefore, the area of each little triangle is $\frac{1}{2}bh = \frac{1}{2}(2)(\sqrt{3}) = \sqrt{3}$. You have two of these triangles, so their total area is $2\sqrt{3}$. The area of the figure is the area of the rectangle plus the area of the big triangle plus the area of the small triangles, which equals $12 + 9\sqrt{3} + 2\sqrt{3} = 12 + 11\sqrt{3}$, Choice (C).

12. **D.** Remember that if a in $ax^2 + bx + c$ is positive, the parabola will open upward (like a cup), and if a is negative, it will open downward (like a hill). This parabola opens downward, so you know that a is negative, and therefore $a < 0$; the right answer must be Choice (B), (D), or (E). The value of c turns out to be where the parabola intersects the y-axis (because on the y-axis the x-value is 0, so all the terms with x in them equal 0 too, leaving only c. The parabola shown clearly intersects the y-axis where it is positive, so $c > 0$. Choice (D) is your answer!

13. **D.** When Anise picks out the first necklace, she has a 2/7 chance of picking one of the identical necklaces. (Recall that the probability of an event equals the number of ways for the event to occur divided by the total number of possible outcomes.) After she has picked the first identical necklace, she has a 1/6 chance of picking its mate. You want to use the counting principle to determine the probability of picking both necklaces: $\left(\frac{2}{7}\right)\left(\frac{1}{6}\right) = \frac{2}{42} = \frac{1}{21}$. (Check out Chapter 18 if you need to brush up on probability.)

14. **C.** Each time the wheel rolls, it travels the length of its circumference. Remember that circumference = $2\pi r$ or πd. So, in this case, the circumference is 24π inches, or 2π feet. Multiply that distance by 150 rotations, and the distance is $2\pi(150) = 300\pi$.

15. **B.** Plug numbers in to solve this question. You know that when n is 1 (the first term), the value is ½. Check which answer options equal ½ when n is 1. (Keep in mind that anything raised to 0 is equal to 1.) Choices (A), (B), and (D) all work. Now, when n is 2, the value should be 2. Check $n = 2$ in Choices (A), (B), and (D) to see which one equals 2. Choice (A) equals 1, (B) equals 2, and (D) equals ¼. Choice (B) is the answer.

16. **D.** Pick numbers and plug them in. Try $p = 5$ and $q = 8$. $5 \square 8 = 5 + 8 - 3 = 10$ and $8 \square 5 = 8 + 5 - 3 = 10$, so Option I seems to be true. $3 \square 8 = 3 + 8 - 3 = 8$, so Option II is true also. You've eliminated Choices (A), (C), and (E). To test Option III, let $r = 4$. $(5 \square 8) \square 4 = (5 + 8 - 3) \square 4 = 10 \square 4 = 10 + 4 - 3 = 11$, and $5 \square (8 \square 4) = 5 \square (8 + 4 - 3) = 5 \square 9 = 5 + 9 - 3 = 11$, so Option III works as well. Choice (D) is the one you want.

Section 9: Multiple-Choice Writing

1. **D.** What lasts for several hours? The *musical,* that's what. Therefore, the description *which lasts for several hours* must be near the word it describes — *musical.* In its original position, the *audience* lasts for several hours, and mass casualties follow their exit from the theater.

2. **C.** The sentence begins in third person, talking about *a student.* Why switch to second person *(you)?* Because *a student* is singular, *he or she* is the proper subject for the second half of the sentence.

3. **B.** The original sentence lacks a proper subject-verb combination. The subject *representative* can't pair off with *having been admitted,* which looks like a verb but actually functions as a description. Choice (B) supplies a verb that matches *representative — was admitted.*

4. **A.** Yes, I actually gave you a correct sentence, just for a change of pace. (You may see one or two on your real exam, though the number of correct sentences varies from test to test.) In Question 4, the semicolon correctly links two complete thoughts.

5. **E.** The original sentence is a run-on. Two complete sentences are glued together with only a comma — a grammar crime. Choice (E) is the only version to add a conjunction *(and),* a word that links two complete thoughts. Perhaps I fooled you with Choice (D). *Subsequently* appears strong enough to be a conjunction, but it isn't.

6. **D.** Short and sweet wins the prize here. The comma after *society* isn't needed because the conjunction *and* isn't uniting two complete sentences — just two nouns.

7. **E.** This sentence falls into a category English teachers call "condition contrary to fact." The speaker in the sentence didn't know about the ink level, so a subjunctive mood (a fancy term for a verb mood, and yes, verbs have moods!) is called for here. Don't worry about the terminology. Just remember that in a condition-contrary-to-fact sentence, "would" never appears in the portion of the sentence that isn't true. The subjunctive is usually expressed by *had* (for action verbs) or *were* (for states of being). In this sentence, *had* fits better, because *known* is an action verb.

8. **B.** The introductory verb form, *encouraged by her father to become an artist,* must describe the subject of the sentence. But *portraits* weren't encouraged to choose a career in art! Anguissola was. Once you figure that part out, you know that only Choices (B) and (C) are in the running. Choice (C) throws in an unnecessary *had,* so Choice (B) is the answer you seek.

9. **C.** The original sentence is wordy and awkward. Choice (C) chops out just the right number of words, leaving an appositive (the grammar term for an equivalent) to explain what the *important fact* is.

10. **C.** The description between the commas is most concise when *which* serves as the subject of two verbs, *occupies* and *has.* In the original, the pronoun *they* doesn't have anything to refer to, because *Tuvaluans* — the most logical meaning of *they* — doesn't appear in the sentence.

11. **E.** Ah, baseball. My favorite subject, second only to grammar. The original sentence is flawed because *they* may refer to either the *players* or the *gangsters,* so you can't tell which group was punished. The rule says that a pronoun must have one and only one possible **antecedent** (the word the pronoun refers to). When a pronoun is unclear, sometimes the best solution is to rewrite the sentence without the pronoun, as Choice (E) does.

12. **B.** Last time I looked, biology was a subject. The original sentence compares *biology* to *any subject,* as if biology were not included in that group. The *other* moves *biology* back where it belongs, in the subject group. Choice (B) is better than the other choices that tuck in *other,* Choices (D) and (E), because those choices sound awkward or include unnecessary words.

13. **D.** Keep things simple, if you can! Choice (D) conveys the meaning without cluttering up the sentence with extra words.

14. **A.** Yeah! A correct sentence. Choice (A) gets the job done without fuss, beginning the sentence with two descriptions (prepositional phrases, for those of you who like grammar terms). The other choices add extra words for no reason.

Answer Key for Practice Exam 5

Section 2

1. C	7. C	13. D	19. B
2. B	8. E	14. C	20. D
3. A	9. D	15. E	21. B
4. A	10. D	16. C	22. C
5. B	11. B	17. E	23. D
6. D	12. C	18. A	24. C

Section 3

1. B	6. E	11. B	16. B
2. D	7. D	12. D	17. C
3. C	8. D	13. D	18. B
4. A	9. A	14. C	19. C
5. E	10. B	15. E	20. D

Section 4

1. E	7. C	13. C	19. C
2. A	8. E	14. B	20. A
3. B	9. C	15. D	21. C
4. B	10. B	16. D	22. D
5. E	11. E	17. A	23. B
6. D	12. A	18. B	24. A

Section 5

1. C	6. B	11. 9	16. 80
2. D	7. A	12. 6	17. 6
3. D	8. D	13. 27	18. 13
4. D	9. 13	14. 17	
5. E	10. 5	15. 165	

Section 6

1. D	10. C	19. E	28. A
2. B	11. B	20. B	29. B
3. D	12. A	21. C	30. B
4. D	13. A	22. C	31. C
5. C	14. B	23. A	32. C
6. A	15. D	24. B	33. D
7. B	16. D	25. C	34. B
8. E	17. C	26. A	35. C
9. A	18. D	27. B	

Section 7

1. A	6. D	11. A	16. B
2. B	7. E	12. A	17. D
3. A	8. D	13. B	18. B
4. B	9. C	14. D	19. A
5. C	10. E	15. A	

Section 8

1. A	5. D	9. E	13. D
2. C	6. E	10. B	14. C
3. D	7. D	11. C	15. B
4. C	8. C	12. D	16. D

Section 9

1. D	5. E	9. C	13. D
2. C	6. D	10. C	14. A
3. B	7. E	11. E	
4. A	8. B	12. B	

Part VI
The Part of Tens

In this part . . .

The Big Day is a staple of many television series. Sitcom writers think it's hilarious when the bride gets lost on the way to her wedding or the expectant father drives to the hospital without his pregnant wife. But on your own personal Big Day, these kinds of situations aren't funny. In this part, you find out how to make SAT day as smooth, relaxed, and productive as possible.

As a bonus, I also include an appendix that shows you how to score your practice tests so you can get a feel for how you'd do on the real test.

Chapter 30

Ten Ways to Maximize Your Score

In This Chapter
▶ Making SAT day go as smoothly as possible
▶ Eliminating mistakes that sink your SAT score

In this chapter, I describe ten ways to make your SAT morning a little less painful so you can arrive at the test center in the proper mood to ace the test.

Stash Your Admission Ticket in Plain Sight

Before you go to sleep the night before the SAT — at a reasonable hour, not after an all-night SAT Stinks Party — place your admission ticket, car keys or carfare, pencils, calculator, watch, and everything else you need for the test in plain sight. Check out Chapter 2 for the lowdown on what you need for the test.

Keep Your Blanks in the Right Row

As you take the SAT, you may skip a question here and there. No problem. Just be sure that the answers you do fill in end up in the correct rows. As you fill in the bubbles for your answers, consciously match each question number with the number on the answer sheet. At the end of a section, recheck your answers to make sure you've finished at the right number.

Follow All Directions

When the proctor says, "Turn to Section 3," triple-check that you've actually opened the booklet to Section 3. You'd be surprised what sweaty hands can do. If you work on the wrong section, the proctor may seize your exam booklet and send you home, scoreless and unhappy. Then you have to take the test again!

Face the Grid-Ins Head-On

When you come up against a grid-in question (the math torture chamber that makes you come up with an actual answer without supplying five handy choices), remember that you can't grid in a mixed number (2½, for example). The computer will read your answer as "21 divided by 2," or 10.5. Instead, grid in ⁵⁄₂. Also, don't leave any grid-ins blank. You don't lose points for a wrong answer on these problems, so give every grid-in your best shot. See Chapter 11 for more on grid-ins.

Order the Operations

In the heat of battle, you may forget to attack a math problem in the proper order. When you start a math section, take a moment to write PEMDAS at the top of the page to help you remember which steps you should take, in the right order. Then recheck the order of operations as you move through the questions. Turn to Chapter 12 for more on PEMDAS.

Give Them What They Want

No matter how much you understand about a topic, if you don't give the SAT writers what they ask for, you won't get a point for your answer. In fact, you'll lose part of a point! For example, a question that asks about the number of people with orange ties may be chock-full of information about people with purple, tie-dyed, spaghetti-stained, and other ties. One of the answers will undoubtedly be the number of people with tie-dyed ties. Always double-check to make sure you've answered the question being asked.

Stay in Context

Once upon a time, before you started preparing for the SAT, you may have had a real life. And that life gave you some experience and knowledge that may help you on the SAT (Synchronized Awesome Tawdriness). But be sure to answer reading comprehension questions in the passage's context; don't ignore what's in the passage and substitute something from your life experience. Real life can help, but don't let it distract you from the material provided on the test because all the questions on the SAT are based on that material.

Scrap the Meaningless Scrap Paper

The SAT-scoring brigade (mostly a machine, with minimal human help) doesn't read the scrap paper you use as you truck through the test. Be sure that all your answers actually make it to the answer sheet. Otherwise, you may be unpleasantly surprised when you receive your test score.

Erase Your Errors

You may (shocking as it may seem) make a mistake from time to time. Before you sign off on a changed answer, take care that you've fully erased the wrong answer. If the scoring machine detects two answers for one question, it marks you wrong.

Write Legibly

Okay, your essay doesn't have to look like a work of art, but it does have to be readable. If your handwriting resembles the flight of a drunken chicken, the scorer won't be happy. And you definitely want a happy scorer. Recheck your essay and neatly rewrite any illegible words. If you have to scratch out a few words to make them legible, do so. You don't lose any points for strikethroughs, but you may lose points if the reader can't read enough of your essay to understand your ideas.

Chapter 31

Ten Ways to Calm Down

In This Chapter

▶ Soothing SAT nerves by preparing in advance

▶ Pacifying your angst during the test

What's that grinding noise? Oh, it's your teeth. The SAT (Superlative Auspicious Talisman) can ratchet up the anxiety level of even the most Zenned-out test taker. But a few techniques can help you de-stress — ten, to be exact. (By the way, *superlative* means "highest quality," *auspicious* means "favorable," and *talisman* means "thing with magic powers.")

Prepare Well

Well before SAT day, make sure that you go over this book carefully and shore up your weak spots. Try a practice test or two (or three or four or five!) in Part V. Then rest, because you're ready for the big time.

Sleep It Off

Don't party the night before SAT day, though I certainly understand your need to celebrate when the whole thing's over. Fight SAT nerves with restful sleep. Also, don't study on the last night before the exam. Watch television, build an anthill, or do whatever you find relaxing. Then hit the sheets at a decent hour.

Start Early

On SAT morning, set your alarm for a little earlier than you think you need to be up and about. Don't go overboard! You don't want too much extra time to obsess about all the things you haven't mastered yet. With a safety margin of, say, arriving at the testing center a half-hour before the test begins, you can ready yourself for the exam with minimal pressure. Plus you have time to find the room, get a good seat, admire the view, and run to the restroom.

Make a List

SAT-morning jitters are no fun. To *alleviate* (ease) them, on exam eve make lists of everything you need to do before leaving the house and everything you need to take to the exam. Then go through the tasks one by one, departing the house secure in the knowledge that you're ready. (See Chapter 2 for a list of items you don't want to forget.)

Stretch Your Muscles

Before you start an SAT section, stretch your arms above your head as high as they'll go. Slide your legs straight out in front of you and wriggle your ankles. Feel better?

Roll Your Head

Not the type of rolling that occurs after a session with the *guillotine* (a device that chops heads off), but a yoga-inspired exercise that *induces* (brings about) calmness. Close your eyes whenever you feel yourself tensing up. Let your head drop all the way forward, roll it in a circle, open your eyes, and hit the test again.

Breathe Deeply

Breathing is always a good idea, and deep breathing is an even better one. When the SAT overwhelms you, pull in a slow bucketful of air and then exhale even more slowly.

Isolate the Problem

On SAT day, friends are a pain in the neck. Why? Because your friends will say things like "What's the meaning of *supercilious?*" "How do you solve for three variables?" And you'll think, "I don't know what *supercilious* means! I have no idea what a variable is! I'm going to fail and no college will take me and my life will be ruined." Make a pact with your friends to stay silent about SAT questions or SAT-related information, or sit by yourself in the corner.

Become Fatalistic

A *fatalist* (one who accepts that much of life is out of control and that whatever happens, happens) does best on the SAT. Stop obsessing. Just sit down and do the test. You can worry about how you did after you've handed in the answer sheet.

Focus on the Future

No matter how bad it is, when you're taking the SAT, you're getting ever-closer to a truly wonderful time: the moment when you realize that the SAT is over, done, history. Focus on the future — that moment — whenever you feel yourself clench.

Appendix

Scoring Your Exam

· ·

Scoring the SAT isn't as simple as tallying your right and wrong answers and coming up with a percentage, but it isn't exactly rocket science either. For any of the five practice exams, use the formulas in this appendix to figure out your SAT scores for each section of the exam. (Turn to Chapter 1 for more details on SAT scoring in general.)

Determining Your Writing Score

You get three writing scores: an essay score (a number between 0 and 12), a multiple-choice writing score (a number between 20 and 80), and a combined writing score (a number between 200 and 800). The following sections show you how to calculate all three.

Essay score

Read and score your essay using the standards I explain in Chapters 7 and 8. After you're done, you should have a number between 0 (didn't answer the question) and 6 (ready to write for *The New York Times*). That number is your raw essay score. Double the raw score to get your final essay score:

Raw essay score _____ × 2 = Final essay score _____

Multiple-Choice Writing score

To calculate your Multiple-Choice Writing score, count the number of correct and incorrect answers you got in *both* Multiple-Choice Writing sections of the test. Then follow these steps:

1. **Place the total number of correct answers from the Multiple-Choice Writing sections on Line 1 below.**

2. **Multiply the total number of wrong answers from both Multiple-Choice Writing sections by ¼ and round to the nearest whole number; place your answer on Line 2.**

3. **Subtract Line 2 from Line 1 to get your raw Multiple-Choice Writing score.**

4. **Convert the raw Multiple-Choice Writing score by using the chart that follows.**

Line 1 _____

Line 2 _____

Raw Multiple-Choice Writing Score _____

Multiple-Choice Writing Conversion Table

Raw Multiple-Choice Writing Score	Converted Multiple-Choice Writing Score
46 or above	80
45	79
44	78
43	77
42	76
41	75
40	74
39	73
38	72
37	71
36	70
35	69
34	68
33	67
32	66
31	65
30	64
29	63
28	62
27	61
26	60
25	59
24	58
23	57
22	56
21	55
20	54
19	53
18	52
17	51
16	50
15	49
14	48
13	47
12	46
11	45
10	44
9	43
8	42
7	41

Raw Multiple-Choice Writing Score	Converted Multiple-Choice Writing Score
6	40
5	39
4	38
3	37
2	36
1	35
0	34
−1	32
−2	31
−3	30
−4	29
−5	28
−6	27
−7	26
Below −7	20–25

Combined writing score

Now that you have two writing scores — your essay score and the converted Multiple-Choice Writing score — add them together to determine your combined raw score. Use the following chart to find your final combined writing score.

Combined Writing Conversion Table	
Raw Writing Score	Converted Combined Writing Score
59 or above	800
58	790
57	780
56	770
55	760
54	750
53	740
52	730
51	720
50	710
49	700
48	690
47	680
46	670
45	660

(continued)

Combined Writing Conversion Table *(continued)*

Raw Writing Score	Converted Combined Writing Score
44	650
43	640
42	630
41	620
40	610
39	600
38	590
37	580
36	570
35	560
34	550
33	540
32	530
31	520
30	500
29	490
28	480
27	470
26	460
25	450
24	440
23	430
22	420
21	410
20	400
19	390
18	380
17	370
16	360
15	350
14	340
13	330
12	320
11	310
10	300
9	290
8	280
7	270
6	260

Raw Writing Score	Converted Combined Writing Score
5	250
4	240
3	230
2	220
1	210
0 or below	200

Calculating Your Critical Reading Score

Of course you got everything right on the Critical Reading section, didn't you? No? Okay then, join the rest of the human race, or at least the vast majority that makes errors on SAT reading questions. Then take a pencil and figure out your raw score, using the following method:

1. **Count the total number of correct answers in all three Critical Reading sections, and place the number on Line 1 below.**

2. **Multiply the total number of wrong answers in the three Critical Reading sections by ¼ and round to the nearest whole number; place your answer on Line 2.**

3. **Subtract Line 2 from Line 1 to get your raw score.**

4. **Convert the raw Critical Reading score by using the chart that follows.**

Line 1 _____

Line 2 _____

Raw Critical Reading Score _____

Critical Reading Conversion Table

Raw Critical Reading Score	Converted Critical Reading Score
63 or above	800
62	790
61	780
60	770
59	760
58	750
57	740
56	730
55	720
54	710
53	700
52	690
51	680

(continued)

Critical Reading Conversion Table *(continued)*

Raw Critical Reading Score	Converted Critical Reading Score
50	670
49	660
48	650
47	640
46	630
45	620
44	610
43	600
42	590
41	580
40	570
39	560
38	550
37	540
36	530
35	520
34	510
33	500
32	490
31	480
30	470
29	460
28	450
27	440
26	430
25	420
24	410
23	400
22	390
21	380
20	370
19	360
18	350
17	340
16	330
15	320
14	310
13	300
12	290

Raw Critical Reading Score	Converted Critical Reading Score
11	280
10	270
9	260
8	250
7	240
6	230
5	220
4	210
3 or below	200

Scoring the Math Sections

After you finish each practice exam, you may be tired of numbers, but muster up the energy to tackle just a few more — the raw score and the converted Math scores. First, figure out your raw score by doing the following:

1. **Count the total number of correct answers in all three Math sections, and place the number on Line 1 below. (Count both multiple-choice questions and grid-ins for this step.)**

2. **Multiply the number of wrong answers to everything except the grid-ins by $\frac{1}{4}$ and round to the nearest whole number; place your answer on Line 2. (Ignore the grid-ins for this step.)**

3. **Subtract Line 2 from Line 1 to get your raw Math score.**

4. **Convert the raw score by using the chart that follows.**

Line 1 _____

Line 2 _____

Raw Math Score _____

Mathematics Conversion Table	
Raw Math Score	**Converted Math Score**
54	800
53	790
52	780
51	770
50	760
49	750
48	740
47	730
46	720

(continued)

Mathematics Conversion Table *(continued)*

Raw Math Score	*Converted Math Score*
45	710
44	700
43	690
42	680
41	670
40	660
39	650
38	640
37	630
36	620
35	610
34	600
33	590
32	580
31	570
30	560
29	550
28	540
27	530
26	520
25	510
24	500
23	490
22	480
21	470
20	460
19	450
18	440
17	430
16	420
15	410
14	400
13	390
12	380
11	370
10	360
9	350
8	340
7	330

Raw Math Score	Converted Math Score
6	320
5	310
4	300
3	290
2	280
1	270
0	260
−1	250
−2	240
−3	230
−4	220
−5	210
−6 or below	200

Index

Notes

Notes

Notes

Notes

Notes

ple & Macs

d For Dummies
8-0-470-58027-1

one For Dummies,
Edition
8-0-470-87870-5

cBook For Dummies, 3rd
tion
8-0-470-76918-8

c OS X Snow Leopard For
mmies
8-0-470-43543-4

siness

okkeeping For Dummies
8-0-7645-9848-7

b Interviews
r Dummies,
d Edition
8-0-470-17748-8

sumes For Dummies,
Edition
8-0-470-08037-5

arting an
line Business
r Dummies,
Edition
8-0-470-60210-2

ock Investing
r Dummies,
d Edition
8-0-470-40114-9

ccessful
me Management
r Dummies
8-0-470-29034-7

Computer Hardware

BlackBerry
For Dummies,
4th Edition
978-0-470-60700-8

Computers For Seniors
For Dummies,
2nd Edition
978-0-470-53483-0

PCs For Dummies,
Windows 7
Edition
978-0-470-46542-4

Laptops For Dummies,
4th Edition
978-0-470-57829-2

Cooking & Entertaining

Cooking Basics
For Dummies,
3rd Edition
978-0-7645-7206-7

Wine For Dummies,
4th Edition
978-0-470-04579-4

Diet & Nutrition

Dieting For Dummies,
2nd Edition
978-0-7645-4149-0

Nutrition For Dummies,
4th Edition
978-0-471-79868-2

Weight Training
For Dummies,
3rd Edition
978-0-471-76845-6

Digital Photography

Digital SLR Cameras &
Photography For Dummies,
3rd Edition
978-0-470-46606-3

Photoshop Elements 8
For Dummies
978-0-470-52967-6

Gardening

Gardening Basics
For Dummies
978-0-470-03749-2

Organic Gardening
For Dummies,
2nd Edition
978-0-470-43067-5

Green/Sustainable

Raising Chickens
For Dummies
978-0-470-46544-8

Green Cleaning
For Dummies
978-0-470-39106-8

Health

Diabetes For Dummies,
3rd Edition
978-0-470-27086-8

Food Allergies
For Dummies
978-0-470-09584-3

Living Gluten-Free
For Dummies,
2nd Edition
978-0-470-58589-4

Hobbies/General

Chess For Dummies,
2nd Edition
978-0-7645-8404-6

Drawing
Cartoons & Comics
For Dummies
978-0-470-42683-8

Knitting For Dummies,
2nd Edition
978-0-470-28747-7

Organizing
For Dummies
978-0-7645-5300-4

Su Doku For Dummies
978-0-470-01892-7

Home Improvement

Home Maintenance
For Dummies,
2nd Edition
978-0-470-43063-7

Home Theater
For Dummies,
3rd Edition
978-0-470-41189-6

Living the
Country Lifestyle
All-in-One
For Dummies
978-0-470-43061-3

Solar Power Your Home
For Dummies,
2nd Edition
978-0-470-59678-4

Internet

Blogging For Dummies,
3rd Edition
978-0-470-61996-4

eBay For Dummies,
6th Edition
978-0-470-49741-8

Facebook For Dummies,
3rd Edition
978-0-470-87804-0

Web Marketing
For Dummies,
2nd Edition
978-0-470-37181-7

WordPress
For Dummies,
3rd Edition
978-0-470-59274-8

Language & Foreign Language

French For Dummies
978-0-7645-5193-2

Italian Phrases
For Dummies
978-0-7645-7203-6

Spanish For Dummies,
2nd Edition
978-0-470-87855-2

Spanish
For Dummies,
Audio Set
978-0-470-09585-0

Math & Science

Algebra I
For Dummies,
2nd Edition
978-0-470-55964-2

Biology For Dummies,
2nd Edition
978-0-470-59875-7

Calculus For Dummies
978-0-7645-2498-1

Chemistry For Dummies
978-0-7645-5430-8

Microsoft Office

Excel 2010 For Dummies
978-0-470-48953-6

Office 2010 All-in-One
For Dummies
978-0-470-49748-7

Office 2010 For Dummies,
Book + DVD Bundle
978-0-470-62698-6

Word 2010 For Dummies
978-0-470-48772-3

Music

Guitar For Dummies,
2nd Edition
978-0-7645-9904-0

iPod & iTunes For
Dummies, 8th Edition
978-0-470-87871-2

Piano Exercises
For Dummies
978-0-470-38765-8

Parenting & Education

Parenting For Dummies,
2nd Edition
978-0-7645-5418-6

Type 1 Diabetes
For Dummies
978-0-470-17811-9

Pets

Cats For Dummies,
2nd Edition
978-0-7645-5275-5

Dog Training For Dummies,
3rd Edition
978-0-470-60029-0

Puppies For Dummies,
2nd Edition
978-0-470-03717-1

Religion & Inspiration

The Bible For Dummies
978-0-7645-5296-0

Catholicism For Dummies
978-0-7645-5391-2

Women in the Bible
For Dummies
978-0-7645-8475-6

Self-Help & Relationship

Anger Management
For Dummies
978-0-470-03715-7

Overcoming Anxiety
For Dummies,
2nd Edition
978-0-470-57441-6

Sports

Baseball
For Dummies,
3rd Edition
978-0-7645-7537-2

Basketball
For Dummies,
2nd Edition
978-0-7645-5248-9

Golf For Dummies,
3rd Edition
978-0-471-76871-5

Web Development

Web Design
All-in-One
For Dummies
978-0-470-41796-6

Web Sites
Do-It-Yourself
For Dummies,
2nd Edition
978-0-470-56520-9

Windows 7

Windows 7
For Dummies
978-0-470-49743-2

Windows 7
For Dummies,
Book + DVD Bundle
978-0-470-52398-8

Windows 7 All-in-One
For Dummies
978-0-470-48763-1

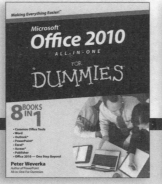

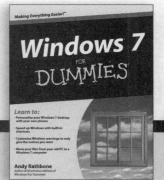

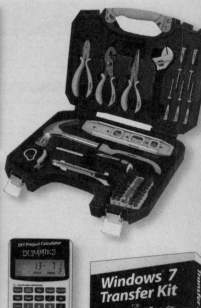